The Latin American Subaltern Studies Reader

A book in the series

Latin America Otherwise: Languages, Empires, Nations

Series editors

Walter D. Mignolo, Duke University

Irene Silverblatt, Duke University

Sonia Saldívar-Hull, University of California at Los Angeles

The Latin American

Subaltern Studies Reader

Edited by Ileana Rodríguez

Duke University Press   Durham and London 2001

© 2001 Duke University Press

All rights reserved

Printed in the United States of America on acid-free paper ∞

Typeset in Carter and Cone Galliard by Keystone Typesetting Inc.

Library of Congress Cataloging-in-Publication Data

appear on the last printed page of this book.

To María Milagros López

(1950–1997)

In memory

Everything has to do with everything else

I lament the demise of my friend and colleague
María Milagros López. Raised in Puerto Rico and
educated in France, she had the grace of
transforming everyday life occurrences and funny
ready-made phrases into serious theoretical questions.
I miss her sharpness of mind and her sense
of pleasure and wit.

Contents

Acknowledgments   ix

About the Series   xi

Ileana Rodríguez

Reading Subalterns Across Texts, Disciplines, and Theories: From Representation to Recognition   1

I. CONVERGENCES OF TIMES: SUBALTERN STUDIES SOUTH ASIA / LATIN AMERICA, MODERN / POSTMODERN

Ranajit Guha

Subaltern Studies: Projects for Our Time and Their Convergence   35

John Beverley

The Im/possibility of Politics: Subalternity, Modernity, Hegemony   47

María Milagros López

Solidarity as Event, Communism as Personal Practice, and Disencounters in the Politics of Desire   64

Alberto Moreiras

A Storm Blowing from Paradise: Negative Globality and Critical Regionalism   81

II. INDIGENOUS PEOPLES AND THE COLONIALITY OF POWER

Marc Zimmerman

Rigoberta Menchú After the Nobel: From Militant Narrative to Postmodern Politics   111

Patricia Seed   No Perfect World: Aboriginal Communities'
Contemporary Resource Rights 129

Sara Castro-Klarén   Historiography on the Ground:
The Toledo Circle and Guamán Poma 143

III. SUBJECT POSITIONS: DOMINANT
AND SUBALTERN INTELLECTUALS?

Doris Sommer   Slaps and Embraces: A Rhetoric
of Particularism 175

José Rabasa   Beyond Representation? The Impossibility of the
Local (Notes on Subaltern Studies in Light of a
Rebellion in Tepoztlán, Morelos) 191

Abdul-Karim Mustapha Questions of Strategy as an Abstract Minimum:
Subalternity and Us 211

IV. UNGOVERNABILITY: AUTHORITARIAN
AND DEMOCRATIC HEGEMONIES

Robert Carr   From *Glory* to *Menace II Society*: African
American Subalternity and the Ungovernability
of the Democratic Impulse under Super-
Capitalist Orders 227

Michael Clark   Twenty Preliminary Propositions for a Critical
History of International Statecraft in Haiti 241

Gareth Williams   *Death in the Andes:* Ungovernability and the
Birth of Tragedy in Peru 260

Javier Sanjinés C.   Outside In and Inside Out: Visualizing Society
in Bolivia 288

V. CITIZENSHIP: RESISTANCE,
TRANSGRESSION, DISOBEDIENCE

Beatriz González Stephan The Teaching Machine for the
Wild Citizen 313

Ileana Rodríguez   Apprenticeship as Citizenship and
Governability 341

Marcia Stephenson   The Architectural Relationship between Gender,
                           Race, and the Bolivian State   367

Marcelo Bergman and   Gender, Citizenship, and Social Protest:
Mónica Szurmuk   The New Social Movements in Argentina   383

Josefina Saldaña-Portillo Who's the Indian in Aztlán? Re-Writing
                           Mestizaje, Indianism, and Chicanismo from
                           the Lacandón   402

Walter D. Mignolo   Coloniality of Power and Subalternity   424

                           Contributors   445

                           Index   449

Acknowledgments

This book was going to be edited by María Milagros López and myself. This book was going to be our book. One of the policies of the Latin American Subaltern Studies Group was that of joining the efforts of social scientists to those of cultural critics. Milli, as we called her, organized the third Subalternist meeting in San Juan, Puerto Rico, in 1994 where some of the papers included in this volume were presented. Sometime after the meeting Milli and I began reading the papers and exchanging ideas. I remember one of her comments particularly. Milli was adamantly opposed to the category of alienation. She thought that was the quintessential way of academicians to look down on the "poor." She also disliked "negation" and "revolution" for reasons she never made explicit to me. She wanted us to read the work of Antonio Negri. These were some of the exchanges we had over the phone.

From her work in this volume, we can gather the directions Milli was moving toward. She was working with very interesting concepts such as the "post-work" society, and the sense of history of marginal people. They had a pressing sense of present and very little sense of future. She certainly was moving in the direction of pleasure. In this, she was our link to other ways of looking at the field, to other colleagues. We were still much centered on pain. But pleasure is one of the fundamental tools that subalterns use to contest hegemony.

Unfortunately, our dialogue was interrupted around 1996 and totally severed with her death in 1997. She did not have time to see all the articles in this volume. I will forever miss her valuable input, but most of all, I missed her company during this journey. Milli's spirit, sense of humor, common sense, and solidarity were with me during these years of waiting. With her collaboration, this introduction would have been substantially richer.

I want to thank Robert Carr, Patricia Seed, Anupama Mande, Derek Petrey, and John Beverley for helping me with the rewrite of this introduction in English. John Beverley, however, did the final and most severe editing. All of them were very generous with their time, and without their editorial corrections this manuscript would have never seen the light of day. I am also indebted to the readers of the volume who examined the manuscript very meticulously. Their thorough reading of the text and their insistence on having all the pertinent corrections made is fundamental to the intellectual success of this production. My editor, Reynolds Smith, has always been very supportive of our work. It was his faith in the manuscript and his patience in dealing with the particularities of intellectuals that ultimately allowed this text to come out in print. We all cherish the support he gives us and are grateful for his formidable friendship and sound advice. Finally, I am grateful to the contributors to this volume who endured the long delay in its production. In this they showed their commitment to Latin American subaltern studies. To me this proves that the source of our strength lies in our collective effort.

About the Series

Latin America Otherwise: Languages, Empires, Nations is a critical series. It aims to explore the emergence and consequences of concepts used to define "Latin America" while at the same time exploring the broad interplay of political, economic, and cultural practices that have shaped Latin American worlds. Latin America, at the crossroads of competing imperial designs and local responses, has been construed as a geocultural and geopolitical entity since the nineteenth century. This series provides a starting point to redefine Latin America as a configuration of political, linguistic, cultural, and economic intersections that demand a continuous reappraisal of the role of the Americas in history, and of the ongoing process of globalization and the relocation of people and cultures that have characterized Latin America's experience. *Latin America Otherwise: Languages, Empires, Nations* is a forum that confronts established geocultural constructions, that rethinks area studies and disciplinary boundaries, that assesses convictions of the academy and of public policy, and that, correspondingly, demands that the practices through which we produce knowledge and understanding about and from Latin America be subject to rigorous and critical scrutiny.

The Latin American Subaltern Studies Reader, edited by Ileana Rodríguez, collects several significant papers emerging from almost ten years of work and debates generated by the Latin American Subaltern Studies Group. This volume brings a new perspective to intellectual and political work that indirectly refashions area studies as well as cultural studies paradigms. It also introduces new problems within the agenda shaped in the past thirty-five years by the Latin American Studies Association.

The volume is at the same time a landmark in the intellectual and institutional relations between North and South, a signal invitation to think Latin American Otherwise and to imagine different possible futures. Within our series, *The Latin American Subaltern Studies Reader* introduces a theoretical dimension that we hope to pursue. At the very moment at which global reorganization is forcing regional reordering (NAFTA, MERCOSUR), and that thirty-three million "Hispanics" live in the United States, the necessity of imagining and theorizing Latin American Otherwise is more than a scholarly imperative. It is mainly an intellectual, ethical, and political necessity.

Reading Subalterns Across Texts, Disciplines, and Theories: From Representation to Recognition

ILEANA RODRÍGUEZ

Numerous voices, deriving specially from the liberal-conservative camp, have insistently argued that Western societies face a crisis of governability and the threat of dissolution at the hands of the egalitarian danger. — Laclau and Mouffe, *Hegemony and Socialist Strategy*

In the wake of the Sandinistas' defeat in the 1990 elections in Nicaragua, a small group of friends and colleagues who despaired over world politics, as well as the politics of public and academic institutions at a moment of changing paradigms, met in Washington, D.C. We were originally a group of five: John Beverley, Robert Carr, José Rabasa, Javier Sanjinés, and myself. With the assistance of Tom Moylan, we held our first meeting at George Mason University. We had met Tom at meetings of Fredric Jameson's long-lasting and fruitful Marxist Literary Group, which was so decisive for our generation. Gayatri Spivak, John Beverley, and I had also belonged to that group. To our first meeting we also invited anthropologists Carol Smith and Roger Lancaster; historians Patricia Seed and Charles Bergquist; Norma Alarcón, Lauro Flores, and Clara Lomas from Latino studies; Julio Ramos; and then-graduate students José Mazzoty and Robert Cohn, who were finishing requirements for doctorates in literature at Princeton. The rest of us were also in literature. What brought us together was a shared intuition that the project launched by the South Asian Subaltern Studies Collective in the 1980s was somehow relevant to our work as Latin Americanists. (Lack of institutional resources prevented us from inviting people from Latin America.)

On the model of the South Asian Collective we decided to be a decentralized and democratic collective with an academic project that would continue the legacy of politically committed scholarship. To this day we stand by our original commitment. All of the founding members of the Latin American Subaltern Studies Group had been involved with the Left in the sixties, so we were used to participating in small study groups to discuss marxism, dependency theory, ethnicity, and feminism. In the sixties the world seemed to be on the verge of revolution, and as students, our struggle was for the inclusion of marxist studies in university curricula. Specifically, we were determined to link literature to politics.

In the sixties there was nothing in the curriculum that could meet our intellectual and political needs. John Beverley and I had done our graduate studies at the University of California, San Diego, whose faculty included Fredric Jameson, Carlos Blanco Aguinaga, Herbert Marcuse, and the late Joseph Sommers. Both John and I worked closely with Jameson, and we joined him in founding the Marxist Literary Group (MLG) in the mid-seventies; John was co-coordinator of the MLG for some years. I took a position at the University of Minnesota in 1974, where some years later, stimulated by the spirit of California, the Institute of Ideologies and Literature (II&L) was founded through the efforts of Hernán Vidal and Antonio Zahareas. The work of the institute provided an enormous and decisive impetus to what, for lack of a better name, we can call in retrospect marxist studies of Latin American culture. The institute's project became one of the most structured attempts at linking politics, culture, and literature. At the institute's symposia we had the opportunity to gain firsthand knowledge of the work of Francoise Perus, Jean Franco, Jaime Concha, Roberto Marquez, Clara Lida, Iris Zavala, Alejandro Losada, and Osvaldo Zunkel. We also met scholars working in institutions such as FLACSO (Facultad Latinoamericana de Ciencias Sociales) and CEPAL (Centro de Estudios para América Latina). Javier Sanjinés was a graduate student at Minnesota during the institute's heyday. I would say that, professionally, the MLG and the II&L were sister structures that formed three of the founders of the Latin American Subaltern Studies Group. The MLG was ad hoc and voluntary, organized and sustained by the prestige and dedication of Jameson; the II&L was affiliated with the University of Minnesota and was organized and sustained by the prestige and dedication of Vidal and Zahareas. José Rabasa came out of the History of Consciousness program at the University of California, Santa Cruz, which was a continuation of similar efforts in the areas of transdisciplinary and multicultural studies. Sanjinés, Rabasa, and I were all at the University of Maryland in 1991–1992. One of Rabasa's students was Robert Carr, who was working toward a Ph.D. in English. Our past struggles with academia can explain why we were attracted to the work of the South Asian group and established with them a kind of unmediated recognition and spiritual affinity. It was what Ranajit Guha calls "a convergence of times" that enabled us to establish a bond with them. Our past had also been one of situated knowledges and participation in the praxis of theory. We started to adamantly oppose the traditional categories of our own academic practices and expressed our discontent with the pervasive role of "statism," both liberal and leftist.

But there is more to it than this. In the nineties, we perceived in the South Asian group a new kind of social sensibility that, coupled with a theoretical stubbornness and a spirit of academic militancy, was very much in agreement with what we called a "new humanism." By "new humanism" we meant a postrevolutionary sympathy with the struggles of the poor at a time when the collapse of socialism had made that posture very unpopular. Many around us had already realigned themselves with the winners. That is why we agree with the views of Florencia Mallon in her article "The Promise and Dilemma of Subaltern Studies: Perspectives from Latin American History," in which she reviews the state of the profession and discusses how major narratives came undone. We also agree with her claim that this undoing triggered a political and intellectual crisis that made us post-marxist intellectuals doubt "a belief in progress and modernity, a commitment to revolution as forward-looking, linear, developmentalist transformation" (1492).[1]

The Latin American Subaltern Studies Group saw subaltern studies as what Spivak calls "a strategy for our times," with two essential postulates. One was to continue placing our faith in the projects of the poor. The other was to find ways of producing scholarship to demonstrate that in the failure to recognize the poor as active social, political, and heuristic agents reside the limits and thresholds of our present hermeneutical and political condition. Like the South Asian Collective, we were also dissatisfied with the realization that the poor had not been recorded in a history of their own, but rather had been subsumed in a narrative which was not exactly their own. Ethnic studies in the United States would label such recording and writing as racist discourses. The ventriloquized nature of the representation of the subaltern (spoken for and spoken about, as Spivak has pointed out) in narratives of the state is particularly and unfortunately pervasive not only in liberal nationalist projects but also in those organized in the name of socialism. In socialist projects the ideology of modernization, the lack of ethnic and feminist criticism and awareness, or even simple sensibleness resulted in postponing people's pressing agendas and contributed to the fragmentation of movements, as well as the defeat of revolutions and revolutionary states. The realization of this absence or neglect was in a way the basis for Antonio Gramsci's analysis of Italy in terms of South and North, of peasants and workers, and the idea of the "passive revolution," which made Italy "not-France" (that is, the noncoincidence of people and [formal] nation in the project of the Italian Risorgimento). Current studies of modernism and modernization in Latin America will state that Latin America is not-Europe. While the South Asian Subaltern

Collective was criticizing the postcolonial liberal state and the nationalist independence and anticolonialist movements from the Left, we were criticizing leftist states and party organizations for their liberalism. It was the same question attacked from pre- and postrevolutionary fronts.

Florencia Mallon, observing the tension in the work of subaltern studies, claims that we are trying to ride the "four horses of the apocalypse"—namely, Derrida and Foucault to underscore technique and genealogy, and Gramsci and Guha to highlight subaltern consciousness and agency. She says, quoting David Hardiman, that "one road leads towards greater concentration on textual analysis and a stress on the relativity of all knowledge; another, towards the study of subaltern consciousness and action so as to forward the struggle for a socialist society" (1498). The point is of considerable importance for the positioning of the South-South, North-North, or South-North debates. Indeed, elucidation of this tension appears to be a major point of her article. Have we, as she argues, reduced subaltern studies "to half of its complexity: the methods and techniques of postmodernism" (1504)? In other words, has our political project been buried beneath our postmodern vocabulary? Are we really capable of "marshalling semiotics and postmodern techniques for emancipatory purposes" (1498)? Can we combine "the politically positive, liberating potential of subaltern histories" (1498) with poststructuralism and deconstruction? Are we capable of maintaining "the irresolvable tension . . . between technique and political commitment, between a more narrowly postmodern literary interest in documents as 'constructed texts' and the historian's disciplinary interest in reading documents as 'windows,' however foggy and imperfect, on people's lives" (1506)? That is what, for Mallon, is at the center of subaltern studies.

The intervention into the historiographical debate by the South Asian Subaltern Studies Collective was triggered by tensions generated within South Asian marxism and leftist parties and organizations. They were unable to account for the realities of an anticolonialist nationalism that had betrayed the masses. Our context has been that of a marxist tradition that was being called into question not only by the collapse of socialist societies but by the unresolved questions raised by the indigenous people and women within the antiimperialist movements and left-leaning nationalist revolutions. Were we all, in effect, rethinking the nature of popular front politics? Is it possible that for each alliance there is a corresponding betrayal? In other words, both South Asian and Latin American subaltern studies were cases of criticism from the Left undertaken at different moments of our modern and postmodern histories. The fact that some of us in the Latin American group, like some in the South Asian group, have had direct experience with nationalist political practices and also with the academies of the West is yet another point of convergence that very few critics have mentioned. A key point of the subalternist intervention has been to stress the "politics of location," which now means the relations between North-South and South-South. The convergence of Latin American and South Asian subaltern studies is a case of South-South dialogue, but paradoxically it passes through the North.

Of the members of the Latin American group, Robert Carr, Michael Clark, and I had firsthand experience with governments that attempted to be popular and democratic: Michael Manley's government in Jamaica, and the Sandinistas in Nicaragua. We all had lived the paradoxes of a politics that demanded a rethinking of theory. Javier Sanjinés defines himself not as an observer, but as an active scholar who has been engaged with questions of politics and representation in Bolivia in the wake of the deterioration of its "national" revolution of 1954. John Beverley had been involved in other types of struggles: in the antiwar movement and New Left in the United States, in Central American solidarity groups, and most recently, in academic politics regarding the content, form, and philosophy of cultural studies. José Rabasa participated in the independent *grillas* (political groups) fighting for the future of the university in Mexico City and the provinces. Patricia Seed also has a history of student activism in Mexico. María Milagros López was involved in the Puerto Rican Socialist Party and the Puerto Rican women's movement. We all were already immersed in the debate over the legacy of the Amerindian and African American populations, and were moving into the hard task of disciplinary and institutional criticism. Most of us had been marxist and were coming from marxist formations. Although we were primarily based in the United States, none of us were happy with what Coco Fusco and bell hooks call the "triumphant multiculturalism" that spoke little to "the decentralization of wealth and the democratization of political power" (2).[2]

The concept of the subaltern itself marks the insufficiencies of, and dissatisfactions with, the concept of class. Class is what Laclau and Mouffe refer to as the "determination in the last instance," the straw that breaks the camel's back. It has been well established that within the realities of peripheral modernities, the concept of class cannot override the categories of ethnicity and gender. The question of ethnicity is very similar to the sense of the subaltern within the South Asian Subaltern Studies Collective. The tension within political movements that mobilize around the notion of class while simultaneously subordinating ethnic and gender agendas creates a theoretical faultline for a revolutionary theory based on emancipation. It begs the question of who belongs and who does not belong to which class. Our question concerns the necessity of redefining the concept of oppression to make it more comprehensive. "Subalternity" seemed a more all-encompassing term than "class" in expressing the fullness of the disenfranchised community. It also seemed a more politicized concept than the sanitized concept of difference promoted by U.S.-style multiculturalism. At this theoretical juncture, our choice as intellectuals was to make a declaration either in support of statism (the nation-state and party politics) or on behalf of the subaltern. We chose the subaltern.

The Latin American Subaltern Studies project involved a radical critique of culture as such and also of its forming, informing, and deforming disciplines in relation to representations of the subaltern. Regarding the relationship between methodologies and politics — the two pairs of horses to which Mallon refers, with Derrida and Foucault on the methodological side and Gramsci and Guha on the political — the question is not one of privileging the political over the cultural but precisely the opposite: of demonstrating the impossibility of disengaging one form of representation from the other. In a critique of postcolonial reason, Spivak sharply demonstrates the limitations of deconstructive technique when it lacks awareness of situational politics. If we take this question seriously and rephrase it, what it entails is the relationship between postmodern, postcolonial, and cultural and subaltern studies. If Gramsci is invoked at this point, it is because his work marks the moment of the slippage of culture and "the history of the subaltern classes" into politics. In turn, this slippage, which results in the blurring of the borders of disciplines, accounts for the appeal of subaltern studies to those engaged in academic politics.

The South Asian project was intended to dismantle the colonial reason permeating all academic fields in order to restore subalterns to their condition as plural, decentered subjects on which the archive of state citizenship and governability was constructed. Subalterns were something alien, different, and preexistent to the Western world, forming a heterogeneous and elusive "civil society." The work of the South Asian group reinforces the possibility of a "history from below" that hears the voices of the oppressed and sees its central task as listening to their concerns. But under colonialism, or in the postcolonial world (and despite the century and a half of independent life that distinguishes most, but not all, Latin American countries from India, Latin America is still, we believe, postcolonial), history from below, is somewhat different from that proposed by E. P. Thompson and Eric Hobsbawm. Knowledge of the colonial subject must take notice first and foremost of colonialism. History from below must be able to register all the diverse and continually changing strategies and to master epistemologies of colonialism in the forms of positivism, modernism, racism, as well as to explain, as Laclau and Mouffe advise, the difference between people and the people. The significance of subaltern studies cannot be limited to its contribution to research methods; its uniqueness lies in its philosophical approach as an inflexion that tries to discern how the world looks when stood on its head.

The Latin American Subaltern Studies Group has had three stages. The foundational moment occurred when the group attended the first meeting at George Mason University, which constituted the historical core. A second stage at Ohio State brought Walter Mignolo, María Milagros López, and Michael Clark to the group. The third stage was formed by the affiliation of new members with the group in Puerto Rico: Alberto Moreiras, John Kraniauskas, Gareth Williams, Josefina Saldaña-Portillo, Abdul Mustafa, Fernando Coronil, Marsh Stephenson, and Sara Castro-Klarén. The Ohio State group introduced the discussion of postcolonialism and insisted in revising issues pertaining to "the determination in the last instance," urging us to move away from theories of alienation and into the living cultures of the quotidian.

The Latin American Subaltern Group has been the object of criticism. One of these criticisms claims that by taking the idea of subaltern studies into the Latin American field, we were disregarding the specificities of Latin America itself. But, as we all know, Latin American studies has always borrowed from European and U.S. theory, and not so long ago was heavily invested not only in following but even in elevating French theory to canonical status. Given, too, almost a century of heavy borrowing from marxism, it was strange, to say the least, to be rejected on the basis of borrowing from the South Asian subalternists. In another version of the same criticism, the tag "traveling theory" was used to mean pan-Americanism, or domination of the Latin American field from North American academic centers. It was implied that we were imperialist because we were trying to impose models from other realities on Latin America. Here, the new normative regulations for knowledge production and the weakening of Latin American academic institutions under the pressure of neoliberal reforms play a fundamental role. To hold a self-subsistent academic collective responsible for a trend that had been restructuring education on a global scale was to totally miss the point. On the basis of these and similar misunderstandings, the idea of the dialogue between North and South was discarded, discredited, and chastised. The idea of a South-South dialogue was proposed in its stead. Thus, in the first Spanish translation of the work of the South Asian group, edited by Silvia Rivera Cusicanqui and Rossana Barragán, *Debates post coloniales: Una introducción a los estudios de la subalternidad* (1997), the editors state that "against the grain of the multidisciplinary postulates of the Indian Group, the North American debate seems only to follow disciplinary lines: from history the theoretical pretensions of literary and cultural studies are criticized. These are the traits of an invisible localization, which the Northern mediation can induce, in the South-South historiographical debates, empowering their theoretical and methodological horizon" (14).[3]

Aside from expressing a desire to discuss the works in Spanish, the views of Rivera and Barragán (to whom I am particularly grateful for including marxism as "one of our traditions" [16]) and our own readings seem to coincide along major lines. For example, the argument that "the works of the [South Asian] group attempt to dismantle that type of enlightened and colonial reason by the simple fact that they attempt to restore to the subaltern (groups, classes) their conditions as plural and decentralized subjects" (11) is also applicable to our work. We also view the subaltern as a heterogeneous and pre-Western subject. Nevertheless, instead of pointing out similarities between the work of the South Asian and Latin American groups, Rivera and Barragán refer to Florencia Mallon's criticism of the "literary character" of the work of the latter. They also express their impatience with what they characterize as North American agendas involved in our project. Hugo Achugar argues that the geographic location of the intellectual influences the meaning, concepts, and interpretation of the text.[4] The perspectives of postcolonialism and subaltern studies are located in the North American academy, or the "new theoretical Commonwealth." Achugar claims that the "terms of the discussion about postcolonialism as well as Subalternity do not have the same meanings" when they are generated "from or in Uruguay or the Rio de la Plata region and even southern Brazil." To use these terms within Latin American fields without paying attention to their specific meanings in local realities is what Achugar means by "the new Pan-Americanist agendas" (386). He concludes that "it is misleading to characterize the Americas following the wars of independence as postcolonial. In short, the Americas were neither Asia nor Africa. Mexico is not India. Peru is not Indonesia. And Latinos in the U.S., although tragically opposed by an exclusionary will, are not Algerians" (385). The claim is echoed by Mabel Moraña, who argues that the "boom of the subaltern" is linked to a market where that notion affirms itself as an ideological trademark of a product incorporated through diverse strategies of promotion for globalized cultural consumption (52).[5]

There are real points of contention we can identify in this type of criticism. The most important concerns our own positionalities as intellectuals. Achugar and Moraña are, like us, located on both sides of the North-South continental divide. They may claim to speak for Latin America, but that claim is rhetorical. Let me partially respond to their geopolitical perplexities with Ranajit Guha's words on the local. In his article in this volume, Guha explains that as knowledgeable as he is of the vast diversity of regional or local materials, his project never claimed a universal validity. He also disclaims comparisons by analogy that are reduced to "a touch of resemblance there and a suggestion of parallelism in yet another respect to produce at best what Wittgenstein has called the 'experience of comparison.'" But he believes there is another kind of comparison that "combines with reflection and abstraction to generate concepts in the process of understanding," which thinks its way through to the ground which is "nothing other than an overarching temporality subsuming local times." It is that temporality, and its connection to the problem of governability, that is the central ground of "convergence."

As Latin Americanists, we cannot be oblivious to the work of scholars in Latin America and other parts of the world who offer radical critiques of Enlightenment and of orthodox marxist paradigms. Jesús Martín Barbero, Nelly Richard, Ernesto Laclau, Néstor García Canclini, Renato Ortiz, Silvia Rivera, Josefina Ludmer, and George Yúdice, among others, have highlighted the pervasive influence and limits of European and North American theoretical paradigms in research. Clearly, their contributions must be acknowledged. Their work has, indeed, enabled us to mark the distinction between an emerging discourse of what might be called Latin American cultural studies and subaltern studies.[6]

Subaltern studies is not, as it has been wrongly presumed, a study of subalterns. Much less is it, as Mabel Moraña has claimed, a "theoretical trafficking which attempts to totalize the Latin American hybrid empirical facts with universalizing and leveling concepts and principles" (2). Latin American subaltern studies aims to be a radical critique of elite cultures, of liberal, bourgeois, and modern epistemologies and projects, and of their different propositions regarding representation of the subaltern. Subaltern studies are postmodern and postrevolutionary attempts to understand the limits of previous hermeneutics by challenging culture to think of itself from the point of view of its own negations. Another goal is to recognize that in the history and culture of "societies' Others" we can find, paradoxically, new ways of approaching some of the riddles created by the incapacity of bourgeois culture to think about its own conditions of discursive production. Subaltern studies positions itself as a radical critique predicated on cross-, trans-, and multidisciplinarity, as well as on a commitment to comparative studies between different post-(neo)colonial situations, in an effort "to provincialize Europe," as Dipesh Chakrabarty puts it.[7]

In "Dominance without Hegemony and Its Historiography," Guha defines the conditions of radical criticism as follows: "To commit a discourse to speak from within a given consciousness is to disarm it insofar as its critical faculty is made inoperative thereby with regard to that particular consciousness. For no criticism can be fully activated unless its object is distanced from its agency. Since the paradoxes characteristic of the political culture of colonialism testify to the failure of the bourgeoisie to acknowledge itself the structural limitations of bourgeois dominance, it is hardly surprising that the liberal historical discourse too should be blind to those paradoxes" (216).[8] Guha locates this idea at the intersection of politics and culture within post(neo)colonial nations to underscore the lack of critical distance between the indigenous elite intellectual and the ruling class. The condition, however, for a radical critique from the point of view of the subaltern is not only to speak from a variety of subject positions, but also to speak in reverse or against the grain—to take into consideration the principle that "no discourse can oppose a genuinely uncompromising critique to a ruling culture so long as its ideological parameters are the same as those of that very culture" (220). Thus, the paradox of knowledge is that one has to learn to think from its own negation, "from outside the universe of dominance which provides the critique with its object" (220). One has to think within the context of an ideology that "is antagonistic towards the dominant culture and declares war on the latter even before the class for which it speaks comes to rule" (221).

Before we move on to the nexus between hegemony and domination, we must turn to the thorny question of the intellectual's role in the constitution of subalterns. In the restatement of "Can the Subaltern Speak?" in *A Critique of Postcolonial Reason,* Spivak takes the poststructuralist scrutiny of the sovereign subject to task.[9] For Spivak, it is impossible to separate the agent from its object. Her point of departure is the positionality of the speaking subject as intellectual alongside a critique of a "concealed Subject" of the West that has pretended to have "no geo-political determinations" (272), however much it may have been narrativized by law, political economy, and ideology. I will highlight three points in her argument in order to explain the paradoxical representation of a problematized Western subject in relation to a Third World subject, and of intellectuals in relation to subalterns. First, Spivak reintroduces the mediation of ideology in the Althusserian sense; second, she distinguishes between representation (*Vertreten* [—as proxy]) and re-presentation (*Darstellen* [—a portrait]); third, she differentiates between descriptive and transformative class consciousness. Keeping the mediation of ideology as part of the analysis allows her to reintroduce "constitutive contradiction" and positionality as a means to reinscribe politics into culture, and to "admit that a developed theory of ideology recognizes its own material production in institutionality" (274). It follows that the condition for a criticism of the subject must include both the complicity of the intellectual and the state, and the intellectual's role in reproducing the international division of labor. The "best prophets of heterogeneity and the Other" (272), Gilles Deleuze and Michel Foucault, proposed to unveil the concreteness of the oppressed subject, which led to their desire to decenter the sovereign subject and propose a theory of pluralized "subject-effects." But this proposition fails because, although it provided the illusion of undermining the sovereign subject (S), it also furnishes a cover that masks this subject (s) of knowledge — that is, their own position of "centrality" and privilege in "allowing" the subaltern to speak.

The difficulty of producing counterhegemonic ideologies leads Spivak to distinguish between representation as "speaking for" ("within the state and political economy") as opposed to representation as "speaking about." One might describe her position thus: that theories of representation offer the only means of making a radical critique of a theory which, under the pretext of valorizing "the oppressed as subject . . . 'to establish conditions where the prisoners themselves would be able to speak,'" argues that the masses can speak for themselves because they *know* perfectly well . . . [that] they know far better than [the intellectual] and they certainly say [what they want] very well" (274). For Spivak, this is tantamount to allowing the signifiers to "look after themselves" (275) and to sever "theory's link to the signifier" (275) — in other words, to efface the relationship between the intellectual and the state, and excuse culture from its participation in politics. To underscore the difficulties of producing a counterhegemonic discourse and to show that the historical machine moves in a dislocated way, Spivak makes the distinction between a descriptive and a transformative class consciousness. Class consciousness is not individual; it is a feeling of community — of the nation, the public arena, the collectivity, the party.[10]

In "Discipline and Mobilize," Guha studies the relationship between the metropolitan imperialist powers and the new nationalist insurgent movements. He uses the distinction between hegemony and domination to introduce the question of a national popular democratic subject as subaltern to show how its political practice constituted itself into a radical critique of elite nationalism. He defines imperialism as the subjugation of one nation by another based on the universal values of reason. He defines nationalism as the ideology of indigenous ruling groups in their struggle for hegemony and their attempt to establish a state that protects their economic, cultural, and political interests. He defines hegemony as rule by consent.[11] For Guha, the critique of elite liberal nationalism lies within postcolonial politics, parties, movements, social projects, and common popular fronts. Dominance is predicated on the double articulation of two types of governance: one by the British and the other by Indians. "Double articulation" is what inexorably ties the politics of the local (national) to the global (international, colonial, imperial). Thus hegemony and domination present themselves as an adjustment to the dysfunctional evolutionary, totalizing, and lineal paradigm of modernity. Because of the constitution of an elite (oligarchic) nation, liberation demands a double disarticulation: one from the colonial power and another from the masses. The question is, does the logic of dominance and hegemony work in tandem with the logic of imperialism (colonialism) and nationalism, and does it explain the relation between classes and subalterns? Guha's criticism of nationalism is that it erases the distinction between hegemony and domination, and focuses on mobilization while still representing domination with the vocabulary of premodern traditions.

Whereas for Guha the notion of hegemony brings up the schooling of the indigenous by the alien, for Laclau and Mouffe it explains the differences between two historical articulations that call into question what is necessary and what is contingent to theory. From the very outset, the logic of hegemony presents itself "as a complementary and contingent operation, required for conjunctural imbalances within an evolutionary paradigm whose essential or 'morphological' validity was not for a moment placed in question" (3). Hegemony, which begins by explaining a disjuncture, ends by becoming a radical critique that reformulates the theory of universal reason and "determination in the last instance." In other words, it constitutes the radical critique of the marxist idea of underlying morphologies of history, of "intelligible totalities constituted around conceptually explicable laws" (3). To formulate new conceptions of politics, we must grasp the logic of this double articulation of power and theory — Guha's within the politics of nationalism, and Laclau and Mouffe's within the politics of internationalism. But there is more to it than this. Once the "determination in the last instance" has been removed, the subject of history is pluralized. The fragmented and disaggragated social groups (the masses, the multitude) will come to constitute the subaltern. The term "subaltern" is employed not because the critical intellectual wants to subalternize the masses, but because s/he wants to point out how in the logic of hegemony and domination, the popular-democratic project becomes subordinated.

How do these questions relate to Latin America subaltern studies? In theory, hegemony is a conceptual device that permits a reading of the national question in transnational terms. In Latin American studies, Julio Ramos calls this disjuncture *desencuentros* with modernity; Beatriz Sarlo, "peripheral modernities"; Roberto Schwartz, "ideas out of place."[12] All of these terms are foreshadowed by Andre Gunder Frank's theories of under- or uneven development.[13] In keeping with the argument of Latin American critics of modernism, Guha questions the "universal" character of bourgeois and socialist theories and categories and highlights the particular. If in India the elite renders the European Enlightenment opaque, in Russia workers' strikes render classical marxist theories of social organization inoperative. This reading of European Enlightenment is very much in agreement with that of Néstor García Canclini. For him, modernity in Europe is the transnationalization of the emancipatory spirit of the Enlightenment. In contrast, in Latin America modernity, the economic strategy adopted by the liberal elites (oligarchies) was to constitute themselves and their nation "by taking care of the intersection of different historical temporalities and trying to elaborate a global project with them" (46).[14] In India, the liberal elite paradoxically used the authorized language of premodern traditions to effect its transition to modernity and thus dimmed "the luminosity of the so-called . . . Renaissance to considerable extent" (17). The liberal elite "makes one wonder whether Indian liberalism, thanks to the rather peculiar condition of its development within colonial power relations, did not indeed belong to an ideological and cultural category altogether distinct from its Western prototype" (16). Laclau and Mouffe's radical critique of marxist epistemologies centers equally on representation of the subalternized masses, whose dislocated position in economic and philosophical theory traces what Spivak calls "the archaeology of silence" (7).[15] This dislocation illustrates for them the transition from the Second to the Third International, from trade unionism to revolution, from classes to masses, and from economic necessity to the politics of contingency and popular fronts.

Guha observes that what is new in (postmodern) studies of peasant insurrections is how theorists connect them not to the nation-state but to colonialism; how they take subaltern agency as a subject of its own history and not the history of something transcendental; how they make evident that subaltern agency becomes a matter of the security of the state; how they link that to the production of history, mainly to the history of bureaucracy; and finally, how they negate the character of spontaneity attributed to it and thus revise accepted notions about peasant consciousness, knowledge, and political organization.[16] The act of recognizing subaltern consciousness moves insurrection away from the terrain of criminality into the political. Guha's debate with Hobsbawm over the rebel as bandit and the bandit as a prepolitical consciousness dovetails with the Communist Party's criticism of peasant insurgencies as spontaneous and disorganized acts.

In resituating the subaltern at the center of his/her own struggle, Guha debunks several mediations simultaneously—those of the intellectual, the party, and the disciplines—calling into question the very concept of the pre- or subpolitical. To this end, he highlights how the subaltern, by altering the logic of order and the syntax of domination and governance, has the power to turn the world upside down. Popular movements must not be "one hundred percent conscious . . . [and] governed by plans worked out in advance to the last detail or in line with abstract theory" (4). Of the many peasant insurrections discussed in his work "there is none that could be said to have been altogether leaderless. Almost each had some sort of central leadership . . . although in no instance was it fully in control of the many local initiatives originating with grassroots leaders whose authority was as fragmented as their standing short in duration. One is dealing here with a phenomenon that was nothing like a modern party leadership but could perhaps be best described, in Gramsci's words, as 'multiple elements of "conscious leadership" . . . no one of them . . . predominant'" (10).

Although Guha continues using words such as feudalism and peasantry, he is using them already within a different space, on the threshold, so to speak, of postmodernity, in the sense Néstor García Canclini gives to this term: "not as a stage or tendency that replaces the modern world, but rather . . . a way of problematizing the equivocal links that the latter has formed with the traditions it tried to exclude or overcome in constituting itself" (9). One way to understand subaltern history is to think of ungovernability as insurrection, disobedience, or indiscipline. Insurrection implies that the subaltern is negating his/her own negation within the established order, inviting punishment through his/her counternegation. The insurgent can lose everything, from his/her sense of self to his/her own body; therefore, rebellions must first pass through the filter of consciousness.

Politically, the disarticulation of elite and subaltern within national insurrections is labeled "mobocracy" or "spontaneism." In India, the Mahatma, who "shared with the colonialists a prejudice common to all elites in regarding any mobilization of the masses on their own initiative as indiscipline" (37), used "mobocracy" to describe the "uncouth, unruly, unheeding to all advice" (35) behavior of the crowds. Discipline—which is the beginning of coercion and authoritarian hegemony (domination)—is the way of regulating, harnessing, instructing, or excising obedience from the people; it is the beginning of subordination. Gandhi, who did not want to "conquer undiscipline by force" (37), believed it is important to "harness" and appropriate the politics of the people

> to a nationalism which would allow the bourgeoisie to speak for its own interest in such a way as to generate the illusion of speaking for all of society. To regulate what defied control, to discipline the undisciplined was to subject it to a critique. The undiscipline Gandhi complained of would seem to amount to a particular style of popular mobilization. . . .
>
> By denouncing such mobilization as "habitual undiscipline" Gandhi was simply owning up to his failure to make the traditional forms of mass mobilization compatible with the new forms which were evolving at the time within the nationalist movement . . . [and that] would resist assimilation to the other domain so long as its immediacy remained intact. (38, 39)[17]

Citizenship and Ungovernability: Latin American Subaltern Studies

If you want your children to become communists, send them to study in a capitalist country.
— a popular saying

The purpose of this volume is to examine the relationship between citizenship and governability through a critical study of dominant cultures and ideologies. In Guha's essay for this volume, I want to highlight his criticism of reason and "its function as a paradox," which "arises out of an iron necessity for reason to have its universalistic drive curbed by history," when "the notion of progress itself comes under question." Guha also considers the "three salient aspects of modernity's intersection with colonialism" that render visible the convergence of temporalities of the South Asian and Latin American fields. These aspects simultaneously illustrate that "since the Enlightenment, in every serious contest with a critique that has belonged to its own time, it is the claims of pure reason that have taken a beating." Guha's three salient aspects are "firstly, that the phenomenon of post-Enlightenment colonialism is constitutive of and presupposed in modernity even if it is not always explicitly acknowledged to be so; second, that postmodernism as a critique can never be adequate to itself unless it takes colonialism into account as a historic barrier that reason can never cross; and third, that the colonial experience has outlived decolonization and continues to be related significantly to the concerns of our own time."

John Beverley's essay, "The Im/possibility of Politics" examines the difference between cultural and subaltern studies. His thesis is that this difference expresses the tension between culture and politics. From the beginning, Beverley recognizes that subaltern representation is very problematic in the context of neoliberalism, and that neither liberal nor leftist nationalisms take into account what Dipesh Chakrabarty calls "radical heterogeneity." Of the three definitions of the subaltern that Beverley revises (Gramsci's, Spivak's, and Guha's), Guha's definition seems to be the only one to open the possibility of representation, simply because it allows construction of the subaltern within the parameters of popular-front politics. Although Beverley believes that both subaltern and cultural studies recognize the limits of the nation-state and converge in thinking of the popular as mass culture, they split in the theoretical and political relevance they assign to consumption.

Beverley believes that cultural studies tends to perpetuate "unconsciously the modernist aesthetic ideology it supposedly displaces by transferring the formalist program of dehabitualization of perception from the sphere of high culture to the forms of mass culture." In recognizing the multiple logics in civil society and in privileging one of its loci—that of a community of consumers (Canclini) separated from national or territorial referents—cultural studies applies the Gramscian concept of the popular to crisis. This makes it impossible to articulate the elite/subaltern opposition through mass culture, to construct the counterhegemonic. Beverley argues instead for the possibility of a radical multiculturalism based on subaltern positionalities, and its political articulation in what he calls a "postmodernist version of the Popular Front."

For Beverley, ungovernability is tied to the construction of the counterhegemonic, which consists partially of the radicalization of "situations of ungovernability through grass root resistance" at a "sub or supra national level," or in the reconstitution of the "people" as a potentially hegemonic bloc. One of the main questions he raises in his essay concerns the possibilities of rethinking the state from the point of view of the subaltern. He argues that culture, as political identity, impedes thinking of subalterns as the people, a precondition for the constitution of popular-front politics. In revising the history of leftist debates about the popular, Beverley finds them to be overdetermined by liberal ideology; the only way of constituting alternative hegemonies is by reproducing the logic of what is already hegemonic. Thus, elite thinking wins even in defeat. The problem is then how to unify subaltern identities into a block, "the people," to oppose the structure of power, grounded in the ungrounded figure of the "nation." As do Laclau and Mouffe, Beverley calls for a "radical democratization." If this could be done, it might still be possible to produce the people / power bloc antagonism, precisely because the subaltern positionalities come to understand that the possibility of realizing their specific demands depends on entering into an alliance with others. This amounts to recognition of heterogeneity as the new image of the nation-state or "people-state."

María Milagros López's contribution, "Solidarity as Event, Communism as Personal Practice, and Disencounter in the Politics of Desire," is an attempt to articulate the relation between intellectuals and subalterns within the thorny question of citizenship and governability. If ungovernability is predicated on the opacity of a social subject, with whom there is no possibility of dialogue because there are no common interests, subalterns are situated beyond the codes of communicative rationality, and ungovernability remains located within negativity. If that is true, subaltern studies must focus on state forms of persuasion rather than on coercion—on the links between pleasure and social justice. Ungovernability permits us to hold on to unedited forms of optimism, which the politics of neoliberalism has negated, and to keep on looking for the places from which contestation is possible.

López engages the notion of contradiction in postmodern rather than modern forms of ungovernability. She thinks not within the sixties-style of insurgency theory but within the contradictory manner in which insurgency inserts itself in a "post-work" society such as contemporary Puerto Rico (where about half the adult population is structurally unemployed). López argues for postmarxist ways of disassembling domination as a precondition for working toward social justice and the end of human suffering. She claims that alienation, false consciousness, and class consciousness for and in itself are the only places where Marx and Engels speak about subjectivity and agency. But theories of consciousness do not lead to democratic devolutions, and even less to insurgency. She therefore welcomes Ernesto Laclau and Chantal Mouffe's displacement of the base-superstructure dichotomy and the "determination in the last instance." She thinks subaltern studies should relate ungovernability to the postfordism, flexible accumulation, and globalization that generate the new contradictions. As the penetration of capital increases, so do the points of contestation. Subalterns are not docile subjects. Docility and alienation are ways of seeing them from the outside, from domination — evident in her invocation of the *"jíbaro's ajá"* — a popular phrase that expresses a form of subalterns' empty acquiescence to elite commands.

Alberto Moreiras's work, "A Storm Blowing from Paradise: Negative Globality and Critical Regionalism," examines several new paradigms of Latin American studies: Antonio Cornejo Polar's notion of heterogeneity or contradictory totality; Beatriz Sarlo's anatomy of different types of intellectuals; Silviano Santiago's need to rethink cultural enjoyment and his call for a new approach in education; Jorge Castañeda and Néstor García Canclini's idea of "regional federalism"; Silvia Rivera Cusicanqui's *"ayllu* democracy"; and Chela Sandoval's "differential consciousness." Moreiras points out the contradictions in each of these paradigms and comes back to his original focus: the "possibility of Latin American cultural studies as an enterprise of productive and not simply reactive knowledge." How does one incorporate "Latin American subaltern difference in the global context"? He then returns to the question of heterogeneity and the systematic effort to account for it as the mark "of a paradigmatic shift in knowledge production." His thesis, which dialogues with Beverley's assumption of identity politics as a form of subaltern agency, is that cultural heterogeneity seems to have been the question of modernity as well, with the difference that heterogeneity today seems to be produced and consumed at the same time, and hence does not "by itself guarantee an appropriate teleology for Latin American cultural knowledge." He offers in its place his idea of "critical regionalism" "as a thinking of cultural consumption from regional perspectives . . . as the thinking of the singular resistance to consumption from within consumption, through which regional and local identity formation happens in global times." For Moreiras, the concepts of "negative globality" and "narrative fissure" are useful for theorizing critical regionalism: "narrative fissure" designates the dialectics of global integration according to processes of modernization and the reversal of its expectations, which produce what he calls "negative globality." For Moreiras, there is no postmodern global integration; globalization rather produces its own counterimage.

In the second part of this volume, Marc Zimmerman's essay, "Rigoberta Menchú After the Nobel: From Militant Narrative to Postmodern Politics," approaches the question of ungovernability as the failure of the state "to totalize all the social relations constituting the nation." In this situation "the state . . . required to maintain and extend given international and local socioeconomic power relations has to exert such pressure over one or more social sectors or social configurations." This type of state agency "strains the government's legitimacy and leads to further oppositions and . . . [the] ungluing of the social fabric." By controlling multiple social contradictions, the state may create the conditions for its opposition and resistance to the given construction of hegemony. His essay focuses on the career of Rigoberta Menchú and her participation in Guatemalan politics, especially her role after winning the Nobel.

The question is, as Menchú moves beyond her identification with the armed struggle and the marxist Left in Guatemala and develops "a propensity for independence of thought" (as well as being interested in "the Lacanian construction of the collective subject and the formation of postmodern movements in search of a radical democracy") can she represent the subaltern social forces in the postmarxist era? His answer is yes. Menchú cannot be boxed into previous marxist or traditional Guatemalan categories but is a mobile signifier that tends to spill beyond the signified. Zimmerman's thesis is that the Indian postholocaust, the military penetration of the indigenous territories, the growing indigenous entrepreneuralism, and the move to military rule gave Menchú her prominence. She has already played a significant role in reconfiguring forces and possibilities, structuring a new period beyond the revolutionary 1980s, a period also characterized by struggles such as those of Zapatistas, which the Italian political theorist Antonio Negri calls "emergent movements of constituent power."

In Patricia Seed and Sara Castro-Klarén's essays, indigenous people's knowledge and the coloniality of power are the inflections that serve to pierce the unity of the universal categories of knowledge, reason, nations, and citizenship, and compel us to look at them from the point of view of subalternity. These two scholars propose hermeneutical models for rearticulating local histories as a condition of possibility for the construction of subaltern globalities. Patricia Seed's essay, "No Perfect World: Aboriginal Communities' Contemporary Resource Rights," is a comparative study of legislation that governs the use of natural resources and defines the identity of indigenous peoples. Her point of departure is a contrast between English and Iberian traditions regarding property, legal soil and subsoil rights, hunting and fishing grounds, and cultural uses of natural substances. The appeal of her analysis lies in the multiplicity of symbolic repercussions it radiates. Legislation on natural resources constitutes the indigenous subject as subaltern (his status as a minor, his identity as a male hunter, the exclusion of women as cultivators of land) and defines and organizes the notions and structures of civic rights from which indigenous people are excluded. It also distinguishes the subject positions of colonial agents and their respective occupations, and territorializes identity, delimiting the place where indigenous and colonial practices can be performed. Seed substantiates aspects of Guha's point about "an overarching temporality subsuming local times" by showing the patterns, consistencies, and inconsistencies of colonialism within a transnational space that includes Australasia, Canada, the United States, and Iberoamerica. The value of her study is its demonstration of how modern nation states reproduce in their practices of governance the legacies of colonialism. In her own words, "Colonial pentimenti are the traces of the original colonizations: outlines from the past that show through the contemporary national law codes, administrative and judicial decisions. Such colonial pentimenti become clearly visible when we look at contemporary aboriginal communities' access to natural resources."

In contrast to Seed's and Zimmerman's concerns about the current situation of indigenous peoples in the Americas, Sara Castro-Klarén's work, "Historiography on the Ground: The Toledo Circle and Guamán Poma," details the workings of the circle of intellectuals created by Viceroy Francisco Toledo to work out the model for colonial government in viceregal Peru. Toledo's strategy was to first organize a coherent group of lawyers, historians, and informants to describe the nature of Inca rule and to conceptualize it as tyranny. These intellectuals were charged with processing the information provided by "native" informants about Inca society and then reframing it according to the assumptions of Spanish-European jurisprudence. The Andean subjects, such as the Inca Garcilaso, Guamán Poma, or "the mysterious anonymous Jesuit Blas Valera," contested Toledo's model of governmentability in turn. They all undertook a tacit or explicit defense of "the Inca and the pre-Inca knowledge and experience in the arts of governing," which implies an Andean rationality "worth preserving and even imitating by the Spaniards," a fact that infuses European categories of governability with a sense of negation.

In part 3, Doris Sommer's piece, "Slaps and Embraces: A Rhetoric of Particularism," engages the "humanist" logic of universalizing readers, readings, and epistemologies—a logic that must be confronted with the limits of the "particular" of ethnically or culturally marked texts. For her, rhetoric is a technology of offense and defense, and she illustrates that, for some writers, a rhetoric of secrecy "is a safeguard to freedom."

Ludwig Wittgenstein may not have had precisely these readers in mind when he exhorted us to "Look, don't think," because propositions (of universality, in this case) are "queer things"; they let one make sense of data, but they also eliminate the details (ethnically marked particularities, for example) that don't fit into propositional patterns. Nevertheless, his advice can yield a recognition of language games that are played alongside and against the game of universalizing the particular into the familiar, games of distantiation and coy seduction that refuse assimilation and that worry privileged readers who may be left with open, but chaste and empty, arms.

The ethical corollary to hermeneutics lies in the relationship Sommer establishes between law and order and the production of cultural artifacts, which enables the reader to read culture in state policies and politics, and state policies and politics in cultural production. This analytical frame constitutes her strategy for crossing the divides between cultures to warn readers against the transparency of texts, to caution them against the productivity of telling secrets, and to suggest that the most productive alliances are premised on respect. What the subaltern invites us to, she suggests, is "not a heart-to-heart but a tête-à-tête."

In "Beyond Representation? The Impossibility of the Local (Notes on Subaltern Studies in Light of a Rebellion in Tepoztlán, Morelos)," José Rabasa approaches the question of the subject positions of dominant and subaltern intellectuals by analyzing his own intervention in the reporting and theorizing of rebellions—in this case, the Zapatista insurgency. In his opening remarks he includes his family in his narrative to translate life into theoretical language. Rabasa then moves to a discussion that is very pertinent to our volume—namely the transition of the notion of subalternity from fascist Italy (Gramsci) to postcolonial India (Guha/Spivak) to postrevolutionary Latin America. He argues for four moments, which, in his opinion, map the transformation of the concept of subaltern in this sequence: "(a) the idea of the organic intellectual in Gramsci functioned as the consciousness and theory of what subalterns did instinctively in the process of acquiring a modern mentality; (b) the intellectual in decolonization history makes allowances for the specific practices of subalterns but still retains the task of furnishing a mirror for the subaltern—that is, to recover the place in history for subalterns; (c) subaltern studies expounds the inadequacy of elite models of intellectual and political protagonism; (d) but this implies the need for a new ethics and sensibility." Rabasa argues that the concept of the subaltern should travel further. In his opinion, subaltern studies has much to learn from the tactics and strategies displayed by subaltern groups in their interactions with the Mexican state.

Abdul-Karim Mustapha's "Questions of Strategy as an Abstract Minimum: Subalternity and Us" raises the question of the place and role of intellectuals within globalization as the referent for a series of discussions aimed at ordering the beginning and ending of the so-called end of communism, an element of a much larger specter, the long Cold War. By bringing the questions of strategy and populism to the pressing dilemmas of politics in a post-Cold War context, Mustapha invites us to discuss how we might begin to think strategy of political futures and their place in the immense theater of democracy. Like Moreiras, Mustapha anticipates a new project on the critique of hegemony, as if hegemony were something like a screen onto which intellectuals project their anxiety about being displaced by the "radical heterogeneity" of an emergent heterogeneous popular subject, what Negri calls "the multitude."

In part 4, Robert Carr, Michael Clark, Gareth Williams, and Javier Sanjinés, approach ungovernability in both authoritarian and democratic hegemonies by bringing the question of the "double articulation" of the national and international to bear on what disengages elite from subaltern in the epoch of neoliberalism.

Robert Carr's essay, "From *Glory* to *Menace II Society:* African American Subalternity and the Ungovernability of the Democratic Impulse under Super-Capitalist Orders," tracks the history, ahistoricity, and historiography of African Americans through the representation of citizenship and ungovernability in two U.S. films. In *Glory,* which is about a regiment of black soldiers in the Union Army during the Civil War, Carr argues that the subjects, once categorized as "slaves," come to assume categorization as "soldiers" as part of the promise of inclusion of blacks as citizens. *Menace II Society,* about gang violence in contemporary Los Angeles, presents the inversion of the paradigm of inclusion proposed by *Glory.* If in *Glory* the antagonism of the state is ubiquitous and directly related to the status of the black population — represented as ungovernable even when the state is acting as a war machine — in *Menace* hope of citizenship is lost, with the newest generation of African Americans still caught up in a war zone. The impossibility of citizenship has led this new generation of ungovernables to devour themselves.

Carr wonders what intellectuals and cultural analysts must do to face the burden of history and "to speak out in the name of democracy as equal rights in human rights." He starts by asking what has happened to the hopes of democracy and equality posited by the Civil Rights movement and the promise of Enlightenment rhetoric, and ends by demonstrating how promotion of the image of a hidden yet public menace to society in the form of war or gangs is the media's contribution to the representation of people as noncitizens. His thesis is that the U.S. Constitution establishes "the equation of democracy with a new kind of oligarchic [global] capitalism" that legalizes violence to protect property and the wealthy against the threat of enemies, "defined in local laws as 'Negroes,' 'Mulattos,' and/or 'Indians.'" Hence, contemporary media and film address two notions of public: one inside (citizens) and one outside ("the struggling coloreds who constitute the global majority"). Carr argues that competing definitions of the state as either "(a) a sovereign body responsible for the welfare of the population living within its borders; or (b) a sovereign body expanding the economy . . . has been resolved in terms of the latter," and that globalization has meant the impoverishment of the people.

In Michael Clark's essay on Haiti, "Twenty Preliminary Propositions for a Critical History of International Statecraft in Haiti," he attempts to interrogate the discipline of "political science" from the disposition of subaltern studies. He also undertakes a radical critique of the discourses of modernization, development, and democratization, studying their displacement in the new project of "postconflict peace building." Clark studies the 1994 international intervention in Haiti by the joint United Nations-Organization of American States International Civil Mission, which was celebrated by the international community as "an effort to support indigenous movements in the struggle for democratization." Its nominal purpose was to help reconstruct the political institutions of the Haitian national state and civil society. Clark argues that the state does not stand apart from social relations; it is not a thing within a structure, governing that very structure but escaping structurality, but a pervasive social field constructed in and through discursive practices. The nature of the state is always international. The outside world is an active and continuous presence trying "to impose its will through an endless variety of modalities — repeated invasion, embargo, indemnity, denigration." Thus, in Haiti, the venality of public officials cannot be understood as "an unbroken chain of bad people, bad policies, and bad luck," but as the ability of tyrants and criminals to comprehend, use, and manipulate existing legal structures and state resources to serve their own needs. In Haiti, poverty, underdevelopment, and ignorance are the products of a strategy of a double articulation of governance that began with the blockade of the Haitian revolution and that has been sustained for two centuries. Haitian ungovernability — that is, precisely the "disorder" of civil society that UN-OAS intervention was intended to correct — can be seen as "a heroic refusal to be overwhelmed," "a protracted struggle to persevere in the struggle for liberty against tremendous natural and human opposition."

Gareth Williams's essay, "*Death in the Andes:* Ungovernability and the Birth of Tragedy in Peru," is a critical approach to what he calls "Creole rationality." Within the panorama of neoliberalism, the Latin American state is disinterested in social and national integration and dedicates its energies to maintaining the marketplace. Williams believes that the intellectual task now is "to engage in an affirmative deconstruction of the epistemological and political limits of neoliberal cultural politics and state practices." Using Mario Vargas Llosa's novel *Lituma en los Andes* (*Death in the Andes*) to examine the question of "agency and cognitive failure and hegemonic inability to reflect upon a zone of epistemic breakdown that nevertheless remains foundational to the successful application of neoliberal thought." *Manchay tiempo,* the "time of fear" invoked by Vargas Llosa, is pivotal to construction of his critique because it refers to the subaltern knowledge of the loss of state legitimacy and the breakdown of the myth of cohesion and unity promoted by the post(neo)colonial Republican state. In Vargas Llosa, says Williams, this is when Peru got "fucked up." He lists the erosion in terms of mass labor, shantytown mobilization, foreign debt, hyperinflation, corruption, guerrilla warfare, and narcotrafficking. The migration of the rural masses to the city gives rise to new identity formation; the hybrid *cholo,* an "outsider within," becomes the new social actor that makes the system fall apart.

An important point argued by Williams is the nature of José Carlos Mariátegui's intervention, in which the figure of the Indian is viewed "as a modernizing revolutionary force." The Indian proletariat was to give Peru its "life-affirming revolutionary spirit." This spirit now inhabits Mario Vargas Llosa's reading of manchay tiempo, the "Andean nether world and the indigenous system of belief, or 'cosmo vision,' that structures the cultural landscape." This world is the "lost object of Creole reason . . . namely the *apus, huancas, chancas, pishtacos* and *nacaqs.*" The struggle of the Dionysian and the Apollonian, reminiscent of Nietzsche's influence on Mariátegui, is in Vargas Llosa the opposite—namely, it is not the "underlying spirit of the Peruvian social classes, but rather the Indians' apparently barbaric relationship to enjoyment" that turns the Creole world upside down and constitutes "an oppositional or subversive relationship with historically constituted hierarchies."

Javier Sanjinés's essay, "Outside In and Inside Out: Visualizing Society in Bolivia," reviews the work of social scientists based on macrodiscursive models of modernization, development, and state formation. He contrasts this with the work of Silvia Rivera Cusicanqui, William Carter, and Javier Albó on "rotating democratic organization." Like them, Sanjinés is interested in "the collision between the concepts of citizenship and ethnicity, and the interaction between modern and premodern categories of thought." In agreement with López's idea of pleasure as a modality of subaltern agency, Sanjinés's positioning of the popular subaltern foregrounds new social movements and their new aesthetics, which are linked not to European or Latin American modernist high art but to the "antistructural" nature of social marginality that erases the center/periphery dichotomy. For the social scientists, governability "relies heavily on the modernization of the political party system," but for communally-oriented intellectuals such as Albó and Rivera, it must be studied in relation to the incomplete modernity of the Bolivian state. Modern citizenship, he argues, is predicated on individual performance and self-determination, at odds with ethnic and cultural commonalities; modernity does not erase subaltern visceral rebelliousness tied to the "long memory" of communal traditions and ethnic pasts. The nation-state is alien to the ideology of community. It undermines the autonomy of the *ayllus* (the smallest unit of social and territorial organization under Inca rule), and denies their territoriality as a jurisdictional space for political representation. Modern citizenship cannot be conceived independent of the centrally administered nation-state disciplined by the rule of law, which lays the foundation for ethnic and cultural homogeneity.

Part 5 continues to analyze the category of citizenship. Marcelo Bergman and Mónica Szurmuk argue in their essay that one cannot expect the nation-state to proffer its promised benefits of citizenship in the form of civil and social rights and services. Neither can it be expected to "channel [social] pressures via deliverable laws, and to then act under the guidelines of those laws." Latin American nation-states can be conceived as functioning within the logic of discipline and coercion (or authoritarian hegemony). The popular democratic national subjects—*cholas, chinitas,* indigenes, rural migrants, *gauchos, jíbaros, turbas*—are theorized as the community. The history of subalterns is then read in any and all other cultural texts, such as the microdiscourses that organize everyday life: households, hygiene habits, clothing styles, foods, and preparations for holidays. The proposition is that only the culture of the everyday—in interaction with popular, industrial, and elite cultures—can express diversity.

The essays in this last section also focus on production of legislation in disciplining the social body. Citizenship is constituted through discipline and coercion, through the mediation of political and pedagogical institutions in charge of changing the habits and customs of urban populations through the correct use of words. These acts of cleansing—often involving submitting popular cultures to criticism through ridicule, derision, and mockery—ensure the viability of the modernizing project. Disciplinary texts are the foundational narratives of the modern. The desired model of civilization demanded by the new urban space is, according to Beatriz González Stephan, predicated on compliance with behavioral rules as yet unknown to illiterate users, whose unrestrained habits must be inhibited: no more hooting, urinating, defecating, or farting in the public space, which demands silence and a sensibility that looks down on the public expression of intimacy and manifests phobias against dirt, disease, and bodily contact.

González's essay, "The Teaching Machine for the Wild Citizen," shows how nineteenth-century programs of compulsory hygiene were combined with a severe and contained morality supported by advances in medicine and biology and aided by grammar. A general hygienic attitude toward bodies and souls is expressed in language. Good habits and health are plotted as the flip side of the struggle against illness and dirt, the physical deterioration of social space, the indeterminacy of vernacular Spanish, the vagrancy of migrant workers, and criminality. González argues that this conjunction shows the workings of a new ethic based on commercial values, which seeks to redirect social energies toward production of profit. González establishes the link between bodies, language, and archives as legality and constitutions constitute them. The anxiety about cleanliness ties legality to culture in manuals of good conduct, grammar books like Andrés Bello's, and "Bibles, hagiographies, almanacs, brochures, and perhaps a book on national history." This "body" or canon of writing comes to form a body of politics policing the human body and, at the same time, the new bibliographies of Latin American studies. Cleanliness, the purging from language of "indecent words," the control of body functions, and circumscription to enclosed spaces are all equated with citizenship. The boundaries established for the body and speech acts measure the boundaries of governability.

In my essay, "Apprenticeship as Citizenship and Governability," I study the tension between masters and slaves, which is exacerbated by the effects of soil deterioration on local agricultural production, the end of British protectionism, and the nature of the slave trade itself. The habits and customs of the subaltern, whose sense of identity and positionality are in transition between slave and free laborer, become strained. Habit and habitat are conflated, and travel literature plays the same role of disciplining the people that grammar, hygiene, and behavioral manuals play in González's work. The difference is that English etiquette is more indirect, carried out through mockery and ridicule. Culture (that is, local culture, or the absence of propriety and/or conscience) is represented through the comic and the picturesque. The picturesque is that physical space in which the magnificence of the natural landscapes, narrated by Christopher Columbus in the high mimetic language of the Bible, and in the nascent tropes of Golden Age literature as the enchanted gardens of Andalusia in April, has become soiled and disorganized by a popular subject. In painting, this space is reduced in size and represented in miniature. In nineteenth-century travel narratives and plantation diaries, this space is narrated as the world of the "barbaresque." The areas of everyday life, mainly those concerning services (lodging, washing of clothes, preparation of food) and public festivities, are submitted to severe scrutiny and harsh criticism. Free blacks engaged in laissez-faire practices are chastised or sneered at. The discussion on freedom as problematic citizenship is collapsed into the discussion of land tenure systems, soil deterioration, and labor. Thus, the literature of travelers and commissioners to the "islands" is the predecessor of "scientific" narratives of research and development. Freedom for the slaves underscores the double disarticulation of national and popular-front politics. Ungovernability, as mobocracy, is "a cultural behavior that does not conform or submit to the norms"; it is, to paraphrase Spivak, "the place where history is narrativized into culture." It is also the moment of cognitive failure, an area that escapes the control of dominant hermeneutics and hence represents an epistemological break. The essay looks for those narrative spaces where "the object of contemplation and understanding renders itself ambiguous to [the master's] gaze." In "disorder" and transgression (in [un]discipline), what is at stake is decolonization, "the possibilities of breaking colonial patterns by contradicting — however mildly, however incompletely, and however topically — the presuppositions of a relationship that are not necessarily unwavering."

In the same vein, Marcia Stephenson studies the space of the house (and the figure of woman and mother) as the troping of state power. In "The Architectural Relationship between Gender, Race, and the Bolivian State," home or the domestic space "constitutes the fundamental core of womanhood." Womanhood and motherhood are "inextricably linked to the socio-spatial arena that is the home." She then links the domestic regime (and the space of the house) to the political regime through the *testimonio* of a domestic worker, Ana María Condori. Condori's work illustrates the ideology of home and family, of the familiar unfamiliar. The crossing of thresholds reveals the relation between property and propriety, which divides people across ethnic lines and perpetuates the subjugation of ethnicities. The distribution of space inside the house is a useful tool to read the relationships "between governability, citizenship, and discourses of modernity in the context of Bolivia." The house is a spatial manifold in which the "unruly play of representations" can be disciplined or domesticated. The house defines the limits between outside (the racially heterogeneous) and inside as a metaphor of the modern/civilized and the uncivilized. "'Normative' houses domesticate individual bodies and families, forcibly bringing them into the realm of the familiar." The "normative" house represents the *criollo* elite order, which Stephenson indicts: "The practices of enclosure are made viable through hegemonic discourses of modernity and citizenship. The underlying architectural rhetoric of the house, in conjunction with the image of the Western white mother depicted as inhabiting this idealized space, functions as the organizing principle of modernity." Criollos re-create identity through the state; Stephenson's wish to delink civilization from the positivist rhetoric that equates participation in the liberal market system with citizenship. Through specific forms of constructing houses, the state constitutes itself and reproduces a tradition that oppresses women and ethnicities.

In "Gender, Citizenship, and Social Protest: The New Social Movements in

Argentina," Bergman and Szurmuk describe the body of an Argentinean woman (a *chinita* — a pejorative expression for a lower-class nonwhite woman) who is raped and discarded, her body polluted by drugs injected after her death, as an example of state abuse that triggers new forms of protest along the lines of the Mothers of the Plaza de Mayo. *El caso María Soledad* and the Marches of Silence it gave rise to question the capacity of local government to deal with social conflict, which sought to supersede that local government when it failed to react. This case is presented as a new social movement in which subalterns struggle for citizenship and demand not only the protection of the law but the accountability of those in power. The narrative of this crime transcended the local papers. The trial of the culprits was nationally televised, and a mistrial was declared "when every single provincial judge was declared incompetent to preside . . . due to suspicious connections to the indicted." In this way, the case of *la chinita,* who "smells of fish," contested the relationship between government and the people, establishing democracy as the only game in town. Martha Pelloni, a charismatic Catholic leader who organized the marches — which grew from 7,000 to 30,000 in a city of 122,000 people — referred to the victim as *la nena* or "Sole." María Soledad's image became that of a teenager who, despite any mistakes she might have made, deserved equal protection under the law and respectful treatment as a citizen. The authors argue that peripheral groups feel entitled to unmet rights; "their struggle represents the counterpart to the state's weakness." Cases such as that of María Soledad "are neither prodemocratic nor antidemocratic, but clearly prorights." They represent the new challenges of new social actors to weak states, and the mobilization of civil society and their new agendas and strategies of resistance attempting to disturb traditional patterns of social control. They are the heirs to the tradition of the Mothers of Plaza de Mayo. Bergman and Szurmuk thus show how a crime becomes a political event, and how self-defense and solidarity press community into justice.

Finally, Josefina Saldaña-Portillo's work, "Who's the Indian in Aztlán? Re-Writing Mestizaje, Indianism, and Chicanismo from the Lacandón," is concerned with the discourses of development and globalization as they interpellate immigrants to the United States from Central America and southern Mexico. Her purpose is to expose the logic of developmentalism. She is interested in the critique of mestizaje and *indigenismo* as the basis for an identity. She argues that in Mexico, citizenship rights and democratic representation involve the concept of mestizaje, which has helped to construct not only the "national" Mexican identity but that of Chicano migrants as well. Her recognition that mestizaje has had moments of radical appropriation throughout the Americas compels her to reconsider the transnational deployment of mestizaje as it intersects the Mexican and Chicano/a indigenous identities. Her thesis is that in mestizaje there is an inherent developmentalism, which in turn is inviable as a model of citizenship: "Mestizaje has served as the biological metaphor for the corporativist government policies of the Institutional Revolutionary Party (PRI), policies that held sway in the country from the establishment of corporativism." The uncritical appropriation of mestizaje by Chicanos/as presumes access to indigenous identity, a tenuous claim of kinship with indigenous populations on both sides of the border. In the works of Gloria Anzaldúa and Richard Rodríguez, she finds a move "toward a more postmodern and politically viable model of Chicano/a identity, albeit they continue to rely on a biologistic interpretation of mestizaje for easy access to 'the Indian within.' "

Zapatismo, she argues, is not an "Indianist movement," although most of its supporters are indigenous peoples. What kind of movement is it then? Saldaña argues that it is a national type of movement defending its supporters' rights as citizens and refusing biological definitions because both indigenismo and mestizaje have proven damaging. One of the important points in Saldaña's essay is her underscoring of the use of technology within social movements that are called premodern but which are indeed modern, and even postmodern, to the degree that they occur within the space of the economic strategies of the neoliberal world order in the NAFTA period. She also makes the point that the Zapatistas' claim is derived not from a position of ethnicity but of citizenship.

In the concluding essay, Walter D. Mignolo brings up the differences between two moments of what he calls the coloniality of power. One of these moments refers to time, the other to space. In turn, they mark the difference between discussing the subaltern project from the position of temporality and modernity, as it has been discussed by modernism and postmodernism, or discussing it from the position of space, as it has been discussed by colonialism and postcolonialism. While the former belongs to the industrial moment of capitalism, the latter belongs to its mercantile stage. These two moments come to explain why the South Asian project is marked by two hundred years of solitude, whereas the Latin American project is marked by five hundred years of solitude.

The time-space distinction also marks the domains in which South Asian and Latin American scholars have contributed to the polemic on subalternities produced by the coloniality of power. Among the distinctions, we can take into account those mentioned above as well as the longer temporal path trodden by Latin America. Space is also important to signal the creation of identities such as those of Indian, Creole, and black as variants of the native that do not exist in the Asian context. Perhaps the notion of caste represents such a division. Tied to this question is the idea of internal colonialism.

The theoretical matrix that articulates these conditions of subalternity, based on domination without hegemony, places us in front of two nondialogical epistemologies marking the divide between two different types of knowledge, one elite and the other subaltern. It is only from the position of the subaltern that hegemony and subordination can be understood. This type of double vision opens up the possibilities of taking people out of their position as victims and Calibans and locating them within the struggle for meaning and the production of knowledge. Mignolo's strategy is to take us back into our own field to retrieve the Latin American discussion on colonialism, dependency theory, and world-systems. From there we can come back to renegotiate theories that, produced by peripheral scholars, come to constitute a kind of subaltern knowledge. This knowledge, with its double take or vision, incorporates, as Mignolo puts it, the concepts of modernist improvement and those of *danda* (punishment by law), two idioms central to the notion of both foreign and indigenous domination.

In this volume, citizenship and ungovernability are indissolubly tied to subaltern positions and positionings. The essays address a wide variety of issues, from the theoretical dilemmas of subaltern and cultural studies, to theories of modernity, to indigenism, Creolism, and mestizaje; from the elite philosophies of hygiene to the carnal and skeletal metaphors used by contemporary social theory, to food, sexuality, and consumption as new ways of organizing societies. One intent of this volume is to see how subalterns live, enjoy life, and organize despite all of the efforts to negate their being. The focus of the volume is, on one hand, the problem of representation, and on the other, what Jesús Martín Barbero would reveal as the desire for recognition. The question is, are we moving away from the politics of representation to those of recognition? That is one inquiry we wish to raise in this volume and with it, to open a debate within the Latin American field. One final word on María Milagros López. She was very correct in thinking that the problem of governability was not a problem of the subaltern but a problem of the state; to this I must add the reverse, that all questions of citizenship are the unmet claims of subalterns.

The impulse behind this book comes out of the brief history of the Latin American Subaltern Studies group (dissolved in 2000) and both the achievements and the limitations of that history are deeply implicated in it. As I stated above, the group came into being in 1992 at a meeting at George Mason University near Washington, D.C. About a dozen or so people participated, most of whom knew personally at least one or more of the other participants. We adapted from the project of South Asian Subaltern Studies not only the idea of subaltern studies as such, but also the organizational model of a small, interdisciplinary academic "affinity group" that would meet together to discuss each others' work and to plan a publication series similar to *Subaltern Studies*. But as the work of the group began to attract more attention, both favorable and negative, in the mid-1990s, it became increasingly difficult to maintain that model.

As this collection demonstrates, many different agendas, some complementary, some competing, crossed the space of the group. We thought and still think of that heterogeneity as a kind of advantage, because it deflected us from the disciplinary or epistemological monism of our own individual projects, always a danger in academic life. We saw the group as representing a kind of unity in difference, and we found that in working together collectively, the impact of what we were doing was more than simply the sum of our individual projects.

At the same time, however, precisely because of that impact, we began to be taken as representing or claiming to represent the implications of subaltern studies for Latin American studies. On one hand, we attracted the interest of scholars who wanted to affiliate themselves with the group, and on the other hand, we increasingly came under attack (sometimes from competing models of what Latin American subaltern studies should be, sometimes from critics hostile to or skeptical about the idea of "traveling theory"). We never thought of ourselves as more than a small part of a much larger paradigm shift taking place around the issue of the subaltern in Latin American studies — and elsewhere, but we came to embody the project as a whole.

The last meeting of the Latin American Subaltern Studies on "Cross Genealogies and Subaltern Knowledges" took place at Duke University and was organized by Walter Mignolo and Alberto Moreiras. After that, the Group as a whole never reconvened again, and although many attempts were made to find a new organizational form that would accommodate the new directions (some members subsequently met at Rice University), all of them were unsuccessful. Two years later, in November 2000, Gayatri Spivak organized a conference at Columbia University around the presence of Ranajit Guha, the founder of the South Asian Subaltern Studies group, bringing together some members of the South Asian group and the Latin American group, together with scholars representing the implications of subaltern studies for other disciplines (including African studies and Near Eastern studies). The title of the conference was "Subaltern Studies at Large," suggesting, among other things, that the project of subaltern studies had begun to escape its former area studies boundaries. One of those boundaries was perhaps the form of the Latin American Subaltern Studies group itself, so it is appropriate to use that event to mark the formal end of the historical group. There is a sadness in this as in all endings, but also a hope: that the work of subaltern studies is indeed, now, as Spivak's title signaled, "at large."

Notes

1 Florencia Mallon, "The Promise and Dilemma of Subaltern Studies: Perspectives from Latin American History," *American Historical Review* 99 (1994): 1491–1515.

2 Coco Fusco, *English Is Broken Here: Notes on Cultural Fusion in the Americas* (New York: New Press, 1995).

3 Silvia Rivera Cusicanqui and Rossana Barragán, *Debates post coloniales: Una introducción a lost estudios de la subalternidad* (La Paz: Editorial Historias, 1997).

4 Hugo Achugar, "Leones, cazadores, e historiadores, a propósito de las políticas de la memoria y el conocimiento," *Revista Iberoamericana* 180 (1997): 379–387.

5 Mabel Moraña, "El boom del Subalterno," *Revista de Crítica Cultural* 14 (1997): 48–53.

6 Mabel Moraña, ed., *Nuevas Perspectivas desde/sobre América/Latina: El desatío de los estudios culturales.* (Santiago de Chile: Cuarto Propio, 2000).

7 Dipesh Chakrabarty, "Postcoloniality and the Artifice of History," in *The Post-Colonial Studies Reader,* ed. Bill Ashcroft, Gareth Griffiths, and Helen Tiffin (London: Routledge, 1995), 383–389.

8 Ranajit Guha, "Dominance without Hegemony and Its Historiography," *Selected Subaltern Studies VI* (London: Oxford University Press, 1989), 210–309.

9 Gayatri Chakravorty Spivak, *A Critique of Postcolonial Reason: Toward a History of the Vanishing Present* (Cambridge, Mass.: Harvard University Press, 1999).

10 "Full class agency . . . is not an ideological transformation of consciousness on the ground level, a desiring of identity of the agents and their interest. It is a contestatory replacement as well as an appropriation (a supplementation) of something that is 'artificial' to begin with. . . . [For Marx] the projects of class consciousness and of the transformation of consciousness are discontinuous issues" (Spivak, 278).

11 For Guha, hegemony stands for a condition of Dominance (D), such that, in the organic composition of the latter, Persuasion (P) outweighs Coercion (C). "Hegemony operates as a dynamic concept and keeps even the most persuasive structure of Dominance always and necessarily open to Resistance. At the same time, it avoids the Gramscian juxtaposition of domination and hegemony (a term sometimes used in the *Prison Notebooks* synonymously with leadership) as antinomies, which has, alas, provided too often a *theoretical pretext* for the fabrication of a liberal absurdity — the absurdity of the idea of an uncoercive state. Since hegemony . . . is a particular condition of D [dominance] and the latter is constituted by C [coercion] and P [persuasion], it follows that there can be no hegemonic system under which P [persuasion] outweighs C [coercion] to the point of reducing it to nullity. Were that to happen, there would be no Dominance, hence no hegemony. In short, hegemony, deduced thus from Dominance, offers us the double advantage of pre-emptying a slide towards a liberal-utopian conceptualization of the state or representing power as a concrete historical relation informed necessarily and irreducibly both by force and by consent" Ranajit Guha, "Discipline and Mobilize." In *Dominance without Hegemony: History and Power in Colonial India* (Cambridge, Mass.: Harvard University Press, 1997). 100–151.

12 Julio Ramos, *Desencuentros de la modernidad en América Latina: Literatura y política en el siglo XIX* (México: Fondo de Cultura, 1989); Beatriz Sarlo, *Escenas de la vida posmoderna: Intelectuales, auge, y videocultura en la Argentina* (Buenos Aires: Espasa Calpe, 1997); Roberto Schwartz, *Ao Vencedor as Batatas* (São Paulo: Livraria Duas Cidades, 1992).

13 Andre Gunder Frank, *Capitalism and Underdevelopment in Latin America: Historical Studies of Chile and Brazil* (New York: Monthly Review Press, 1967).

14 Néstor García Canclini, *Hybrid Cultures: Strategies for Entering and Leaving Modernity* (Minneapolis: University of Minnesota Press, 1995).

15 Spivak, op. cit.

16 Ranajit Guha, *Elementary Aspects of Peasant Insurgency in Colonial India* (Delhi: Oxford University Press, 1992).

I. CONVERGENCE OF TIMES: SUBALTERN STUDIES — SOUTH ASIA/LATIN AMERICA, MODERN/POSTMODERN

Subaltern Studies: Projects for Our Time and Their Convergence

RANAJIT GUHA

When the first volume of *Subaltern Studies,* the journal named after our project, was published in 1982 in Delhi, we did not count on any readership abroad. For throughout the long period of colonial rule we were always represented by the colonizers, and it is through them — their academics and other intellectuals, their publications and other media — that the West had come to know about us. The fact that the colonized in the subcontinent had been writing about themselves not only in their own languages but also in English since the beginning of the nineteenth century made little difference, and the legacy of that alien representation seemed destined to continue even after decolonization. We had accepted this as a sort of fate. It was therefore with a degree of genuine surprise and delight that I came to learn of the interest taken in our work by scholars concerned with Latin American studies in Latin America and the United States. Some of them have done our project a singular honor by allowing it to take its place alongside theirs under a common designation. It is gestures like these which, more than anything else, make it possible for us to break out of our containment in two hundred years of solitude. I am deeply moved and dedicate this essay to my colleagues of the Latin American Subaltern Studies Group as a token of our solidarity.[1]

Our project, Subaltern Studies, had its genesis in the South Asian experience. Informed by the immediacy and urgency of the subcontinent's political and social conditions, it identifies itself by such names, thematizes itself according to such problems, chronicles itself in terms of such events, and expresses itself in sentiments that are all unmistakably South Asian. This may, of course, make one wonder whether it is at all possible to make something so area-specific comprehensible to those who do not belong there. Doesn't the very concreteness of its regionality make this project useless to scholars, such as Latin Americanists, with no specialized interest in that part of the world? The answer, I think, is no. For it is not territoriality that relates our project to theirs in a bond of mutual relevance, but temporality.

Our project belongs to our time. It made its debut at a time of turbulence marked by the difficulties facing India's new nation-state, by acute civil disturbances that occasionally threatened to tear it apart, by a common anxiety in which the frustration of the "Midnight's Children," those born since independence, blended with the disillusionment of older generations to produce an explosive discontent. One could go on adding to this list, but what is curious about it is that not one of its items has only local time as its referent. In each instance, a "when" assigned to it within the Indian experience has a corresponding "when" in a global register in which phenomena of longer duration designated as eras and ages (e.g., the age of superpower rivalry or the electronic era) have been contemporaneous with a countless number of relatively short-term events, ranging from the Cuban missile crisis and the Vietnam war to fluctuations in world commodity prices and race riots in Britain. In other words, our time in the Subaltern Studies project concerned with South Asia is one that has been thoroughly overdetermined by global temporalities.

This is also true for the time of the Latin American Subaltern Studies project, a time it can legitimately be called "our time," as witness the periodization that provides the group's formation with a historical background in its founding statement, and the observation in the introduction to the anthology, *Subaltern Studies in the Americas* that connects "the specific nature of [that] project" to "such historical and geographic determinants as the so-called demise of socialism after the fall of the Berlin Wall in 1989 and the loss of the elections by the Sandinistas in Nicaragua in 1990."[2]

Such a collapsing of local and global times — the time of the Naxalbari uprising in India and that of the Cultural Revolution in China, the time of the Nicaraguan elections and that of the fall of the Berlin Wall — is of course one of the most salient features of capital's "self-realization process" (*Selbstverwertungsprozess*), in the course of which it strives to annihilate space with time, as Marx has argued.[3] Since this process underlies all that has gone into the making of the modern age as the age of capital, its intensification in our time is designated, justifiably, as the condition of postmodernity in much the same way as an aggravated phase sometimes acquires a special name in the diagnosis of a prolonged illness. This goes to show, among other things, that the phenomenon of postmodernity stands no less for a movement of capital than for a movement of ideas.

It is in this overarching temporality that "our time," with all its South Asian specifications, intersects with a distinctively Latin American "our time." And since comparison between any two terms requires a third term in which both can be expressed, we have in this particular phase of global temporality — call it postmodernity, if you like — the ground that should suffice to compare these projects. However, before proceeding any further in this direction, it may be worthwhile to pause for a moment and consider whether the significance of this intersection is best grasped by a comparative exercise, for the latter often tends to degenerate into a sort of contestatory evaluation that is as gratuitous as it is unhelpful for any genuine understanding of the entities compared.

In numerous instances, our humble project, with no claim at all to universal validity, has been summoned to stand trial by comparison and has been found wanting as measure or model for studies based on very different regional material. I have come to doubt the value of such an approach, which usually relies on the most slender trace of an analogy here, a touch of resemblance there, and a suggestion of parallelism in yet another respect to produce, at best, what Wittgenstein has called the "experience of comparison," indicating that one is only "inclined towards a comparison," that one is inclined "to make a paraphrase."[4] There is nothing wrong with such an inclination in itself; however, it is not the same thing as a comparison that combines with reflection and abstraction to generate concepts in the process of understanding.[5] Yet this is not always kept in mind. On the contrary, superficial inclination is too readily accorded the status of conceptualization, allowing it to sit in judgment over works concerned with widely disparate phenomena before thinking its way through to the ground where these may be brought together for a proper consideration of what is unique about each of them and what they share.

That ground, as we have already observed, is nothing other than an overarching temporality subsuming local times. We shall try to approach it not in a spirit of comparison and competition, but of convergence. To converge is to meet in a point as lines do in a figure, or to approximate as numbers do in a mathematical series, toward a given limit. Generally speaking, it is one thing to incline toward another in a specified direction and approach it closely enough to verge on it. There is nothing in these meanings shown for the phrase in the *Concise Oxford Dictionary* to impute to it any presupposition of similarity or to tie it to the notion of parity, as in comparison. For tendencies can be dissimilar and unequal in important respects and yet share an orientation toward some horizon each can recognize as its own. What is of crucial significance here is the dynamics of "towardness," with its characteristic movements of inclining, approaching, and approximating. It is these that make it possible for drives, initiatives, and ideas to coalesce without any of them compromising the identity and originality of the projects to which they belong. There is room enough in such coalescence for all such tendencies to come alongside each other and let their borders touch in a lateral solidarity. None of these has to race against any of the others. As neighbors they are free to look over the fence, inspect each other's gardens, engage in mutual criticism, and do so, as it befits good neighbors, without mutual antagonism.

Indeed, criticism anchored in convergence will find all the strength it needs to overcome the petty jealousies and rancor that so often usurp its place in academic discussion.

However, for any such solidarity to take effect in a convergence, it is essential that the ground for the latter is clearly delimited. How is that to be done? There is no single formula to guide all tendencies in dealing with that task in a uniform manner for they differ in their formulations, inclinations, and paths to convergence. I see the delimiting done for our project by all those considerations that the Latin Americanists and other scholars have brought to bear on our writings, which is to acknowledge straightaway that convergence relies on reciprocity as the very condition of its possibility.

It is the interest taken in our work on South Asia by intellectuals engaged in the study of other regions and within other tendencies which alone enables us to reach out to them. All their questions addressed to us, all expressions of doubt or approval, all suggestions including even those which signal nothing more than the merest "experience of comparison," are indeed so many points where their concerns touch ours. To join up those points of contact in an outline, however irregular, broken and roughly sketched, would be to map out a space for all ways of thinking on the problem of subalternity to gather in a congress of critical exchange. That would make a rather large map no doubt judging by the range and volume of discussions on Subaltern Studies amongst the Latin Americanists alone, not counting the numerous interventions made by other regional specialists. I can't chart all that extensive territory in a talk of this length and must be selective in my exploration of the delimited ground visiting, on this occasion, only a few of its many interesting sites. I make no claim however for my itinerary as either the best or the only possible one.

Let us start with postmodernism. I choose this rather than any other as my point of departure not only because our project has been drawn into some of the recent debates among Latin Americanists themselves on this problem, but also because of its timeliness. For one thing, it highlights the intersection of our time with theirs. Furthermore, the question "What is postmodernism?" is timely in much the same way as was that other question "What is enlightenment?" asked over two centuries ago. That, too, was asked from within its own time as the articulation of an actuality, of a present, a "now" to which the philosopher, its contemporary, related as if to a predicament and was driven by his doubts to inquire, "What is it that we call enlightenment? Where does it come from and where is it taking us?"

The contemporaneity of Kant's essay "An Answer to the Question, 'What is Enlightenment?,'" is fairly well documented in all its circumstantial aspects. It was a partisan intervention published in *Berlinische Monatsschrift,* the principal organ of the Berlin school of enlightenment philosophy with which he had allied himself. Joining the battle of ideas against political and intellectual reaction in Prussia, "he had gathered up all the threads clustering around the name of this party" in this article, says Ernst Cassirer, "and endeavoured to define their one most integrating tendency," namely, the conception of autonomy.[6]

This local battle of so long ago, and with so provincial an air about it, would have mattered little to us had it not been for the fact that its challenge, "Have courage to use your own reason," has not spent its force even today. To the contrary, it appears to have gained not merely in urgency but also in complexity and scope. Of the many different aspects of its continued importance, at least one bears directly on our present discussion.

This aspect concerns the question of autonomy, that is, what Kant calls "man's release from his self-incurred tutelage" so that he can "make use of his understanding without direction from another."[7] Insofar as such direction had traditionally been the prerogative of institutional or individual authorities exercised in the name of an age-old wisdom, to rebel against it would be to assert the primacy of the present as a time reclaimed from its assimilation to tutelary pasts and made entirely one's own. The moment of such self-assertion, with humanity proclaiming the autonomy of reason, would be the moment of the critique, as Foucault observes in a brilliant reading of this text.[8] For it was only a critique that could define the legitimate use of reason. "The critique is, in a sense, the handbook of reason that had grown up in Enlightenment; and, conversely, the Enlightenment is the age of the critique" (Foucault, 38). He echoes in these words Kant's own characterization of his time in his preface to the first edition of the *Critique of Pure Reason,* "Our age is, in special degree, the age of criticism, and to criticism everything must submit."[9]

What, from our point of view, is important about that critique is its function as a paradox. It heralds the advent of reason and upholds its sovereignty, and yet ends up by defining the limits of the latter. This is nowhere more obvious than in the philosopher's own attempt to reconcile the freedom of political argument with an unquestioning obedience to the enlightened despot, Frederick II of Prussia — an ingenuity described by Foucault as "a sort of contract . . . the contract of rational despotism with free reason" (Foucault, 37). The irony of this compromise does not lie in the contingencies of political tact alone. It arises out of an iron necessity for reason to have its universalist drive curbed by history — a point that seems not to have received the emphasis it merits in Foucault's overly actualist reading of the text.[10] He sees reason hurtling against insuperable limits ever since its formation, but does not push the limit attitude to the point where the notion of progress itself comes under question. For it is precisely there that human progress "must be connected to some experience," according to Kant, in much the same way that a certain outcome can be "predicted in general as in the calculation of probability in games of chance," although "that prediction cannot enable us to know whether what is predicted is to happen in my life and I am to have the experience of it." Progress still retains its place in this perspective "as an inevitable consequence" but is left "undetermined with regard to time," that is, with regard to history, which as we know from *Logic,* is another name for experience.[11]

These ideas, elaborated by Kant in *The Conflict of the Faculties* (1798) were already anticipated in his 1784 article in the form of a cautionary statement: "If we are asked, 'Do we now live in an *enlightened age?,'* the answer is 'no,' but we do live in an *age of enlightenment.*"[12] Indeed, this gesture of a gaze turning away from the immediate present toward the still unexplored vistas of time helps us to grasp the significance of the copula in the question "What is enlightenment?" For the "is" has for its referent here, one can say, following Heidegger, "not only the currently actual, which affects us and which we stumble upon." It refers also to "the possible, which we expect, hope for, and fear, which we only anticipate, before which we recoil and yet do not let go."[13] With actuality projected thus on a horizon of possibility, that historic question would serve no purpose merely as a cue to some well-rehearsed apology for reason. On the contrary, reason would henceforth have all its certainties invested by an unremitting anxiety, and Enlightenment, racked by self-doubt — a Pangloss haunted by an unhappy consciousness, would herald an epoch for a melancholy optimism characteristic of all that modernity was to stand for.

The encounter between reason and experience that provoked the Enlightenment's interrogation of itself is also what enables us to ask today, "What is postmodernism?" An echo of a sort, it is still by no means an exact reproduction. No echo ever is. For the interval that separates it from the original is also what reduces it to a mere fraction of the latter, constituting, thanks to Juno's curse, a rather different sound.[14] Our question, too, has become unmistakably our own by virtue of its deferral. It no doubt shares a distinctive ethos of criticism with its eighteenth-century forebear, but differs so utterly from the latter in manner and content that the fears expressed about its role as a secret agent of high modernism are perhaps grossly exaggerated.

Since the Enlightenment, in every serious contest with a critique that has belonged to its own time, it is the claim of pure reason that has taken a beating. Undetermined by the historicism of Herder in the study of the human past, by romanticism in aesthetics, by Marxism in political economy — to name only a few among a host of its younger adversaries — it has been pursued relentlessly since its inception by a critique that moves with time and corrodes it by the relativities of an inexhaustible and always rechargeable contemporaneity. If criticism has not amounted to a revolutionary challenge in every instance of such an engagement, it has still been unsettling enough to sustain and intensify the "constant revolutionizing of production, uninterrupted disturbance of all social conditions, everlasting uncertainty and agitation," which "distinguish the bourgeois epoch from all earlier ones," according to that other founding statement dated 1848.[15]

The importance of this reflection on the ontology of capital and the age named after it is hard to exaggerate, for it teaches us to valorize and cherish any critique whatsoever that contributes to this process of "constant revolutionizing," "uninterrupted disturbance," and "everlasting uncertainty." Whether such a critique is oriented or not toward a utopia of ultimate liberation, I do not see how it can be denied a place on the agenda for changing the world for those who still believe in doing so. It should therefore be radical enough for us if only because it does not allow reason to forget the pain of that historic carbuncle that, metaphorically speaking, could stimulate such thoughts even in an age of unquestioning faith in the inevitability of progress.

I am therefore quite happy to have postmodernism be the ground of our convergence. On that ground we—that is, projects called Subaltern Studies and others with different names but similar orientations—come together with concerns specific to our time. Our time is, in this context, the time of our being with others in the world. Insofar as the latter is local as well as global, to converge implies our being alongside others in an extended world and seeing ourselves in the light emitted by them. It is a light that illuminates differences between regional experiences no less than their agreements. Consequently, the specificity of each converging instance is spelled out in such cases as a narrative plotted in its own time, as witness the introduction to the special issue of *boundary 2* called *The Postmodernism Debate in Latin America* in which temporal markers of the Latin American engagement with postmodernism are displayed clearly enough to make it stand well apart from similar engagements, such as the Anglo-European and South Asian ones.

The latter is of course easily recognized by its temporality, designated as postcolonial. It indicates the path we have taken to the convergence. As part of that trajectory merges with postmodernism, but does so without losing its identity as one that has been trodden by a two-hundred-year-long colonial occupation. In what sense does that experience lead our project to take its stand alongside other postmodernist critiques? For an answer, one could consider that experience in the light of three salient aspects of modernity's intersection with colonialism that, stated briefly, are as follows: first, that the phenomenon of post-Enlightenment colonialism is constitutive of and presupposed in modernity even if it is not always explicitly acknowledged to be so; second, that postmodernism as a critique can never be adequate to itself unless it takes colonialism into account as a historic barrier that reason can never cross; and third, that the colonial experience has outlived decolonization and continues to be related significantly to the concerns of our own time.

Of the numerous questions that could arise from the colonial experience connecting thus with modernity, one assumed a good deal of urgency for us in the 1970s. It was a question about the structure of politics under colonial rule, on which much had already been written during the raj and since Independence by nationalist and neocolonialist academics in India and abroad. The domain of politics was conceptualized in this vast literature invariably as one that was unitary and undifferentiated. All schools of thought appeared to have been bound by a tacit agreement on this issue despite their differences on other matters as colonialists, nationalists, Marxists, or whatever.

For our part, we came up with an answer radically opposed to the dominant view. The domain of politics in colonial India, we argued, was structurally split. To interpret it as homogeneous was elitist and unhistorical. As we said in an inaugural statement, "For parallel to the domain of elite politics, there existed throughout the colonial period another domain of Indian politics in which the principal actors were not the dominant groups of the indigenous society or the colonial authorities but the subaltern classes and groups constituting the mass of the labouring population and the intermediate strata in town and country—that is, the people. This was an *autonomous* domain, for it neither originated from elite politics nor did its existence depend on the latter."[16]

That insight has been of foundational importance for our project. Everything that distinguishes it from all other positions within South Asian studies follows from this thesis. It informs the entire range of our work in many different aspects of history, politics, and culture, much of which is, of course, regionally specific. However, such regionality does not take away from the relevance of that thesis for a more general postmodernist critique, which is where we join other projects and tendencies. On the contrary, it helps to emphasize what is uniquely South Asian and postcolonial in our approach. This can be demonstrated by a review of the conditions that made it possible for the elite to be so blind toward the structural split in the domain of politics and regard the latter as unitary.

One of those conditions was based entirely on the idea that there was nothing to politics apart from what concerned the state, and since all that concerned the colonial state in South Asia were the transactions between the colonial and indigenous elites, there was no politics other than elite politics. Defined in terms of this double exclusion—that is, the exclusion of whatever was nongovernmental and nonelite—from the realm of politics, the latter could indeed be considered as an integral and undifferentiated space. As such, it could serve as a secure, if narrow, base to an autocracy dependent entirely on the collaboration of a minority of dominant elements for its survival. Since the colonial regime in South Asia was in all important respects precisely such an autocracy, it had no use for a political domain that was structurally split.

However, the image that the raj liked to project of itself was far from that of a narrowly based autocracy. It claimed to rule by the consent of the subject population. The theme of loyalty was prominently displayed in all its official policies and institutions, and used as an exorcising mantra against the specter of nationalist opposition during the last fifty years or so of its career. Mountains have indeed been made of molehills of native collaboration in all kinds of colonial discourse ranging from the crude official propaganda of the First World War to the more sophisticated histories produced by neocolonialist scholars since the Second World War. The nonantagonistic relationship of colonizer and colonized presumed in such discourse requires the elitist view of power to postulate an integrated and unified politics, and to persist in its blindness toward the structural split in that domain.

It has been up to us, following the logic of our insight, to expose the hollowness of this presumption. We have traced the latter to its source in the colonial state's desire to model itself on the liberal bourgeois state of metropolitan Britain, the Mother of Parliaments, the world's first and foremost democracy. However, what, the raj, for all its emulation, ended up with was tawdry caricature. An autocracy eager to pass itself off as a rule of law, a state without citizenship trying unsuccessfully to legitimize itself by the approval of its disenfranchised subjects, a master craving desperately for the bondsman's love, the raj — with the moment of consent outweighed by that of coercion in the organic composition of its power — was a dominance without hegemony.[17]

The colonial state in South Asia, we have argued, stood thus for a historic failure of reason. There was nothing in its record to justify the latter's promise of a steady progress toward the happiness of all humankind. Neither capital nor liberalism, the twin engines of reason, proved powerful enough to overcome local resistance in the subcontinent's indigenous economy and culture. Colonialism in South Asia therefore gives the lie to the universalist pretensions of reason. This, I believe, is the essence of a postcolonial critique as it developed in our work. It goes to show how that critique overflows the boundaries of mere regional experience to converge with all the other currents of postcolonial and postmodern thinking on the question, "What is Enlightenment?"

We have effectively adapted that question for our own time by dropping the sign of interrogation and setting it up as an affirmative sedimented by two hundred years of doubt and ready for translation into a new interrogative, "What is postmodernism?" as Lyotard has formulated it for us.[18] It confronts us today with a host of other questions that have been waiting until now to be asked. One of these, related directly to the postcolonial condition, must be heard at once: *How is our critique going to be adequate to our time if it continues to speak in the language of those post-Enlightenment critiques whose time is gone?*

Those critiques, too, had contested reason in their own different ways and had shown how reason had compromised its principles in its colonial project. The tolerance of autocracy in Europe's overseas empires in an age when new republics were replacing the older absolutist states nearer home; the narrowly Eurocentric character of her so-called civilizing missions operating in the other continents; the promotion of white supremacist ideas and practices by the Western imperial agencies in their colonies — blatantly contradicting the ideals of equality and fraternity professed, if not fully achieved, by the metropolitan governments — have all been cited again and again as evidence of the nonuniversality of reason in its career abroad. Indeed it was liberals firmly committed to reason themselves who were the first to join issue thus with reason, and they came from both sides of the colonial divide, from the colonizing as well as the subject nations — Tagore and Gandhi among the latter.

The range and power of that critique cannot be overestimated, yet as a critique of reason circumscribed by the statism inherent in reason itself its adequacy for our own time is far from clear. The state trusted by reason to serve as the vehicle for human progress is left unquestioned not only in the classical political philosophy of the Enlightenment, but even in the more interventionist of rationalist theories such as utilitarianism and socialism. The failure of colonialism to live up to that progressivist agenda has been interpreted even by the severest of liberal critics either as an instance of bureaucratic lapse remedied easily by measures of improvement and efficiency in the administration of the regimes concerned, or as just a case of colonizers being unreasonable in their opposition to the colonized peoples' demand for self-determination, which, once conceded, would solve all problems by converting colonial states into sovereign nation-states. The latter continue thus to inspire the same sort of faith as did that historic "Event of Our Time," Kant's name for the French Revolution when he celebrated it as the demonstration of a universal "moral tendency of the human race" (Kant, *Conflict,* 153), not only in its predisposition to hope for progress but also in its ability to achieve it.

That faith has lost the freshness of dawn by now and has curdled into a dogma. It takes the universality of reason in statehood for granted even where the latter is conspicuous for its contingency and particularity, as it was in India under British rule. The colonial state there did not arise out of the indigenous society but was foisted on it by conquest and condemned to live in utter isolation. A dominance without hegemony, it never succeeded in penetrating the civil society of the subject population deeply enough to absorb it to itself. Consequently, vast areas of the South Asian experience remained beyond the reach of governmental apparatus and the range of official vision. Yet such inaccessibility of society to state, which gave colonialism its distinctive character, failed to register in the discourse of reason either as a matter of fact or as a phenomenon to be apprehended by theory. This becomes obvious when one considers the writing of history as an instance of rationalist discourse par excellence. It would be no exaggeration to say that all the major tendencies of Indian historiography—colonialist, nationalist, and Marxist—have been seriously afflicted by statism, entrenched so well in the post-Enlightenment critique of reason. The primacy of the state in the histories they produced left no room in them for the complexity, diversity, and multitude of experience located within the still-unassimilated parts of civil society. The result has been to leave unheard myriad stories in the life of our people and to deny them the history to which they are fully entitled.[19]

Our project calls upon us to unshackle the critique of reason from its tutelage to statism. For no state, even the sovereign nation-state that was so dynamic two hundred years ago when the world was still young, can be trusted to act as an unstoppable engine of progress today. Indeed, the new states that emerged after the Second World War out of the old colonial empires under the rulership of indigenous elites have in most cases a long way to go before they can claim to have their dominance endowed with hegemony. They rely a great deal on the authority of elitist discourse and its philosophical, methodological, and narratological strategies to sustain and propagate the statist ideologies that they need to keep themselves in power. It is for us to stand up to that authority and enable the small and silenced voice of history—the subaltern voice—to be heard again. That is no mean challenge. The convergence of the South Asian and Latin American Subaltern Studies projects and other such initiatives gives me the courage to believe that the time for such a challenge has come.

Notes

1 This essay was originally presented as a lecture at a meeting of the Latin American Subaltern Studies Group at Rice University, Houston, Texas, October 1996.

2 José Rabasa, Javier Sanjinés, C., and Robert Carr, eds. *Subaltern Studies in the Americas,* special issue of *Dispositio/n* 46 (published in 1996), p. vi.

3 Karl Marx, *Grundrisse,* trans. Martin Nicolaus (Harmondsworth: Penguin Books, 1973), p. 539.

4 Ludwig Wittgenstein, *Remarks on the Philosophy of Psychology* (Oxford: Basil Blackwell, 1980), # 316, and generally # 316–20.

5   For the concept-forming functions of comparison, reflection, and abstraction, see Immanuel Kant, *Logic*, trans. Robert S. Harman and Wolfgang Schwartz (Indianapolis: Bobbs-Merrill, 1974), pp. 100–101.

6   Ernst Cassirer, *Kant's Life and Thought*, trans. James Haden (New Haven: Yale University Press, 1981), p. 367.

7   Immanuel Kant, "What is Enlightenment," p. 3. This and all other references to Kant's essay "An Answer to the Question: 'What is Enlightenment?'" are to its translated version published under the title "What is Enlightenment" in Immanuel Kant, *On History*, edited by Lewis White Beck (Indianapolis: Bobbs-Merrill, 1963), pp. 3–10.

8   Michel Foucault, "What is Enlightenment," in *The Foucault Reader*, ed. Paul Rabinow (Harmondsworth: Penguin, 1984), pp. 32–50.

9   Immanuel Kant, *Immanuel Kant's Critique of Pure Reason*, trans. Norman Kemp Smith (Houndmills: Macmillan, 1990), p. 9.

10 Foucault writes: "In the text on *Aufklärung* [Kant] deals with the question of contemporary reality alone. He is not seeking to understand the present on the basis of a totality or of a future achievement" (34).

11 See Kant, *Logic*, 78: "Empirical certainty is original (*originarie empirica*) as far as I am certain of something *from my own experience*, and *derivative* as far as I become certain of something through others' experience. The latter is also commonly called *historical* certainty."

12 Immanuel Kant, *The Conflict of the Faculties*, trans. Mary J. Gregor (Lincoln: University of Nebraska Press, 1992), p. 151.

13 Martin Heidegger, *Basic Concepts*, trans. Gary E. Aylesworth (Bloomington: Indiana University Press, 1993), p. 21.

14 John Sallis, *Echoes* (Bloomington: Indiana University Press, 1990), pp. 1–14.

15 Karl Marx and Frederick Engels, *Collected Works* (London: Lawrence and Wishart, 1976), vol. 6, p. 487.

16 Ranajit Guha ed., *Subaltern Studies I* (Delhi: Oxford University Press, 1982), p. 4.

17 Ranajit Guha, *Dominance without Hegemony: History and Power in Colonial India* (Cambridge, Mass.: Harvard University Press in 1997).

18 Jean-François Lyotard, "Answering the Question: What is Postmodernism?" In *The Postmodern Condition: A Report on Knowledge*, trans. Geoff Bennington and Brian Masumi (Manchester: Manchester University Press, 1987), pp. 71–82.

19 For some discussion on this question, see Ranajit Guha, "The Small Voice of History," *Subaltern Studies IX*, eds. Shahid Amin and Dipesh Chakrabarty (Delhi: Oxford University Press, 1996), pp. 1–12.

The Im/possibility of Politics: Subalternity, Modernity, Hegemony

JOHN BEVERLEY

One of the things that could be said to define postmodernity as such is the collapse of communism. Would it be possible, however, to reimagine the possibility of communism not only in the context of postmodernity but also in some sense *from* postmodernity? The question seems at once perverse and quixotic. Perverse because of everything we know about the Gulag, the crimes of Stalin and all the little Stalins, the killing fields of Cambodia, the constant stifling of expression and initiative even under conditions of what was known euphemistically as "socialist normality." Quixotic because of the simple, inescapable fact of the historical failure of a system that justified those crimes and that repression in the name of building a more egalitarian and democratic human future.

Most of us would agree that the regimes that have emerged as a result of the collapse of communism have been, on the whole, a mixed bag, with especially disastrous results in the cases of the former Soviet Union and Yugoslavia. This has provoked both within and outside the postcommunist world a nostalgia for at least the illusion of a golden age of post-World War II Stalinism, not unlike the nostalgia for the fifties in contemporary U.S. culture. But the restoration of regimes of a Stalinist type or the implantation of new ones (such as might have happened in Peru if Sendero Luminoso had prevailed), even if this were still in fact possible, would simply lead in time to the same impasse that the regimes of "actually existing socialism" experienced in the 1980s. This is because the seeds of that impasse were present in the very form of economic, political, and cultural centralization and modernization practiced by these regimes, which we may now recognize as a peculiar form of dictatorship of the bourgeoisie.

There are many good reasons to oppose the U.S. blockade of Cuba or to think that the Chinese model of *perestroika* is yielding better results than the Russian one. But no one—beginning with the Cubans and Chinese themselves—is going to claim that Cuba or China offer a compelling model of a new type of postcapitalist society. (Indeed, this loss of socialist normativity is precisely what the Cuban concept of "special period in times of emergency" expresses.) Instead, the strategic projection of the regimes in both countries is to use the Communist Party's monopoly of political and bureaucratic power to facilitate integration into globalization without the sort of meltdown that the Soviet Union and Yugoslavia experienced.

Paradoxically, a similar synergy between the Left and globalization also occurs with contemporary variants of social democracy, such as Tony Blair's New Labour in Britain or Renovated Socialism in Chile. Like Clinton, who is to some extent their model, they represent the reconfiguration of the various forms of the historical Left into what the late Michael Harrington, the main spokesperson of U.S. social democracy, called "the left wing of the possible." But that reconfiguration consists, in the end, in accepting the actual hegemony of globalized capital and its requirements for modernization.[1] They do not propose an alternative to that hegemony, but rather more-progressive ways of designing national or regional policy in relation to globalization. They do not have a vision of radically other forms of history, community, value, production, democracy — that is, of the possibility of another mode of production. They reproduce the traditional function of social democracy of adjusting blue- and white-collar working-class and middle-strata demands to the requirements of capital and vice versa.

We know that the projects of both historical communism and social democracy were subordinate in many ways to the project of modernity. Indeed, the argument between capitalism and communism that defined the Cold War could be seen as essentially an argument about which of the two could best carry forward the possibility of a political, scientific, cultural, and economic modernity latent in capitalism itself. The basic premise of Marxism as a modernizing ideology was that bourgeois society could not complete its own promise of emancipation and material well-being given the contradictions inherent in the capitalist mode of production — contradictions above all between the social character of the forces of production and the private character of ownership and capital accumulation. By freeing the forces of production from the fetters of capitalist relations of production, so the familiar argument went, the state socialist or quasi-socialist regimes inspired by the Soviet model would soon overcome these limitations, inaugurating an era of unprecedented economic growth which in turn would be the material precondition for socialism and eventually the transition to communism. The (ultimately triumphant) response of capitalism was that the force of the free market would be more dynamic and efficient in the long run in producing modernity and economic growth.

What was not in question on either side of this argument was the desirability of modernity as such and the idea of a teleological historical process (involving "stages" of one sort or another) necessary to attain that modernity. Modernity implies the possibility of a society that is (or that could become) transparent to itself. This is what Habermas's concept of communicative rationality expresses. What opposes transparency or the universalization of communicative rationality, however, is not only the conflict of tradition and modernity — that is, the incompleteness of modernity, to borrow Habermas's own phrase — but also the proliferation of forms of social heterogeneity and difference produced in part by the very process of capitalist modernity itself, involving as it does colonialism, slavery, genocide, demographic catastrophe, mass immigration, combined and uneven development, boom and bust cycles, the reproduction of sexism and racism, and so on.

But can one imagine the project of the Left as detached from a *telos* of modernity? How would such a project legitimize itself ideologically? What the concept of ungovernability expresses is the incommensurability between what Dipesh Chakrabarty calls the "radical heterogeneity" of subaltern social subjects and the "reason" of the modern nation-state. Ungovernability is therefore the space of resistance, opposition, and insurgency in globalization. But ungovernability also designates the failure of politics as such — that is, of hegemony. Gramsci writes in the *Prison Notebooks:* "The subaltern classes, by definition, are not unified and cannot unite until they are able to become a 'State'" (57). That aphorism is, of course, also a way of describing the project of communism, since it is the (necessary) function of the party to enable the subaltern to take state power. But if in order to gain hegemony the subaltern classes or groups have to become essentially like that which is already hegemonic — that is, modern bourgeois culture and the existing forms of the state — then the ruling class will continue to win, even in defeat. This paradox defines the crisis of the project of communism.

Subaltern studies is born directly out of that crisis.[2] It is not only a form of academic knowledge production, then; nor is its field of vision limited to the premodern. It is also a way of intervening in the present on the side of the subaltern. What is at stake in this intervention is a sense of the failure or limits of previous paradigms of intellectual and political radicalism, like communism, combined with the need and desire to continue the project of social liberation that those paradigms expressed, however inadequately. As such, subaltern studies exists in a tension between a project that is deconstructive of the claims of formal politics to represent the subaltern, and a constructive articulation of emergent and residual forms of political and cultural agency in the context of globalization. It entails both a critique of hegemony and the possibility of a new form of hegemony. What would be the point, after all, of representing the subaltern *as subaltern?*

Gramsci believed that hegemony is organized in civil society, but despite his own suggestion that "the history [of the subaltern classes] is intertwined with that of civil society" (52), the subaltern is not necessarily commensurate with civil society. That is because the idea of civil society in its usual sense (Hegel's *burgerlich Gesellschaft*— actually, that is, more bourgeois than civil) society is itself tied to a normative sense of modernity and a narrative of necessary "development" or "unfolding" (*Entwicklung*), which by virtue of its own requirements (formal education, literacy, nuclear family units, attention to party politics and business news, property or a stable income source) excludes significant sectors of the population from full citizenship or limits their access to citizenship. That exclusion or limitation is what constitutes the subaltern. It follows that what Chakrabarty calls the "politics of despair" of the contemporary subaltern is often driven by a resistance to or skepticism about modernity and "development."

What, then, is the relation between subalternity, modernity, and hegemony? Is hegemony itself a form of (capitalist) modernity, such that the project of subaltern studies must necessarily think of itself, deconstructively, as posthegemonic? And how does this question, in turn, bear on the prospects for renewing the project of the Left? What is at stake in these questions is the relationship between subalternity and the time of capital, as it is understood by Marxism. Chakrabarty formulates the problem in the following way:

> Subaltern histories written with an eye to difference cannot constitute yet another attempt, in the long and universalistic tradition of "socialist" histories, to help erect the subaltern as the subject of modern democracies, that is, to expand the history of the modern in such a way as to make it more representative of society as a whole. . . . Stories about how this or that group in Asia, Africa, or Latin America resisted the "penetration" of capitalism do not, in this sense, constitute "subaltern" history, for these narratives are predicated on imagining a space that is external to capital—the chronologically "before" of capital—but that is at the same time a part of a historicist, unitary time frame within which both the "before" and "after" of capitalist production can unfold. The "outside" I am thinking of is different from what is simply imagined as "before or after capital" in historicist prose. This "outside" I think of, after Derrida, as something attached to the category *capital* itself, something that straddles a border zone of temporality, something that conforms to the temporal code within which "capital" comes into being while violating that code at the same time, something we are able to see only because we can think/theorize capital, but something that also reminds us that other temporalities, other forms of worlding, coexist and are possible. . . . *Subaltern Studies,* as I think of it, can only situate itself theoretically at the

juncture where we give up neither Marx nor "difference," for, as I have said, the resistance it speaks of is something that can happen only *within* the time horizon of capital and yet has to be thought of as something that disrupts the unity of that time. ("Time of History," 56–57)

As Chakrabarty himself suggests in his passing allusion to Derrida, the philosophical-critical activity of deconstruction might be seen as something like the "theoretical correlative" of the project of subaltern history. In the image produced by subaltern studies historiography, including Chakrabarty's own work, the subaltern is the subject that "interrupts" the modern narrative of the transition from feudalism to capitalism, the rise of the nation-state, and the passage through the stages of capitalism (merchant, competitive, monopoly, imperialist, global). That narrative involves centrally the idea of the "people" and the capacity of the state to integrate the people into its own desired modernity. "The people" designates a heterogeneous collectivity, including social agents with identities unmarked, or partially or ambiguously marked, by their position in the relations of production. What constitutes the "national-popular" for Gramsci is the putative identity between the people and the form of the nation-state. But the appeal to the unity of the nation (for example, in the context of anti-imperialist or anticolonial struggles) stabilizes the category of the people around a vision of common values, interests, community, tasks, sacrifices, and historical destiny that its heterogeneous components may or may not share to the same degree. It rhetorically sutures over the gaps and discontinuities of "the people," and it is precisely in those gaps and discontinuities that the subaltern appears. The deconstructive task of subaltern studies, then, is to undo that suturing.

In Spivak's well-known articulation, the subaltern is akin to what Julia Kristeva understands by "the abject": that which is beyond the possibility of representation because simply by emerging into representation — the Symbolic in the Lacanian sense — it loses the character of subalternity. Thus, for example:

> Especially in a critique of metropolitan culture, the event of political independence can be automatically assumed to stand between colony and decolonization as an unexamined good that operates a reversal. But the political goals of the new nation are supposedly determined by a regulative logic derived from the old colony, with its interests reversed: secularism, democracy, socialism, national identity, and capitalist development. Whatever the fate of this supposition, it must be admitted that there is always a place in the new nation that cannot share the energy of this reversal. This space has no established agency of traffic with the culture of imperialism. Paradoxically, this space is also outside organized labor, be-

low the attempted reversals of capital logic. Conventionally, this space is described as the habitat of the *subproletariat* or the *subaltern*. (Spivak, *Outside*, 78)

Or:

[T]he arena of the subaltern's persistent emergence into hegemony must always and by definition remain heterogeneous to the efforts of the disciplinary historian. The historian must persist in his efforts in this awareness, that the subaltern is necessarily the absolute limit of the place where history is narrativized into logic. (Spivak, *In Other Worlds*, 207)

But since deconstruction has no politics specific to it, its activity must also "interrupt" the constitution of the subaltern as a subject-of-history. It follows for Spivak that a politics of the subaltern (assuming such a thing is possible in the first place) can happen only in a process of continual displacement marked by conjunctural but precarious possibilities of collaboration between intellectuals, such as Spivak herself, working in the postcolonial or metropolitan academy and the subaltern.

While subaltern identity is performative in the sense Judith Butler gives this term, it is not clear that it is deconstructive. That is because it least thinks of itself and acts in the world as a subject-of-history, via what Spivak characterizes as a metalepsis—the rhetorical figure of substitution (in this case, the substitution of subject-as-effect for subject-as-cause) that nevertheless inescapably characterizes it, since its alterity is bound structurally to forms of subordination and exploitation that cannot be "unfixed" except by a radical change in social relations.[3]

What is at stake in the deconstructive model of subaltern studies is a sense of the subaltern as a subject that is not totalizable as the "people-as-one" of nationalist or populist discourse (or, for that matter, as the "citizen-subject" of Habermas's communicative rationality), but which nevertheless acts in history and has effects on power. In this view, hegemony, any form of hegemony, is simply a screen onto which elites or would-be elites project their anxiety about being displaced by a heterogeneous, multiform popular subject that always escapes being "represented" (in the double sense of representation that Spivak articulates; that is, of being spoken for and spoken about) completely by the political. That subject is akin to what the Italian political theorist Paolo Virno understands by the "multitude."

One of the forms of the multitude is, of course, mass culture in the way it is apprehended by cultural studies. The negative reaction of traditional intellectuals of all political stripes to mass culture is in part a reaction to democracy and its effects. In this sense, market liberalism is perhaps better equipped to serve as an ideologeme of mass culture, and thus of cultural studies, than Frankfurt School-style negative critique (I will come back to this point). The equation between civil society, culture, and hegemony in Gramsci runs up against the problem that subaltern negativity is often directed precisely against what is understood and valued as "culture" by dominant groups. For example, subaltern groups tend to affirm the authority of orality against processes of cultural modernization and transculturation that privilege literacy and written literature as norms of expression. By contrast, Gramsci's idea of hegemony corresponds to a stage of modernity in which citizenship and cultural author-ity cannot be separated from formal education and literacy, since the values and information required to exercise citizenship are available only, or pri-marily, through print media. (That is, why, for example, he saw the produc-tion of popular serial novels such as existed in nineteenth-century England and France as a necessary condition for the emergence of an Italian national-popular culture.) With the advent of mass audiovisual culture, however, the masses can make the transition from the primary orality of precapitalist peas-ant or rural culture to what Antonio Candido calls (despairingly) the "urban folklore" of the media, detouring around, so to speak, print culture and its special requirements and pleasures. Like Gramsci's idea of hegemony, de-construction is text-centric (as in Derrida's deconstruction of the writing/speech binary in *On Grammatology*), and in this sense it, too, belongs to the regime of modernity.

The point here is not to celebrate difference in yet another form of primitiv-ism, magic realism, or fundamentalism. (Indeed, the surge of religious funda-mentalism in the contemporary world — and the "clash of civilizations" it may portend, in the view of Samuel Huntington — must itself be understood as an effect of capitalist modernity rather than as something that existed in the same way prior to it.) The subaltern has no more reason to celebrate tradition than modernity as such, since both of these time frames can be the conditions of its subalternity (or its liberation). It may be defined as a subject position by a resistance to modernity, as Chakrabarty suggests, but it may also involve a *desire for modernity.*

Cultural studies shares with subaltern studies a deconstructive sense of the narrative of state formation and modernization. Where it differs from sub-altern studies is that in its concept of a civil society defined in part by the operations of mass culture, it also seeks to deconstruct the strong binary implied in the hegemonic/subaltern dichotomy. The privileging in current social theory of the concept of civil society is undoubtedly connected to a postmodernist disillusion with the capacity of the state to organize society and to produce modernity in either a capitalist or socialist form. But, above all, the concept has served as an explanation of the dynamics that led to the demise of communism (in that, in the absence of other political parties, "civil society" becomes the space of political opposition to the regime) and, to some extent, as an advertisement for the desirability of that demise.

What a cultural studies theorist like Néstor García Canclini realizes, however, is that contemporary capitalist societies also confront the problem that the narratives that legitimize and organize the state do not coincide, or no longer coincide, with the multiple logics of civil society. In fact, it is the crisis or sense of inadequacy of the nation-state provoked by globalization and transnational mass audiovisual culture that allows the category of civil society to appear in its full light: that is, as what Canclini calls "interpretive communities of consumers," partially detached from a national referent (since the circulation of cultural consumer goods has become supra- and subnational at the same time). The nation and a historicist narrative of national development no longer serve to design and maintain cultural citizenship.

This line of thought might seem at first sight to be a variation of Gramsci's point that the nation-state is not fully commensurate with the "people" (that noncommensurability, to repeat, is what the concept of the subaltern designates for him). But the crisis of the nation-state is also, for Canclini and cultural studies, the crisis of the Gramscian concept of the national-popular. Canclini explicitly rejects the subalternity/hegemony dichotomy, seeing it as founded on an outmoded distinction that links subalternity to premodern forms of culture and hegemony to modern ones. In contemporary societies, the tradition/modernity binary dissolves, and thus along with it, subalternity/hegemony. The category that expresses the dynamic of popular culture for Canclini is hybridity rather than subalternity, in that hybridity designates sociocultural forms in which the traditional and the modern, the subaltern and the dominant, popular and high culture are "mixed."[4]

If hybridization is, in effect, coextensive with civil society in Canclini's argument, the binary that is not deconstructed in it is the one that is constitutive of the concept of hybridity itself: that is, the state/civil society antinomy (where civil society is seen as the place where cultural hybridity appears, as against the supposedly monological and homogenizing narrative of the nation-state). However, in making this identification—which seeks democratically to displace hermeneutic authority from the bourgeois high culture to popular reception—cultural studies paradoxically ends up in some ways legitimizing the market and globalization. The very logic of heterogeneity and hybridity it seeks to represent points in the direction of assuming that hegemony is no longer a possibility because there no longer exists a common cultural basis for forming the collective national-popular subject required to exercise hegemony. There are only deterritorialized identities or identities in the process of becoming deterritorialized. In the manner of Foucault, power is seen as disseminated in all social spaces instead of being concentrated in the state and the state ideological apparatuses.

Jameson explains magic realism as entailing the coexistence in a given social formation of temporalities and value systems corresponding to different modes of production that bleed through each other in the manner of a palimpsest. Canclini's idea of hybridity depends on a similar concept of "mixed times"—*tiempos mixtos* (the subtitle of Canclini's *Hybrid Cultures* is *Strategies for Entering and Leaving Modernity*). But the generalization of the time of capital portended by globalization tends to produce instead a single, overarching temporality—that of the circulation of commodities and "the end of history"—in which other historicities continue to exist simply as elements of pastiche. In Jameson's argument, postmodernist historicist pastiche or *mode retro* is possible only because history has lost its power to represent the subject and the national-popular. Mixed times are, by contrast, times, implying values, languages, states of mind, desires, and needs that are not subject to dialectical "sublation."

If in the earlier Latinamericanist idea of mestizaje or transculturation there was an explicit teleological narrative of the adaptation of the people to the postcolonial state (and vice versa), a similar, but now postnational (and unacknowledged), teleology operates in the concept of hybridity/hybridization, since it designates a dialectical process—seen as both inevitable and providential—of the "overcoming" of antinomies that are rooted in the immediate cultural and historical past, including the past of high modernism itself. Despite its gestures to postmodernism, then, Canclini's argument runs the risk of simply transferring the dynamic of modernization from the sphere of bourgeois high culture and the state ideological apparatuses to mass culture, now seen as more capable of producing cultural citizenship. In this sense, the project of cultural studies does not break with the values of modernity and does not, in itself, point beyond the limits of neoliberal hegemony.[5]

We come back, therefore, to the question of the radical heterogeneity of the subaltern. Is that radicalism simply related to its anachronism, or does it represent a contradictory alterity within modernity—"something that conforms to the temporal code within which capital comes into being while violating that code at the same time," to recall Chakrabarty? Provisionally, I would like to name this heterogeneity—which represents different logics of the social and different modes of experiencing and conceptualizing history and value within the time of capital and the territoriality of the nation-state—multiculturalism. I say "provisionally" because the concept of multiculturalism has a very different connotation than that of the subaltern. The problem, of course, is that multiculturalism appears on the contemporary scene not only as coincident with the hegemony of global capital but also as, in a sense, *requiring* that hegemony in its own demands for rights and recognition. (In turn, multiculturalism often serves as an ideologeme for globalization, as in the United Colors of Benetton advertising campaigns.) This coincidence has been a reiterated theme in recent Marxist discussions of globalization. Thus, for example, Slavoj Žižek remarks that multiculturalism is "the ideal form of ideology of . . . global capitalism" (44). But it is not enough simply to note, and lament, the synergistic relation of multiculturalism and globalization, because embedded in it is one of the most fundamental ideological challenges neoliberalism poses to the renewal of the project of the Left.

It is well-known that neoliberal theory (and here it is important to make a distinction between neoliberalism and neoconservatism) does not presuppose any hierarchy of cultural value apart from that expressed in individual market choice. It follows that the market is in principle more egalitarian than the state or previous forms of cultural hegemony that do, in fact, entail such hierarchies of value, since it does not presume to know or dictate in advance what is right or proper for anyone. The commodity creates its own hegemony, so to speak, or rather no longer requires hegemony in the historical-cultural-moral sense as understood by Gramsci. In turn, since subaltern identities are, by definition, founded on the negation or resentment of existing forms of cultural hierarchy and value, it becomes possible, paradoxically, for them to cathect the principle of market liberalism (and the market may have less compunctions about recognizing and catering to difference than the state or the state ideological apparatuses). Finally, if market choice is essentially rational and free — that is, not subject to external normative constraints — and if, in turn, the forces of opposition to the system represented by subaltern alterity have been enveloped by the logic of the system itself (as Herbert Marcuse envisioned back in the sixties), then Habermas's communicative rationality is already implicit in globalization, and with the extension of the principle of the market to all social spaces we are, indeed, for all practical purposes at the end of history.[6]

Would it be possible, however, to derive from multiculturalism a more radical possibility given that what is expressed in the various forms of identity politics that emerge from multiculturalism are relations of inequality, subordination, repression, and exploitation that derive, in the last instance, from the requirements of capitalist modernity itself? This question might be seen as a variation of the question we started with: Is it possible to imagine a politics of the Left that is not tied to a telos of modernity? To paraphrase what I take to be Ernesto Laclau and Chantal Mouffe's central argument in *Hegemony and Socialist Strategy:* Multiculturalism conforms to liberal pluralism because the identities in play in multiculturalism find in themselves, rather than in a transcendental social principle or goal, the principle of their validity and rationality. On the other hand, what fuels identity politics — its material base, so to speak — is resentment of and resistance to inequality and discrimination as such. Identity demands are heterogeneous to one another, but at the same time involve collectively what Laclau and Mouffe call an "egalitarian imaginary." If the demands of identity politics are not only for formal equality within the parameters of bourgeois legality but also for concrete epistemological, cultural, economic, and civil equality and self-determination, then the logic of multiculturalism will begin to enter into contradiction with the limits of neoliberal hegemony.

This makes it theoretically possible to produce from the recognition demands of identity politics not only the serialized interest-group politics of what Laclau and Mouffe call a "democratic subject position," but also a "popular subject position" — that is, a position that would tend to divide the political space into two antagonistic blocs: that of the people and that of the elite or ruling class. The idea inherent in this argument is that one can derive the possibility of a new form of hegemony from the principle of multiculturalism. I imagine the political form of this possibility as something like a postmodernist version of the Popular Front — the idea (perhaps more than the reality) of the Rainbow Coalition or the Brazilian Workers' Party (PT) are two cases that come to mind. But here we return precisely to the problem of the fictive unity of the people and its noncoincidence with the subaltern. Cultural studies recognizes the limits of hegemony, and thus the failure or limits of a traditional politics of the Left in both socialist and nationalist forms; but that recognition leads, in turn, to a kind of quietism or acquiescence with globalization. What might be envisioned instead is a new kind of politics that would be informed by the theoretical work of "studies" (cultural, subaltern, postcolonial, feminist, ethnic, queer, and so on). Such a politics would seek to articulate the people as a historical bloc, in Gramsci's sense, but not as a unitary, homogeneously modern subject (the subject of Habermas's communicative rationality or of rational-choice marxism, for example). Rather, the people (and so, too, the nation) is itself internally fissured, heterogeneous, multiple. This people-multitude or people-as-many would be the political form of the egalitarian imaginary inherent in multicultural heterogeneity.

This means that the people is essentially multicultural (in the manner of Spivak's idea of "strategic essentialism"); that is, multiculturalism is a necessary rather than a contingent aspect of its identity as such. It does not mean, therefore, the generalization of the principle of multiculturalism to the whole social space, such that existing economic, racial, class, and gender differences (or, for that matter, difference itself) require market liberalism for their expression. Rather, the possibility of heterogeneity is internal to the bloc of the people, which in turn has to be articulated against that which it is not — its "constitutive outside," to use Laclau's term. What could that outside be other than the logic of acculturation or transculturation of capitalist modernity and the nation-state, and the law of value itself, seen in the last instance as incompatible with the recognition/redistribution claims of both class and multicultural identity politics?

To put this another way, the unity and mutual reciprocity of the elements of the people depends (as the idea of the Rainbow Coalition meant to symbolize) on a recognition of sociocultural difference and incommensurability — a recognition, that is, of contradictions among the people, without resolving them into a transcendent or unitary cultural or political logic.

Some final observations in this regard:

1. Laclau and Mouffe note that multiculturalism can point either in the direction of the proliferation of democratic subject positions of an advanced liberalism, or in the direction of the popular-subject position of a potentially counterhegemonic historical bloc. But it should be immediately evident that what is operative in both political alternatives is essentially the same socialcultural logic. This argues for a convergence, or tactical alliance, between the forms of advanced liberalism (for example, contemporary feminist and queer theory, critical legal studies, human rights discourse, ecological movements) and the project of reimagining the possibility of the left, a convergence that would in some ways pass beyond the limits expressed in the Third Way or (in the United States) New Democrat politics.

2. If, as the passage from Chakrabarty quoted earlier demonstrates, one of the characteristics of the poststructuralist intervention that deeply marks subaltern studies has been the insistence on the overdetermination of class identity by other identities, by the same token it is necessary to insist in turn on the overdetermination of those identities by class identity. But this is also to ask how class itself functions as an identity rather than assuming that politicalcultural agency flows from its positioning.

3. Jameson has argued the "systematic incompatibility" between the principle of the market and socialism, noting the enormous destructive force, both economic and cultural-ideological, of the reintroduction of capitalist market relations in postcommunist societies. But the recognition of the relation between the market and democratization in the neoliberal critique of state planning does not necessarily imply an identification of markets with capitalism or, for that matter, of markets as such with the free market. That identification depends rather on the ideological function of neoliberalism in assuring the hegemony of global capital, since markets are not practices exclusive to capitalism, nor do market relations as such define capitalism. (There can be modes of production that depend on markets but that are not capitalist, as in the case of petty commodity production, and by the same token, there can be social regimes of class exploitation — for example, feudalism — that do not depend

on the market.) The question then is not whether markets are better or more rational than state or communal planning, but rather whose class and group interests and values are hegemonic in the operations of both the state and the economy; that is, it is a political and cultural question. State ownership of the means of production does not in itself imply noncapitalist relations of production; vice versa, noncapitalist relations of production are not necessarily dependent on state ownership and control of the means of production.

4. The deconstructive attention in subaltern studies and postcolonial studies to the limits of the nation-state coincides with the effective weakening and deterritorialization of that state by globalization. Nevertheless, the space of hegemony in political and cultural terms is still the nation-state (conversely, the nation is an effect of hegemony). To construct the people/power bloc antagonism today, under conditions of globalization and in the face of the neoliberal critique and privatization of state functions, may in some circumstances, therefore, require a *relegitimization* of the nation-state. But, of course, such a relegitimization also would require a new concept of the nation, of national territoriality, identity, and interests, of citizenship and democracy, of the national-popular, and of politics itself. All existing nation-states are deeply tied to the history of capitalism, but it would be a form of essentialism to argue that the idea of the nation as such is limited to only one form of class rule. What would it mean to create a sense of national "belonging" in which instead of the many becoming one, the one would become many? Would that mean the end of the nation (and/or the state) as such, or is rather the anxiety about multiculturalism the same sort of anxiety expressed in the idea of homosexual panic in queer theory (that is, an aversion to something that is always/already the case)?

5. I am aware that my invocation of "contradictions among the people" may not do justice to the kind of *intra-subaltern* antagonism that is evidence in the cases of, for example, the genocidal conflict between Tutsis and Hutus in Rwanda; the violent clashes between Islamic fundamentalists and secularists in Algeria, or Catholic and Protestant workers in Northern Ireland; the continuing communal violence in South Asia; the resentment between African American and Latino communities in the United States; or the persistence of male chauvinism and violence against women in many, perhaps all, subaltern groups. These antagonisms are due in part, as Mahmood Mamdani argued at a recent conference on subaltern studies at Columbia University, to the fact that subaltern identities are shaped not only by a precapitalist or precolonial past, but also by the forms of discrimination and segregation of populations introduced or reinforced by colonialist and imperialist policies of "divide and rule" — for example, the separation between racial and tribal identity enforced by colonial regimes in Africa. Identity politics, in turn, tends to "ethnicize"

politics, to found its demands on some real or imagined (but always unredeemed) historical injury, grievance, or deprivation attributed to an ethnic or racial other, constituted or reconstituted as such by colonial or capitalist biopower itself. To avoid another Rwanda, Mamdani asks, is not a "sublation" rather than a simple affirmation of subaltern identity what one should be aiming for? But that suggestion returns us to Hegel and the question of modernity's limits, for it is entirely possible that to produce something like the citizen-subject of the sort Mamdani has in mind (one who would not be drawn into genocidal violence of the Tutsi/Hutu sort) out of the immense variety of populations in the world today would require a violence easily as great—if not greater than—as intra-subaltern violence. It might be argued that many instances of intra-subaltern violence, including the Rwandan genocide, have their roots precisely in efforts to "sublate" subaltern particularities—via nationalism, the formation and consolidation of nation-states, statesponsored or imposed development schemes, and the like. The failure of Soviet policy in Afghanistan, which was "enlightened" in many respects (for example, on women's rights) is exemplary in this respect (and presaged the collapse of the Soviet Union itself).

One needs to ask in reply to Mamdani, then, not only sublation to what but also sublation *by whom?* It is doubtful that any class or group would enter into an alliance with others in a project of resistance or hegemonic articulation if it thought it was going to be "sublated" in the process — that is, lose precisely the values, desires, and sense of itself that led it into struggle in the first place. The trick would seem to be, as I have tried to argue here, finding a commonality in subaltern particularity, and posing that commonality—which is what I understand by Laclau and Mouffe's idea of the egalitarian imaginary—against the global hegemony of capital. To achieve real multicultural equality would require the defeat of that hegemony. But that, of course, is something easier said than done.

6. For reasons that will be obvious, the project of reimagining the left will have to be, for the time being, more a project in the field of culture than in the sphere of practical politics or economics. It will depend on the work of contemporary cultural and social theory, art practice, history and ethnography, developments in cybernetics, media and communication systems, and, above all, on the multiple forms of struggle and creativity of subaltern classes and social groups. But one of the characteristics of postmodernity itself is precisely the breakdown of what José Joaquín Brunner has usefully called "the 'cultural' conception of culture"—the concept that identifies culture essentially with high culture, the academic humanities, or the arts supplement of the Sunday paper.

However, the new centrality of culture in globalization also marks a new sense of limit, a limit that concerns our own role and responsibility as intellectuals. In a process of hegemonic articulation, it is not clear in advance what the interests and demands of the individuals, parties, groups, or social classes involved will be. This is because they modify their interests and demands in the process itself since the possibility of hegemony by definition modifies or inverts the structure of subordination that defined their identity in the first place. If, however, the subaltern is to "become" the state (to recall Gramsci's formulation), it is not only the subaltern, but also the state—and along with it, the state ideological apparatuses, including the education system—that will have to undergo a transformation. The necessity of that transformation is what the concept of cultural revolution designates. It will require not only a radically new political imaginary but, at the same time, a critique of the forms of academic knowledge as we practice them; that is, a critique of our own complicity in producing and reproducing relations of social and cultural inequality.

Notes

This paper extrapolates some themes from my recent book, *Subalternity and Representation: Arguments in Cultural Theory* (Durham, N.C.: Duke University Press, 1999). An earlier version appeared in *boundary 2* 26, 3 (1999): 39–46, and in translation in the Cuban journal *Revolución y Cultura* 4, 5 (1999): 50–53.

1   Blair himself is explicit on this point. In his speech at the twenty-first Congress of the Socialist International in 1999, he states that "the debate today is no longer about whether we modernize but how, and how fast. In history the Left always wins when it is not just about justice but about the future too" (cited in Mason, "A Report").

2   On the relation between the project of the South Asian Subaltern Studies Collective and the Naxalbari movement in India, see Guha, *Introduction,* ix–xv. The "Founding Statement" of the Latin American Subaltern Studies Group includes the following: "The present dismantling of authoritarian regimes in Latin America, the end of communism and the consequent displacement of revolutionary projects, the processes of redemocratization, and the new dynamics created by the effects of the mass media and transnational economic arrangements: these are all developments that call for new ways of thinking and acting politically. . . . Indeed the force behind the problem of the subaltern in Latin America could be said to arise directly out of the need to reconceptualize the relation of nation, state, and people in the three social movements that have centrally shaped the contours of Latin American studies (as of modern Latin America itself): the Mexican, Cuban, and Nicaraguan Revolutions" ("Founding Statement," 1, 3).

3   Spivak's provisional solution to this problem is her notion of "strategic essentialism," but she locates strategic essentialism in the discourse of subaltern studies rather than in the discourse—and practices—of the subaltern itself.

4   In *Hybrid Cultures* (145–146), Canclini says: "The bibliography on culture tends to assume that there is an intrinsic interest on the part of the hegemonic sectors to promote modernity and a fatal destiny on the part of the popular sectors that keeps them rooted in tradition. From this opposition, modernizers draw the moral that their interest in the

advances and promises of history justifies their hegemonic position: meanwhile, the backwardness of the popular classes condemns them to subalternity. . . . [But] traditionalism is today a trend in many hegemonic social layers and can be combined with the modern, almost without conflict, when the exaltation of traditions is limited to culture, whereas modernization specializes in the social and economic. It must now be asked in what sense and to what ends the popular sectors [also] adhere to modernity, search for it, and mix it with their traditions."

5 Thus, for example, George Yúdice, in a recent statement, argues for a model of cultural studies that will be "a useful corrective to the Gramscian-inspired view of cultural practice as a process of hegemony," and in his own project for the Rockefeller Foundation, *The Privatization of Culture*, proposes to examine "the ways in which the partnership between government, non-profit organizations, and the corporate sector may be salvaged, or if that is not feasible, then redesigned in order to ensure a more democratic access to resources and participation in decision-making" (217, 219).

6 Žižek's argument against multiculturalism eventually turns back on itself and ends in a defense of Enlightenment rationalism and the principle of what he calls "reflective knowledge." But if the class struggle is to be waged on the terrain of the rationality, then liberalism — whose roots are precisely in the Enlightenment — will always win.

Works Cited

Brunner, José Joaquín. "Notes on Modernity and Postmodernity in Latin American Culture." In *The Postmodernism Debate in Latin America*, ed. John Beverley, José Oviedo, and Michael Aronna. Durham, N.C.: Duke University Press, 1995.

Chakrabarty, Dipesh. "Postcoloniality and the Artifice of History: Who Speaks for the 'Indian' Past?" In *A Subaltern Studies Reader*, ed. Ranajit Guha. Minneapolis: University of Minnesota Press, 1997: 263–294.

——. "The Time of History and the Times of the Gods." In *The Politics of Culture in the Shadow of Capital*, ed. Lisa Lowe and David Lloyd. Durham, N.C.: Duke University Press, 1997: 35–60.

Chatterjee, Partha. *The Nation and Its Fragments: Colonial and Postcolonial Histories*. Princeton, N.J.: Princeton University Press, 1993.

García Canclini, Néstor. *Hybrid Cultures: Strategies for Entering and Leaving Modernity*. Minneapolis: University of Minnesota Press, 1995.

Gramsci, Antonio. *Selections from the Prison Notebooks*, ed. and trans. Quintin Hoare and Geoffrey Nowell. New York: International Publishers, 1971.

Guha, Ranajit. *Elementary Aspects of Peasant Insurgency in Colonial India*. Delhi: Oxford University Press, 1983. Reprint, Durham, N.C.: Duke University Press, 1999.

——. Introduction to *A Subaltern Studies Reader, 1986–1995*, ed. Ranajit Guha. Minneapolis: University of Minnesota Press, 1997: i–xvii.

——. Preface to *Selected Subaltern Studies*, ed. Ranajit Guha and Gayatri Spivak. New York: Oxford University Press, 1988: 35–36.

Jameson, Fredric. *Postmodernism, or the Cultural Logica of Late Capitalism*. Durham, N.C.: Duke University Press, 1991.

Laclau, Ernesto, and Chantal Mouffe. *Hegemony and Socialist Strategy*. London: Verso, 1985.

Latin American Subaltern Studies Group. "Founding Statement." In *The Postmodernism De-*

bate in Latin America, ed. John Beverley, José Oviedo, and Michael Aronna. Durham, N.C.: Duke University Press, 1995.

Mamdani, Mahmood. "Remarks," Conference on Subaltern Studies at Large. Columbia University, November 10–11, 2000.

Mason, John G. "A Report from the Twenty-first Congress in Paris: DSA and the Socialist International." *Democratic Left* 27, 4 (2000): 4–6.

Spivak, Gayatri. *In Other Worlds.* New York: Methuen, 1987.

——. *Outside in the Teaching Machine.* New York: Routledge, 1993.

Virno, Paolo, and Michael Hardt, eds. *Radical Thought in Italy: A Potential Politics.* Minneapolis: University of Minnesota Press, 1995.

Yúdice, George. "Cultural Studies Questionnaire." *Journal of Latin American Cultural Studies* 6, 2 (1997): 216–219.

Žižek, Slavoj. "Multiculturalism, or the Cultural Logic of Multinational Capitalism." *New Left Review* 225 (1997): 28–51.

Solidarity as Event, Communism as Personal Practice, and Disencounters in the Politics of Desire

MARÍA MILAGROS LÓPEZ

The discussion among progressives in so-called First World countries seems to have shifted in recent years from an orthodox politics of class toward the contemporary debates about the politics of pleasure.[1] Simultaneously, the working class as a historical agent proportionally loses its ability to renegotiate the social wage, and the class struggle loses its explicative and mobilizing power. While the essentialist narratives of social movements dominate the social landscape, identities are reconfigured. Paradoxically, this occurs as social conditions are increasingly precarious, and income polarities grow. In their wake, diverse notions appear, both empirically and conceptually, that offer explanations for social conflicts. If we are optimistic, we accept the idea that the contestatory struggle against multiple oppressions has affected the entire social fabric, both displacing and amplifying the labor/kapital contradiction without either abandoning it or negating its importance.

Diverse subject positions engage in different behaviors and modes of confronting power: e.g., mothers, fathers, sons and daughters, entities subject to environmental contamination, subjects before the so-called fiscal crisis, consumers, gender, and different appropriations of gender/sexuality.

The appearance in progressive mediums of efforts to reconstruct the socialist or communist discourses leads us to the examination of social practices seldom considered by the Left, particularly those associated with the domestic, the subjective, and the quotidian spheres. These authors make a call to the communitarian, communitarist, and egalitarian impulse, as well as to the notion that individual salvation does not exist. Salvation, as a possibility, occurs collectively or not at all. This is not to deny libertarian rights and libertarian subjects who operate from their own needs and desires. The material, ecological, and subjective conditions of humanity do not permit other emergency exits for those who presume themselves to be individuals. The goal of these reevaluations is to rearticulate well-being as a function of an increased sociality and of a higher quality of life where goods are shared and our sense of privacy and property is transformed. For example, for Etienne Balibar property lacks meaning if the conditions for its enjoyment are not closely linked to a conception of common good, even a universal well-being. Is it possible to practice communism this way — as a utopic horizon — autonomously, personally, and communitarially? In the presence of an apparent political inertia in the forces of the Left of so-called First World countries, and that of our own, many seem to think so.

Communitarianisms

In light of the collapse of the international socialist project, an increasingly important effort on the part of progressive sectors appears to move toward reclaiming the notion of community. "Community" replaces the notion of "class," and hopes are focused on cooperation, personal agency, and empowerment through communitarian activism. Regrettably, it is arguable that this intention is already part of right-wing projects that have been successful in reviving family values, the church, and communitarian work. The communitarian terrain seems to have been appropriated before, and with more mobilizing effect, by conservatives in Puerto Rico and the United States. In Puerto Rico, for example, the neighborhood security councils have organized around the fears and insecurities created by criminality. Undoubtedly, the communitarian fiber is reconstituted, and the panopticons reproduced, under the safeguards of relations of solidarity. This is why the convergence between the Right and Left in their interest in proposing communitarian activism merits a brief reflection.

For the communitarians of the Right, it is about defending their bourgeois conception of individual rights in response to what they perceive as an increased intervention of the State in "private affairs." This is related to a notion of "character" that is developed through the institutions of the family, school, religious and ethnic groups, and even possibly the labor unions inasmuch as they revive the work ethic. The strengthening of these rights implies larger responsibilities and duties, such that these rights would imply sacrifice. Critics of conservatives argue that this perspective blames the victim without understanding the corrosive effects of the unequal distribution of wealth and the evils this inequality engenders. The focus of this conservative vision is the family as the anchor for the development of moralities, which the challenge of citizenship requires. As a result, conservatives suggest making divorce proceedings more difficult. Paradoxically, they also maintain the necessity for increased state aid for child rearing (in the style of Nordic countries), the extension of maternal and paternal work leaves, and flextime during the workday. Further, a return to the local and the strengthening of the public sphere are also on their agenda. For Konner communitarianism as the new political project in the United States looks like part religious sermon, part the reaffirmation of the "old morality," part political platform, and part social movement. This does not constitute a negative critique. On the contrary, it captures the manifold nature of the proposal. Conflictualities disappear beneath the cloak of immediate necessities that are more urgent and more concrete or, in any case, always subject to the quick fix of the therapeutic democracy of communal consultation promoted by all who are well-intentioned.

Randy Martin (1995) alerts us, from a leftist perspective, of the temptations and dangers of these proposals. In light of Edward Said's (1983) and Stanley Aronowitz's (1993) work, among others, he criticizes the renewed interest in the local and the tribal. But we understand the importance of focusing on the immediate necessities in our proximity, the local, as a way of ensuring the interpelation of subjects and a greater condensation in our understanding of forms of oppression in quotidian life. If class exploitation, although lived on a day-to-day basis, turns out to be more opaque, the environment, education, public services, and sexual freedom manage to convene people in heterogeneous ways.

The tribal, on the other hand, particularly notable in the works of Michel Maffessoli (1988) in France, adds to the new forms of social aggregation where emphasis is placed on socialization for the sake of socialization, and on the multiple insertions and identifications of subjects who resist rigid identities. Neotribes are not configured on the basis of familial or formally communitarian institutions; rather, they participate in a search for the intimacy of a sociality without work or justification, which permits an affective nomadism that foments multiple solidarities that do not demand long-term commitments. Paradoxically, within these conceptions, communism represents "the largest underdevelopment of the ethical responsibility which sustains solidarity because it is the State which assumes the administration of universal reason" (Martin 16). That is to say, the State appropriates the collective desire and renders ineffective particular group initiatives in its attempt to administrate social relations.

Localism and tribalism, however, leave structures of domination intact and are satisfied with isolating a space of individual freedom that does not threaten the established order in any way and is easily tolerated by the centers of power. The global is assumed unchangeable and abstract relative to immediate concerns. So far, the political imaginary of the virtues of resistance on a small scale seems to be the primary proposal from the Left. Perhaps this is accompanied by another phenomenon on a theoretical order. In similar ways, even when the dichotomy between base and superstructure seems, fortunately, to have been overcome, its substitutes continue to be validated. In the same way that access to technology is seen as democratizing, the disappearance of infrastructure or of the economic base as the final analytic instance is celebrated. However, Julie Graham (1995) suggests that the economic base has been displaced as a concept by the notion of a technological globalization, which then becomes the determining and fantasmatic instance that justifies a return to economic determination in the last instance. For the social sciences, the notion of globalization has been essentialized and has become a deus ex machina, capable of explaining all of our previous analytical failures. How could we not have recognized this before? Martin pleads for a conception from the Left of a globalization that does not result in another overdetermining instance.

Other examples from the Right, but more in tune with our purposes here, from the Left, are to be found in works such as that of Curtis (1995) on the possibilities of a sustainable economy, based on the suggestive writing of Wendell Berry in his book *Sex, Economy, Freedom, and Community* (1993). Berry's eco-local perspective is praised not only for reinvigorating the agentive capacity of the microcommunity, but also for including nature as a social actor.[2] In this way, agentive and democratic aspirations merge and are rearticulated with the growing conservative conquests and the abandonment of contestatory projects that do not seem to acknowledge increasing social polarization.

In Puerto Rico, for example, the recent creation of community schools presents, paradoxically, a democratic yearning that converges with a need to transfer the responsibilities of the State to civil society. Sociologists have skillfully pointed to the coincidences between progressive aspirations and the needs of the State for increased privatization of public education, more communitarian action, and the reduction of fiscal costs. The involvement of parents in educational spheres — as teaching assistants in the classroom, for example — reflects the diminished employment of personnel. In every way, self-help initiatives are good ideas if it were not for their clear correspondence with neoliberal politics and the dismantling of the welfare state, which are detrimental to the same communities.

Another variation in the paradoxical leftist experience of the United States is current attempts to recuperate the roots of U.S. history and culture (the democratic roots of the Constitution, for example) — which have traditionally been territories appropriated by the Right — as a way of looking for an exit from increasing conservatism. Strategic attempts are made to extend bridges of shared histories that escape the stereotype of the Left in the United States as anti-American, admiring and fearful of the European and Third World Left. It is also a critique of the Eurocentric epistemology and Europeans' devalorization of the "absence of theorization and even culture" of many American intellectuals.

The intellectual terrain of cultural studies (previously in England and later in the United States), where cultural criticism is often radical, can be seen as one such instance of the reorganization and revalorization of history, tradition, and memory of the American from the American Left. In its extremes, we are dealing with the revalorization from the beginnings of the twentieth century of the social labor of corporations based on a conception of "corporate socialism." The corporation is presented in its best moments, and the demonization of these by an intolerant and rigid Left is questioned. For me, it is about a search for departures from the impasse of the Left in the United States, which attempts to find in its midst the anticapitalist and democratic virtues of quotidian life in the United States as well as the need to wield an intrinsic radicalism (according to these groups) in the founding history of their country. It is about an essentialism of the democratizing capacities of this country in its interior coexistences.

The imperialist politics of the United States, however, constitute a separate chapter that should be understood in a different way, perhaps as a glance to the interior that minimizes what the processes of globalization impose. In 1995, the right-wing armed militias were exposed. These also take refuge in history. Tocqueville and Baudrillard have described this as the phenomenon of theoretical and political "flattening" of North American society, as well as the implacable ingenuity of the North American masses in the face of inequality, and a naturalization of the social as an ontological event. Simultaneously, a sort of spontaneous rebellion against injustice and the pretensions of European high culture persists.

Solidarity as Event

The concept of an individual socialism that, as a sort of "frosting on the cake," has subversive effects is severely criticized by David Harris (1992). His critique is centered on the complacency and political paralysis that results from these postures, as well as the dissolution of the organizational instance. If it is necessary to validate his concerns, it is also important to advance other interpretations. It is possible to observe, within our context, personal practices that assume a transpersonal dimension and appear to presuppose an awareness of the collective. This is so, as the collective appears and disappears in that which could be called "solidarity as event," following the linearities of when "class" was referred to as "event." This is to say that class, community, or collective consciousness emerges, submerges, and reappears in particular circumstances as if it were potential if not present. The alliances between communities of different interests disappear as soon as the event that convokes them culminates. It is not ontological data, nor essence, nor positivism easily susceptible to quantification, though its social power is felt and palpable in diverse social spaces.[3]

This proposal contains a critique of the essentialization of the notion of class in diverse approximations of a marxist order. It is possible, however, to think that class as an overdetermining and contestatory instance appears to multiply and fraction itself instead of disappearing. Or better yet, it disappears, submerges, and then is roused once again in the interest of a group of circumstances. In the presence of the apparent organizational incapacity of progressive sectors, it is possible to ask if the instances of organization, within informational and televised societies like our own, is displaced by the flow of information in the media — in other words, whether what feels at times like the impossibility of continuity in reference to the organizational has to do with the extension of information, which allows people to conglomerate when they consider it "necessary," and where the convocation is spearheaded through the media to sectors that presume themselves to be convoked. This would decrease the interest in confrontational organizational initiatives and their requirement of a more continuous and demanding militancy.

I do not pretend to celebrate here the lacks involved, but rather am asking questions that invite us to new optimisms and that anticipate possibilities for different activisms within the transformations of information society itself. At present, where technology allows us to assume other identities (for sectors of the elite, of course), to reclaim the authenticity of our political compromises in terms of a corporeal presence seems, perhaps, too much to ask. Could it be that the new convocatories are to be found, for some sectors, in cyberspace? For these, the neutral identities capable of a metamorphosis of identity permitted by technology seem to be particularly attractive, or perhaps more feasible. I insist, as do other more knowledgeable people, that cyberspace is populated by political consequences unknown but comprehensible on the basis of a driving idea that if the subject is interested, if it wants to, it can enter the webs of desire and technodemocracy through a recycling of the work ethic and individual motivation. For these increasingly conservative sectors of contemporary industrial societies, ultimately the politics of cyberspace have to do with a return to individual interest and a digital expertise that depends on personal achievement, and within which there is no reason for differing economic classes, genders, or races to exist. For them, in this cyberspace, the end of ideologies is consolidated. The technological experience is presented as a direct democracy whose only prerequisite is access to the machine.[4]

If technological expertise understands itself as heir to a democratic impulse, it is also necessary to ask, as Samira Kawash does (1995), if this does not clearly coincide with the allegedly hegemonic moments of international capital and its democratic claims. The capitalist hegemony seems to encourage these cyberspaces without confronting immediate threats because of it; as a matter of fact, it declares them to be achievements. The extension of the socialities of the Internet—inasmuch as they are regulated, promoted, selective, and competitive—do not manage to subvert the capitalist ways of life. Perhaps they are another instance of solidarity as event, as we have been discussing them. Would these groups surface if the pleasure of the Internet was threatened, or if the situation warranted it?

Kroker and Weinstein (1994), Francfurtian in their impulses, insist in theory about the virtual class of the information age in the conservative and nihilistic values of the telematic networks. History is dissolved, and interactions suffer an even larger abstraction. The computer, far from establishing the conditions of technodemocracy, is an instrument of the growing authoritarianism of advanced capitalist societies. The information superhighway destroys the public dimension that the Internet promotes and emphasizes individualist gains. If it is true that, as did Marx, they recognize the emancipatory and enslaving contradictions of technological innovations, these authors place their bets on the reifying elements. Refusing to submit to technological digitalization implies becoming rapidly obsolete and is a direct line to the historical trash can. For these authors, when knowledge is reduced to information, it is undressed of its live connections to history, critical evaluation, and experience. This is obstructed by the parameters of a programming that pretends to be universal in its contours. It could be speculated that, in the 1990s, capitalism and/or communist ideologies were subsumed by a will to virtuality that proposes a common language and a consensus of the new posttechnological elites of postcapitalism and postcommunism.

So, in light of the recent fall of socialist regimes, is there a reason to think that this aspiration has perversely transited to the private sphere in insidious ways? Even while the authoritarianism of the so-called liberal democracies grows, has there been an accentuation of a generalized feeling of ill-being, a sensibility to human suffering that, without pretending itself a program, has re-created the public sphere? If this optimism seems unjustified, it can be argued that sensibilities have emerged that configure themselves around the conquest of the present from where life is lived "in spite of it all." The prevalent cynicism or fatalism regarding the honesty or efficacy of the political instance is substituted with a more immediate fraternity. Instead of contributing to more-abstract causes that foresee a better future, the human being that occupies the nearest space of necessity is granted the gesture of solidarity, the collective interest and impulse.

The boom of fundamentalist, evangelical, and Pentecostal religions signals an increased interest in a spirituality that is lived day to day in direct contacts and supports, and which appears uninterested in the affairs of dogmas. Thought of from the perspective of more-institutionalized religions as proof of the ignorance of the masses, catharsis, like intimacy, is redefined as an atheoretical religiosity that mistrusts the coldness or impersonality of churches. Religious populism gains territory in the very same places where encounters in cyberspace propose their narratives — which is not to say that the project is progressive in itself with respect to the social order. It is subversive only of a certain ordering of spirituality that places emphasis on control, asceticism, and existence as being in the service of progressivist abstractions. For example, although financial contributions to the party or political organization in charge of the great social transformation was demanded from the militants of the 1970s, acts of corruption have led us to favor direct contributions to those who ask for them in our streets over those to long-term projects. And why not? It is the face-to-face interaction with human suffering that takes precedence over progressivisms whose promises have not always borne fruit. The solidarity as event that happens every day during our trajectories on foot or in cars seem more worthy, although not incompatible with sustenance of organizational instances.

More Disencounters

A second purpose of this chapter is to examine the new contradictions that facilitate social movements and their discourses — contradictions not usually anticipated in our analyses. For example, consumption has been seen, more or less, as a regulating process that hides class conflicts and permits and encourages social consensus. This is so even though, at the same time, it stratifies differences. On the other hand, women's experiences allow us to consider the space of consumption as a space of liberty conditioned to women. Although they are subjects to the realization of the merchandise, women also discover a space of choice, though regulated, and a way to subvert, within the terms of the contract, the isolation that their conditions submit them to. The socialities that emerge from consumption have been the object of multiple defamations: women go to the store to spend money without thinking and to *chismear* (gossip). If, indeed, consumerism obeys the requisites of capital and the media, it is also possible to say that it configures new socialities that open spaces of movement and conflict. Going shopping makes possible a space where subjection, the search for companionship, validation, and entertainment interweave. Gossip itself is transformed into a literary medium in that place where other creative options are invalidated. Through the quotidian medium of gossip, women reproduce the world, their world, of values, anxieties, and aspirations. To call the quotidian articulations and interactions of women gossip exposes the devalorization to which female conversation is submitted.

Consumption is also an instance of confrontation with a market that accentuates distrust simultaneously with our attempts to exact a victory over the

mercantile objects that seduce us. It is about developing the ability to anticipate sales and discounts, cutting and using discount coupons, communicating
with other consumers about current sales, anticipating the opinion of the
"Other" in the face of perspicacity, and managing to feel that one is astute in
the ways of the growing abstraction and commodification of the social arena.
It supposes, generally, a consumer who discerns between commercial advertising and the comings and goings of fashion. Attaining this capacity is transformed into a feminine virtue that can be put into use in different social
instances and even to give way to a movement of organized consumers. Elderly women show great tenacity in these affairs. To get one over on the
market or, more concretely, on the stores, even if only in insignificant ways,
creates an effect of self-valorization and control in a life full of devaluing social
situations.

Another instance that calls for attention in Puerto Rico is the motor clubs
organized around possession of certain kinds of cars. The Toyota owners clubs
meet to organize caravans and plan parties and Sunday outings under the
pretense of exchanging parts, skills, and evaluations of the cars themselves.
The object, or car—which should function toward the end of confirming
individual property and the isolation of the consumer in respect to his or her
object—functions instead as an excuse or justification for a new form of social
aggregation not previously contemplated. Alienation or reappropriation?

The official discourses, including that of the Left, condemn consumerism
and point to its capacity to debilitate the social fiber. Consumption as the new
opium of the masses would be the slogan. For authors like Néstor García
Canclini (1995), however, consumption has come to be constructed as the
way to produce citizens. Objects under whose significations the occasion is
marked accompany familial and communitarian rites. Euphoria as well as
sadness is often remedied through compensatory or supplementative con-
sumptions. Consumption as dignity, in the interiors of poverty, designates a
function of self-valorization where the labor force and its skills have been
expelled and disqualified. If people cannot value themselves through the production of goods, they will do so through consumption as an expression of a
longed-for individuality in the society of masses. From there, García Canclini
would say, we go to the most acute observation of the ways in which consumers act to protect themselves from or conform themselves to the processes
of the global restructuring of capital.

Consumption as a fallible form of mediation between bodies and structures
demands from us new reflections on the process. If citizenship is a site of
struggle—a space of differing memories and an encounter of unequal voices,
as García Canclini argues—then consumption as intermediary offers us an

entrance into a sociocultural analysis in which the appropriation and uses of commodities are realized. The representation of the self, personal style, increases in importance as a way to assert oneself and extract from urban anonymity a space of personal re-creation and a sense of interlocution with respect to either a concrete or imagined community.

As it is possible to anticipate, the preoccupation here is with the way in which the diverse demands of social movements and the contradictions that they generate are articulated or made possible. In what way does it position them elliptically face to face with domination to accede to or to negate desire? If social movements, support systems, and groups of friends proliferate within the growing abandon of the State or, even more plurally, civil society, they find themselves with new/old questions to be asked. Is the dependence on State subsidies the new form of an insidious imperialism? Is consumption, so notable in Puerto Rico, an indication of submission and alienation, or a recuperation of spaces of new kinds of necessities that open the way for new claims in the face of an increasingly precarious situation? Has environmentalism become, paradoxically, a new form of regulation and the politically necessary creation of the subject? Is "individual socialism" the pious communitarianism that shifts from Right to Left a reappropriation or a growing subversion?[5] Can solidarity be thought of, postmodernly, as a phenomenon that aspires only to its own fleeting nature? Perhaps the easiest reference to invoke is that of the French Situationists of the past few decades and their call to the revolutionary and contingent act that resists theorization.

To think about desire always implies confronting a fallible and elusive category. Authors who attempt it propose the reappropriation of a notion relatively absent from the leftist discourses of the sixties and seventies, in which sacrifice marked the contract of social commitment. In actuality, desire is marked, under the Lacanian sign, as the driving force that, with the brute force of the subconscious, nears the subversion of the phallus. There is, however, no direct line. The comings and goings of desire — as well as of rebellion in response to frustration of the same — moves us, if only partially, toward the collapsing of oppressions. The subject is perversely displaced and permits a duplicity in the face of power: the capacity to confront power inasmuch as it is an inevitable situation, and a permanent subversion that distances the subject from these regulations. The phrase *Sí, usted es el/la que sabe* [Yep, you're the one who knows best] on the part of the Caribbean subaltern consolidates this duality, which presupposes a long history of alternate consciousness that, though it might not manage to escape the ideological constructs, questions the so-called modern rationalities. It is then that the speaking subject knows that she/he does not know.

The implicit subject of environmentalist discourses, most of the time, has not been assumed a problematic one. To be ecologically conscious and acting on it is thought of as a virtue in itself. Right away, this presupposes ownership of "the truth." The claim here is that the environmentalist discourse has proposed another aspect of the regulation of the subject and her/his actions. If it is true that people's quotidian practices are of the utmost importance, it is likewise true that there has been an installment of a more restrictive State machinery. There is, too, a consciousness of a more ascetic citizenship, quasi-monastical at times, that conforms, knowingly or otherwise, with the demands of the ethics of work and productivity, and which ultimately does not generate major contradictions on a political level except for occasional minimalisms in the sphere of consumption.

The environmentalist subject aspires to recuperate the spaces of nature as they are understood contemporarily. To him/her, the relativity of the very discourses on nature seem repulsive; it is preferable to think of oneself as part of an a priori natural truth, of a homeostasis between human beings and nature that precedes the linguistic and social constructions of the same. But, more important to our considerations, environmentalism on occasions secretes thick racism. Urban minorities and subaltern subjects are thought of as predators in respect to the environment. The new environmentalist ethic reports it, ambivalently so. Ross (1994), in his provocative book *The Chicago Gangster Theory of Life: Nature's Debt to Society,* discusses how most environmentalist sectors risk subscribing to a return to a sort of neobiologicism as a model for social well-being. For example, the problem for those who argue for bioregionalism as the communitarian alternative is that the laws of the bioregionalist economy are intimately tied to a geographically delimited economy. Within the logic of these sectors, the social lives of these autonomous communities are determined by the local rules of nature itself to which it is necessary to adapt. Local resources would, in turn, limit the contours of social and political liberties. To praise the beginnings of small-scale economies, decentralization, and democracy face to face with eco-anarchist thought, bioregionalism turns to small communities and their tribal and rural past. The oppressive aspects, especially for minorities, are excluded from the analysis because they are presupposed as convoked by the same interest.

When the environmentalist subject is seen within North American or European contexts, and that of local sectors, we would seem to be dealing with an almost 100-percent-cotton elite. Their diets are found only in more-exclusive and expensive establishments. To be vegetarian and macrobiotic, to dress in natural fibers and ethnic fashions, and to practice tai chi is not a cheap way of life. The implicit disdain for the diet of the masses is not hard to identify, even when environmentalists appear as intrinsic defenders of local diets (a kind of neofolklorization of the local that permits its insertion into the transnational sublime; see Beverley 1994). The return to the "natural" results in new forms of cultural stratification. Perhaps it is about a return to a mythical idea of nature — one that is romantic or, even worse, exclusive.

If this characterization appears unjust with respect to other sectors within environmentalism — such as the movements for ecological justice, ecofeminism, or those of communities directly affected by the effects of contamination — it is no less true that these environmentalist vanguards maintain a connection, directly in relation to their class status, with the disencounters that operate in the interiors of social movements. Consequently, they are frequently observed with tolerance as an alien cultural phenomenon that does not recognize its classist insertion or its illuminist vision. This rendering of ecological phenomena as universal tends to lose sight of the local issue, and also of its contradictions with respect to other needs and claims — for example, those having to do with gender and the welfare state.

If the working hypothesis I have previously formulated (in terms of understanding Puerto Rico as a post-work society) has any validity, then the processes pointed out here must assume a different contour in the Puerto Rican context.[6] The extension of the welfare state in Puerto Rico, especially since the 1970s, has fomented, much to the chagrin of the Left and Right, a sense of entitlement, of necessary claim, of a right to demand that is similar to that of societies of the First World. For conservatives from both the Left and Right, the struggles for reclaiming the social salary result only in dependencies and abandonment of the work ethic, even when operating within extremely high levels of unemployment. This is to say that those who live without working and depend on the handouts of the welfare state are criticized without taking into account that for large sectors of the population, there is no employment. In contrast, it could be supposed that this sense of entitlement is a reclaiming of rights and a consequence of the mobilization of a population during the last century toward the satisfaction of necessities promised by consumerist society itself. It is a negativity produced in reaction to past poverties and to the promises for the future made by illuminism and the illusions about the State prevalent since the nineteenth century in Europe and since the middle of this century in Puerto Rico.

After the international crises of capital during 1971–1972 and 1982–1983, labor, always a fragile experience in the poor colony, continues to lose its importance for many Puerto Ricans as the central experience in their lives. There is not much employment to be found, and what there is pays very little. As Vázquez Calzada claims (1989), Puerto Rico shows the highest rate of idleness in the world, if by this we mean the 70 percent of people between the ages of 16 and 65 who do not sustain a formal relationship to the structure of labor and salary. The processes of industrialization by invitation have created fewer jobs than anticipated. "Manos a la Obra" (Hands on the Job) suffered its checkmate with the advent of globalization and the initiative of the Cuenca del Caribe (Caribbean Basin), so far a failure that, in conjunction with the 936 law of the U.S. Department of the Treasury, has permitted a waiting period.[7]

Fortunately, in my opinion, these conditions have generated in the population of Puerto Rico expectations of consumption and of rights that underscore the contradictions of the simultaneous presence of colonial and postcolonial forces. The conditions of Puerto Ricans are singular in this particular sense inasmuch as they show a desire for continued U.S. citizenship while at the same time they participate in the struggles of subaltern classes in the United States and in Puerto Rico to gain spaces of protection from the appetite of corporate gains.[8]

The desire to consume, the sense of entitlement, the expectation that the government owes us something in terms of satisfying immediate needs are, in my understanding, already anchored in the subjectivity of the masses. In other words, the democratic predisposition already exists. Those of us who want a more egalitarian society cannot receive this idea with anything but approval, even if the contradictions always complicate our disposition. For some of us, the fear lies in the waiting period for the 936 regulations in the U.S. Congress, as well as in the conservative spirit of the United States. Recent steps taken toward reducing and contracting the welfare state may send large sectors of the population into situations of despair. Over here, the need is for a reformulation of the independentista and socialist discourse as well as (why not?) an openly communist one. By "communist" we mean a society of equality between genders, races, and ages, and of the creation of and democratic access to goods, including, but not restricted to, sexual, aesthetic and intellectual freedom for all of its participants.

The crisis of the work ethic in Puerto Rico has been a subject of discussion since Spanish colonization and right up to our days under diverse nomenclatures and traditions: the passivity of the Taíno, the passive resistance of African slaves along with their yearnings for freedom, the stupidity of campesinos (country folk), the docility of Puerto Ricans, the psychology of the colonized, the tropical laziness and stupor, the Caribbean *relajo y gufeo* (jovial slacking off and joking around), the culture of poverty, homelessness, the post-work identities described by this author, and the underclasses. Is it possible to understand these various discourses as part of an effort to account for a political economy of pleasure in our population? Are these originary myths supposed to explain the insubordination of the population?

It is in this sense that the movement from a discussion centered on class struggle to one centered on pleasure (heir to a Gramscian tradition, misunderstood or not) manages an appeal to the academic Left. What touches upon surely decentered lifestyles is perhaps a late involvement with the attempts of populations to rescue life and sociality in spite of it all. *Matar el tiempo antes de que el tiempo nos mate* (To kill time before time kills us) seems like a slogan many times appropriated in our space of high disoccupation and tendency towards *la jueyeria* so looked down upon by some.

To reiterate, the task at hand is to try to understand the correspondences and/or disencounters between various personal practices and lifestyles, and the discourses that try to explain them. The attempts on the part of social movements to articulate conflicts and revindications create antagonisms that must be recognized. For example, if feminism does not manage to incorporate the struggle for the social salary because of a strategy that emphasizes equality in the job sphere and an emancipatory hope for insertion in salaried work, we confront serious difficulties for the 70 percent of the population who are unsalaried in Puerto Rico. This is to say, if incorporating women into salaried work is a central axis for the feminist program, how is that reconciled with expansion of the social salary and valorization of nonsalaried work? Likewise, this happens with anti-imperialist struggles when these present dependence on State subsidies as an instrument of domination. "Los cupones [food coupons] as a medium of exacting control and dependence" is constituted with a shortsighted glance at the conditions of the country and the multiple resistances of the subaltern classes. Perversely, this points to the comfortable-class accommodations of those who announce themselves as spokespeople or vanguards; perhaps they have not had to be direct clients of the welfare state.

The social salary, the guaranteed minimum wage, the shortening of the workday, the democratization of consumption, the increased security in spaces of employment, paternal and maternal leaves — all become necessary claims that recognize and amplify the horizons of the exercises of resistance. This is particularly important in those moments where capital and the State pretend to submit us to the labor conditions of the nineteenth century, belittling so the struggles of this century to gain spaces of possibility.

It is not possible for us to discern with absolute certainty if these aspirations represent ways of transgressing or accommodating, of dealing with the carnivalesque and its populist utopia, or if they approach Nietzsche's politics of resentment. In any event, I subscribe to them, even if these forms suppose the "good" ways of resistance (taking us categorically to a more just and democratic society) or if, on the contrary, they deal with "bad" forms of unorganized resistance (lacking a long-term vision) — victories constituted through negativity (the slave morality). It would be the triumph of impermeability, silence, indifference, and sabotage to question insistently our notions of what appear to be contemporary contestatory practices. The general understanding of the struggle, with a capital S, as a phenomenon that is rational, linear, organized, and quantifiable on occasion blinds us to social processes that do not necessitate us. The role of intellectuals, in this sense, inasmuch as they are administrators or ideologists of the social movements, is reduced. The sectors, increasingly professionalized, in charge of managing quotidian life under the directive of the State are left disconcerted. The facilitators of participation, regardless of their good intentions, are left bewildered by impenetrable subjects in their schools, work spaces, and communities. These subjects do not show themselves to be grateful for the "contributions" of these leaders because they feel themselves heirs to a historical debt that has not been theorized, and which they insist on collecting, for which it is not necessary to justify themselves.

To conclude, the shift of some sectors of the Left toward a politics of pleasure, the conditions of socialism on an international level, the sense of entitlement in the face of the State on the greater part of the populations, including in principal ways the right to consume, seem to invite a personal appropriation of equitable practices. Technology promotes new forms of convocation and sociality. The study of popular culture and the dissolution for progressive sectors of academia of the distinction between high culture and popular culture are attempts to revindicate popular democracy as an analytic axis.

For some optimists, including me, in spite of the disencounters and contradictions between contemporary social movements, the transit toward a more ample horizon of conflictualities in civil society seems to announce other definitions not of communitarianism, but, perhaps, of communism.

Notes

1   We understand "politics of pleasure" to be all of those acts, practices, and ideas that justify the pursuit of pleasure as a transgressive disposition against domination. Where the body is submitted as an instrument of work, pleasure surfaces as vindication. The body becomes the topography of the battleground between the subject and society.

2   Wendell Berry does not assume a strictly marxist perspective. His work, however, complements contemporary ideas about the need for an approach to the production of values. According to Berry, sustainable agricultural production is only possible on a small scale. His notion of community preserves the requisites of geographical proximity, which assume the stability of space and the dedication or commitment of the producers to an amicable relationship with nature.

3   The multiple gestures of solidarity in Puerto Rico that occurred in 1989 during and after Hurricane Hugo amazed a population that thought itself immersed in indifference and distrust.

4   If this proposal appears to contradict the politics of identity that affirms points of particular political insertions, the wish for multiple identities and for neutral spaces not socially

demarcated seems to be equally contemporary, according to certain investigators such as Cingolani in France. It is difficult to anticipate the extent of the contradiction, as well as its consequences, in the presence of efforts for social mobilization by groups, mostly youth groups, that conglomerate in favor of different "causes."

5   We understand "individual socialism" to be those practices that visualize as their horizon the transpersonal and collectivizing aspiration: an attempt to attain social justice and equality through individual actions that strive to reach the communist ideal during the course of personal life.

6   María Milagros López, *La luz de 'alante es la que alumbra, or Post-Work Selves and Society in Peripheral Post-Industrial Puerto Rico* (Minneapolis: University of Minnesota Press, forthcoming).

7   Section 936 is a provision of the Tax Code. The Tax Code is a very large series of regulations made by the Internal Revenue Service (Code of Federal Regulations, Title 26, Parts 1.936-1 to 936-11).

8   If our nationalist discourse sometimes desires not to recognize these gains, it is because, in our country, the colonial contradiction takes precedence in our analysis.

Works Cited

Aronowitz, Stanley. "The Situation of the Left in the United States." *Socialist Review* 93, 3: 5–80.

Balibar, Etienne. "Ownership and Membership." Seminar at the Center for the Critical Analysis of Contemporary Culture, Rutgers University, New Brunswick, N.J., February 1995.

Berry, Wendell. *Sex, Economy, Freedom, and Community*. New York: Pantheon, 1993.

Beverley, John. *Against Literature*. Minneapolis: University of Minnesota Press, 1993.

Chun, Wendy. "The Extropians: Sex in the Age of Fiber Optics." Presented at the conference Stages of the Virtual, Princeton University, Princeton, N.J., April 1995.

Curtis, Fred. "The Economics of Community, Place, and Land: Wendell Berry's Alternative Critique of Capitalism and Globalism." Presented at the conference Marxism and the Politics of Anti-Essentialism, University of Massachusetts, Amherst, April 21–22, 1995.

Debord, Guy. *The Society of the Spectacle*. New York: Zone Books, 1995.

Ehrenreich, Barbara. "The Problem of Abundance." Seminar at the Center for the Critical Analysis of Contemporary Culture, Rutgers University, New Brunswick, N.J., February 1995.

García Canclini, Néstor. *Consumidores y ciudadanos: Conflictos multiculturales de la globalización*. Mexico City: Grijalbo, 1995.

García, Estela. Personal testimonial. San Juan, P.R., March 1995.

Graham, Julie. "Capitalism, Community, and Nature: Possibilities for a Postmodern Politics of Environment and Class." Presented at the Center for the Critical Analysis of Contemporary Culture, Rutgers University, New Brunswick, N.J., March 1995.

Harris, David. *From Class Struggle to the Politics of Pleasure*. London: Routledge, 1992.

Kawash, Samira. *Dislocating the Color Line: Identity, Hybridity, and Singularity in African-American Narrative*. Stanford, Calif.: Stanford University Press, 1997.

Konner, Melvin. *Why the Reckless Survive—and Other Secrets of Human Nature*. New York: Viking, 1990.

Kriv, Arleen. "Incorporating Domesticity: Capital, Reform, and the Public Sphere." Presented at the Center for the Critical Analysis of Contemporary Culture, Rutgers University, New Brunswick, N.J., March 1995.

Kroker, Arthur, and Michael Weinstein. *Data Trash: The Theory of the Virtual Class.* New York: St. Martin's, 1994.

Maffessoli, Michel. *Les temps des tribus.* Paris: Meriden, 1988.

Martin, Randy. "Resurfacing Socialism: Resisting the Appeals of Tribalism and Localism." *Social Text* 44 (Fall-Winter 1995): 97–118.

Negri, Antonio. *Marx beyond Marx.* South Hadley, Mass.: Bergin and Garvey, 1984.

Prezworski, Adam. *Capitalism and Social Democracy.* London: Cambridge University Press, 1985.

Ross, Andrew. *The Chicago Gangster Theory of Life: Nature's Debt to Society.* New York: Verso, 1994.

Said, Edward. *The World, the Text, and the Critic.* Cambridge, Mass.: Harvard University Press, 1983.

Steinfels, Peter A. "Political Movement Blends Its Ideas from Left and Right." *New York Times,* 24 May 1994, late edition, 6A.

Vázquez Calzada, José L. *La población de Puerto Rico y su trayectoria histórica.* Río Piedras, P.R.: Escuela Graduada de Salud Pública, Recinto de Ciencias Médicas, Universidad de Puerto Rico, 1988.

A Storm Blowing from Paradise: Negative Globality and Critical Regionalism

ALBERTO MOREIRAS

A Critical Regionalist Teleology

A sufficient counterpart to the notorious affirmation of the end of modernity's macronarratives does not exist yet. Instead mirages abound, and a lot of those mirages have been conceptualized, as mirages, in terms of micronarratives of difference and heterogeneity. Difference and heterogeneity permanently run the risk of being understood, and of understanding themselves, as simple negations *within* a false dialectic of consciousness imposed by the supremacy of what we could understand as the neo-imperial avatar of imperial reason: the culture-ideology of consumerism. "Narrative fissure," "negative globality," and "critical regionalism" are concepts that attempt to preserve a historical legacy, to deconstruct a historical legacy, and, immodestly enough, to open up a discursive field where the possibility of new forms of reflection can be prepared.

Michael Geyer and Charles Bright use the expression "narrative fissure" to refer to the experienced contrast between expectations of modernization and the realities of the course of events, understanding them in every case as "arising out of world-wide processes of unsettlement (the mobilization of peoples, things, ideas, and images and their diffusion in space and time) and out of the often desperate efforts both locally . . . and globally . . . to bring them under control or, as it were, to settle them" (1053). These reversals of expectations, because they are planetwide and affect everyone, produce a sort of *negative globality* that must be culturally ciphered in the various impossibilities, everywhere observable, of narrative closure and cultural self-understanding.

It is not that modernization has not happened or is yet incomplete. It is rather that modernization has not happened in the sense it was supposed to have happened. A rupture at the level of consciousness has taken place — and it has taken place everywhere. That rupture could perhaps be represented, allegorically, using Louis Althusser's notion of a "materialist theatre." Commenting upon melodramatic consciousness, Althusser says of the subaltern characters that share it:

the motor of their dramatic conduct is their identification with the myths of bourgeois morality: these unfortunates live their misery within the arguments of a religious and moral conscience: in borrowed finery. In it they disguise their problems and even their condition. In this sense, melodrama is a foreign consciousness as a veneer on a real condition. The dialectic of the melodramatic consciousness is only possible at this price: this consciousness must be borrowed from outside (from the world of alibis, sublimations and lies of bourgeois morality), and it must still be lived as *the* consciousness of a condition (that of the poor) even though this condition is radically foreign to the consciousness. (*For Marx*, 139–140)

Let me attempt to read these words as if "modernization" were the same thing as "melodramatic consciousness." "Modernization" would then be "melodramatic consciousness," always lived by subaltern subjects as such, in the terms used by Althusser, as a "foreign consciousness . . . on a real condition" (139). The analogy might permit us to understand the underlying connections between imperial reason and modernization; and it permits us to understand modernization as the empty signifier for a certain kind of imperial hegemony at the planetary level.[1] This is a condition for the emergence of what I am calling critical regionalism.[2]

We are all now in the position of Nina, the main character in the play Althusser analyses: we have undergone a world-historical experience that ended with the collapse of so-called "actually existing socialism" and the ongoing destruction of the welfare state, allowing us potentially to break with a form of melodramatic consciousness whose destruction is, as Althusser puts it, "the precondition for any real dialectic" (138). "Actually existing socialism" was no enemy of modernization and imperial reason. The conflict between the so-called First and Second Worlds was an internal episode in a dialectic of consciousness that has now come to reveal itself as the false dialectic of modernization. The rupture with such false dialectic is a historical moment of denarrativization. It has been widely understood as signaling the end of modernity's macronarratives. But it is simultaneously more and less than that. It is not so much an end of particular macronarratives as it is a fissure in modern consciousness itself, a monumental moment of arrest not just for macronarratives but for any and all supplementary narratives, no matter how "micro-" they claim themselves to be.

The rupture with the false dialectic of modernizing consciousness is also ultimately a rupture with all false dialectics, with all melodramas, with all narratives of identity, and with all narratives of difference, and it is so to the extent that these latter narratives depend for their own constitution upon a negation of the macronarrative of modernization, which is the great narrative of Western identity itself. Narrative fissure has to be understood, objectively, in the sense of "the fissure in narrative" (that is, not as "the fissure of narrative"). It affects all narratives and not selectively so, including all (post)modern narratives of difference and all (post)modern narratives of identity, and including subaltern narratives wherever they exist. I would like to endorse John Kraniauskas's definition of subaltern studies, which as the proper thinking of the narrative fissures in the discourse of globalization, is "the critique of the total apparatuses of development" whose ground of necessity is its refusal to be complicit with the hegemonic production of narratives of heterogeneity as a product of the movement of capital.[3]

Negative globality is the underside of the great narrative of global modernization, or, even more than its underside, negative globality is the "other than itself" through which the false dialectic of melodramatic modern consciousness comes to an end *in every case;* that is, not just at the abstract level defined by the hegemony of metropolitan, neo-imperial reason, but also in its innumerable subsumptions in subaltern consciousness throughout the planet, wherever "a foreign consciousness" developed "as a veneer on a real condition." It has been a long time since there was an outside to Western imperial reason — and it may no longer be possible to think *without* it.

If modernization, from the point of view of the subaltern, is nothing but "a foreign consciousness as a veneer on a real condition," could we then invert the proposition and define "negative globality" in terms of "a real consciousness as a veneer on a foreign condition"? Can negative globality be understood as "genuine" subaltern consciousness? If so, then we would probably want to say that negative globality, like Nina in Althusser's interpretation of Bertolazzi's play, "is for us the rupture and the beginning, and the promise of another world and another consciousness, [which] does not know what [it] is doing. Here we can say that consciousness is delayed — for even if it is still blind, it is a consciousness aiming at last at a real world" (142).

Because our critical narrative is also fissured, we cannot know if negative globality (which is the formal concept to design the blockage for any reconstruction of melodramatic consciousness at the level of social totality and which is, therefore, an absolute condition for the possibility of "a real consciousness" or of "a consciousness of the real") is in itself already seized by a return of melodramatic consciousness at the level of critical argumentation. The possibility that "narrative fissure" and "negative globality" are, as critical concepts, nothing but a ruse of reason, another mirage in themselves, is however the very motor of the notion of critical regionalism, and the very basis of its effective dialecticity. In other words, critical regionalism already contemplates the possibility that it constantly runs the risk of developing into melodramatic consciousness.

The universal phenomenon of consumerism must be understood not merely at the anthropological level, as a primary mechanism of socialization, but at the sociological level, as a secondary or symbolic mechanism of socialization into the culture-ideology of global capitalism. I am thinking of a consumerism that goes beyond the lure of the market: a consumerism that is no longer an effect of the market, but its very cause in contemporary terms. I am thinking of commodity consumption, or of its deprivation, as the very basis of a relation to the world, the primary form of worlding in the present, including the present of knowledge production, of university discourse: knowledge as commodity, university discourse as a discourse of the market.[4] If so, could we then establish the theoretical possibility of a nonconsumptive singularity? Nonconsumptive singularity would be a code word for the singularly resistant modality of subjective presence within global capitalism: it would be the name for the theoretical possibility of a residual outside to global consumerism, of an "outsid-ing" trace. Whatever its possibilities, they would have to be thought without, and not within, the game of identity/difference, for the dialectics of identity and difference have been exhausted and should rather be understood today as the latest avatar of melodramatic consciousness at the global level. Difference, in other words, is no longer an "other than itself," but it has been made into more of the same through the expanding power of cultural commodification that defines our regime of capital accumulation.

A subalternist critical regionalism is the systematic exploration of the fact that no systematic exploration can be understood today as something other than a ruse of universal reason—even if and when such (latter) systematic exploration believes itself to be merely local or subaltern. "Critical regionalism" is therefore the name for an enterprise of thinking that takes the subaltern perspective, formally defined as the perspective from the constitutive outside of hegemony, as the starting point for a critique of contemporary consciousness. Its goal is twofold: on one hand, to continue the enterprise of deconstruction of melodramatic consciousness—whether local, regional, national, or global—understood as the false consciousness of a real situation; and on the other, to move toward alternative, nonhegemonic local and regional histories that will seek to constitute themselves as the real consciousness of multiple and always false situations. I think this is a strong teleology for critical practice, and one that could perhaps sustain a certain historical realignment in the production of knowledge.

The Difficulty of a "Major Realignment"

The Gulbenkian Commission report on the restructuring of the social sciences associates the development of so-called cultural studies with the ongoing challenge to "the tripartite division of knowledge" (64) between the natural sciences, the social sciences, and the humanities that had been thoroughly institutionalized in the Western Academy by 1945.[5] For the commission, the rise of cultural studies, which originated in the humanities field, has "undermined the organizational divide between the superdomains of the social sciences and the humanities" to such an extent that it has produced the possibility of "a major realignment" (68, 73) in scientific and disciplinary boundaries. Although the commission never makes the link explicit, such epistemic shifts are strongly related to changes in the geopolitics of knowledge. So-called "area studies" have also been undergoing a grave crisis. What is at stake is the substitution of area studies by another global enterprise or epistemic apparatus geared to the production of "area-based knowledge."[6] In the words of a former president of the Social Science Research Council, Kenneth Prewitt, "from United Nations agencies to international corporations, from nongovernmental organizations to the State Department, the traditional region-by-region approach is found to be poorly aligned with the tasks and opportunities of the contemporary world" (10).[7]

The traditional intellectual aim of "understanding the foreign other," which was always defined from a U.S.- or Eurocentric perspective that became consubstantial to the area studies enterprise, is to be replaced by a new goal: the code words refer to the integration of problem-oriented scholarship and area-based knowledge in the context generated by the exponential increase in the speed and spread of processes of global integration and fragmentation. Traditional area studies were excessively dependent on reflection on local cultures in view of their particularity and uniqueness. Their reconfiguration as area-based knowledge purportedly promotes the critical and dynamic study of historical localities in terms of the processes of globalization and fragmentation that affect them. The linkage between cultural studies and area-based knowledge is essential, and it is, as such, already implied in the very definition of cultural studies provided by the Gulbenkian Commission: "The three themes that have come together in cultural studies are: first, the central importance of gender studies and all kinds of 'non-Eurocentric' studies to the study of historical social systems; second, the importance of local, very situated historical analysis, associated by many with a new 'hermeneutic' turn; third, the assessment of the values involved in technological achievements [read: modernization] in relation to other values" (65).

Cultural studies is, from this definition, centrally concerned with the activities that have historically occupied area specialists, whose mission was to study the uniqueness or particularity of non-Eurocentric social formations within the previous epistemological paradigm of global modernization. The epochal shift connecting cultural studies to the end of area studies as we know it genealogically tied to the exploration and theorization of social difference in a globally integrated world from which the allure of modernization as ultimate teleology has vanished. But the study of social difference, when it is deprived of teleology — that is, when done for its own sake — is in itself unproductive, unless the very pleasure of epistemological consumption is considered productive. In the words of Jacob Heilbrunn, in view of current epistemological changes, "to examine area studies itself is to realize that it has become a field without a mission" (50). The disciplines most seriously affected by the rise of cultural studies today — fundamentally, literary studies, history, anthropology, and communication studies — also find themselves deprived of a clear historical mission for the near future. Even if we accept the epistemological hegemony of cultural studies within area studies, its teleological determination remains fundamentally obscure. This essay attempts to argue that a radicalization of cultural studies in the sense of subaltern studies, of a subalternist critical regionalism, can indeed offer the possibility of a perhaps complex solution to the impasse of the current configuration for critical practice.

According to the definitions given above, which I will use tactically, the basic thrust of cultural studies would be the incorporation of the experiences of dominated groups into the discourse of knowledge. This obviously includes an attention to local and historical singularity. Prewitt insists that "globalization does not render the specifics of place inconsequential. Whatever may be meant by the term 'globalization,' the phenomenon to which it points is clearly constructed from dozens to thousands of separate places, not all marching in some lock-step pattern" (10). The Gulbenkian Commission finishes its report by referring to the "arduous task of demonstrating how incorporating the experiences of [dominated groups] is fundamental to achieving objective knowledge of social processes" (88). But the crucial question is arguably not "what our understanding of social processes gains once we include increasingly larger segments of the world's historical experiences" (88), but rather why we should want to include those experiences into our knowledge; that is, for what purpose.

Geyer and Bright point out a fundamental problem that seems to threaten contentions in favor of the possibility of a "major realignment" in knowledge production as something other than a simple continuation of imperial reason: "[the] century began with the expectation of a modern and thoroughly homogeneous world that would become one as a result of the expansion of the West and the consolidation of its power at the center of an integrated human experience. It ends with people asserting difference and rejecting sameness around the world in a remarkable synchronicity that suggests, in fact, the high degree of global integration that has been achieved" (1036–37) — except, of course, that the achieved global integration does not respond to the admittedly Eurocentric expectations of progress toward modernity, or to any other expectations. As Geyer and Bright say, "The world we live in has come into its own as an integrated globe, yet it lacks narration and has no history" (1037). This lack of historicity, this pointed moment of denarrativization, must on one hand be associated with the disciplinary absence of mission Heilbrunn has mentioned. On the other hand, however, it might guard a critical potentiality having to do with the unfathomable excess of singularity itself: the moment when a narrative, any narrative, breaks into its own abyss is also a moment of flight in which subjectivity registers as noncapturable; indeed, it is a moment of pure production without positivity that will not let itself be exhaustively defined in the name of any heterogeneity.

I will start my argument by raising some questions about the metacritical justification of area-based cultural studies for the specific case of Latin American studies. Latin American cultural studies — and let me insist that I am using this term accepting the Gulbenkian Commission definition of "cultural studies" for tactical reasons — must emphasize Latin American singularity and heterogeneity even as it attempts to place them in the context of global events beyond Latin America's geographic borders. The first critical question, on which the very constitution of Latin American cultural studies as a kind of critical regionalism in the global context might depend, is then to wonder up to what point Latin American cultural studies, and its particular fostering of the production of regional difference, is a genuinely productive enterprise and not the mere by-product of a global phenomenon that is reading us all: the stealthy and radically totalizing "culture-ideology of consumerism," in Leslie Sklair's formulation.[8]

An often quoted remark by Fredric Jameson referring to what he calls the "temporal paradox" of postmodernity might serve as an epigraph for my argument: "[There is an] equivalence between an unparalleled rate of change on all the levels of social life and an unparalleled standardization of everything — feelings along with consumer goods, language along with built space — that would seem incompatible with just such mutability" (15). We do not yet know whether the intellectual work that may go under the name of Latin American cultural studies might avoid falling into the trap of (re)producing local difference for the sake of a merely regionally diversified consumption of sameness. But the cultural studies enterprise, in its foundational appeal to a dialectics of difference and identity, may in fact not be as protective of subaltern subject positions as it pretends. I would like to propose what I see as a necessary reframing of cultural studies work under the twin concepts of hegemony and subalternity as an alternative to the traditional conceptualization in terms of identity and difference.[9] I will suggest that a certain historical exhaustion of the critical productivity of the dialectics of identity and difference must be put to work at the service of an alternative understanding of critical reason that makes of subalternity, as the "constitutive outside" of hegemonic consciousness, a privileged reference.

Heterogeneity and Fissured Globality

Even as late as 1990, when Antonio Cornejo Polar published his essay "Nuevas reflexiones sobre la crítica latinoamericana," he could not have anticipated how quickly the epistemological ground was going to shift. It remains his merit to have insisted then on the fact that a *"cambio de paradigma"* (a paradigm shift) in literary-historical reflection was at the same time coming and long overdue. What he could not have known was that his cambio de paradigma (in the midst of which we presumably still are) was going to alter the conditions of possibility of literary-historical reflection to such an extent that the very viability of the literary-historical discipline — insofar as its goal is to produce knowledge about a bounded geocultural system — would come under serious questioning (231).

Cornejo's recommendations were radical enough. Drawing on the work of scholars such as himself, Rolena Adorno, Martin Lienhard, and Walter Mignolo, Cornejo called for a complete redrawing of Latin American literary history on the basis of the heteronomy of its objects: "el gran tema del pensamiento crítico e historiográfico es sin duda el de la heterogeneidad y los contrastes de la literatura latinoamericana" [the great theme of historiographic and critical thought is without a doubt the theme of heterogeneity and the contrasts in Latin American literature] (235). His notion that Latin American literary historiography had to attempt to reconstruct itself on the basis of the concept of *"totalidad contradictoria"* [contradictory totality] went beyond all previous historiographical efforts in the respect it showed in all of its implications for the irreducibility of cultural difference and historical heterogeneity in the hemisphere: "totalidad . . . porque [los modos de producir literatura] están insertos en la gran corriente de la historia social de nuestra América, que los articula sin desdibujarlos, y contradictoria porque se trata de la reproducción, sesgada pero fidedigna, de la muy disgregada, conflictiva y beligerante realidad socio-étnica de la vida americana." [A "totality" . . . because [the modalities of literary production] are inserted into the great stream of our America's social history, which articulates them while keeping their specificity, and "contradictory" because we are dealing with the faithful if indirect reproduction of the disaggregated, conflictive, and belligerent socioethnic totality of American life] (230).

And yet Cornejo was still calling for a totalizing historiography whose main normative category, Latin America, was arguably as much of a historical construct as anything. A fundamental preoccupation with the past and future destiny of Latin America as a historical unit pervades Cornejo's essay even as the thrust of his thinking is to argue for the contradictory, irreconcilable character of "Latin American" culture as such.[10] This is a subtle but not unnoticeable contradiction that necessarily contaminates his whole argument. In Cornejo's thesis, Latin America, explicitly named "our America," remains or becomes a privileged object of critical reproduction and consumption.

A residually organicist conception of Latin America as a contradictory *totality* is the dominant subtext in "Nuevas reflexiones." Its inaugural gesture is to oppose an operating notion of "our" America to a supposedly foreign postmodernity that must remain outside the circle of legitimate conceptual categories with which to think of Latin America. However, this undesired postmodernity may, at the same time, have managed to creep inside, into the supposedly endotopic, bounded horizon of Nuestra American modernity, through what Cornejo seems to consider either the stupidity, the frivolity, or the corruption of some. Cornejo asks, self-reflectively: "El encuentro con nuestra beligerante multiplicidad ¿es el resultado orgánico del autoexamen de América o más bien responde a ciertas ideas — como las relativas a la crítica del sujeto o a la heterogeneidad del discurso literario — de filiación indudablemente postmoderna?" [The encounter with our belligerent multiplicity, is it the organic result of America's self-examination, or does it rather respond to certain ideas   such as the critique of the subject or the heterogeneity of literary discourse — of an undoubtedly postmodern filiation?] (225–226).

I am interested in this latter anxiety, which I will not hesitate to call the moment of truth of the essay. Cornejo's anxiety symptomatically reaffirms the residual resistance of the old paradigm by reinvoking the organicity of a geocultural "us" — that is, a tradition of cultural and geographical self-sameness whose main feature would have been to provide for historical articulation and continuity. His project is to foreground, within this self-sameness, its internally contradictory and heterogeneous nature for the sake of subaltern subjectivities in Latin America. But Cornejo's heterogeneity, at the very moment it is formulated, always goes too far, seeming to step out of bounds, and he must then contain it. Thus, the question itself ("Is the critical concept of heterogeneity a result of self-examination, or is heterogeneity the result of postmodern, hence foreign, influences?" where we can already see that the question within the question would be how to embrace the former and reject the latter) reveals a decisive experiential ambiguity according to which such organicity would have always been seemingly fissured, not only by interior constraints, but also by an aggressive and destructive outside. For Cornejo, what is particularly significant about the present situation is that postmodernism would purportedly speak about heterogeneity and the end or the rupture of organicity, which makes undecidable to what extent the fissure in organicity comes from within the historically organic — that is, from Latin American history itself, now understood as a contradictory totality — or, on the contrary, whether it is the result of a phantasmatic internalization of a presumably postmodern, but certainly always already imperial, outside.

This undecidability is crucial for Cornejo because it opens up the bothersome possibility that the thinking of heterogeneity may depend upon the postmodern situation itself. Heterogeneity, then, as the limit or the goal of thinking, would be nothing but a mask of neocoloniality — that is, the direct opposite of what was intended. Whatever the case, Cornejo lucidly affirms that such an undecidability will only make itself more undecidable, "con todas las ventajas y desventajas que tienen estas hibridaciones en el desarrollo de la crítica hispanoamericana" [with all the advantages and the disadvantages that these hybridizations have for the development of a Hispanic American critique] (227). This paradoxical affirmation of a fissured and heterogeneous globality from within which it remains necessary to retrieve a lost historical sense of the Latin American multiple singularity is, in my opinion, the starting point of the new cultural-historical paradigm Cornejo is proposing. It is also a striking formulation for the possible starting point of a Latin American critical regionalism, where the word "critical" finds centripetal and centrifugal references to the multiplicity of regional localities within Latin America and the various global mappings within which the concept of Latin America is to be understood today.

I have, of course, pointed out that Cornejo's formulation does not solve but rather opens up a fundamental problem; namely, that all attempts to circumscribe the local are bound to run into their conceptual impossibility, even when the local is understood as a contradictory instance. Cornejo's attempt to limit the ceaseless reproduction of contradiction by the ambiguous appeal to a historically constituted totality that would arrest the spread of the virus and produce a thinkable object is ultimately arbitrary, to the extent that it is not a sanction of the sheer facticity of modernity's hold on our reason. His notion of Latin American cultural heterogeneity has been an important part of Latin Americanist critical discourse since it was first proposed in the early 1980s.[11] In "Nuevas reflexiones," far from recommending that heterogeneity should serve as some kind of wedge to set the new critical paradigm loose, Cornejo insists that, given the great magnitude of the proposed change, it is imperative "vencer las tentaciones del adanismo y rescatar los valores de la tradición crítica latinoamericana: solamente así el cambio será en la historia y dentro de ella, y no en el espacio autoespecular de la pura abstracción" [to overcome the temptations of Adanism and to rescue the values of the Latin American critical tradition: only then will change happen in history and within it, and not in the self-specular space of pure abstraction] (231). In the name of concrete politics and against pure speculation, Cornejo oversubscribes the importance of the redemptive value of a "Latin American critical tradition." Indeed, if heterogeneity could be taken to express the mark of a Latin American cultural and historical singularity, then those vague "valores de la tradición crítica latinoamericana" would be nothing but the precipitate of the numerous historical attempts to come to terms with it—that is, to erase it, more or less successfully: in other words, they are themselves the residue not only of a presumed "Latin American" resistance to imperial reason, but also of the cultural regimes of rule that the Latin American(ist) intellectuals have dreamed up to produce historical sense *against* internal heterogeneity.

Why does Cornejo need to avoid the thought that his "valores" of the Latin American critical tradition are something other than the ideological counterpart to the various hegemonic articulations in the region as historically constituted? Now, as a new round of historical sense-production is called for, the complementary notions of contradictory totality and heterogeneity would seem to be encompassing enough that they could, on one hand, account for past regimes of rule, and on the other, inaugurate a fresh one. But would this new regime of rule be anything other than a reconstitution of the ideological grounds of hegemonic power under a new world configuration? In other words, can the new regime of sense that Cornejo is proposing be something other than a new version of the old dialectics of singularity and totality? The local and the global do not relate merely dialectically when the local is said to remain resiliently heterogeneous to any notion of globality, and when the (postmodern) global is already a fissured, ruptured global of (mostly) negativity.

The anxiety about "postmodern filiations" that Cornejo's essay registers is part and parcel of the old resistance of Latin American left-wing intellectuals to modernization theory, which was the dominant and largely uncontested global paradigm more or less up until the 1973 oil crisis. So-called "three worlds theory" was inextricably connected to modernization, as Carl Pletsch showed in his remarkable 1981 essay.[12] As Geyer and Bright put it,

> the paradigm of global modernization . . . predicted, first, that in dominating the world through its mastery of the technical and material means of global integration, the West would actually control the world and be able to shape the course of global development, and second, that in shaping the world, the West held secure knowledge, positive empirical proof in its own development, of the direction and outcome of world history. The world would become more like the West in a protracted period of modernization, and, as the rest of the world moved toward

uplift and progress, the division between "the West" and "the rest" would diminish. (1051)

But globalization has not followed that course. Global integration has, in fact, proceeded in spite of the collapse of various modernizing projects and ideologies throughout a very large part of the planet. Geyer and Bright use the expression "narrative fissure" to designate the various dissonances between the expectations of modernization and the realities of the course of events, understanding them in every case as "arising out of world-wide processes of unsettlement (the mobilization of peoples, things, ideas, and images and their diffusion in space and time) and out of the often desperate efforts both locally . . . and globally . . . to bring them under control or, as it were, to settle them." These reversals of expectations (including industrial destruction, the failure in the constitution of political regimes of global order, diasporic migrations, and the weakening of the nation-state) produce what could be called a negative globality that must be culturally ciphered in the various impossibilities, everywhere observable, of narrative closure and cultural self-understanding.

Narrative fissures are thus a constituent feature of the new regimes of rule, from postmodernism to fundamentalism in its various guises.[13] The announcement of a Latin American historical heterogeneity or contradictory totality that Cornejo offered us is thus only the acknowledgment of such narrative fissures; left there, it is in fact, at a certain critical level, a predictable kind of acknowledgment, "for the progress of global integration and the attending struggles among would-be hegemons have persistently set loose contests over identity . . . and for autonomy that, time and again, have renewed difference in the face of integration and thus continued to fragment the world even as it became one" (Geyer and Bright, 1044).

Narrative fissure, in the general sense, has produced, following a logic of negativity, a vindication of difference and a rejection of sameness whose synchronicity with postmodern global integration should make us see how they are in fact but the latter's counterpart at the local level. Heterogeneity may be the code word for the cultural paradigm of global postmodernity. But already Pletsch — as he detected the structural anomalies in three-worlds and modernization theory that also in his opinion foretold the necessity of a "scientific revolution" and a paradigmatic shift — was warning us that "it may be more appropriate to put ourselves on guard against whatever new conceptual scheme may grow up to replace the three worlds than to congratulate ourselves upon having seen through modernization theory and the three worlds" (587). This brings me closer to the heart of my intent in this essay.

Counterconsumptive Consumption

In *Escenas de la vida posmoderna,* Beatriz Sarlo identifies three dominant intellectual emphases in the contemporary world, respectively related to the culture industry, to the ruins of popular culture such as they are, and to high aesthetic reflection. The neoliberal intellectual would be more or less loosely but always fundamentally connected with the cultural industry in her or his role as advisory expert. The neopopulist intellectual would have some claim to dwell among the ruins of popular culture from a redemptive perspective. And the critical intellectual would be an individual committed to a nonmediating, nonredemptive reflection on social and aesthetic values, and would thus be genealogically linked to the figure of the enlightened intellectual in the best tradition of negative thinking. What happens, however, when negative thinking must be understood — as it must be understood today, in the face of global capitalism — within the sphere of a thinking of practices of consumption? One has to wonder whether it is not, in fact, the case that the critical intellectual must necessarily incorporate into herself the basis defining features of what Sarlo calls the neopopulist and the neoliberal intellectuals.

To conciliate those conflicting or contradictory attitudes — cultural-industry adviser, redemptive populist, and nonmediating, nonredemptive negator — is not an easy task, but it might well be the task one is called upon to assume. In any case, it represents as good a definition as any of the task that goes under the name of cultural studies. The problem is compounded when cultural studies are pursued from a regional perspective, such as the Latin American one, since regionalist intellectual labor is doubly obligated to confront the paradoxical role of mediation between localities and totality in global times.

In an essay titled "Reading and Discursive Intensities: On the Situation of Postmodern Reception in Brazil," Silviano Santiago insists upon the need "to rethink radically the problem of cultural enjoyment and evaluation in mass society" (201). Santiago calls for an alternative approach to education in Latin America that will foster, at the very point of intersection between the state and civil society (the educational apparatus), a different understanding of cultural consumption. Santiago turns decades of negative thinking against itself by suggesting that the only negativity significantly available today is the one potentially exercised not by intellectuals against mass culture, nor by intellectuals against the cultural industry, but by consumers at different levels of literacy as they receive, experience, and interpret the cultural object in its very disappearance into, or resistance against, exhaustive consumption.

For Santiago, it is precisely not a matter of turning consumption against itself. It is rather a matter of coming to terms with the fact that the culture-ideology of consumerism constitutes the inescapable horizon for thinking in our time. Thinking consumption is therefore one of the most urgent tasks for the critical intellectual. Part of that task is, of course, figuring out ways of teaching it: if that suggested change in the educational field were to be implemented, Santiago implies, then the educational field would turn into the most proper and promising site for a productive, and not merely reproductive, cultural politics.

Santiago's particular proposal is germane to the proposals made by Jorge Castañeda and Néstor García Canclini regarding what they understand as "regional federalism."[14] The proper understanding of this notion—to be thought of as the guided regional response to U.S.-led globalization from an anti-neoliberal perspective—implies a turn away from any rushed idealization of local difference, from all kinds of national-popular statism, and from any celebration of the cosmopolitanism of transnationalization as such. In Castañeda's words, regional federalism is, simply and soberingly enough, "an intermediate solution between a largely unsustainable status quo and a largely harmful progression toward the dissolution of [local] sovereignities" (313; qtd. in Yúdice, "Civil Society," 18). The purpose of regional federalism is the creation of regulatory policies that would help, in this case, Latin American civil society so that what Yúdice calls "the affective aspects of cultural interpellation—identity formation" are not, in his words, "so overwhelmingly determined by U.S.-identified transnational corporations nor by particular nationalist ideologies" (18). Yúdice agrees with Santiago, and with García Canclini's model as proposed in *Consumidores y ciudadanos,* about the need to think of consumption as the inevitable road to the construction of citizenship in global times: "societies may have reached a historical threshold in which it is no longer possible to think such ideas as citizenship and democracy in the absence of consumption" (20).[15]

For all these thinkers, what is now at stake is not primarily the self-conceptualization of critical practice as different from mass-cultural practice, but rather the former's insertion within mass-cultural consumption, and the particular role it is fated to play there. What is at stake is the possibility of theorizing, and then implementing, what we could call a counterconsumptive, negative instance within cultural consumption itself; that is, the preservation of a sort of residual subject sovereignty or local singularity within the totalizing process of consumption. By "counterconsumption" I do not mean "anticonsumption": it is not a matter of opposing mass-cultural consumption, precisely since we are always already immersed in it. Rather, "counterconsumption" refers to a particular mode of relation to consumption from within consumption: an adequate analogy would be, for instance, Homi Bhabha's implicit notion of "contra-modernity" as a form of constitution "otherwise than modernity." For Bhabha, "[the] cultures of a postcolonial *contra-modernity* may be contingent to modernity, discontinuous or in contention with it, resistant to its oppressive or assimilationist technologies; but they also deploy the cultural hybridity of their borderline conditions to 'translate,' and therefore reinscribe, the social imaginary of both metropolis and modernity" (6). Counterconsumption is perhaps not an "otherwise than consumption," but it refers to an "otherwise in consumption": a trace of discomfort, the fading memory of an experiential otherwise which can also be taken to be the anticipation of an alternative future.

But there are two ultimately divergent ways of thinking about this problem. One of them sets off from the militant, substantive affirmation of counterconsumptive singularity. The second takes a dimmer view, judging that any affirmation of counterconsumption, any supposed resistance to consumption, is nothing but a ploy of consumption, a coy niche-marketing of the product for a more or less elite segment of the consumer population. The difference is a matter of emphasis, perhaps: it is one emphasis to affirm the moment of counterconsumption within consumption, and it is another emphasis to state its predictable destiny as a merely more exquisite or sophisticated kind of consumer's behavior. The former would be insisting on the need for a categorical (and then practical) distinction between consumption and counterconsumption within the cultural object's paratext, and claiming the critical potential of the second in its very materiality as an event. The latter would reduce counterconsumption to ideology and say that counterconsumption is only self-concealing or alienated consumption.

John Beverley's differentiation between two possible intellectual projects within cultural studies follows similar lines. For Beverley, the option is not merely a matter of philosophical deduction, but must be articulated along a political cleavage that will determine either the hegemonic or nonhegemonic destiny of cultural studies itself. He focuses on García Canclini's notion of cultural hybridity to note that it has descriptive and normative possible uses, and that the latter use may end up acquiring an unwelcome ideological character whose main function would be to cover up the very possibility of counterhegemonic articulation: "¿No sería [el] concepto central de 'hibridez cultural' precisamente una contra-respuesta al binarismo fuerte implícito en la noción de lo subalterno?" [Wouldn't the central concept of 'cultural hybridity' be a counter-response to the strong binarism implied in the notion of the subaltern?] (20). Similarly, an excessive emphasis upon the totalization or suture of consumption — the notion that there is no anthropological trace of an escape from it, no remainder to the disappearance into it — would indicate a kind of ideological complacency under the pretext or mask of lucidity.

The regulatory policies that Castañeda and García Canclini advocate are, in effect, elements of statist cultural politics. Santiago's call for a renewed form of education is also part of it. They run counter to the neoliberal state and try to set some controls over the terms of global integration. By the same token, however, they can be understood as excessively timid reformist attempts. They can even be understood, counterintentionally, as neoliberal social policy in the sense explained by Carlos Vilas. After establishing that in the neoliberal model, "the state has abandoned its role as an agent of social development and integration [in order to merely] help define winners and losers in the marketplace," Vilas calls neoliberal social policy any (semiparadoxical) neoliberal state intervention "intended to compensate for the initial negative effects of structural adjustment among certain sectors of the population" (18). In other words, neoliberal social policy has a minimalist mediating function, describable as "putting out fires so that situations of extreme social tension do not become larger political problems" (18).

Once it is understood that neoliberal social policy does not consist, as is habitually suggested, of the lack or rejection of any kind of social policy, but that it does exist and that it has an *in extremis* compensatory character, it will also be understood that there is little in the logic of statist social policies that we have ciphered under the name of regional federalism that will keep them from eventually being swallowed by global integration and made radically indistinguishable from neoliberal structural compensation. Even if, at the cultural level, those social policies did manage to control "the affective aspects of . . . identity formation" (Yúdice), it may well be because a degree of identity diversification — that is, a degree of difference production — remains irreducibly essential for the global marketplace and its mechanisms of cultural consumption. Castañeda's "intermediate solution," in other words, would become just another structural part of the neoliberal order: the always surpassable limit on which it will ceaselessly grow.

It would seem to be essential to look for ways of upholding counterconsumptive singularity in its first emphasis. If education is to form citizenship, it will have to incorporate into itself, as its main theoretical justification, the teaching of counterconsumptive consumption, as it were, or how to consume while resisting the total disappearance of the historical subject into consumption: the total exhaustion of the historical subject into practices of consumption. It will have to find its own ideological resources, not necessarily in local traditions, although it would not exclude them, but rather in the negative force of historical disjunction, of social difference, of regional solidarity. In this modified sense, federal regionalism could be the social and political articulation of what in educational, intellectual, and cultural terms would better be called "critical regionalism." Critical regionalism, as a thinking of cultural consumption from regional perspectives, is necessarily then a thinking of the singular resistance to consumption from within consumption through which regional and local identity formation happens in global times. It does not point to the production of any kind of counteridentity; rather, it moves beyond identity as well as difference in order to interrogate the processes of their constitution. It dwells at the border of hegemony in order to break its circle for the sake of attaining not a new identification, not even a disidentification, but rather a recalcitrant production of subjectivity as something other than subjection to history: not what obtains at the intersection of historical timespace, but what exceeds it. Critical regionalism is, then, a regionalism against itself: a savage atopics. At this point the question is whether that notion can be something other than political desire; that is, whether it is intellectually and practically viable in any strong sense. And, if so, which one?

From Recognition to Compulsion

The critical question would be how to theorize a tactical engagement of heterogeneity, and how to develop it in the intellectual practice of a Latin American cultural studies, without falling into the regulatory trap of proposing, as an alternative to global or dominant ideological interpellations for consumption, particular ideological interpellations for counterconsumption that end up producing counterconsumption as yet another consumer's (compulsive) choice. Arjun Appadurai's words on "the fetishism of the consumer" should be kept in mind: "the consumer has been transformed, through commodity flows [which include not just mediascapes, but also ideoscapes], into a sign, both in Baudrillard's sense of a simulacrum which only asymptotically approaches the form of a real social agent; and in the sense of a mask for the real seat of agency, which is not the consumer but the producer and the many forces that constitute production" (286).

Take Silvia Rivera Cusicanqui's work on *ayllu* democracy in northern Potosí as an example of the difficulties of Latin Americanist work on singularizing practices. Speaking from the collapse of the Bolivian national-populist state, Rivera argues in favor of a new anti-integrational concept of citizenship within Bolivia whereby the ayllus would be left alone to develop their own ways of communal democracy. Her fundamental hypothesis is that the Bolivian ayllus are the potential locus of "a richly democratic communal life," whereas "attempts by liberals, populists, and leftists to impose liberal democratic models on the *ayllus* have actually hindered the emergence and consolidation of democratic practices and institutions" (102). Rivera's proposal is for the Bolivian state and hegemonic classes to keep their hands off the ayllus, since "no human right will be fully recognized so long as the indigenous peoples are denied the right to autonomy in their decisions to continue or transform, by themselves, their forms of organization and collective life and their conceptions of the world" (117).

Rivera's call for a politics of "recognition of the right to be different as a fundamental human right" has ample resonance in the context of a history of secular oppression of the ayllus by the Bolivian mestizo/creole population (117). And yet things become conceptually and ethically complicated when we find out that "tensions have grown between the older and the younger generations: the latter have seen the NGOs as a way to escape collective social controls and to seek individual subsistence alternatives, such as migration, which have a direct, negative impact on the communities' productive potential" (112).

Rivera's notion of multicultural citizenship in Bolivia is akin to what Nancy Fraser has called a "post-bourgeois conception" of the public sphere. According to Fraser, it is necessary to realize, against the "bourgeois conception" (26), that "public spheres are not only arenas for the formation of discursive opinion; in addition, they are arenas for the formation and enactment of social identities . . . [P]articipation means being able to speak 'in one's own voice,' thereby simultaneously constructing and expressing one's cultural identity through idiom and style" (16). But Fraser, who, like Rivera, is engaged in the theorization of "democratic possibilities beyond actually existing democracies" (26), fails to take account of the fact that, as Judith Butler puts it, "identity categories tend to be instruments of regulatory regimes, whether as the normalizing categories of oppressive structures or as the rallying points for a liberatory contestation of that very oppression" (13–14).[16] It is easy for any regulatory regime of truth to slip over, perhaps inevitably, from recognition into compulsion. We do not know that, given the fact of a rearticulation of Bolivian citizenship in the multicultural sense proposed by Rivera, the "younger generation" of ayllu inhabitants would no longer wish, through migration or otherwise, to escape collective social controls within the ayllu. Thus the emphasis on the defense of a cultural and social difference secularly reluctant to accept the parameters of the national state can inadvertently move into a contrary emphasis on compulsive identity consumption, even if for the sake of communal redemption.

How, then, to engage, from the perspective of the intellectual producer at odds with the institutional mandate for social reproduction, with a politics of recognition without stepping over into a politics of compulsion? The identitarian claims that Rivera and Fraser promote as necessary to the construction of a post-bourgeois public sphere involve, in the current configuration, a "fetishism of the consumer," in Appadurai's sense, which remains blind to the possibility that such claims are not in fact *produced* by the subject, but only *consumed* by him or her. Is this not the case as well for so many other theoreticians of subaltern identity?

Differential Consciousness

Dreamed alternative singularizations of thinking are a different kind of "global dream," to mimic Richard Barnet's expression, but not separate from it.[17] Those singularizing dreams today orchestrate the panoply of antiglobal discourses within global discourse. They are more and more thought of as microdiscourses, places where a singularity is enacted and an intensity is affirmed, sites of a resistance which is also a withdrawal, a monadic pulsion, a punctual, discardable identity, or a customized difference, in any case, whatever can be salvaged as the sheer possibility of an alternative articulation of experience outside global homogenization. Even Appadurai seems to concede that much when he mentions the "brighter side" of global culture today. If its central feature is "the politics of the mutual effort of sameness and difference to cannibalize one another and thus to proclaim their successful hijacking of the twin Enlightenment ideas of the triumphantly universal and the resiliently particular" (Appadurai, 287), then the brighter side of global culture would reveal the possibility of an enactment, however fleeting, of the singular difference within totality.

These singular dreams are not only the dreams of urban squatters and Third World feminists, of U.S. queers or Muslim fundamentalists, of neo-Zapatista guerrilla leaders or German cyberpunks, of Catalán greenheads, Galician rockers, or Bangkok S&M practitioners: they are also the dreams of (former) academic area-studies intellectuals as they resist their reconversion into corporate intellectuals at the very instant of their absorption by the global university. They are also the metacritical dream as it informs this essay that I am writing, here and now — and thus the dream of a critical Latin Americanism.

All dreams of singularization are virtual expressions of a certain distance, a certain inadequacy, a felt disjunction vis-à-vis global incorporation. They can be tenuous dreams, as in the kid who fantasizes her identity as one of the players in Mortal Kombat, or strong dreams, such as the ones at the basis of the Zapatista rebellion or the Río *arrastões,* such as nationalist dreams, or Rigoberta Menchú's understanding of the particularity of her people as a people with secrets. But they all express a singular intensity. As Jean Franco puts it, "in the age of global flows and networks, the small scale and the local are the places of the greatest intensity" (21). Franco is placing intensity at the service of an experience of what I would call "distance-toward-the-global." Such an experience can only be categorized as an instance of self-reflexivity: a particular arrest of the process of consumption, or even self-consumption, or the emergence of what Chela Sandoval calls "differential consciousness" (3).

Sandoval's 1991 article on oppositional consciousness in the postmodern world provides a concise theoretical formulation of the possibility of a self-redemptive practice through tactical singularization. But Sandoval's theory reveals, in spite of itself, a constitutive lack of closure. It is perhaps not so much a theoretical inconsistency or a flaw as rather itself an expression of how tactical singularization is a reactive practice against homogenization: nothing but an alternative consumptive move from within consumption. Sandoval's differential consciousness is based on a formal movement of self-reflexivity, where self-reflexivity is not to be conceived in terms of a synthetic move of the Hegelian spirit but in terms of a self-reflexivity of affect—of intensities or affective tonalities.

For Sandoval, her theory "focuses on identifying forms of consciousness in opposition, which can be generated and coordinated by those classes *self-consciously* seeking *affective* oppositional stances in relation to the dominant social order" (2, my emphasis). "Differential consciousness" is, for Sandoval, the self-reflective affect which alone becomes the necessary and sufficient condition for the constitution of a new subject position. She makes a grand claim for it: "Differential consciousness is the expression of the new subject position called for by Althusser—it permits functioning within yet beyond the demands of dominant ideology" (3). The status of that perhaps surprising "beyond" stands in need of questioning; as it is, if the essay's logic is to make sense, the keystone of its articulation.

Within Sandoval's topography of consciousness, the place of that "beyond the demands of dominant ideology" is a function of self-reflexivity: "Any social order which is hierarchically organized into relations of domination and subordination creates particular subject positions within which the subordinated can legitimately function. These subject positions, once self-consciously recognized by their inhabitants, can become transformed into more effective sites of resistance to the current ordering of power relations" (11). The crucial move for Sandoval consists in positing *differential* consciousness as the only effective locus of resistance: that is, the liberatory dimension of difference is the mere form of the subordinated but resistant subject position as such, and not its positive content. Yet, without a strong refusal of any positivization—that is, without an active, self-reflective commitment to a radical restraint in the face of any temptation to substantivize subaltern identity—she cautions that "any liberation movement is destined to repeat the oppressive authoritarianism from which it is attempting to free itself and become trapped inside a drive for truth which can only end in producing its own brand of domination" (14). She is interested in arguing not just against homogenization, but also against presumed heterogenizations that ultimately resolve themselves into more of the same; in the terms used above, she is opposed to any forms of compulsive recognition.

Sandoval's attempt to escape a politics of compulsion consists of positing a "tactical subjectivity" whose articulation would be purely formal: this tactical subjectivity would open the possibility of a "beyond the demands of dominant ideology" because it would situate itself, by definition, in an oppositional beyond, always in a "variant" site, formally defined as a given differential possibility "emerging out of correlations, intensities, junctures, crises" (14). But, if her "beyond" is always a formal punctuality, always arising out of the negation of the dominant, always an oppositional stance whose very possibility is orchestrated by the dominant, then her "beyond" is just another formulation of the impossibility of an outside to the dominant. From Sandoval's own postulates, in effect, the dominant exhaustively constitutes the non-dominant as a merely formal negative relationship to itself, and negation lives only as a function of what it negates.

Sandoval's theory of oppositional discourse can only justify itself on the basis of a previous acceptance of the claim of the global dominant to a complete saturation of the discursive field. It would only be possible to step, from within the saturated field, into its formal negation through an extreme self-reflexivity or differential consciousness, but at the cost of a thorough renunciation of any substantive endowment of the content of the differential consciousness as such. If differential consciousness is to be understood as "a [tactical] movement between ideologies along with the concurrent desire for [oppositional] ideological commitment" (Sandoval, 15), then oppositional desire is the only positive characteristic of differential consciousness. A radically tactical subjectivity, whose content can only be mimetic negation even as it seems to be affirming something or other, comes close to no subjectivity at all. The negativity of differential consciousness cannot but preempt the very possibility of its affirmative emergence.

Paul Smith, discussing the "theoretical task . . . of coming to an understanding of how the ideological force of interpellation can fail (and often) to produce a compliant 'subject' for a discourse," understands self-reflexivity as always already produced by ideological interpellation (39). For him, what is crucial is not only the development of a differential consciousness in Sandoval's sense ("a conscious and deliberate refusal of particular interpellations and the meanings they proffer for subject positionings") but also the theorization of "a radical heterogeneity in the subject-positions which are constituted in the human agent through interpellations" (39). The fine line here resides, of course, in the difficulty of theorizing a radical heterogeneity while at the same time avoiding the call for a self-conscious appropriation of it for the sake of an apparently contestatory practice always already produced by ideological inter-pellation. Smith does not solve this metacritical difficulty, and his dream of radical heterogeneity does not therefore abandon its dream character. There is, to say it once again, a short step between the recognition of heterogeneity and a compulsive consumption of heterogeneity as a kind of counterconsumption commodity: heterogeneity then becomes a commodified fetish. Sandoval's "U.S. Third World feminism," once endowed with self-conscious recognition as the purveyor of differential consciousness, runs the risk of turning into yet another cultural fetish, as does, for instance, Guillermo Gómez-Peña's brand of border performance, the "coming-out" discourses of closeted sexualities, or even indigenous identities in times of negative globality.

If subject positions are produced through their actual performance, if there is no essential subject before social practice, but only subjects whose partial identities must be enacted in order to "be" at all, and if the field of social practice itself is produced by ideological interpellations, then what does it mean to dream of theorizing "radical heterogeneity in subject positions"? If heterogeneity can only be a function or a result of performance, and if perfor-mance always already produces a subject position within ideological inter-pellation, then heterogeneity must necessarily be self-conscious in order to be at all. But self-reflexivity immediately reduces heterogeneity into yet an-other produced, and therefore not-quite-heterogeneous, subject position. The mechanism becomes a merely formal practice of contestation insofar as its concrete contents are constantly being voided or reabsorbed into consump-tion, no matter how illusorily rebellious or disjunctive.

The Negative Ground of Critical Regionalism

Practices of singularization, or the formation of a differential consciousness, can only be understood as practices *produced* by the very ideological interpella-tion that frames them and, by framing them, also performs them. Singulariz-ing practices offer, in that sense, no beyond to the ideological apparatus of interpellation in response to which they arise, which brings us full circle back to the question with which this essay started. The question concerned the very possibility of Latin American cultural studies as an enterprise of productive and not simply reactive knowledge.

In the wide definition of the Gulbenkian Commission, cultural studies was to be understood as a systematic effort to incorporate subaltern difference into both nomothetic knowledge (that is, the normative knowledge proposed by sociology, economics, or political science in their best moments) and herme-neutic knowledge (the sort of knowledge which is proper to idiographic disciplines such as literary studies or anthropology). Latin American cultural studies, then, is to be amply understood as the systematic effort to incorporate Latin American area-based knowledge into both nomothetic and hermeneutic science as primarily knowledge of the Latin American subaltern difference in the global context. The systematic effort to account for subaltern difference is hailed by the Gulbenkian Commission as introductory of a paradigmatic shift in knowledge production.

Although knowledge of cultural heterogeneity was instrumental in undoing the old dominant paradigm that went under the name of modernization theory, in times of postmodern global integration it is no longer clear that an emphasis on heterogeneity can be made to fulfill the secular requirement for knowledge to be productive, as opposed to having it merely be at the service of social reproduction. Heterogeneity, particularly when used as a critical banner, cannot but become yet another market option in the marketplace of subjectivities. There is, as we have seen, a certain understanding of local singularity that serves the reproductive interests of the neoliberal order by fostering consumption of (and thus, not coincidentally, annihilating) difference. Heterogeneity, whatever it may have been in previous historical times, is today produced in advance by a social interpellation that at the same time consumes it, or prompts its consumption. The consumption of heterogeneity does not guarantee by itself an appropriate teleology for Latin American cultural knowledge.

The concept of critical regionalism offers a potential resolution of this theoretical impasse. Critical regionalism, as a thinking of cultural consumption from regional perspectives, was understood as the thinking of the singular resistance to consumption from within consumption through which regional and local identity formation happens in global times. But the concept was simply offered as a potential solution, and the question of its practical viability remained open. It is one thing to understand a problem and make a claim for its solution, and it is altogether different to show that the solution works. The examples of Rivera and Sandoval—as well as, in a different sense, my comments on Cornejo—were meant to raise substantial objections to an all-too-quick acceptance of that possibility.

The twin concepts of negative globality and narrative fissure are pertinent to a theorization of critical regionalism. If critical regionalism refers to the very possibility of simultaneously thinking through the contradictory totality of global integration and fragmentation, then negative globality is to be understood as the structural ground of critical regionalism; within that ground, narrative fissure is the figure of its negativity. Critical regionalism has a necessarily negative ground, for it must necessarily proceed through the systematic exploration of its impossibility to constitute itself as something other than a ruse of reason. The theoretical foundation of a radicalized critical regionalism is not constituted by a posited heterogeneity between any world area and hegemonic homogenization. *It is constituted by the very impossibility of thinking heterogeneity beyond the processes of globalization that always already determine it as heterogeneity for consumption.*

As critical regionalism, therefore, a possibility opens up for Latin Americanist reflection that will no longer reduce it, as the Gulbenkian Commission would perhaps seem willing to do, to the systematic study of Latin American subaltern identities in the global context: it is also, and perhaps primarily, the study of the historical fissures through which the "valores de la tradición crítica latinoamericana" disappear into material constraints. It is the study of the aporias of identity formation, and thus also of what could dwell beyond identity formation. And it is, last and not least, the study of the geopolitical fissures through which any kind of cultural universalism will show itself, from a subalternist perspective, as a figure of dominant ideology. These may seem contradictory purposes, but their very tension keeps open the possibility of a productive knowledge of the social totality, even if such a totality is only accessible in negation and from negation. They point toward a materialist thinking that can adjust to present reality without a fear of either postmodern filiations or neoliberal entrapment.

Notes

1 I follow Ernesto Laclau's application of the linguistic notion of empty signifier to the sphere of political theory in *Emancipation(s)* (36–46, passim).

2 I first found the notion of "critical regionalism" in Fredric Jameson's *Seeds of Time.* Jameson takes it from Kenneth Frampton. The notion of "region" designates "not a rural place that resists the nation and its power structures but rather a whole culturally coherent zone (which may also correspond to political autonomy) in tension with the standardizing world system as a whole" (*Seeds* 191–92). See also my book *Tercer espacio,* especially chapters 1 and 4.

3 John Kraniauskas offered the definition of subaltern studies as "the critique of the total apparatuses of development" at the meeting on "Cross-Genealogies and Subaltern Knowledges," Duke University, October 1998.

4 On the relationship between contemporary epistemologies and the market, see Brett Levinson's unpublished typescript, "The State/Market Duopoly," which I read after completing this essay. My argument, however, is indebted to numerous conversations with Levinson.

5 The commission makes the case that cultural studies challenges the division between the humanities and the social sciences. But John Guillory presents an interesting argument that cultural studies should pay particular attention to systems theory, one of whose merits is to have a claim to dissolving the difference between natural science and social

science: "Systems Theory has a beachhead in the university now in the new discipline of Cognitive Science, which may be the first discipline to overcome the distinction between social science and natural science" (18). See also Wallerstein, 6.

6   On "area-based knowledge" see the Social Science Research Council's "Proposal to the Ford Foundation for Core Support of a New Joint International Program": "Traditional area studies is primarily knowledge *about an area*. Area-based-knowledge starts with knowledge about an area, but then applies that knowledge to processes, trends, phenomena that transcend any given area" (2).

7   For a more detailed presentation of the New York-based Social Science Research Council's new position on area studies, see Prewitt's "Presidential Items."

8   Sklair, 75; see 75–77 and 129–69 in particular.

9   It is perhaps unnecessary to say that others have already initiated the critical examination of the ideology of identity and difference within cultural studies. See, in particular, Lawrence Grossberg, "Identity," revised and expanded as "Cultural Studies in/and New Worlds" for an analysis that departs from the position that identity/difference have become more central to cultural studies than they originally were given, the influence of "so-called postcolonial theory and critical race theory" ("Identity," 87). See also my "Hybridity and Double Consciousness" for additional references. At the moment of sending this text to press, Gareth Williams's typescript "The Other Side of the Popular," which engages with these issues in many fascinating ways, is finished and awaiting publication.

10 Something similar could be said about Cornejo's concept of "literature," despite his effort and marked interest to include within it oral symbolic productions. See Mignolo, "La lengua, la letra, el territorio" and *The Darker Side of the Renaissance* (passim) for a thorough questioning of the concept of "literature" as an adequate category to account for the complexity of Latin American symbolic-verbal production.

11 See, for instance Cornejo, *Sobre literatura y crítica latinoamericanas,* and also *Escribir en el aire.* The first pages of the latter repeat the "anxious" formulation about postmodernity I have been discussing. "Heterogeneity" in Cornejo's sense has recently generated some important essays: see Schmidt; Moraña; and Achugar.

12 According to Pletsch, "Modernization theory is almost inextricable from the idea of the three worlds" (571), and "modernization theory is not merely some adventitious appendage of the idea of three worlds, it is constituent to the structural relationship among the underlying semantic terms" (576).

13 A strong case could be made, in my opinion, that the notion of "narrative fissure" is more productive than the well-known and overabused Lyotardian notion of "the end of meta-narratives" to discuss postmodern phenomena.

14 George Yúdice refers to both Castañeda and García Canclini in connection with the concept of "regional federalism" (explicitly formulated by Castañeda) in "Civil Society, Consumption, and Governmentality in an Age of Global Restructuring" (17). See Castañeda, *Utopia Unarmed;* and García Canclini, *Consumidores y ciudadanos.*

15 Yúdice has pioneered work in this, to my mind, decisive conceptual area in Latin American cultural studies; see "Consumption and Citizenship," 8, and also "Globalización y nuevas formas de intermediación cultural."

16 A fascinating discussion of the dangers of a compulsive politics of identity in the context of minorities' cultural survival can be found in several of the essays included in Gutmann; see especially the essays by Appiah, Taylor, and Habermas.

17 See Richard Barnet's *Global Dreams: Imperial Corporations and the New World Order.*

Works Cited

Achugar, Hugo. "Repensando la heterogeneidad latinoamericana (a propósito de lugares, paisajes, y territorios." *Revista Iberoamericana* 62 (July–December 1996): 845–861.

Althusser, Louis. *For Marx,* trans. by Ben Brewster. New York: Pantheon Books, 1969.

Appadurai, Arjun. "Disjuncture and Difference in the Global Cultural Economy." In *The Phantom Public Sphere,* ed. Bruce Robbins. Minneapolis: University of Minnesota Press, 1993: 269–295.

Appiah, Kwame Anthony. "Identity, Authenticity, Survival: Multicultural Societies and Social Reproduction." In *Multiculturalism: Examining the Politics of Recognition,* ed. Amy Gutmann. Princeton, N.J.: Princeton University Press, 1994: 149–163.

Barnet, Richard. *Global Dreams: Imperial Corporations and the New World Order.* New York: Simon and Schuster, 1994.

Beverley, John. "Sobre la situación actual de estudios culturales." Manuscript. 1996.

Bhabha, Homi. *The Location of Culture.* London: Routledge, 1994.

Butler, Judith. "Imitation and Gender Insubordination." In *Inside/Out: Lesbian Theories, Gay Theories,* ed. Diana Fuss. New York: Routledge, 1991: 13–31.

Castañeda, Jorge. *Utopia Unarmed: The Latin American Left After the Cold War.* New York: Knopf, 1993.

Cornejo Polar, Antonio. *Escribir en el aire: Ensayo sobre la heterogeneidad sociocultural en las literaturas andinas.* Lima: Horizonte, 1994.

——. "Nuevas reflexiones sobre la crítica latinoamericana." *De Cervantes a Orovilca: Homenaje a Jean Paul Borel.* Madrid: Visor, 1990: 225–235.

——. *Sobre literatura y crítica latinoamericanas.* Caracas: Facultad de Humanidades y Educación, Universidad Central de Venezuela, 1982.

Franco, Jean. "What's Left of the Intelligentsia? The Uncertain Future of the Printed Word." *NACLA Report on the Americas* 28, 2 (1994): 16–21.

Fraser, Nancy. "Rethinking the Public Sphere: A Contribution to the Critique of Actually Existing Democracy." In Robbins, 1–32.

García Canclini, Néstor. *Consumidores y ciudadanos: Conflictos multiculturales de la globalización.* Mexico City: Grijalbo, 1995.

Geyer, Michael, and Charles Bright. "World History in a Global Age." *American Historical Review* 4 (October 1995): 1034–1060.

Grossberg, Lawrence. "Cultural Studies in/and New Worlds." In *Bringing It All Back Home: Essays on Cultural Studies.* Durham, N.C.: Duke University Press, 1997: 343–373.

——. "Identity and Cultural Studies: Is That All There Is?" In *Questions of Cultural Identity,* ed. Stuart Hall and Paul du Gay. London: Sage, 1996: 87–107.

Guillory, John. "System without Structure: Cultural Studies as Low Theory." Manuscript. n.d.

Gulbenkian Commission. *Open the Social Sciences: Report of the Gulbenkian Commission on the Restructuring of the Social Sciences.* Stanford, Calif.: Stanford University Press, 1996.

Gutmann, Amy, ed. *Multiculturalism: Examining the Politics of Recognition.* Princeton, N.J.: Princeton University Press, 1994.

Habermas, Jürgen. "Struggles for Recognition in the Democratic Constitutional State." In Gutmann, 107–148.

Heilbrunn, Jacob. "The News from Everywhere: Does Global Thinking Threaten the Social Sciences? The Social Science Research Council Debates the Future of Area Studies." *Lingua Franca* (May/June 1996): 49–56.

Jameson, Fredric. *The Seeds of Time.* New York: Columbia University Press, 1995.

Laclau, Ernesto. *Emancipation(s).* London: Verso, 1996.

Levinson, Brett. "The State/Market Duopoly." Manuscript 1999.

Mignolo, Walter D. *The Darker Side of the Renaissance: Literacy, Territoriality, and Colonization.* Ann Arbor: University of Michigan Press, 1995.

——. "La lengua, la letra, el territorio (o la crisis de los estudios literarios coloniales)." *Dispositio* 11, 28–29 (1987): 137–60.

Moraña, Mabel. "*Escribir en el aire:* Heterogeneidad y estudios culturales." *Revista Iberoamericana* 51 (January–June 1995): 279–286.

Moreiras, Alberto. "Hybridity and Double Consciousness." *Cultural Studies* 13, 3 (1999): 373–407.

——. *Tercer espacio: Duelo y literatura en América Latina.* Santiago: ARCIS/Lom, 1999.

Pletsch, Carl E. "The Three Worlds, or the Division of Social Scientific Labor, circa 1950–1975." *Comparative Studies in Society and History* 23 (1981): 565–587.

Prewitt, Kenneth. "Presidential Items." *Items: Social Science Research Council* 50 (June–September 1996): 31–40.

——. "SSRC, ACLS, and the Reexamination of Area Studies." *LASA Forum* 27, 1 (1996): 10–12.

Rivera Cusicanqui, Silvia. "Liberal Democracy and Ayllu Democracy in Bolivia: The Case of Northern Potosí, Bolivia." In *The Challenge of Rural Democratization: Perspectives from Latin America and the Philippines,* ed. Jonathan Fox. London: Frank Cass, 1990: 97–121.

Robbins, Bruce, ed. *The Phantom Public Sphere.* Minneapolis: University of Minnesota Press, 1993.

Sandoval, Chela. "U.S. Third World Feminism: The Theory and Method of Oppositional Consciousness in the Postmodern World." *Genders* 10 (spring 1991): 1–24.

Santiago, Silviano. "Reading and Discursive Intensities: On the Situation of Postmodern Reception in Brazil." In *The Postmodern Debate in Latin America,* ed. John Beverley and José Oviedo. A special issue of *boundary 2* 20, 3 (1993): 194–202.

Sarlo, Beatriz. *Escenas de la vida posmoderna: Intelectuales, arte, y videocultura en la Argentina.* Buenos Aires: Ariel, 1994.

Schmidt, Friedhelm. "¿Literaturas heterogéneas o literatura de la transculturación?" *Nuevo Texto Crítico* 14–15 (1994–1995): 193–199.

Sklair, Leslie. *Sociology of the Global System.* Baltimore: Johns Hopkins University Press, 1991.

Smith, Paul. *Discerning the Subject.* Minneapolis: University of Minnesota Press, 1988.

Social Science Research Council. "Proposal to the Ford Foundation for Core Support of a New Joint International Program." Ts. New York: SSRC, 1996.

Taylor, Charles. "The Politics of Recognition." In Gutmann, 25–73.

Vilas, Carlos M. "Neoliberal Social Policy: Managing Poverty (Somehow)." *NACLA Report on the Americas* 29, 6 (1996): 16–25.

Wallerstein, Immanuel. "Open the Social Sciences." *Items: Social Science Research Council* 50, 1 (1996): 1–7.

Williams, Gareth. "The Other Side of the Popular: Neoliberalism and Subalternity in Latin America." Book ts. 1999.

Yúdice, George. "Civil Society, Consumption, and Governmentality in an Age of Global Restructuring." *Social Text* 14, 4 (1995): 1–25.

——. "Consumption and Citizenship." Paper presented at the "Conference on Globalization and Culture," Duke University, Durham, N.C., November 1994.

——. "Globalización y nuevas formas de intermediación cultural." *Mundo, región, aldea: Identidades, políticas culturales e integración regional,* ed. Hugo Achugar and Gerardo Caetano. Montevideo: FESUR-Goethe Institut, 1994: 134–157.

II. INDIGENOUS PEOPLES
AND THE COLONIALITY OF POWER

Rigoberta Menchú After the Nobel:
From Militant Narrative to Postmodern Politics

MARC ZIMMERMAN

In a now well-known essay, Doris Sommer (1991) argues that in the growing consciousness and shifting articulations of Rigoberta Menchú's testimonial narrative are to be found the bases for exploring multiple oppositional possibilities—not tied to or determined by state, party, or class-centered agency—that could constitute a model for the very kind of coalition politics that Laclau and Mouffe had registered with respect to the advanced capitalist world.

For Sommer, Latin America's incomplete and uneven modernization confirms a social complexity as great as in any place on the globe. The struggle to establish oppositional coalitions and to pursue ideological and political lines of any coherence and efficacy has been revealed as being far more difficult to map than the furthest reaches of Menchú's own metonymic significations, and takes us through testimonial or postliterary discourse to subaltern subject positions and resistances beyond standard theoretical constructs.

My goal, then, in what follows, is to see if Sommer's sense of alternative interpretative possibilities is borne out in regard to Rigoberta Menchú in her metaphorical, metonymic, imaginary, symbolic, and supposedly "real" roles in Guatemala, but also in regard to recent Mexican contexts.

This effort involves contemporary questions about the constitution of civil society and of civic action among subaltern social groups and movements, which can end by constituting "ungovernability." This situation is one in which, as Laclau and Mouffe put it, "a society constructs the image and management of its own impossibility" (1995: 191).

Latin American ungovernability can be defined as a situation in which the state systems and apparatuses required to maintain and extend international and local socioeconomic power relations have to exert such pressure over one or more social sectors or social configurations that oppositions develop. These oppositions can only be contained by adjustments that unsettle the relations that the state is supposed to maintain, or by repressive violence that strains the government's legitimacy and leads to further oppositions and ungluing of the social fabric. The formally democratic states that emerged in the 1980s are not able to totalize all the social relations constituting the nation — above all, those ignored in the process of previous hegemony construction, and those emerging and countering national orders in the wake of globalizing pressures. The revenge of the repressed, ignored, manipulated, and marginalized (the subaltern) is frequently configured and limited in the "weapons of the weak." However, contemporary social formations — by their control over class, race, ethnicity, gender, and other contradictions — may well create the very preconditions for more radical opposition or direct confrontational resistance to the given construction of hegemony.

Currently, neoliberal and controlled democratization without a resolution of basic social conflicts leads to new social movements, as well as new modes of citizenship and resistance as legitimate activities within civil society. The results are conflicts and threatened breakdowns that the state can only resolve by force or by further concessions, which begin to erode its reason for being and its legitimacy.

In Guatemala, the modern state representing criollo power ran into snag after snag as it sought to maintain and build a criollo-dominated multiethnic nation able to deliver goods to the market and to provide the basis for future development. In the 1944–1954 revolution, the Arbenz government sought to establish the bases for agrarian reform and make some inroads into rural indigenous problems, but in so doing, it progressively lost ground with dominant sectors and their primary client-state. Thirty years of guerrilla warfare and indigenous unrest came to a head in the early 1980s through a partial rapprochement between a Ladino marxist guerrilla group attempting to penetrate the indigenous world and a radical indigenous sector ready to take on Ladino marxist perspectives. The conjuncture of Indian-Ladino concerns and discourse projected in the crucial testimonial texts of Mario Payeras and Rigoberta Menchú pointed to deeper levels of convergence, only to be thwarted by the weight of military power (see Zimmerman 1995; Zimmerman and Rojas 1998). By 1982 and 1983, the military had terrorized whole communities; once relatively secure, it was able to engineer its "democratic transition" with Marco Vinicio Cerezo as president. Meanwhile, the transition that emerged was a contradictory affair, with all democratizing gestures countered and ironized by persisting military hegemony and the efforts of a greatly weakened guerrilla movement that had retreated into the mountains. Entering into sporadic forays in a kind of low-intensity civil war, the guerrillas, now formalized as the URNG, sought to maximize an appearance of strength to negotiate a peace that would leave them some maneuvering room and chances for development in the new social order.

In the context of Esquipulas II and the gradual abatement of the Central American crisis, the new government sought a new arrangement of civil society. However, even with efforts toward some minimal degree of participatory democracy, the government's inability to hold the military in check and adequately meet popular demands led to growing ungovernability as given social sectors began to organize, demonstrate, and threaten the social order. The new social movements of the 1990s threatened the powers that be and also transcended the perspective of the marxist guerrillas, speaking to new configurations of power and resistance beyond the usual dichotomies of capital and labor, capitalist and marxist, Ladino and indigenous.

The Guatemalan situation of ungovernability and social insurgency in the early 1990s is my subject here. In this context, I focus on Rigoberta Menchú. But not she of the famous text, nor she out of whom the text came, but she who came out of the text, she who was able to make a new history because of the space created by the reception of her text, and the religious and political narratives that her text incorporated and disseminated. The space in question has to do with the articulation of microstruggles in the peripheral context of postmodern / post- and perhaps once again premarxist life of Latin America. It also has to do with borders and the discourse of borders: as well as with a shift in sociohistorical gravity, first from the central to the north of Mesoamerica, and second from one side of the Guatemalan-Mexican border to the other. Other geographical and conceptual borders are involved, and all of these not so micro stories and struggles that cross borders and frontiers are, of course, part of the shifting patterns generated by internal and global tremors, and transformations that affect and characterize our times.

Menchú's Many Roles

Even before the Nobel, Menchú was on the road to becoming an icon or symbol, or even a symbolic good or commodity from which the left and leftist intellectuals could profit. Rigoberta the Indian, the woman, the human rights defender: these three products opened new lines that quickly won a niche in the market. Even when she agreed to dictate her story, she knew she was making a commodity. But she applied the same correct logic here as she did in favoring the adoption of Spanish by her country's indigenous groups: Under capitalist hegemony, you must enter into market relations. If you're outside the circuit of commodities, if you do not have a commodity or cannot become one, you do not signify and you do not exist. Even if your goal is to destroy the circuit, there is, as Nelly Richard reminds, "no outside of power" from which to negotiate (1990: 9). Rigoberta Menchú was somehow aware of this. So she agreed to narrate her story as dramatically as possible and promoted it in its bookish commodity form on a global level; she campaigned actively for her cause; and she campaigned avidly for her prize. She knew its value. The general question resulting from this is not only if the subaltern can speak, but if they can remain subaltern when their lives and what they say brings them to the Nobel. More specifically, would Rigoberta Menchú continue to represent the URNG, or would she represent the broader definition of her referentiality as conferred by the Nobel, even if this definition might sometimes conflict with more partisan concerns?

While the Guatemalan military worked with other sectors to engineer its civilian transition, Menchú, in exile, became an international spokesperson for indigenous rights, appearing at forums throughout the world. These appearances reached a new level of intensity in the mobilizations arranged around the quincentennial of Columbus's New World arrival and Menchú's successful Nobel Peace Prize campaign. As the years came and went — as the Cold War ended, the Central American revolutionary crisis abated, and 1992 grew closer at hand — Menchú grew in skills, experience, and perspective. She became a writer of speeches and analytical texts, a subject of government campaigns, a target of racist and sexist jokes, a leader of indigenous and women's organizations, a symbol of the subaltern and, especially, indigenous peoples, a figure in the concrete political life of her country. To be sure, Menchú received support even from conservatives in their effort to create a broader political democracy. As she campaigned for the Nobel, rightwing Ladinos proposed an alternative candidate, and certain indigenous groups questioned her representativity.

Also involved in this story is the question of postinsurgency political mobilization in Guatemala, and Menchú's relation to Guatemala's guerrilla groups and mass organizations during and after her Nobel campaign. Of course the Nobel gave her a new space under President Jorge Serrano-Elías, as she came and went and wove her way into the Guatemalan politics. And the post-Nobel conjuncture particularizes questions about the status of her organization, CUC, as an independent mass organization or one fronting for and controlled by the leftist organization with which it is allied. Of all the questions, the most important has to do with Rigoberta's relation to CUC — as a guerrilla popular front operative or as a figure related to but above and beyond a specific filiation. The question goes to the overall grid of structures and organizations established in the wake of the 1992 Centennial and Menchú's Nobel campaign — primarily, the Vicente Menchú Foundation, dedicated to the worldwide defense of indigenous peoples.

Finally, the crucial questions were raised ever so sharply in the dramatic events of May–June 1993, when Serrano attempted a military-backed Fujimori-style "self-coup" known as the Serranazo, and the questions have mounted in relation to other events since then. I shall turn to those events, but first I wish to contextualize them in terms of the narratives of postmodernity in Latin America, and in Guatemala, involving shifts in groups, forces, modes of governance and resistance, and modes of discourse under the weight of globalization.

Ultimately, the key question is whether the military-initiated democratic transition achieved any qualitative change. I would argue that it did, and that the failure of the Serranazo consolidated the change. That I use the term "postmodern" for that changed context is quite debatable, but it at least ties us to overall world and hemispheric contexts, and also suggests links between the recent Central American crisis and the Mexican one that now stares us in the face.

Recent Developments and the Postmodern Condition

What some of us have characterized as Latin American postmodernity has come to mean a new ambience marked by the conjuncture of the end of the Cold War, "the exhaustion" of the "grand narrative" of marxism, and adrift toward democratization, the transformation of the directly militarized state in function of democratization, involving at least limited and partial popular participation, which ultimately spells integration in a U.S.-centered transnational free-market economic and cultural system (Achugar 1990: 18).

No matter how unique Guatemala might be, can it not claim some similarities with countries marked by formal, controlled "democracy and dis-exile, but also of broken or truncated dreams" (ibid.)? For its ethnic formation, and its economic and political structuration, Guatemala has posed severe problems for those, right or left, who have dreamed of the nation's entry into modernity, and the superimposition of postmodern norms further complicates the picture. But modernization processes — including narcotraffic, ecological struggles, democratization, Protestantism, economic globalization, Miamization, and the undermining of older military patterns through their integration with neoliberal capitalist norms — are all very much part of the contemporary landscape. To apply a postmodernist scale to Guatemalan cultural reality means viewing the nation's present in terms of the tentative creation of a new order as it extends out to the fragmented sectors that constitute an unintegrated national aggregate. The revolutionary and repressive conjunctures extending from 1944 to the early 1980s represent efforts of modernization culminating in the current period of democratization.

The attempt by Serrano-Elías to oppose the new emergent forms of social opposition and mobilization through a return to the past via his Serranazo produced a result that is more parallel to the coup against Gorbachev than Fujimori's effort. This is because the new government system — including many in its legislative, military and other sectors — responded readily both to internal popular and external (indeed, global) pressures (not the least of which were the moves toward NAFTA, which were also to register their effects in Chiapas). Thus, the fragile and threatened patterns of Guatemala's precarious and clearly idiosyncratic postmodernity were, in the last analysis and however provisionally, affirmed, and a potentially new social pact involving the quite-possible emergence of a new historical period in Guatemala has become a plausible, if constantly threatened, hypothesis.

Even more so perhaps than under Cerezo or Serrano-Elías, as the nation lived through a period balanced by the timid initiatives of its human rights president and a military that felt it had made all the concessions it could, Guatemala continued to live its own strange, tentative, insecure, peripheral, and paranoic encounter with postmodernity in a world of new-wave shopping malls and chain restaurants, selective killings, ecological blight and narcocapitalism, Ladino left and right flirtations and accommodations, and Indian entrepreneurs commuting on business flights to Houston and taking faxed orders for huipils and ceremonial dolls in thousands of units in the colors, sizes, and styles determined by external demand. But it was also a time of growing animation and participation of popular and middle-class, Indian and Ladino, student and professional sectors (including journalists and professors/writers) in forging a new public sphere and civil society that (why not?) we may as well call postmodern.

What are some of the global and focal factors conditioning this Guatemalan emergence? What development in Central American and Guatemalan history had situated Rigoberta Menchú as one who would be important in the social conjuncture that led to May–June 1993, then January 1994, and on into the Guatemalan elections of 1995? And what are the implications of this strange and contradictory Guatemalan postmodernity for our consideration of Rigoberta as cultural and political actor? Such questions become acute in an era in which, until Chiapas, a writer like Jorge Castañeda could argue that armed resistance hardly seemed a convincing agenda (1994), and in which oppositional culture seems to involve "a play of positions in the struggle of interests sustained by significations of the sectors in dispute" (Richard 1990: 8).

With respect to Indian and other social questions, one would have to underline the postholocaust situation of the Indian population, their penetration by the military, the intensified alternative of Protestantism, and, above all, the supposed move from forced to hegemonizing military controls, as well as growing indigenous entrepreneuralism. The military now lived in close contract with the Indians in most areas, and the question of Indian resistance had supposedly become more problematic. But then, according to Suzanne Jonas (1991), Indians' incursions into the cities and their modernization fed into a context of their growing politicization and the capacity of many of them to organize. Indeed, whereas Protestant evangelism seemed to imply Indian quietism, even the evangelical practices were now leading to reversals. And instead of Indian sectors tying their fate to a guerrilla vanguard, they were showing the way in terms of new patterns of resistance. Serrano-Elías sought to tap and throttle this development, but popular movements emerged with some force and were the key factor in his attempted coup and fall.

Menchú's struggle of the 1980s continued on its own and was also a prelude to the struggles of the Zapatistas in the 1990s. However we see that struggle, as subaltern discursive formation or action on the real, it should be related to developments in the middle sectors, best articulated and exemplified by the works and activities of Guatemala's writer-intellectuals, into whose discourse world Menchú's testimonio had been inserted as a core, transformative force.

Privatization, the Writers, Rigoberta Menchú, and the Articulation of a New Discursive Space

As Serrano came to power in 1990, all public discourse, literary or otherwise, began to enter more fully into the neoliberal orbit of privatization. Writers involved in privatized projects experienced a new sense of freedom and diversity as the spaces for expression were decentralized and multiplied. Expression, especially in the (yes, privatized) journalistic work undertaken by many writers became more dissident as part of the rising tide of mobilized discourse vis-à-vis the economic and social consequences of Serrano's neoliberal project and such questions as the dialogue process and human rights. Most writers, however, experienced increased fragmentation, alienation, and vulnerability as Serrano officials retaliated against the growing "ungovernability" of civil society and the lettered sectors thereof. Perhaps most emblematic of literary change at this juncture was the death of the great patriarch of Guatemalan leftist resistance literature, Luis Cardoza y Aragón, at the age of 89 — especially because of the heated discussions which his death incited in relation to the importance of the 1944 Revolution and the role of Guatemalan writers as journalists, poets, and overall contributors to cultural politics.

Older generation figures filled new spaces, as Mario Monteforte Toledo came home and quickly established his presence with some of the younger writers, above all, the emerging indigenous poet Humberto Ak'Abal. Arriving at a time of growing student activism and military repression under Serrano, Mario Roberto Morales raised questions about Guatemala's revolutionary past and its place in a new order where the older Left-Right categories and perspectives no longer had meaning, and the indigenous issue became a central consideration. Morales pointed to postmodernist perspectives as he viewed Guatemalan conflicts in terms not of old Left-Right divisions but of multiple and contradictory forces involving shifting constellations and relations of power in which popular sectors evolving with ever greater independence took on the leading roles. Furthermore, he raised the question of increased testimonialization and indigenization of Guatemalan literature as the logical direction in response to the changed historical conjuncture. Above all, and however his subsequent positions may now be considered, his intent began as an effort to constitute a critique of the Left from within the Left, to forge a vision of hybrid, microgroup alliances and ideological constructs that might be important for the nation's full entry into a new phase, which might well be postmodern.

Writing in 1992, Morales saw the new configuration of world power in terms of electronic interdependence, multinational megamarkets, new democratization patterns — all within a context conditioned by North-South power relations and potential free-trade structures under the aegis of neoliberalism, which both conditioned and potentiated indigenous and broader patterns of resistance. The Central American crisis was the last major conflict to be resolved before the emergence of the new world order of globalization and hybridization (Morales 1992a).

Clearly, in this emergent order, leftist revolutionary parties and popular movements played their part, Morales insisted, even if they could not fulfill their dream of actually coming to power. The Serrano government attempted to give lip service to the necessities Morales underlined, but its main goal was to maintain the basic military-governmental pact that kept it and its interests afloat (even as it sought to throttle, but actually incited, further resistance). As long-hard-put popular sectors' demands crescendoed for democratization (at a time when the hegemonic North no longer feared a massive international rival and could only be strengthened by democratization), the government faced a growing "crisis of ungovernability" that it sought ultimately to overcome by attempting to crack down in the most decisive way: the self-coup of May 1993.

As events moved toward confrontation, Morales, from his emergent critical perspective, proposed to now kill Cardoza—this in an article written just before and published just after Cardoza's death (1992b). Morales argued that the Guatemalan intelligentsia should go beyond Cardoza's literary model; they should not obviate, denigrate, or forget Cardoza, but receive the lesson that Cardoza provided and go beyond him—just as Cardoza had done with the models of a previous generation. Guatemalan writers had to make a new literature corresponding to a reality in which the old categories no longer functioned, and in which themes of ethnicity and gender identity have a weight they had never been given before.

Contemporaneous with the campaign for Menchú's Nobel Prize and the rise of new, redefined indigenous organizations led by figures such as Rosalina Tuyuc, these were matters that attracted attention to Humberto Ak'Abal, the writer who seemed to best express the era and anticipate a future when, as many argued, indigenous dimensions would finally achieve full articulation in national discourse.

Ak'Abal culminated a development in twentieth-century Guatemalan letters from *indigenista* Ladino writers to ones more specifically Indian. A key aspect to his emergence was his relationship with Monteforte, who championed indigenous concerns in the 1944 revolution, and above all, his overt relationship with Menchú as a symptom of indigenous emergence after their supposed vanquishment in the mid-1980s. It is surely no accident that the most exciting new poet in Guatemala had his work heralded in 1991–1992, and that that work had a certain resonance in the magic month of October, when, four days after October 12, Menchú was accorded the Nobel Peace Prize. Among the avalanche of poetic texts to appear in homage to Menchú is one by Ak'Abal himself, which makes my point emphatically.

> You uprooted a testimony of blood
> and spread it throughout the world;
> your sandals traversed
> the roads of the earth
> and now the world knows the truth;
> the Indian sees, hears and thinks. . . .
> Sister by blood, race and tongue:
> *sib'alaj kij ki'kotik,*
> *ke b'ixon ri tukmux. . . .*
> 500 years weigh,
> 500 years hurt,
> and your cry of peace, Rigoberta,
> returns hope to us.
> (Ak'Abal, "Rigoberta Menchú Tum,"
> 1992 my translation)

Finally, in that same ever-so-symbolic year, a new volume by Menchú and her organization, CUC, began to circulate in Guatemala (1992). A collection of essays about peasant struggles, this book included two poems written in 1990 by Menchú herself. Some may balk at the idea of Rigoberta Menchú as a poet and writer, and it is true that some supporters insisted that she try her hand at poetry. Are these poems profoundly Menchú's, and do they express her Indian past as much as her Ladinization process? Are they Indian poems translated into Spanish? Or are they the product of Ladinization, Westernization?

It is not surprising in the face of this conjuncture that writer-anthropologist

Carlos René García Escobar should then publish the essay "El abrazo histórico de Cardoza y Rigoberta" (1992), which examines crucial political and cultural dynamics. This essay, framed by pictures of Cardoza and Menchú and one of Ak'Abal's poems, connects literature and the popular movements, literature and testimonio, literature and the indigenous question as the Serrano government was entering its final phase. Pointing to 1992 as a significant year for the peoples of the world, García Escobar notes that "a world reordering has begun that has still not been consolidated, . . . but that is already having repercussions in all sectors of the earth's societies." Guatemala is hardly an exception, he remarks, and the awarding of the Nobel Peace Prize to Menchú for her stances on human, women's, and above all, indigenous rights is a demonstration that Guatemalan concerns are also international ones.

García then couples this occurrence with the death of Guatemala's greatest poet some weeks before the announcement of Menchú's prize. Cardoza died, leaving the Guatemalans with "a lesson of dignity . . . and authentic love for . . . what is ours," he says.

> In dying, . . . Cardoza salutes Rigoberta and passes to her the historical baton of social revindication. It's the embrace of generations. It's the assumption of a centuries'-old commitment. Cardoza ended the five hundred years in an uncompromising attitude. Rigoberta begins the new five hundred years with the same posture and with the same hope in the future. . . . Now everything begins to change. We can't see reality with the same eyes as before. The Nobel Prize permits Rigoberta and the popular Guatemalan Indian organizations to level the road, always and when efforts combine the common interests and the pluri-ethnic and pluri-cultural collectivity of oppressed Guatemalans. Our recent past . . . weighs over the present with a gravity of pain and humiliation and the irreversibility of death. . . . Rigoberta's triumph is ours, that of all of us who have been and are participating in the defense of the most cherished interests of our people. . . . This recognition is as great as the context of popular demands; the October Revolution of 1944 begins to fade now because we see the future with greater conviction and security. . . . The usual pitfalls persist but something begins to change. The criminal impunity against the population should be eliminated along with the infamous bloodshed, and so we should all prepare so that with our emerging social consciousness, we can obtain social justice in all its dimensions. The imaginary historical embrace of Cardoza and Rigoberta, of generation to generation, is our guarantee for the future. (my translation)

These words envision a new conjuncture in which the most progressive writers of respective generations have a certain affiliation and are linked not only to Menchú but to such women as Nineth García, Mirna and Helen Mack, and Rosalina Tuyuc. The movement from Cardoza to Menchú is a movement from Ladino to Indian, from man to woman, from "high modernist" macroliterature to postmodernist testimonial microtext. It is also a movement from older forms of leftist politics to the new post-Gramscian, Laclau-Mouffean alliance politics, which would seem the only possible, if however fragile and vulnerable, route toward transformative social change in the new era. It is in relation to this hope that we are to understand Morales's critiques of past revolutionary projects and cultural-political models; it is in relation to this hope that García Escobar champions Humberto Ak'Abal as one who points us toward Guatemala's future, and that he and Mario Roberto see indigenous testimonials as crucial in the country's future literary development after all.

Clearly, the writings of García Escobar, Morales, and others bespeak the effect of Menchú on their work; for such writers, "in the future, testimonial will be stronger in Guatemala" (García Escobar 1993). Surely, the best testimonial-inflected texts will continue Guatemala's recent tradition of experimentation, forays into Asturias's magic realism, or Cardoza's Latin Americanized surrealism; they will be Bakhtinian, multiple, mixtures of document and imagination, prose and poetry, expression, yes, and denunciation. But clearly they will also be testimonial and will embody indigenous and feminist dimensions that will be important to a discursive system fully expressive of those who have heretofore been silenced.

The Serranazo and Rigoberta Menchú

Spring 1993 was a time marked by questioning of military impunity and judicial integrity. Mexican-based refugees, accompanied by human rights workers, returned to their home areas only to suffer harassment and murderous attack from the army; popular organizations and their supporters marched past the government palace, shouting their protests. Attacks on protesting students and an increasingly confrontational press increased. The shadow of growing economic woes and charges of corruption provoked shows of resistance by mass organizations, and conspiratorial plans by a president who studied the moves of Fujimori and discussed with uniformed friends whether or not he could repeat history. What he achieved wasn't even a farce, but a pastiche.

By mid-May 1993, several students had been abducted, and word spread of the assassination of a University Student Association leaders; student, teacher and worker groups took to the streets. As the social climate heated up, Serrano-Elías, backed by the military Right, moved to install martial law, suspend the Congress, and hold the Supreme Court under house arrest. By the second day of the self-coup, all of Guatemala's newspapers were placed under strict censorship, and two television stations were closed. Ramiro de León Carpio, human rights ombudsman, went into hiding to avoid arrest.

So began the culminating crisis of the controlled democracy established by the military as part of its counterinsurgent strategy. The popular mobilizations of indigenous and Ladino workers joined with the intellectuals (students, teachers, and writers, especially reporters) and other sectors to precipitate the power play by Serrano and members of the military hierarchy in an effort to save the regime. But mounting public opposition in Guatemala, along with international opinion and the specific role of the United States in the Organization of American States (OAS), forced key military leaders to abandon Serrano and negotiate a civil restoration—clearly, as time has shown, with certain guarantees that would make democratic advance very difficult, but rather resistance all but inevitable.

How can we measure Rigoberta Menchú's participation in the Serranazo? It was not without controversy. How could a Nobel Peace Prize winner work to overthrow a government? The negative campaign was ferocious, and in the recent book by Alvaro Vargas Llosa and Santiago Aroca (1995: 166), Ramiro de León Carpio criticizes Menchú's activity, questioning her representativity with respect to Indian groups, saying that she withdrew from the struggle and took on an almost completely negative posture—that in this, as in other matters, she had not acted at the level of her Nobel Prize, but had followed the totally unacceptable line of the URNG. Of course, here the question of interpretation becomes crucial, for the guerrilla leaders attacked her deviations from an official line that just days later they themselves had to criticize. And in this matter the problem of Indian-Ladino understandings and priorities indicate a different perspective.

First, the growth of the popular movement in which Menchú had played a crucial role was the prime reason for Serrano's self-coup, and it would also be a major reason for its failure. Menchú was in Guatemala to participate in the first Indigenous Peoples World Summit meeting when the Serranazo began. She immediately joined with other leaders to form the Coordinating Committee of Civil Sectors (the CSC), a coalition of more than sixty groups that met and decided to form a national front calling for the restoration of the Constitution. Menchú also operated as a member of the Representación Unitaria de la Oposición Guatemalteca (RUOG), overcoming the doubts of some about her participation on the national level after years of work in Mexico and participation at international conferences, acting now with commitment as "a woman disposed to fighting within her own country" ("Editorial," *Crónica* June 12, 1993: 13).

In the first days of the struggle, Menchú announced a religious service for peace, demanding that the international community enact sanctions against the Serrano regime. She also organized a worker rally against the coup outside the court building where Serrano was to swear in his new handpicked Supreme Court. When the rally was broken up with tear gas, Menchú announced a protest mass at the cathedral. Several thousand demonstrators attended and then marched to the government palace, where Menchú delivered a letter to Serrano demanding constitutional restoration. These acts of defiance in the face of complete suspension of legal guarantees helped galvanize popular opposition. A few days later, a petition Menchú penned condemning the coup was read from the pulpits of churches throughout the country. The petition, which also circulated internationally, called for the resignation of Serrano and company and the prosecution of corrupt representatives. When Clinton representatives indicated their clear opposition to the Serranazo and warned that all aid and trade would be cut off, this "crisis of globalization processes" divided those who supported the coup and helped bring together the final coalition against Serrano.

With the military clearly divided and rendered ineffective, popular protest grew, and Serrano, shown the writing on the wall, resigned and left the country. The army then jockeyed for some kind of transition, selecting an ultraconservative military ally, Vice President Gustavo Espino Salguero, as the new president. But Menchú's group protested bitterly that the majority of the population had been excluded from the decision making. On June 2, 1993, thousands gathered outside the national palace to hear Menchú issue a declaration saying that the removal of Serrano and the subsequent high-level machinations were yet another coup d'etat. The military accused her of polarizing society and, by their railing, confirmed her "significance in publicly voicing the demands of the popular sectors in the crisis and assuring that they would be heard, by those in power and the international press" (ibid.).

On June 4, the Supreme Court ruled that Espina could not be president because of his role in the coup. Some claim that there was an effort to form a triumvirate with Menchú, Helen Mack, and Ramiro de León Carpio, which proved too radical to be accepted, but popular pressures were adequate to promote Congress's election of León Carpio into the presidency. This election was not without the military's acceptance, with León Carpio assuring that he would maintain his human rights emphasis while seeking to resolve the country's economic problems, advance a pro-indigenous agenda, and negotiate an end to armed struggle in the country. León was acceptable to the Left, but the way he was selected was not.

The URNG and Menchú's CUC organization gave cautious recognition to the new government, while many intellectuals and writers began comparing

León Carpio's statements and goals with those of Juan José Arévalo in the period from 1944 to 1951. Indeed, many of the writers whose news stories and columns had attacked Serrano-Elías's government time and again now joined formally to help create an environment that would give the new government a chance. The question was what compromises had he made in exchange for his coming to office. The answer now seems evident: that he would not interfere with the military. Meanwhile, Menchú returned to exile to wait and watch developments in the new, emergent era.

That Serrano and the military could not sustain the coup in the face of the North's economic pressures, as well as firm internal opposition, confirmed the possibility that Guatemala was indeed entering a new historical period in which still-existing military hegemony was hedged and qualified by an odd alliance of global and areawide, U.S. and national, business and popular interests that had to be in some way appeased. As the military yielded to the pressures, it did not capitulate fully but sought some middle ground to stem the tide. Whether or not the new presidency would be able to counter the military's potential for violence, coup, and atrocity, and continue building the "democratic infrastructure" needed for the construction of civil society would be the challenge of the day.

The Serranazo was part of a structure of events and relations tied to globalization processes and impacting the national process in that many military leaders were also entrepreneurs affected by the social disturbances. Above all, however, attention should be given to the role of the popular groups and their "organic leaders," including Rigoberta Menchú. While the URNG leaders remained disoriented and indecisive, the popular organizations reacted rapidly to the events, escaping URNG categories and agendas and leaving official representatives of the Left in the position of attempting to catch up, and seeking how to rehegemonize the opposition as a supposed vanguard—an effort in which they have not been successful to this day.

This leaping of bounds puts Rigoberta Menchú and the CUC beyond the EGP or another political group, in a position outside the existing structures and norms of the Left, in that Laclau-Mouffean space that Doris Sommer referred to beyond existing leftist paradigms and norms, constituting the possibility of still newer social subjects generating ever newer social movements.

After the Serranazo

The role of Rigoberta Menchú — related but not tied to the guerrilla Left, developments in Mexico, and also the events north of the Guatemalan border — was to enter a new phase following the Serranazo. From the beginning, León Carpio struggled to find a legalist path for improving Guatemala's economic and social conditions under pressure from NAFTA and other forces emerging in the area. His trade-off was a low prioritizing of the peace talks, a matter which, while understandable as he sought to withstand the military, did imply increasing criticism from Rigoberta and others. CUC, GAM, and other organizations were vehement in their protests against the civilian patrols as a source of human rights atrocities, but Carpio argued that many of the indigenous people wanted the civil patrols to protect them against the guerrillas and the military. In late August 1993, Menchú wrote a letter to Carpio saying it was incomprehensible that he continued to support them, and calling for their dissolution and national demilitarization. She also spoke out against Carpio's slowness in resuming any peace talks with the URNG. Protest was also registered against the military's harassment of the thousands of Guatemalans seeking to relocate from Chiapas. Then Menchú attacked Carpio's "National Plan for Peace" for demanding that the URNG disarm before talks resumed. She claimed that Carpio's proposal was no advance over Serrano's ninety-day peace plan.

The violations of indigenous rights connected with these matters spilled over into questions that did not respect strict nation-state formations, borders, or ethnic divisions. Just days before the Serranazo, Menchú had named Chiapas bishop Samuel Ruíz as one of fourteen leaders in defense of the indigenous peoples. Then, on November 1, after all her efforts to exert pressure on León Carpio, she used her position to call on the pope to prevent the transfer of Ruíz, whom she credited with helping thousands of Guatemalan refugees to escape the widescale repression of the 1980s and, she added, "with continually defending the human rights of Mexican indigenous living in Chiapas."

In January 1994, after the Zapatista uprising, Menchú departed from her usual caution in criticizing the government that had offered her refuge for more than a decade and spoke out "in her role as Nobel Prize winner," affirming her solidarity with the religious organizations and concerns relating to the people and Bishop Ruíz. She called for dialogues leading to a negotiated settlement respecting the just complaints of Chiapas's indigenous population, and also for an end to the bombing of civilian living areas, so much a part of her Guatemalan experience.

As if to ensure the attention of the Mexican and Guatemalan governments, she then accompanied almost nine hundred refugees crossing from Chiapas en route to Guatemalan relocation, and she was party to Guatemalan government–URNG efforts to reopen peace talks with an eye to a negotiated peace by the end of the year. The next week, Menchú announced plans to lead an international group of indigenous leaders to Chiapas to press for and monitor a peaceful and negotiated settlement of the crisis — this at a time when Guatemalan military officials were, officially or not, offering to help the Mexican military deal with insurrectionists. Menchú's pressuring role was clear as León Carpio moved toward a more negative stance regarding the civilian patrols and, almost simultaneously, offered asylum to Mexico's indigenous who might be fleeing from the military.

With the initial Mexican agreements and the reopening of Guatemalan peace talks, it became clear that Menchú would be playing a significant role in the configuration of forces and possibilities structuring a new period beyond the revolutionary 1980s and its theoretical frames. This assessment applies to the effort on the part of many social actors to construct a new public sphere consonant with a postmodern pluralism and able, at least for the moment, to contribute to making at least a hopeful transition for Guatemala. Rigoberta's way was no longer the road of armed struggle leading to the socialist millennium that previous resistance writers had imagined. But it was the road of the possible in an era in which mass organizations led the way for the supposed vanguard, and in which new literary modes could relate to new social ones involving the new social subjects and movements which older discourses were at loss to fully project. Whatever happened with León Carpio's particular government (and the disappointment was so great that so little had happened to spur the peace process and resolve the nation's problems of ungovernability that Efraín Ríos Montt's candidate almost won the 1996 elections), and whatever happens with the new government of Arzú and other regimes to come, it is still in the new space of new positions, relations, and representations that Guatemalan civil society and its discourses will greet the new century.

In expressing this viewpoint, then, we are no longer in the overt political turf of EGP-CUC (Leninist/liberationist) syncretism, nor are we in the terrain simply of a Laclau-Mouffean (post-Leninist/post-Gramscian) alliance politics, but rather, as Sommer would have it, in some unexplored new space beyond current theorizations. The process by which Menchú projects and shapes her public, revolutionary identity is also the process by which a new, nonreducible collective subjectivity begins to emerge (Brittin 1994: 96). It is by internalizing all she has experienced and learned that Menchú has come to embody and represent transformative possibility and hope in her country and region in the epoch of globalization. The controversies surrounding her name, including all the questions raised by David Stoll, cannot erase what she has accomplished.

Note

This essay is partially based on materials appearing in Zimmerman, *Literature and Resistance in Guatemala* (Athens: University of Ohio Press, 1995); a longer, Spanish version of the essay appeared in Zimmerman "Rigoberta Menchú después del Nobel: Desde la narrativa militante a la lucha postmoderna," in *Revista Canadiense de Estudios Hispanicos*. vol. 23, 3. (spring 1999): 499–519. I am responsible for all translations from the Spanish. A note on the acronyms which appear: CUC, Comité de Unidad Campesina (Committee for Peasant Unity) has been Guatemala's primary indigenous peasant organization, often associated with the EGP, the Ejército Guerrillero de los Pobres (the Guerrilla Army of the Poor), one of the more radical guerrilla groups that believed in close relations with the indigenous populations and that eventually joined with other revolutionary organizations to form the URNG, Unión Revolucionaria Nacional Guatemalteca (Guatemalan National Revolutionary Union). Another important organization mentioned is the women's organization, GAM, the Grupo de Apoyo Mutuo (Mutual Support Group), which dealt with questions of disappeared persons and political repression.

No version of the essay takes into account Menchú's narration of post-Nobel prize events in her book of 1998, nor the claims made by David Stoll (1999), although my book contains a discussion of the earlier versions of Stoll's arguments, answered partially by Stoll (p. 241). A recently published interview with Arturo Taracena gives considerable background into the circumstances leading to the first volume. The book I edited with Raúl Rojas, *Voices from the Silence* (1998: 305), drafted before the publication of Stoll's famous text, summarizes my own take on the questions at stake: "Menchú's account may well be colored by traumatized memory, learned biblical tropes, her interlocutor's interviewing and editing orientations, and, not least of all, Menchú's own interest in promoting the guerilla-Indian, or more specifically, the EGP/CUC alliance." What is important to note here is that even if Menchú's testimonio contains key distortions and untruths in part attributable to her political agenda and that of the EGP (Stoll's thesis), that conclusion would only strengthen the argument in this essay about her text and indeed her public identity as commodity. On the other hand, her more recent activities would point to her growing independence from party lines and older narratives, even in terms of the "fundamental contradictions" governing Guatemalan society. For my most recently published position on the Stoll/Menchú controversy, see Zimmerman, "Medio siglo de sueños de utopías destruidos." *Arena Cultural* 18 (September 2000): 11–13.

Works Cited

Achugar, Hugo. 1990. "Postmodernidad y postdictadura: Fin de siglo en Uruguay." *Revista de Crítica Cultural* 1, 1 (May): 18–19.

Ak'Abal, Humberto. 1992. "Rigoberta Menchú Tum." *La Hora Cultural*, 14 November, 7.

Brittin, Alice A. 1994. "Me llamo Rigoberta Menchú in the Politics of Poetics in Central American Testimonio." Ph.D. diss, University of California, Berkeley.

Castañeda, Jorge G. 1994. *Utopia Unarmed: The Latin American Left after the Cold War*. New York: Vintage.

"Editorial." 1993. *Crónica*, 12 June, 14–15.

García Escobar, Carlos René. 1992. "El abrazo histórico de Cardoza y Rigoberta." *La Hora Cultural*, 31 October: 7.

———. Interview with Marc Zimmerman. 1993. Spring Hotel, Guatemala City, 22 March.

Jonas, Suzanne. 1991. *The Battle for Guatemala*. Boulder, Colo.: Westview.

Laclau, Ernesto, and Chantal Mouffe. 1995. *Hegemony and Socialist Strategy: Towards a Radical Democratic Politics*. London: Verso.

Menchú Tum, Rigoberta. 1985. *Me llamo Rigoberta Menchú y así me nació la conciencia*. Ed. Elisabeth Burgos-Debray. Mexico City: Siglo XXI.

——. *Rigoberta: La nieta de los mayas.* 1998. With the collaboration of Dante Liano and Gianni Mina. Madrid: Aguilar.

Menchú Tum, Rigoberta, and Comité de Unidad Campesina. 1992. *Trenzando el futuro: Luchas campesinas en la historia reciente de Guatemala.* [Bilbao, Spain]: Terser Presa. Reprint, Hirugarren Prentsa: S.L., 1992.

Morales, Mario Roberto. 1992a. "Autogestión, desradicalización, y autonomía." *El Cauce* 1, 1 (July): 8–10.

——. 1992b. "Ahora matemos a Cardoza: A fuego libre." *Prensa Libre,* 6 September, 22.

Richard, Nelly. "De la rebeldía anarquizante al desmontaje ideológico (crítica y poder)." *Revista de Crítica Cultural* 2, 1 (8 November 1990): 8–9.

Sommer, Doris. 1991. "Rigoberta's Secrets." *Latin American Perspectives: Voices of the Voiceless in Testimonial Literature,* pt 1. 18, 3 (issue 70) (summer): 32–50.

Stoll, David. 1999. *Rigoberta Menchú and the Story of All Poor Guatemalans.* Boulder, Colo.: Westview.

Vargas Llosa, Alvaro, and Santiago Aroca. 1995. *Riding the Tiger: Ramiro de León Carpio's Battle for Human Rights in Guatemala.* Miami: Brickell Communications.

Zimmerman, Marc. 1995. *Literature and Resistance in Guatemala: Textual Modes and Cultural Politics from El Señor Presidente to Rigoberta Menchú.* Athens, Ohio: University of Ohio Press.

——. 1999. "Rigoberta Menchú después del Nobel: Desde la narrativa militante a la lucha postmoderna." In "Pequeños Relatos y globalización. Debates sobre identidades en el mundo hispánico. Revista Canadiense de Estudios Hispánicos, 23, 3 (spring: 499–519).

——. 2000. "Medio siglo de sueños de utopías destruidos." *Arena Cultural* 18 (September): 11–13.

Zimmerman, Marc, and Raúl Rojas, eds. 1998. *Voices from the Silence: Guatemalan Literature of Resistance.* Athens, Ohio: University of Ohio Press.

No Perfect World: Aboriginal Communities' Contemporary Resource Rights

PATRICIA SEED

Indigenous peoples remain the world's most subaltern despite the major advances in health, living standards, and political rights over the last five hundred years. Initially decimated by diseases from foreign invaders, natives died off in record numbers during successive waves of European colonization. Indigenous people who survived either had to move to vacate the space for invaders — or else were required to live nearby so that they might be forced to toil for them.

Nineteenth- and twentieth-century revolutions catapulted a new anticolonial political elite to power throughout Asia, Africa, and the Americas. Yet in these newly independent anticolonial states, aboriginal peoples usually continued to reside in isolated communities or in labor reservoirs as basic economic rules instituted by European colonizers remained in place. And as the twentieth century drew to a close, aboriginal peoples remained impoverished, dwelling on the margins of sleek new nation-states.

In the final decade of the twentieth century, aboriginal peoples' rights began to be a significant international issue, spurred in part by the awarding of a political prize for peace to a Guatemalan native woman, Rigoberta Menchú, in 1992. The world over, indigenous communities saw her award as signaling an opportunity that might restore to them some measure of economic dignity. Many indigenous communities turned to the United Nations to find allies in their search for a form of economic justice. Yet two decades before, the United Nations had determined that national, not international, policies would define sovereignty over natural resources.[1] While seemingly uncontroversial on its surface, this accord legitimates denying access, use, or profit from any natural resources to aboriginal communities. Furthermore, the agreement prevents the world's indigenous people from claiming ownership of specific resources in an international forum. National, not international, criteria fix indigenous peoples' rights to own or to manage even their resources in their own territories.

The central trouble for many contemporary indigenous communities lies in the unnoticed colonial legacy of the rules governing resource ownership. In many formerly colonial nations, the economic rules imposed by European colonizers were never overturned during the revolution for independence. Therefore, these formerly colonial economic rules for access to natural resources still prevail among dozens of independent nation-states. Thus the United Nations accord allowing nations to control natural resources has legitimated colonial traditions of unequal access to natural resources in these states. Furthermore, it has perpetuated the different colonial traditions of England and Iberia, which denied aboriginal communities' right to own either land (England) or valuable buried minerals. In former English colonies the world over, indigenous people remain unable to assert sovereignty over land, while in former Spanish and Portuguese colonies, it preserves the same indisputable sovereignty over mineral deposits.

The political and economic consequences for the world's indigenous people are continuing economic pressures to sustain their subaltern status. And under international agreement they remain unable to challenge the basic ownership of land in former English colonies, and of mineral deposits in former Iberian colonies. The rules governing such ownership form part of "sovereignty," the internationally guaranteed right of national autonomy in allocating ownership of natural resources. How and what indigenous people can argue for remain constrained by colonial English and Iberian parameters, as illustrated by the following examples.

In 1963 in the Australian Northern Territories, a group of senior aboriginal men wrote a petition in the Gumatj language to the House of Representatives in Canberra claiming that an Australian government concession of 363 square kilometers in an aboriginal reserve to a French bauxite mining concern contained sites sacred to aboriginal peoples.[2] Five years later, after mining had begun, they submitted a demand for compensation and for the right to be consulted regarding future mining contracts on their soil. Although their petition was initially turned down in the House of Representatives, in 1976 a law was passed (amended in 1987) that secured aboriginal rights to compensation for mining activities in the Northern Territories.[3]

Two decades later, on the other side of the globe, another Southern Hemisphere controversy erupted over indigenous peoples' rights to regulate mining. During the debates over ratification of the 1988 Brazilian Constitution, a nongovernmental organization, the Indian Mission Council, proposed a constitutional prohibition on mining in Indian lands. The most controversial of all proposals regarding indigenous peoples, it was targeted by a sharp political attack orchestrated in the nation's four major newspapers. To ban mining (or suggest that Indians might be given the right to do so) was to undermine the sovereignty of the Brazilian state. To even make such a suggestion, the newspapers claimed, constituted bad faith. The proposal was swiftly withdrawn, and the final draft of the 1988 constitution (art. 176) specifically excluded indigenous peoples from exercising any rights, including payment from mining activities in their territories. The regulation of mining remains solely in the hands of Congress, and only the national government can be paid for mining.[4]

Although it was politically impossible even to suggest that Indians should be consulted about, let alone paid for, mining activities on their land in Brazil, it was feasible both to discuss and obtain compensation in Australia.[5] In Canada, Australia, New Zealand, and the United States, native communities (or a government official representing them) can request compensation for mining done in their terrain.[6] Yet in former Iberian colonial states, such an idea is unconscionable. Valuable mineral resources belong to the nation, which alone has the right to profit from mining. These Iberian traditions regarding minerals operate powerfully today, and not just for the world's aboriginal peoples, for in this fuel-powered era, there is an additionally valuable subsoil resource: oil.

One of the great ironies of global geological processes is that most of the world's oil and natural gas reserves lie beneath the surface of lands governed by legal principles of Islamic origin. Today, in Saudi Arabia, Yemen, Iran, Iraq, Kuwait, Libya, the United Arab Emirates, Qatar, Algeria, Indonesia, Ecuador, Mexico, Venezuela, Argentina, and Nigeria, the people hold inalienable title to all petroleum resources.[7] And in most of these states, the national government manages these resources for the community.[8] Sharing this Islamic tradition of communal ownership of mineral resources has made possible the only successful commodity consortium possible, the Organization of Petroleum Exporting Countries, or OPEC.

Venezuelan leaders originated the idea and initial meeting of this highly successful multinational organization in 1960, but its success has been possible because the many past and eleven current members of OPEC share not simply a natural resource, but a common legal understanding of its ownership and management.[9] Even within modern Nigeria, many citizens remain convinced that oil is a gift from God to their nation or people.[10] Because of shared beliefs in popular sovereignty over valuable minerals, private ownership of petroleum resources is not only wrong, but also unthinkable. *Governments* alone can set national production levels and quotas without fear of private interference or competition.

While multinational corporations can dictate terms for the extraction of less-valuable minerals such as bauxite and copper, they have been unable to do so for petroleum because geological processes and historical accident have united to produce a common cultural understanding of sovereignty and management of much of the world's petroleum. OPEC's success as an international league of governments, however, springs both from its member nations' common geological fate and shared (and originally identical) set of legal and moral beliefs about communal ownership and management of this resource.

The situation could not be more different in the regions colonized by England, where a hodgepodge of rules prevails. Whoever owns the surface land also usually (but not always) owns the minerals.[11] As a result, individuals, corporations, and state and national governments can own the petroleum beneath the surface. The landowner usually negotiates separately with international mining concerns, thus frequently giving the latter (holding greater information) the upper hand; however governments, native tribes, as well as individuals in former English colonies have requested compensation for mining.[12] But in a remarkably ironic twist, one twentieth-century U.S. judge defined oil in a way that facilitated Native American rights to income from it. Following the first discoveries of oil in the early twentieth century, lengthy debates about its legal status in the United States ensued. In 1934, a celebrated judged decided that natural gas behaved like wild animals (ferae naturae) and therefore was owned by the person who snared it.[13] While controversial in legal circles, the definition of oil as a wild animal reinforced Texas and Oklahoma Indian communities' ownership of oil and natural gas. The laws of capture allowed Indians ("hunters") to ensnare petroleum as well.

If the aboriginal people of former Iberian colonies can neither own nor benefit from the yellow or black gold found in their soil, then aboriginal groups in former English colonies can neither own nor benefit significantly from their land.[14] To regain lands that have been taken away is only possible when the nation believes such land will never be employed for profit. Only land that the natives will never use because they consider it sacred is ever returned in former English colonies.[15] The Taos Pueblos regained their sacred Blue Lake along with 48,000 acres of the Carson National Forest—land already set aside for nonproductive use. In 1972 part of Mount Adams in Washington State was restored to the Yakima Indians, but only because it was a place in which the Yakima would undertake no economic activity because it was sacred.[16] The Canadian province of British Columbia today allows native retention of "cultural heritage resources," meaning an "object, a site, or the location of a traditional society practice of historical cultural or archaeological significance to the Province, a community, or an aboriginal people."

Resource Rights: Land

Just as in former Iberian colonies in which the nation owns mineral resources, in former English colonies the nation owns the land on which they reside.

Native people are only entitled to reside on, but not own, the land, a practice called "native" or "aboriginal title."

Aboriginal or "tribal" peoples are restricted to what is called "native title" in the United States, Australia, and New Zealand, and "aboriginal title" in Canada.[17] The U.S. Supreme Court declared that "aboriginal interest simply constitutes permission from the whites to occupy the land and . . . [is] not specifically recognized as ownership by Congress."[18] The Canadian Constitution Act of 1982 similarly defines aboriginal title as "the right to exclusive use and occupation of the land," not ownership. The celebrated Australian Mabo case (1992) describes native title as preserving only "entitlement to use or enjoyment under the traditional law or custom,"[19] but not the right to own. In New Zealand, a leading Maori chief, Nopera Panekareao, explained native title more poetically: "The shadow of the land passes to the Queen, but the substance remains with us."[20]

Claims of ownership of land are usually immediately denied throughout the former English colonies. When hereditary chiefs of the Gitksan or Wet'suwet'en from British Columbia in 1994 sought ownership of 58,000 square kilometers, the Canadian court transformed this claim into a request for aboriginal title.[21] But the right merely to use land severely limits how native peoples can earn a living, since in this legal tradition land ownership is the key to raising capital. Denying Indians ownership actually eliminates their ability to use either the land or the valuable assets that it contains as collateral for loans for their own economic development.

When substantial quantities of highly profitable resources are discovered in Indian territories today, governments of former English colonies frequently rush to take the lands away, thus once again eliminating future native economic development. The Alaska Native Claims Settlement Act in 1971 extinguished Yup'ik and Inuit claims to aboriginal hunting, fishing, and land rights, thus clearing access to Prudhoe Bay and North Slope oil reserves.[22] In Canada, one-quarter of the remaining discovered petroleum and one-half of the country's estimated potential are located north of 60 degrees latitude. In order to obtain ownership of these hydrocarbon rich parts of otherwise desolate tundra, the Canadian government agreed to create an indigenous Canadian province called Nunavut, meaning "Our Land." The Inuit now control only 770,000 square miles of ice and snow.[23]

In 1974 a previously undiscovered treaty signed by George Washington surfaced in Maine granting half of the state to two tribes, the Passamaquoddy and Penobscot. The federal government instantly and without any explanation reduced the area from 12.5 million to 3 million acres, excluding from consideration both the populated coast and valuable timber regions that George Washington had granted them in the treaty.[24] The Department of Justice was able to do so because there exists a cultural and political consensus in the United States that Native Americans are still not entitled to own any highly profitable land. In exchange for 10–12.5 million acres of what had become valuable timberland, the tribes received only 300,000 acres of "average quality timberland," plus the option to purchase an additional 200,000 acres of such timberland at fair market prices.[25]

Rarely are natives of former English colonies permitted in theory to receive significant profits from income-producing resources, and when they are allowed to do so, there is usually a reason. National governments customarily permit native communities to retain the right to compensation for allowing access to a resource when seeking an additional bargaining chip in negotiating with multinational corporations.[26] Because corporations control mining and marketing of natural resources such as copper, zinc, and bauxite (for aluminum), governments often remain at a distinct disadvantage in such negotiations. Introducing another arm of the government that claims to represent native peoples (as in Canada and the United States) or the natives themselves (in Australia and New Zealand) provides national or provincial governments an additional card to play in negotiating payments with multinational corporations seeking to mine bauxite, zinc, or copper.

Evidence that governments in former English colonies customarily see the native communities principally as bargaining chips shows up initially in their securing only a nominal portion of the revenues for these communities, and later failing to exercise reasonable care in seeing that natives receive what is owed them.[27] In 1998 a federal court judge found that U.S. government officials, including an internationally famous economist in charge of the nation's treasury, were unable to account for more than $4 billion in revenues owed Native Americans from oil and gas exploration in Oklahoma.[28]

Aboriginal communities in former English colonies can occasionally retain rights over resources when development will likely cause major environmental damage. Underneath Native American lands in the United States, for example, are most of the country's uranium supplies, and a coal mine on the Navajo reservation requires enormous amounts of water—and has polluted great expanses of the region. Navajos in the southwestern United States are permitted to run the profit-making Navajo Forest Products Industry, whose environmental policies closely resemble those of Peabody Coal in the same region. Environmental damage from uranium mining usually also ensures that the natives will never again be able to use the land for profit.

A further constraint is that without legal ownership, natives lack the freedom to sell their resources to the highest bidder.[29] Native peoples cannot take advantage of the market in order to receive a fair price for their land. From Jefferson to Carter, U.S. presidents have fixed an arbitrary figure—considerably less than fair market value — as compensation to natives seeking to sell their lands to the federal government.[30] Similarly, in 1994 the New Zealand government fixed the fiscal or settlement envelope of NZ$1 billion dollars to settle Maori land claims.

In addition to not having access to a fair market for their land, in most former English colonies the natives cannot invoke standard legal requirements for consent to sales of their land. Consent by verbal or written agreement, acquiescence, or other conduct must be present for binding real estate transactions under law, but native consent to the sales is not required.

The disregard for natives' refusal to consent to "sales" of their land is particularly apparent when the land has even a minimal or marginal economic value for ranching or farming. In the Nevada desert or the Dakota badlands, natives' repeatedly expressed desires to hold on to marginal pasture or agricultural land are usually unapologetically ignored, while consent must be considered for all others. For over a quarter of a century, the Western Shoshone have been struggling to hold onto their land — a battle they keep losing, but refuse to give up on. Their land is arid and rough scrub. The brush is prickly and hard to digest even for most animals. A large stretch of this desert nourishes just a few animals. But despite the land's lack of minerals or anything else of significant economic value, the U.S. government has steadfastly insisted since the 1970s that the Western Shoshone may not keep their marginal rangeland. Two Shoshone sisters have repeatedly taken their case to the Supreme Court; in its most recent decision, the court has said unequivocally that holding onto their pasture land was not an option for the Dann sisters.[31] The unwritten rule of former English colonies is that aboriginal people can only retain lands lacking potential for farming or ranching, and furthermore, they lack the right of refusal to sell.[32]

Since 1975, however, one former English colony, New Zealand, has taken present and past native consent to such transactions seriously. Even under these conditions, Maori cannot regain ownership of valuable land lost in earlier eras; they must settle for compensation. But in contrast to U.S. law, they can exercise authority (rangatiratanga) in managing some of the country's rivers, and have a right of first refusal when traditional Maori terrain leased to others becomes available.[33]

The contrasts with the Iberian world are striking. In Spanish America, popular opinion widely holds that native communities are firmly entitled to own, not merely use, farming and pasturelands as well as other profitable resources (except, of course, for mineral deposits). Several national constitutions and presidential decrees throughout Spanish America in the 1980s and 1990s have reinforced indigenous ownership (not just use) of traditional lands. The Indigenous Communities Statute of Paraguay (1981), the Peruvian Native Communities Act of 1974, and the Colombian Constitution of 1991 all recognize indigenous land ownership. A series of ministerial resolutions in Bolivia in the 1990s, the 1994 Constitution, and land grants in the 1980s by the Ecuadorian government all were passed with widespread public approval. Even the 1987 Philippine Constitution also recognizes native ownership and not merely occupation. The major cultural assumptions that operate automatically for citizens of former English colonies do not usually occur to citizens of former Spanish colonies. No assumption operates that natives are only entitled to unproductive or worthless land.

Among the most politically popular aims of the 1993 indigenous uprising in the southern Mexican state of Chiapas was their demand that owners of profitable farms return land to indigenous communities. "All poor-quality land in excess of 100 hectares and all good-quality land in excess of 50 hectares will . . . [be] taken away from them [landowners] . . . [who] may remain as small landholders or join the cooperative farmers' movement, farming societies, or communal lands."[34] The demand for the return of privately held agricultural land (with or without compensation) to the indigenous communities was widely popular even with urban Mexicans.

Yet such moves are decidedly unpopular in the United States. The Maine congressional delegation on February 28, 1977, stated, "There is simply no equitable way of forcing a return of land which has been settled, developed and improved in good faith by Maine people for two centuries."[35] Claiming to have "settled, developed and improved" constitutes neither a legally nor a culturally acceptable reason for refusing to return indigenous land in Ibero America.

A second distinguishing assumption found in former Spanish colonies concerns the treatment of written evidence or pictorial evidence of native ownership. Such writing creates an entirely different legal environment. In Ibero America, discovering documentation of a native claim shifts the burden of proof from the native community to the current owners, who then must prove that they and other non-Indians have acquired the land legitimately. Some national governments are even committed to helping natives recover written or pictorial evidence of old titles. The National Archives of Mexico, for example, has full-time staff fluent in native languages available to help Native Americans who regularly visit in search of documentary evidence of lands that they owned as recently as twenty years ago or as long ago as the sixteenth century.

Yet the contrary attitude toward natives' written documentation persists in the United States. When it was discovered that George Washington had, in writing, granted large sections of Maine forests to the Passamaquoddy and Penobscot tribes, Frank Trippett wrote in *Time* magazine that observing the treaty and returning land to Indians would result in an "unthinkable unraveling of society" that was an "inherent absurdity."[36] Yet in contemporary Spanish America, such sentiments would rarely, if ever, be voiced because the presumption (given written evidence) would be that natives had a right to their lands, and it would be up to the purchasers to prove to the contrary.

While the original covenant with subjugated indigenous communities only applied to agricultural communities, the tradition guaranteeing land ownership has created a contemporary presumption in favor of such rights, even in regions of mixed nomadic and sedentary peoples. Thus formerly nomadic communities on the periphery of Mexico, Chile, and Ecuador, for example, then as now can rely upon a tradition (not originally established for their own communities) that views native communities' retention of their traditional lands favorably. Thus the nomadic Mapuche have been able to obtain more than 185,000 acres in a recent settlement from the government of Chile.

The most interesting contrast in the contemporary Americas occurs in Brazil. Native peoples there are neither entitled to own their mineral resources, nor are they permitted to own their land. While it would seem that Brazil's native peoples would have the worst of all possible worlds, this is not entirely true, because aboriginal peoples are not entitled to own their lands for different reasons than in the former English colonies. Not finding any large-scale agricultural communities, Portuguese officials never implemented the Islamic-inspired Iberian covenant protecting indigenous ownership. But, unlike those in former English colonies, Portuguese-speaking citizens did not question natives' holding potentially profitable terrain. Thus it was possible in the 1990s to have lengthy political debates over the natives' right to possess (but not own) profitable terrain in Brazil, which resulted in the 1993 restitution of exclusive land-use rights for the Yanomami in the gold-bearing region of the Amazon Basin. In Maine, no discussion was ever possible over the Passamaquoddy and Penobscot's potential right to occupy valuable timberland.

Finally, the dominant themes of historical studies of aboriginal peoples in these respective areas of the Americas continue to differ depending on the nation's colonial past. Studies of aboriginal labor dominate the scholarly agenda in Ibero-America — yet just the opposite is true for studies of aboriginal peoples in Anglo North America. Alice Littlefield and Martha C. Knack write, "Studies of North American Indian economic life have largely ignored the participation of indigenous people in wage labor, even though for over a century such participation has often been essential for the survival of Native individuals and communities."[37] The predominant topic in the study of aboriginal peoples and communities in Anglo scholarship is land, although the professional groups in the United States that study Latin America usually focus also on the labor of aboriginal peoples.

Throughout the Americas, nationalists often assert that their colonial and/

or present treatment of natives was superior to that of others. Not only are they vying for the dubious honor of proving the advantages of one colonial project over another, but they are also unquestioningly assuming the validity of their own judgments about the proper path to riches. The belief that certain goods belonging to others can be expropriated while others remain untouchable rests on nothing more solid than historically and culturally constructed judgments about economics. Yet for modern nationalists, the only legitimate route to riches is their own; objectives and methods remain as valid today as they were in the time of their ancestors. Until citizens of both former English colonies and Iberian colonies understand that national traditions still follow colonial ones, there will be no possibility of overcoming the still-colonial position of native peoples within the nations of the Americas. But for the indigenous peoples of the Americas and Australia, there was, and still is, no perfect world.

Notes

A different version of this chapter appears as the conclusion of *American Pentimento: The Invention of Indians and the Pursuit of Riches* (Minneapolis: University of Minnesota Press, forthcoming).

1 Kamal Hossain and Subrata Roy Chowdhury, eds., *Permanent Sovereignty over Natural Resources in International Law: Principle and Practice* (London: Pinter, 1984); Gerhard Brehme, *Souveranitat der jungen National-staaten uber Naturreichtumer* (Sovereignty of the young nation-States over natural resources) (Berlin, Staatsverlag der Deutschen Demokratischen Republik, 1967), 71, 266; Ian Brownlie, *Legal Status of Natural Resources in International Law,* 162; *Principles of Public International Law* 4th ed. (Oxford: Oxford University Press, 1990), 287; G. A. Res. 626 (1952), reprinted in *United Nations Resolutions: General Assembly,* ed. Dusan J. Djononvich, vol. 4 (1973), 106; G. A. Res. 837 (1954), reprinted in ibid., vol. 5 (1973), 137; G. A. Res. 1314 (1958), reprinted in ibid., vol. 7 (1974), 121.

 For reflection on the United Nations debates of the 1970s that declared permanent national sovereignty over natural resources, see George Elian, *The Principle of Sovereignty over Natural Resources,* trans. Andre Bantas (Alphen aan den Rijn, The Netherlands; Germantown, Md.: Sijthoff and Noordhoff, 1979), 83–139. Stanley Hoffmann, forward to *State Sovereignty: Change and Persistence in International Relations,* by Sohail H. Hashmi (University Park: Pennsylvania State University Press, 1997), vii; for the slippery and changeable nature of sovereignty, see Thomas J. Biersteker and Cynthia Weber, eds., *State Sovereignty as Social Construct* (Cambridge: Cambridge University Press, 1996).

2 L. R. Hiatt, "Aboriginal Land Tenure and Contemporary Claims in Australia," ed. Edwin N. Wilmsen, *We Are Here: Politics of Aboriginal Land Tenure* (Berkeley: University of California Press, 1989), 100–101.

3 Aboriginal Land Rights (Northern Territory) Act, pt. 1, sec. 3, "Traditional Aboriginal Owners," pt. IV, sec. 44, 8 sec. 48D, sec. 63, 150.191.80.20/legislat/2b6e.htm.

4 Mining or hydroelectric projects must be approved by the Brazilian Congress rather than by indigenous communities (*Constituição . . . do Brasil,* art. 231, 3; Manuela Carneiro da

Cunha, "El concepto de derecho consuetudinario y los derechos indígenas en la nueva constitución de Brasil," in *Entre la ley y la costumbre: El derecho consuetudinario indígena en América Latina,* ed. Rodolfo Stavenhagen y Diego Iturralde [Mexico: Instituto Indigenista Interamericano, 1990], 299–313, esp. 304–306, 309; *Constitução da república federativa do Brasil* (Río de Janeiro, 1995), art. 176.

5 The Native Title Act of 1993 provides parties holding native title the right to negotiate with the government and the mining company about any proposal for mining, including exploration (sec. 51; www.austlii.edu.au/au/legis/cth/consol_act/nta1993147/. See also "Procedures under the Right to Negotiate System Issued by the National Native Title Tribunal, June 7, 1995." The URL is www.arts.uwa.edu.au/Anthropwww/negotiat.htm. For the Northern Territories legislation, see Aboriginal Land Rights (Northern Territory) Act, pt. VII, sec. 69.

6 While native communities can negotiate directly with multinationals in New Zealand and Australia, government officials represent them in Canada and the United States. First Nations are entitled to full economic benefit from metallic minerals only on reserves created before 1930 in Alberta, Saskatchewan, and Manitoba; Yukon; and the Northwest Territories. In other areas the resources belong to the Crown or the province. But they still are entitled to lesser economic benefits in British Columbia reserves created after 1930 in Alberta, Saskatchewan, and Manitoba under the Natural Resources Transfer Agreement (Constitution Act, 1930); Ontario; Quebec (where the province claims mineral rights); Nova Scotia; New Brunswick; Newfoundland; and Prince Edward Island.

7 John D. Martz, *Politics and Petroleum in Ecuador* (New Brunswick, N.J.: Transaction, 1987); Jonathan C. Brown and Alan Knight, eds., *The Mexican Petroleum Industry in the Twentieth Century* (Austin: University of Texas Press, 1992); Gustavo Coronel, *The Nationalization of the Venezuelan Oil Industry: From Technocratic Success to Political Failure* (Lexington, Mass.: Lexington Books, 1983); Luis Vallenilla, *Oil: The Making of a New Economic Order: Venezuelan Oil and OPEC* (New York: McGraw-Hill, 1975).

8 In Argentina, the provinces and national government own the resource. Carl E. Solberg, *Oil and Nationalism in Argentina: A History* (Stanford, Calif.: Stanford University Press, 1979).

9 The eleven OPEC members are Saudi Arabia, Iraq, Kuwait, the United Arab Emirates, Iran, Venezuela, Libya, Nigeria, Algeria, Indonesia, and Qatar, all of which (save Nigeria, which has a modified version of this idea [see note 10 below]) share the same political perspective on subsoil ownership. Furthermore, of the next five largest non-OPEC oil producers — Mexico, Norway, Egypt, Oman, and Yemen — only Norway does not share the Islamic heritage regarding subsoil ownership. In Iran the mullahs claim that the Iman owns the resources. Former OPEC member Ecuador, which withdrew in 1992, shared this assessment, but Gabon, which resigned in June 1996, did not.

10 In Nigeria, whose leadership is Muslim, oil fields are located in the Christian regions of the country.

11 The exceptions are the areas of the southwestern United States that were either conquered or purchased from Mexico. In those areas (under the influence of Mexican and originally Islamic law) the separate sale of surface and mineral rights has become possible.

12 The 1072 Mining Law, which still governs the United States, states that "all valuable mineral deposits in lands belonging to the United States . . . are hereby declared to be free and open to exploration and purchase."

13 Commissioner Osso Stanley of the Court of Appeals, in Hammonds v. Central Kentucky Natural Gas Co. (*Southwestern Reporter,* 2d vol. 75 [1934], 204).

14 Hiatt, "Aboriginal Land Tenure"; Henry Reynolds, *Law of the Land* (New York: Penguin, 1987); Paul Tennant, *Aboriginal Peoples and Politics: The Indian Land Question in British Columbia, 1849–1989* (Vancouver: University of British Columbia Press, 1990); Claudia Orange, *Treaty of Waitangi* (Wellington, N.Z.: Allen and Unwin and Port Nicholson Press, 1987); Hugh Kawharu, ed., *Waitangi: Maori and Pakeha Perspectives of the Treaty of Waitangi* (New York: Oxford University Press, 1989). Indians could not even sue to regain lands until the twentieth century, and even then only during a twenty-five-year period (Petra Shattuck and Jill Norgren, *Partial Justice: Federal Indian Law in a Liberal Constitutional System* [New York: Berg, 1991, distributed exclusively in the United States and Canada. 1991]).

15 The set-aside for hunting and fishing of the James Bay Cree also ensures the continuance of a sacred relationship. See Adrian Tanner, *Bringing Home Animals: Religious Ideology and Mode of Production of the Mistassini Cree Hunters* (New York: St. Martin's Press, 1979).

16 Donald Worcester, *Under Western Skies: Nature and History in the American West* (New York: Oxford University Press, 1992), 147–48.

17 Aboriginal title encompasses the right to exclusive use and occupation of the land — not ownership of land (Section 35[1] of the Constitution Act, 1982). Aboriginal title in Canada was created by the Royal Proclamation of 1763, the common law which recognizes occupation as proof of possession (Delgamuukw v. British Columbia [1997] 3 S.C.).

18 *Tee-Hit-Ton Indians v. United States,* 348 U.S. 272–295.

19 Canadian Constitution Act of 1982, Section 35(1). The statement is by Deane and J. J. Gaudron to Mabo (no. 2) in *CLR* 175 (1992), 109–10. The Native Title Act (1993) does not state so clearly that no ownership is meant — only "use." Even the dissenter from the decision, J. Dawson, considered that "native title, where it exists, is a form of permissive occupancy at the will of the Crown."

20 "Ko te atakau o te whenua i riro i a te Kuini, ko te tinana o te whenua i waiho ki nga Maori." Waitangi Tribunal Reports, Muriwhenua Fisheries Claim (1988), 10.3.3 Legal Perspectives of the Maori Context (h) citing Shortland to Hobson, 6 May 1840, CO 209/7. The tribunal report continues "the natives kept to themselves what Vattel calls the 'useful domain' while they yielded to the Crown of England the 'high domain.'" *Victoria University Law Review* 14 (1984): 227, 240.

21 Territories were claimed by the seventy-one Houses representing all of the Wet'suwet'en people, and all but twelve of the Gitksan Houses. The Nisq'a recently received a fee simple title in a landmark British Columbia case.

22 Joseph G. Jorgensen, *Oil Age Eskimos* (Berkeley: University of California Press, 1990); Gary Anders, "A Critical Analysis of the Alaska Native Land Claims and Native Corporate Development," in *Native Americans and Public Policy,* ed. Fremont J. Lyden and Lyman H. Legters (Pittsburgh: University of Pittsburgh Press, 1992), 85–98; David Rich Lewis, "Native Americans and the Environment: A Survey of Twentieth-Century Issues," *The American Indian Quarterly* 19 (1995): 423–51.

23 John Merritt, *Nunavut: Political Choices and Manifest Destiny* (Ottawa: Canadian Arctic Resources Committee, 1989), 35. The recent Canadian cases include the 1975 James Bay and Northern Quebec Agreement, followed by the Inuvialuit Final Agreement (1984), the Gwich'in Comprehensive Land Claims Agreement (1992), the Sahtu Dene and Metis Comprehensive Land Claims Agreement (1993), the Yukon Final Agreement (1993), and the Nunavut Claims Agreement (1993). Completed concurrently with the Yukon Final Agreement: Champagne were Aishihik First Nation, Nacho Nyak Dun First Nation, and Teslin Tlingit First Nation agreements.

24 The original case was *Passamaquoddy v Morton*. The Department of Justice reduced the claim to 5–8 million acres and, of course, excluded the heavily populated coastal areas.

25 Maine Settlement Treaty of 1980; U.S. Commission on Civil Rights, *Indian Tribes: A Continuing Quest for Survival* (Washington, D.C., 1981), 130.

26 They are also used as bargaining chips in internal political disputes. Thus federal support for the James Bay Cree provided a powerful counter to the independent-minded Quebecois intent on building a hydroelectric dam in the early 1970s. Public support for the James Bay Cree continues for the same reason among those opposed to Quebec separatism.

27 "Five years after the signing in 1981, it was clear that the federal government had neither budgeted any special funds to meet its new obligations under the agreement, nor had established any agency with responsibility for overseeing its role in the implementation processes. . . . In 1984, after three additional years of negotiation, the Cree-Naskapi Act was signed and passed into law, establishing local self-government for Cree (and adjacent Naskapi) communities, thereby fulfilling one of the obligations from the 1975 agreement." Harvey A. Feit, "Hunting and the Quest for Power: The James Bay Cree and Whitemen in the 20th Century," in *Native Peoples: The Canadian Experience,* ed. R. Bruce Morrison and C. Roderick Wilson (Toronto: McClelland and Stewart, 1995).

28 The economist is the former treasury secretary and noted MIT scholar Richard Rubin. The case (*Corbett v Babbitt*) has yet to be resolved. The Indian Minerals Development Act of 1982 — passed without significant controversy — gives tribes a larger role in managing petroleum rights. The legal presupposition is that unless otherwise specified, subsoil rights belong to indigenous communities, but the federal government, which often fails to observe basic rules of competitive bidding, manages the income. Felix S. Cohen, *Handbook of Federal Indian Law* (Washington, D.C.: Five Rings Press, 1986). In fact, even within petroleum-bearing reservations there is a mix of headright, allottee, and tribal ownership. See BIA, "Oil and Gas Opportunities," 1996. U.S. Indians own approximately 3–4 percent of oil and gas reserves, 10 percent of the coal, as well as 5 percent of the phosphate and all of the uranium. Monroe Price and Robert Clinton, *Law and the American Indian: Readings, Notes, and Cases* (Charlottesville, Va.: Michie, 1983), 755–56. For the lawsuit to force the U.S. government to hand over revenue owed Native Americans, see Timothy Egan, "Poor Indians Who Own Rich Lands Try to Break Out of Vast Federal Maze," *New York Times*, 9 March 1999.

29 Ao contrario do sistema brasileiro o sistema juridico norteamericano exige ser proprietario *antes* de poder vender-o.

30 For Jefferson, see Anthony F. C. Wallace, *Jefferson and the Indians: The Tragic Fate of the First Americans* (Cambridge, Mass.: Belknap Press of Harvard University Press, 1999). For Carter, see U.S. Commission on Civil Rights, *Indian Tribes: A Continuing Quest for Survival* (Washington, D.C., 1981), 133.

31 Since 1972 the Western Shoshone have spurned requests by the U.S. government to surrender lands in exchange for payment. When presented with $26 million, which the Indian Claims Commission has determined was the value of the terrain, the Shoshone refused to accept any funds. The federal government then placed the money into a U.S. Treasury account and declared that the government owned the land. The Shoshone argued that placing funds into a U.S. Treasury account failed to constitute "payment" under section 22(a) of the Indian Claims Commission Act, but the courts disagreed (*United States v. Dann*, 470 US 39 [1985] and *United States v. Dann*, 873 F.2d 1189 [9th Cir., 1989], cert. den., 493 US 890 [1989]). Recently, in *United States v. Nye County*

(Nevada), a case currently (1998) on appeal in the Ninth Circuit, the Shoshone are arguing that "payment" does not automatically transfer title.

32 Even in New Zealand, Maoris largely hold two categories of nonarable land: those with moderate limitations and hazards when under a perennial vegetation cover (34 percent) and land that only supports extensive grazing or erosion control forestry (32 percent) ("Maori Land Use Capability, New Zealand 1996, Ministry of Maori Affairs).

33 "The 'full exclusive and undisturbed' possession of properties connotes all rights of authority, management, and control" (Whanganui River Report, Waitangi Tribunal, chapter 11, 28 June 1999). Note that this does not include a possibility of alienation or sale, which would mean ownership.

34 *Viento primero,* rendered in English as *The Southeast in Two Winds* (by Subcomandante Marcos Selva Lacandona, agosto de 1992); Declaration of War, 1993.

35 U.S. Commission on Civil Rights, *Indian Tribes,* 107.

36 Even the article title screams "Should We Give the U.S. Back to the Indians?" (*Time* 109 [11 April 1977]: 5).

37 Alice Littlefield and Martha C. Knack, eds., *Native Americans and Wage Labor: Ethnohistorical Perspectives* (Norman: University of Oklahoma Press, 1996), 3.

Historiography on the Ground:
The Toledo Circle and Guamán Poma

SARA CASTRO-KLARÉN

As regards the question of Peru . . . nothing that comes my way has caused me greater embarrassment than the corruption of benefices and the affairs of the Indies which freeze the very blood in my veins.
— Francisco de Vitoria, 1534 (quoted in Pagden, 65)

My purpose in this essay is to delve into the construction of subalternity of American polities and peoples by the Spanish discourse of discovery, conquest, and coloniality. Focusing specifically on the "writing" of Inca history under the gaze of Viceroy Francisco de Toledo (1515–1582) — the supreme organizer of Andean colonial rule — I intend to show that the deauthorizing of the Andeans' own narratives of the past relied on the conjugation of at least three discursive operations. First, it was necessary to deploy a systematic gathering of "facts" under the observation of the forces of the Spanish Crown. The "facts" themselves were the result of "observations" conducted by Spanish agents of the Crown who decoded the observed cultural practices in the light afforded by the transportation of the "facts" to a cultural matrix other than their own grid of signification. Second, the confusion, disjunction, and contradiction that resulted from observational practices were resolved by the juxtaposition of hermeneutic operations in which translation — cultural and linguistic — played a paramount role. Third, when the assumption of European practices as normative failed to provide sufficient ground for "othering" Andean accounts of the past as a foundation for claims to self-government, coded readings of classical Greek and Roman antiquity were deployed in order to estrange Andean discourses of self-knowledge and produce a generalized deauthorization of local knowledges. Such deauthorization of local knowledges — historiography on the ground — became the keystone for colonial governability.

The connection of this essay to the historiographic work of the South Asian Subaltern Studies group is one of affinity and recognition. Inasmuch as Ranajit Guha and others have questioned the discursive and universal capacity of

History — a local European modality of dealing with memory and the past — I find my inquiry into the writing of coloniality reaffirmed. The problem of the writing of history was recognized in the Andes from the inception of the deployment of writing as the principal epistemological paradigm. Ever since, Latin American intellectuals — most notably Guamán Poma, José Carlos Mariátegui, Edmundo O'Gorman, novelists, and anonymous writers — have examined the paradoxical positions of postcolonial writing subjects, their modes of cognition, and the conflict-ridden elaboration of the past that ensued. There is, then, a convergence of postcolonial perspectives encompassed by the problematic of the writing of history and processes of subalternization as expressed by the South Asian group and the thinking of many Latin Americans across the centuries.

By March 1572, Tupac Amaru, the last direct successor of the Incas and head of the reigning *panaca*,[1] was dead. Viceroy Francisco de Toledo had the young man executed, on charges of conspiracy against the Spanish state, in the central plaza of Cuzco before the eyes of most members of the twelve royal panacas and thousands of loyal subjects. One of the many roles of the panacas was to conserve the memory of their deceased royal ancestors in rhymed songs, narratives and probably also paintings. Barely a month before, the viceroy had gathered together the descendants of the twelve panacas for a viewing of the "árbol genealógico pintado"

> y se les leyese la *Historia índica* y lo escrito sobre los cuatro paños preparados para enviar al rey como un resumen de los hechos y de la sucesión de los Incas. . . . Y para concretar, se hizo una nueva información, a la que fueron convocados únicamente los primitivos conquistadores, y a ellos se volvió a pedir testimonio sobre todo lo que sabían y habían oído decir a los indios desde cuarenta años que vivían en el Peru. (Levillier, 285)

The lawyer Polo de Ondegardo (?–1575), who had barely completed his *Notables daños de no guardar a los indios sus fueros* (1571), was also to be present at the reading.[2] His task was to lend his expertise on Inca history to the proceedings so that if questions arose with regard to the truth of the *Historia índica* (1572) by Pedro Sarmiento de Gamboa (1532–1592), Polo could put them to rest.[3] The version of Inca history composed by Sarmiento de Gamboa, to some extent gathered and written during the early part of the viceroy's inspection of the Inca Empire (1569–1572), was never questioned by the members of the twelve panacas. Some of the members merely uttered (in Quechua?) the noncommittal phrase: "Así será pues." In the presence of the notary public, they heard the history. They listened to the interpreter's rendition of what was being read aloud in Spanish. The reading of Sarmiento's

Historia índica took two days and the work of many interpreters. When it concluded, the members of the royal panacas were asked to declare in public, and to certify before the appointed notary public, that what they had heard constituted a complete and accurate account of the history of their ancestors and the manner of government employed by them in the empire.

Toledo knew that one of the key roles of the panacas was to devote their energies to the conservation of the memory of their deceased ancestor's deeds in songs and narratives. Much of what was known about the past was committed to memory in songs that were sung and acted out in dance-theater processionals in the many ritual celebrations that marked the Inca calendar. The *amautas* and *quipucamayoc,* or intellectuals, were perhaps the most important members of the panacas in terms of their historical function. Thus Toledo was pitting one set of intellectuals against another, one set of records against another. He was making sure that Spanish law, power, and historiography gained, once and for all, the upper hand.

Toledo had asked Sarmiento de Gamboa to draw from the material being compiled in his *Informaciones*[4] a history of the Incas that would prove that they were not "natural lords" of the Andeans but rather usurpers and tyrants.[5] Although the document known as the *Anónimo de Yucay,*[6] sent to Toledo in 1571, had already advanced the same thesis on the illegitimacy and tyranny of the Incas, and Polo's own study on the origin of the Incas could "prove" that the Incas were not autochthonous to Cuzco, Sarmiento's "history" was more highly authorized, inasmuch as its author was part of Toledo's inner circle of intellectuals, and the contents were supposedly based on the notarized depositions and answers made by many *curacas* to the questions posed by the *Informaciones.*[7]

Toledo's decision to mount a whole juridical and historiographic assault on the Incas seems redundant for he had already decided that "conviene acabar este debate por guerra" (Valcarcel, 6). His aim was not only to end the debate on the legitimacy of Inca rule but also to remove the Incas physically in order to proceed to the confiscation and distribution among his supporters of the lands, treasures, subjects, and *pallas* still held by the reigning panaca.[8] In fact Polo de Ondegardo was accused by the Anonymous Jesuit of having no other motive for writing on Inca religion than to ascertain the location of the tombs of the royal mummies in order to be the first to sack them.

With the scene of the panacas signing their names and thus authorizing the historical theses of *Historia índica,* the viceroy — that is, the colonizing state — intervened directly once again.[9] The games of truth played by the Spanish Crown and its *letrados* were an effort to extract visibilities upon which to lay the foundations of a colonial order.[10] The Spanish conquest of the Andes required, in order for power to traverse and invest the dominated, their "help."

The scene in which the panacas certify the Spanish interpretation and therefore valuation of their culture constitutes a critical achievement in the production of the Indian in the Andes. As the viceroy sought to acquire a strategic space to position the forces of the nascent colonial state, he seized on the power of discursive formations — law, civil ordinances, dictionaries, university curricula, language policies, population statistics, state intellectuals, the Inquisition, and above all, historiography — as a central tactic in his plan to "organize and pacify" the "land."

However, as the viceroy moved about with complete confidence in his ability to defeat the Inca nobility both militarily and legally — spaces and maneuvers which he controlled exclusively — and while he instituted practices by which the Incas were to be watched at all moments, "and their seed to be eradicated for ever,"[11] he seemed unaware of the fact that his understanding of the power/knowledge relation was also being observed, analyzed, and problematized by those *subjected* by the power of writing which he deployed.[12] Toledo had made the Indians subject to his control, but as Foucault has argued (in Dreyfus and Rabinow 1983: 212), that control and dependence appear also tied to the subject's identity, conscience, and knowledge. The colonial subjects — Toledo, the letrados, the panacas — appear in the grid of power that subjugates them also makes them subject to and enables a specific cognitive productivity.

Having set the scene, from here on I will analyze the discursive modes, strategies, practices, and disciplines that colonial rule, as epistemic violence, deployed in the Andes when Toledo's forces elaborated the histories of the Andeans as a prelude to his *Ordenanzas*. Toledo authorized a blueprint for a new world organized by the forces of writing, power, and the law that took the form of a panopticom. From the compilation of the *Informaciones* to the minute regulations of everyday life in the *Ordenanzas,* the ensemble of knowledge that Toledo brought together and developed as he entered the land and consciousness of the Andeans aims at thinking and producing a model of governmentality that will subject the Amerindian population while at the same time transforming their cultural constitution into a replica of the Christian novitiate subject.[13] Moreover, the Toledan discursive panoply would be indeed incomplete if it were severed from the objects and objectives of its discursive maneuvers: the Andean subjects.

While Toledo compelled the diverse set of curacas to speak the "truth" under the force of his questionnaire in order to produce an Inca history with appropriate subjects (tyrants), other members of the Andean polity, touched by and aware of the far-reaching power of Toledo's examination of their past and memory, prepared responses which, in a manner of speaking, took the place of the silence of the panacas. As is well known, the most distinguished and "famous" of the post-Toledan Andean chroniclers — Inca Garcilaso de la Vega, Guamán Poma, and the mysterious Anonymous Jesuit (Blas Valera? 1551–1597?) — replied, critically, and with maneuvers of their own, to Toledo's idea of inventing a past and, consequently, a future on the ground.[14]

No response was more vigorous and detailed than Guamán Poma's *El primer nueva córonica y buen gobierno* (1615), in which we fing a microhistory of the Andes together with a utopia for self-government. Conceived, in a way, to respond to the charges of tyranny, Guamán Poma's enormous work also registers the historiographic dilemma brought about by the irreparable, and all too visible, rupture and end of one order and the birth of another. The sense that the new order is based on falsified, deceptive facts elaborated on the grounds of governamentality only deepens the post-Toledanos understanding of the idea that governability is a game that conjugates the tactics of writing institutions in the production of knowledge to an arena that extends to the struggle of the battlefield. As if anticipating Foucault, the post-Toledan authors seem to understand governability as "the ensemble formed by the institutions, procedures, analyses and reflections, the calculations and tactics that allow the exercise of this very specific, albeit complex form of power, which has as its target population, as its principal form of knowledge, political economy, and as its essential technical means an apparatus of security" ("Governmentality," 102).

The post Toledan chroniclers contested Toledo's thesis on the Inca models and practices of governability. Their own versions of the histories of Andean empires were based on personal and collective memories as well as what was left of the quipu recording system. The lost Latin manuscript of Blas Valera, a major source for Garcilaso's *Comentarios reales* (1609) and Guamán Poma's *El primer nueva corónica y buen gobierno* (1615), undertakes a minute display, a "thick description," of both the Inca and pre-Inca knowledge and experience in the arts of governing.[15] The most ambitious of these texts dares to offer the Inca ensemble of economic and political measures as a model of governmental rationality, as a structure of practices worth preserving and even imitating by the Spaniards. As the post-Toledan intellectuals wrote the Andean "conduct of conduct" (Gordon, 2), they inaugurated a doubled discursive space that infused European categories of governmentality with a sense of alterity that needed to be recognized as it embodied practices which challenged the idea — Inca, ayllu, curaca, acllas, hanan/hurin, reciprocity — and questioned the notion of referent. The post Toledan intellectuals used their study of practices to intensify thought, and in their hands, the models or ideas that Spanish intellectuals ventured forth suffered certain wear and tear, resembling eventually what Deleuze has termed a "philosophy of the phantasm" behind which the real truth does not lurk (xliii). The challenge that mestizo and Indian intellectuals mounted to the power of Spanish colonial historiography wrote in indelible ink the idea that "the law is always a structure of illegalism" (Deleuze, 29).

The Books of the Brave

As soon as Toledo arrived in Peru in 1569, he sought to gather around him a group of intellectuals who could lend the expertise and authority necessary to his goals: to end all possibility of shared rule with the Incas, to discredit Andean culture, and to organize "the conduct of conduct" in Peru. In order to do so, he needed to counter not only Las Casas's objections to the encomienda system and the many arguments advanced in "Las doce dudas" (1552),[16] but even more urgently he needed to defeat the theory of the Incas' right to rule by virtue of their being "señores naturales" (autochthonous lords), advanced a generation earlier by the Dominican theologian Francisco de Vitoria (c. 1492–1546) in Salamanca.

Vitoria had argued that being in mortal sin does not detract from the ability to rule in civil matters. Infidelity to the Christian faith was no impediment to legitimate rule, as demonstrated by the existence of Protestant and Jewish rulers. Toledo brought into his circle the adventurer Pedro Sarmiento de Gamboa; the *licenciado* (civil lawyer) Polo de Ondegardo; the jurist Juan de Matienzo (1520–1588), who had a long residence in Peru; and the friar Cristobal de Molina, el Cuzqueño, who knew Quechua very well and assisted Tupac Amaru on the day of his execution.[17] Toledo also approached José de Acosta (1540–1600), but the Jesuit kept his distance. Whether Toledo and his circle of intellectuals hatched a conspiracy to defame the Incas or whether the ideological dovetailing of the histories and plans for government of the Andes that they authored were part of the spirit of the times became a heated polemic during their lifetime and has remained so for many later students of the period.

The publication of the *Informaciones,* along with much of Toledo's correspondence, in 1940 has enabled historians to recover evidence of a well-thought-out set of theses that the viceroy wanted to advance both by discursive and practical methods and tactics. It seems that Toledo carried out a campaign among the Indians themselves to demonstrate the illegitimacy of Inca rule over the empire. The historian Raúl Porras Barrenechea, an admirer of Toledo, denies that any such conspiracy ever occurred but does admit and identify the five major "tendencies" or ideological determinants that universally mark the historical work of the Toledo circle:

> 1. The Inca Empire came about suddenly. It was the product of violence and force of arms deployed during the reigns of Pachacutec and Tupac Yupanqui.

2. The Incas were warring tyrants whose culture was based on cruel rites, military structures, and human sacrifice.

3. The Incas developed an admirable economic and social system.

4. The Spaniards should conduct, as they were doing, intensive study of Andean religion in order to forbid and condemn their moral ideas and religious practices.

5. The historiographic assumptions of the Toledo circle rested on the thought of the Spanish intellectuals, theologians and civilians, who argued for the sustained supremacy of the Spanish Empire over the entire globe (Porras, in Valcarcel, 39).

In fact, the convictions that animated Toledo and his intellectuals were not really that far away from the theses developed earlier by Ginés de Sepúlveda, the famed "loser" to Las Casas in the Valladolid debates (1550–1551) over the Indians' questioned humanity. Toledo and his circle proceeded into their inquiry assuming that it was legel to conquer and kill all Indians due to the gravity of their sins and crimes, the crudeness of their minds ("crudeza de su ingenio"), their extensive practice of human sacrifice, and their ignorance of Christianity.

The *Historia índica,* the *Gobierno del Perú,* Toledo's *Ordenanzas,* and many other texts produced then in the Andes entered the various doors of the Spanish imperial bureaucracy but were not to see the light of day until late in the nineteenth century, when scholars searching in archives found them and published them for the first time.

The recognition that such historiographic practices, while convenient to the state, were also dangerous to Spanish interests, is best expressed in the 1577 decree issued by Philip II. The Spanish king forbade all further inquiry into Amerindian religion and history, and ordered the colonial authorities to confiscate all manuscripts dealing with such topics. The possibility of producing and working on a countermemory was officially foreclosed. As David Brading has put it in *The First America:* "The past constituted too dangerous an arsenal to be left open for random or ill-intentioned inspection" (143). And this referred to both the archives, which buried many things, as well as to the minds of the "natives," for they were to be watched, examined, and regulated at all times. It is in this atmosphere of prohibition, discipline, and fear that the post-Toledans carried out most of their rewriting of the Andean past by wresting out of quipus and quipu-camayoc a rationality of the past which then lay in shards.

Furthermore, the truth claims of the Toledo circle did not limit themselves to the ruling imperial families or Incas. After all, with the death of Tupac Amaru, their participation in history was thought to have been canceled. In their attempt to make history useful for governing the present, to reemploy elements of the living past into the construction of the present, these letrados also produced and placed on the ground a crucial portrait of the common Amerindian population. For Matienzo, the Andeans were timid, melancholic, pusillanimous, "born to serve," cruel, given to all kinds of sexual excesses, and not very bright. It did not matter that this portrait did not coincide with the simultaneously drawn warlike and conquering image of the Inca armies and administrators. Above all, Matienzo assured his readers that the Indians were lazy. They had to be compelled to work. "Compeler a los indios a que tra- baxen" (19) becomes a leitmotif in his *Gobierno del Perú* for, according to the jurist, they were sworn enemies of work. Matienzo seems unaware of the fact that a few chapters later, when he recommends that the Indians be taught European crafts but be forbidden from making gunpowder and using arms and horses, he justifies this by remarking on the Indians' exceptional clever- ness and ingenuity. "Los indios de este reino son tan hábiles que ninguna cosa les enseñan que no aprendan bien, como no sean cosas que requieran pruden- cia, que esto no cabe en sus entendimientos" (69).

Both Matienzo and Polo felt comfortable arguing that some of the Incas' great architectonic achievements resulted from a combination of their cruelty and the laziness of the common people. Furthermore, according to these observers, this is so because if not compelled to work, the Indians would get lost in their love of festivals, drunken idleness, and devilish worship of the *guacas*. The Spanish Conquest, it was thus argued, actually freed the Andeans from the tyranny of the Incas—the tyranny of work and the tyranny of their rites. Endowed with the new freedom that the conquest had brought them, they were now at liberty to enter the world of labor in the mines and the repartimientos that the Spanish offered in the name of the new Christian pastoral order that Toledo compiled under the title of *Ordenanzas*.

This plan for governing, or rather incarcerating, this new population was convincingly portrayed as the freeing of a population from its native tyrannical and thus "false" rulers. This erasure of the past, this preparation of a portal for the inauguration of empire, relied on certain angular readings of both Plato's *Republic,* first prepared by Matienzo, the lawyer, and Aristotle's thesis on natural law. It bent to the service of empirical governmental theories embrac- ing the idea of citizens, and not vassals, as the center of a just polis.

On the Pleasure of Tyranny

The Spanish claims to rule America would have been lost (on paper) without the catapult that tyranny, as elaborated by Plato and read by the letrados at the Spanish universities, afforded them in surmounting the walls set up by Las Casas and the plain doctrine of natural right.

Arguments on natural law, human rights, and the right to local rule has been stretched dangerously thin, twisted and turned to the point of the risible, in order to justify not just the conquest and subsequent destruction of the people, but also the right to legal enslavement of entire populations. It seemed that somehow, every time the answer on which to rest Spanish claims was found, another problem cropped up and new ground had to be elaborated out of the ensemble of knowledges available. Francisco de Vitoria (c. 1492–1546), a theologian and major player in the School of Salamanca, took up the "need to describe and explain the natural world and the place of man within it, in the same rationalistic terms as Aquinas himself had used in the *Summa contra gentiles*" (Pagden, 61). In his attempt to understand the place of man in nature, Vitoria, rather than opting for the self-reflection arrived at by Montaigne (1533–1592) in "Des cannibals" (1580), assumed without question the primacy of Christian behavior.[18] For Vitoria, European social and political institutions were normative. Thus the only comparison possible, as with José de Acosta, would be one of unequal terms. Comparison meant hierarchy.

Blind to his assumptions, Vitoria labored on the exegesis of Aristotle's and Aquinas's theories of natural law. Aquinas's theory held out great promise as a tool for explaining the "strange" or "depraved" costumes and thinking of the Amerindians because it involved finding a rationality in the laws of nature. For the Scholastics, the "law of nature was the efficient cause which underpinned man's relationship with the world about him and governed every practice in human society" (Pagden, 61). The law of nature constitutes a system of ethics. There could not be a doctor of natural law for it is not a codified body of precepts. Natural law, as Toledo and his circle were to learn from Vitoria and utilize in their historiography, was a "theory in part epistemological, in part sociological, about the mechanisms which permit men to make moral decisions. In its simplest form it consists of a number of 'clear and simple ideas', the *prima praecepta* implanted by God at the creation of *in cordibus hominum,* to enable man to accomplish his end *qua* man" (Pagden, 61).

Such simple and clear ideas were, theoretically, granted to all men. They are an instrument of cognition which allows man to "see" the world as it is. These primary precepts were later translated into secondary precepts that constitute the basis for all the codes that regulate social behavior. Practically the entire ensemble of patterns of beliefs and behavior—culture—fell within the scope of natural law, and since the normative primacy of European costumes and beliefs was never questioned by the School of Salamanca, it followed that all differences were to be identified and interpreted as an insufficiency in the capacity for cognition, and a weakness in the ability to "see the world as it is." Simple and clear ideas functioned, as we shall see later, in a way similar to an uncritical idea of "common sense." Thus Toledo and Matienzo felt on safe and holy ground when they formulated regulations expressing the tutelage theory that colonial labor and religious law affirm and detail. The theory of natural law constitutes the first philosophical step by which it can be held that all men are natural creatures. However, some, due to the "observed" differences of their dress, food, labor patterns, and languages, constitute an enfeebled breed apart. The idea that God had created all men equal — as the same species — was thus turned on its head by the colonial situatedness in the structure of domination, and it would be several centuries before it could be taken seriously again.

Moreover, Vitoria's disquisitions on natural law and the American Indian were not univocal. In fact, while Toledo may have found his thesis on the Indians' feebleness of mind suitable, he found many other aspects of Vitoria's thinking troublesome. If he sought to prove publicly that the Incas were tyrants, it was in part to bring closure to the multifarious juridical aspects of the natural law exegesis. In 1537 Vitoria authored his *De indis* (printed in 1557), with which he sought to bring closure to the ever exasperating question of just title to the Americas. Vitoria argued that the question was not juridical. He reasoned that only theologians were prepared to discuss divine law. The Indian question devolved on the nature of man, and therefore it was a subject for theologians to solve. Although the force of Aristotelian premises would leave Vitoria to conclude that the Incas, as "señores naturales," had the right to rule their land and the people on it — the very notion that Toledo aimed to disprove with the maneuver of the *Informaciones* and the public reading of the *Historia índica* — Vitoria's reasoning ended up giving Toledo and his circle the most efficacious thesis for charges against the Indians, which in turn were used to justify the rigor of the *Ordenanzas*. That Vitoria did not bring a satisfactory end to the discussion is evident in the fact that the Emperor Charles V, on learning of the substance of Vitoria's arguments, ordered him not to deal with the question any further.

Slipping back onto juridical ground, Vitoria isolated four reasons for thinking that the Indians could legitimately be deprived of their natural rights. Either they were (a) sinners, (b) infidels, (c) feeble-minded (*dementes*), (d) irrational, or all of the above. Vitoria found that the first two were not really impediments to rule. Despite much argument to the contrary, Vitoria found that the Indians were rational creatures capable of building cities (Aristotle's indispensable test for deserving inclusion in the category of civilization) and establishing commerce amongst themselves. Where they failed was in loving the Spanish. Anthony Pagden explains that for Vitoria, as with Cicero and Aristotle, trade was a means of establishing communication and knowledge, the foundation of the noblest of human virtues: friendship. "One of the just titles for conquering the Indians might be . . . that by refusing to 'receive' the Spaniards the Indians were attempting to close those natural lines of communication. By so doing they had revealed the full extent of their barbarism" (Pagden, 77). Further, by denying the Christians access to their lands without good reason, the Indians were *refusing to be loved* and hence violating the law of nature, for no man may love another without knowing him (Pagden, 77).

Despite the all-too-visible elasticity of natural law, or perhaps precisely because of it, in the second part of *De indis,* Vitoria took back—that is, *retracted*—all the empirical, ocular evidence he had mustered to demonstrate that the Indians lived in full civil societies and could not in any way be considered barbarians in the Aristotelian sense of the word (Pagden, 79). In the second part of *De indis,* which deals directly with the "just" right to conquest, Vitoria offered the contra-argument demanded by the Scholastic method and the reality of forces in place. In this text he focused precisely on the perception of absence of certain European—that is, *normative*—social and political traits in Indian societies. According to Vitoria, the Indians did not have adequate laws nor magistrates that would enable them to govern their households satisfactorily. Vitoria's idea of the visibility of law was, of course, pegged to the practice of a written, visible archive. Without writing (European script), the materiality of Indian law and rights (*derecho* in Spanish means both "law" and "right") was inconceivable to Vitoria and his contemporaries. It followed, therefore, that not only was Indian law invisible, but what there may be of it was inadequate. How then could their rulers be wise or competent? The best visible proof of such absences and inadequacies was, for Vitoria, the Indian's human sacrifice and cannibalism. Therefore, in *De indis,* the whole edifice of theology's superior qualifications for investigating the nature of mankind collapsed before the force of what Greenblatt has called mimetic blockage and eucharist anxiety.[19]

Such blockage or theory of irreversible difference ironically puts a stop to the very circulation of communication and exchange that Vitoria faulted the Indians for impeding when they did not receive the Spaniards with love as the Spaniards entered their territories to sack them and convert them. The pliability in the theologian's discourse on the Indian's humanity and, therefore, on their human right to self-rule reenacts the modes of cultural blockage operating at the heart of the Spanish Conquest. Greenblatt has identified the idea of a principle of blockage—"the principle by which homologies are resolved into antithesis, brothers into other" (138)—as the agent at work in the misrecognition and destructiveness of the discourse of the Spanish Conquest. Vitoria's commitment to mimetic blockage, "a radical differentiation that is a constitutive feature of the destructive enterprise and of *the text that records and apologizes for the enterprise*" (139, my italics), harbors within its pleats the violence of Toledo's panopticon.

In the end, Vitoria provided two contradictory pictures of the Amerindian mind, and this is because both the Andean and the Aztec cultures offered a substantial challenge to the hierarchical cultural classification deployed by the Scholasticism of the School of Salamanca. Vitoria's theology held that while the Indians were rational men, they had no right to rule because of the depravity of their costumes, sodomy, cannibalism, and human sacrifice. Such depravity, such absence of virtue, could only be explained by the notion that their minds were feeble, degenerate, and unable to "see" the world correctly.

Perhaps, like Philip II, tired and weary of the twists and turns of the discourse of conquest, Toledo chose another, less apologetic and more effective set of tactics. His gamble was to leave in place all the suspicions raised by the natural man and slavery discussion while at the same time focusing on "tyranny" as the final chapter on the right to rule the Amerindians. His hopes were high, for as we shall see below, Toledo's thesis on tyranny treaded on very solid ground. He wrote to Philip II that it was his wish:

> Cese tanta variedad de opiniones en cosa de tan grande importancia por no estar los hechos de estos reinos claros sino fingidos . . . cada uno como se le antoja para fundar los derechos que desea con tanta turbación y confusión de conciencia así de su Majestad como de sus ministros y moradores de estas provincias tan escrupulisadas que cualquier ignorante ha osado hasta aquí poner la boca en el cielo. (Valcarcel, 23)

Toledo had become convinced that the greatest service he could provide the king was to remove all scruples from his/their conscience so that they could proceed to distribute wealth among his valuable Spanish subjects, place the Indians under the iron rule of fear and obedience, and collect tribute and taxes. All this could be accomplished with a deeply layered psychological portrait: the Incas were tyrants, and the Indians lacked prudence. Once this thesis was proven with the assistance of the Indians themselves, caught in yet another instance of their lack of wits, then the king could accept and implement his role as "tutela y defensión de los indios naturales" (Valcarcel, 23). Such a plan called for nothing less than Plato's theory of governability in the *Republic* and *Statesman,* and Toledo found that both Matienzo and Sarmiento de Gamboa, obviously familiar with Plato's ideas on geography and governability, had already been advancing the tyranny thesis. Matienzo's opening remarks for his *Gobierno* identify the marks of "tyranny" in the Incas: "Otra señal de tiranos . . . ser pusilámines . . . son mentirosos y traicioneros. . . . eran tan crueles" (Matienzo, 8–10).

From the outset of *The Republic,* the reader learns that the dialogues intend to argue that justice is tantamount to life in the city governed by temperate and wise men who rule for the benefit of temperate and prudent citizens. In the course of the dialogue it is shown why tyranny, oligarchy, democracy, and aristocracy are defective forms of government. The central idea is that these forms of government reflect the personality or character of the men who become the state and thus proceed to set up the laws that reflect or resemble their psychology. What is needed, according to *The Republic,* is an arrangement by which the rulers, like physicians, are men specialized in the knowledge and art of governing, men so trained in their art as to be capable of *separating* their character from their craft. These men would be capable of making a key distinction between subject (self) and object (the government) for, as in medicine—which does not consider the interest of medicine, but rather the interest of the body (301)—the philosopher king, versed in the rationality of government, would not govern only for his own benefit. While the pastoral model is eventually discarded in the *Dialogues,* the argument continues its movement assuming that if "the states are as humans are [for] they grow out of human character" (402), the objective is to discover how to distinguish among the various types of men's characters so as identify the marks of the philosopher-king.

The soul is divided into three principles, and one "principle prevails in the souls of one class of men, another in others" (421). The three principles correspond to three classes of pleasures. The first is the faculty to learn, and it corresponds to the love of wisdom and the capacity for self-government; it is the intelligent part of the soul. The second principle involves the passions and corresponds to the love of honor; men ruled by the second principle are ambitious and contentious, and they love money. The third principle of the soul involves the appetites, and it corresponds to the love of food, drink, sex, money, and all other sensual desires.

The first principle of the soul rules the capacity for self-discipline, discretion, order, and prudence. Temperance allows the philosopher to keep *separate* the three principles of the soul. That is why the perfect guardian of the city must be a philosopher in whose steadfast nature, stoic practices, and love of truth the state can grow as a firmly structured ensemble of categories of peoples specializing in their various arts and social functions. Such a state would be a reflection of his own disciplined and stable character (369). This first principle of the soul corresponds to the perception and cognitive faculties of the head and the face, and pleasures approved by the lover of wisdom are the truest (422) for they entail the absence of pain. This higher form of man regulates his body and his mind in order to preserve the harmony of the soul. As a ruler, he will look at the city that is, within him, and regulate its resources and forces to produce the balance and harmony of civility.

The second principle prevails in the souls of men who rule oligarchies and democracies. These types of states are unruly, and their citizens are fed by either the excessive love of money or freedom, or both. The second principle of the soul is tied to the faculties that arise from the organs housed in the trunk of the body, especially the heart and the liver.

The third principle, the appetites, gives rise to tyranny. It is associated with the functions of the lower part of the body, the abominable digestive and sexual functions that place the body (self) in contact with otherness. The "transgressions of the tyrant reach beyond the spurious; he has run away from the region of law and reason and taken his abode with slave pleasures" (424). The state ruled by the tyrant resembles his person, and he only grows worse with the increment of his power. The nature and unlawful character of his appetites cannot be controlled by either the law or reason, for these lower-third (body) appetites "awaken the wild beast within us [which] gorged with meat and drink, starts up and having shaken off sleep goes forth to satisfy his desires, and there is no conceivable folly or crime. . . . when he has parted company with all shame and sense, a man may not be ready to commit" (416).

Plato's tyrannical man, "purged away from temperance and brought into full madness" (417), does not of course coincide with the order of Andean governmentality, which by definition no European ever "saw." Andean religion, like Christianity itself, addressed the realm of Plato's third principle. The move that the Toledo circle made was to posit the tyrannical man generated by drunkenness, lust, obsessive love of feasts, reveling, and frenzy, the tyrannical man given to a succession of pleasures and the eating of forbidden fruits, as the man to be understood by Andean governmentality. The Toledo circle, prepared by Vitoria's exegesis on natural law, conflates the realm of the sacred with the realm of political and economic administration. The tyrannical man that Polo de Ondegardo, Matienzo, Cristobal de Molina, and Sarmiento left dispersed in the pages of their descriptions of Andean belief — "ritos y fabulas de su origen" — represents religious visibilities in Andean cosmology together with what today we understand as the play of desire. The inclinations of the lower third of the body appear indelibly inscribed in their accounts of "idolatries" — that is to say, the ground of the sacred.[20]

It is clear that the charges of Inca tyranny went far beyond the defects of an absolutist form of government practiced by a dethroned elite. Perhaps that is why Philip II sought to compensate with a total denial of all pleasure for his own absolutism, or, in the same vein, Toledo sought to acquire the reputation of an ascetic man moved only by political ambition and money.[21] As such Toledo fell within the ranks of the second principle but stayed well away from the very charges of tyranny from many of his contemporaries.

At any rate the resemblance between the state, the tyrant, and its subjects informed not only the insatiable curiosity of the Spaniards for Andean religious practices but also justified the link between them and the thesis on the unredeemable character of the Indians, who could thus never be allowed to wander away from the vigilant eye of the colonial Christian state. For Plato, as well as for Matienzo, who often refers to *The Republic,* tyrannical men (or, for Matienzo, the feeble-minded Indians) occupy a place so far from the king, aristocrats, or letrados that even the pleasures they crave and their experiences of them are, as Plato put it, "shadow pleasures" (425). To the Spaniards, the Indians appeared to be ruled by the third principle of the soul: they knew nothing, and their cognitive powers were so diminished by the shadow pleasures of the lower third — sodomy, anthropophagy, incest — that they, as Vitoria argued, "could not see the world as it is," much less arrive at a body of written law. At best they may have seen shadows.

As Matienzo put it, Indians lacked prudence and common sense. In José Rabasa's critique of Gramsci's category of the folkloric, he argues that common sense stands for an "uncritical understanding of the world where the signifier bypasses the signified and is thus identified with referents." Rabasa further points out that for Gramsci, common sense continually transforms itself as it incorporates scientific ideas and philosophical opinions into everyday life. As such, common sense could then be regarded as the folklore of philosophy.[22] It is in this sense that we must understand Matienzo's statements on the Indians' lack of prudence as well as Vitoria's judgment about the Indians' inability to "see" the world. Therefore, we can see that prudence and common sense are nothing other than sedimentation of the Western philosophical tradition and which in colonial situations pass for natural signs.

Bartolomé de Las Casas (1484–1566) succeeded in dismantling the Aristotelian globalizing category of "barbarian," and in doing so he proposed the first comparative ethnology by dispersing in time and space an evolutionary, *cultural* set of four types of barbarians, a scheme which accounted for the diversity of Amerindian cultures as well as the differences in their behavior (Pagden, 119–145). But Las Casas's *Apologetica historia* (written after 1551) as well as his *Argumentum apologiae* (1550) remained unpublished during his lifetime, and the psychological portrait advanced by Plato continued to be ascendant in the discourse dealing with Amerindian cultural differences. Despite claims to the contrary,[23] the work of José de Acosta (1540–1600), who left Spain for Peru in 1571, affirmed the tyranny and thus the tutelage thesis.[24] Acosta was critical of the evangelizing manner of the orders that had preceded the Jesuits in America. He also did not believe in the use of force against the Indians, and in harmony with the politics of his order, he sought to position himself as a third, neutral force in disputes over the Indians' bodies and souls between the Spanish state and the various evangelizing orders. In his calculations, Acosta looked for points where the interests of the state could coincide with those of the Jesuits (Shepherd, 104).

In 1577, while in Lima, and before he wrote his more famous but perhaps less influential *Historia natural y moral de las indias* (1590), Acosta penned his manual for evangelization and indoctrination of the Indians into the Christian faith. Despite the fact that *De procuranda indorum salute* was written in Latin, it made the rounds in the Andes quite quickly. Since his arrival in Lima, Acosta had delivered several major sermons on the ways to indoctrinate and govern the Indians. He had been a prominent voice in the 1576 Councils of Lima and Cuzco. Acosta joined the viceroy's court in Chuquisaca and accepted a post as an adviser. During this time he met Polo de Ondegardo, Matienzo, and Sarmiento de Gamboa. Therefore, it should come as no surprise that the ideas informing the pedagogy recommended in the manual assume an Indian subject impaired by much the same cognitive disabilities drawn by Vitoria, encapsuled in Plato's tyrant, and deployed by all the intellectuals of Toledo's circle. George Shepherd writes that: "Many of the programs initiated by Toledo resurfaced in *De procuranda* (198).

"*De procuranda* does *not* employ a comparative reasoning for understanding the different behavior of the Indians. It recognizes the difference, but it does not explain it. In fact, in this work Acosta departs from the Aristotelian claims on the primacy of experience in the making of cognition. Despite the fact that he recommends that "missionaries should attempt to understand Indians in their own terms and not by means of simple comparison with other races" (Pagden, 154), Acosta nevertheless falls back into the psychological model of government and cognition, and accepts the tyranny category as descriptive of the Amerindians' highest capacity for civilized organization and for understanding of the preaching of the gospel.

The tyrant thesis, however, turned out to pose a major challenge to the idea of preaching the gospel, for it proposed Indian subjects so blinded by deep cognitive disabilities as to be rendered incapable of understanding notions such as God and the Eucharist. It came dangerously close to promoting a doctrine of complete psychological and cultural incompatibility between Indians and Europeans. The remedies necessary to bridge the gaping chasm between the first and third principles of the soul needed thus to engage not only the dimension of the soul but the corporeal space, as Toledo and Matienzo recommended. The care of the body — disciplined work, food, clothing, movement, sleep, hygiene — needed to be brought within the scope of doctrine.[25] In practical terms, *De procuranda*'s rationality was not that different from Matienzo's *Gobierno del Perú* (1569), and the similarity was not lost on Toledo, who although resentful of the Jesuits for founding universities without his permission, nevertheless claimed Acosta and his ideas as part of his organization.

Governmentality: Ordenanzas *and* Gobierno del Perú

Having cleared all the discursive obstacles, Toledo, relying heavily on the *Gobierno del Perú* (1567) prepared by Matienzo, proceeded to order the chaos brought about by the conquest and the ensuing wars between the Spaniards and Andeans after the events of Cajamarca in 1532.[26] Nathan Wachtel has proposed the notion of "destructuration" to describe the Andean situation in Toledo's hands not simply as the destruction of the local order by the colonizing power but rather "the survival of ancient structures displaced from the relatively coherent context in which they used to function" (135).[27]

The climate that Toledo found of resistance, revolts, accommodation, and even attempts to bring back the Inca order despite the Incas' demise involved, of course, the whole Andean population (Spaniards and Andean) in a collective act of boundless cultural translation and accommodation.[28] The conquest wove in a single strand the discursive work of evangelization and the work of the legal system as the twin forces in the emergence of a new economic system that took over the conception of the body, its labor, and its relation to the means of production as well as the fruits of that production. Therefore, *lenguas,* or interpreters, were necessary with almost every step that Toledo took to control the overlapping relations.[29]

Integrating the myriad of official and unofficial, bad and good and even censored translators was Guamán Poma. By his own account, he was present at all discussions, *informaciones,* map makings, interrogations, Inquisitorial trials, sermons, and civil trials going on in the Andes then. Although very little is known about his identity, it is certain that he worked as a court interpreter and that, as he himself tells us, he worked for the zealot Cristobal de Albornoz in one of his campaigns "against idolatries" at the time when Albornoz discovered the Taqui-Oncoy movement in 1564 (Castro-Klarén, "Dancing," 162–66).[30] A comparison of the method, the strategy of the questions in the *Informaciones* (1572), the governmental plan devised by Matienzo in his *Gobierno del Perú* (1567), and the contents and organization of *El primer nueva corónica y buen gobierno* (1615) shows clearly that Guamán Poma had intimate knowledge of the preparation of the Spanish texts and their intent. His own multilingual, "illustrated" letter to the king attempts a total and globalizing response to most, if not all, the tactics and strategies of the Toledo circle and those who had prepared the way for the tyrant (Plato's lower one-third of the soul/body) thesis.[31] I cannot here offer the details of the comparison but must limit myself to identifying two central points.

All three proposals for a governmental model are examples of destructuration. Guamán Poma's model basically would have kept pan-Andean labor and social institutions intact. The rulers would have been a set of enlightened, temperate, and prudent curacas, local Andean lords who, having adopted Christianity and reading and writing, would *continue* the Andean world on behalf of the Spanish king, who would, of course, receive tribute. The chief qualification for these curacas would have been their experience gained in the Andean tradition of good government. As Guamán Poma endeavors to show, they knew how to run an ordered and very productive society. The curacas scored high marks in economics, ethics, and common sense. Guamán Poma shows that they had even devised a social system that embodied all the chief principles of Christianity as an ethics of living. Thus there was no need for Spanish juridical or political thought. Regarding the "vices" and "evils" that the Spaniards saw in Andean rites and religion, Guamán Poma formulated a very adept answer. Such "tyrannical" behavior was indeed the work of the devil, a Christian, not Andean, gnoseological category, with which the Spaniards, as he pointed out, had ample experience. The objectionable behavior of the Andeans did not stem from within, from their character or psychology; the lack of temperance was the work of an external force. The devil and his temptations were omnipresent, and thus Guamán Poma was willing to accept that Christianity be preached in the Andes.

Matienzo and Toledo, having perhaps calibrated better the extent to which the interjection of Spanish cultural practices into the Andean world would result in structural changes, devised a model by which to control the Indian population through new and old institutions — *reducciones* (or Indian towns), encomiendas, and colonial *mita* (or forced labor) — which would also serve as appropriate vehicles to wear down the Indians' affection for and loyalty to their pan-Andean cultural practices, especially religion. Following Matienzo's advice, the viceroy's plan was to discipline the bodies and souls of the Indians so completely as to keep them physically and psychologically exhausted.

Toledo and Matienzo differed on the kind and quality of the ruler. Implicit in the *Ordenanzas* is the idea that the ruler, as representative of the king, would be a member, like Toledo himself, of the Spanish nobility. Matienzo had other ideas. He thought that the only appropriate and capable rulers for the colony would be Spanish letrados, in his mind the closest thing to a philosopher-king. Quoting Plato, Matienzo writes: "No dexará de haber males y desventuras en la república hasta que la manden y gobiernen filósofos, esto es hombres sabios" (197).

Assuming the idea of the tyrant, Toledo's program, like Acosta's, entailed a two-stage process of conversion: the regulation of the body, building good habits, would in time produce the prescribed and desired mental habits. Thus Toledo's *Ordenanzas* regulated the minutiae of the concreteness of the body — twenty lashes to anyone who took away an Indian's cloth that covered his coca basket — as well as the minutiae of the social and political order. His aim was, as he put it, to continue "to specify the punishments needed in order to ensure the execution of order . . . so that each person could carry on with his business" (37).

Toledo goes on to theorize his ideas on the relation of punishment and justice as the foundation of government. Justice is practically synonymous with punishment, for to "punish the evil man is great mercy [*misericordia*] indeed. Justice is the greatest pity [*piedad*] that can be carried out inasmuch as to forgive a bad man is to be cruel to all others" (38). Toledo states his conviction about the fundamental role of rigorous punishment for small transgressions in the constitution of the republic and good government (38). Just punishment or order depends on the division of the population and behaviors into infinitesimal categories. The detection of the smallest infraction of the law demands a very large corp of observers and listeners—witnesses, clergymen, *alcaldes,* corregidores, *auditores,* translators, scribes, confessors, interrogators, visitors, tax collectors—capable of entering their observations in the multilayered archives of punishment that Toledo set up at the heart of all the institutions he regulated.

Proper consideration of the nature of an infraction and the assignation of a fitting punishment were both facilitated and dependent on the written record. Aware of the dependency of the Toledan order on the written word and on the archival system of government it deployed, Toledo set many ordinances requiring corregidores to employ letrados for the cabildos to keep written records of everything, and for scribes and notaries to be present in almost every transaction; of course, translators were required to swear to translate and interpret accurately and to observe the prohibition of receiving gifts from warring parties (40–66).

Toledo is particularly clear in forbidding the use of quipus in any official transaction. Guamán Poma would not destroy the quipu, but would agree with Toledo about the need to keep a written record of every transaction; in Guamán Poma's view, only the detailed archival record could keep the Spaniards from cheating on the Indians. Thus both sides understood and sought the manipulation of dimensions of writing as the engine of the law and an instrument of power.

Matienzo's observation of Andean social and political practices had furnished Toledo with the main categories for the organization/destruction of Peru. Acosta had contributed the notion of building a new pastoral order from the ground up; that is, from the smallest corporeal habits to mentalities. Together with Sarmiento de Gamboa and Polo de Ondegardo, and through the types of questioning and situations of the witnesses interviewed in the *Informaciones,* Toledo had managed to press his own political thesis: That the Incas, as tyrants and usurpers of the "right" of the local lords or curacas, had no legitimate claim on Andean government. Toledo, unlike Guamán Poma, had no wish to preserve the curacas' native authority. The study of Andean religion — the guacas, origin myths, rites — carried out by Cristobal de Molina, el Cuzqueño, the civil lawyer Polo de Ondegardo, and the "cosmógrafro del rey" Sarmiento de Gamboa contained all the necessary information-cum-interpretation to extend the tyranny thesis to the curacas and thus place them under the gaze of suspicion and vigilance. Although the curacas were deployed by Matienzo as the political link between the old Andean order and the new colonial administration, their authority on myriad things had to be drastically curtailed to produce the appropriate circumstance for conversion in the fields of belief and authority.

With a series of prohibitions, Toledo sought to disempower the curacas and take away all illusion pertaining to the power invested in the ceremony of their persons. For each infraction, the curacas could receive one hundred lashes or be brought to trial, be imprisoned, and lose their office. They could also be accused, before the Inquisition, of idolatry or relapses into the old religion. Toledo forbade them to offer other Indians any assistance or favors. They could not seek the help of the Audiencia or file any lawsuits. They could not receive tribute. They could not keep the company of Spaniards in order to curry favor. They could not ride horses or be carried in litters (330–373). More charitably, Matienzo thought that they should be allowed to wear Spanish clothing. In that way they would spend their money on the purchase of Spanish goods and "learn to love us, for they would love our clothing and begin to look like men" (69).

Toledo's indictments against Andean culture were monumental, and they were certified by the studies of his circle of intellectuals and the power of his office. By the time he was finished with the *Ordenanzas,* the viceroy had not only executed the last Inca, but he had placed a historiography on the ground with the full force of the most important knowledge of the time: cosmography, jurisprudence, theology, "informaciones," Renaissance political theory, ocular observation, testimony and verification, and, on the ground, the public assent of the panacas. In organizing "the conduct of conduct" in the former Inca Empire, Toledo and his circle came up with a potent mixture of the pastoral model — the tutelage by the Christian shepherd of his sheep — with Machiavelli's reason of state. The Anonymous Jesuit, widely believed to be the mestizo Jesuit Blas Valera, and Guamán Poma, in separate or perhaps coordinated ways, endeavored to contest the viceroy's claims on the "tyrannical" qualities of Andean culture and government, as well as to devise a blueprint in which conversion would take place, but only at the level of the gods. In the plan of the post-Toledanos, the habits of the Andeans, already the product of immense corporeal and mental discipline, would stay in place—as a Christian order avant-la-lettre. What would change would be the identities of the divinities and the ways of worshipping. Blas Valera, Garcilaso de la Vega, and Guamán Poma advanced a revolutionary thesis on which the right to autonomous rule could be based: *a truly comparative ethnology.* Their method and tactics would show that the Andeans' ethics and law, and thus their entire social and political organization, espoused more strictly and consistently the ideal Christian ethics than any observable behavior of the Spaniards, especially that of most of the friars and high bureaucrats in charge of the conversion, who in fact engaged in the most libidious behavior Plato could have ever imagined.

The effect of their writing was, of course, nil on the policymaking of their contemporaries, but Garcilaso's *Comentarios reales* (1609) had a tremendous impact both in Europe and the Americas long after his death. For a long time it stood as the only known reconstruction of life in the Inca Empire, and it was fundamental in the later construction of nationhood in the Andes.[32] Only more recently has the work of Guamán Poma come to join the ranks of the subaltern's disputation with Toledo. I do not have space to enter here into their arguments and rationality of government; suffice it say that they offered an economic and social model—the disposition of things—in a rather "modern" and complex way of thinking in which the relation of men/women to things was the ground of governmental administration. Guamán Poma seems to have been particularly aware of the distinction between government and sovereignty, a distinction not made in Europe until the idea of government as economic administration appears in the work of Guillome de La Perrière (*Mirrorir politique* [1567]; see Foucault, "Governmentality," 89–97). Curiously, both in La Perrière and Guamán Poma, government is defined as the right manner of the disposition of things and people, and their imbrication with other things such as wealth, resources, and institutions. Government is not the imposition of laws on men, as Toledo ordained, but rather the management of things, and as Foucault has pointed out in the case of La Perrière, it is the arrangement of multiform tactics (95).

In summary, when Toledo arrived in Peru, he understood his service to the king in strictly Machiavellian terms: "The objective of the exercise of power is to reinforce, strengthen and protect the principality, but with this last understood to mean not the objective ensemble of its subjects and its territory, but rather, the prince's relation with what he owns, with the territory he has inherited or acquired, and with his subjects" (Foucault, "Governmentality," 90).

Thus his statements regarding the need to protect the Indians from destruction have to be understood in the sense of protecting the king's property and not as humanitarian feelings or policies. In the hands of Toledo, whose mission and measures encapsuled rather neatly Machiavelli's reason of state (the state is a holding-out provision to retain sovereignty, however acquired), governing the Andes took the form of the logical result of the pedagogic and pastoral discourse of Scholasticism (Gordon, 9). Such theory of tutelage could only be based on deployment of a myriad of disciplinary techniques. The Toledan order kept its subjects physically and mentally exhausted at all times: it was a nightmarish version of a limitless and unforgiving novitiate. When Matienzo, Vitoria, Sarmiento, and Acosta speak of making *men* of the Indians (they are not speaking of human rights, as some have claimed), they are calling for and justifying a desire for extreme uses of what Foucault has called biopower, or the excessive deployment of power over persons understood as living beings. Toledo's regulations exemplify, anachronistically, the observation that Foucault makes of "modern" man as an "animal whose politics places his own existence into question."[33] The double movement that took place in Europe at the end of the sixteenth century—the state centralization coupled with the dispersion of religious dissidence (Foucault, "Governmentality," 88)—registered in the Andes under colonial rule as a level of repression which Europe was spared until later, when the combination of the pastoral model and reason of state would produce the totalitarian regimes of this century.[34]

Notes

1. A panaca was made up of the descendants of the last reigning Inca. It excluded the person chosen to occupy the throne, who went on to form a new panaca. The panaca's charge was to conserve the mummy of the deceased Inca and the memory of his deeds in songs and narratives. Following Zuidema, María Rostworowski writes that "cada Inca nacía en una panaca y pasaba a otra cuando recibía la mascapaycha, de ahí también que tenía que cambiar de nombre. Cambiar de ayllu no signficaría la creación de un nuevo grupo sino el paso de un linaje a otro. . . . Este hecho daría una enorme importancia al ayllu o panaca de la madre de un soberano y nos hallaríamos ante una práctica particular de los linajes incaicos" (143). See María Rostworowski, *Estructuras andinas del poder: Ideología religiosa y política* (Lima: Instituto de Estudios Peruanos, 1983). Zuidema explains that the word "panaca" derives from "pana," which means "sister of a man." "Panaca" in Cuzco designates noble ayllus (55), and means "group descending from a man's sister" (56). The panacas have a calendrical function, with each assuming the celebration of monthly rites in the agricultural calendar (65). See Tom R. Zuidema, *Inca Civilization in Cuzco* (Austin: University of Texas Press, 1990), 23–24 and 51–61.

2. The text authored by Polo de Ondegardo was not intended for publication. It was found with the papers that belonged to Francisco de Avila, known for his "mission" among the Huarochiri and his connection to *Ritos y tradiciones de huarochirí,* ed. Gerald Taylor (Lima: Instituto de Estudios Peruanos, 1987). The *Relación de los fundamentos acerca del notable daño que resulta de no guardar a los indios sus fueros* lay in the Spanish Archivo de

Indias until it was published for the first time by Torres de Mendoza as part of the *Colección de documentos inéditos del Archivo de Indias* (tomo XVII, Madrid, 1872). A year later Sir Clement R. Markham published it in London with a title more descriptive of its contents: *Relación del linaje de los incas y como extendieron ellos sus conquistas.* Polo's work was printed along with other texts by the Hakluyt Society in London as part of *Narrative of the Rites and Laws of the Incas.* The most recent edition, based on the manuscript housed in the Biblioteca Nacional in Madrid and which does not differ from the text edited by Torres de Mendoza, has a new title: *El mundo de los incas,* ed. Laura González and Alicia Alonso (Madrid: Historia 16, 1990). All translations from the *Ordenanzas* of Toledo, the *Gobierno del Perú* by Matienzo, *De procuranda* by Acosta, *El primer nueva corónica y buen gobierno* by Guamán Poma, and the writing of the Anonymous Jesuit are mine.

3.   The *Historia índica* is the title generally used for the manuscript that Pedro Sarmiento de Gamboa (1532–1592) presented to Viceroy Toledo and which was read to the members of the twelve panacas. Sarmiento planned to write three books on the Incas, but it appears that he only put down the *Segunda parte de la historia general llamada índica.* It was sent to Spain along with the genealogical paintings ordered by Toledo. The Council of the Indies buried it. At the end of the eighteenth century, a manuscript copy was found in the library of Abraham Gronov in Leiden. In 1906 the German scholar Richard Pietschmann published it for the first time in Berlin with a long preliminary study. This same version was later published by Ángel Rosenblat with a long study on the life and works of Pedro de Sarmiento, "nigromántico," poet, censor, captain, royal cosmographer, and prisoner of the Huguenots in Mont-de-Marsan in 1586. See Pedro Sarmiento de Gamboa, *Historia de los incas,* ed. Ángel Rosenblat (Buenos Aires: Emecé Editores, 1943).

4   For a more or less full text of the *Informaciones* see Roberto Levillier, *Don Francisco de Toledo, supremo organizador del Perú: Su vida y su obra (1515–1582),* T. II, *Sus informaciones sobre los incas (1570–1572)* (Buenos Aires: Biblioteca del Congreso Argentino, 1935).

5   The *Informaciones* were not published at the time of Toledo. It lay in the Archivo de Indias in Seville. In the nineteenth century, various historians, among them Clement Markham and Jiménez de la Espada, published partial texts from archival sources. Roberto Levillier, in his *Don Francisco de Toledo, supremo organizador del Perú: Su vida y su obra (1515–1582)* (Buenos Aires: Biblioteca del Congreso Argentino, 1935), published summaries from parts of the *Informaciones.* His purpose was to correct the meagerness of the previous partial publications (204).

6   The *Anónimo de Yucay* has left a deep mark on Peruvian historiography. In 1571, the anonymous author wrote the *Dominio de los incas en el Perú y del que su magestad tiene en los dichos reinos,* known as *El anónimo de Yucay.* This text articulates in the clearest way Toledo's own ideology: it was a mistake (*engaño*) to give to the Incas true and legitimate lordship over this kingdom, great damages had already ensued as a consequence of this falsehood, and there was a need to establish that the only true and legitimate domain and lordship of these kingdoms resided in the Spanish king and his successors. This *cronista* launches an impassioned attack on Bartolomé de Las Casas. Finally, the *Anónimo* makes a case for the great virtue in killing these Indians "y alancearlos porque [eran] idólatras, [adoraban] piedras, [comían] carne humana, [sacrificaban hombres] y no eran teólogos." See Francisco Carrillo, *Cronistas del Perú antiguo: Enciclopedia histórica de la literatura peruana* (Lima: Editorial Horizonte, 1989), 4: 15–16.

7   Roberto Levillier has published the entire body of Francisco de Toledo, *Ordenanzas.* See volume 8 of *Gobernantes del Perú: Cartas y papeles del siglo XVI,* ed. Roberto Levillier

(Madrid: Imprenta de Juan Pueyo, 1925). In his *Don Francisco de Toledo,* Levillier offers a summary of the questions put either to individual curacas or groups of them, which ranged from five to eighty men called to declare before a notary public with the aid of an interpreter in meetings called by Toledo which lasted two or three days. The same fifteen questions were asked both of Jauja (ethnic groups friendly to the Spaniards) and Guamanga (longstanding enemies and rivals of the Incas). These questions were later modified for the Cuzco and Yucay assemblies. The questions were designed based on a linear idea of the past that did not at all coincide with Andean temporal concepts nor with the "historical" categories employed by the amautas or quipucamayoc. The questions had two aims in mind: to determine if the Incas had gained control of those (local) territories by conquest, and if the Incas had appointed the curacas or if they had allowed the local ayllus to elect them. The inquiry not only reflected a European concept of the past foreign to the Andean peoples, but it assumed idealized principles of governmentality that not even the most "advanced" European kingdoms practiced. Here is a sample of the fifteen questions: "1. ¿Descendía el testigo de caciques o capitanes antiguos? ¿Cuál era su calidad? 2. ¿Sabían como era el gobierno de los pueblos del Perú, antes de que los incas los conquistasen y sometiesen? 4. ¿Gobernabase cada pueblo por si a manera de behetería? 5. ¿A esos capitanes o principales los elegían los pueblos por reconocerles valentía y entendimiento, o tiranizaban ellos mismos a esos pueblos y se hacían mandones? See Levillier, 206–207. Carrillo notes that often the required answer was to be either yes or no.

8   There is no question that part of the high motivation of those surrounding the viceroy in the march on Vilcabamba in search of the eighteen-year-old and *uti* (retarded) Tupac Amaru — Martin de Loyola and Pedro Sarmiento de Gamboa — was the promise of fabulous riches to be obtained in *encomiendas,* treasure from the royal mummies, and appointments. As "usurpers," the descendants of the panaca in Vilcabamba would not have rights to anything. See Luis Eduardo Valcarcel, *El virrey Toledo, gran tirano del Perú: Una revisión histórica* (Lima: Imprenta del Museo Nacional, 1940), 13.

9   See the account of the debates between Juan Ginés de Sepúlveda and Bartolomé de Las Casas in David Brading, *The First America: The Spanish Monarchy, Creole Patriots, and the Liberal State, 1492–1867* (Cambridge: Cambridge University Press, 1991).

10   See Gilles Deleuze, *Foucault,* 63.

11   Toledo's letters provide ample evidence of the intent of his campaign against the uti Inca in Vilcabamba. He takes credit for "Haber sacado toda la raíz y pretención de derecho de este reino y fuera de él y crédito; de poder perderlos y castigarlos" (Levillier, 28).

12   Foucault explains that "there are two meanings to the word subject: subject to someone else by control and dependence, and tied to his own identity by conscience or knowledge. Both meanings suggest a form of power which subjugates and makes subject to." See Foucault, "The Subject and Power," in Hubert L. Dreyfus and Paul Rabinow, *Michel Foucault: Beyond Structuralism and Hermeneutics* (Chicago: University of Chicago Press, 1983), 212.

13   I use the term "governmentality" in the sense developed by Michel Foucault in his "Governmentality." The conquest of the imaginary in the Andes cannot be understood as a parallel to the situation in Mexico. For an illuminating analysis of the elaboration of the questionnaire that produced the *Relaciones* in Mexico and a study of the capture of Aztec memory by the Spaniards, as well as the harnessing of the Christian supernatural by the Mesoamericans, see Serge Gruzinski, *The Conquest of Mexico: The Incorporation of Indian Societies into the Western World, 16th–18th Centuries* (Cambridge: Polity Press, 1993).

14 Blas Valera was born in Chachapoyas in 1551 and is believed to have died in Spain in 1597. He has often been identified as the author of texts otherwise attributed to the Anonymous Jesuit. The *Relación de las costumbres antiguas de los naturales del Perú,* finished in 1578 (Porras, 471), was first published by Jiménez de la Espada in 1879 and reprinted in Lima in 1945. Blas Valera is also believed to be the author of the extensive *Historia occidentalis,* written in Latin and lost during the sacking of Cádiz by the English. Fragments of this manuscript were read and cited by Garcilaso in his *Comentarios reales.* The Anonymous Jesuit revealed a great sense of self-identity with Inca culture. He rejects the version of Inca ritual practices established by Polo de Ondegardo and Sarmiento, and he especially attacked Polo for his weak knowledge of Quechua and his inability to understand the ample semantic shadings of the language. The Anonymous Jesuit pointedly rejects the claims made about the practice of human sacrifice, and seriously details the similarities between Catholic belief and rites and Andean religion: confession, belief in the resurrection, bishops, nuns, anchorites.

15 The Italian scholar Laura Laurencich Minelli has described a manuscript she has found in the family papers of the Neapolitan historian Clara Miccinelli. Laurencich believes the manuscript to be a seventeenth-century Jesuit text that contains detailed information on the coding of the quipu and especially on their use for literary purposes. According to the author of the document, Quechua is "a language similar to music and has several keys: a language for everyone; a holy language [which] was handed [down] by the knots; and another language which was handed down by means of woven textiles and by pictures on monuments and by jewels and small objects" (52). Included in the document are three half pages of drawings signed "Blas Valera." They purport to show how a poem was written with woven symbols and knotted strings. According to Joan Anello, the author of this document, Blas Valera, did not die in Spain. He survived the English attack on Cádiz and secretly returned to Peru in 1598. While in Spain, because of his quarrel with Cardinal Aquaviva, he was supposed to live as if dead. During that time he wrote his *Historia occidentalis,* but he could not publish it. So he sent it to Garcilaso de la Vega, who lived in Córdoba, who used it extensively in his *Comentarios reales* (1609). Back in Cuzco, Blas Valera undertook a plan for the secret publication of yet another version of his book. Always in hiding, he and his friends looked for a ghost writer who would want to lend his name to the book. They settled on Guamán Poma, who boasted titles of Indian nobility and was well known for his pride and vainglory. See Viviano Domenici and Davide Domenci, "Talking Knots of the Inka: A Curious Manuscript That May Hold the Key to Andean Writing," *Archeology* (November–December 1996): 50–56.

The finding has been received with skepticism. Quechua scholars have raised questions regarding the Quechua used in the manuscript, which is clearly associated with Chachapoya uses and therefore not consistent with Guamán Poma's writing in Ayacucho usage, and it includes eighteenth-century Quechua usage.

16 See Bartolomé de Las Casas, *Aquí se contiene una disputa o controversia entre el obispo don fray Bartolomé de Las Casas o Causas y el doctor Ginés de Sepúlveda* (Seville, 1552; qtd. in Pagden, *The Fall of Natural Man*).

17 Cristobal de Molina penned three manuscripts: *Historia de los incas* and *Relación de las juntas,* both lost, and *Fabulus y ritos de los incas,* which survived and was published in 1943 as *Crónicas de los Molinas* (Lima: Francisco A. Loayza).

18 Montaigne began to revise his *Essays* almost immediately after their first publication in 1580. For "On Cannibals," see *Essays,* 91–98.

19 See Stephen Greenblatt, *Marvelous Possessions: The Wonder of the New World* (Chicago: University of Chicago Press, 1991), 119–151:

> But if for the Spaniards absolute blockage occurs around the images of cannibalism and idolatry, there still has to be some point of contact for understanding to occur, some basis for communication and negotiation. Otherwise the whole encounter would be a complete blank, a brute clash of bodies, in which the invaders, hopelessly outnumbered, would certainly be destroyed. The Spanish need to facilitate the improvisational manipulation of the other." (139)

20 In *De procuranda* (1577), José de Acosta argues that while it is not licit to punish the "infieles" or destroy them by force, it is indeed legal to make war upon them ("es licito hacer guerra a los bárbaros") so that they will abandon their idolatries and their abominable sacred rites: "el trato frequente con el demonio, el pecado nefando con los varones, los incestos con las hermanas, y madres, y demas crimenes de este género" *Obras del padre José de Acosta,* ed. Francisco Mateos (Madrid, 1954), 2:3, 432. See also Shepherd, 194.

21 Toledo brought with him from Spain a good number of pages. He remained single throughout his life, but on more than one occasion, his enemies in Peru murmured and even brought public charges concerning homosexual relations with the pages in his household (Valcarcel, 10–11).

22 See José Rabasa, "Of Zapatismo: Reflections on the Folkloric and the Impossible in a Subaltern Insurrection." Forthcoming in *Other Circuits,* ed. David Lloyd and Lisa Lowe (Routledge).

23 Anthony Pagden's careful study of Acosta argues that *Historia natural y moral de las indias* (1590) continues the comparative ethnology done by Las Casas in *Apologetica historia* (146–197).

24 Acosta wanted to inaugurate an order that was not based on lies and did not rely on the violent destruction of the Indians and their possessions. But he did not agree with Las Casas's thesis of restitution, nor with the idea of self-rule. He saw the Jesuit mission as an enlightened system of tutelage in which the king could discharge his responsibilities to his Indian vassals. See Shepherd, 104.

25 Following Aristotle's discussion of incontinence in the *Nicomanchean Ethics* — in which he identifies "three causes for incontinent behavior: (1) genetics, (2) natural depravity, (3) the influence of habit in one's mental state" (Shepherd, 173) — Acosta regards the formation of new bodily habits in the Indians as crucial to his plan of acculturation.

26 Guillermo Lohmann Villena has shown in great detail the close relationship of *Gobierno del Perú* to Toledo's *Ordenanzas.* On the whole, it is clear that the *Ordenanzas* would not have had the same scope nor precision and clarity for which they are known without the work of Matienzo. See Lohmann Villena's "Étude préliminaire" to Matienzo's *Gobierno del Perú.*

27 See Wachtel, *Los vencidos.*

28 See Castro-Klarén, "Dancing and the Sacred in the Andes: From the Taqui-Oncoy to Rasu-Ñiti."

29 It has already been noted that in the trial that the Audiencia de Lima set up against the prosecutor Loarte, who had been in charge of Tupac Amaru's own "coarse and precipitous" trial, Loarte was accused of employing the services of Gonzalo Jiménez, or Jimenillo, known for his inaccurate and even insidiously false interpretations. After being accused of sodomy, Jimenillo was put to death by order of the viceroy, despite the fact that he was one of his pages. In Arequipa, in 1575, three years after Tupac Amaru's execution, Toledo engaged Gonzalo Holguín, an expert in Quechua, Aymara, and Puquina, as

"lengua *general*," or chief official interpreter of the state. In the ordinance establishing this position, Toledo included a series of regulations on the expertise of interpreters, the quality of the person who may hold governmental positions, and made it mandatory that the viceroy and other officials keep interpreters available for all functions. In the stipulations for Holguín's appointment Toledo tells his interpreter that "habeis jurar de guardar ante mí y de usar bien y fielmente el dicho oficio y no dejeis de cumplirlo así por ninguna manera, so la dicha pena y a más quinientos pesos para la cámara de Su Majestad." The interpreter must keep records "hacer memoria . . . Que no reciba dávidas, ni cohechos de los indios" (*Ordenanzas*, 300–302).

30   See Guamán Poma, *El primer nueva corónica y buen gobierno* (1583–1615), ed. John Murra and Rolena Adorno (Mexico City, 1981), 282, 285, 689–690.

31   The work of Guamán Poma has received abundant and serious examination. For his engagement with Andean and European discourses, see Juan Ossio 1973; Nathan Wachtel 1973; Franklin Pease 1973, 1995; Manuel Burga 1988; Rolena Adorno 1986; Sara Castro-Klarén 1989, 1995.

32   To gauge some of the *Comentarios*' impact on the formation of another historiography, see Manuel Burga and David Brading. Of course, the work of Garcilaso, like that of Las Casas, provided some of the key information for the main charge of the Spanish "black legend": the wanton and cruel destruction not only of individual Indians, but of their civilizations.

33   See Michel Foucault, *History of Sexuality*, vol. 1, *An Introduction* (New York: Random House, 1980), 143.

34   In his *A History of Latin America: Empires and Sequels, 1450–1930* (Oxford: Blackwell, 1997), Peter Blakewell writes that Toledo's policies on restricting the physical movement of the Indian population largely failed (233). Through a quirk in Toledo's legislation that exempted those living away from their communities from service in the *mita*, Indians found the loophole that enabled them to flee the reducciones and dreaded mita. On the matter of population decline, Blackewell reports that the Toledo census of 1570 showed 1.3 million Indians. By 1620 the Spanish authorities reported 700,000. The population continued to decline through the epidemic of 1720. The total estimated decline for the Andes is 48.5 percent, and for central Mexico 85 percent.

Works Cited

Acosta, José de. *De procuranda indorum salute.* 1577. Reprint, Madrid: Consejo Superior de Investigaciones Científicas, 1984.

———. *Obras del padre José de Acosta.* Ed. Francisco Mateos. Madrid: Ediciones Atlas, 1954. Vol. 73 of *Biblioteca de Autores Españoles.*

Adorno, Rolena. *Guamán Poma: Writing and Resistance in Colonial Peru.* Austin: University of Texas Press, 1986.

Blakewell, Peter. *A History of Latin America: Empires and Sequels, 1450–1930.* Oxford: Blackwell, 1997.

Brading, David A. *The First America: The Spanish Monarchy, Creole Patriots, and the Liberal State, 1492–1867.* Cambridge: Cambridge University Press, 1991.

Burchell, Graham, Colin Gordon, and Peter Miller, eds. *The Foucault Effect: Studies in Governmentality, with Two Lectures by and an Interview with Michel Foucault.* Chicago: University of Chicago Press, 1991.

Burga, Manuel. *Nacimiento de una utopía: Muerte y resurrección de los incas.* Lima: Instituto de Apoyo Agrario, 1988.

Carrillo, Francisco. *Cronistas del Perú antiguo: Enciclopedia histórica de la literatura peruana.* Vol. 4. Lima: Editorial Horizonte, 1989.

Castro-Klarén, Sara. "Dancing and the Sacred in the Andes: From the Taqui-Oncoy to Rasu-Ñiti." In *New World Encounters,* ed. Stephen Greenblatt. Berkeley: University of California Press, 1993: 159–176.

——. "El orden del sujeto en Guamán Poma." *Revista de Crítica Literaria Latinoamericana* 41 (1995): 121–134.

——. *Escritura, transgresión, y sujeto en la literatura latinoamericana.* Mexico City: Premia, 1989.

Deleuze, Gilles. *Foucault.* Ed. and trans. Seán Hand. Minneapolis: University of Minnesota Press, 1988.

Domenici, Viviano, and Davide Domenici. "Talking Knots of the Inka: A Curious Manuscript That May Hold the Key to Andean Writing." *Archaeology* (November–December 1996): 50–56.

Dreyfus, L. Hubert, and Paul Rabinow. *Michel Foucault: Beyond Structuralism and Hermeneutics.* Afterword by and interview with Michel Foucault. Chicago: University of Chicago Press, 1983.

Flores Galindo, Alberto. *Buscando un inca: Identidad y utopía en los Andes.* 4th ed. Lima: Editorial Horizonte, 1994.

Foucault, Michel. "Governmentality," In *The Foucault Effect: Studies in Governmentality, with Two Lectures by and an Interview with Michel Foucault,* ed. Graham Burchell et al. Chicago: University of Chicago Press, 1991: 89–97.

Garcilaso de la Vega, Inca. *Comentarios reales de los incas.* 1609. Reprint, 2 vols. Ed. Aurelio Miró Quesada. 2d ed. Caracas: Biblioteca Ayacucho, 1985.

Gordon, Colin. "Governmental Rationality: An Introduction." In *The Foucault Effect: Studies in Governmentality, with Two Lectures by and an Interview with Michel Foucault,* ed. Graham Burchell et al. Chicago: University of Chicago Press, 1991: 1–50.

Greenblatt, Stephen. *Marvelous Possessions: The Wonder of the New World.* Chicago: University of Chicago Press, 1991.

——, ed. *New World Encounters.* Berkeley: University of California Press, 1993.

Gruzinski, Serge. *The Conquest of Mexico: The Incorporation of Indian Societies into the Western World, 16th–18th Centuries.* Trans. Eileen Corrigan. Cambridge: Polity Press, 1993.

Guamán Poma de Ayala, Felipe. *El primer nueva corónica y buen gobierno.* 3 vols. Ed. John Murra and Rolena Adorno. 1615. Reprint, Mexico City: Siglo XXI, 1981.

Las Casas, Bartolomé de. *Aquí se contiene una disputa o controversia, entre el obispo don fray Bartholomé de Las Casas o Casaus y el doctor Ginés de Sepúlveda.* Seville: N.p., 1552.

Levillier, Roberto. *Don Francisco de Toledo, supremo organizador del Perú: Su vida y su obra, 1515–1582.* Buenos Aires: Biblioteca del Congreso Argentino, 1935.

Lohmann Villena, Guillermo. "Étude préliminaire" to *Gobierno del Perú,* by Juan de Matienzo. Paris: Institut Française d'Études Andines, 1967.

Matienzo, Juan de. *Gobierno del Perú.* Ed. Guillermo Lohmann Villena. 1567. Reprint, Paris: Institut Français d'Études Andines, 1967.

Montaigne, Michel. *Essays.* Ed. Carew Hazlitt. Trans. Charles Cotton. Vol. 25 of *Great Books of the Western World.* Chicago: Encyclopaedia Britannica, 1952.

Ossio A., Juan M. "Guamán Poma: Nueva corónica o carta al rey. Un intento de aproximación a las categorías del pensamiento del mundo andino." *Ideología mesiánica del mundo andino.* Ed. Juan M. Ossio A. Lima: Ignacio Prado Pastor Editor, 1973: 153–213.

Pagden, Anthony. *The Fall of Natural Man: The American Indian and the Origins of Comparative Ethnology*. Cambridge: Cambridge University Press, 1982.

Pease G. Y., Franklin. *Las crónicas y los Andes*. Lima: Pontificia Universidad Católica del Perú; Mexico City: Fondo de Cultura Económica, 1995.

———. *El dios creador andino*. Lima: Mosca Azul Editores, 1973.

Plato. *The Dialogues of Plato: The Seventh Letter*. Ed. Robert Maynard Huthcins. Trans. Benjamin Jowett and John Harward. Vol. 7 of *Great Books of the Western World*. Chicago: Encyclopaedia Britannica, 1952.

Polo de Ondegardo, Juan. *El mundo de los incas*. Ed. Laura González and Alicia Alonso. Madrid: Historia 16, 1990.

Rabasa, José. "Of Zapatismo: Relections on the Folkloric and the Impossible in a Subaltern Insurrection." In *Politics of Culture in the Shadow of Capital*. Ed. Lisa Lowe and David Lloyd. Durham: Duke University Press, 1997: 399–431.

Rosenblatt, Ángel. Nota preliminar. *Historia de los incas*, by Sarmiento de Gamboa. Ed. Ángel Rosenblatt. 2d ed. Buenos Aires: Emecé Editores, 1943. 9–66.

Rostworowski de Diez Canseco, María. *Estructuras andinas del poder: Ideología religiosa y política*. Lima: Instituto de Estudios Peruanos, 1983.

Sarmiento de Gamboa, Pedro. *Historia de los incas*. Ed. Angel Rosenblatt. Buenos Aires: Emecé Editores, 1943.

Shepherd, George. "José de Acosta: Reading the American Past and Programming the Future toward the Christianization of Amerindians." Ph.D. diss, Georgetown University, Washington, D.C., 1996.

Taylor, Gerald, ed. *Ritos y tradiciones de huarochiri: Manuscrito quechua de comienzos del siglo XVIII*. Lima: IFEA/IEP, 1987.

Toledo, Francisco de. *Ordenanzas*. Ed. Roberto Levillier. Vol. 8 of *Gobernantes del Perú: Cartas y papeles del siglo XVI*. 14 vols. Madrid: Imprenta de Juan Pueyo, 1925.

Valcarcel, Luis E. *El virrey Toledo, gran tirano del Perú: Una revisión histórica*. Lima: Imprenta del Museo Nacional, 1940.

Wachtel, Nathan. *Los vencidos: Los indios del Perú frente a la conquista española, 1530–1570*. Trans. Antonio Escohotado. Madrid: Alianza Editorial, 1976.

———. *Sociedad e ideología: Ensayos de historia y antropología andinas*. Lima: Instituto de Estudios Peruanos, 1973.

Zuidema, Tom R. *Inca Civilization in Cuzco*. Trans. Jean-Jacques Decoster. Austin: University of Texas Press, 1990.

III. SUBJECT POSITIONS:
DOMINANT AND SUBALTERN
INTELLECTUALS?

Slaps and Embraces: A Rhetoric of Particularism

DORIS SOMMER

A few years ago, I wrote a book about the mutual construction of Eros and Polis in the novels that helped to consolidate Latin American republics. Founding fathers wrote passionate fictions that slipped allegorically between personal and public desires to inflame citizens with the double ardor that would engender nations. Readers identified with the frustrated lovers who wanted to cross regions and races to consolidate modern states, and those readers conspired in the patriotic work of getting together. This was a mirror effect that survived mass distribution to required readers who were taught that their differences from the elite lovers did not really matter. My project, in other words, was to explore national foundations in their own foundational language, which conjugated imagined communities with shared dreams of love.

While I wrote that, I was also reading Rigoberta Menchú. She startled me by what she refused to share in her 1983 testimony about Guatemala's war on Indians. Here was an exposé that insisted on keeping secrets. Why proclaim secrets? I wondered. Why flaunt them instead of keeping them, discreetly? One result was that no amount of information she gave could establish a mood of intimacy or conspiracy between us. It slowly dawned on me that this might be the point of the performance. It was to engage readers without surrendering herself. A formidable lesson. Still illiterate, in newly learned, occasionally incorrect Spanish, a young woman managed to turn a possibly condescending interrogation into a platform for her own leadership.[1]

Rigoberta withholds intimacy while she speaks at length about herself, her community, the struggle. Many readers have presumed that this amounts to candor, despite knowing that her voice was recorded, synthesized, processed, and despite her redundant restrictions of access. Could our ardent interest, and best intentions toward the informant, come from construing the text as a kind of artless "confession," like the ones that characterized surveillance techniques of colonizers? Maybe empathy for an informant is a good feeling that masks a controlling disposition, what Derrida calls "an inquisitorial insistence, to extort it a secretless secret" (Derrida, 87). The possibility should give us pause. Natives who remained incalculable, because they refused to tell secrets, obviously frustrated colonial control (Bhabha, 99).

Rigoberta might have guessed at the passively aggressive, while her sentimental readers miss the point. She frustrates demands for confessions. Think of Dinesh D'Souza's tirade when Stanford University made her testimonial part of a required curriculum. He would have allowed scientific information about genuine Indians, stable objects of investigation, but not this protean subject of multiple discourses in Indian disguise (D'Souza, 71–73). Those of us who dismiss his inquisitorial demand for knowable data should worry that the demand may linger in us, in our sentimental interest and solidarity. Sympathetic readers can be as reluctant as D'Souza to accept insincerity in a life story; they are reluctant, as well, to question their own motives for requiring intimacy.

"What draws the reader," in Walter Benjamin's scornful observation, "is the hope of warming his shivering life with a death he reads about" (101). The projections of presence and truth are less than generous here. Empathy is hardly an ethical feeling, despite the enthusiasm for identifying with Others in some political activists. In effect, the projections of intimacy allow for appropriations that shorten the stretch between writer and reader, disregarding the text's rhetorical (decidedly fictional) performance of keeping us at a politically safe distance. To close in on Rigoberta would threaten her authority and leadership.

The stunning message sent me back to recognize other tactics that distance and disturb readers. There was the absence of intimate details from slave narratives, El Inca Garcilaso's dizzying tour of Peru, Toni Morrison's refusal of confession in *Beloved,* the narrator's rebuffs in Elena Poniatowska's testimonial novel, the theatrics of incompetence in white narrators who tell stories about blacks, even the cold shoulder that Richard Rodriguez turns to his Anglo allies. The list of examples that drew me back and brought me up short is almost arbitrary; I happened to have read them. Anyone can think of different or overlapping lists.[2] The point is that refusals to fit into a reader's agenda can get in the way, if we stop to notice.

The refusals discriminate between the author's audience, full of curious outsiders, and the author's community (which will not read Menchú, is avoided by Rodriguez, and has no monopoly on Morrison). They target readers who speculate "If I were a . . . , I would. . . ?" and forget how positionality helps to constitute the subject.[3] Asking about the place from which one speaks, the locus of enunciation, is a question sometimes put to narrators and characters, but hardly ever to readers. The asymmetry of positions, though, restricts travel, despite readers' fantasies of mutuality. "Ideal" or target readers need not be the coconspirators that standard literary criticism would make of us. Instead, we are sometimes targets of the text. Rather than pander to "competent" readers with guided tours of one's intimacy, some ethnically marked writers produce a "Cordelia effect" to cripple authority by refusing to submit to it.[4] Vargas Llosa's fictional informant turns away; Elena Poniatowska's heroine purposefully bores her readers to distraction; Cortázar's black musician contradicts his meticulous biographer, just to keep him nervous. The moves show up even in assimilationists (Garcilaso and Rodriguez) who flaunt their "exoticism" to become the center's unconquerable object of desire. All of these books locate traditionally privileged readers beyond impassable borders. From there readers can be "ideal" — paradoxically, because they are excluded.

Subject positions, we know, are not fixed through time. But in the war of positions that reading so often is, historically specific circumstances matter.[5] If we are used to assuming the virtues of overstepping the frontier between self and other, we may need to consider the differential effects of liberal and universalist principles when the other is magnanimously absorbed into the greater self.[6] The condescending generosity, for example, in Tzevtan Todorov's *The Conquest of America* provokes conflicting responses. Universalists are guilt-ridden about the Aztecs, who were unequal to the more advanced Spaniards, and particularists are angry at the invidious comparison that laments the disaster by explaining its inevitability. Like Mexico's first Jesuit chroniclers and catechists, Todorov assumes that the catholic or universal Self already inhabits the particularist pagan other, and that history is a process of necessary accommodations.[7] In *The Morals of History,* he (Todorov) will argue again that relativism leads to solipsism (Montaigne's "I say others the better to say myself") in order to side with Montesquieu, who held on to universal values that he tried to coordinate with particular cultural norms. Sometimes they fit badly. Respect for Aztec and Inca cultures, Todorov glosses, made Montesquieu predict their doom. The only thing that could have saved them was what they could not possibly have had: European rational philosophy. "If a Descartes had come to Mexico. . . ."[8] It may surprise some well-meaning readers to find that particularists do not imagine their cultures to be static. Nor do they welcome offers of redemption from difference.

Liberal campaigns for empowerment have offered just that, and demanded enlightened transparency, reciprocity, intimacy, "breaking the silence." The assumption is that the truth will set us free, that we can achieve, for example, a "feminist dream of a common language."[9] Silence, however, is not simply a prison in this asymmetrical world. Sometimes it's a sanctuary, or a tactic. Long ago, Sor Juana Inés de la Cruz claimed obedient silence when the Church demanded it of her, and then she explained silence, at great length, in a published letter.[10] Her baroque ingenuity of insubordination is matched by Rigoberta's ploy. It claims secrecy to interrupt her role as informant and affirm her role as leader. If the privileged reader can learn to listen, she will hear creative refusals.

To listen, we will have to resist the embrace of sisters who celebrate "breaking silences."[11] By this point of women's movements (and of this essay), we should doubt whether all classes and races of women are equally served by candid disclosures. Some feminists still cringe at hierarchies and prefer to wish them away. Consider philosopher Drucilla Cornell. She urges women — all of us — to overcome apparent social limits. Limits are merely disabling fictions, she claims on the authority of Wittgenstein. And she coyly uses Lacan's empty concept of "the feminine" to imagine endless meanings for the word. Liberties have been taken with Wittgenstein in Cornell's slide from one discourse to another.[12] Because meaning, he insisted, was the particular use that words have inside limited circumstances. Boundaries are flexible and rules change constantly, but they are, literally, the enabling circumstance of meaning (99–100).

Wishful overreading of Lacan and Wittgenstein fuels this feminist empathy for other women.[13] Limitlessly, Cornell hopes for "mimetic identifications [as] a rhetorical and artistic device for both the engagement with and the displacement of the boundaries that have limited our imagination."[14] The trouble is that metaphoric identification is a murderous trope that reduces two to one. Paul de Man noticed this danger and named autobiography as the strong case of metaphoric substitution when readers take the place of writers.[15] Rigoberta shored up boundaries to prepare for metonymic association and to forestall metaphoric overlap.[16] Cornell wants more, an empathic, ethical, "Levinasian" impulse that leaves aggression behind as barriers fall away. But empathy is the egocentric energy that drives one subject to overtake another, the catastrophic dismissal of politics by feeling in Arendt's critique of the French Revolution.[17] And Levinas has been evacuated, too, along with the sacred difference of the Other that his work tirelessly defends. The expansive subject is precisely the target of his attack on philosophy.

Levinas warned Western readers about the self-promoting solipsism of a philosophical tradition that strives to overcome mystery with clarity. Ours is a culture that presumes to reduce the experience of Self and Other into a neat totality. If everything fits into the One, of which the ego is an expression, then the other fits inside the self with no remainder, no loose, particular, or incompatible features. It is the promise of ultimate fit that drives traditional universalism forward. "This primacy of the same was Socrates's teaching: to receive nothing of the Other but what is in me, as though from all eternity I was in possession of what comes to me from the outside — to receive nothing, or to be free."[18]

This profound lesson resonated with my reading of some Latin American books. They had prepared me to read Levinasian sentences like this critique of Socratic arrogance. But were I to conjecture a reversal of encounters, I doubt that reading Levinas first could have predicted my engagements with particularist texts. His Other is absolute, not a particular strategist. He exhorts us to venerate the mystery of a face, not to improvise a response based on another's provocation. He stares at alien ground on which the Other remains largely imaginary, always already known as mystery. Unable himself to give up the endless speech of submissiveness, Levinas may have suspended the Other's chance to talk by imagining him/her as divinely nonviolent enough to keep silent. Or Levinas is not listening.[19]

It is one thing to read an inscrutable face and to conclude that attempting to understand it would be a violation; it is another (though related) thing to hear a foreign accent set the terms for respectful distance. In Levinas, different voices do not jar the subject. The consistency of his posture is suspiciously like that of Eurocentrist theorists from Montesquieu to Barthes, Kristeva, Todorov. And the dissymmetry of a meek self (prostrate before the transcendent, divine Other) can turn out to be a mirror inversion of the older dissymmetry of the voracious subject before its objects of knowledge. Humility is not the result of recognizing oneself as the Other's other, as the potential object of another (asymmetrical) desire.[20] Instead, it is an injunction that presumes a greatness that can be humbled. What gesture would follow if a subject could not presume advantages over another? Would humility be ethical? Or would underrepresented subjects do damage to themselves and to democratic process if they deferred to powerful interlocutors? The self-limitation that assumes privilege suggests what Jewish mystics called *tzimtzum* to describe God's loving self-diminishment to make room for creation.[21]

A break, a destabilizing eruption outside the self, is what I learned to miss in Levinas from having read particularist books.[22] When others speak, their appeal is not an entreaty;[23] it brooks no subordination and wants no empathy or murderous mutuality from the reader.[24] By "appeal" I mean attractiveness, the books' capacity to play on our desires and to frustrate them with a limiting subject-effect. The life-and-death game is to stop us short of conquest. Sometimes I think that Rigoberta Menchú, Jesusa Palancares, the nameless narrator of *Balún Canán,* and Richard Rodriguez write at length about their apparently private selves precisely to withhold the anticipated intimacy that would invite conquest.

I learned to be careful of some books. They can sting readers who feel privileged to know everything as they approach a text, practically any text, with the conspiratorial intimacy of a potential partner. Readers bent on understanding may neglect a different engagement that would make respect a reading requirement. The slap of refused intimacy from uncooperative books can

slow readers down, detain them at the boundary between contact and conquest, before they press particularism to surrender its cultural difference for
the sake of universal meaning. The very familiarity of universalism as a measure of literary worth, while its codependent term "particularism" sounds new
to literary studies, shows how one-sided interpretation has been, even when
we read "minority" texts. If learning makes the distance between writers and
readers seem superficial or circumstantial, mere interference on the way to
understanding, particularist writing puts circumstance to work, resurfacing
the stretch with fresh stop signs. Those signs go unnoticed and have no rhetorical names because the study of rhetoric has generally assumed cultural
continuity between writer and reader.[25]

Naming some figures of discontinuity is one purpose of my new book, to
contribute toward a rhetoric of particularism that will appreciate artful maneuvers for marking cultural distance. Why should distance be marked? Why
not overcome limits through empathy and learning? Because, as I have been
saying, overcoming makes the writer and reader finally redundant. One will
do. Contemporary criticism is hardly scandalized by readers who disappear
authors, even when texts resist. The reduction cheats readers, too, as they
override a specific charm or bite in some books. More seriously, they miss
opportunities for dialogue with texts and with citizens in public arenas where
presumptuous habits of reading cannot prepare us to listen. Learning and
teaching to read literature in ways that acknowledge difference can be the
most basic training for democratic imaginations. Yet children usually learn
one-sided approaches that ask them to identify with favorite characters, without also asking what interferes in the process. And critics continue to "collaborate" with authors, rather than to pause at uncooperativeness.

This is not to give up the promise of universalism. After all, differently
positioned citizens have to share a polity, and all of us share a world. But
universalism's promise today depends on difference, Ernesto Laclau argues
provocatively along with some critical legal scholars.[26] It has survived classical
philosophy's dismissal of particularity as deviation, and has outlived a European Enlightenment that conflated the universal (subject, class, culture) with
particular (French) incarnations. Today's universalism is a paradox for the
past, because it is grounded in particularist demands. They unmoor it from
fixed cultural content and keep it open to an "always receding horizon."[27]
Politics needs dissonance which is not useless noise, but the breaks in rhythm,
unpredictable sounds, the "performative contradictions" that call attention to
the assumptions at play. Think of Gloria Estefan's recording *Mi tierra*. The
tellingly generic homeland of the title counts on our collective nostalgia,
despite the fact that *mi tierra* may not be *la tuya*, while one of the songs,
"Hablemos el mismo idioma," wants to move the feeling of unity toward a

better future. Played to a salsa mix, it translates as "Let's Speak the Same Language" in the bilingual booklet, an apparently ecumenical accompaniment to make good on the lyric's call for racial rainbows and musical fusions (colores de un arcoiris, acordes de un mismo son). But after listening, one irritated colleague said, "Universalism isn't what it used to be." And he is right, because the appeal to get beyond differences is pitched to decidedly Latin locutors. After the first few lines, the song disinterpellates some listeners when the "us" turns out to be "los hispanos." They are literally put off, even though Estefan had accounted for differences from the very first lines of her call to unity. She admitted that differences constitute her as a subject ("A pesar de las diferencias que me hacen quien soy"), as she enjoined us to think about how much we have in common ("respiramos el mismo aire, despertamos al mismo sol, nos alumbra la misma luna, necesitamos sentir amor").

But then her rhythm of moving from outside to inside falters. It skips a beat, breaks the movement to freeze it in a "syncope," a term that Catherine Clément takes from musical notation (and from its medical meaning of "apparent death") to name a political or philosophical interruption of predictability. "The queen of rhythm, *syncope is also* the mother of *dissonance;* it is the source, in short, of a harmonious and productive discord. . . . Attack and haven, collision."[28] (It's what Toni Morrison calls "slaps and embraces" when she describes *Beloved* in terms of African American music.) The pause between strong beats, between unity and selective solidarity, is a break for reflection. Readers who may feel the sting of exclusion do not necessarily stop to think about it — not if they are too quick on the uptake.

Estefan's pitch for pan-Hispanic solidarity rehearses what Puerto Rican Willie Colón, Panamanian Rubén Blades, and Cuban Celia Cruz have been intoning for years, a "trans-Latino" identity that now characterizes urban centers like "the New Nueva York."[29] Improvising on the themes of sameness and difference, the way that musical mixes make salsa from different national styles, Latinos are also saying that universalism is not what it used to be. They are saying it with relief, because they had fit so badly into milky homogenizations. "Racism as Universalism" is one result of the colorless abstraction.[30] But universality has renewed hope, say defenders of the public sphere and pragmatists, if democracies can tune in to discord in order to develop an "interactive" politics. Discord among culturally and economically situated subjects locates gaps as the space of democratic negotiation.[31] Without gaps, negotiation would be unnecessary. And because of them, listening is not easy, it requires patience at the syncope of communication in a country where citizens do not always speak the same language. Even when we do speak English, Mari J. Matsuda argued in the *Yale Law Journal*, the range of culturally inflected accents fissures the language community — happily, she adds, because our accents safeguard American diversity from the meanness of one standard sound. Cultural difference is something for democracy to celebrate, not just to tolerate.[32] Theodor Adorno appreciated the "negativity" inside communities as boundary markers that resist the subject's "greedy thirst for incorporation" of difference into sameness.[33] If there were no difference, there could be no recognition of one subject by another, but only the identification that reduces real external others into functions of a totalizing self. Yet the very gap that allows for enough autonomy to make mutuality possible also risks misrecognition and violence. The risk is worth taking, because without it we allow the violence of forcing sameness on others. Either they are forced to fit, or they are forced out.[34] The necessary risk of breakdown that democracies defend as the negative (autonomous) moment of mutuality surely gives some universalists pause about the possibility of a coherent culture and a cohesive policy.[35] But pause is not a bad thing if it gives time for one to listen to another.[36] Breaks risk liberal improvisation between the "apparent deaths" of the polity. Precisely because citizens cannot presume to feel, or to think, or to perform alike, their ear for otherness makes justice possible.[37] That is why political philosophy and ethics, from Benjamin and Arendt to Bakhtin and Levinas, caution against empathy, which plays treacherously in a subject-centered key that overwhelms unfamiliar voices to repeat sounds of the self.[38]

The very fact that I am able to call self-critical attention to our culture-bound appetites is a sign that I have been reading Rigoberta. When I began, her refusals to satisfy my interest woke me to the possibility that the interest was being cultivated so that I could feel the rebuff. Concerns about the text's authenticity seemed beside the point as I began to appreciate the evident manipulation. Perhaps the informant was being more active and strategic than our essentialist notions of authenticity have allowed. Then I noticed other particularist tactics that distance readers in order to engage them as allies.

To read particularist works in *their* ideal terms needs a paradigm shift from the foundational fictions that would make lovers and siblings of potential citizens. A model of inclusive communities cannot read books or times that stretch society into a map of competing particularisms. To read them, our critical vocabulary would strain after antifoundationalist terms. It would struggle because the vicious hermeneutic circle of familiarity and predictability makes unanticipated lessons hard to read. How can the books teach reading effectively if our training strives to overcome the lessons? If training assumes that learning is a progression, that it always learns something, how does interpretive reticence make sense? At our most modest, we have been assuming, with the New Critics and then with deconstruction,[39] that ambiguity cannot be conquered. But an ethical distance from the object of desire? Confessed ignorance of that object? Prohibition against trespassing? We have yet to acknowledge the enticement of a hand outstretched to keep us at a distance.

Notes

For more provocative suggestions, see my latest book, *Proceed with Caution When Engaged by Minority Writers in the Americas* (Cambridge, Mass.: Harvard University Press, 1999), in which a more developed version of this piece appears.

1 For an excellent discussion of these anthropological traps, see Frederick Cooper and Ann Laura Stoler's introduction to *Tensions of Empire: Colonial Cultures in a Bourgeois World* (Berkeley: University of California Press, 1996).

2 They might include urban musical innovations made to leave the competition behind. "A style nobody can deal with" is the goal, says Fab 5 Freddy, an early rapper and graffiti artist. See Tricia Rose, "A Style Nobody Can Deal With," in *Microphone Fiends: Youth Music and Youth Culture,* ed. Andrew Ross and Tricia Rose (New York: Routledge, 1994), pp. 71–88, excerpted from Tricia Rose, *Black Noise: Rap Music and Black Culture in Contemporary America* (Middletown, Conn.: Wesleyan Press, 1994). I thank Arnaldo Cruz Malavé for this suggestion.

3 Michel Foucault gives a strong formulation in *The Archaeology of Knowledge,* trans. A. M. Sheridan Smith (New York: Pantheon, 1972). Of course, John Rawls derives his sense of justice as fairness in *A Theory of Justice* (Cambridge, Mass.: Harvard University Press, 1971) from the fictional device of "original position" and the socially unmarked "veil of ignorance." Some political philosophers find embeddedness to be unavoidable. These are lessons that Homi Bhabha develops in *The Location of Culture* (London: Routledge, 1994).

4 In George Steiner's pithy indictment, "Like murderous Cordelia, children know that silence can destroy another human being. Or like Kafka they remember that several have survived the songs of the Sirens, but none their silence." See his *After Babel: Aspects of Language and Translation* (London: Oxford University Press, 1975), p. 35.

5 I borrow the term loosely from Antonio Gramsci, for whom the war of position is a process of ideological disarticulation (of bourgeois hegemony) and rearticulation (of a hegemonic workers' bloc). It is the ideological struggle between the fundamental classes over elements that could serve either one, a struggle that precedes military confrontation. See Gramsci's *Selections from the Prison Notebooks,* ed. and trans. Quintin Hoare and Geoffrey Nowell Smith (New York: International Publishers, 1971), pp. 238–39. See also Chantal Mouffe, "Hegemony and Ideology in Gramsci," in *Gramsci and Marxist Theory,* ed. Chantal Mouffe (London: Routledge/Kegan Paul, 1979), pp. 168–204.

6 Derrida's remarks on Levinas underline that war of positionality: "One would attempt in vain . . . to forget the words 'inside,' 'outside,' 'exterior,' 'interior,' etc. . . . for one would never come across a language without the rupture of space" (113). See Derrida, "Violence and Metaphysics: An Essay on the Thought of Emmanuel Levinas," in *Writing and Difference,* trans. Alan Bass (Chicago: University of Chicago Press, 1978), pp. 79–153.

7 See, for example, Fernando Coronil, "Mastery by Signs, Signs by Mastery," a review essay in *Plantation Society* 2, 2 (December 1986): 201–207; and José Piedra, "The Game of Critical Arrival," *Diacritics* (spring 1989): 34–61. See also Myra Jehlen, "Why Did the Europeans Cross the Ocean? A Seventeenth-Century Riddle" in *Cultures of American*

Imperialism, ed. Amy Kaplan and Donald Pease (Durham, N.C.: Duke University Press, 1993), pp. 41–59. Consider also Gayatri Spivak's general indictment of "the ferocious standardizing benevolence of most U.S. and Western European human-scientific radicalism (recognition by assimilation)" in her "Can the Subaltern Speak?" in *Marxism and the Interpretation of Culture,* ed. Nelson and Grossberg (Urbana: University of Illinois Press, 1988), p. 294. See also Simon Gikandi, *Writing in Limbo: Modernism and Caribbean Literature* (Ithaca, N.Y.: Cornell University Press, 1992), where Todorov's book figures as the condensation of Eurocentric assumptions about the Conquest.

8   Tzvetan Todorov, *The Morals of History,* trans. Alyson Waters (Minneapolis: University of Minnesota Press, 1995); see especially chap. 4, "The Conquest as Seen by the French," pp. 34–46, 41.

9   Donna Haraway, "A Manifesto for Cyborgs: Science, Technology, and Socialist Feminism in the 1980s," in *Coming to Terms: Feminism, Theory, and Politics,* ed. Elizabeth Weed (New York: Routledge, 1989), p. 173.

10   Silence "explains a great deal through the very stress of not explaining, we must assign some meaning to it that we may understand what the silence is intended to say." *Sor Juana Inés de la Cruz, a Woman of Genius: The Intellectual Autobiography of Sor Juana Inés de la Cruz,* trans. Margaret Sayers Peden (Limerock, Conn.: Limerock Press, 1982), pp. 18–20.

11   The quote continues: "in the words of Beverly Tanenhaus, this is in itself a first kind of action. I wrote *Women and Honor* in an effort to make myself more honest, and to understand the terrible negative power of the lie in relationships between women. Since it was published, other women have spoken and written of things I did not include: Michelle Cliff's 'Notes on Speechlessness' . . . led Catherine Nicholson . . . to write of the power of 'deafness,' the frustration of our speech by those who do not want to hear what we have to say. Nelle Morton has written of the act of 'hearing each other into speech.' How do we listen?" Adrienne Rich, "Women and Honor: Some Notes on Lying (1975)," in *On Lies, Secrets, and Silence: Selected Prose 1966–1978* (New York: Norton, 1979), p. 185.

12   Slavoj Žižek seems inspired by that flattened, weblike image of meaning. In *The Sublime Object of Ideology* (London: Verso, 1989), he argues against Freudian psychoanalysis that desire is not hidden, but is on the surface and attached, between the thought and the dream text: "the real subject matter of the dream (the unconscious desire) articulates itself in the dream-work, in the elaboration of its 'latent content'" (13).

13   This seems different from the playful love that moves María Lugones's "schizophrenic" trips between culturally differentiated worlds. See Lugones, "Playfulness, 'World'-Travelling, and Loving Perception," *Hypatia* 2, 2 (summer 1987): 3–19. I thank Keja Valens for this reference.

14   Drucilla Cornell, "What is Ethical Feminism?" chap. 4 of *Feminist Contentions: A Philosophical Exchange,* by Seyla Benhabib, Judith Butler, Drucilla Cornell, and Nancy Fraser, intro. by Linda Nicholson (London: Routledge, 1995), pp. 75–106, 97.

15   "The autobiographical moment happens as an alignment between the two subjects involved in the process of reading in which they determine each other by mutual reflexive substitution." Paul de Man, "Autobiography as De-facement," in *The Rhetoric of Romanticism* (New York: Columbia University Press, 1984), pp. 67–82. Ross Chambers points out that the contemporary Greek use for the word "metaphor" is quite literally as transportation, in a bus or a shuttle, for example. See his "Meditation and the Escalator Principle (On Nicholson Baker's *The Mezzanine*)," *MFS* 40, 4 (winter 1994): 765–806, 773.

16   See G. Spivak's skepticism, based on assuming that coalitions are always organized from

the elite participants: "Even if the absurdity of the nonrepresenting intellectual making space for her to speak is achieved. The woman is doubly in shadow . . . there are people whose consciousness we cannot grasp if we close off our benevolence by constructing a homogeneous Other referring only to our own place in the seat of the Same or the Self. . . . To confront them is not to represent (*vertreten*) them but to learn to represent (*darstellen*) ourselves. This argument would take us into a critique of a disciplinary anthropology and the relationship between elementary pedagogy and disciplinary formation." G. Spivak, "Can the Subaltern Speak?" in *Marxism and the Interpretation of Culture,* ed. Nelson and Grossberg (Urbana: University of Illinois Press, 1988), pp. 288–289.

17 Arendt calls her reliance on compassion a "misplaced emphasis on the heart as the source of political virtue" (92); "Because compassion abolishes the distance, the worldly space between men where political matters, the whole realm of human affairs, are located, it remains, politically speaking, irrelevant and without consequence. . . . Jesus's silence in 'The Grand Inquisitor' and Billy Budd's stammer indicate the same, namely their incapacity (or unwillingness) for all kinds of predicative or argumentative speech, in which someone talks *to* somebody *about* something that is of interest to both because it *interest,* it is between them. Such talkative and argumentative interest in the world is entirely alien to compassion" (81). Hannah Arendt, *On Revolution* (New York: Viking, 1963).

18 Emmanuel Levinas, *Totality and Infinity: An Essay on Exteriority,* trans. Alphonso Lingis (The Hague: M. Nijhoff, 1979), p. 40.

19 For Jacques Derrida, the contradiction (or paradox) derives from the "nonviolent urgency" of Levinas's ethics, which proposes "a language without phrase," while at the same time speech is privileged over sight as the safeguard for exteriority. "Violence appears with *articulation*"; and yet righteousness is only possible through discourse. Derrida observes the hypocritical use of speech against speech: "The very elocution of nonviolent metaphysics is its first disavowal." Derrida, "Violence and Metaphysics: An Essay on the Thought of Emmanuel Levinas," in *Writing and Difference,* trans. Alan Bass (Chicago: University of Chicago Press, 1978), pp. 147.

20 See Derrida's comparison with Husserl, whose ethics begin precisely from the assumption of mutual alterity. Ibid., pp. 128–133.

21 This choice is like the liberal's self-constraint on reading "fragile" minority literature, advocated by Peter J. Rabinowitz. See his "'Betraying the Sender': The Rhetoric and Ethics of Fragile Texts" (*Narrative* 2, 3 [October 1994]: 254–267), where he worries about his reading of Nella Larsen's *Passing* for having "tampered with a finely wrought text in such a way as to damage it" (202). He understood the book's secret (that it was about lesbians passing for heterosexuals) and divulged it. Thanks to Irene Kacandes for this article.

22 Enrique Dussel makes a similar objection from his position as a Latin American philosopher of liberation. See Dussel and Daniel E. Guillot, *Liberación Latinoamericana y Emmanuel Levinas* (Buenos Aires: Editorial Bonum, 1975).

23 Hannah Arendt said this before on Billy Budd in *On Revolution* (New York: Viking, 1963).

24 I am apparently siding with Kant against Schopenhauer, according to Robert Gooding Williams, in their debate about the basis of ethics. For one, it was respect for rational beings (the demand for respect constituting, it seems to me, a sign of rationality); for the other, it was compassion.

25 See, for example, Richard A. Lanham's useful *Handlist of Rhetorical Terms,* 2nd ed. (Berkeley: University of California Press, 1991).

26 See Neil Gotanda, "A Critique of 'Our Constitution is Color-Blind,'" *Stanford Law Review* 44, 1 (November 1991): 1–68. Citing Robert Paul Wolff (in "Beyond Tolerance," in *A Critique of Pure Tolerance,* ed. Robert Paul Wolff, Barrington Moore Jr., and Herbert Marcuse [Boston: Beacon Press, 1965], pp. 4, 17), Gotanda defends racial-cultural diversity as a positive good in the polity, rather than something to be merely tolerated and benignly overlooked (53). Gotanda also quotes Justice Brennan, whose decision in *Metro Broadcasting v FCC* draws from *Regents of University of California v Bakke:* "Just as a 'diverse student body' contributing to a 'robust exchange of ideas' is a 'constitutionally permissible goal' on which a race-conscious university admissions program may be predicated, the diversity of views and information on the airwaves serves important First Amendment values. The benefits of such diversity are not limited to the members of minority groups; . . . rather, the benefits redound to all members of the viewing and listening audience" (57). Thanks to Susan Keller for directing me to this article.

27 Ernesto Laclau, "Universalism, Particularism, and the Question of Identity," in *The Identity in Question,* ed. John Rajchman (New York: Routledge, 1995), pp. 93–108, quote from p. 107. Judith Butler cautiously agrees that universality can be a site of translation. See Seyla Benhabib, Judith Butler, Drucilla Cornell, Nancy Fraser, intro. by Linda Nicholson, *Feminist Contentions: A Philosophical Exchange* (London: Routledge, 1995): "the universal is always culturally articulated, and that the complex process of learning how to read that claim is not something any of us can do outside of the difficult process of cultural translation. . . . the terms made to stand for one another are transformed in the process, and where the movement of that unanticipated transformation establishes the universal as that which is yet to be achieved and which, in order to resist domestication, may never be fully or finally achievable." See also Butler's "Sovereign Performatives in the Contemporary Scene of Utterance," forthcoming in *Critical Inquiry,* where she argues for the efficacy of "performative contradictions" in the contestatory translations of "universal." "Performative contradiction" is a term Habermas had used to discredit Foucault's critique of reason via reason. Also, see Jürgen Habermas, *The Philosophical Discourse of Modernity* (Cambridge, Mass.: MIT Press, 1987). I'm not sure, however, how different in practice is Butler's project of open-ended translation from Habermas's pursuit of the universal as an ideal. Who could ever reach an ideal? And yet, in the heuristic spirit of Seyla's Benhabib's work, how can one have a political engagement without imagining ideals? Homi K. Bhabha also makes translation the site of the movable nature of modernity in general. Translation is the favored strategy for keeping the promise of modernity usably alive. See Bhabha, *The Location of Culture* (New York: Routledge, 1994), pp. 32, 242.

28 Catherine Clément, *Syncope: The Philosophy of Rapture,* foreword by Verena Andermatt Conley, trans. Sally O'Driscoll and Deirdre M. Mahoney (Minneapolis: University of Minnesota Press, 1994), p. 4.

29 For an excellent review of the sociological literature, see Juan Flores, "Pan-Latino/Trans-Latino: Puerto Ricans in the 'New Nueva York,'" *Centro* (Journal of the Center for Puerto Rican Studies), 8, 1–2 (1996): 171–186.

30 Etienne Balibar, "Racism as Universalism," in *Masses, Classes, and Ideas,* trans. James Swenson (New York: Routledge, 1994), pp. 191–204. See also Marc Shell's excellent *Children of the Earth: Literature, Politics, and Nationhood* (New York: Oxford University Press, 1993). "All men are brothers" is the slogan that Shell considers throughout the book. The danger is that if some are not brothers, or do not want to be, then they are not "men" and can be eliminated.

31 See Seyla Benhabib, *Situating the Self: Gender, Community, and Postmodernism in Contem-*

porary Ethics (New York: Routledge, 1992), pp. 3, 5. See also Richard Rorty's *Objectivity, Relativism, and Truth* (New York: Cambridge University Press, 1991) in his defense of Dewey as clearing the ground for liberal democracy (13).

32   Mari J. Matsuda, "Voices of America: Accent, Antidiscrimination Law, and a Jurisprudence for the Last Reconstruction," *Yale Law Journal,* 100, 5 (March 1991): 1329–1407. She celebrates cultural difference beyond the tolerance that liberals like Rorty defend. I am grateful to Susan Keller for this reference.

33   The greedy subject is Freud's formulation. T. W. Adorno, *Negative Dialektic* (Frankfurt: Surkamp, 1966), pp. 172. See also Diana Fuss, *Identity Papers* (New York: Routledge, 1996).

34   Jessica Benjamin, "The Shadow of the Other (Subject): Intersubjectivity and Feminist Theory," *Constellations* 1, 2 (1994) (Basil Blackwell): 231–254, 245. Her entire discussion is most useful. I am grateful to Kerry Riddich for the reference.

35   See, for example, Naomi Schor, *Bad Objects: Essays Popular and Unpopular* (Durham, N.C.: Duke University Press, 1995), p. xiv.

36   Emmanuel Levinas, *Totality and Infinity:* "The real must not only be determined in its historical objectivity, but also from interior intentions, from the secrecy that interrupts the continuity of historical time. Only starting from this secrecy is the pluralism of society possible" (57–58). Also see Jean-François Lyotard, "The Other's Rights," in *On Human Rights: The Oxford Amnesty Lectures 1993,* ed. Stephen Shute and Susan Hurley (New York: HarperCollins, 1993), 136–147. How to share dialogue with *you,* requires a moment of silence. "Aristotle said: The master speaks and the pupil listens. For that moment, the status of *I* is forbidden to me. . . . 'The suspension of interlocution imposes a silence and that silence is good. It does not undermine the right to speak. It teaches the value of that right' " (142).

37   This is a commonplace of political philosophy, one that Mari Matsuda develops for the practice of law in note 32 above. See John Rawls, "Justice as Fairness: Political Not Metaphysical," *Philosophy and Public Affairs* 14 (1985): 223–251. "Liberalism as a political doctrine supposes that there are many conflicting and incommensurable conceptions of the good, each compatible with the full rationality of human persons" (248). See also Robert Dahl, *Dilemmas of Pluralist Democracy: Autonomy Versus Control* (New Haven, Conn.: Yale University Press, 1982); and Milton Fisk, "Introduction: The Problem of Justice," in Fisk, *Key Concepts in Critical Theory: Justice* (Atlantic Highlands, N.J.: Humanities Press, 1993), pp. 1–8. "There has to be at least a conflict based on an actual lack of homogeneity for what is distinctive about justice to become relevant" (1). See also Benhabib, *Situating the Self,* p. 2.

38   In thesis VII of "Theses on the Philosophy of History," Benjamin disdains historicism for cultivating empathy, that lazy attachment to the past that has survived in documents, necessarily to the oppressive winners. See Benjamin, *Illuminations,* ed. and with an introduction by Hannah Arendt, trans. Harry Zohn (New York: Schocken, 1969), pp. 253–264. Also see the long section in chap. 2, "The Social Question" (69–90) of Hannah Arendt's *On Revolution* (New York: Viking, 1963): "Because compassion abolishes the distance where politics can happen, it is irrelevant for worldly affairs" (81), and worse, "speaking for (weak) others may be a pretext for lust for power" (84). See also M. Bakhtin, *Art and Answerability: Early Philosophical Essays,* ed. Michael Holquist and Vadim Liapunov (Austin: University of Texas Press, 1990), pp. 64, 81, 88; and Emmanuel Levinas throughout *Totality and Infinity: An Essay on Exteriority,* trans. Alphonso Lingis (The Hague: M. Nijhoff, 1979) and *Otherwise Than Being,* trans. Alphonso Lingus (Dor-

drecht: Kluwer, 1981). For a proceduralist critique of grounding politics in positive feeling, see, for example, Robert Dahl, *Dilemmas of Pluralist Democracy: Autonomy versus Control* (New Haven, Conn.: Yale University Press, 1982), esp. chap. 7, "Changing Civic Orientations," pp. 138–164: "To love a member of one's family or a friend is not at all like 'loving' abstract 'others' whom one does not know, never expects to know, and may not even want to know" (147).

39 Steven Mailloux on Stanley Fish in *Rhetorical Power* (Ithaca, N.Y.: Cornell University Press, 1989), p. 43.

Works Cited

Adorno, T. W. *Negative Dialektic.* Frankfurt: Surkamp, 1966.

Arendt, Hannah. *On Revolution.* New York: Viking, 1963.

Bakhtin, M. M. *Art and Answerability: Early Philosophical Essays.* Ed. Michael Holquist and Vadim Liapunov. Austin: University of Texas Press, 1990.

Balibar, Etienne. "Racism as Universalism." In *Masses, Classes, and Ideas.* Trans. James Swenson. New York: Routledge, 1994.

Benhabib, Seyla. *Situating the Self: Gender, Community and Postmodernism in Contemporary Ethics.* New York: Routledge, 1992.

Benjamin, Jessica. "The Shadow of the Other (Subject): Intersubjectivity and Feminist Theory." *Constellations* 1, no. 2 (1994): 231–254.

Benjamin, Walter. *Illuminations.* Edited and with an introduction by Hannah Arendt, trans. by Harry Zohn. New York: Schocken, 1969.

Bhabha, Homi K. *The Location of Culture.* New York: Routledge, 1994.

Chambers, Ross. "Meditation and the Escalator Principle (On Nicholson Baker's *The Mezzanine*)." *MFS* 40, no. 4 (winter 1994): 765–806.

Clément, Catherine. *Syncope: The Philosophy of Rapture.* Foreword by Verena Andermatt Conley, trans. by Sally O'Driscoll and Deirdre M. Mahoney. Minneapolis: University of Minnesota Press, 1994.

Cooper, Frederick, and Ann Laura Stoler. *Tensions of Empire: Colonial Cultures in a Bourgeois World.* Berkeley: University of California Press, 1996.

Cornell, Drucilla. "What is Ethical Feminism?" In Seyla Benhabib, Judith Butler, Drucilla Cornell, Nancy Fraser, eds. *Feminist Contentions: A Philosophical Exchange* (Routledge, 1995).

Coronil, Fernando. "Mastery by Signs, Signs of Mastery." *Plantation Society* 2, no. 2 (December 1986): 201–207.

Dahl, Robert. *Dilemmas of Pluralist Democracy: Autonomy Versus Control* (New Haven, Conn.: Yale University Press, 1982).

de Man Paul. "Autobiography as De-facement." In *The Rhetoric of Romanticism.* New York: Columbia University Press, 1984).

Derrida, Jacques, "Living On the Border Lines." In Jacques Derrida, Paul de Man, J. Hillis Miller, Harold Bloom, and Geoffrey Hartman, eds., *Deconstruction and Criticism.* London: Routledge, 1979.

——. "Violence and Metaphysics: An Essay on the Thought of Emmanuel Levinas." *Writing and Difference,* trans. Alan Bass. Chicago: University of Chicago Press, 1978.

Dussel, Enrique, and Daniel E. Guillot. *Liberación Latinoamericana y Emmanuel Levinas.* Buenos Aires: Editorial Bonum, 1975.

Fisk, Milton. "Introduction: The Problem of Justice." In *Key Concepts in Critical Theory: Justice.* Atlantic Highlands, N.J.: Humanities Press, 1993.

Foucault, Michel. *The Archaeology of Knowledge,* trans. A. M. Sheridan Smith. New York: Pantheon, 1972.

Fuss, Diana. *Identity Papers.* New York: Routledge, 1996.

Gikandi, Simon. *Writing in Limbo: Modernism and Caribbean Literature* (Ithaca, N.Y.: Cornell University Press, 1992.

Gotanda, Neil. "A Critique of 'Our Constitution is Color-Blind.'" *Stanford Law Review* 44, no. 1 (November 1991): 1–68.

Gramsci, Antonio. *Selections from the Prison Notebooks,* ed. and trans. Quintin Hoare and Geoffrey Nowell Smith. New York: International Publishers, 1971.

Habermas, Jürgen. *The Philosophical Discourse of Modernity.* Frederick Lawrence (Cambridge, Mass.: MIT Press, 1987.

Haraway, Donna. "A Manifesto for Cyborgs: Science, Technology, and Socialist Feminism in the 1980s." In *Coming to Terms: Feminism, Theory, and Politics,* ed. Elizabeth Weed. New York: Routledge, 1989.

Laclau, Ernesto. "Universalism, Particularism and the Question of Identity." *The Identity in Question,* ed. John Rajchman. New York: Routledge, 1995.

Lanham, Richard A. *Handlist of Rhetorical Terms.* 2d ed. Berkeley: University of California Press, 1991.

Levinas, Emmanuel. *Totality and Infinity: An Essay on Exteriority,* trans. by Alphonso Lingis. The Hague: M. Nijhoff Publishers, 1979.

———. *Otherwise than Being, or Beyond Essence,* trans. Alphonso Lingis. Dordrecht: Kluwer Academic Publishers, 1991.

Lugones, María. "Playfulness, World-Travelling, and Loving Perception." *Hypatia* 2, no. 2 (summer 1987): 3–19.

Lyotard, Jean-François. "The Other's Rights." In *On Human Rights: The Oxford Amnesty Lectures 1993,* eds. Stephen Shute and Susan Hurley. New York: HarperCollins, 1993.

Mailloux, Steven. *Rhetorical Power* (Ithaca, N.Y.: Cornell University Press, 1989.

Matsuda, Mari J. "Voices of America: Accent, Antidiscrimination Law, and a Jurisprudence for the Last Reconstruction." *Yale Law Journal* 100, no. 5 (March 1991): 1329–1407.

Mouffe, Chantal. "Hegemony and Ideology in Gramsci." In *Gramsci and Marxist Theory,* ed. Chantal Mouffe. London: Routledge, 1979.

Rabinowitz, Peter J. "'Betraying the Sender': The Rhetoric and Ethics of Fragile Texts." *Narrative* 2, no. 3 (October 1994): 254–267.

Rawls, John. *A Theory of Justice.* Cambridge, Mass.: Harvard University Press, 1971.

———. "Justice as Fairness: Political, Not Metaphysical." In *Philosophy and Public Affairs* 14 (3) (1985): 223–51.

Rich, Adrienne. "Women and Honor: Some Notes on Lying (1975)." In *On Lies, Secrets, and Silence: Selected Prose, 1966–1978.* New York: Norton, 1979.

Rorty, Richard. *Objectivity, Relativism, and Truth.* New York: Cambridge University Press, 1991.

Rose, Tricia. *Black Noise: Rap Music and Black Culture in Contemporary America.* Middletown, C.T.: Wesleyan Press, 1994.

Schor, Naomi. *Bad Objects: Essays Popular and Unpopular.* Durham, N.C.: Duke University Press, 1995.

Shell, Marc. *Children of the Earth: Literature, Politics, and Nationhood.* New York: Oxford University Press, 1993.

Sor, Juana Inés de la Cruz. *A Woman of Genius: The Intellectual Autobiography of Sor Juana Inés de la Cruz,* trans. Margaret Sayers Peden. Limerock, Conn.: Limerock Press, 1982.

Spivak, Gayatri Chakravorty. "Can the Subaltern Speak?" In *Marxism and the Interpretation of Culture,* ed. Cary Nelson and Lawrence Grossberg. Urbana: University of Illinois Press, 1988.

Steiner, George. *After Babel: Aspects of Language and Translation.* London: Oxford University Press, 1975.

Todorov, Tzvetan. *The Morals of History,* trans. Alyson Waters. Minneapolis: University of Minnesota Press, 1995.

Žižek, Slavoj. *The Sublime Object of Ideology.* London: Verso, 1989.

Beyond Representation? The Impossibility of the Local (Notes on Subaltern Studies in Light of a Rebellion in Tepoztlán, Morelos)

JOSÉ RABASA

To the old women of Tepoztlán who faced
down the riot police with wooden sticks

(I open and close this essay with parentheses to situate its emphasis on the *now* of the rebellion in Tepoztlán — a small village a forty-five minutes' drive from Mexico City — and to provide an update at the end. I wrote this essay in Tepoztlán while on leave from my U.S. academic institution in 1995. The rebellion in Tepoztlán began the morning of August 24, 1995, which I witnessed as I was getting on a bus to go to San Andrés Sacamch'en de los Pobres, Chiapas (officially known as San Andrés Larráinzar) for the conversations "Larráinzar VI" between the government and the Ejército Zapatista de Liberación Nacional (EZLN). The EZLN, an army composed mostly of Indians, surprised the world on January 1, 1994, when it took over several cities in Chiapas.[1]

As I read this essay today in Ann Arbor, I cannot fail to feel a distance from the intensity I felt that morning when I left my wife, Catherine, and two children, Magali and Pablo, in an intense political situation in which the residents of Tepoztlán barricaded the town and armed themselves with wooden sticks. Catherine eventually lent her solidarity by making the rounds of the barricades with large containers of coffee. Magali, thirteen at the time, had the fortune of having a social science teacher who not only supported the rebellion but discussed it in class to impart invaluable lessons on citizenship. To date I wonder about how this experience helped shape a politically committed fifteen-year-old who attends school board meetings, cooks for Food Not Bombs, and has participated in the organization of a student political action group in her high school. I also wonder about the experience of Pablo, who played with his friends in the plaza during the nightly town meetings when new guards of the Municipal Palace assumed their post, leaders summarized the events of the day, and the people of Tepoztlán expressed their views on the rebellion and the appropriate politics to follow.

Given that such personal notes are commonplace in recent self-reflexive modes of writing ethnography, I should dispel the illusion that what I am doing in this essay is ethnographic. I am not an anthropologist by training, nor do I want to be one. I am writing on this rebellion because of my interests in subaltern studies and, more particularly, on the Zapatismo of the EZLN. Tepoztlán, in this respect, is an exemplary instance of a subaltern struggle and assertion of a new politics of citizenship that try the government's commitment to democracy. For both the Zapatistas in Chiapas and Tepoztlán, the Mexican state—as identified with the Partido Revolucionario Institucional, the PRI—is an *outlaw state* whose credibility depends on living up to its promises of democratic reform. Thus, ungovernability is a category that speaks less about "others" living outside or resisting the national project than about a breakdown of state institutions.)

One of the most amusing benchmarks of the beginnings of modern philosophy—in particular, of philosophies concerned with current events, *la philosophie de l'actualité* (as the French like to call it)—is Hegel's statement that "reading the morning paper is a kind of realistic prayer" (quoted in Descombes, 3). Newspapers, however, situate our prayers in local interests, whether these might be school board decisions, the latest rapist in the community, or, from an international point of view, the collapse of the Mexican peso and its impact on the U.S. economy. Hegel's observation assumes that one must read the news (the compulsion to *see* the morning news on TV is today's equivalent) in order to fully function in our immediate context, which might very well mean making decisions about investments in today's highly volatile "emergent" economics. Newspapers (especially those in metropolitan centers of power) reify the local as universal inasmuch as they make sense of the world selectively, according to particular interests. If it is in the nature of things to be localocentric, only the metropolis can afford to fetishize a particular perspective. Other news, in other circuits of information, until very recently were the realm of area studies specialists—one cannot pray with last week's papers. One could always call friends and get a briefing on events, but the call is motivated by an awareness of being limited to reading partial truths and lacks the religiosity that accompanies our morning consumption of the *real*. The circulation of newspapers today on the Internet has opened new sites of "prayer" and also has made possible the dismantling of the control of information by press agencies. It is worth remembering that only a few years ago the United States pulled out of UNESCO because of its insistence (due to what was perceived as overtly political: maintaining a Third World bias) on creating an international bank of information (the New International Order). This circulation of information, however, does not exclude forms of control that do or may yet come to exist over e-mail and the World Wide Web.

The Internet was thus conceived by the Zapatistas in Chiapas as one of the channels to convey their communiqués to an international community. Cyberspace became a means to disseminate information since the early days of the uprising in 1994, but also a place where members of the international community could contribute to their cause. The effectiveness of the Zapatistas as a subaltern group in building solidarity in Europe, the United States, Latin America, Australia and other parts of the world is a unique phenomenon. They have managed to internationalize their local struggle. It is also worth remembering that this most modern form of communication does not contradict ancestral, Indian communal forms of social organization that emphasize consensus and the participation of the whole community—men, women, and children. If the Zapatista use of the Internet globalizes the local, the insurrection in Tepoztlán, as I will argue below, localizes the global. In both instances, Hegel's highly individualized prayer metaphor gives place to collective forms of action and reading.

In another version of this essay (actually, by now, another essay), I have examined the nature of the *impossible* and the *folkloric* inherent to the subaltern character of the Zapatista insurrection (Rabasa, "Of Zapatismo"). The impossible and the folkloric refer respectively (1) to a *complete liberation*—i.e., to redress five hundred years of injustice against Indians (in Antonio Negri's terms, of constituting communism as a critique of capitalist and socialist stateforms), and (2) to the *compatibility of modern and nonmodern political and cultural forms*—i.e., to build international solidarity by means of the Internet while evoking the pre-Columbian Votán, the heart of the people (in Reynaldo Ileto's terms, of accepting the reality of other conceptual systems). This earlier essay was conceived and written, as it were, in cyberspace, in Ann Arbor, reading local news on the Internet. This situation has changed in the last few months since I am currently writing these lines in Tepoztlán, Morelos, a village of approximately eighteen thousand located forty miles southeast of Mexico City.

The people of Tepoztlán—an old bastion of Zapatismo during the 1910 Mexican Revolution (John Womack's *Zapata and the Mexican Revolution* is the classic, though somewhat dated, study of the life of Emiliano Zapata and Zapatismo in general)—have overthrown their elected government for not consulting the town in their dealings with a transnational enterprise that sought to build a golf course, eight hundred luxury homes, and a GTE communications center in communal lands (which were, according to the Tepoztecos, illicitly sold thirty years ago) and a protected natural refuge. The village has been barricaded, and its youth guards the town with big wooden sticks. More recently the town has called for the election of a new mayor and city council, and has defined itself as a free municipality (*municipio libre*)—

that is, not bound to the authorities of the state of Morelos. The old Zapatista motto *mandar obedeciendo* (to rule obeying) led not only to the ouster of the mayor and city council but also, perhaps more important, to an election of a new government following the ancestral democratic traditions and customs of the town, and a tightened vigilance of the new officers. Though I am now located in the field, in the local, my connection to the Internet still remains central—no longer as a space to gain information, but as a tool to reach hundreds of networks in case of an emergency, in the eventuality of a repression by the army or the riot police. My "immersion" in the local, however, has made manifest to me that the local, like the subaltern, is an elusive concept that becomes meaningful only as a relational term. Local or subaltern vis-à-vis what? I still read the newspapers religiously to learn about the events of Tepoztlán; in fact, I read the relevant articles published in different newspapers and magazines on the bulletin boards that display them in the main plaza of Tepoztlán.

One would assume that these *representations* (articles "describing" the events and "speaking" for the people) function as mirrors, as if the self-consciousness and identity of the people of Tepoztlán would depend on them. This eerie feeling disappears once we view this display of representations not as informative of what is occurring in the town, but as mirrors of the outside world. Beyond representing the Tepoztecos (a function of dubious value to the citizens of Tepoztlán), these news items manifest cracks in the narrative of neoliberalism and the inevitability of globalism. For the Tepoztecos, and the purposes of this essay, representations of the events are significant in what they convey about changes in the *structures of feeling* of those who make it their business to report and interpret the events surrounding the emergence of the Tepoztecos as subjects of their own history. Rather than providing one more account of the events (though to some extent this is inevitable), I will reflect here on the intertwining of the local and the global. Beyond representation, the local manifests its impossibility in its bind to the global. Ultimately, the local must be seen as a catachresis for the national and the global in all their contradictions. Local and regional identities, as well as nationalisms not subsumed under the nation-state, have evolved in Tepoztlán, as in the case of Chiapas, as points of contention for bending the humdrum of globalism. The global might very well be a determinant of local communities and contribute to their deterioration, but it lacks the symbolic elements to institutionalize an alternative community (see Lomnitz, "La decadencia," 90–91).

In this article I would like to relate this uprising in Tepoztlán to the Zapatistas of Chiapas and dwell on the need to move beyond representation and explore the impossibility of the local in subaltern movements. These tasks, however, call for a critique of subaltern studies, as well as the need to trace the transformations the concept of the subaltern has undergone as it has traveled from the Italy of Antonio Gramsci in the 1930s, to the South Asian Subaltern Studies Group in the 1980s, to the emergent Latin American group in the 1990s. Tepoztlán and Chiapas force us to make the concept of the subaltern travel from the metropolitan centers of power in the U.S. academy to the local/regional sites of struggle, and to resist the temptation of reading these insurrections through Gramsci, the Indian group, or even the Latin American proposals. We must, on the contrary, outline the insufficiencies of these metropolitan-based theoretical formulations from the point of view of Tepoztlán and Chiapas.

This essay consists of two parts: the first traces the transformations that the concept of the subaltern has undergone as it has traveled (geographically and historically) from Italy to Latin America. The discussion will emphasize how Gramsci's blindness to the "folkloric" has been superseded in both the Indian and the Latin American Subaltern Studies groups. There is, however, a need to critique signs of a creeping vanguardism in both the Latin American and South Asian discourses. This discussion of Gramsci (and, to a lesser extent, the South Asian group) further elaborates some of the points I have addressed in "Of Zapatismo." As I have pointed out, there is a continuity between this essay and the earlier piece, whereas changes in the location of writing as well as the emergence of new events accent the differences. These changes correspond to a physical as well as an intellectual movement from the global to the local, to invert the title of a recent conference in Mexico (García Canclini et al.). The gist of my critique of subaltern studies aims precisely to trace in the evolution of the concept a transition from understanding subalterns as objects of study in global contexts to subjects of history in local practices. The second part of the essay consists of a series of notes that suggest the possibility of giving serious consideration to the indigenous discourse of Chiapas and Tepoztlán. Furthermore, these notes underscore how Zapatismo, as manifest in these regions of Mexico, constitutes a new vanguard that is precisely grounded in its self-conscious subalternity; that is, as an instance of the hegemony of the diverse.

In what follows I would like to identify what is usable in the evolution of the concept of the subaltern. Clearly, I am more interested in the transformations the concept of the subaltern has undergone than in assessing how Gramscian or, for that matter, un-Gramscian are the expansions of thematics, the elaborations of the category, and the emergent sensibilities in the Indian group in the eighties and the Latin American in the nineties. These instances of traveling cultures/theories have less to do with the circulation of a specific theory than with the formation of a discourse on subalternity (see Rabasa, "Of Zapatismo").

Antonio Gramsci first used the term "subaltern," beyond military referents, in his *Notes on Italian History.* His writings also inaugurated the concept of hegemony as a new mode of understanding ideology. Although readings of Gramsci have a long history in Latin America (including Laclau's early work [*Politics and Ideology*]), they have tended not to be critical of his understandings of Culture (the capital "C" marks an elitist conception) and the corresponding counterhegemonic blocs.[2] Gramsci's notion of the folkloric, which he opposes to the modernist conception of the historical emergence of national Culture, in particular, needs to be critiqued in order to understand subaltern movements. What is at stake in this critique is the compatibility of modern and nonmodern forms of culture and politics, and not the celebration of some sort of pristine indigenous community. We must keep in mind that the possibility of critiquing the ideology of progress is a recent phenomenon not readily available to Gramsci.

For Gramsci, notions of popular culture and indigenous knowledge were incompatible with his understanding of a Culture that could be established as a counterhegemony. As Gramsci put it in *The Modern Prince,* one must study elements of popular psychology "in order to transform them, by educating them, into a modern mentality" (Gramsci, 197). His understanding of cultural politics unavoidably privileged Western conceptions of knowledge, art, and ethics — evidently, of History. The elaboration of a counterhegemonic culture signified an alternative modernity that would transform premodern subjects. In "On Education," Gramsci wrote, "The first, primary grade should not last longer than three or four years, and in addition to imparting the first 'instrumental' notions of schooling — reading, writing, sums, geography, history — ought in particular to deal with an aspect of education which is now neglected — i.e. with 'rights' and 'duties,' with the first notions of the State and society as primordial elements of a new conception of the world which challenges the conceptions that are imparted by the various traditional social environments, i.e. the conceptions which can be termed folkloristic" (ibid., 30).

The "folkloristic" would reduce all forms of knowledge not bound by Western criteria of truth to superstition at worst, and to unexamined "common sense" at best. "Common sense," in this regard, would parallel what semioticians call natural signs; that is, an uncritical understanding of the world where the signifier bypasses the signified and is thus identified with referents. The history of philosophy, in itself, would be a chronicle of the institutionalization of "common sense": "Every philosophical current leaves behind a sedimentation of 'common sense': this is the document of its historical effectiveness" (this passage from *Gli intellectuali e l'organizzazione della cultura* is quoted in

n. 5 of Gramsci, 326). For Gramsci, common sense continually transforms itself as it incorporates scientific ideas and philosophical opinions into everyday life: "'Common sense' is the folklore of philosophy, and is always half way between folklore properly speaking and the philosophy, science, and economics of the specialists" (ibid.). This understanding of common sense as the folklore of philosophy enables us to turn this concept against Gramsci by pointing out that the reduction of what he terms "traditional social environments" to folklore is in itself a manifestation of philosophical folklore. I term this critical gesture a form of *enlightened de-enlightenment.*

Although common sense and folklore were clearly inferior forms of knowledge in Gramsci's assessment, their role in rebellions and insurrections, especially of the peasants, cannot be ignored. If he was critical of voluntarism, of instinct (and called for a transformation of peasant mentality by modernity), subaltern insurgencies would call for a theoretical reflection rather than a dismissal on grounds of insufficient consciousness — lacking plans in advance or not following a theoretical line. Theory, then, should hold a dialectical relation with movements of revolt that fall out of the schema of historico-philosophical outlooks. The task of subaltern studies, as I define it in this essay, would be to conceptualize multiple possibilities of creative political action rather than defining a more mature political formation. Subaltern studies, therefore, would not pretend to have a privileged access to subalterns but, rather, would define intellectual work as one more intervention in insurgent movements. In developing practices, the intellectual would grow parallel to the emergent social actors and their interventions in everyday life. *Protagonism* would thus be subjected to infinite deconstruction.

We may now consider this last observation by Gramsci in the context of Gautam Bhadra's analysis of the 1857 rebellion in India. Bhadra concludes his study with a brief allusion to fragmentary leadership in peasant insurrections: "Yet this episodic and fragmentary narrative points to the existence in 1857 of what Gramsci has called 'multiple elements of conscious leadership' at the popular level" (173–174). We have seen that Gramsci would use this historical event as a means to further prove his theory. For Gramsci, the task would consist of translating life into theoretical language. Our question would now be: What changes does subaltern theory undergo as Gramsci travels from fascist Italy in the 1930s to postcolonial India in the 1980s? Guha's preface to the first volume of *Selected Subaltern Studies* suggests a difference between Gramsci's project and that of the Indian group: "It will be idle of us, of course, to hope that the range of contributions to this series may even remotely match the six-point project envisaged by Antonio Gramsci in his 'Notes on Italian History'" (35). It is fair to say that the main difference, and the modesty of Guha, is less academic than political. The political urgency and concreteness of Gramsci's historiography, which never left out the immediate significance of his examples to praxis, are impossible to match given the different historical moments and loci of writing. The historiography of the Indian group in exchange supplies a richness of detail and methodology that were not available to Gramsci, who might still surprise us in "The Modern Prince" with such statements as "it never occurs to them [subalterns] that their history might have some possible importance, that there might be some value in leaving documentary evidence of it" (*Prison Notebooks*, 196). We have learned in the aftermath of deconstruction to distrust the preeminence given to the written letter. We must pay special attention to the (post)colonial element at play in the Indian group. We must also attend to theoretical changes, as well as to emergence structures of feeling. Let's go on and read Bhadra's concluding thoughts.

Bhadra's account works against dismissals of the indigenous leaders' role in the insurrection as "minor incidents" by academic historians such as S. N. Sen in *Eighteen Fifty-Seven* (Delhi, 1957), or mockeries such as "mushroom dignities" by soldier historians such as R. H. W. Dunlop in *Service and Adventure with the Khakee Ressalah or, Meerut Volunteer Horse, during the Mutinies of 1857–58* (London, 1858). In Bhadra's account, the indigenous leaders played an integral role in the popular insurrection. The four leaders shared ordinariness and had learned to use the logic of insurrection in the practice of everyday life: "The consciousness with which they all fought had been 'formed through everyday experience'; it was an 'elementary historical acquisition'" (175). Bhadra's analysis of this rebellion differs in the tone and the details of the insurrection from Gramsci's historical examples: "It was the perception and day-to-day experience of the authority of the alien state in his immediate surroundings that determined the rebel's action" (ibid.). Though one could argue that the situation of Sardinia and the Italian South in general was one of internal colonialism, Gramsci's counterhegemonic State and project of modernity would reinscribe them within a narrative that posits historical continuity. In the case of the British Empire, the colonial situation foreclosed a connection, and the consciousness on the rebels was one of insurgency against a colonial power—not against a landed aristocracy, as in the case of what Gramsci conceptualizes as a progressive peasantry, i.e., one that does not align itself with the local landlords against the urban leadership of both South and North. In this regard the work of the South Asian subalternists falls within a postcolonial subject position that is fully aware of the colonial impulses that accompany the modernist project.

This call for a radical transformation of historiography, however, still believes that the task of tertiary discourse is to recover the place in history *for* subalterns. Its task is to prove that the insurgent can rely on the historian's performance and not that the performance of the insurgent itself can recover his or her place in history. This faith in the historian has less felicitous moments among other members of the Indian group, as I will point out below. Given this sort of conclusion regarding tertiary discourse, we need not wonder why Gayatri Spivak raised the question "Can the subaltern speak?" in the title of her famous essay. For better or worse, the Latin American Subaltern Studies project bears the imprint of Spivak's critique of Guha and the Indian historiographical project in general ("Subaltern Studies"). I point to the shortcomings of the Indian group to foreground the critical process that has led them to address insurgent formations that Gramsci would reduce to "folklore" or undeveloped consciousness.

In a key moment in her critique of the subaltern group, Spivak suggests an internationalization of historiography that would include "the political economy of the independent peasant movement in Mexico [the Zapatistas of the 1910 revolution!]" (ibid., 211). She has in mind Partha Chatterjee's comparative studies of Indian communal power with European *history* and African *anthropology*. Spivak makes a parenthetical remark — "(an interesting disciplinary breakdown)" — that should be pursued more closely. I will return to Zapatismo later. For now I would like to underscore that the disciplinary breakdown is commonplace in Western constructions of Otherness. Implied in Chatterjee's examples, in what he calls the evidence, drawn from studies of European feudalism and African "tribal" societies (I retain his scare quotes over tribal), is a *universal* narrative of the transition from feudalism to capitalism (Chatterjee, 375 and passim). Whereas anthropology would study the "Other" of capitalism in contemporary Africa, and by implication India, medieval and early modern European history would provide the categories to understand *communalism* as existing in an earlier temporality. Not only is Chatterjee repeating, as Spivak points out apropos of Guha, "that tendency within Western Marxism which would refuse class-consciousness to the precapitalist subaltern, especially in the theaters of imperialism," but also the denial of coevalness in the production of anthropology's object of study. Thus, Chatterjee repeats a series of commonplaces regarding marxist definitions of communalism that tend to see it "as 'the negation of capital'. Communalism was thus defined as 'what capital is not,' and was assumed to have 'an antithetical relation' to capital, so that the establishment of capitalist commodity relations required the destruction of community relations" (Ranger, 221).

I cite this passage from an essay by Terence Ranger to underscore the critical impulse that informs the subaltern group and the fruitfulness of their debates, rather than to further document the conventionality of Chatterjee's essay. But it also foregrounds the continuation of imperialism and neocolonialism in nonsuspect quarters of Western marxism and poststructuralism. By moving "back" into a colonial situation, into a moment in the production of African communalism as Other, not by marxist but by colonial experts such as "missionaries, native commissioners, mining compound and municipal medics, and employers," Ranger further establishes the ways in which Western marxism repeats forms of subjection characteristic of colonialist discourses.

One of the defining positions of the Latin American Subaltern Studies Group (perhaps under debate, but nevertheless new vis-à-vis the starting motivations of the Indian group) is the questioning of the adequacy of intellectuals to represent subalterns. As John Beverley has put it: "What was at stake in our move to subaltern studies was, in other words, a growing sense of the inadequacy of the models of intellectual and political protagonism in which many of us were in fact formed" ("Writing in Reverse," 273). I would like to suggest that this radical questioning of the adequacy of intellectuals is a logical consequence of the Indian group's critique of bourgeois, as well as some of forms of Marxist, historiography. The implications of a poststructuralist critique of humanism are overdetermined in the case of the Latin American group by a post-1989 situatedness. Only from that locus of enunciation could the founding statement address the following epistemological as well as ethico-political issues of subaltern studies: "Clearly, it is a question not only of new ways of looking at the subaltern, new and more powerful forms of information retrieval, but also of building new relations between ourselves and those human contemporaries whom we posit as objects of study" ("Founding Statement," 146).

This statement suggests that epistemology, the positing of new ways of looking and constituting objects of study, must be tempered by an ethos that knows how to respect silences in subaltern discourses. It is not a coincidence that the founding statement concludes by citing Rigoberta Menchú's final words in her testimony: "I am still keeping secret what I think no-one should know. Not even anthropologists or intellectuals, no matter how many books they have, can find out all our secrets." Doris Sommer's identification of silence as an ethico-aesthetic strategy is obviously pertinent to subaltern studies: "Announcing limited access is the point, not whether or not some information is really withheld. Resistance does not necessarily signal a genuine epistemological impasse; it is enough that the impasse is claimed in this ethico-aesthetic strategy to position the reader within limits" (409). Sommer advocates a new sensibility, an awareness of the restrictions that texts of resistance place on readers. Readers must first learn to recognize figures that mark gaps before an ethic of respect can be implanted. Equally dangerous to missing the gaps is the tendency by professional readers who, because of a shared space, hastily fill in the gaps. Subaltern discourse, as exemplified by Rigoberta Menchú's denial of complete access to her culture, aims, as Sommer points out, to create conflictive or incommensurable positions. Thus, this incommensurability blocks assimilationist impulses in Western discourses, while paradoxically underscoring the compatability of modern and nonmodern forms of life in subaltern texts and insurrections.

The transformations that the concept of the subaltern has undergone as it has traveled from 1930s Italy to 1990s Latin America entail radical revisions of the place of the intellectual. Four major positions can be singled out: (1) the organic intellectual in Gramsci functioned as the consciousness and theory of what subalterns did instinctively in the process of acquiring a modern mentality; (2) the intellectual in tertiary history makes allowances for the specific practices of subalterns but still retains the task of furnishing a mirror for the subaltern; i.e., to recover the place in history for subalterns; (3) Beverley expounds the inadequacy of the models of intellectual and political protagonist; (4) Sommer and the founding statement call for a new ethics and sensibility. These theoretical transformations in subaltern studies have had a felicitous correspondence in the insurrections of Chiapas and Tepoztlán. The new ethics of respect for silence and gaps in what Sommer calls resistance texts now faces a new subaltern practice that strategically deploys silence—the subaltern cannot speak syndrome—to make manifest the racism and parochialism of dominant discourses: Dialogue as a learning process in which the government representatives must *learn how to speak to subalterns* and the Tepoztecos and Zapatistas in Chiapas *gain consciousness of their power to assert their demands* in peace negotiations.

From the Global to the Local

The communiqueés from Subcomandante Marcos; the Comité Clandestino Revolucionario Indígena, Comandancia General del Ejército Zapatista de Liberación Nacional (Clandestine Indigenous Revolutionary Committee, General Command of the Zapatista Army of National Liberation, or CCRI-CG); and the Indian comandantes David, Tacho, Trini, and Ramona, among others, address the prejudices that have hindered the reception of calls for justice, democracy, and liberty. The representatives of the government as well as certain sectors of the Mexican intelligentsia were forced to learn about the prevailing racism in Mexico from these subalterns who emerged from the Selva Lacandona on 1 January 1994. Up to the present writing of this essay, the attitudes of the government and some members of oppositional parties (from both the Right and Left) continue to endanger the peace negotiations and dialogue with EZLN in which members of numerous Indian ethnic groups participate as advisers.[3] If one wonders at times about the sincerity of the learned lessons regarding respect for Indian proposals, the new politics based on civil society have gained a momentum and theoretical sophistication that bring shame on those who balk at the dialogues.[4]

The sketchy notion of an emergent hegemony of the diverse that I have identified above with recent developments in Latin American subaltern studies gains a full articulation in the discourse of the Zapatistas and other resistance movements that have emerged in Mexico during the last year— among them, the rebellion in Tepoztlán, the strike by the independent union of the public bus system Ruta 100, the association of small and middle-size businesses called El Barzón whose members refuse to pay banks overcharges due to outrageous changes in interest rates, and the movement of students who were not admitted to the Universidad Nacional Autónoma de México (the National Autonomous University of Mexico) and have denounced a flagrant corruption in the administration of admission exams. Luis Javier Garrido, in his article "La resistencia" for *La Jornada,* has written that if globalism and neoliberalism "have proven to be a challenge for intellectuals, who up to the present have not been able to address the issues with clarity, because they fail to grasp the significance of the events, broad cross-sections of society are fully mobilized because they live in their flesh the effects of these politics" (22 September 1995, p. 20).

This new politics calls for a full participation of all sectors of the nation in an alternative social and economic project that, as Pablo González Casanovas has put it, "would change the system of a State party, and the State, for a system of national organization of civil society" (*La Jornada,* 29 October 1995, p. 13). We must recall, moreover, that González Casanovas's tentative theorizations on a new system of national organization depend on and draw their inspiration from the subaltern politics of the EZLN (see his article "Causas de la rebelión in Chiapas" in the special section "Perfil de La Jornada," *La Jornada,* 5 September 1995, I–IV). Central to the new politics of Zapatistas are an autonomy from political parties and a struggle that does not aspire to take over the State. The learning processes involved in the dialogue the Zapatistas have promoted between different sectors of civil society (as exemplified in the Consulta Nacional e Internacional [National and International Consultation] of last August, where more than one million participated in the discussion of six points that would define the kinds of politics and issues that should guide their struggle) has a deeper modality in the emphasis on consensus and communalism that underlies all the decisions of the EZLN (see Rabasa, "Of Zapatismo"). The Zapatista emphasis on building *a hegemony of the diverse* implies the formation of strong subjectivities as a constituent power (the impossible as the condition of the possible) and the exercise of cultural and political practices that up until very recently were seen as in conflict with modernity (the folkloric as the space for the articulation of local struggles). Let us now examine the role of the folkloric and the impossible in the Tepoztlán rebellion.

The tendency to dismiss forms of popular culture as folklore (used as a pejorative term that obviously ignores Gramsci's technical use) bars an understanding of how Indian communities organize and perpetuate themselves. Folklore is a key component of the Tepoztlán uprising and the stories we tell about it. In telling these stories, there is a danger of making caricatures of local struggles and their folklore for a capitalist, metropolitan consumption (see Lomnitz, *Las salidas*, 34). Indeed, a good-willed lament over the disappearance of traditional forms of life, which, in the same breadth, confirms an iron-fisted logic of the invincibility of transnational power, often accompanies this tendency to turn local struggles into caricature. The stories from all over the world in Linda Wertheimer and Robert Siegel's program "All Things Considered" on National Public Radio (Washington, D.C.) provide a place to examine how local folklore and struggles turn into caricature and lost causes.

David Welna opens a story on the rebellion in Tepoztlán for "All Things Considered" with the remark (which includes a sound track for *ambiente*): "In the Mexican town of Tepoztlán nothing of any importance ever begins without a curtain-raiser of noisy firecrackers and nothing ever develops without a brass band to move it along" (7 September 1995). Welna goes on to mention that the particular occasion is the seizure of the Presidencia Municipal (town hall) and ouster of the city council and mayor. Welna recorded speeches by and interviews with several important people in the town, ranging from a fiery speech by one of the most respected elders (Welna's terms; he fails to give his name) to an interview in English of Germán Almazán, a multilingual (French, German, English) fruit vendor in the plaza. He complements this local perspective with the opinion of Juan Kladt Sobrino, who leads the development project of Grupo KS; Homero Aridjis, a poet and environmentalist from Mexico City; and concludes with a brief interview of Tomás Cajiga, an architect who lives in Tepoztlán. Cajiga, who once supported the project, is now critical because it will destroy the tranquil lifestyle he enjoys with his family. But Cajiga also predicts that the project will go through because "they have enough support from government agencies, they have enough permits to really justify the use of force in the construction of this golf course, if need be." This assessment of the situation repeats Kladt Sobrino's prepotent and self-assured assertion earlier on in Welna's story that he is not worried about Tepoztecos invading "his" lands because "anyone entering private property can be punished." Cajiga deplores the inevitability of globalism and the incapacity to resist transnational interests supported by the government. By closing the story with Cajiga's pessimistic assessment, Welna would seem to confirm Cajiga's view of an inevitable defeat of the Tepozteco rebellion. The story thus opens with a caricature (clearly sympathetic) of folklore and closes with a lamentation over a world that is doomed to vanish.

The folklorism of brass bands, firecrackers, and effigies hanging from the roof of the town hall has its match in a perhaps equally folkloric view of a Mexico ruled by corrupt officials willing to be bought by transnational enterprises. But more annoying than the folkloric opening (firecrackers and brass bands) and closing (corrupt Mexican official supporting transnational interests), remarks that frame the story between caricature and lament, are Robert Siegel's introductory comments to Welna's story: "In Mexico, the construction of a golf course is causing a rebellion in the rural town that borders the project. Residents of Tepoztlán say they do not want the golf course because it will change their traditional way of life and put too great a demand on their scarce water supplies. Over the weekend, there were violent demonstrations and the mayor quit. The standoff has pitted international developers backed by the government against Mexicans who are deeply suspicious of change." Seigel's categories defining the town as bordering the project, the defense of the town's sovereignty as a violent demonstration, and the reverence for ancestral traditions as a suspicion of change are, to say the least, offensive to the people of Tepoztlán. Seigel's objective tone obviates the town's perspective: The project plans to build on communal lands that were illegally sold thirty years ago, the riot police invaded the town, and the government's and developer's "modernism" destroys traditional communal forms of organization and consensus politics. In Welna's story and Seigel's introduction, the culture and dignity of Tepoztlán become a caricature in the global context of NPR. The struggle to death of a people amounts to little more than quaint cultural practices hopelessly bound to disappear with the onslaught of modernity.

Even when critics of folklore are correct in condemning the curiosity that outsiders have for Indian art and cultural practices — a fascination which, as in the case of the NPR story, conveniently brackets a complicity with the oppression of Indians — these same cultural practices must be understood as forms of cultural endurance and social reproduction. If Rosa Rojas, in her book *Chiapas: La paz violenta,* quite correctly sees the press's fascination with the mask of the Zapatistas as one more folkloric item that exemplifies how reporters systematically exclude news regarding the oppression of Indians (as it were, only armed Indians deserve the attention of journalists), we should not overlook that the masks, like the traditional costumes, fulfill other functions than satisfying a craving for the exotic or the outlaw (17). Needless to say, while masks protect individual identities, costumes assert cultural patterns; there is a felicitous coexistence of the two in the Zapatistas from Chiapas. Likewise, beyond "condiments" of social occasions, firecrackers are forms of communication (calls to action, signals of alert), and brass bands are forms of social reproduction (every barrio of Tepoztlán has its particular kind of musical ensemble). There is more than an entertainment value when, for instance, the contingent from the Barrio de la Santísima appears at the evening change of guard at the Presidencia Municipal with a drum and a *chirimía* (a flageolet) that accompanies the chanting of slogans. Music functions as an intensifier of solidarity and a definer of a particular barrio identity.

Hanging in the main room of the Presidencia are an image of the Virgen of Guadalupe, a photograph of Emiliano Zapata, and an icon, which follows pre-Colombian pictorial conventions, of El Tepozteco, El Señor de los Vientos (The Tepozteco, The Lord of the Winds). Whereas the first two figures are ubiquitous in the state of Morelos, El Tepozteco is particular to Tepoztlán. Every September 8, as part of the feast that celebrates the Virgin of the Natividad (Virgen de la Natividad), the patroness of Tepoztlán, the town stages a play that reenacts the conversion of the ruler of Tepoztlán at the time of the conquest. It is a play that at once reinforces the Christian identity of the Tepoztecos and asserts a continuity with the pre-Columbian beliefs as the god of Christianity is accommodated within the old pantheon. We must recall that on this feast of the Virgin of the Nativity, the people traditionally ascend the mountain to render offerings to El Tepozteco on the remains a pre-Columbian temple.

In a popular assembly on October 1, when Lázaro Rodríguez Castañeda was sworn in as the first mayor of the "municipio libre, constitucional y popular de Tepoztlán" (free, constitutional, and popular municipality of Tepoztlán), a personification of El Señor de los Vientos, El Tepozteco handed down, in a symbolic act, the *bastón de mando* (the staff of command) to the new mayor. El Tepozteco spoke the following: "You shall not attempt to undo our region by allowing yourself to be deceived by light that are not stars, because they are moons, nor will you allow the imposition of something that is alien to the will of the people, because if you allow it, the people itself will demand your heart for sacrifice to soothe the wrath of the gods." This symbolic act, which perhaps could be easily dismissed as an atavistic and quaint resurgence of pre-Columbian rituals, institutes a popular vigilance over the new mayor and council under the threat of being sacrificed to the gods. Traitors will be sacrificed, if not by cutting out their hearts, then perhaps by hanging in the manner of the effigies hanging from the roof of the Presidencia. El Tepozteco and his speech form part of what Antonio García de León has described as a permanent carnival in rebellious Tepoztlán, "where the children, the youth and the women constitute the most combative sectors, the most decided to defend at whatever cost a territoriality that in Tepoztlán is not a written law, but a millenarian tradition" (*La Jornada,* 20 September 1995,

p. 19). These clearly nonmodern political practices and claims of territoriality define the impossibility of the local in the Tepoztlán uprising. This is not to say that they are incompatible with modern practices, such as appealing to Articles 39 and 115 of the Mexican Constitution to legitimate the legality of their municipio libre — that is, its constitutionality — since for the Tepoztecos, nonmodern forms only recognize their claims at the expense of its authority. In this regard, the rebellion in Tepoztlán forms part of an emergent new politics that I have defined with González Casanovas as a call to "change the system of a State party, and the state, for a system of national organization of civil society."

González Casanovas's proposal defines the "local" as the site of resistance to transnational interests and processes of globalization. Beyond representation, the impossibility of the local resides in the emergence of strong subjectivities and a hegemony of the diverse. The EZLN's politics of dialogue — as a learning process in which the Indian communities define and debate concepts of autonomy, demand respect for their traditional cultures, and give prominence to women issues — has gained an unexpected (by the government) momentum that increasingly brings into play multiple, diverse sectors of civil society. In the process, the locale named Chiapas has become a catachresis for a national, if not an international, struggle against neoliberalism. The transformations that the concept of the subaltern has undergone warn us against reading the new insurgencies through the lenses of Gramsci or even of the more recent Southeast Asian and Latin American subaltern groups. The evolution of subaltern studies that I have traced above concluded with the dissolution of the intellectual as a privileged agent in the articulation and definition of social change. Furthermore, this line of analysis would reveal how intellectuals tend to play integral roles in processes of subalternization. Intellectual work would now be a practice that runs parallel to insurrections but does not dictate their meaning or define their direction; rather, it would make manifest how these processes of appropriation erase the diverse. Ultimately, the impossibility of the local faces the likelihood of repression as the State might refuse to give place to a new system of national (and international) organization of civil society. If the citizens of Tepoztlán listened to the NPR story, they would not find a mirror of their struggle, but of an opinion that considers as inevitable the imminent danger that the State could lose (that is, be willing to wage losing) its commitment to peace and democracy. The willingness of the people to sustain a struggle to death is, paradoxically, the only deterrent of violence.

Tepoztlán, November 1995

Although Tepoztlán has warded off an invasion of the town, the struggle to assert its sovereignty unfortunately has had its toll. Two Tepoztecos have died since I wrote the last sentence of the essay, and members of Central Unica de Trabajadores (CUT) have been systemastically accosted, harassed, and kidnapped by the police when doing their business outside the village. Some incidents:

On 3 December 1995, Pedro Margarito Barragán Gutiérrez, a supporter of the development project, was accidentally murdered, shot in the back by fellow supporters who fired their guns at a multitude of Tepoztecos. Three opponents of the project—including one named Gerardo Demesa Padilla, a founding member of CUT and a leading thinker of civil defense strategies in Tepoztlán—were arrested and charged with the homicide. Witnesses and forensic reports failed to establish a connection between them and the crime, but nearly three years after the event, on 19 September 1997, Demesa Padilla was sentenced to eight years in prison for *homicidio simple;* the judge found that even though Demesa Padilla did not shoot Barragán Gutiérrez, he had provoked the incident that led to the homicide. Demesa Padilla has appealed the verdict.

The Morelos police ambushed a caravan of eight hundred Tepoztecos on April 10, 1996, when they were traveling to the town of Tlaltizapán to present a petition to President Ernesto Zedillo Ponce de León, who was presiding over a commemoration of the seventy-seventh anniversary of Emiliano Zapata's assassination. Under the orders of Governor Jorge Carrillo Olea, several police units attacked the Tepoztecan caravan, which included children, women, and elders; several Tepoztecos were wounded by gunshots and sixty-four-year-old Marcos Olmedo Gutiérrez was found dead a few hours later with clear signs of torture and a bullet in his neck. Two foreign journalists from France and Spain and an amateur from Tepoztlán with a video camera witnessed and recorded the events, contradicting Carrillo Olea's version of armed Tepoztecos attacking the police. Zedillo was thus forced to fault the police, and as a result of a wise press coverage of the massacre, Grupo KS, unable to justify the murder and violence against the Tepoztecos, canceled the megaproject on April 13, 1996. Nevertheless, KS continues to claim its right to the plots, and in the words of one of their vice presidents, José De los Ríos, they canceled because "no hay gente interesada en invertir donde no hay gobernabilidad" (Nobody is interested in investing where there is no governability] (*La Jornada,* 14 April 1996). Obviously, De los Ríos has in mind the people of Tepoztlán as the ungovernable and not Carillo Olea, the governor of the state of Morelos, who instructed his police to assault the caravan. Ironically, two years after the rebellion, the Tepoztecos claim a 60 percent reduction of crime in spite of, or more likely as a result of, the absence of a police force.

On a happier note: On September 11, 1997, Tepoztlán received with firecrackers and music the caravan of 1,111 Zapatistas from Chiapas in their last stop before marching into Mexico City. Three thousand Indians from the area joined the caravan from Chiapas. Tepoztlán remains barricaded and continues its struggle in solidarity with other Indians in Mexico.

In June 1999 I visited Tepoztlán and interviewed Asciano Cedillo Méndez, Regidor de Educación (Education Regent) of Tepoztlán, who informed me that the town had agreed to hold elections in March 1997. In order to receive federal funds from the State, the Tepoztlán had to renounce to its status of Municipio Libre. The CUT, however, agreed to hold elections and abide by the State's requirement that only members of officially recognized political parties could run for office. The CUT made an agreement with the Partido Revolucionario Democrático (PRD) to use this party to present a *planilla* (voting ballot) of officers who were elected according to the community based juridical norms, the so-called *usos y costumbres* in a public assembly of the town. Thus, they retained the right to use their own legal traditions and comply with the State's requirements to receive federal funds.

I returned to Tepoztlán last summer and found the town immersed in a celebration. When I inquired on the reason for celebrating, an old man in the plaza told me that the PRI had been defeated. At first, I thought he was speaking of Fox's recent election, but no, the reason was the election of the new mayor, Lázaro Rodríguez Castañeda (who had already served as mayor during the uprising), and the planilla the town had elected according to their juridical norms. Tepoztlán citizens have dismantled the barricades and given up their status as Municipio Libre, but they also have invented a way to circumvent the requirements of the State to gain access to federal funds without giving up their own legal and political forms. In a word, their autonomy is a fact even if the State does not recognize in yet.

Notes

> Early versions of this paper were read at the symposium on "Private Culture/Public Policy," organized by Norma Alarcón, at the University of California at Irvine Humanist Research Institute, June 8–12, 1994; the colloquium on "Other Circuits of Theory," organized by David Lloyd and Lisa Lowe, at the University of California at Irvine Humanist Research Institute, July 13–16, 1994; the colloquium on "Gloca-Cola: World Theories, Pictures, Subjects," organized by Terry Smith, at the Chicago Humanities Institute, May 19–20, 1995; and at the Latin American Subaltern Studies meeting on "Ingobernabilidad y ciudadanía," hosted by María Milagros López, Universidad de Puerto Rico, Río Piedras, March 2–6, 1996. I benefited greatly from the comments at these gatherings.
> 1 For accounts of the rebellion, the historical roots, and the new revolutionary politics of the EZLN, see, for example, Barreda et al.; Le Bot; Ross; Rojas; Collier. *La palabra* and EZLN reproduce documents and communiqués written by the EZLN.
> 2 My critique of Gramsci has many affinities with David Lloyd's critique of Gramsci's view that the history of subaltern groups is episodic and fragmentary (127 and passim).

3   In the conversations at "Larráinzar VI" last September, the government and the EZLN finally agreed on the formats for the discussion of particular issues in specific tables. Five tables have been established and have met in San Cristóbal and San Andrés Sacamch'en de los Pobres, as the Indian people prefer to call the town officially known as Larráinzar. The five groups address issues pertaining to: (1) community and autonomy: indigenous rights; (2) guaranties of justice for Indians; (3) participation and political representation of Indians; (4) situation, rights, and culture of indigenous women; (5) access to communication media. For a summary of the first round of discussions, see the communiqué by the CCRI-CG of 19 October 1995 published in *La Jornada*, 20 October 1995, p. 12.

In February 1996, the Mexican State and the EZLN signed the Acuerdos de San Andrés, which committed the government to a reform of the State's policies toward Indian peoples. These accords established a radical redefinition of the status of Indian peoples in Mexico that would grant them political as well as economic self-determination. The government was apparently blind to the implications of granting Indian communities the right to determine the rational use and the benefits to be derived from the exploitation of natural resources within their territories. Beyond cultural and juridical freedoms recognized by the State, I single out this economic freedom because of its radical implications and the ultimate inability of the government to live up to its agreements. If the accords of San Andrés pose the question of reforming the State, the specific changes entail a revolutionary process in which the Indian peoples of Mexico would find in the language of reform the elements for the implementation of a constituent power. The EZLN published a communiqué on 3 September 1996 declaring that they had stepped out of the negotiations and demanded minimal conditions for the renewal, among which were the liberation of imprisoned Zapatistas, a credible governmental interlocutor with the authority to make decisions, and an end to persecution and military harassing of Indians in Chiapas. As I write this note on 6 November 2000, the Mexican press speaks of the commitment of the recent president elect, Vicente Fox, to open the discussion on the terms for a dialogue over the agreements—hardly a promise of recognizing the signatures of the representatives of the previous administration. For the Acuerdos de San Andrés, see Hernández Navarro and Vera Herrera 1998. I derive the concept of *constituent power* from Negri 1999 and 1994.

4   For an assesment of the government's hypocrisy and manipulation at the dialogues, see Armando Bartra, "Chiapas: El diálogo sobre el tema indígena. 'No podemos hablar con palabras blandas,'" in the special section "Del Campo," *La Jornada*, 1 November 1995, pp. 1–2.

Works Cited

Barreda, Andrés, et al. eds. *Chiapas*. 4 vols. Mexico City: Instituto de Investigaciones Económicas, Universidad Nacional Autónoma de México, 1995–1997.

Beverley, John. "Writing in Reverse: On the Project of the Latin American Subaltern Studies Group." In Rabasa, Sanjinés C., and Carr, *Subaltern Studies*, pp. 271–288.

Beverley, John, and José Oviedo, eds. *The Postmodernism Debate in Latin America*. Durham, N.C.: Duke University Press, 1995

Bhadra, Gautam. "Four Rebels of 1857." In Guha and Spivak, *Selected Subaltern Studies*.

Chatterjee, Partha. "More on Modes of Power and the Peasantry." In Guha and Spivak, *Selected Subaltern Studies*.

Collier, George A. *Basta! Land and the Zapatista Rebellion in Chiapas*. Written with Elizabeth Lowry Quaratiello. Oakland, CA.: Food First, 1994.

Descombes, Vincent. *The Barometer of Modern Reason: On the Philosophy of Current Events.* New York: Oxford University Press, 1993.

EZLN: Documentos y comunicados. 2 vols. Mexico City: Ediciones Era: 1994–1995. "Founding Statement/Latin American Subaltern Studies Group." In Beverley and Oviedo, *Postmodernism Debate.*

García Canclini, Néstor, et al. *De lo local a lo global: Perspectivas desde la antropología.* Mexico City: Universidad Autónoma Metropolitana, 1994.

Gramsci, Antonio. *Selections from the Prison Notebooks,* ed. and trans. Quentin Hoare and Geoffrey Nowell Smith. New York: International Publishers, 1971.

Guha, Ranajit. Preface to Guha and Spivak, *Selected Subaltern Studies.*

Guha, Ranajit, and Gayatri Chakravorty Spivak, eds. *Selected Subaltern Studies.* New York: Oxford University Press, 1988.

Ileto, Reynaldo Clemeña. *Pasyon and Revolution: Popular Movements in the Philippines, 1840–1910.* Quezon City, Metro Manila: Ateneo de Manila University Press, 1979.

Laclau, Ernesto. *Politics and Ideology in Marxist Theory.* London: New Left Books, 1977.

Le Bot, Yvon. *Le rêve zapatiste: Sous-commandant Marcos.* Paris: Seuil, 1997.

Lloyd, David. *Anomalous States.* Durham, N.C.: Duke University Press, 1993.

Lowe, Lisa, and David Lloyd, eds. *The Politics of Culture in the Shadow of Capital.* Durham, N.C.: Duke University Press, 1997.

Lomnitz, Claudio. "La decadencia en los tiempos de la globalización." In García Canclini et al., *De lo local a lo global,* pp. 88–101.

——. *Las salidas del laberinto.* Trans. Cinna Lomnitz. Mexico City: Joaquín Mortiz, 1995.

Negri, Antonio. *Insurgencies: Constituent Power and the Modern State,* trans. Maurizia Boscagli. Minneapolis: University of Minnesota Press, 1999.

Negri, Antonio, and Michael Hardt. *Labor of Dionysus: Communism as Critique of the Capitalist and Socialist State-Form.* Minneapolis: University of Minnesota Press, 1994.

La palabra de los armados de verdad y fuego. 3 vols. Mexico City: Editorial Fuenteovejuna, 1994–1995.

Rabasa, José. "Of Zapatismo: Reflections of the Folkloric and the Impossible in a Subaltern Insurrection." In Loyd and Lowe, *Worlds Aligned,* n.p.

Rabasa, José, Javier Sanjinés C., and Robert Carr, eds. *Subaltern Studies in the Americas. Dispositio/n* 46 (1994, published in 1996).

Ranger, Terence. "Power, Religion, and Community: The Matobo Case." *Subaltern Studies.* Vol. 7. Ed. Partha Chatterjee and Gyanendra Pandey. Delhi: Oxford University Press, 1992.

Rojas, Rosa. *Chiapas: La paz violenta.* Mexico City: La Jornada Ediciones, 1995.

Ross, John. *Rebellion from the Roots: Indian Uprising in Chiapas.* Monroe, Maine: Common Courage Press, 1995.

Sommer, Doris. "Resisting the Heat: Menchú, Morrison, and Incompetent Readers." In *Cultures of U.S. Imperialism,* ed. Amy Kaplan and Donald E. Pease. Durham, N.C.: Duke University Press, 1993.

Spivak, Gayatri. "Can the Subaltern Speak?" In *Marxism and the Interpretation of Culture,* ed. Cary Nelson and Lawrence Grossberg. Urbana: University of Illinois Press, 1988.

——. "Subaltern Studies: Deconstructing Historiography." In *In Other Worlds: Essays in Cultural Politics.* New York: Routledge, 1988.

Womack, John. *Zapata and the Mexican Revolution.* Harmondsworth, England: Penguin, 1972.

Questions of Strategy as an Abstract Minimum: Subalternity and Us

ABDUL-KARIM MUSTAPHA

What was the meaning of the call to the way?
Its closer meaning was destruction's destruction.
Its closest meaning: the search for pathes to that
necessary beginning.
— Ayi Kwei Armah, *Two Thousand Seasons*

I

The era of subaltern studies has been, for me, the moment of intense concentration on one issue: how do we understand the rules and functions of
subalternity on the way to eradicating its many passages? Because answers to
this question never seem close, we have tended to make gestures toward it
within debates about such topics as globalization, populism, civil society, and
neoliberalism. In and through these debates, however, the ground of subalternity is quite often displaced with and even deflected by a host of theoretical
claims whose injunctions are said to hail from the experiences of subalterns.
Paradoxically, and in light of the diffusion of subalternity (through practices
of war, consumption, and technobiological reproduction all over the globe),
it appears that no claim, however rigorous its measures, can ground itself
without opening up to the gift of strategy. That gift, whose figuration is
always a repetition of the contradictions that emerge between thinking and its
incorporation or dis-incorporation of the people, must now come to be the
central problem of any subaltern studies. With this, I am attempting to reflect
modestly on a series of conjunctures that the political and theoretical vacilla-
tions emerging from this central problem have produced. In this regard, subaltern studies always operates with some sense of strategy, or rather it is driven
by a strategy. Thus, throughout this reflection I never settle on a single notion
of strategy. Rather, I insist on its openness and destructive character as I
engage Latin American Subaltern Studies, globalization, populism, the critique of statism made by Ranajit Guha, and of course my own secret trope,
which is Marx's idiomatic reference to the "fantastic standing," addressed in

the *Communist Manifesto*. By all means, I understand that subaltern studies is still necessary, and that it will always be, to the extent that that necessity is the rational kernel of a thinking that exhaustively feels the force of subalternity at an ever larger scale.

The founding statement of the Latin American Subaltern Studies Group provides a characterization of the directions and intentions of the group in order to situate its practice within several regions of knowledge such as Latinamericanism, American postcolonial theory, and cultural studies.[1] According to the statement, those regions of knowledge lack a strategic valuation of the relationship between historiography and struggling people, and between the politics of representation and the politics of action. Hence, underlying the group's diversion from these regions of knowledge, as Moreiras, Williams, and Beverley, among others, have suggested, was a genuine effort to rethink the question of intellectual production as a way of actualizing the immanent possibility of a common interest sheltered in the dialogue with subalterns, or rather within the remainders of subaltern political and cultural expressivity. The question of intellectual production is construed here as a moment of either prying open the inner essence of a novel philosophical operation or a situation wherein the motivation to ground a question is already in the midst of constructing an idea, a consciousness. In what continues to unfold as the work of Latin American Subaltern Studies, generally speaking, that grounding question is never apart from and is not the limit of this field of knowledge itself. Intellectual production as the guiding question of subaltern studies has come to constitute the study of the subaltern as a permanent constraint on the existence of subalternity, therefore leading the subalternist closer to the effects of the inexhaustible grounding question of what subalternity is vis-à-vis the singularity that any form of intellectual production would wish to inaugurate as a sign of its own originality.

For Latin American Subaltern Studies, even when the many heterogeneous statements of its members contradicts the work (we should realize after Foucault that a work and a statement are two different processes of intimating knowledge), the logic of the work is primed with what we could call a conditioned intersubjective destitution, through and against which the subalternist must come to accept that "there is no a priori, no preceding intelligibility: there is only the a posteriori truth of what comes to pass."[2] In a corollary statement, José Rabasa and Javier Sanjinés C. argued that it is precisely through an "ethics of epistemology" that this subaltern studies group can raise to the level of permanent visibility the faint boundary between "the subject of historical knowledge" and "the subject of political action."[3] This obvious distinction, registered and conceived as the site of the usual pitfalls of voluntarism and theoretic misapprehension, is recognized by Rabasa and Sanjinés, as an impasse for innovation and a confrontation with the question of intellectual production as a guiding question. And yet their call to embrace an ethics of epistemology over and against a nonidiomatic epistemology is close to something like a nonposition, but made available within the structure of a position. This nonposition is a provisional if not infinitely temporary basis for commanding the sense and openness of the question of subalternity. The consequence of their call can thus be read in the following manner: for them subalternity is a totalizing event that circumscribes the question of intellectual production and, consequently, the rhythm of exchange between subalternists and subalterns in that their congruity and dissonance always anticipates a new outlook on what constitutes the thought of subalternity and its function in any project that wants to think beyond the limits of globalization.

The question of what subalternity is sets a precedent by opening the way to a nearly complete reconstruction of the values, meanings, and structures of intellectual practice as it is presently constituted. By ascertaining the question and its consequences, we begin to unveil what is essential to intellectual life, hence also to intellectual production. Again, this is the reason why Rabasa and Sanjinés also made a further claim that "Subaltern Studies would not aspire any longer to a new history nor, for that matter, a new ethnography, but a new theoretical practice."[4] The practice is new precisely because it presents the question of what is subalternity as the grounding question, the question that will enable us to question further. Subalternity has become important for philosophy and the passages for this importance are subaltern studies. We must be clear that there is no philosophy of subalternity and no potential to subalternize the philosophical; subalternity stands in front of philosophy. The question of subalternity institutes a turning point within philosophy. It wrests philosophy's categories out of their traditional contexts and relocates them in a new space where the breaks, fissures, and gaps in Gramsci's thinking about the subaltern are never neutralized, but reconditioned as the premise of the question of what is subalternity.

I am not suggesting that previous considerations of the subaltern have not been philosophical. Rather, my aim here is to clarify that only subaltern studies, in its current configuration, has attempted to posit the question of what is subalternity as the grounding question. This is decidedly different from those approaches that would claim to understand the subaltern as a descriptive subject, from a sociological, historical, economic, and psychological point of view. While these approaches maintain a distance from subaltern studies as such, subaltern studies continually thinks through their differences and similarities on the way to thinking the question. What follows is my modest attempt to locate subaltern studies in debates on globalization and to postulate the question of subalternity as a strategy. In developing this question as a strategy within and among recent political discourses, we must remember that we are only at the beginning of an expression.

II

The question of globalization is reflective of and a marker of the dispersed referent for a series of discussions aimed at ordering the beginnings and endings of the so-called end of communism, an element within a much larger period, the long cold war. We are implying that there is a time consciousness to be delineated as a measure of approaching the final form of our theme. We have stated that globalization is not independent. It is not an autonomous system. It establishes continuity at the point of decline of another theme, communism, and yet it does not stop there. Its formation is proper to something larger than itself. If this is our itinerary, the order of our speculation must begin not within globalization, but within the cold war. We must suspend the historical distance that has been the privilege of globalization, by subsuming it within the cold war. The order of globalization is singularly the continuity of the problematics and diversions imminent in the cold war. This would make sense if we accept the possibility that globalization, like the cold war, is an operation by which the international nature and context of political reason is condensed and narrowed to the internal sociocultural substructure of one or several nation-states. But the presence of this double function characterized by the means of the internationalization of politics and the brutal compression of national cultures (or essentializing the local, what Arjun Appardurai calls culturalism, to meet the demand of the global and emphasizing the global as difference in sameness), also places us at the point where the intrinsic valuation of a discourse of globalization is contradicted by the interests that it produces. Perhaps this is what Boris Frankel means when he argues: "If internationalism denies the finite, then localism is too narrow, cutting off humanity from the infinite."[5] The consequences of this denial and narrowness go beyond mere political naiveté and faulty economic speculation. It places the vanquished means and ends of power mongers under the temptation of class hegemony, on the path of hopeless resignation to the contrivances of "lived experience" as the absolute negation of the existential-political demands of "common interest," as defined by Marx.

The proper identity of globalization is to always conceal and deny the thought of communism, what Marx and Engels suggested as the constitutive imbrication of the knowledge of justice alongside new regimes of labor — by which they meant the moment when the figure of the worker becomes an emblem in the redistribution of the thematic of solidarity. This is a thematic that instructs us eternally that the figuration of work, and hence, the human figure of the worker, is already a double determination over against the ideality of property. For work itself, whenever it is carried out under the pressure of intense domination counter to the energies and aspirations of the worker, sets up a new epistemology for the distribution of equality and justice in the element of community, and over against property. Property is understood here as the thing that communism wants to abolish, however, as symbolic capital, property is the dream of egalitarian life, a life of giving and taking, a life of lack and fulfillment, and a life of belonging and nonbelonging. Ironically, though, it is this last article of the democratic consensus, the particular vacillation of this article as a political axis in either liberal-democratic or socialist communities that constantly threatens to undo the quality and effect of citizenship, and therefore our "anthropological situation," which "never ceases its progressive dramatization of his History, never ceases to render it more perilous, and to bring it closer to its own impossibility."[6] Isn't the first lesson of C. L. R. James's *The Black Jacobins* how the diminished circumstances of the imperial world led them to overturn their self-proclaimed universal principles? In other words, it is the lesson of how the figure of the worker became property. It is also the determined instance of racial bigotry that chastened the narrative of modern democracy itself. Consequently, at the time of the emergence of the modern politics of the rights of man and other stories, we have the persistent dispersal of regressive seedlings, not at home but abroad among the aboriginal Occidential, Oriental, and African other. Simply put, the circuits and moods of exchange inherent in the modern experience of democratic life have not changed much, least perhaps the commitments to oppress.

Perhaps the prejudicial narratives of the end of communism must stand not simply as facts in themselves, but as the barometer of the "waning terrain of effective reality" in critical thought and of the speciousness that abounds in such thoughts. Thus, the question of globalization, and its sister, the question of the end of communism, negatively invoke less the complete overhaul of the internal structure of capital than the rise of populism among intellectuals. The question might keep us closer to the parameter of the finitude of intellectual production, a question whose epistemic singularity vitiates the tragic results of George Lukacs's double incommensurability: "either the world is narrower or it is broader than the outside world assigned to it as the arena and substratum of its actions."[7] In this statement we can recognize that the archeological work of collecting signs of incompletion, as is evident in various globalisms, localisms, internationalisms, and cosmopolitanisms (all varieties of practical populism) marks a complicity with the very frontiers of danger that are so gallantly fought off in packaged manifestoes ridiculing the "reality" of such structures, while losing sight of the quality and orientation of effective resistance and opposition. Here it would seem that the quiet interiority of intellectual desire in the face of questions of globalization points away from strategy, and more toward a space where political stakes are wrapped around adventurism, and responses to the purported crisis are bound by spontaneity, ideology, and conventionalism treated in the form of critical readings. To restate this problematic in light of Lukacs's critique of the modern novel and its hero would be to suggest that the intellectual "thinks that reality is bewitched by evil demons and the spell can be broken and reality can be redeemed either by finding a magic password or by courageously fighting the evil forces."[8] Our current password is globalization from below, and the enterprises that carry the elucidation of the movement and structure of this globalization compound the "capacity of the world to be misunderstood."

What is most explicitly missing in recent claims to populism — derived in part from Gramsci's meditation on the national-popular and other strands of political thought as evidenced in the work of Paul Piccone, Paul Hirst, and Barry Hindness — is a dynamic relationship between consent and force, a relationship at the heart of the very conditions of possibility of populism. Populism is force qua force, dressed in that stained and perfumed overcoat called consent. For Marx, populism is the elusive simulation of common interest. Populism has become a measure of realizing common interest in a neoliberal way, revitalizing the welfare-state discourse as the single object of the people and the private sector, displacing the antagonistic sphere of reform, the negotiation of rights and security on to the people under that suspicious and the rigid banners of "realpolitik" and "alternative politics," exclusive of a robust political economic base. Populism is the closest thing to a postmodern realization of "common interest" in the idiom of communist thought, insofar as its ideologues would argue that it constitutes a heavy critique of a promising detour away from "corporate cynicism and dominant cultural political elites."[9] Alberto Moreiras has suggested that populism wants to do the unthinkable; it wants "to change the hegemonic relation as presently constituted. Only a populism can aspire to do that, whether of the dominant or the dominated. But any populism, precisely because it conceives of itself as a hegemonic tool, will proceed to a seizing of the social in whose closure the subaltern . . . will emerge as such."[10] As a subalternist myself, I would subscribe and distance myself from this position, as Moreiras has done in the rest of his essay. In the meantime, we must affirm that it is the belated awakening to the present crisis, the rush to settle accounts with the present in order to structure the future, that marks the blindness of populist thinking. In other words, it lacks strategy. It has misunderstood the rule of contemporaneity, "to dwell within the working of history, as its goal is to establish a new hegemonic rule."[11]

Recall the paratactical character of a hidden and forbidden passage in the

Communist Manifesto. Recall it and steer away from its "messianic formalism." It is a warning:

> The significance of Critical-Utopian Socialism and Communism bears an inverse relation to historical development. In proportion as the modern class struggle develops and takes definite shape, this fantastic standing apart from the contest, these fantastic attacks on it, lose all practical value and all theoretical justification. Therefore, although the originators of these systems were, in many respects, revolutionary, their disciples have, in every case, formed mere reactionary sects.[12]

For populism to understand itself as the clear road to hegemony, it must apprehend presence from the wrong end, while clandestinely working overtime to reserve the inversion, which is proper to the workings of history. In all likelihood, populism is always late. It is the opposite of the reason required by communist thought and specifically common interest. The ground of negativity, says Marx, is promise, it is what is to come, and keeps coming from nowhere. In this regard, Jacques Derrida would confirm and conform to the specificity of the "fantastic standing" in *Spectres of Marx:*

> Without lateness, without delay, but without presence, it is the precipitation of an absolute singularity, singular because differing, precisely and always other, binding itself necessarily to the form of the instant, in immanence and urgency: even if it moves toward what remains to come, there is the pledge (promise, engagement, injunction and response to the injunction and so forth). The pledge is given here and now, even before, perhaps, a decision confirms it. It thus responds without delay to the demand of justice.[13]

Without delay to the demand of justice! Populism wants to suture the gap between the juridical and cultural subject. It was to deny the fact and existence of the juridical constitution in the activity of a new subject for a new society. Social law, or common interest, situates the code and order of responsibility between subject and society as a will to will, always approaching and reproaching injustice. It is this Heideggerian inflection of the law, that poses a serious challenge to the efficacy and capacity of populism as the rule of the average, hegemonic power. Populism as it is currently performed by a disillusioned Left in a desperate secretive dialogue with the Right, as a corrective to a common interest, embarks on a Hobbesian political anthropology that exercises a double fixing: the suppression of class articulation and difference, or rather it uses difference in a way that allows it to account for difference as simply one more element in the machinery that is populism itself. If populism is seen as the clear road forward to a new constitution of social relations, we must seriously reconsider the place of intellectual strategy as an experience of hegemony and a bipartisan encounter with common interest. For the political reason of populism would turn out to be the very moment of cancellation of the spontaneity of subaltern action and homogenization of the nonconsensus active within the sphere. If populist will seeks to broker the normative, then subalternity is never within its grasp and in that case the political future will ascend to the position of the regulated ideal of its exterior. In other words, there is no democratic vision akin to any style of populism.

III

At the front of my thinking is the attempt to understand a conjuncture within a conjuncture — the thinking about the thought of globalization — and how we might begin to think strategically of political futures and their place in the immense theater of democracy as promise without allocating to the latter the moribund form of contemporary identity politics that tends to muster the support of both toilers and idlers. This is an infinite task. And subalternity is the dark light of that infinity. This is an old story.

Now, let us start over, strategically, thinking strategically about strategy. What is strategy? For Gramsci, the enabler and poet of subaltern studies, the question of strategy appears as the very edifice upon which the intellectual reconstitutes the topography of subalternity. Does strategy imply a meaningful guidance of thought, does strategy imply caution, does it imply refrain, does it imply finally a radical suversion of the temptations of subalternity as an empty signifier? By thinking strategically about the question, do we annul the singularity of the risk that comes along with philosophical thought itself? Furthermore, what, if anything can this question allow us to inherit and disown by adhering to a single or multiple traditions of strategy?

The strength of strategy is never at the vanishing point, but precisely in the moment of its appearance, when it masters its own historicity as a lesson in becoming. Becoming, learning to be with, and to be from, is within the order of strategy. In becoming, strategy is understood as relating to what comes before and after it, encompassing both the interior and exterior. It calculates its own sense as being near and far, here and there. Strategy interrupts. It displaces one strategy, only to rescue and recapture another. It is an indifference that places strategy before and after the human question (the anthropological situation that focuses on producing the reproducing democracy as experience and promise). This figuration of succession, one strategy for another, hegemony after hegemony, destroys any ideal proper to strategy. Strategy has no ideal. It is the reiteration of an ideal to the point of erasure. Where, then is the practicality of strategy? If and when a strategist claims to strategize in order to thwart the immediate, that claim would simply impress a total-itarian logic of subjectivization upon the sphere of politics. Herein lies the truth that Gramsci wants to underscore about hegemony.

> Consciousness of being part of a particular hegemonic force (that is to say, political consciousness) is the first stage towards a further progres-sive self-consciousness in which theory and practice will be one. Thus the unity of theory and practice is not just a matter of mechanical fact, but part of the historical process, whose elementary and primitive phase is to be found in the sense of being different and apart, in an instinctive feeling of independence, which progress to the real possession of a single and coherent conception of the world. This is why it must be stressed that the political development of the concept of hegemony represents a great philosophy advance as well as a politico-practical one.[14]

I am trying to ground strategy and in the process I hear traces of Marx in the voice of Gramsci. The unity of theory and practice is not in advance of hege-mony; rather, strategically speaking, the unity achieves sovereignty in the midst of the contest for hegemony. This is why Marx would claim that at the moment of intensity, there is a loss of "practical value and theoretical justifica-tion" in the fight for hegemony. This does not mean, however, that all is madness; instead, it points to the fact that strategy always retracts its own existence merely to show the nonessence of the objects in its path.

Understood in this manner, the relationship between strategy and hege-mony would appear to contradict hegemony as deployed by populist logic — populism views hegemony as a finitude, thus cutting off the excesses and reminders that, according to Gramsci, would made hegemony worth fighting for. The fight for hegemony is a process by which the excluded can consoli-date their desires, and minimize their needs in order to arrest and confiscate hegemonic power, the silent motivation for migrating from the position of the dominated to that of the dominant. This fight is precisely the politico-philosophical problem at the core of the question of strategy. The disposition to maximize interests, the injunction to rehabilitate the order of things (to put into permanent disrepair the order of language, labor, life) must exasperate the fundamental character of the proportion of history to the historical pro-cess, and thus amend the modest practices and institutions of truth as being of historicality. What, then, is the occasion for strategy beyond the declining future as the ruse of present political uncertainty, beyond the immediate neces-sity of self-assertion, and finally beyond domination? Can the conditioning of strategy be said to begin with the flesh, and yet never reducible to that sub-stance? If strategy is conceived as a counterpart to the transparency of populist causes and actions, can we conclude that strategy does not appeal to or bargain with the given, that it is in itself giving without the given?

The tradition of subalternist strategy would seem to confirm this predicament, albeit that confirmation itself is bound by strategy. As Guha has shown recently by destroying "ordinary historiography" and assembling a more robust "critical historiography" that unbridles orientalist, masculinist, and statist reasoning "by bending closer to the ground in order to pick up the traces of a subaltern life in its passages through time," is the predicative of hegemony as the design according to which history is unhinged from the state, as the privileged site of insurgent memory. In "The Small Voice of History," Guha argues that there is a pattern of thought particular to Europe and passed on to the Third World through elite colonial education, whose constancy and consistency manages and repeats a law that affirms that history is the good story of the state.[15] By priority, according to Guha, subalternism would seek to disentangle history from the state and turn it over to the cause of the people and their struggles. This retrievalist stance, after disclaiming its own authority and allegiance to institutions of power, might assist the dominated in their efforts to coordinate their interest. But it is uncertain whether or not this effort on the part of the subalternist is collusive with the agenda of populism as I have described it. Let us return to this very quickly. For now, we must make way for what I understand to be one of Guha's central points: "The study of history developed into a sort of 'normal science.' . . . It now acquired a place of its own in the increasingly expanding space where hegemonic process often appealed to history in order to realize itself in the interaction between citizens and the state. It was here, again, that the study of history found its public — a reading public, progeny of the printing technology and avid consumers of such of its products as catered to a new bourgeois taste for historical literature of all kinds." Is Guha suggesting here that the transmission of history from one person to another, one generation to another, became, through a process of institutionalization, the principled and correlated form of common interest? "So it was as a highly institutionalized and statist knowledge that the study of history was introduced by the British in nineteenth-century India."[16] "The institutionalization," he writes further, "was therefore of little help to the rulers in their bid for hegemony. It was, on the contrary, simply a measure of the containment of this knowledge within the colonized elite who were the first to benefit from western education in our subcontinent."[17] The philanthropists of nationhood, having inherited "Statism in Indian historiography," as "a gift of [elite] education," were abruptly disarmed in their adventure to secure power by the absence of a collective body called citizens, upon whose favor, flesh, and mentality the state would rush to appropriate the past.[18]

The inadequacy of statism for a truly Indian historiography follows from its tendency to forbid any interlocution between us and our past. It speaks to us in the commanding voice of the state which by presuming to nominate the historic for us leaves us with no choice about our own relation to the past. Yet the narratives which constitute the discourse of history are dependent precisely on such choice. To choose means, in this context, to try and relate to the past by listening to a conversing with the myriad of small voices in civil society.[19]

In the sphere of education, within life as pedagogy, if we follow Guha's argument, the state is always at work normalizing its form of subjugation to the point where all relations of power become ephemeral. However, civil society, which is as yet uncontaminated by the malaise of statism, according to Guha, holds the key to the reconstitution of history and it is toward that sphere of exchange that the subalternist must strategically conspire with the subaltern to wither the state. This appeal to civil society, which is also common to populist rhetoric, is an error in political judgement and a weak philosophical operation. Here it seems that Guha, with a sly governmentalist critique of the colonial and postcolonial relationship between historiography and the state, surrenders to a communitarian ideal that advocates civil society as the locus classicus of free will. Civil society, to the extent that it is part of the passage to the hegemonic, excludes the subaltern. If, however, the achievement of unhinging history from the state adheres to the complexity and compelling vision of justice, of democracy as promise, then perhaps the incorporation of history by the body politic or civil society would necessitate a history for and by the people determined and invested with an ethico-ontological priority beyond the need and destiny of subalternist intellectual strategy. Yet as paradoxical as it would appear, this revitalized and subalternized history, can animate within the subalternist's theoretical practice not an orientation toward hegemony, but one toward equality. As Guha says, the equality of choice, the freedom and ability to choose and relate to the past unsystematically, is the goal of history retrieved. This is strategy.

I want to insist on the endurance of the theme of democracy as promise, for it is the concourse on which subaltern studies meets the history of philosophy and there, in the immediacy of that encounter, it breathes new life into the reading and writing of the philosophy of history. In this regard, I would agree with Guha that it is necessary to unhinge the philosophy of history, even at the expense of academic security and commitment, from that fully perverse statism. With the question of strategy collaborating with Guha's insistence (to unhinge history from statism), it is fair to say that by burrowing into the philosophical possibilities of common interest and its incalculable valuation, we are aspiring to abolish the distance between knowledge and the people, or rather the reappropriation of knowledge by the people. This distance is never neutral. In fact it is the stuff of politics, of democratic thought. The question takes us beyond this limit, forcing us to confront the anomalous character of politics as the pursuit of justice and equality, as in the words of Jacques Ranciere:

> Politics assigns itself an edifying purpose. Stripped of its theatrical fancy dress, democracy is introduced into this programme as the dialogue, the collective search for homonomoia, which Plato counterposed to the seduction of rhetoric as of noise assemblies to popular theaters. But Plato will not accept payment in such cheap coin. For him, the difference between dialogue and rhetorical persuasion cannot define any conceivable correction of democracy. Rather, it defines philosophy's radical difference from democracy. Democracy cannot be redeemed by philosophy. And it is most certainly farcical to posit its dialogic redemption through discussion of the more and the less or the weighing of interests in the balance. Imparity is an essential part of democracy. The only kind of dialogue compatible with democracy is one where the parties hear one another but do not agree with one another.[20]

Here is then an example that would confirm Guha's retrievalist position of returning history, stolen and reappropriated from the state, back to the people. It is an act of restoration and not restitution, which is edified by the ungovernability of the subaltern or multitude. Thus, one cannot overlook nor escape a glaring dimension of the problem of subalternity, related as it is to that of strategy; it is this logic of disagreement introduced by Ranciere it supposes while also revealing the tenacious nature of the mask that is populism (recoded, for instance in Guha, in the name of civil society). Perhaps under the question of strategy, the undeniable relationship that we ought to begin to consider or approach as an absolute manifestation of what Guha poses as the relation between knowledge or history and the state is the relationship between subalternity and the Real. One cannot, at least from an exterior position of interpretation, describe either subalternity or the Real. What we do describe and speculate on are either the expressivities of both or their subsidiary, which appears to us as a theoretical operation that is being yielded in this paper as the question of strategy. Here are further diversions for the question of strategy, if it seeks to restore equality in the pursuit of hegemony, between the dominant and the dominated (with the intellectual situated between them) would anticipate a new interrogation of the renewed possibility of philosophical anthropology, namely organized in the horizontal difference of *Menschenkunde* and *Erkundbar.* However we shape and reshape the latter, subalternity does not seem to fit well into the scheme. In the constitution of the problem of history, it seems that in rebuilding the terrain of values between people and knowledge we have already excluded subalternity at the very beginning of the initiation of the act to correct this injustice. Or is it that subalternity is beyond the apparent, the difference of difference? If this is the case, the question of strategy as an appendage of subaltern studies requires us to redraw the dividing line between knowledge and the people. Strategy is of course a wager! The question of strategy is therefore not a medication, a moment of silencing the instances of ungovernability in the texts of the modern experiences of democracy, but the obverse. Strategy is a symptom of democracy as promise.

The dream of a strategy for subaltern studies is not my way of anticipating closure. All forms of closure, whether populist or not, would never think strategically, or rather it would never dream to think of its own existence as already conditioned by multiple strategies. My call, this thinking that thinks strategy and in effect subalternity as a grounding question can only make mention of the twin effects of adversity and pleasure as other passages inform us of the profound relationship between subalternity and us.

Notes

1   Latin American Subaltern Studies Group. "Founding Statement," *boundary 2* 20:3, 1993.
2   Antonio Negri, "Twenty Theses on Marx." In *Marxism Beyond Marxism,* edited by Saree Makdisi, Ceseare Casarino, and Rebecca Karl (New York: Routledge, 1996), 158.
3   José Rabasa and Javier Sanjinés C. "Introduction." In *Subaltern Studies in the Americas,* edited by José Rabasa, Javier Sanjinés C., and Robert Carr. Special issue of *Dispositio/n* 46, 1996, v–xi.
4   Ibid.
5   Boris Frankel, "Post-Marxist Populism," *New Left Review,* 226/1997, 66–67.
6   Michel Foucault, *The Order of Things* (New York: Vintage, 1980), 259.
7   Georg Lukacs, *The Theory of the Novel* (Cambridge: MIT Press, 1971), 99.
8   Ibid.
9   See Frankel, "Post-Marxist Populism."
10   Alberto Moreiras, "Populism in a Double-Register," unpublished ms., 1997.
11   Ibid.
12   Karl Marx and Friedrich Engels. *The Communist Manifesto* (New York: Peguin, 1967), 117.
13   Jacques Derrida, *Spectres of Marx* (London: Routledge, 1994), 65.
14   Antonio Gramsci, *Prison Notebooks* (New York: International Publishing House, 1971), 334.
15   Ranajit Guha, "Small Voice of History," in *Subaltern Studies X,* edited by P. Chatterjee (London: Oxford University Press, 1997), 10.

16 Ibid.
17 Ibid.
18 Ibid.
19 Ibid.
20 Jacques Ranciere, *On the Shores of Politics* (London: Verso, 1995), 16.

IV. UNGOVERNABILITY: AUTHORITARIAN AND DEMOCRATIC HEGEMONICS

From *Glory* to *Menace II Society:*
African American Subalternity and the
Ungovernability of the Democratic
Impulse under Super-Capitalist Orders

ROBERT CARR

The obvious nature of the impact of globalization has led to an increasing dialogue among progressive intellectuals and a rethinking of the investments — geographic, economic, historical, political — undergirding their arguments as they situated those terms. Certainly, the collapse of the Second World has made obvious that global capitalism as the only option is now the only terrain on which practical political-economic debates can even begin to find a functional vocabulary. Capitalism, meanwhile, is backed up by economic deprivation and a massive, aggressive U.S. military apparatus, itself predicated on becoming more extreme in its capacity for destroying its prey. In the wake of this, Third World–driven theories of underdevelopment — themselves political attempts to adapt critiques of hegemonic European economic narratives to democratize and "rationalize" Caribbean realities — have also become endangered.[1]

In his article published, revealingly, in *Poetics Today,* Fernando Coronil sums up what has happened to the hopes of democracy in the "other" Americas, which constitute the geographic and demographic majority of the Western Hemisphere. In Venezuela, which defined itself as Latin America's neoliberal capitalist vanguard, even neoliberal definitions of democracy would conflict with the secondary status that he argues is given to democracy by the state apparatus. Analyzing particular speeches addressed to the Venezuelan National Assembly in 1988, Coronil points out that the interlocutor for this "model" Latin American state is neither a literal definition of democracy nor the *pueblo* — the people as a national community — but its own simulacrum. He argues that "development" in Latin America is predicated on charming the international media as a fundamental element of the state's foreign policy. That is, the interlocutor is not the pueblo so much as Venezuela's coverage by CNN and the world press, "the public . . . outside Venezuela, in the United States and Europe" (Coronil, 651). Turning the neoliberal state's military forces on the Venezuelan people (who are taking to the streets in a rejection of state concessions, and are marking an exceptional break from the public passivity of neoliberal democracy) is an embarrassment to the state by the state in global forums. The city streets easily become occupied zones kept hidden from the world.

The stories told by the bourgeoisie and its corporate agents become the state's national-developmental narratives. For Latin Americans and, I will argue, African Americans, the dialectic between the streamlining of global power politics and the threat of direct and violent military action abroad to protect the United States is of the utmost importance. Within this dialectic, African Americans have been striking back from the belly of the beast.[2] U.S. gay studies has underscored for us that the center of U.S. state policy as male-male interaction is underwritten by bodily violence as an imminent threat.[3] These cultural analysts have argued that the U.S. audience must be lulled into believing that war, a key axis of my analysis, is now reinvented as a media event, while its realities are hidden. This mass marketing of war is supplemented by sentimentality grounded in newly redefined "family values": we may not support the state's slaughter of an unknown people, but we support our sons, daughters, fathers, mothers, sisters, brothers at risk. The rhetoric of family values as allegiance to the state acts within the United States to cover for that threat of violence. The threat, however, is overt for those outside U.S. information control, citizenship, and governability, who would otherwise feel that they have the right to sovereignty.

The Latin American Subaltern Studies Group is dedicated to examining the state's responsibility toward all the people, ferreting out the elisions which support the omnipotence of the elite. Such an adventure in the ongoing experiment in democracy was cut short within the United States as soon as elite consensus was possible after the Declaration of Independence.[4] Historically, the U.S. agenda dedicated itself to equating democracy with a new kind of oligarchic capitalism. Property and wealth were to be protected from the threat of violence from external and internal enemies, the latter defined in local laws as "Negroes," "Mulattoes," and "Indians." After such a burden of history, what then can we do to expose the legacy of strategic hypocrisy and speak out in the name of democracy as equal rights in human rights?

Reading New World Subalternity

Apocalyptic post-marxist Jean Baudrillard puts it well for my analysis of both *Glory* and *Menace II Society*: "Capital doesn't give a damn about the idea of the contract which is imputed to it — it is a monstrous unprincipled undertaking, nothing more. . . . Capital in fact has never been linked by a contract to the society it dominates. It is a sorcery of the social relation, it is a challenge to society and should be responded to according to moral and economic rationality, but a challenge to take up according to symbolic law" (Baudrillard, 29–30). This, perhaps, is the best starting point for my analysis of the nature of subalternity in the Americas, from the Civil War as a mid-nineteenth-century military crisis documented in *Glory*, to the twentieth-century fin-de-siècle military crisis in *Menace II Society*.

Subaltern studies in the New World concerns itself with the history of those constituted by the terms of the state, in laws as much as in quotidian social practice, as ungovernable, menacing sociopolitical noise. And it is on the backs of their subalternization that order, government, state, as much as progress, have continually been predicated. African Americans have left us a centuries-old legacy of strategies and tactics against U.S. hegemony. Against all odds, they have written and battled, if not bickered, themselves into history. As a byproduct of this, *Glory* attempts to underscore the terms of African American commitment to the federal agenda in nineteenth-century history, and thus the possibility of rights for people of color under U.S.-policed citizenship. *Glory* also documents the struggle to rend what W. E. B. Du Bois called the veil that lies between African Americans and their neurotically fearful and antagonistic compatriots. In *Menace II Society*, I will argue, the terms of entry are still war, but the system to be accessed is global, open to and dominated by Latin Americans and subalterns in the New World—that is, the global megatrade in drugs. The convergence of these strategic struggles for citizenship—national in *Glory* and then global in *Menace II Society*—with ungovernability will be an axis of my analysis.

Glory

I want to begin by respecting the optimistic promise of the title of the film. The progression of colonial and postcolonial U.S. laws continuously investing the category of "Negro"—ultimately codified as subaltern in the laws of the southern U.S. with "Mulattoes," pregnant indentured servants, "Indians," and so on—makes what constitutes their development very clear.[5] On one hand, then, establishing who owns smooth access to the increase of development is ensured as foundational to the constitution of order; on the other, the excising of those designated as "Negroes," "Mulattoes," and "Indians" from those rights becomes equally foundational. These laws are very explicit, and those ratifying them felt no reason to be ashamed; at stake was the formation of controls over a vast economic opportunity. These men would kill to control it, with legal backing. Eventually they engendered a revolution to claim all profits for themselves. It is here that the rhetoric deployed to turn people into killers (militia, troops) and the need of the state to invent the nation come head to head.[6] In the years between this revolution and the ratifying of the Constitution, democracy meant reinventing local politics; Rhode Island, for example, redistributed its wealth. The Constitutional Convention brought such nonsense to a close; at the local as much as the federal level, it was engaged directly in the definition of the citizenry hand in hand with controlling subjects and objects of markets, and in that act, the crisis-ridden legislative definition of the subaltern.

As Coronil sees it for modern-day Venezuela, "Dominance and subalternity are not inherent, but relational characterizations. Subalternity defines not the being of the subject, but a subjected state of being" (649). When the proponents of slave labor (that is, most of the southern United States) lost their patience with the proponents of wage labor (that is, the northern U.S. oligarchy), territories began to be reclaimed, and since political and macroeconomic borders were at stake, this meant war. It also meant that enslaved African Americans, whose lives and labor built the tremendous wealth of the South and, to a lesser extent, the North, were suddenly thrown out of the prison-house of "slaves" and became a legally contradictory mass who could be reconstructed as "troops." For African Americans, engagement in full-scale war had been a long time coming.

Reading Glory

In this film's opening moments, the Civil War is established in our hero Robert's voice-over as the crescendo of U.S. history. All the men of states east and west, the lushly sentimental voice of our central narrator tells us, come together to enforce the might of Northern-controlled federal will. As an axis of the film's ability to know, Robert (Matthew Broderick) writes to his mother to establish that she need not worry for his life, for as in the American Revolution, "thousands of men" are massing together for a war to "make a whole country, so that all can speak."[7] The "all," of course, is meant to sign Robert-cum-the audience's belief that this is a war over black subalternization versus black macropolitical speech.[8] In this opening moment, the film is thus predicated on a lie and a caesura. The exhausted, straggling lines of "Negroes" predicated as the center of the struggle are, he tells us as they pass the white Northern troops going in the opposite direction, "the dispossessed," those who will soon rise to write "their own poetry" which "has never been written" — again his naïveté is inscribed.[9]

Here, then, reading against the grain in the name of "the dispossessed," we can say that the film attempts an arc it cannot complete, plotted through the equations education = knowledge = culture = whiteness = Europe = the enemy, and slave culture = creolization = resistance = rebellion = independence = sanity, which is not equal to freedom or citizenship. The film's logic reproduces a series of politicized non sequiturs with life and death implications for the African American body politic. Charles, the well-spoken black man who addresses Robert at the party of the Northern elite, as much as the cameo inclusion of a Frederick Douglass, embodies the film's contradictions of knowledge and race in legitimating ethnicity. The straggling mass of freed blacks is excluded from such erudition and access to elite parties.

The unjamming of the film's politico-cultural logic will be predicated on the creolization of the film's white hero, as the white man is put to rationalizing, leading, and thus inventing a black regiment. What has come home to roost is the march of colonial and postrevolutionary labor laws that have created the group "Negroes" as a homogenous chattel category, reduced from subjects to objects of law.[10] This reading of colonial legal history into postrevolutionary nation-constitution will come back in the film's version of a boot camp for blacks. Only within the context of the Civil War can the possibility of African American citizenship be contemplated given the terms of the U.S. state, although the answer to black inclusion will inevitably be "no."

The film, speaking the historical African American subject, smoothes over such crises just as it apologizes for the silence of the state that in fact speaks its policy—the "freed" slaves at the center of the film are renegades who reconstitute themselves as expectant citizens on the Northern side of the war. They enter in as the lie at best, Union patsies at worst, in a war over paradigms in which sociopolitical justice for blacks is strategically, if not tactically, irrelevant. The black soldier community is the slave community using escape from slavery to confront the Union and its fear of "Negroes" as irretrievably ungovernable, according to the science of the time.[11] If "the men need help" as black men, it is because they are below the standard of *Homo sapiens;* that is, their inscription as soldiers is an experiment in species development. The risk sets in that the war may lead to a promise of citizenship for ungovernables. The security of the category "Negro soldier" as "an ugly as chimp" now "in a blue suit," to quote Denzel Washington's character, immediately locates all other citizens north and south in the nation-state's sociopolitical hierarchy, and acknowledges a key to the power of the Southern landed aristocracy. The black people who were now committed to the terms of citizenship, which could include their death, stumble toward their future en masse as tactical units in a war conducted by a federation that considers them baggage. The crisis of black citizenship converges with the crisis of the war up to the point where the world cracks; therefore, black men, and only men, can scramble to negotiate full-scale armed rebellion into state-sanctioned war. The postwar Northern nation-state will romanticize it; the South will never forget it.

Governability

African American hopes for citizenship, predicated on governability, depended on their capacity to please the genteel Northern elite, an elite come face to face with implications of the steady crisis built around legislating African Americans as objects rather than subjects of law. The boot camp exercises of these soldiers thus take on an added burden: African Americans must prove themselves as "men" (i.e., *Homo sapiens*) as much as soldiers. Faith in African Americans as troops is excess baggage found in rhetoricizing and marketing the Civil War — pitting white brother against white brother, rendering the racial politics of the Mason-Dixon line irrelevant.[12] Yet the war of economic strategies finally enables African Americans to enter into a mutated citizenship, irretrievably coded ethnically as well as racially. In the rhetoric of black men as maximum-men, black soldiers (and thus black men deserving consideration for citizenship and human rights) are abused in their new constitution as not to be "Mexican whores" and not "Hindus," the terms against which their boot camp commander demands they reconceive themselves into troops. I'll leave that morass alone.

Governability: From Nigger/Coon to Soldier

The use of ungovernable "runaway slaves" as troops allowed the state to define them. As do those of prisoners, soldiers' bodies belong to the state. Denzel Washington's character confronts this pseudodemocratic inclusion — the military's assurance of boots, uniforms — but not immediately. In search of shoes that fit to ease his festering sores, he is declared a deserter by the liberal Colonel Robert. "Deserter" here becomes the Northern military equivalent of the South's chattel "runaway" when Washington's character is whipped as punishment. The scars of Southern slavery on his back speak volumes as they are added to in the name of Northern military order. Either way, African Americans lose in the strain of national cohesion, hence the military tenor of Reconstruction and its resolution in Jim Crow laws.

If for the colonel the readiness of the troops is a vexed question, then the troops' blackness is what is centrally intervening. White troops' access to boots, uniforms, and guns is a necessity for the Union administration to consider itself coherent. Black troops beg. Citizenship is being issued to the troops, and it is telling that the black men's shoes are secured by ransacking the supply station, and the idea of equal wages for equal risk respected by strike.

To *Glory*'s credit, this endless struggle is registered as explicitly political. *Glory* is thus explicit as it walks toward the conditional fiction of the line of order — the resolution of the war = the resolution of defining the amorphous mass. The socius reconceives itself not through black American citizenship but in idealism, an idealism lingering on, hinging on the pact between the black troops and their white commanders.

Black Nationalist Regrouping

Denzel Washington's character functions as the black nationalist voice contesting the reorganizing strictures of the Northern state. The Northern-educated black character Charles signifies accession to Northern incorporation into order, which means federal success as white success, which means, here, white supremacy. Again, in the film, education = knowledge = culture = whiteness = Europe = the enemy, and slave culture = creolization = resistance = rebellion = independence = sanity, which is not equal to freedom or citizenship. Slave culture's political debates are transposed to military debates because the amorphous mass of black Americans must recast itself.[13] The Northern government's tactically mocking disdain for its black regiment is obvious, and the film's subtitled historical markers of time and place only underscore the irony, for as the black troops march forward, African American access marches back.

We may see the black regiment win, but in tandem with an ironic unraveling. The black casualties are characterized as victories, as accession to the political requirements for humanity. Late in the film, Washington's character seeks permission to tell his white commanding officer that it is a farce to see this war as a war over black American rights. Men die in escalating numbers, but for nothing. Subalternity persists; he rejects the "honor" of being chosen to bear the regiment flag.

The military reassures itself by reciting its cachet, might and intention. Winning is synonymous with "character," cast as foundational resolution of the black troops. Black subaltern culture enters: suddenly we are in the midst of singing, harmonica playing, praying, men steeped in black Southern culture committing themselves to victory or death, congregating together to that end as banned explicitly by Southern law. Success in battle means success in citizenship, and the Bible comes to be the means by which hope, as order, is ensured within an apocalyptic universe. Morgan Freeman's character, the unstinting integrationist, seconds the motion before the black gathering. He speaks as a man who has left all family ties in the hell of that other bondage, which has not been shown here; that is, the hell of slavery. Success, governability, means liberation in God as much as the fulfillment of the promise of the nation.

Washington's character comes to tell another story, of family as much as of history as historylessness. "Y'alls is my family, no matter what happens tomorrow," he tells the community, knowing they are being sent into a suicide mission in the name of citizenship. The war is not history here, for it means no progress, no development, no citizenship, no hope. There is the community of the ungovernables seeking governability; this is the insight the character brings with him from subalternity. With hindsight, we find prisons and ghettoes and menaces to society articulating that gap in the social pact.

The struggle for citizenship is managed within the terms of the U.S. military. The ungovernable exist to the extent that they conform to the parameters proffered by the state. As the film progresses, there is less and less choice. "Nobility," in the end, is the only option left in a fight for a fort never taken, an option they tie to heroism in blackness, governed by white spokespeople addressing the white leadership (Colonel Robert, for example) in the name of something beyond the interests of the nation-state: African American humanity, African American citizenship. Nobility in the form of patriotism as obedience stands in for petitions to enter into the national body; hurling their bodies into a death struggle in the name of what they know to be a lie is the best way out—mass suicide of the black regiment (marking the climax of the film) in the name of abstracted philosophical concepts such as "strength" and "character."

If this war is in the name of *Glory,* then against whom it is fought remains obfuscated—that is, the racism of the United States. If this war is indeed the extreme of the United States breaking the bonds of brotherhood, nation as family, who now, we may ask, is the enemy? *Glory*'s focus is the range of subaltern black political positions united, governable, in the name of a battle against an enemy dramatically never named as the enemy, yet constitutive, endemic, systemic, home. After the images of black men at war, the solemn closing captions tell us that black troops were authorized after the regiment's mass suicide, and that Lincoln credited these troops with turning the tide of the war. At the end of the film, after the debacle at the fort, the bodies of citizens and noncitizens are piled into a mass grave, but as Washington's character prophetically has put it, in the name of what?

Menace II Society

We can turn, then, in contexts of readings after globalization, to Rodríguez's rethinking of the "subaltern" in the Americas. "In [Robert] Reich's opinion," she writes, "the present day workings of capitalism are hypothesized in terms of the global economy which casts doubt on nations as functional units of analysis, consequently repositioning governments and citizenry. He believes the global is tearing the ties binding citizens together" ("Rethinking," 16).

She sets up some initial parameters for a reading of *Menace II Society* under the terms of ungovernability, subalternity, and the quality of the U.S. nation-state's social pact with the African American body politic. In *Glory* that pact was premised on war and suicide to prove blacks deserving of citizenship. We can reread, then, *Menace*'s precredit scene in which Kevin, one of the central black characters, murders an Asian American shopkeeping couple and takes the surveillance videotape. No social pact binds these two groups of citizens, as their suspicious and volatile interaction amply demonstrates. There is no nation here, only a dysfunctional economic pact.

Moreover, in Kevin's obsessive playing and replaying of the video of the murder to entertain his friends, we can identify at least two forces (implications?) of the historic failure of state representation as national inclusion: (1) that this act and this tape write this man, somehow, into history by his own hand (history in globality as a media event); and (2) that the void filled by martyrdom in *Glory*'s attempt at writing black Americans into history's archive is now filled by something else—murder, we need say in the beginning.

But if, briefly following Ranajit Guha and Rodríguez, we read this "crime" against the grain as a "speech act," we can glimpse something else: revenge? agency? jealousy, perhaps? But against whom or what? What is the purview of this world, what is its horizon against which we could measure meanings of this act? I would argue that it is the death of the concept of nation, of nation as family, of previously functional units of analysis central to African American as to U.S. societal comprehensibility. Hence these men indeed form a *Menace to Society* in the terms under which society has been understood. Here, then, the one interlocutor is the horizon preceding globalization, the horizon of the Civil Rights and the Black Power movements. This also means the horizon of faith in capitalist or socialist world orders, in which the nation-state, patriotism, and citizenship were functional units of analysis. The subaltern rewrites the meaning of the state.

This, perhaps, is what the Hughes brothers mean in their after-comment for the home video of the film that "understanding" is what is at stake, and that "the trigger has no heart." Such a comment cuts both ways, for it refers to those killed by the police as a military wing of the state as much as to ungovernable African Americans killing each other. The trigger of automatic weapons now straddles the social pact between nation and nation, family and nation, nation and state, thus chaos and the order let loose by the state—which is to say, following Hobsbawm, "patriotism," "order," "society." "If patriotism means self-interest," writes Rodríguez, "within the boundaries of nations and the formation of citizenship in accordance with national prowess, or even [to quote Reich] 'looking out for ourselves by looking out for our company,' globalism means the dissolution of that bond. With the disappearance of political organizations, parties, and utopian thinking, people have lost their moorings and become politically adrift" ("Rethinking," 16).

In Charles S. Dutton's introduction to the video of the film, he advocates the Institute of Black Parenting as the answer to a nation whose future is at risk because "guys who think they're cool use a gun to settle every argument." As in *Glory*, "character" again is offered to resolve the question of citizenship. In the absence of other functional units, we return to the family, antithetical here to the military, as the building block of order in chaos, which here means the quotidian. The simple financial transaction, buying two beers, took place in the opening murder scene. It is only, somehow, when the Asian American shopkeeper says that his mother would be ashamed of him that all hell breaks loose. "Go in to buy a couple beers," notes Cane, the protagonist and Kevin's friend, in voice-over, "and come out an accessory to murder and armed robbery."

To constitute its narrative, the film follows its credits with the Watts riots — the birth pains of the Black Power movement and the death of the ethos of nonviolence — presented as an eruption of another civil war. Rather than love, prayer, and church, the axis of the black political subject is here represented in rage, war, and prison. "When the riots stopped," says Cane's voice-over, "the drugs started." The people, he tells us, are "either just out of prison or on their way to prison." If war and militarism constitute the politics of the new community, the drug trade constitutes its political economics at the cultural level. The drug trade immediately puts us in the space of the transnational global marketplace, in which subalterns can find access to dreams of getting paid and profit sharing, or at least psychological escape. What the U.S. state defines as criminality becomes economic viability. Cane's dead father apprenticed him in the production and selling of drugs. The minimum wage, he tells us, was never his style. Access to money substitutes for citizenship.

Weaponry and alcohol consumption become the terms of pride and honor (glory) in manhood in place of the threat of armed violence that protects the citizenry and is delegated to the armed forces (nation as man-nation). It is women's function throughout the film to advocate another kind of social order, one in which violence is kept away from children and women (nation as family-nation) in defense against madness — what we could call sustainable development. The film's establishing shots show housing projects as stolid as prison blocks. Cane makes it clear that he believes that the educational system advocates "bullshit," and he graduates with half of it. The other half of what he knows is learned on the street, selling drugs to make real money — patriotism in subalternity versus capital accumulation.

The nation as an army at war becomes a nation feeding on itself. The grandparents as the representatives of black American would-be citizens come to represent the defining opposite of these man-boys' public political identity, and even for the grandparents, religious faith replaces citizenship. The Black Panther Party would have organized these man-boys as cadres, and, under Elaine Brown at least, put them to work building model schools or free breakfast and lunch programs.[14] Guha's distinctions between crime and insurgency prove extremely valid here:

> What differentiates a . . . rebellion from . . . crime is not its inversive function [turning things upside down] which is common to both and leads people often to mistake one for the other. The confusion . . . is particularly acute during that twilight phase which separates the actual outbreak of an insurrection from its precursor — the wave of "preliminary outrages" as it is called in official language. But insurgency soon extricates itself from the placenta of common crime in which it may be initially enmeshed and establishes its own identity as a violence which is public, collective, destructive and total in its modalities. Each of these constitutes a distinctive feature in the sense that it has its antithesis in crime, so that the opposition between two types of violence may be represented as a series of binary contrasts thus — public/secretive, collective/individual-istic, destructive/appropriate and total/partial. (Guha, 108)

It is the absence of any commitment to the entire ghetto community that renders Kevin and his ilk indeed a menace. Their alignment with the individu-alistic attack leaves a void filled with drinking and killing. For their actions to register as rebellion, their victims would need to follow a political logic — not a beer, not a car hotshopped for a quick buck, not an addict shot in the head as a nuisance.

Dutton's appeal to the restoration of the black kin structure to bring order in chaos — of rendering the ungovernable governable — turns in on itself when assaults on family ties consistently lead to violence or alienation. The desire for revenge in defense of cousins, mothers, homeboys is synonymous with death and murder as the means for reinstating order. Cane's cousin's girlfriend and son, along with the devotion he shows in engaging with them in his cousin's place, establish the alternative paradigm of family relationships and, from there, a manhood that can survive. The new son's growth into the language of the man-streets ("punk," "punk-ass," etc.) as well as training in how to shoot, and Cane's dismissal in his function as father-substitute-cum-military trainer, breadwinner, and man of the streets, set up the defining oppositions necessary for a political incarnation of deconstruction at work — with life, death, and apocalypse at stake. The only way to survive this vicious game cycle is to get out. Survival, as all "menaces" realize — military and civilian, official and subaltern — is the final interlocutor. The only question is the value attributed to it. From martyr to *Menace,* the black subject lives the arc of apartheid's dead end. Police brutality becomes redundant.

Labor, Markets, Culture

Having the place of the "subaltern" and Latin American realities founda-tionally in mind, Rodríguez writes that it "is evident that both capitalism and socialism, for different reasons . . . outgrew their political-organizational forms, but as a consequence, the organizing principles of consciousness, law and order, finances, etc., became dysfunctional. The terms of the debate dis-cussing hegemonies and hierarchies are security, defense, wars, killings, mar-kets, identity, subalternity. Since nations can no longer be the defining princi-ples, labor, markets, and culture are being proposed as central" ("Rethinking," 17). Hence the Hughes brothers grapple with a reality that finds an interlocu-tor in South-South analyses of subalternity in the Americas as they turn their lens to the inner-city streets. Sutton's appearance as father figure tries to rescue the black subaltern community back into the black social body (patriarch → *patria*) to argue "that the way we grew up is bullshit," as Cane's cousin tells Cane in the end. This attempt falls apart, however, under the rigorous indoc-trination of the streets, and the fact that money is citizenship. Returning to Baudrillard, "Capital doesn't give a damn about the idea of the contract which is imputed to it" (29). And yet, still, fatherhood — kinship as the best hope of survival for "my niggers" — is at stake.

Notes

1   See World Bank, *World Development Report* (1997).
2   See, for example, a May 1723 Virginia law further recodifying the category of a slave as subaltern, which begins: "I. Whereas the laws now in force for the better ordering and governing of slaves and for speedy trial of such of them as commit capital crimes are found insufficient to restrain their tumultuous and unlawful meetings or to punish the secret plots and conspiracies carried on amongst them and known only to such as by the laws now established are not accounted legal evidence. And it being found necessary that some further provision be made for directing and punishing all such dangerous combinations for the future." See Hening, 7:126–134. Or again, the October 1670 law banning the purchase of "Christian Servants" by "Indians or Negroes" "though baptized and enjoined in their own freedom," though they are "not debarred from buying any of their own nation" (Hening, 2:280–281.
3   See Kokopeli and Lakey, "Masculine Sexuality and Violence."
4   See Ollmann and Birnbaum, *The United States Constitution.*
5   See Higgenbotham, *In the Matter of Color.*
6   See Hobsbawm, *Nations and Nationalism.*

7   For analyses of family metaphors as national metaphors, see Rodríguez,) *House/Garden/Nation;* and Sommer, *Foundational Fictions.*

8   See MacKinnon, "The Liberal State," in *Toward a Feminist Theory of the State;* also "The Sexual Politics of the First Amendment," in *Feminism Unmodified.*

9   I refer here to the mass of writings by Africans in the Diaspora in the eighteenth and nineteenth centuries, Olaudah Equiano among them. The *Heath Anthology* (vol. 1, ed. Lauter) gathers together important speeches, petitions, poetry, and other writings. See, for example, selections of late-eighteenth-century work by Jupiter Hammon (1711–1792?), Phyllis Wheatley (1753–1784), and Lemuel Haynes (1753–1784).

10 See MacKinnon, *Toward a Feminist Theory of the State.*

11 See Jefferson, *Notes on the State of Virginia,* especially "Query VI" on degeneracy, "Query XI" on "Aborigines," "Query XIV" on "Laws," and "Query XVIII" on "Manners" and the "Effect of Slavery."

12 See the endings of Frederick Douglass's first autobiography and Harriet Jacobs's *Incidents.*

13 See the "Confessions of Nat Turner," in which he discusses transforming the "slaves" into "men" as "soldiers." Included in Tragle, *The Southampton Slave Revolt.*

14 See Brown, *A Taste of Power.*

Works Cited

Baudrillard, Jean. *Simulations.* New York: semiotext(e), 1983.

Brown, Elaine. *A Taste of Power: A Black Woman's Story.* New York: Pantheon, 1992.

Coronil, Fernando. "Listening to the Subaltern: The Poetics of Neocolonial States." *Poetics Today* 15, no. 4 (winter 1994): 643–658.

Douglass, Frederick. *Narrative of the Life of Frederick Douglass, an American Slave.* 1845. Reprint, New York: New American Library, 1968.

Guha, Ranajit. *Elementary Aspects of Peasant Insurgency in Colonial India.* Delhi: Oxford University Press, 1992.

Hening, W. W., ed. *Statutes at Large of Virginia.* 13 vols. Richmond: printed by and for Samuel Pleasants Jr., printer to the Commonwealth, 1809–1823.

Higgenbotham, Leon, Jr. *In the Matter of Color: Race and the American Legal Process: The Colonial Period.* New York: New York University Press, 1980.

Hobsbawm, Eric. *Nations and Nationalism Since 1780: Programme, Myth, Reality.* 2nd ed. Cambridge: Cambridge University Press, 1992.

Jacobs, Harriet. *Incidents in the Life of a Slave Girl Written by Herself.* 1861. Reprint, New York: Harvard University Press, 1987.

Jefferson, Thomas. *Notes on the State of Virginia.* Ed. William Peden. Chapel Hill: University of North Carolina Press, 1996.

Kokopeli, Bruce, and George Lakey. "Masculine Sexuality and Violence." In *A Certain Terror: Heterosexism, Militarism, Violence, and Change,* ed. Richard Cleaver and Patricia Myers. Chicago: Great Lakes Regional Office, American Friends Service Committee, 1993.

Lauter, Paul, ed. *The Heath Anthology of American Literature.* 2 vols. 2nd ed. Lexington, Mass.: D. C. Heath and Company, 1994.

MacKinnon, Katherine. *Feminism Unmodified: Discourses on Life and Law.* Cambridge, Mass.: Harvard University Press, 1987.

——. *Toward a Feminist Theory of the State.* Cambridge, Mass.: Harvard University Press, 1989.

Ollmann, Bertell, and Jonathan Birnbaum, eds. *The United States Constitution: Two Hundred*

Years of Anti-Federalist, Abolitionist, Feminist, Muckraking, Progressive, and Especially Socialist Criticism. New York: New York University Press, 1990.

Rodríguez, Ileana. *House/Garden/Nation: Space, Gender, and Post-Colonial Latin American Literatures by Women.* Durham, N.C.: Duke University Press, 1994.

——. "Rethinking the Subaltern: Patterns and Places of Subalternity in the New Millenium." *Dispositio/n 46: Subaltern Studies in the Americas.* José Rabasa, Javier Sanjinés C., and Robert Carr, guest editors. 19, 46 (1994, published in 1996): 13–25.

Sommer, Doris. *Foundational Fictions: The National Romances of Latin America.* Berkeley: University of California Press, 1991.

Tragle, Henry Irving, ed., *The Southampton Slave Revolt of 1831: A Compilation of Source Material.* Amherst: University of Massachusetts Press, 1971.

World Bank. *World Development Report: The State in a Changing World: Selected World Development Indicators.* New York: Oxford University Press, 1997.

Twenty Preliminary Propositions for a Critical History of International Statecraft in Haiti

MICHAEL T. CLARK

"Haiti, where negro means man." — Creole saying

The essay that follows is largely theoretical and speculative. Its focus is conceptual: it seeks to deconstruct a central discursive figure in mainstream historical narratives about colonial and postcolonial politics: the nation-state as historical subject. What little it has to say about the concrete history of the state and statecraft in Haiti is largely derived from interpretive English-language sources, is based on limited travel in the country, and, in any case, is meant to be illustrative. How does such an essay fit within the defining concerns of subaltern studies?

At least four distinctive preoccupations characterize the South Asian subaltern studies project and have been carried over into the Latin American context — all within a defining moral and political disposition we have characterized as a "preferential option for the poor." First, the project has been concerned to recover and valorize the agency of subalterns as history-making subjects. Presenting the subaltern as a knowing and capable, if disadvantaged, strategic actor, subaltern studies prepares the ground for a new interpretation of the history of "subject peoples." It deconstructs those histories, usually written by foreign elites, that depict subaltern action and consciousness as "pre-historical" (i.e., insufficiently Westernized), and it surpasses narratives of victimization and exclusion. It also, at least implicitly, critiques political projects that pretend to speak for, or in the enlightened interest of, subaltern groups and classes.

Second, the subaltern studies project has been characteristically preoccupied with the operation of power in all its myriad forms and processes. The very concept of subalternity is charged with the sign of relative power; the concept's plasticity rises from the vast multiplicity of power's contexts and contours. The colonial and postcolonial contexts define one range of analytic variables, while situations of class, caste, identity, and gender present another.

Third, all of subaltern studies has been concerned, to a degree that is more or less explicit, with the problem of "the sources." The issue here is less one of the accuracy or reliability of the historical record, but rather an awareness of a systematic discursive bias operating in all phases of past and present "documentation." Fourth, subaltern studies has been characteristically concerned with exploring the interdependence of, to put it roughly, the ideational and the material. As much as anything else, it is the clash of mental worlds—and above all an iron refusal to privilege the Western and colonizing formations in the historical process—that characterize the distinctive political and moral stance of subaltern studies. At the core of subaltern studies is a recognition of, and an attempt to recover for contemporary political support, the value claims of subaltern agents.

A fifth element of style and approach has been so finely developed with the subaltern studies project that it has also become virtually characteristic. This is, of course, the general preference for the concrete and specific. Through close and rigorous examination of particular cases, informed and motivated by all four of the preoccupations listed above, the South Asian group has demonstrated an extraordinary capacity to mine from the dusty, often desiccated detritus of history luminous pearls of human action and meaning. The method, elevating the lowly and obscure to the center of historical focus, seems to model the ambitions of the project. But there never has been within subaltern studies a commitment to a particular focus, method, or style. "There is no one way of investigating this problematic," Ranajit Guha wrote in the introductory essay of the very first volume of *Subaltern Studies*. "Let a hundred flowers bloom and we don't even mind the weeds" (reprinted in Guha and Spivak, 43).

Nearly two decades and nine volumes later, Guha's successors observed: "We have expanded our critical focus to include elite texts and practices, our interests have ranged beyond the discipline of history, and we have tackled issues of contemporary politics and the politics of knowledge. These moves may have not pleased our critics who wish us to place the subaltern within a clearly defined domain, and object to our straying beyond the strictly defined disciplinary practices of history. On our part, however, we have always conceived the presence and pressure of subalternity to extend beyond subaltern groups; nothing—not elite practices, state policies, academic disciplines, literary texts, archival sources, language—was exempt from the effects of subalternity" (Bhadra et al., v). In these terms, I would present the essay below as motivated by the same concerns and commitments that have motivated the South Asian project and wholly consistent with its broad methodological license.

The following twenty points outline the core structure of a complex argument about the historical development and present condition of "the state" in Haiti. Each point represents an assertion whose demonstration requires a substantial essay in its own right, so that the complete argument can only find adequate expression in a monograph of considerable length. In their present form these points stand as theoretical preliminaries, a prolegomenon, to a history of the Haitian present that remains to be written, but which cannot be written in the terms of contemporary political discourse, beholden as it is to a concept of state that serves to mask and obliterate the real history of the Haitian subaltern's continuous engagement with the West. Integrating dispersed threads of post-structuralist theory to present an alternative conception of the state as social relation, I then deploy this perspective to adumbrate a reconstructed narrative of the historical process of state-making in Haiti. This synopsis is offered as a challenge to the dominant assumptions and premises of U.S. officials and international organization representatives. If the alternative premises of this analysis are correct, the Haitian people can be expected to reject, sooner rather than later, the self-styled "altruism" of the international agencies that have attempted to reconstruct the Haitian state from the ground up during the period of July 1994 to July 1997. This essay is also offered to anticipate and meet the recriminations that are certain to be made against Haitians when, as now seems inevitable, upon the scheduled departure of U.S. military forces, "things fall apart."

The Critique of "the State"

1. The indispensable task of any theoretical approach with pretensions to analytical rigor is an adequate specification of the object of study — in this case, "the state." The extraordinary advance of the natural sciences in this century has been first and foremost a history of the critique and replacement of common-sense understandings of visible and invisible phenomena.[1] In the social sciences, where categories and analytic frameworks serve not only as modes of representation for social relations but are themselves the medium of those relations, such a critical stance toward common sense is imperative. As an initial premise of any investigation of the historical development and present possibilities of the Haitian state, I want to propose a decisive departure from received notions of what states are and how they "work" as social forces. The break I have in mind is to reconceive the state as a pervasive social field constructed in and through discursive practice. The essential analytical move can be described by analogy with a similar "event" that Jacques Derrida noted more than thirty years ago in Claude Lévi-Strauss's evolving understanding of discursive structure: "In effect, what appears most fascinating in this search for a new state of discourse is the stated abandonment of all reference to a *center*, to a *subject*, to a privileged *reference*, to an *origin*, or to an absolute *archia*" (286).

2. Conventional views, both mainstream and marxist, tend to understand

the state in just these terms: as center (capital) subject (sovereign actor), privileged reference (public authority), origin (founder, legislator), and absolute archia (institution with a monopoly on the legitimate use of force). This general view of the state as a more or less ("relatively") autonomous social entity, governing social relations but somehow also standing apart from them, is deeply rooted in common sense and the "experience" common sense produces, from which the conventional view derives its apparent "realism." This common-sense view also sets the problem for theory—how to relate (functionally, organically, instrumentally, or structurally) this putative center (the state) to its surrounding social structures (whether that milieu be conceived as "civil society," nation, social formation, or elite and subaltern groups)—and it defines the "necessary" task of political action: resist or seize control of (by subterfuge, hegemonic alliance, coup, "regular, democratic process," or revolutionary force) this primordial power, "that very thing within a structure which, while governing the structure, escapes structurality" (Derrida, 279).

3. The rudiments for an alternative, decentered approach to the state have already been fashioned in an emerging body of social theory, and while the transformation is far from complete, the fundamental direction of the shift is sufficiently clear, and its general force, carried by leading scholars across a wide range of disciplines, is already quite impressive.[2] Summarizing a broad trend, what the new approaches have in common is the deconstruction and problematization of the image of governments as unitary actors acting within and upon, but somehow separate from, "society";[3] the abandonment of the idea that the state is the ultimate arbiter, if not primary font, of social power;[4] and the decentering of "the state" within the fields of national and transnational social relations.[5] The field of social power, in this view, is diffuse and pervasive both within and across "societies," which themselves lack any coherence or unity apart from the diverse, complex, and changing networks of power relations that operate through them.[6] There are two distinct but overlapping moves here: on one hand, taking away the idea that the state is a unified, neatly bounded, and coherent social entity and bringing into question its putative autonomy or, indeed, its efficacy as an actor in its own right; on the other, preserving the state as a vital social presence (as idea and practice), but repositioning it as only one of many sites implicated in the production, and contestation, of social power and relations.

4. Vocabulary is a problem; even among those who have moved to rethink the state in the way I am describing, there is no consensus on how and when to use the term "state" to refer to governments, and when to use it to refer to the wider field of social power in which governments are embedded and from

which they draw their apparent capacities. It is sometimes useful to conceive of the state (following Foucault) as a kind of "meta-power" that "is super-structural in relation to a whole series of power networks that invest the body, sexuality, the family, kinship, knowledge, technology and so forth" (1980: 122) — or (following Bourdieu) as a kind of "meta-capital" that is "capable of exercising a power over other species of power, and particularly over their rate of exchange" (Bourdieu and Wacquant 1992: 114). In other words, what is familiarly called "the state" refers to a kind of power among powers, or relation of relations, that cannot be simply reduced to those other relations. In this sense, the state is a kind of power that stands above (or below) other forms of power in society. But this power, real and irreducible as it is, cannot be located at any single point (or side of a relationship) in society. Rather, what is implied is a mutual conditioning and dependency of groups and actors in a variety of spaces and levels — *all* constituted relationally through a pervasive social field. The state may operate in ways that are analytically distinguishable from other kinds of fields, but it cannot be contained in any closed or separate social space. To simplify, I will use the term "state" to refer to the expansive view of the entire complex and contradictory field of social antagonism and power, and will reserve the term "government" for the formal, "visible" institutions of governance. The conventional concept of the state corresponds to the restricted view, what I am calling (institutionalized) government, and is based, I believe, on a category mistake, a misrecognition of the tip of the iceberg for the whole, an error on which many great projects of political analysis and reconstruction have foundered.

5. Once we depart from the common-sense understanding of the state, a very serious concern emerges. There is a great fear that once we begin to characterize the state in a poststructuralist mode as decentered, as a pervasive social field, as contested discourse, as operating in and through micromechanisms at every level of the social process, as an indeterminate space, as a structuration measurable only through its effects, as a text open to deconstruction, as a practice of mask and illusion, and, in the words of Michael Mann, "a patterned mess," we have effectively rendered the state unanalyzable and have lost sight of the differential distribution of social power, forsaking any hope of effective strategic intervention. My view, on the contrary, is that each of these transformations in our understanding of what states are and how they work is indispensable precisely for rendering the state as an object open to analysis.[7] It is only once we begin to ask how the "text" of the state is inscribed and produced in social relations, how power is organized and reproduced, and through what specific mechanisms, that we open the state to theorization and to critical and effective reconstruction.

6. Extending the analogy with language, we can describe the state quite usefully as a complex discursive formation (or rather, an ensemble of linked but not systematically unified discursive formations) and assert, with Philip Corrigan, that the state is "the grammar of politics" (1994: xix). As such, the state is the medium of social action and, more specifically, the medium structuring a social relation (i.e., a structuration), but it is also the outcome of an antagonism and hence a result and form of the operation of unequal social power. We can summarize this move by asserting that the state is a relation, or rather a complex system of relations—nothing more, nothing less. Not a condensation, an outcome, or residue of some preexisting social relationship; it simply *is* the relation. These relations do not exist independent of the discursive formation, but in and through it. As a structuration, the state affords to social actors rules and resources for their activities, but it *exists* only as ideas and practices, strategies and repertoires. It is both the outcome and medium of activities undertaken by agents constituted and situated in a field of power, but it has no materiality of its own. Rather, it is what imparts to material objects their use and significance. What must be done to abandon every move toward materializing the state, toward mistaking the tokens of state power for the power of the state, toward fetishizing the material objects whose significance is not determined by any intrinsic properties of the objects themselves, but from their relative positions in a field of relations.

7. The view of the state that results from this kind of displacement can be described as neither a monism nor a dualism; instead, the state is comprehended as a single field of structur(at)ed difference *constructed through and constructing social antagonism*. This last qualification, of course, is supremely important: if the state is a kind of discursive formation, this does not mean the relations of antagonism and difference constituted within it are mere relations of meaning. At this point, we should accept Foucault's injunction that "one's point of reference should not be the great model of language (*langue*) and signs, but to that of war and battle. . . . Neither the dialectic, as logic of contradictions, nor semiotics, as the structure of communication, can account for the intrinsic intelligibility of conflicts" (1980: 14). By the same token, however, the antagonisms of social life cannot be comprehended, as indeed the whole of Foucault's opus demonstrates, apart from the work of discourse. Bourdieu made the point quite clearly when he observed, "The power of imposing a vision of divisions, that is, the power of making visible and explicit [or concealing] social divisions that are implicit, is the political power *par excellence:* it is the power to make groups, to manipulate the objective structure of society" (1991b: 138). But to go further, to examine how the state operates recursively as a discursive field to both structure and be structured by social antagonisms, we need to move toward the concrete.

8. Every state must be comprehended in its own space and time as well as in its coevalness (Fabian) with other spaces and times. This assertion is an entailment of the view of the state I have outlined. If a state were not constituted according to its own particular social logic of splitting and distancing, it would scarcely be a state of its own but would be, literally, a part of something else. To "stand" (have *status*) or operate as a social field, it must be both internally divided and externally separated. In a sense, however, this "action" of dividing and separating is illusory. Because this division and separation are not given by the natural order of things, but are constituted through a discursively ordered field of social relations, what divides and separates — the very system of relations I am calling the state — also connects. Untangling this seeming paradox is key to understanding both what states are and how they do what they "do": they are fields of power in and through which diverse elements are not only brought together in a specific relationship, but they also "produce" the specific relations of difference and opposition through which the identities of the particular "units" are constituted.[8] Carrying this idea further toward the concrete, the concept of state as a decentered but agonistic and differentiated discursive field of unequal relations helps us to integrate within a single perspective three distinctive features of the Haitian social landscape: (1) the long-standing and continuing prevalence of peasant agriculture in Haiti and its distinctive "economically irrational" pattern of land tenure, (2) the pervasiveness and centrality of vodoun in all facets of Haitian life and society, and (3) what economist Mats Lundahl has labeled Haiti's "tradition" of predatory government (1992: 3). These three phenomena are usually viewed as incidental or peculiar to Haiti, consequential in their effects, but essentially unrelated to the nature of the state. Comprehended in accord with the social logic I have outlined, however, these three phenomena are not only intimately related to each other, but they all owe this connection to the state. Let us briefly consider each in turn.

9. First, land. Its significance is determined within a relational order of signification that transcends and pervades the materiality of the thing itself. I have proposed to conceive of the state as a discourse, understanding discourse, with Laclau, as "a structure in which meaning is constantly negotiated and constructed." On this model, "material things, external objects as such, also participate in discursive structures. This is not unlike Wittgenstein's concept of language games, which involves the constitution of a signifying order in which the materiality of things themselves participates" (1988: 254). Land — including its edaphic characteristics, its fertility, its use value, its limited exchange value, its place value, its significance for kinship, and its sacrality — thus

has a significance that we can only comprehend within the historically structured order of practice and signification particular to Haitians; or to put it another way, the particular significance of land in Haiti cannot be understood apart from the broader social field of which it partakes.

10. Substantively, it is clear that land has a significance in Haiti that extends far beyond, and indeed limits, its economic use value. The history of the Haitian slave revolt, and of more than two hundred years of political struggle since, can and must be read as a struggle over the rights of former slaves and their descendants to escape the servitudes of coerced collective labor. The emergence of the Haitian peasantry — the abandonment or active destruction of the plantation in favor of smallholdings, in other words — must be understood as "*a mode of response* to the plantation system and its connotations, and *a mode of resistance* to imposed styles of life*" (Mintz 1974: 132–133). In Haiti, the only place where slaves ever succeeded fully in overthrowing their masters, the result of these struggles was one of the most thorough redistributions of landholding ever undertaken, a movement whose dynamism came entirely from below and which was only grudgingly and partially recognized by the postcolonial elites who understood perfectly well that the disappearance of Haiti's once fabulous wealth was the concomitant of the former slaves' newly found economic independence. What development economists regard as the average Haitian's "obsessive" attachment to the land — that is, their refusal to treat land as an alienable commodity — is the consequence of a memory as well as a strategy fashioned during more than two centuries of social struggle. In Haiti, possession of land has been the marker of freedom, the core of identity, and the basis of economic independence. Alienation of land, conversely, has implied economic dependence, abandonment of identity, and loss of freedom.

11. In Haiti, the massive redistribution of land that took place in the revolutionary period and the first decades of the nineteenth century resulted in neither the yeoman-farmer republic of the Jeffersonian imaginary, nor the steady aggrandizement of an emergent "kulak" class. To get at the Haitian difference, we must contextualize the utilization and discursive appropriation of land in that broader metaphysical system of belief and practice known to unbelievers as voodoo. The attachment to land, patterns of social aggregation (kinship, economic partnership, political alliance), the obligations of marriage (or *placage*) and of parenting, the significance of place and locale — all are locatable only in the distinctive religious practices of Haitians. Vodoun "emerged" in the course of the revolutionary struggle simultaneously with peasant agriculture as an insurgent political consciousness, an alternative social imaginary, an esoteric code of communication and intelligence, and the constitutive discursive field of a novel collective identity.[9] It was eventually taken up, worked, and reworked by all Haitians during the course of the

revolutionary war and its aftermath. Its esoteric nature is part of its political history: "born" of struggle against slavery, often actively opposed by state elites and their foreign allies (including the once largely foreign Roman Catholic hierarchy and later U.S. occupiers), Vodoun spread, flourished, and survives today as a mode of organizing social power, including both resistance and domination. Culture, conceived as practice (not reified as form) and as practical strategy, is produced through *activity* and perdures as a mode of social adaptation, with a history and consequences of its own. In the operations of vodoun practice — which includes not only the formal rites of ceremony and "possession" but also the everyday practices of kinship and the "experience" of emotional response — the processes of cultural construction (what Lévi-Strauss described as "bricolage" without a "bricoleur") are enacted. Relationalized, Vodoun practice involves simultaneous sociopolitical representation, performance, contestation, and negotiation.[10] As a lived practice, Vodoun constitutes a vital dimension of the habitus, the structuration of consciousness, embodied history. It is, in short, a deeply embedded cultural resource and practical strategy, simultaneously a mode of being and doing through which the world is both experienced and made. Within this field of discursive practice, the land is invented with a value far beyond its productive value: it is, among many other things, the home of the ancestral spirit-gods, the point of reference for kin relations, the focal point of identity, the "ground" (both source and limit) of obligation, as well as a vital source of livelihood. It belongs to no one person and so cannot be alienated by any one person. Nor can any one person assert rights of property except on behalf of, and with the active (and hence rare) consent of, all those who "belong" to that land as much as it "belongs" to them.

12. The violence, corruption, and venality of Haitian public officials, and most notably the heads of government, are notorious. Often the condition of Haiti is said to owe to the emergence of a predatory state.[11] The suffering of the vast majority of Haitians, on this common view, is made to depend upon an unbroken chain of bad people, bad policies, and bad luck. But how to explain two hundred years of bad luck, a run that predates the revolution and that was continued even by the very fathers of the Haitian struggle for independence? (The racist has an answer and thereby, unintentionally, reminds us that racism has been a decisive factor in the history and formation of "Haiti.") To explain the constants of Haitian statecraft, we need to ask what it is about the Haitian state that constantly produces or selects for tyrants and criminals. Vague appeals to traditions and the moral failures of individuals or an elite class do not serve. The constraints and "immobility" of Haitian society penetrate far deeper. Reflecting on Norbert Elias's analysis of the web of relations surrounding the Sun King in his court, Bourdieu has observed that "Louis XIV was so

totally identified with the position he occupied in the gravitational field of which he was the Sun, that it would be futile to try to determine which of all the actions occurring in the field is or is not the product of his volition, just as it would be futile to distinguish in an orchestral performance between what is done by the conductor and what is done by the players" (1981: 306–307). Taking the case of Papa Doc Duvalier, a stock figure of Third World tyranny, many observers have mistaken his virtuosity with the "grammar" of Haitian politics (that is, his ability to work within the determinate but flexible field of relations that is here called the state) for a kind of omnipotence and draw attention away from the broader field of relations that Duvalier simply acted to preserve and exploit. To summarize the main idea here, it is the state relation that shapes the possibilities and personalities of those who enter the field and not the other way around. Or to be even more to the point, the Haitian state, as a structuration of a field of power between the Haitian peasantry and the outside world, is inherently a relation of violence. If we imagine overt political activity within the field of the state relation as a game, a very serious and lethal game, then we understand why "no one can take advantage of the game, not even those who dominate it, without being taken up and taken in by it" (ibid.: 307–308). Conceived as an international relation, we can understand the violence of the Haitian state as the enactment or performance of a relation of violence between the Haitian subalterns and the outside world.

Three Displacements

13. Once we make this basic move, conceiving the state as a relation of relations, we can no longer view Haiti as a world apart, but rather must inquire into the violent processes by which we (Haitians and their "others") have come to make it appear so, forced the imagining of separateness, constructed our mutual alienation. We can no longer understand the history of the Haitian state as a function merely of the nature or "character" of the persons who occupy its locations within the field of relations, and we can no longer see the Haitian peasantry as just victims but as active constructors of an identity and position for which they have come to pay a heroic but excruciating price. We can sketch the rough outlines of an alternative imaginary relief of Haiti through these three necessary displacements in the received vision of the Haitian social topography.

14. Against the illusion of separateness: The state relation is always international; it operates as a system for managing and containing as well as denying a *copresence*. Contrary to the orthodox state-centered image, international relations is not about the relationship of two or more atomistic subjects but is a struggle, always a combat, over the nature and shape of states. The state

itself — in both the restricted sense and the wider sense — is the outcome and medium, the structuration, of international relations, not their subject. In short, states don't *have* international relations; they *are* international relations. International war, civil war, and revolution are all inherently international (as well as domestic) processes, the stabilizing of which is accomplished by the formalization of a status (i.e., state formation). State-craft is a contested process of constructing eternalities. Returning to our focus, it is not, and never has been, accordingly, "the Haitians themselves" who have been responsible for the state of Haiti. In the contestation to define the Haitian state, the outside world has been a persistent presence, actively and continuously striving to impose its will through an endless variety of modalities: repeated invasion, embargo, indemnity, denigration, nonrecognition, trade, regular interference and outright occupation, receivership, quarantine, military training, economic advice and (conditioned) support, destabilization, the cultivation of agents of influence, embargo, "intervasion," reform, and on and on.[12] The formation, or rather the deformation, of the Haitian state fosters an illusion of separateness, a mode of containment and manipulation of a copresence. What we call the government *of Haiti* is not necessarily a government *by Haitians,* and has never been a government by Haitians alone. There has never been an effective (I use the term in the minimalist legal sense) government in Haiti (or anywhere else) that is not a compromise with outside powers. The very form of the state has been the negotiated outcome of a power struggle, and the structure of government at any given moment registers the current balance of power in a continuous struggle.[13] In other words, what we call the state, including the institutions of government, is itself the crystallization, the form, of a complex power relation between peoples.

15. Furthermore, as a structuration, the government of Haiti is the medium/outcome of a relation of only putative exteriorities. In fact, the formation of states is intrinsic to the formation of two cultures' separate identities. On the Haitian side, formal "recognition" of the Haitian government and state, always conditional and revocable, has meant the enforcement of a boundary, a limit whose minimally obscured reverse face has always been some form of subordination (indemnity, intervention, occupation, and beginning in 1994, "intervasion" and externally mandated liberalization and "democratization"). Today, as in the past, recognition of statehood, the juridical constitution of separateness, proceeds on the basis of what statehood seems to deny — a convergence of (elite) interest. Haitian independence is predicated on elite interdependence. Haitian elites benefit from a power container that cages Haitian masses in semi-insular isolation; the narrow boundaries of Haitians' life chances are fixed territorially. On the American side, restoration of Haitian "sovereignty" implies the repair of a social and political boundary, the

reconstitution of a limit to complicity, obligation, and responsibility. Haitian "sovereignty" becomes a solution to the refugee problem, the economic problem, the problems of epidemic contagion. What Paul Farmer (1994: 232) has called the "uses of Haiti" — "Haiti as a source of infection or boat people, Haiti as stereotypical other, Haiti as confirmation of one's worst racist theories, Haiti as exemplifying a 'cultural problem,' Haiti as all-around whipping boy" — are unending.

16. International state-making in Haiti has been based on a fundamentally flawed premise: that by changing the nature of the persons who occupy the space of government, you change the nature of the state. The common sense behind recent international statecraft in Haiti has been the assumption that the problem is rooted in character. The root cause of the failure of Haiti's governments, according to a widely shared premise, is moral failure — the failure of Haiti's elites to take responsibility for ending the corruption and violence that have long plagued public life and, ultimately, the failure of Haiti's people to demand anything better. Haiti's sheer intractability, the massive inertia of its political institutions and the incorrigibility of its economic and political leadership, are taken to be symptomatic of the depth of corruption into which the Haitian people have fallen. That the practices and habits that predominate in Haiti's civil and political spheres have their roots in a structured field of social relations extending far beyond the island of Hispaniola, that they may reflect perduring patterns of international conflict and local repertoires of strategic action formed and reinforced during two centuries of struggle with the world beyond, and that those structures and that struggle were little transformed by the events of the 1990s — these possibilities find no place in the imagination of Haiti's observers and critics.

17. If we understand the inalienability of land and the spirituality of vodoun as rooted in subaltern strategies of resistance, then the consequences of this strategic preference appear in a new light. What we outsiders typically describe as poverty and underdevelopment are actually the manifestations not of a lack, but of a positive assertion, a choice, an act of will and strategic intelligence developed and sustained during two hundred years of struggle. What we regard as the symptoms of ignorance and poverty, and of ungovernability, are rather the consequences, unintended but accepted as necessary, of a heroic refusal to be overwhelmed and of a protracted struggle to persevere in the struggle for liberty against tremendous natural and human opposition.

The Limits of International Statecraft

18. Something "new": the definition and practice of international statecraft in Haiti. The latest and most ambitious effort by the outside world to transform

the state of Haiti began the morning of September 19, 1994, with the arrival of a "multinational force" of ultimately about 30,000 (mostly U.S., 1 percent other) military personnel. While explicitly disavowing any pretension or responsibility for "nation-building," the international community undertook to reconstruct the visible apparatus of the Haitian state from the ground up. During the two years that followed the "intervasion," and while U.S. operational control over the successive UN mission was preserved, the international presence could count a number of successes: general conditions of personal security was restored, and the legitimate, democratically elected president returned to office; the Haitian army was disbanded; a new national police force of 5,300 was recruited and trained; the notorious *chefs de section* system of officially sanctioned rural thuggery was eliminated, and local government placed in the hands of 2,000 elected officials; a new school for magistrates was established to develop competency in administering justice, training for prison staffs was provided, and new rules were promulgated for assuring transparency and minimal guarantees of due process and respect for basic rights.[14] Less touted—indeed, not mentioned at all in the many self-congratulatory pronouncements issued by Clinton administration officials in the several months following the intervention—was the repatriation of more than 75,000 boat people who had sought refuge in the United States, and scores of thousands more from the Bahamas and elsewhere in the Caribbean. But, of course, this too was part of the restoration of the "integrity" of Haiti, and perhaps its most enduring accomplishment.

19. The error of formalism: failure to transform the social field. The international community seems to have fallen prey to an illusion, an illusion with a motive, that by changing the form of government, it has transformed the state. As I have argued, basis of the power of government (like that of language) is contextual; the energy and power of government rest not in the government itself, but in the nature of the wider field of social power in which it is embedded. A change of governmental form is of enormous potential importance. In Haiti it led to a moment of great hope and to the first election of a popular leader. But without a fundamental change in the wider field of power, there can be little hope of a change in the pattern of Haitian politics. The relation between the Haitian subaltern masses and the outside world remains one of violence; the democratic moment actually reveals this. The hope of the self-styled agents of the international community has been that by bringing democratic form to Haiti's government, the Haitian people would willingly begin to dismantle strategies they had developed during two centuries of struggle. When instead they chose to make the institutions of government instruments of their own purposes during the first months of the Aristide administration, the "international community" hesitated, opening

the door to a coup d'état, and then blamed Aristide's Lavalas government for bringing on the coup with its imprudent and irresponsible policies. The restoration of democratic government three years later did not bring the restoration of popular government, but the restoration of popular figureheads for a government whose basic policies were determined from outside by those who exercised the effective monopoly of the legitimate use of force.

20. Denouement: repression, revolution, or degeneration. If Haiti's state is to be transformed, it follows from the foregoing analysis that there must be a radical transformation of both the micro and macro frameworks of everyday life, both the domestic and international relationships that define Haiti's "state." To achieve such revolutionary change, there are two roads ahead: one liberal and capitalist, the other more democratic. If the liberal capitalist road — the path preferred by Haiti's would-be rescuers in the "international community" — then there needs to be a radical transformation of social relations, particularly with respect to the inalienability of land.[15] Title and property must be established, and land must become a tradable commodity in order for the economic "medicine" to work effectively.[16] Of course, powerful forces are working toward a restructuring of social relations in the countryside. The ecological limits of the land have imposed a powerful constraint on the Haitian subalterns' time-worn strategies. Today those limits have imposed a bleak choice: progressive malnourishment, migration to the city, or both. But even such powerful natural forces do not produce the capitalist revolution in land tenure that is desired by so many powerful outsiders as a fix for Haiti's problems. For that, a great deal of coercive force would be necessary, which would meet with extraordinary resistance and require massive repression. No such effective force exists in Haiti, and the international powers have shown little desire to take on the job themselves. Since the late 1980s a second alternative has taken the form of a far-reaching popular democracy. Yet such a transformative restructuring of social power was/is bound to invite violent resistance — in this event, a military coup. Since 1994, the "international community" has held the balance in its hand. Unwilling to employ the force required to reconstruct Haiti in their own image, and unable finally to let go, Haiti's fixers have been engaged in a practical and moral balancing act. The result has been a progressive dwindling of options and hope, along with the recrudescence of the familiar and tragic patterns of violence and counterviolence — in short, the preservation of Haiti's state.

Notes

The chapter epigraph is a Creole saying, quoted in Dayan 1995: 97. In preparing this essay and learning about Haiti, I have been most profoundly influenced by the work of Joan

Dayan (1991, 1995), Michel-Rolphe Trouillot (1980, 1990, 1995), and Drexel Woodson (1990) — and by brief visits I made to Haiti in October 1996 and April 1998. Because this essay, or rather this beginning of an essay, would have been impossible without the visit, I dedicate it to my sister, Sofia Clark d'Escoto, who not only bought the plane tickets but, leading Dana Gaboury Clark and me by the hand, utterly transformed the sensorium of our lived world.

1   Bourdieu et al. 1991, especially "Part One — The break" and "Part Two — Constructing the object."

2   The basic move, labeling the state the "*res publica* — the public reification, no less," was first crystallized in an essay by Philip Abrams (1988). Michael Taussig (1992) has extended this analysis to show how reification is followed by deification.

3   Here I have in mind not only the scattered remarks of Bourdieu (e.g., 1981; Bourdieu and Wacquant 1992) and Foucault (1980, 1984) on the state, but the broader analyses of fields and relations of power in which these remarks are set.

4   See Michael Mann's displacement of state power (1993, especially pp. 1–91) in a historically variable four-fold field of social power and his characteristic assertion that "*the state need have no final unity or even consistency*" (56; emphasis in original).

5   Besides the contributions of the "world-systems" school (e.g., Arrighi; Wallerstein) and the Latin American dependency theorists, neither of which have until recently focused on the state as the *form* of the relation, there is also the unexploited insight of Anthony Giddens that "the development of the sovereignty of the modern state from its beginnings depends upon a system of reflexively monitored set of relations between states. . . . 'International relations' are not connections set up between pre-established states, which could maintain their sovereign power without them: they are the basis upon which the nation-state exists at all" (1987: 263–264).

6   It is now commonplace in social theory to deny that "societies" actually exist. But see Touraine: "In point of fact, what classical sociology calls society is nothing but the confusion of a social activity — which can be defined in broad terms as industrial production or the marketplace — with a national State. The unity of a society proceeds from the legitimate power with which it endows itself. Its boundaries are not theoretical but real: they are marked by its border customs office. Society is a pseudonym for fatherland" (1988: 4).

7   For examples of the many different kinds of empirical analysis that become available, see Corrigan and Sayer; Coronil; Elias; Ferguson (esp. pp. 272–274); Gupta; Hale; Taussig; and the essays in Joseph and Nugent.

8   Compare Marx: "Society does not consist of individuals, but expresses the sum of interrelations, the relations within which these individuals stands. As if someone were to say: Seen from the perspective of society, there are no slaves and no citizens: both are human beings. Rather, they are that outside of society. To be a slave, to be a citizen, are social characteristics, relations between human beings" (*Grundrisse* [London: Penguin, 1973], pp. 264–265; quoted in Corrigan and Sayer, *The Great Arch,* p. 6. One cannot simply substitute the term "society," as Marx uses it above, for my notion of state. It is the state, understood as pervasive social field, that defines (or rather creates the illusion of) "society."

9   Both vodoun and smallholding agriculture existed before the slave insurrection, operating within the interstices of the plantation system, and elements of both can clearly be traced to African practices. Yet both were thoroughly reworked, incorporating many new elements (Amerindian names, beliefs, and materials; Roman Catholic saints and liturgies; plantation technologies and crops) and reconfiguring many ostensibly continuous "elements" of belief and practice within a new form.

10 See Dayan 1991; Bellegarde-Smith 1994.

11 See, for example, Lundahl (1992: 3):

> Superimposed on the purely economic mechanisms is the factor of government quality. A central theme in several of the essays in the present volume is that Haiti has never had an honest government. During the course of the nineteenth century a predatory state, run by a variety of kleptocratic cliques, gradually emerged. The foundations were laid for a tradition that is still very strong in Haiti. This, in turn, means that the government has done very little to further technological change, education, health and nutrition, and credit in rural areas. The peasants have been subject to heavy taxation without receiving anything for their money. In rural Haiti, the state is a distant entity, one which had better be avoided if at all possible.

> The proposed future study of Haiti would seek to reevaluate and displace the keywords "superimposed," "honest," "tradition," and "distant."

12 Just as the outside world has been a persistent presence in Haiti, so has Haiti (so feared that Jefferson dared not speak its name) been in the history of the United States. See Mathewson; Hunt; Dash; Egerton; Farmer; Zuckerman; and Tucker and Hendrickson.

13 This struggle has both internal and external dimensions, but internal and external should not be viewed as marking out different struggles. The internal struggle is overdetermined by the question of the degree of accommodation to outsiders — as, for example, in the primordial struggle over plantation and peasant agriculture — while the external struggle is profoundly shaped by the internal contest — as in the continuance by former plantation slaves of the revolutionary war against France despite the capitulations of the elite black military leaders Toussaint Louverture, Jean-Jacques Dessalines, and Henry Christophe. The presence of the internal contest within the external one, what Michel-Rolph Trouillot has called "the war within the war," is regularly suppressed in nationalist historiographies. For a compelling description of the ways in which this active silencing works in the case of Haiti, see Trouillot's "The Three Faces of Sans Souci: Glory and Silences of the Haitian Revolution," in his *Silencing the Past*.

14 See the following, all from the *U.S. Department of State Dispatch:* Madeleine K. Albright, "Keeping Faith with the People of Haiti," vol. 6, no. 7 (February 13, 1995): 93; President Clinton, UN Secretary General Boutros Boutros-Ghali, President Aristide, "Haiti: A Time of Peaceful Transition," vol. 6, no. 15 (April 10, 1995): 283–285; Secretary Christopher, "Honor and Respect: The Watchwords of Haiti's Democratic Police Force," vol. 6, no. 24 (June 12, 1995): 493; James F. Dobbins, Special Haiti Coordinator, "Elections in Haiti: An Important Milestone," vol. 6, no. 29 (July 17, 1995): 567–569; and "Assessing the Progress of Haitian Democracy," vol. 6, no. 39 (September 25, 1995): 709–710; Vice President Gore, "Haiti: Celebrating One Year of the Return to Freedom and Democracy," vol. 6, no. 44 (October 30, 1995): 792–793; Alexander F. Watson, Assistant Secretary for Inter-American Affairs, "Support for Democracy and the Rule of Law in Haiti," vol. 7, no. 14 (April 1, 1996): 169–172.

15 For more than a decade, U.S. agencies have been concerned about the political risks of any attempt to transform the Haitian economy by transforming property relations in the countryside. As William Robinson reports: "A 1985 World Bank report stated that domestic consumption had to be 'markedly restrained in order to shift the required share of output increases into exports . . . [emphasis should be placed on] the expansion of private enterprises. . . . Private projects with high economic returns should be strongly supported [over] public expenditures in the social sectors [and] less emphasis should be placed on social objectives which increase consumption.' An AID [U.S. Agency for International

Development] report was candid: 'AID anticipates that such a drastic reorientation of agriculture will cause a decline in income and nutritional status, especially for small farmers and peasants. . . . Even if transition to export agriculture is successful, AID anticipates a "massive" displacement of peasant farmers and migration to urban centers' " (271).

16   Consider the observation of Mats Lundahl (1996: 120–121): "The Haitian peasant is well-known for the ability to ingratiate him or herself with outsiders. In so doing, many basic facts of rural life may be deliberately concealed. Thus, it is never quite clear to the potential intruder just where the real centers of authority and power lie. The importance of voodoo is consciously downplayed, and the inner workings of the secret societies are not revealed. Technical advisors who attempt to enter into a dialogue with the peasants may find themselves suddenly dealing with all kinds of committees, apparently organized spontaneously, in which it is difficult to ascertain just who is really exerting authority, so that development projects are often left to decay as soon as outside observers have left the scene. Finally, when intrusion threatens to take place, verbal skills (dissuasion, mockery, and the like) are mobilized and brought to bear, and, if need be, violence as well. Thus, to conclude, for a concentration of land to take place, a number of obstacles — *most of deliberate design* — have to be overcome." I have added emphasis to stress the acknowledgment of the peasants' agency in resisting outside efforts to restructure the Haitian economy.

Works Cited

Abrams, Philip. "Notes on the Difficulty of Studying the State." *Journal of Historical Sociology* 1 (1988): 58–89.

Arrighi, Giovanni. *The Long Twentieth Century: Money, Power, and the Origins of Our Times.* London: Verso, 1994.

Bellegarde-Smith, Patrick. "Renewed Traditions: Contrapuntal Voices in Haitian Social Organization." In *Imagining Home: Class, Culture, and Nationalism in the African Diaspora,* ed. Sidney J. Lemelle and Robin D. G. Kelley. London: Verso, 1994.

Besson, Jean. "Symbolic Aspects of Land in the Caribbean: The Tenure and Transmission of Land Rights among Caribbean Peasantries." In *Peasants, Plantations, and Rural Communities in the Caribbean,* ed. Malcolm Cross and Arnaud Marks, Department of Sociology, University of Surrey, and Department of Caribbean Studies, Royal Institute of Linguistics and Anthropology. Leiden: Netherlands, 1979.

Bhadra, Gautam, Gyan Prakash, and Susie Tharu, eds. *Subaltern Studies X: Writings on South Asian History and Society.* New Delhi: Oxford University Press, 1999.

Bourdieu, Pierre. *Language and Symbolic Power.* Trans. Gino Raymond and Matthew Adamson. Cambridge, Mass.: Harvard University Press, 1991a.

——. "Men and Machines." In *Advances in Social Theory and Methodology: Toward an Integration of Micro- and Macro-Sociologies,* ed. K. Knorr-Cetina and A. V. Cicourel. Boston: Routledge, 1981.

——. "Social Space and Symbolic Power." *In Other Words: Essays Towards a Reflexive Sociology.* Trans. Matthew Adamson. Stanford, Calif.: Stanford University Press, 1991b.

Bourdieu, Pierre, Jean-Claude Chamboredon, and Jean-Claude Passeron. *The Craft of Sociology: Epistemological Preliminaries.* Berlin: de Gruyter, 1991.

Bourdieu, Pierre, and Loïc J. D. Wacquant. *An Invitation to Reflexive Sociology.* Chicago: University of Chicago Press, 1992.

Coronil, Fernando. *The Magical State: Nature, Money, and Modernity in Venezuela*. Chicago: University of Chicago Press, 1997.

Corrigan, Philip. "State Formation." In *Everyday Forms of State Formation,* ed. Gilbert Joseph and Daniel Nugent. Durham, N.C.: Duke University Press, 1994.

Corrigan, Philip, and Derek Sayer. *The Great Arch: English State Formation as Cultural Revolution*. 2nd ed. Oxford: Blackwell, 1992.

Dash, Michael J. *Haiti and the United States: National Stereotypes and the Literary Imagination*. New York: St. Martin's Press, 1988.

Dayan, Joan. *Haiti, History, and the Gods*. Berkeley: University of California Press, 1995.

——. "Vodoun, or the Voice of the Gods." *Raritan* 10, 3 (1991): 32–57.

Derrida, Jacques. "Structure, Sign, and Play in the Discourse of the Human Sciences." *Writing and Difference*. Trans. Alan Bass. Chicago: University of Chicago Press, 1978.

Egerton, Douglas R. *Gabriel's Rebellion: The Virginia Slave Conspiracies of 1800 and 1802*. Chapel Hill: University of North Carolina Press, 1993.

Elias, Norbert. *The Civilizing Process: The History of Manners and State Formation and Civilization*. Oxford: Blackwell, 1994.

Fabian, Johannes. *Time and the Other: How Anthropology Makes Its Object*. New York: Columbia University Press, 1983.

Farmer, Paul. *The Uses of Haiti*. Monroe, Maine: Common Courage Press, 1994.

Ferguson, James. *The Anti-Politics Machine: "Development," Depoliticization, and Bureaucratic Power in Lesotho*. Minneapolis: University of Minnesota Press, 1994.

Foucault, Michel. "Afterword: The Subject and Power." In *Michel Foucault: Beyond Structuralism and Hermeneutics,* ed. Hubert L. Dreyfus and Paul Rabinow. 2nd ed. Chicago: University of Chicago Press, 1983.

——. *Power/Knowledge: Selected Interviews and Other Writings, 1972–1979,* ed. Colin Gordon. New York: Pantheon, 1980.

Giddens, Anthony. *The Nation-State and Violence*. Berkeley: University of California Press, 1987.

Guha, Ranajit, and Gayatri Chakravorty Spivak, eds. *Selected Subaltern Studies*. New York: Oxford University Press, 1988.

Gupta, Akhil. "Blurred Boundaries: The Discourse of Corruption, the Culture of Politics, and the Imagined State." *American Ethnologist* 22, 2 (1995): 375–402.

Hale, Charles. *Resistance and Contradiction: Miskitu Indians and the Nicaraguan State, 1894–1987*. Stanford, Calif.: Stanford University Press, 1994.

Hunt, Alfred N. *Haiti's Influence on Antebellum America: Slumbering Volcano in the Caribbean*. Baton Rouge: Louisiana State University Press, 1988.

Joseph, Gilbert, and Daniel Nugent. *Everyday Forms of State Formation: Revolution and the Negotiation of Rule in Modern Mexico*. Durham, N.C.: Duke University Press, 1994.

Laclau, Ernesto. "Metaphor and Social Antagonisms." In *Marxism and the Interpretation of Culture,* ed. Cary Nelson and Lawrence Grossberg. Urbana: University of Illinois Press, 1988.

Larose, Serge. "The Haitian Lakou: Land, Family, and Ritual." In *Family and Kinship in Middle America and the Caribbean,* ed. Arnaud F. Marks and Rene A. Romer. Leiden, Netherlands: Institute of Higher Studies, Curaçao, Netherlands Antilles, and Department of Caribbean Studies of the Royal Institute of Linguistics and Anthropology, 1978.

Lundahl, Mats. "Income and Land Distribution in Haiti: Some Remarks on Available Statistics." *Journal of Interamerican Studies and World* 38, 2/3 (1996): 109–126.

——. *Politics or Markets? Essays on Haitian Underdevelopment*. London: Routledge, 1992.

Mann, Michael. *The Sources of Social Power.* Vol. 2, *The Rise of Classes and Nation-States, 1760–1914.* Cambridge: Cambridge University Press, 1993.

Marx, Karl. *Grundrisse.* Trans. Martin Nicolaus. New York: Vintage, 1973.

Mathewson, Tim. "Jefferson and Haiti." *Journal of Southern History* 61, 2 (1995): 209–248.

Mintz, Sidney W. *Caribbean Transformations.* Chicago: Aldine, 1974.

Robinson, William I. *Promoting Polyarchy: Globalization, U.S. Intervention, and Hegemony.* Cambridge: Cambridge University Press, 1996.

Taussig, Michael. *The Magic of the State.* New York: Routledge, 1997.

———. "Maleficium: State Fetishism." *The Nervous System.* New York: Routledge, 1992.

Touraine, Alain. *Return of the Actor: Social Theory in Postindustrial Society.* Trans. Myrna Godzich. 1984. Reprint, Minneapolis: University of Minnesota Press, 1988.

Trouillot, Michel-Rolph. "Discourses of Rule and the Acknowledgment of the Peasantry in Dominica, W.I., 1838–1928." *American Ethnologist* 16 (4) 1989: 704–718.

———. *Haiti, State against Nation: The Origins and Legacy of Duvalierism.* New York: Monthly Review Press, 1990.

———. Review of *Peasants and Poverty,* by Mats Lundahl. *Journal of Peasant Studies* 8, 1 (1980): 112–116.

———. *Silencing the Past: Power and the Production of History.* Boston: Beacon, 1995.

Tucker, Robert W., and David C. Hendrickson. *Empire of Liberty: The Statecraft of Thomas Jefferson.* Oxford: Oxford University Press, 1990.

Wallerstein, Immanuel. *The Modern World System.* 3 vols. New York: Academic Press, 1974, 1980, 1988.

Woodson, Drexel. *Tout Mounn Se Mounn, Men Tout Mounn Pa Menm: Microlevel Sociocultural Aspects of Land Tenure in a Northern Haitian Locality.* 3 vols. Ph.D. diss., University of Chicago, 1990.

Zuckerman, Michael. "The Power of Blackness: Thomas Jefferson and the Revolution in St. Domingue." *Almost Chosen People: Oblique Biographies in the American Grain.* Berkeley: University of California Press, 1993.

Death in the Andes: Ungovernability and the Birth of Tragedy in Peru

GARETH WILLIAMS

The bourgeoisie, by the rapid improvement of all instruments of production, by the immensely facilitated means of communication, draws all, even the most barbarian, nations into civilization. . . . It compels all nations, on pain of extinction, to adopt the bourgeois mode of production; it compels them to introduce what it calls civilization into their midst; ie., to become bourgeois themselves. In a word, it creates a world after its own image. — Karl Marx and Friedrich Engels, *Manifesto*

Todo blanco es, más o menos, un Pizarro, un Valverde o un Areche. — Manuel González Prada, "Nuestros indios"

As the new century begins, it appears that we are obliged to invert Marx's famous opening to *The Manifesto of the Communist Party* and state, now, that a specter is haunting the twenty-first century — the specter of neoliberalism. Given the events of recent years, the original adage ("A specter is haunting Europe — the specter of communism"), taken up by Derrida in *Specters of Marx,* has apparently become subsumed under the free-market economic and social doctrines that seem to be taking the world by storm. As Joseph Collins and John Lear inform us in the opening of their book *Chile's Free-Market Miracle: A Second Look:* "By millenium's close, free-market ideology is likely to have radically altered the lives of far more people and nations than any other ideology in history. The best government is the least government, we are told. Government planning, government regulation, government corporations and government social programs are all losers. Let private enterprise, market forces, and free trade reign!" (3).

Yet free-market ideology does not signify the dismantling of state practices, nor the state's desire to no longer intervene in the social arena, which is what it always likes to tell us. Rather, the contemporary restructuring of the social sphere through market-based control depends for its success on state-sponsored "deregulation" and the masquerade of a division between the state and the Darwinist workings of the postmodern marketplace. As Hernando de

Soto puts it in his Peruvian handbook for neoliberal governability, *The Other Path* (for which the novelist Mario Vargas Llosa, wrote the foreword): "Deregulation involves depoliticizing the economy in order to protect the state from the manipulation of redistributive combines, and the economy from politicians just as the church was separated from the state" (249). It is the state that takes it upon itself to maintain the illusion of a division of state and politics from economic life, and this illusion provides the foundations for the neoliberal success story: namely, the increasing "casualization" of the labor force, the free-floating logic and endemic poverty of the informal economy, the increasing "feminization" of poverty as young women and adolescents are increasingly integrated into the unskilled workforce through the *maquiladora* system of production, and enormous state intervention designed to manage potential conflict by constantly sticking state fingers into the dike of never-ending social antagonisms, rather than actually dealing with the terrain from which antagonism emerges.

All of this presupposes an ideally irreversible transformation of relations between state and society under neoliberalism that alters governmental configurations and the means of governability perhaps forever.[1] The overriding power of the market to mediate and control the lives of millions is consolidated by a state that now legitimates itself in the face of transnational capital by advocating the collective benefits of corporate downsizing: reducing public spending, redirecting social policies, decentralizing and debureaucratizing state apparatuses, and increasing the efficiency of state practices. All of this leads to the redimensioning of the limits of the state and, in particular, of public policies that no longer confront the question of social or of national integration, but interest themselves rather more in the maintenance of the marketplace as the principal form of managing social interactions and potential conflicts between classes, genders, ethnicities, and regions. As Norbert Lechner puts it, within the logic of World Bank and IMF-sponsored development, the systemic competitivity of the nation in the world market means that local or national political decisions now become "overdetermined" exclusively by their eventual economic impact (65).[2]

Of course, the passage to neoliberalism — to the dominance of late capitalism's privileged ideology — has not come without a price. The last twenty years on the capitalist periphery are best characterized by crisis and catastrophe. As Joseph Collins and John Lear inform us, the United Nations in 1990 estimated that in many Third World countries the percentage of citizens deprived of jobs, adequate food, housing, health and education was higher than even during the worldwide depression in the 1930s (4). And in Latin America, of course, the 1980s is now referred to the "lost decade."

The current dilemma for contemporary reflection, then, is grounded precisely in the ungroundedness of contemporary experience and in the seemingly impossible demand to seek out zones of critical practice that might allow us to imagine a desirable future order of experience, a point of historical transcendence somewhere beyond the logics of the omnipotent market and the current casualized order of things. But while it is obvious that neoliberalism and the workings of the neoliberal state are the horizons of a new political and intellectual task in Latin America, as Fredric Jameson puts it, "We do not have the terms and categories ready to describe what succeeds civil society as such, when the latter's collapse is not a regression, but rather the accompaniment of an even more advanced form of economic development" (155).

The redefinition of the public sphere is structurally indispensable to postmodern capital itself. It is also the slippery ground that brings us to the limit-experience of contemporary thought and of its ability to think past the end of the end. Neoliberalism and the increasingly transnational restructuring of collective experience, hailed by Francis Fukuyama as a felicitous post-Cold War "end of History," mark the experiential and political limit to our ability to map out the conditions of possibility for a theory of future change. In order to carry out such a task, perhaps *the* intellectual demand of our times is to engage in an affirmative deconstruction of the epistemological and political limits of neoliberal cultural politics and state practices; to question the limits of the neoliberal knowledge-machine and its production of the world, in order to reveal regions of discontinuity between the advanced countries' projects on the periphery and the latter's uneven assimilation of those projects; to call attention, in other words, to the limits of postmodern singularity and irreducibility that stubbornly persist and occasionally rise to the surface of contemporary geopolitical configurations.

If we consider subalternity, as Gayatri Spivak suggests, as "necessarily the absolute limit of the place where history is narrativized into logic" (16), then our task might well be to try to reflect further on the cognitive and agential boundaries of the subaltern in order to strive to produce a new form of reading and thinking contemporary state practices, together with those cultural configurations that intertwine and impact upon them, and are produced by them. Since, as Edward Said reminds us, subaltern or popular practices cannot be extricated from elite or hegemonic practices, but rather construe themselves as different but overlapping and curiously interdependent territories through history (viii), then an effective subalternist practice would have to analyze the means by which the dominant objects of hegemony are thought through, constructed, and represented at the present time. One has to wonder whether it is only by reading from *within* the grain of hegemonic culture's archive — of literature, for example, and of intellectual history — that one can read against it and engage subaltern knowledge production in light of its negative potentiality (if, indeed, there is any).

This, then, would not require merely a separatist or essentialist practice of subaltern "voice" restitution, agency recuperation, or identity restoration (which has become so typical of many forms of identity politics in recent years), but rather would require reflection on the subaltern as an allegory of the predicament of thought and of deliberative consciousness itself (Spivak, 12), a locus of subaltern enunciation that would demand a subalternist reading deeply imbued with the potentiality of deconstruction: "A theory of change as the site of the displacement of function between sign-systems ... is a theory of reading in the strongest possible general sense. The site of displacement of the function of signs is the name of reading as active transaction between past and future. This transactional reading as (the possibility of) action, even at its most dynamic, is perhaps what Antonio Gramsci meant by 'elaboration', *e-laborare,* working out" (Spivak, 4–5).

My intention in this essay is to propose Mario Vargas Llosa's recent novel, *Lituma en los Andes* (*Death in the Andes*) — his first novel published after running for president in the Peruvian elections of 1990 — as an indispensable (yet an unintentionally indispensable) intervention into the cultural logics and political terrain of peripheral neoliberalism, an essential document for reading and "working out" the limits of neoliberal governability and ungovernability in contemporary Peru. By calling attention to certain impasses in the transcultural "contact zone" between Creole and indigenous cultural practices, my reading will lead us inevitably to the question and agency of cognitive failure, and to Creole hegemony's inability to reflect upon a zone of epistemic breakdown that nevertheless remains foundational to the successful application of neoliberal thought. This, in turn, will lead us to the counterpointal elaboration of a popular "primal scene" of colonialism that is actively "worked through" by the subaltern masses as a collective political language that remains beyond the workings of the state, and remains foundational to the development of semiautonomous pockets of collective expression in Lima. It is the haunting existence and return to everyday urban life of this colonial primal scene — indicative of a modern "cholo" historical consciousness conjuring up, re-presenting from beyond the workings of commodity fetishism, the sedimented ghosts of communal and kindred dismemberment — that potentializes the unleashing of popular ungovernability and points inevitably to the elaboration of possible future challenges to the institutional logics of neoliberal control, governmentality, and crisis management in contemporary Peru.

To describe Peruvian social existence over the last couple of decades, we could easily conjure up the spirit of Walter Benjamin, particularly the phrase from his famous essay "Theses on the Philosophy of History," in which he states that "the tradition of the oppressed teaches us that the 'state of emergency' in which we live is not the exception but the rule" (259). In Peru there is an expression for the popular experience of the "state of emergency" of recent years: *manchay tiempo*. As Starn, Degregori, and Kirk inform us, this is a hybrid of Quechua and Spanish meaning "time of fear," which, while emerging after the Sendero Luminoso's declaration of war on the Peruvian state and the latter's efforts to counter it in the first two years of the 1980s, refers rather more to the period beginning with the war's intensification in 1983, and to its continuation through to the end of the eighties (339).

"Manchay tiempo" refers, then, to subaltern knowledge of the cultural politics of the "Lost Decade" in Peru, to a time characterized by the popular experience of terror, the Latin American debt crisis, hyperinflation, the imposition of IMF austerity programs (Starn et al., 419), and the horror and anxiety with which these *paquetazos* were received by the urban poor, particularly migrant Indian and cholo populations. It refers to a time characterized by the increasing perception among the poor that the state had lost all legitimacy, and to the knowledge that Creole notions of urban culture and national identity were being systematically eroded by the Andean migrant populations' flooding of Lima's streets. It points to a period in which the number of Indian and cholo poor exploded in the capital city while roads, hospitals, and communications systems fell apart at the seams, thereby prompting the ever-diminishing middle classes to look back nostalgically to the years following the Second World War as the halcyon days of Peruvian modernity (Starn et al., 419).

Even back in the late sixties, the sense of something having fallen apart reigned supreme. In the opening lines of Mario Vargas Llosa's 1969 novel *Conversación en la catedral,* Santiago (the protagonist) expresses with eloquent pathos the sense of bewilderment and hopelessness that has come to epitomize what might be called "the Peruvian condition": "¿En qué momento se había jodido el Perú?" (13) [At what moment did Peru fuck up?]. One could only conjecture as to what this sane character would say today, thirty years later, after living through the years of mass labor and shantytown mobilization promoted in the late sixties and seventies by the military regimes, after the stalemate of redemocratization in the early eighties, the onslaught of foreign debt, hyperinflation, rampant corruption, a brutal guerrilla war, so-called "liberated zones," *narcotráfico,* mass internal migration, and the relentless Andeanization of the capital, and all of this on top of a disastrous El Niño in 1983, and in 1990 a novelist, Mario Vargas Llosa, running for president, fully backed by national and international capital, fully armed with the Reaganite/Thatcherite rhetoric of the eighties, who nonetheless lost to a complete unknown who then proceeded to close Parliament, to install authoritarian neoliberal eco-

nomic reforms, to ally himself to the more conservative factions of the Peruvian military. As Starn, Degregori, and Kirk put it, over the last decade and a
half "no country has shared Peru's sheer quantity of calamity, recorded in line
graphs of health, social welfare, and productivity indicators pitched as steeply
downward as the Andes themselves" (419).

The history of Peru, it seems, is the history of repeated failed attempts to
form a nation-state capable of constituting itself as the bearer of what Marx
called the "illusory communal interests" of society (*German Ideology*, 54). If
the state can be conceived, as Philip Abrams puts it, as the device by which
subjection is legitimated in society, then we must recognize that a successful
state-forming ideology must take it upon itself to form an image or a myth of
cohesion, of purpose, independence, common sense, and morality (Abrams,
68). An effective state constructs a mythical illusion, an absence, as "a bid to
elicit support or tolerance of the insupportable or intolerable by presenting
them as something other than themselves, namely, legitimate, disinterested
domination" (Abrams, 76). Yet due to the abject nature of its colonial legacy — to the persistence and pervasiveness of neocolonial social relations and
practices of domination — the Peruvian state has never been capable of mysti-
fying things to such an extent that it ever appeared to be anything other than
what it is: the historically constituted Creole monopoly on domination, a
war machine deeply invested in the continued reproduction of regional-, eth-
nic-, class- and gender-based difference. The Peruvian nation-state has been
plagued by its own self-evidence precisely because it has not been able to
construct the mythical illusion that originates in the central philosophical
paradox of Enlightenment thought; namely, the state as the embodiment, at
one and the same time, of both the particular *and* the universal.

The great irony of the modern Peruvian state is that the colonial regime
promoted a sense of unity that the postcolonial republic was incapable of
reinforcing (Matos Mar, 22). Organized exclusively around the existence of
external demand, the colonial economy's mining and export networks created
a series of links that articulated the distinct regions of the territory and even
integrated the indigenous and Hispanic worlds into a certain asymmetry of
social relations. The colonial state was not a legitimate state by any means, as
Guamán Poma de Ayala so eloquently testifies to, but it was, as José Matos Mar
tells us, an omnipresent entity functioning in its role of directing and organizing society (22–23). The Creole republic, however, could never constitute
itself upon the basis of the integration of historical legacies, cultures, and
regional differences. It could never provide that illusory communal interest
that founds modern nation-states with a veil of mythical complementarity or
commonality. Rather, the postcolonial Peruvian state inevitably constructed itself on the terrain of a white-Indian/colonizer-colonized duality that founded

Peruvian modernity, its political thought, cultural production, and the collective tragedy that is postmodern Peru.

Yet, as Matos Mar informs us in *Desborde popular y crisis del estado,* the foundational presuppositions of modern thought in Peru are becoming increasingly redefined in recent years by the emergence of new social actors and political identities, alternative popular practices, and epistemologically undefinable cultural configurations that can no longer be conceptualized through the rubric of a strict white-Indian, colonizer-colonized, *costeño-andino,* city-country, modern-traditional, or civilization-barbarism duality. The mass indigenous migrations of recent decades have flooded the city streets, producing the hybrid cholo as an urban surplus element, an "outsider within," a new political and socioeconomic agent whose unpredictability is increasingly a force to be reckoned with. These are actors who, while calling attention to the epistemological and political limits of neoliberal cultural politics and state practices, equally test modernity's notions of urban and national culture, and its pervasively dualistic or separatist conceptualizations of Peruvian national identity; they remain modernity's limit-experience, perhaps even at times the potentially threatening specter of an uncontrollable, ungovernable, and unintelligible "other." And it is precisely in the question of ungovernability and incomprehensibility that Mario Vargas Llosa comes into the picture — on one hand as a vehement critic of contemporary Peruvian social configurations, yet on the other as a critic intimately linked to upholding the thought and logic of the dualistic Creole state.

Neoliberalism has unleashed on the public sphere populations, labor practices, and informal organizational forms that inevitably undermine the authority of the state that unleashed them, thereby producing local areas of practice and intervention that challenge the institutional logics of neoliberalism. This unleashing also produces the need for the state to control, co-opt, or depoliticize the specters of uncontrollability that constantly haunt its existence. It is from within this need to exorcise itself of its evil spirits that neoliberal discourses on the art of governing and of controlling its supplementary impulses take on a hue that is uncannily reminiscent of Sarmiento's "civilization versus barbarism," and of the social logics that would later give birth to modern *indigenismo,* and communism, in the 1920s.[3] Thus it is that before engaging Vargas Llosa and the scope of his portrayal of manchay tiempo in *Death in the Andes,* we need to lay the interpretive groundwork by thinking through the Peruvian novelist's connection to Nietzsche's *The Birth of Tragedy,* and his problematic relationship to José Carlos Mariátegui, the founder of Latin American marxism, modern indigenismo, and Peruvian communism.

Mariátegui, of course, sought to authorize the parameters of a singular cultural and national identity, and strived to lay the epistemological and political foundations for Peru's insertion into the major ideological currents of modernity by means of a compensatory regeneration of the figure of the Indian as a modernizing revolutionary force.[4] As Ofelia Schutte remarks, one of the most interesting aspects of Mariátegui's work, and of his *Seven Interpretive Essays on Peruvian Reality* in particular, is the state of debt that he immediately establishes with the work of Nietzsche. As she notes, apart from heading the book with a Nietzschean aphorism from the period of *The Wanderer and His Shadow* (27), in his preface to *Seven Interpretive Essays,* Mariátegui refers to the German philosopher as an author whose spirit is intimately linked to his own: "I bring together in this book, organized and annotated in seven essays, the articles that I published in *Mundial* and *Amauta* concerning some essential aspects of Peruvian reality. Like *Escena contemporánea,* therefore, this was not conceived of as a book. Better this way. My work has developed as Nietzsche would have wished. . . . And if I hope to have some merit recognized, it is that—following another of Nietzsche's precepts—I have written with my blood" (xxxv).

Indeed, in "El hombre y el mito" ["Man and myth"] Mariátegui's debt to Nietzsche is heightened, though remaining implicit, as he comes to identify the underlying spirit of the Peruvian social classes:

> What most clearly and obviously differentiates the bourgeoisie and the proletariat in this era is myth. The bourgeoisie finally has no myth. It has become incredulous, skeptical, nihilist. The reborn liberal myth has already aged. The proletariat has a myth: the social revolution. It moves toward this myth with a vehement and active faith. The bourgeoisie denies; the proletariat affirms. The bourgeois mind amuses itself with a rationalist critique of the methods, the theories, the technique of the revolutionaries. What incomprehension! The revolutionaries' power is not their science; it is in their faith, their passion, their will. It is a religious, mystical, spiritual power. It is the power of myth. (in *Heroic and Creative Meaning,* 144–145)

Mariátegui's creative, life-affirming social myth of proletarian passion, transgression, and unconstrained revolution in Peru appears to construct itself upon the appropriation and reworking of Nietzsche's *Birth of Tragedy* and the distinction that the latter establishes between the Apollonian and the Dionysian spirits. This famous distinction, as Steven Cresap informs us, refers to the conflict of two classical world structures that can perhaps be taken to stand for the originary political conflict of the West: the antagonism between two opposing formulations of communal life, of the state, and of civil society (107). Apollo—the founder of states, etymologically the "shining one," the deity of light, *principium individuationis,* the limits of a single image of the world, a restraining boundary, freedom from wilder impulses, the promise of civilization, repression; Dionysus — the forgetting of the self, the destruction of individuality, a mystical sense of commonality, transgression, the orgiastic spirit, the nether world, the ecstasy of ceremonial bloodletting, the experience of "union through primordial sundering." As Nietzsche puts it, in the rites of Dionysus, "the slave is a free man, now all the rigid and hostile boundaries that distress, despotism or 'impudent fashion' have erected between man and man break down" (17).[5] Marx and Engels also presented the underlying conflict of modern life as differential and liberational impulses emerging inevitably from within the constraints and boundaries of the nation-state under capitalism: "Modern bourgeois society with its relations of production, of exchange and of property, a society that has conjured up such gigantic means of production and of exchange, is like the sorceror who is no longer able to control the powers of the nether world whom he has called up by his spells" (*Manifesto*, 11). Thus it is that Mariátegui's definition of the Indian proletariat as a life-affirming revolutionary spirit inevitably ties the birth of Peruvian modernity, the birth of the Peruvian tragedy, let's say, to the struggle between those forces of social production that originated in, and imposed, the constraints and restraining boundaries of colonialism, of neocolonial governmentality, and those ungovernable collective and liberational impulses that emerge as primordial sundering from within the hostile boundaries of colonialism's order.

Moreover, these are precisely the forces that come to inhabit Mario Vargas Llosa's reading of manchay tiempo in Peru. As we shall see, however, Vargas Llosa, like Mariátegui before him, recuperates the specter of Nietzsche's distinction between the Apollonian and the Dionysian spirit as foundational to the Peruvian tragedy, yet he does so by completely sidestepping Mariátegui's revolutionary appropriation of the indigenous "labor of Dionysus" (Hardt and Negri). Rather, Vargas Llosa wipes the founding father of Latin American marxism off the political and cultural map, and returns to Nietzsche in order to filter the Apollonian and the Dionysian through a "hispanista" reappropriation of Sarmiento's civilization and barbarism paradigm, perhaps as a means of finally laying the body and history of indigenismo — and of Peruvian marxism, of course — to rest for once and for all. But the specters of Mariátegui and of the labor of Dionysus inevitably return to haunt Vargas Llosa, for he cannot account for the power of the subaltern imaginary as a locus of sedimented negativity and historicity.[6]

Death in the Andes is a murder mystery without a crime, without a body or a weapon, and therefore with nothing to investigate; in other words, it is detective fiction without the power of reason and intervention. The representative of Creole state law, Corporal Lituma, has been posted to Naccos, a frontier encampment uncomfortably close to one of the Sendero Luminoso's so-called liberated zones in the Andean highlands. There he finds himself enmeshed in a series of inexplicable disappearances for which no one has the answers—particularly not the Indian laborers who inhabit Naccos, constructing a road to no one knows where.

The object of Lituma's investigation is ultimately the "beyond" of Creole rationality—namely, the Andean nether world and the indigenous system of belief, or cosmo-vision, that structures the cultural landscape. Through his repeated contact with the mysterious shamanistic figures of Dionisio (the bisexual tavern owner and instigator of nocturnal high jinks) and Adriana (Dionisio's wife, a witch and slayer of evil spirits who, Lituma suspects, gives herself over to the orgiastic spirit with men other than Dionisio), Lituma becomes increasingly convinced that the disappearances belong not to the realm of the modern world's material interests of production and exchange, nor to resistance to those interests as seen in the agency of the Sendero Luminoso, but rather to the mysterious experience of the ritualistic and the sacred in what is portrayed as everyday Andean life. In fact, the disappearances belong simultaneously to the realms of the material and to the sacred. As a means of placing the evil spirits of the Andes who have become offended by the construction of a road through the mountains—the road being an obvious symbol of national integration, progress, and interregional communication taken from foundational texts of indigenismo such as Arguedas's *Yawar fiesta*—Dionisio and Adriana incite a series of human sacrifices to the gods aimed at avoiding the apocalypse, thereby keeping the Indian laborers in a job, and keeping intact the community that keeps their carnivalesque tavern open.[7] The victims, it is suggested, are outsiders or social marginals who are thrown down a mine shaft in a state of intoxication, the same state in which the anonymous executioners perform their transgressive functions. *Death in the Andes* is, then, an investigation into the logics of the always already lost object of Creole reason, law, morality, and state intervention: namely, the *apus*, *huancas*, *chancas*, *pishtacos*, and *nacaqs* of the Andean cultural landscape.

The narrative of Lituma's somewhat pathetic attempts to unlock both the mystery of the disappearances and the secrets of the Andean people, language, and culture are interspersed with narrative sequences depicting the barbarism of terrorist violence and persecution against the civilizing forces of white, educated innocents, state representatives, a merchant, and foreign capital. Thus, we are presented with a couple of French students who are bludgeoned to death as they travel by bus to Cuzco; with a Belgian ecologist who is captured in a "liberated zone" while carrying out research and is interrogated and stoned to death at dawn; with a herd of *vicuñas* belonging to a foreign enterprise who are mercilessly destroyed by the Sendero way up in the Andean highlands; with the respected governor of Andamarca, who escapes a Sendero attack by the skin of his teeth and witnesses the violence of Maoist popular justice, only to be later disappeared in Naccos under a pseudonym; and with an albino merchant who has sex with a young indigenous girl on his travels who is confronted by a Sendero death squad led by the now adolescent victim seeking revenge. The merchant escapes miraculously but then disappears in Naccos under suspicion of being a pishtaco, a bloodsucking evil spirit.

Throughout the novel the Andean cultural terrain is portrayed as a place of apocalyptically perverse enjoyment. The civilizing boundaries and foundational restraints of the "state-forming, homeland-producing Apollo"—the idealistic dream-state of the "shining one," in other words—here become translated into the perverse nightmare of the Shining Path's dogmatic war machine against the state and its inevitable ties to international capital. On the other hand, those Indians not directly linked to the Sendero—"innocent" Indians, in other words—congregate in Dionisio's tavern late at night and engage in drunken reveling, shadowy orgiastics, spirit-worship, sacrifice, and ultimately even cannibalism. The logics of the Sendero, suggests Vargas Llosa, can only be understood within the broader context of transgressive Indian practices. What is at stake in the reappearance of the Appollonian and of the Dionysian in *Death in the Andes,* then, is no longer the transformative or modernizing potentiality of the Indian, as in Mariátegui's portrayal of the underlying spirit of the Peruvian social classes, but rather the Indian's apparently barbaric relationship to enjoyment—an enjoyment viewed by Lituma, the incarnation of Creole state reason, to be a lack of enjoyment, a deprivation, an enjoyment in what is profoundly displeasurable or perverse to decent Creole culture. And this Indian pleasure in the profoundly displeasurable is played out through both guerrilla and nonguerrilla practices. It would seem to be all pervasive, omnipresent, and natural to the barbaric forces of Andean life.

In the novel, the Andes are always a space beyond the limits of Creole intelligibility, a frontier landscape in which language, morality, reason, law, and nation transgress their boundaries and disintegrate into an undefinable and unthinkable Indian commonality. The Andes thus stand for the apocalyptic horizon of epistemological breakdown and cognitive failure that undermines modernity, the nation, the state, and civilization. Quechua is little more than "barbaric music" (11), while the apparent inevitability of abject violence only serves to stereotype indigenous ties of kinship and community as they actively exclude the "gregarious" Creole from their logics: "'All of those deaths were like water off a duck's back for these highlanders' thought Lituma. The night before in Dionisio's tavern he had heard the news of the attack on the bus in Andahuaylas and not one of those laborers who were there, drinking and eating, even passed the slightest comment. 'I'll never understand a fucking thing that goes on around here' he thought" (35; translation mine).

Potentially wild, brutish, devoid of selfhood, and ultimately unrepresentable in their threatening commonality, the *andinos* become the Creole heart of darkness to be constituted exclusively through effacement: "'Do you believe in pishtacos? — Lituma asked the men at the next table. Half smothered in their shawls, the four faces that turned towards him were *those* faces, cast from that same mould that he had such difficulty differentiating: burned by the sun and by the cold, elusive unexpressive eyes, nose and lips bruised by the weather, uncontrollable hair. Finally one of them answered — Who knows. Maybe" (66; translation mine).

Throughout this Creole condemnation of all things Andean, the only redemptive space in the Andes is to be found in the sections of the narrative recounting Lituma's only contact with the outside, non-Andean world. Lituma's assistant, Tomasito, is a *serrano* who nevertheless looks like a Creole (13) and speaks both Spanish and Quechua. Tomasito lies in bed at nights and recounts his one-sided love affair with a young prostitute from Lituma's home town of Piura. After a series of picaresque adventures that carry the couple to the verge of criminal excess, the *costeña* prostitute finally abandons Tomasito and takes his savings with her. However, at the end of the novel she reappears in Naccos, deus ex machina, searching for the Creolized Indian who had been so devoted to her well-being. The final coming-together of an acculturated Indian and a now redeemed (i.e., an inherently good costeña) woman, comes to represent the only space in the novel somehow beyond the logics of impending Andean apocalypse. But, of course, this beyond-space is nothing less than a re-presentation of nineteenth-century hispanista-styled romanticism: redemption through the love of a good (non-Indian) woman.

Ultimately the novel is the repeated revelation of the unintelligibility of Andean cultural practices and belief systems, which are invariably portrayed as naturally violent, ancestrally antidevelopmental, and profoundly illogical. But of particular importance in the novel is the persistent paranoia with which the Creole portrays the threat of impending urban Andeanization. At one point Lituma reflects on the cataclysmic consequences of mass Andean migration to the capital, and of the translation to city life — historically equated with civilizing forces, of course — of collective practices and beliefs emerging from within the Andean nether world:

> I'm sorry Tomasito. . . . That article that we read in the Lima paper about those guys stealing kids' eyes has really gotten to me. . . . The paper didn't mention pishtacos, but "sacaojos" or "robaojos." . . . But you're right, Tomasito, they're like the highlander's pishtacos. What I can't understand is how it is that even in Lima people are beginning to believe in that stuff. In the capital of Peru, how can that be? . . . Something serious is happen-

ing in this country, Tomasito. . . . How could a whole Lima shantytown be overtaken by such a tale? Gringos putting five-year-old kids into luxury cars so as to take their eyes out with ultradynamic scalpels. It's unbelievable! . . . It's like an epidemic. . . . It's as if that couple of savages [Dionisio and Adriana] were right, and civilized people were wrong. Knowing how to read and write, wearing a jacket and tie, going to school and living in the city are useless now. Only the shamans understand what's going on. (185–189; translation mine).

What is in danger of extinction in contemporary Peru, it seems, is the Creole notion of the city as progress, of the nation as universal singularity, and of self-government as the foundation of a morally grounded national culture. Eminently ecstatic, orgiastic, barbaric, the Andes is a space that inevitably inaugurates the end of the history of Creole-led modernity and of modernization in Peru, a space beyond thought, not even a limit-experience of Creole historical knowledge but rather of knowledge rendered ahistorical, overrun by rumors and superstitions that are creeping into the very moral fabric of the Creole nation-state and undermining the civilized polis from within.

"So what is to be done with the Andes?" seems to be the underlying question of the whole novel, as it also is in the neoliberal order of things. In the end Lituma reveals what could be either an implicit solution to the question, or perhaps the knowledge of the impossibility of the liberal art of Creole government in Peru. After discovering the truth that he has been looking for — that of sacrifice and cannibalism, of an Andean barbaric ungovernability that can only lead to Creole cognitive failure — he simply walks away, dumbfounded, incapable of further reflection or further intervention. The Creole state's unraveling of the mystery cults of the highlands, it appears, can only lead to cognitive failure and to the state abandoning the sierra to its own devices, since its practices can be of no value in the cultural logics of modern governmentality. Within the novel's configuration, then, the indigenous and indigenismo as modernizing forces within Peruvian society are rendered obsolete: of no value at the "end of History." Yet it is precisely in Lituma's inability to comprehend the collective political language of the Dionysian, the revelation of its truth, and in the silence of epistemic breakdown that is foundational to the logics of the text that negative reflection begins, for the novel unwittingly opens itself up to history and to the question of subaltern historical knowledge at a time of cataclysmic emergency.

After all, it was from within the midst of manchay tiempo that a series of truly remarkable events took place in the shantytowns — the *pueblos jóvenes* — of Lima. And we would do well to examine these events in greater detail than Vargas Llosa does or can, since they represent not something as simplistic as the power of indigenous superstition — to be condemned as ungovernable barbarism and rendered obsolete for the purposes of neoliberal progress and Creole civilization — but rather portray what Walter Benjamin calls "a sign of a Messianic cessation of happening, or, put differently, a revolutionary chance in the fight for the oppressed past" (264–265). It is through these events — which in the novel remain as little more than the ancestral and inaccessible "outside" to "civilizing" forces — that we shall begin to examine the contemporary struggle over the signifying processes of the past, and the creative ungovernable subaltern knowledge of Dionysus as it is appropriated into contemporary urban political practice and put to work in popular forms of organization and resistance in Peru. In other words, we will bring the sedimented specter of Mariátegui back to the question of the Dionysian as a means of displacing Vargas Llosa's "end of civilized History," replacing it, rather, with a phantasmatic subaltern rendering of historicity.

As Gonzalo Portocarrero informs us, between the end of November and mid-December 1988, all hell let loose in the poorest sectors of Lima. At a time of enormous economic and social hardship, with Sendero Luminoso already active in the city and the government incapable of doing anything about it, and on the eve of a suspected paquetazo of austerity-based reforms that promised to halve the buying power of the urban poor almost overnight, an incredible rumor circulated among Lima's popular classes: gringo doctors with black aides or bodyguards were entering the shantytowns, kidnapping children, and extracting their eyes in order to sell them abroad. Some rumors had the gringo doctor and his aides driving around the streets in an ambulance or a yellow Volkswagen; others stated that the doctors left the children blindfolded on a particular street corner with a princely sum of money left in dollars in an envelope. Other rumors even described the machine that the doctors used for the macabre extraction. Others stated that they also extracted the children's kidneys or their body fat. All agreed that the doctors existed and that they were gringos, white, armed, diabolic, and exporting the children's body parts.[8]

On November 29–30, hundreds of mothers — all of them first- or second-generation cholas, daughters or granddaughters of migrant Indians and obviously, as Kraniauskas puts it, "new political subjects" (15) in the capital's public sphere — took to the streets in almost all of the shantytowns of Lima and congregated vociferously around local schools in order to get their children out and home as quickly as possible, for their lives were endangered by the actions of the white gringo doctors and their black assistants. Populations organized nightly patrols, *rondas nocturnas,* through neighborhood streets. People remained in a state of alert, and the authorities could do nothing to quell the tension of the situation. As Nathan Wachtel informs us, far from appeasing the population, the incredulous or ironic articles that appeared in the press, together with the televised denial of the Peruvian minister of health, only aggravated the problem (85). On December 9, three young French tourists engaged in *turismo social* in José Carlos Mariátegui shantytown, were detained by the local residents and almost lynched for kidnapping twenty local children. The tourists were rescued by the police and taken to the Canto Grande police station, where hundreds of mothers soon congregated, shouting, "Poke their eyes out, burn them, child-killers" (Portocarrero, 48–49). On December 10, local neighborhood leaders in Atusparia shantytown met with the people to discuss means of protecting themselves from the sacaojos. On the evening of December 12, a medical team from El Instituto de Investigación Nutricional was attacked by a raging crowd, most of whom were, once again, chola women, and they were saved from a lynching only by the presence of three police tanks and one hundred fully armed civil guards (49–53). From this point on, the rumor began to lose strength but did not disappear, for many believed that the sacaojos had gone into hiding because they had received too much publicity, but that they would return when the time was right.

According to Portocarrero, the sacaojos is a modernized, urbanized cholo transfiguration or stylization of the Andean figure of the nacaq or pishtaco, an evil spirit from the Andean nether world that attacks lone figures on mountainous roadsides, throws a magic powder in their face, and then proceeds to suck their body fat out through the anus, or simply rips them apart. The victim can die immediately, or it can take days before he or she simply disappears or wastes away as the result of a lack of body fat. As Michael Taussig informs us, back in the early 1950s Efraín Morote Best discovered that the nacaq almost invariably extracts fat from bodies in order to sell it to pharmacies, where it is used in medicines, or to people who use it to grease machines, cast church bells, or shine the faces of the statues of the saints (238). The nacaq or pishtaco is nearly always said to be white or mestizo.[9]

Events similar to those of Lima had been reported a year earlier in Huamanga in the Andean province of Ayacucho, this time at the heart of the conflict between Sendero Luminoso and the Peruvian army. Once again, the image of modernity nourishing itself with the bodies of Indians is perpetuated. In Huamanga a number of mutilated bodies were found, and rumors of pishtacos and nacaqs immediately began to circulate. The perpetrators were believed to be nacaqs who had been released on the populace by the government and had been seen to be carrying "an ID card signed by 'presidente Alán' [García]" (Portocarrero, 54). According to local newspaper reports, it was believed that the nacaqs were extracting fat from their victims for export in order to create a medicine that could only be made with human fat. The money from this export was believed to be used to pay off the nation's astronomical foreign debt. In other versions, the victims' meat was to be sent to restaurants particularly frequented by representatives of the state; in this case, members of the armed forces (Portocarrero, 54). In Huamanga, one young merchant was stoned and hacked to death with machetes because, when confronted by a large crowd of people, he could not prove that he could speak Quechua and was immediately identified as an outsider, as a nacaq (54).

Of course, the question now is: what does all of this mean? Obviously we cannot resort to models of Andean savagery or wildness since they merely represent the developmentalist logics of neoliberalism, and of *Death in the Andes* — the unintelligibility and absolute unrepresentability of an indigenous cultural landscape dominated by ancestral "backwardness" and "barbarism." Like Vargas Llosa's novel before it, such an interpretation would simply fail to account for the extent to which such occurrences are capable of articulating oppositional or subversive relationships to historically constituted hierarchies, no matter how momentary.

Neither can we view them as a Macondo-like representation of cultural authenticity or of identitarian difference since these events, probably the degree zero of magic realism, are perhaps even the point at which magic realism breaks down as an adequate mode of representation and merely falls back into Creole romantic folklorism. Neither can we fall into discourses of female hysteria or of irrational insurrectional spontaneity since these interpretations inevitably deny the subaltern the ability to forge the minute functioning of her own philosophical and political world (Spivak, 3). It would be beneficial, then, to propose a critical genealogy of subaltern knowledge, a particular cartography of conflict and discontinuity in order to gain a greater sense of a specifically sedimented subaltern account of colonial history and of contemporary historicity.

These astounding events in one way or another have their roots in colonial relations and in the perpetuation of a subaltern colonial imaginary that succeeds in articulating anticolonial protest at a time in which the subaltern sectors of Lima were becoming increasingly cornered by the transition to neoliberalism. Thus, instead of considering the spread of rumor to be an ahistorical expression of ancestral traditionalism, superstition, and backwardness, as Lituma does, perhaps we would do well to consider it as "a relay of something always assumed to be pre-existent" (Spivak, 24), as a spectral account in the present of a subaltern prior-knowledge that returns to haunt us with the voices of common anonymity. It is very much a collective democratic working through, or laboring, in the present of a knowledge of colonialism grounded in subaltern history: a rememberance, a labor of mourning, a mourning for labor, as Derrida might put it.[10]

In *Shamanism, Colonialism, and the Wild Man,* Michael Taussig points to a common practice on the battlegrounds of the Spanish Conquest which perhaps nourishes the collective re-memberance that came to fuel this anti-neoliberal, anti-gringo, and anti-state chola insurrection. This battleground scenario provides us with the ghost of an originary terrain of loss and dismemberment from which sediments of subaltern historical knowledge emerge and rise to the surface of contemporary political realities: in his *Historia verdadera de la conquista de la Nueva España,* Bernal Díaz del Castillo recounts the opening up of a dead Indian in order to use his body fat to cure the wounds of injured Spanish soldiers: "and with the fat of a fat Indian whom we killed and opened up there, we salved our wounds, since we had no oil" (quoted in Szeminski, 171). Hernando de Soto, states Taussig, "was also reported to have used the fat of Indians slain in combat, as in his expedition against one of the Inca's captains holding out in the Sierra de Vilcaza in the Peruvian Andes" (237). As early as the sixteenth century, as can be seen in Cristobal de Molina's *Relación de las fábulas y ritos de los incas,* dating from 1574, Peru's Indians feared that Spaniards wanted their body fat for medicinal purposes: "It had been put about, wrote Father Molina, that Spain had commanded that Indian body fat be amassed and exported for the curing of a certain illness there, and though nobody could say with certainty, it was probably the sorcerers of the Inca . . . who were responsible for this tale designed to sow enmity between Indian and Spaniard. Now the Indians were loath to serve the Spanish, fearing that they would be killed and their body fat extracted as a remedy for the people of Spain" (Taussig, 238).

It appears that, far from being merely a surface on which power relations are inscribed, the Indian body, as seen in this urban chola conjuring-trick — this re-membering rememberance of the dismembered body of originary subjugation — is historically construed as a central and active site for the appropriation and expansion of white colonial power. The extraction of fat, or of other body parts, through more technologically advanced means comes to be viewed as a form of obtaining power or of wielding it over others, and inevitably attests to the popular knowledge that the subaltern body — with fat as its "excess of vitality" (Taussig, 237), and the eyes as the initial vehicle for bearing witness to contemporary collective dismemberment — is modernity's fetishized commodity par excellence that painfully joins and separates colonizer and colonized, white and Indian, gringo and cholo on the multifarious battlegrounds of colonial and postcolonial history.

What the Lima episode brings to us is an uncanny subaltern conjuring-trick in which the invisible specters of the Dionysian past — of Indian bloodletting on the colonial battlefields, of the becoming-body of collective indigenista insurrection, of José Carlos Mariátegui and the foundation of the Peruvian

Left—return in ghostly fashion as a carnal form to haunt the social corpus of neoliberalism with their very invisibility, with their spectrality, and do so while actively contesting the discourse of Andean "ungovernability as barbarism" that lies at the heart of Creole-inspired modernity, of the transnational logics of neoliberal governability, and of Vargas Llosa's *Death in the Andes*.[11] Manchay tiempo, understood by the subaltern sectors of urban society as the traumatic transition to a new stage in national and local social organization and state intervention into everyday life, comes to be read and disputed through the agency of the historically constituted knowledge that this is yet another chapter in a haunting history of dismemberment, corporeal expropriation, deterritorialization, and exploitation.[12] The chola's performative re-presentation of historical mutilation—the spectral *revenant* to the present of originary disarticulation—bears witness to the popular knowledge that neoliberalism, as a return to the present of the specters of colonialism, desynchronizes the past and the present as history once again nourishes itself with the corpus of the Indian polis, thereby rendering subaltern historicity in postmodern times quite literally, as Derrida puts it, "out of joint."

Historicity is, in this case, the knowledge of the contemporary as the traumatic recombination and haunting revenant of an externally imposed backwardness and progress that constantly reveal and redefine the experiential horizons and hostile boundaries of the condition of subalternity. Subaltern time, then, becomes not simply the question of the relation between two unsynchronized drives within a singular evolution—it is not and can never be a process of potential resynchronization as a passage from backwardness to progress, or from past to future, or from dismemberment to rememberment—rather, it is the constant confrontation with the disjunction and inequality that are internal to the experience of time, when it is understood as inherited obstruction. Subaltern time heals no wounds, in other words, and re-membrance only serves to keep them open. Thus the internal limit of subaltern historicity is its inherited disjointedness, its quality of being always already out of joint. Indeed, it is at this point that my analysis also becomes internally unhinged. After all, my analysis of subaltern ungovernability has served to bring subalternity and its spectral revenants back from the abyss of unknowability, in order to return them to the fold of a more "civilized" hermeneutic. One has to wonder, then, what is it that is promised by such a return within subaltern studies?

My analysis in these pages rides on an internal tension between the neoliberal positioning of subalternity as the absolute outside of logic and knowability (and therefore of neoliberal notions of civilization, and the subaltern as the absolute limit of the place where history can be narrativized into logic. The subaltern, then, is the limit-experience of knowability which is, within the successful unraveling of subaltern studies, dutifully returned to the civilizing fold of the knowable, so to speak, and hence inevitably to the nonsubaltern metropolitan space of the epistemologically governable. "Subalternist" practice, it would appear, intervenes on the side of governmentality and governability — of state-sponsored knowledge-accumulation about the subaltern and about subaltern culture — even when it promises to uncover the logics of governmentality's undoing. Since this is the inevitable underlying logic of all subalternism, and in particular of any group of essays given over to tracing the limits of subaltern ungovernability, then we are left with the question of what the subaltern, and subaltern agency such as that recounted above, and indeed subaltern studies, can actually promise other than the logics of a transnational reproduction of neoliberal governability through knowledge-management.

Indeed, the question of the promise of subalternism and of the messianic that lies at the heart of the promise founds any intellectual practice that construes itself as subalternist. Perhaps more so than any contemporary intellectual engagement with Latin America, Latin American subaltern studies — to be understood as a radical reading and critique of disciplinary traditions and of intellectual inheritances — is a practice deeply imbued with promise and with a particular critical investment in the question of future covenants and the conditions of possibility of a theory of change. It is therefore explicitly invested in the promise of promise. Yet one has to wonder what the nature of the promise that underlies subalternism actually is, or can be, when the analysis of ungovernability inevitably reproduces, in one way or another, the logics of knowability, of knowledge-governability, and ultimately of control.

Up to this point I have, I believe, traced the limits of neoliberal discourses on subalternity and have presented a case for the underlying historical logics of a singular example of subaltern ungovernability that contests the logics installed by neoliberal ideology. But one has to wonder, what does this analysis actually work toward?

Of course, it is overly premature to state that, through the events that I have re-presented above or through the logics of this analysis, or indeed through the examination of ungovernability as a whole, one can somehow imagine or foresee the ways in which subaltern ungovernability or the subaltern's spectral knowledge of the past and of the present can translate into a desirable negative critical practice or order of experience in the future, into a point of historical transcendence beyond the logics of a neoliberal state incapable of thinking beyond its own cognitive failure and epistemic breakdown. Neither can one foresee whether the active application of subaltern knowledge, or the sedimented transfiguration of historical knowledge into contemporary spectral interventions such as those mentioned above, can force a meaningful reform

of the structure of the Peruvian state, a redefinition of Peruvian national identity, or a new period of dialogue designed to relegitimize state practices and
the authority of the notion of the nation (Matos Mar, 104). No such messianism is immediately self-evident from within a subalternist analysis of subaltern ungovernability within Peruvian neoliberalism.

But as a practice that is deeply invested in the question of futurity and in
thinking past the end of the "end of History," in thinking historicity, in other
words, subalternism inevitably returns at one point or another to the thinking
of the limits of historical sedimentation and to the ghostly conjuring-tricks of
subaltern knowledge. After all, it is probably only through our relation to
subaltern specters — to the dismembered, ghostly identities and phantom
epistemologies of colonialism and its very often irrecuperable histories and
fragmented subject positions; to the supplements, cultural remnants, and social leftovers of production and exchange in Latin America; and to those
surplus elements that contaminate and haunt intellectual history apparently
from outside, yet that nevertheless emerge from within the Western knowledge machine and its history of development on the capitalist peripheries —
that we can begin to think the possibility of theorizing historical sedimentation, multiplicity, spectral commonality, differential modes of production, and
ungovernability as components of *another* historicity, of a subaltern historicity,
or of a historicity experienced *otherwise*. And it is only by opening intellectual
practice up to the spectral otherwise of history that one can perhaps redefine
the notion and experience of emergency, of the emergent, and of Benjamin
"state of emergency" that has come to characterize the hostile boundaries of
the contemporary.

Yet perhaps in order to embark on such an adventure in theory we would do
well to reflect further on the subaltern not just as the absolute limit of the place
where history is narrativized into logic, but equally as allegory of contemporary thought and of deliberative consciousness itself (Spivak, 12). If we accept
Ernesto Laclau's take on the contemporary, that "the dissolution of the metaphysics of presence is not a purely intellectual operation [but] is profoundly
inscribed in the whole experience of recent decades" (82), then perhaps contemporary intellectual practice would do well to reflect further on subaltern
spectrality, sedimented historicity, and the leftovers of historical dismemberment: on the possible strategies of a subalternism deeply imbued with the
knowledge of a deconstruction capable of thinking a theory of change as the
site of the displacement of function between sign-systems, as an active transaction between past and future, in other words (Spivak, 4).

In *Specters of Marx*, Derrida calls attention to the need to rethink the inheritance of marxism at the present time, an inheritance that obviously lies at the
heart of subaltern studies: "Marxism remains at once indispensable and struc-

turally insufficient: it is still necessary *but* provided it be transformed and adapted to new conditions and to a new thinking of the ideological, provided it be made to analyze the new articulation of techno-economic causalities and of religious ghosts, the dependent condition of the juridical at the service of socio-economic powers or States that are themselves never totally independent with regard to capital" (58–59). In order for such a transformation to become thinkable, continues Derrida, marxism needs to redefine its relationship to the messianic and hence to the formal structure that it shares with religion, in order to then rethink a new condition of possibility for the intervention of promise, and thus of futurity, into the contemporary:

> If analysis of the Marxist type remains, then, indispensable, it appears to be radically insufficient there where the Marxist ontology grounding the project of Marxist science or critique *also carries with it and must carry with it, necessarily* . . . a messianic eschatology . . . We will not claim that this messianic eschatology common both to the religions it criticizes and to the Marxist critique must be simply deconstructed. While it is common to both of them . . . it is also the case that its formal structure of promise exceeds them or precedes them. Well, what remains irreducible to any deconstruction, what remains as undeconstructable as the possibility of any deconstruction is, perhaps, a certain experience of the emancipatory promise; it is perhaps even the formality of a structural messianism, a messianism without religion, even a messianic without messianism, an idea of justice — which we distinguish from law or right and even from human rights — and an idea of democracy — which we distinguish from its current concept and from its determined predicates today. (59)

As Laclau states in his excellent discussion of these passages, the "messianic" in Derrida should be understood not as something related to actual messianic movements in the past or the present, but rather as something belonging to the general structure of experience, and intimately linked to the idea of "promise" (73). This is no longer, for example, a Mariátegui-style revolutionary faith in the romantic messianic force of the Indian proletariat, since, as Laclau continues, "this does not mean this or that particular promise, but the promise implicit in an originary opening to the 'other,' to the unforeseeable, to the pure *event* which cannot be mastered by any aprioristic discourse. Such an event is an interruption in the normal course of things, a radical dislocation" (73–74). The promise, then, as that of a coming aperture to the unforeseeable other, to the structural failure or "primordial sundering" that produces the dislocating event of time out of joint promises messianism without eschatology and therefore "without a pre-given promised land, without determinate content" (Laclau, 74), and therefore without a final "human emancipation fixed in its contents by a full-fledged eschatology" (80): "It is simply the structure of promise which is inherent in all experience and whose lack of content—resulting from the radical opening to the event, to the other—is the very possibility of justice and gives its meaning only to the democracy to come" (74).

The promise of subaltern studies grounded in the terrain on which the dissolution of the metaphysics of presence has become inscribed in recent decades. Indeed, it is this very inscription—read, invariably, as "the death of the Subject"—that grounds the emergence of hybrid subjectivities, the generation of multiple centers and peripheries, the multifarious locations of contemporary identities, and of course the dissolution of the metanarratives of modernity. In this sense the dissolution of the metaphysics of presence provides us with a privileged terrain within subalternism from which to think, perhaps, freedom in the present and the singularity—the negative potentiality of the singular—that freedom presupposes.

Moreover, since "singularity as the terrain of justice involves the radical undecidability which makes the decision possible" (Laclau, 74), then by definition the promise of subalternism ultimately entails the radicalization of the ethico-political decision. The promise of subalternism, in other words, can take us in various directions: either nowhere, toward an opening up to justice by thinking radical contingency and the sedimentation of historicities from within the recent collective experience of the dissolution of the metaphysics of presence, or equally toward epistemological totalitarianism and the absolute subsumption of the subaltern to metropolitan knowledge management. But in order for subalternism to decide—to act on a promise in its decision taking—perhaps it first needs to cultivate the constitutive incompletion of social relations and of cultural histories, and thereby guarantee the drive of radical undecidability that lies at the heart of the democratic experience. Perhaps it could be said, then, that the promise of subalternism is constantly "to *reactivate* the moment of decision that underlies any *sedimented* set of social relations" (Laclau, 78). Indeed, if, as Laclau puts it, "deconstruction . . . faces the challenge of reinscribing the Marxian model in this complex experience of present-day society" (82), perhaps we could add that subalternism faces the challenge of reinscribing the dissolution of the metaphysics of presence into the complex experience of engaging and thinking its modes of intellectual engagement. Perhaps it is this labor of reinscription that nourishes our subalternist critical becoming-body as we inevitably return to the question of inheritance—to our own intellectual and political specters, in other words—in Latin America, and do so in order to think past the end of the "end of History."

Notes

1   Thus the passage to neoliberalism emerges from within the latest mutation of the international capitalist system. This mutation has inaugurated a generalized crisis in governmental institutionality and the notion of the nation-state, producing a further erosion of the paradigms of civil society, which in Latin America were always uneven at best. As Gilles Deleuze reminds us, the contemporary restructuring of the public sphere — spearheaded by market-oriented social policies — guarantees the progressive and dispersed installation of new systems of domination that emerge from within a move *away from* Foucauldian enclosure and discipline:

> Nineteenth century capitalism is a capitalism of concentration, for production and for property. It therefore erects the factory as a space of enclosure. . . . But, in the present situation, capitalism is no longer involved in production, which it often relegates to the Third World. . . . It's a capitalism of higher-order production. . . . This is no longer a capitalism for production but for the product, which is to say, for being sold or marketed. Thus it is essentially dispersive, and the factory has given way to the corporation. . . . The operation of markets is now the instrument of social control and forms the impudent breed of our masters. Control is short-term and of rapid rates of turnover, but also continuous and without limit, while discipline was of long duration, infinite and discontinuous. (6)

The neoliberal production of informal labor practices, together with the emergence of new populations and political identities created by mass migration, have produced a predominantly urban populace in Latin America which is, on one hand, largely controlled by market forces, yet on the other is characterized by a significant *potential* for ungovernability. After all, this is a populace that is invariably obliged to exist, work, and organize on the margins of legality. Thus the neoliberal state needs to both promote a continued and sustainable flexibility in labor practices and interregional market accessibility, yet must constantly manage and/or incorporate informal labor and its transformational potential into the realms of state lawfulness and control. The informal economy, then, is what gives neoliberal ideology its energy and force, and it is equally the terrain that produces the potential end of governmentality. Thus the questions of the art of governing, of governability, and of the control of potential ungovernability in neoliberalism appear to be intimately linked to questions of state security, to governmental knowledge of population behavior and cultural specifics, and to questions that arise from the interplay between labor/consumer behavior, regional difference, local conceptualizations of territory and "region," and the ways in which these notions penetrate urban centers and modify the workings of primary markets.

2   On the cover of Lawrence E. Harrison's recently published book, *The Pan-American Dream: Do Latin America's Cultural Values Discourage True Partnership with the United States and Canada?* Samuel P. Huntington provides us with a brief synopsis of what is at stake for neoliberal ideology and the globalizing forces of late capitalism in contemporary Latin American cultural politics and underdevelopment: "the Pan-American dream will remain just that unless and until Latin American culture converges with North American culture." "Culture" is construed as a thorny obstacle to market transnationalization and to neoliberal notions of development and governability, it seems, and hence is a new space of intervention for the hemispheric social doctrinaires of neoliberalism. Indeed, for Huntington, "culture" lies at the heart of the "New World Order." He concludes *The Clash of Civilizations and the Remaking of the World Order* with a reworking of Sarmiento's "civili-

zation versus barbarism" paradigm, which is particularly interesting since it uncovers the underlying gang logic of much of neoliberal foreign policy and its moral crusading for market-based "freedom": "In the clash of civilizations, Europe and America will hang together or hang separately. In the greater clash, the global 'real clash,' between Civilization and barbarism, the world's great civilizations, with their rich accomplishments in religion, art, literature, philosophy, science, technology, morality, and compassion, will also hang together or hang separately. In the emerging era, clashes of civilizations are the greatest threat to world peace, and an international order based on civilizations is the surest safeguard against world war" (321). In Harrison's book, Chile (for obvious reasons) is put forward as a showcase of economic and cultural "convergence" between North and South, and presumably of "Civilization." Peru (for reasons that lie at the heart of this essay) is not.

3   The rise in recent years of the urban cholo, together with the Andeanization of what used to be exclusively Creole spaces, immediately raises the question of neoliberal wisdom and its ability to "know" its new populations in order to better control them. The cholo, the outsider within, is the great unknown of the contemporary political field since (s)he marks the end of territorial and cultural binarisms that were foundational to Creole modernity, and brings to those traditionally Creole spaces (such as the urban centers) customs, habits, ways of acting and thinking — forms of self-government, in other words — that question the historical foundations of Creole sovereignty as they call attention to the limits of what has been established by the modern state as the communal interest of all. It is in this sense that cholo self-government, which is inevitably connected to questions of morality and to the so-called barbaric cultural practices of the Andes, takes center stage in Vargas Llosa's portrayal of manchay tiempo in *Death in the Andes*.

4   In 1926 Mariátegui founded the journal *Amauta* upon returning to Peru from Europe. Taking its title from the name of the Incan educators, *Amauta* was designed to advance thought on the possible unifying imaginary of a new postcolonial nation-state and national identity. The discussions that Mariátegui sought to redefine were the "indigenista/hispanista" debates that had been initiated toward the end of the nineteenth century by Peruvian thinkers such as the romantic liberal indigenistas (Manuel González Prada and Julio Tello) and their conservative hispanista counterparts (José de la Riva Agüero and Víctor A. Belaunde) (Arguedas, 189). What Mariátegui proposed was the means of putting Peru on the map for Peruvian thought and finally bringing to a close the dualistic liberal-conservative, indigenista-hispanista debate, which had not really advanced beyond the paradigms founded by Sarmiento's civilization-barbarism debate in Argentina. Thus Mariátegui sought to end the duality of Creole notions of national culture by channeling the collective force of the Indians and refounding the Peruvian polis on a politics no longer grounded in the production of indigenous subalternity and colonial exploitation. The underlying irony of this project, of course, is that Mariátegui's "Peruvianization of Peru" — its proposed political, philosophical, cultural, linguistic, and economic process of "de-Creolization" — was grounded inevitably in the very European frameworks that had given meaning to colonialism for centuries. Indigenismo and the future of the Peruvian subaltern, in other words, could only be theorized through the archive of Western science and thought.

5   For an excellent analysis of Nietzsche's *Birth of Tragedy* in its relation to the philosophical and aesthetic foundation of state practices, see Josef Chytry, *The Aesthetic State: A Quest in Modern German Thought*.

6   Indeed, as we will see in the course of this essay, there is probably no "true" accounting for

such subaltern knowledge or for so-called Dionysian zones of agency. Having said this, however, this essay intends to uncover the ways in which they do exist, or at least can be formulated, retroactively. The difference between neoliberal renderings of subaltern emergence and those of a subalternist thought grounded in the notion of negativity is that neoliberal thought actively banishes the subaltern in the name of continuity, homogeneity, and "rational choice" in order to reimpose its illusory discourses of social, institutional, and cultural hegemony. On the other hand, a subalternist rendering maintains the possibility of a radical heterogeneity beyond rational choice (though not necessarily spontaneous) and beyond the thought of hegemony's positivist constructivism in such a way as to disrupt the continuity and homogeneity of neoliberal control.

7   Without a doubt, this representation is about the policing and the governability of the social, about the survival of the reason of the Creole state, state security, and its means of experiencing and confronting Andean society as an alien force that is beyond cognition, and therefore potentially uncontrollable in its multilayered "excessiveness." The underlying question of Lituma's investigation is: "What are these people capable of?" And this is a question that lies at the heart of liberal governmentality, and of a neoliberal capitalism threatened by cultural practices that do not fall immediately within the rubric of consumerism, but rather locate consumption within the realm of the sacred or the redemptive. "What are these people capable of?" denotes a Creole calculation of risk—a paranoid fantasy scenario of potential threat—that emerges from the increasing Andeanization of urban culture and the inevitable intensification of Creole contact with serrano culture. As Colin Gordon puts it in *The Foucault Effect: Studies of Governmentality,* "In modern liberal societies the social is, *characteristically,* the field of government security considered in its widest sense. . . . The rationality of security is, in Foucault's rendering, an inherently open-ended one: it deals not just in closed circuits of control, but *in calculations of the possible and the probable.* The relation of government with which it corresponds is not solely a functional, but also a 'transactional' one: it structures government as a practice of problematization, a zone of (partially) open interplay between the exercise of power and everything that escapes its grip" (35–36; emphasis mine). It is precisely the problematization of the possible and of the probable in their relationship to population, territory, and deterritorialization, as well as the cultural logics that escape state lawfulness and reason, that structures both Lituma's policing of the social in *Death in the Andes* and the internal workings of the novel itself.

8   I am particularly grateful to John Kraniauskas for bringing these events to my attention in his forthcoming essay "*Cronos* and the Political Economy of Vampirism: Notes on a Historical Constellation."

9   For further analysis of the interregional and transcultural appropriations of the Andean pishtaco, and in particular of its translation to the Peruvian Amazon, see Michael F. Brown and Eduardo Fernández, *War of Shadows: The Struggle for Utopia in the Peruvian Amazon,* in which the authors state that "pishtaco fear lives on today as a powerful metaphor for the experience of Andean people, whose lives have been twisted and foreshortened by what they see as the mysterious power emanating from the gringo world" (143).

10   In Brett Levinson's reading of Freud's essay on "Mourning and Melancholy," he states that Mourning . . . hinges on rememberance. Rememberance, the representation through images, words, sounds, etc. of the past, indicates that a former or dead object/event is indeed of the past: to *re-present* a loss is already to offer testimony to the fact that the lost (dead) object is no longer *present.* Rememberance is hence not only the acknowledge-

ment of loss, but also the marking of the distinction between now and then, memory and actual event, the living self and the dead other. Mourning belongs, in other words, to the self's gradual, often painful attempt to separate itself from loss, and thus move towards the future. It is a condition for temporality: the present's release of the past, as well as its opening towards the future. (99)

It probably goes without saying that mourning, as a labor of re-memberance and internalization, lies at the heart of this subaltern re-presentation. For excellent analyses of the thought of mourning as foundational to contemporary social and philosophical processes, see Alberto Moreiras's "Transculturación y pérdida del sentido: El diseño de la posmodernidad en América Latina" and *Tercer espacio: Literatura y duelo en América Latina*.

11 For Derrida, "the specter is a paradoxical incorporation, the becoming-body, a certain phenomenal and carnal form of spirit. It becomes, rather, some 'thing' that remains difficult to name: neither soul nor body, and both one and the other" (6). The specter marks a point of contamination between past and present, and a point of convergence between body and spirit, between materiality and immateriality, thereby rendering the difference indistinguishable: "For it is flesh and phenomenality that give to the spirit its spectral apparition, but which disappear right away in the apparition, in the very coming of the *revenant* or the return of the specter. There is something disappeared, departed in the apparition itself as reapparition of the departed. The spirit, the specter are not the same thing . . . but as for what they have in common, one does not know what it *is*, what it is presently" (6). The knowledge of the specter, then, is the knowledge of a radical, perhaps constitutive, undecidability: "*It is* something that one does not know, precisely, and one does not know if precisely it *is*, if it exists, if it responds to a name and corresponds to an essence. One does not know: not out of ignorance, but because this nonobject, this non present present, this being there of an absent or departed one no longer belongs to knowledge. At least no longer to that which one thinks one knows by the name of knowledge. One does not know whether it is living or if it is dead" (6).

12 For John Kraniauskas, these events mark the elaboration of a particular political fantasy in which pishtacos or eye-snatchers "are clearly postcolonial and transcultural signs of contemporary social processes, evoking as they do the cultural memory of changes in the social experience of the body and its perceived invasion and colonisation by new institutions (medical) and regimes (technologies): modern doctors having taken the place of colonial priests in an ongoing history of dispossession. From this subalternist point of view, the 'vampire' becomes a kind of 'anti-shaman,' capital's wicked medicine-man, the equivalent of the colonial church's priest: 'converting' subjects and bodies in the name of a new order" (16).

Works Cited

Abrams, Philip. "Notes on the Difficulty of Studying the State." *Journal of Historical Sociology* 1, 1 (1988): 58–89.

Arguedas, José María. *Formación de una cultura nacional indoamericana.* With a prologue by Angel Rama. Mexico City: Siglo Veintiuno Editores, 1989.

Benjamin, Walter. "Theses on the Philosophy of History." In *Illuminations,* ed. Hannah Arendt. Trans. Harry Zohn. With an introduction by H. Arendt. New York: Harcourt, Brace and World, 1968: 255–266.

Brown, Michael F., and Eduardo Fernández. *War of Shadows: The Struggle for Utopia in the Peruvian Amazon*. Berkeley: University of California Press, 1991.

Chytry, Josef. *The Aesthetic State: A Quest in Modern German Thought*. Berkeley: University of California Press, 1989.

Collins, Joseph, and John Lear. *Chile's Free-Market Miracle: A Second Look*. Oakland, Calif.: Institute for Food and Development Policy, 1995.

Cresap, Steven. "Nietzsche as Social Engineer: *The Birth of Tragedy*'s Critique of Action." *Rethinking Marxism* 6, 3 (1993): 102–116.

Deleuze, Gilles. "Postscript on the Societies of Control." *October* 59 (1992): 3–7.

Derrida, Jacques. *Specters of Marx: The State of the Debt, the Work of Mourning, and the New International*. Trans. Peggy Kamuf. With an introduction by Bernd Magnus and Stephen Cullenberg. New York: Routledge, 1994.

Soto, Hernando de. *The Other Path: The Invisible Revolution in the Third World*. Trans. June Abbott. With a foreword by Mario Vargas Llosa. New York: Harper and Row, 1990.

González Prada, Manuel. "Nuestros Indios." In *Conciencia intelectual de América*, ed. Carlos Ripoll. New York: Eliseo Torres, 1974: 193–205.

Gordon, Colin. "Governmental Rationality: An Introduction." In *The Foucault Effect: Studies in Governmentality*, ed. Graham Burchell, Colin Gordon, and Peter Miller. London: Harvester Wheatsheaf, 1991.

Hardt, Michael, and Antonio Negri. *Labor of Dionysus: A Critique of the State-Form*. Minneapolis: University of Minnesota Press, 1994.

Harrison, Lawrence E. *The Pan-American Dream: Do Latin America's Cultural Values Discourage True Partnership with the United States and Canada?* New York: Basic Books, 1997.

Huntington, Samuel P. *The Clash of Civilizations and the Remaking of World Order*. New York: Simon and Schuster, 1996.

Jameson, Fredric. *The Seeds of Time*. New York: Columbia University Press, 1994.

Kraniauskas, John. "*Cronos* and the Political Economy of Vampirism: Notes on a Historical Constellation." In *Cannibalism and the Colonial Order*, ed. Francis Barker, Peter Hulme, and Mary Iverson. Cambridge: Cambridge University Press. 1998: 142–157.

Laclau, Ernesto. *Emancipation(s)*. New York: Verso, 1996.

Lechner, Norbert. "¿Por qué la política ya no es lo que fue?" *Nexos* 216 (1995): 63–69.

Levinson, Brett. "Trans(re)lations: Death, Dictatorship, and Literary Politics in *Artificial Respiration*." *Latin American Literary Review* 25, 49 (fall 1997): 91–118.

Mariátegui, José Carlos. *Seven Interpretive Essays on Peruvian Reality*. Trans. Marjory Urquidi. With an introduction by Jorge Basadre. Austin: University of Texas Press, 1971.

——. *"The Heroic and Creative Meaning of Socialism": The Selected Essays of José Carlos Mariátegui*. Ed. and trans. Michael Pearlman. Atlantic Highlands: Humanities Press International, 1996.

Marx, Karl, and Friedrich Engels. *The German Ideology, Part One*. Ed. and with an introduction by C. J. Arthur. New York: International, 1970.

——. *The Manifesto of the Communist Party*. Trans. Paul M. Sweezy. New York: Monthly Review Press, 1964.

Matos Mar, José. *Desborde popular y crisis del estado: El nuevo rostro del Perú en la década de 1980*. Lima: Instituto de Estudios Peruanos, 1984.

Moreiras, Alberto. "Transculturación y pérdida del sentido: El diseño de la posmodernidad en América Latina." *Nuevo Texto Crítico* 8, 6 (1990): 105–119.

——. *Tercer espacio: Literatura y duelo en América Latina*. Santiago de Chile: LOM Ediciones, 1999.

Morote Best, Efraín. "El degollador (makaq)." *Tradición: Revista peruana de cultura*. 2, 4 (1952): 67–91.

Nietzsche, Friedrich. *The Birth of Tragedy*. Trans. Shaun Whiteside. Ed. Michael Tanner. London: Penguin, 1993.

Portocarrero Maisch, Gonzalo, Isidro Valentín, and Soraya Irigoyen. *Sacaojos: Crisis social y fantasmas coloniales*. Lima: Tarea, 1991.

Said, Edward. Foreword to *Selected Subaltern Studies*. Ed. Ranajit Guha and Gayatri Chakravorty Spivak. New York: Oxford University Press, 1988: v–x.

Schutte, Ofelia. *Cultural Identity and Social Liberation in Latin American Thought*. Albany: State University of New York Press, 1993.

Spivak, Gayatri Chakravorty. "Subaltern Studies: Deconstructing Historiography." In *Selected Subaltern Studies*, ed. Ranajit Guha and Gayatri Chakravorty Spivak. New York: Oxford University Press, 1988: 3–32.

Starn, Orin, Carlos Iván Degregori, and Robin Kirk. *The Peru Reader: History, Culture, Politics*. Durham, N.C.: Duke University Press, 1995.

Szeminsky, Jan. "Why Kill the Spaniard? New Perspectives on Andean Insurrectionary Ideology in the 18th Century." In *Resistance, Rebellion, and Consciousness in the Andean Peasant World, 18th to 20th Centuries*, ed. Steve J. Stern. Madison: University of Wisconsin Press, 1987.

Taussig, Michael. *Shamanism, Colonialism, and the Wild Man: A Study in Terror and Healing*. Chicago: University of Chicago Press, 1987.

Vargas Llosa, Mario. *Conversación en la catedral*. Barcelona: Seix Barral, 1969.

———. *Lituma en los Andes (Death in the Andes)*. Barcelona: Planeta, 1993.

Wachtel, Nathen. *Gods and Vampires: Return to Chipaya*. Trans. Carol Volk. Chicago: University of Chicago Press, 1994.

Outside In and Inside Out:
Visualizing Society in Bolivia

JAVIER SANJINÉS C.

The skeletal, the carnal, and the visceral are three important bodily metaphors of how the social sciences envision contemporary Bolivia. In this essay, I will concentrate on each of them as I go explore their relation with the way Bolivian social researchers understand modernity, postmodernity, and "internal colonialism." However, I must indicate from the beginning that subaltern epistemology responds only to the process of viscerality. One could well argue that my approach to subaltern sensibilities does not integrate the skeleton and the visceral with the muscular and the carnal in a kind of dialectical unity of perspective. By using these three social metaphors, I intend this essay to displace the centrality of the eye. In my view, subaltern epistemology does not have a post-Kantian vision of totality nor a privileged point of view capable of solving in a dialectical unity the antinomies of reality. I should add here that, as actors of their own decolonization, the Andean subaltern cannot hold, as of now, a unified vision of corporeality. Indeed, the dismembered body has been the symbol of Bolivian indigenous rebellions since the insurgency of Tupac Katari (1780) against Spanish colonial rule and remains so up to our present days.

How, then, do the social sciences see contemporary Bolivia? Why focus on bodily metaphors that do not give a unified view of society? Attempting to answer these questions, I will first deal with the modernization model that studies the incomplete construction of the Bolivian national state, particularly in the face of the recurrent political and social crises the country has experienced since the revolution of 1952. From a cultural perspective, this modernization model gives particular attention to the vertebral institutions that serve as a skeleton or backbone of civil society; these institutions — structures capable of incorporating into a new system key social sectors such as organized labor, peasants, and the middle class — define the striae of social space.

Lines of power or lines of resistance, these structures of civil society (political parties, in particular) support the figure of the social body.[1] Consequently, their weak or insufficient constitution is a major setback in attempting to build a strong national state. Vertebral, structural, and systemic, this modernization model relies heavily on the political party system as the key solution to the mediatory relationship between the state and civil society. As I shall discuss later, the actual functioning of this mediatory relationship has important implications for the complicity between literature and modernization. In other words, if the institutional structure fails to mediate between the state and civil society, this failure at the political level will have its necessary repercussions at the cultural level. We are talking then not only of a legitimation crisis, but also of a motivation crisis that permeates the production of "high culture" and pulverizes the idealization of literature as an instrument of national formation.[2] By clinging to the analysis of an "institutional engineering" that shows very little interest in culture and in the peculiarities of everyday life, political societies, however, think of governability as a rational operation that is culture neutral.

Second, the interrogation of the respective spheres (culture, ethics, politics, etc.) of modernity begins to question the modernization model based on the rational operations of institutional governability. This interrogation has made social scientists — particularly political sociologists — more concerned with subjectivity and identity, and more aware of the ethnic and cultural plurality of Bolivia. Intellectuals such as Fernando Calderón, who formerly headed the Latin American Council of Social Sciences (CLACSO) in Buenos Aires, and Carlos Toranzo, the most visible researcher at the Latin American Institute for Social Research (ILDIS), have started to question governability as exclusively political and are now introducing into their research new cultural practices that are popular, "horizontal," and prone to overcome the distinctions between elite and popular (mass) cultures. Consequently, new relations between intellectuals and both new and traditional social movements are emerging with the redefinition of political agency suggested by postmodernist perspectives. The distinguished Bolivian sociolinguist Xavier Albó aptly describes these new relations when he indicates that "we do not doubt the importance and necessity of continuing to do analysis based on the social classes and their interaction . . . but we should also seriously question about the exclusivity of such analysis. *It is like a skeleton without flesh. To delineate our identity as a people the silhouette is as important as the skeleton*" (Albó, "Our Identity," 20).

How is Albó's bodily metaphor different from the one applied by the political scientists? Well, as Albó pointed out to me not too long ago: "One does not fall in love with the skeleton. Only the silhouette can give charm and substance to the bones." Indeed, the class-based institutional analysis promoted by political science seems to be too stiff when attempting to overcome the crisis of state capitalism as the incomplete project of modernity in postrevolutionary

Bolivia. If Albó is correct, we should be paying equal attention to other social and cultural aspects related to gender and ethnicity, particularly to the new forms of mass communication that summon the migrants and the parvenus by stepping outside the established political mechanisms and by leaving behind the traditional forms of representative democracy. These new aspects of everyday life, often neglected by structural analysis, constitute an essential part of the silhouette.

Third, the relationship between society and the state no longer exclusively involves the mediation and organization of political institutions; it also sets civil society in motion directly through the circuitry of its mass-media production. We should be careful to point out, however, that the passage from a "vertical" society to a "horizontal" society also entails dangers and limitations. The metaphors of the skeleton and the silhouette can also give us an indication of the nature of the perils involved in this passage.

If we agree that the images of the skeleton that characterizes the political structures of the organized social classes is not sufficient for our understanding of everyday contemporary Bolivian society, we should also be careful with the changing silhouette of ethnic festivities and the undulating waves of radio-television performances and talk shows. No longer oriented toward political position and class identity, the sphere of popular culture, prone to the flexible and mobile performances of contingent identities, may end up promoting the production of simulacra. And this, John Beverley warns us, "may involve the aesthetic fetishization of its social, cultural, and economic status quo (as abject, chaotic, heterogeneous, carnivalesque, etc.), thereby attenuating the urgency for radical social change and displacing it into cultural dilettantism and quietism" (*Against Literature*, 107).

Unfortunately, the smoothing of social space and the acceptance of Bolivia's heterogeneity as a pluricultural, multilingual, rather somewhat carnivalesque "messy culture" does not bring an end to social injustice and to disciplinary deployments.[3] On the contrary, as sociologists and anthropologists such as Silvia Rivera Cusicanqui would point out, the silhouette is a bordering concept that modern political scientists overlook in their analyses, and postmodern political sociologists palliate through the "pluri-multi" constitution of Bolivian society. I am talking here about the research on the history of the Aymara, research that indicates how indigenous communities have been forced to adapt since colonial times to the economic and social standards imposed by the dominant criollo/mestizo class. Discussing the possibilities of a communal "*ayllu* democracy," Rivera explains this traumatic process, characterized by a constant redefinition of values and transformation of economic modes of production. As I will discuss in the final part of this essay, this notion of "internal colonialism" is central to the writings of intellectuals who not only challenge the construction of political institutions, but also go beyond the festive charm of the silhouette to give us the experience of the limit itself, the visceral experience of reading the "insides out." It is from this perspective that I now judge the carnal and the skeletal.

In the structural analysis of Bolivia's uncompleted project of modernization, few political scientists are as important as James Malloy. Well known for his research on Latin America's authoritarianism and corporativism, Malloy teamed up with Eduardo Gamarra, the well-known Bolivian social scientist at Florida International University, to write *Revolution and Reaction: Bolivia, 1964–1985* (1988). Casting an eye over the past decades in Bolivia after the revolutionary process was initiated in 1952, the authors study the main aspects of national political life from the military coup of 1964 to the return of the National Revolutionary Movement (MNR) in 1985.

Let me call the reader's attention to the set of images political scientists use to describe the continuous crisis of Bolivian contemporary society. "Structure" and "vertebra," often mentioned by Malloy and Gamarra, are skeletal metaphors that help define and support the mediatory relationship between state and society. They are therefore useful metaphors for this vertical model of analysis that seeks to open the way for representative democracy after more than thirty years of authoritarian and quasi-authoritarian rule. To "structure," "vertebra," and "system," I would add "institutional engineering," a metaphor political scientists use in the attempt to surpass the dual economic and political crisis of present-day societies.

A key concept in this "engineering" endeavor is "governability," the notion that indicates the political and social conflict-solving capacity of any representative state by means of democratic procedures. At the institutional level, governability may only be achieved through modernization of the existing political party system, gearing it away from the populist reformist ideologies that predominated not only in Bolivia but throughout Latin America during the past decades. Consequently, governability is a form of institutional engineering that relies heavily on modernization of the political party system. And the model of modernization rests upon the premise that the process of institutional reform needs to strengthen the party system more than ever to avoid the dangerous possibility that it may become prey of micropolitical subjectivities that are allegedly not rational enough.

I would like to introduce two criticisms into this framework of analysis. First, a persistent strain through contemporary social and political theory is the sharp division between "lifeworld" and "system." As Harry C. Boyte has indicated, "We experience this division as the difference between the terrain of the immediate, familiar, everyday, and close to home, on the one hand, and the large institutions and systems that tower over us, like granite mountains of the social landscape, with a seemingly immutable logic and force of their own" (340). Boyte's observation applies well to the model of modernization that I have discussed so far. It seems to me that in Malloy's analysis, particularly in his vertical disengagement between state and society, the middle ground of pragmatic motive and action found within civil society disappears. Even in settings of sharp inequality and political clientelism and corruption, as the one Malloy discusses, the entire people, self-consciously or not, participates to some degree in the maintenance and reproduction of social life at every level. Malloy's model of modernization pays very little attention to such agency and to a series of other crucial questions for political and theoretical investigation, such as the sense in which ordinary people feel themselves to be participating in history, not simply observing it.

Moreover, this midground understanding of public as creator and public as problem solver also provides a key to new forms of democratic political renewal and participation. For example, new migrations from the countryside into the city have created an informal economy that has reworked political relations over the past decade and also created new "public knowledge" across communal and even national boundaries. New political parties were closely connected, moreover, to the development of a vibrant *cholo*/Indian urban culture that formed a spatial environment for an alternative public sphere: the marketplaces, the festivities, the rituals, and the like. Associated with such changes was an already-existing vigorous infrastructure of social information created through institutions such as the radio stations and the television networks, with their talk shows and other forms of horizontal social participation. Clearly, these are not the Western institutions of the traditional public sphere theorized by Habermas, but they are the pragmatic institutions of popular politics that the model of modernization leaves behind.

Second, Malloy and Gamarra leave untouched the cultural aspects of social movements. Indeed, the economic crisis weighed so heavily on the urban middle classes that by 1956 they had lost trust in the revolution. This loss of confidence and reliance—which was soon to affect organized labor as new economic policies turned the costs of the revolution on them—is at the root not only of the legitimation crisis that the authors aptly describe in the book, but also of the motivation crisis that they do not study at all, due to the "culture-neutral" nature of their research.[4] I have indicated before that this motivation crisis is of particular interest to "high culture," particularly to contemporary literature. Let me say that it is impossible to explain the literary production after the revolution of 1952 without relying on this notion. And the motivation crisis, in turn, can be theorized as a consequence of Malloy's pathbreaking political analyses on the lack of mediatory institutions between state and society.

Let us see then how culture is related to trust and to the motivation crisis that permeates the social world of postrevolutionary Bolivia. A particular type of confidence, trust is bound up with contingency. According to Anthony Giddens, "trust implies reliability in the actions of individuals or the operations of systems, where that confidence expresses faith in the probity of another or in the correctness of abstract system" (82). In conditions of modernity, attitudes of trust toward abstract systems are usually routinely incorporated into the continuity of day-to-day activities and are enforced by the circumstances of daily life. But the loss of basic trust generates an existential anxiety that I think explains the motivation crisis of the Bolivian middle class after the revolution of 1952.

An earthquake is to nature what the revolution is to the middle class. Years of hyperinflation, of economic and social disarray, left a lasting impression in the emotional behavior of this sector of society. Harassed by the peasant militias first, and traumatized by military authoritarianism later, the Bolivian middle class lost confidence in its identity and in its "being-in-the-world." Indeed, the emotional disarray can be traced with particular acuteness in the realm of literature. Few have paid attention, for instance, to the countless times that novels, poems, and short stories repeat the idea that "nothing is known here," an expression that projects mistrust, ontological insecurity, and the insufficient personal and collective motivation to participate in the construction of a meaningful world. This "inner exile" of the middle class is rightly described, in the context of Spanish authoritarianism, by Paul Ilie as "the antitype of community. Since the community, like a living body, is composed of members . . . the exile which cuts off the allegedly sick member is a sanitizing force to the point of castration and sterility. Exile becomes the condition of nonintercourse. . . . It expresses the being outside" (70).

Finally, how does all this relate to nation-state formation? Traditionally, Latin American literature has been one of the institutions crucial to the development of an autonomous creole and then "national" culture. As Beverley puts it, Ángel Rama, probably the most important Latin American literary critic of the twentieth century, argued that a "republic of letters" and the consequent role of the writer as a political-moral leader are forms of institutional continuity between colonial and contemporary Latin America. This high function of literature involves a socially and historically "overvalorization" that does not apply well to literatures that do not seem to model the national. Indeed, the analysis of "minor literatures" and their literary tropes reveals the progressive construction of an apocalyptic vision where metaphors of death outweigh any human motivation to act on life. Consequently, and in contrast with the motivation crisis of high culture, I venture the hypothesis that popular cultures "in transition" to democracy may have left behind the vertical expressions of nation-state formation for the smoothing, undulating, horizontal forms of postmodernism, where, as Beverley indicates, "its facile repudiation is as impossible as any equally facile celebration of it is complacent and corrupt" (*Against Literature,* 108).

It is essential to recognize the importance of the systemic and structural factors of society. But just as crucial as the skeleton — and indelibly linked to it — is the carnal silhouette of the ethnic identities that give content to the institutional framework. In the next two parts of the essay, my discussion of culture will contemplate the ethnic movements that seek recognition in the social and political arenas. As I have indicated before, the migrant indigenous populations struggle over meanings as well as material conditions that are tied to culture. Consequently, there is a cultural politics that must be examined away from the conventional forms of analysis. The new theoretical guidelines come from sociology and from anthropology, making the terrain in everyday life the key source of knowledge. I am interested in the micropolitical analyses that study ethnic diversity as part of the conceptualization of Bolivia as a "messy culture." By giving critical attention to everyday life, micropolitics interrelates with political practice and economic achievement. It is therefore difficult to access the behavior of migrant populations without linking their rituals and festivities to the rise of new political movements and to the rapidly growing informal sectors of the economy. But while some politologists explore the more festive aspect of contemporary social movements, other rural sociologists and anthropologists still see them as part of the unsolved colonial nature of Bolivian society.

Arturo Éscobar has expressed that "the relationship between the practice of everyday life, collective action, and politics is not yet well understood" (69). Indeed, it is difficult to say if cultural resistence to vertical state intervention in communal affairs does amount to anything politically, or whether we have found indisputable forms of protest that may be interpreted as "decolonizing." One thing, however, is certain: it is insufficient to study contemporary social movements relying exclusively on models of modernization, such as those couched in terms of political parties, organized labor, and so forth.

We have seen so far that most models of social production have focused their attention on the macro aspects of society, particularly on the structures and mechanisms of domination. Malloy, Gamarra, and René Mayorga, to name three of the most salient political scientists, have concentrated their research on the strategies through which the revolutionary elites, the military, and organized labor dictated the course of political life for the past forty years. But unlike the strategies of domination that, according to Éscobar, "structure the world into 'readable spaces' that dominant institutions can understand and control" (74), the production of migrant groups and other local organizations operates through "tactics" — rituals and festivities, among others — that come from the joys and sorrows of everyday life. As Éscobar indicates, we know from the work of Michel de Certeau that "strategies seek to discipline and manage people and institutions, whereas tactics constitute a sort of 'anti-discipline,' an 'art of making' that proceeds by manipulating imposed knowledge and symbols at propitious moments" (74). Produced by vertebral and anonymous institutions, strategies seem to be deadly serious; tactics, by contrast, have a smoothing nature that introduces play into the system of power. These reflections mix well with Carlos Toranzo's research on the diverse and multicultural nature of present-day Bolivia.

In his prologue to the proceedings of the seminar organized by ILDIS on "Lo pluri-multi o el reino de la diversidad" [The pluri-multi or the realm of the diverse] Toranzo writes quite candidly that it is an illusion to think of Bolivia in purely vertebral and homogeneous terms. He says: "Así como hay un impulso de los sujetos a sentirse inmaculadamente puros ya sea en su fuente ibérica o en su orilla de pueblo originario, del mismo modo existe y existió un empuje a construir la homogeneidad" (Prologue, 8). [Just as subjects have an impulse to feel immaculately pure, be it by virtue of their Hispanic or Indian origin, so too do we have a proclivity to construct homogeneity.] For Toranzo, homogeneity has to do with living in a world of both oligarchic and working-class dogmas and prejudices. These class-based misconceptions and illusions have finished producing ideal models of society that have nothing to do with the real world: "A fuerza de homogeneidades, en los tiempos modernos también la revolución de 1952 quería la suya, invocaba a la construcción de un modelo mestizo homogéneo, donde se borre el rastro de la heterogeneidad, donde se pierda la huella de la diversidad" (ibid.). [So persistent were these homogeneities that in modern times also the revolution of 1952 wanted a homogeneity of its own. Consequently, it is with the model of a homogeneous mestizo that the traces of heterogeneity and diversity got lost.] The revolution, then, wanted us to be culturally the same, and this was its biggest mistake. According to Toranzo, one thing is to be democratically equal in the political sphere, but in no way should this equality erase the plurality and multiple character of ethnic, regional, and cultural diversities.

Openly distrustful of any model of modernization that attempts to see society detached from everyday life, Toranzo believes that only culture can explain diversity. He writes:

> Es tal vez por el lado de la cultura y, claro está, no por la vía del poder político, por donde se ha ido construyendo y explicitando la mezcla; es quizás por esa senda por donde se fue edificando la diversidad. Esa fineza de la multiculturalidad brevó de todo lo diferente que posee el país, su resultado no ha sido sepultar a nadie, a pesar de que todos querían sepultar a todos; antes bien, su producto fue la reproducción de multiples culturas, pero embarazadas mutuamente, enlazadas la una por la otra. (Prologue, 12)

> [Maybe it is through culture and, obviously, not through political power, that hybridity and diversity started to shape up. The finesse of multiplicity got the best from everything that implies difference in this country. Its result has been not to bury anyone, though everybody wanted to bury everybody. Moreover, its product was the reproduction of multiple cultures, linked together, mutually intertwined.]

Detached from the abstract systems of power, this political sociology is not interested in constructing a monolithic "ideal" society, but in exploring the "real" articulation of the diverse components of everyday life.

From food and alcohol to soccer, popular culture, money, and modes of social behavior, Toranzo brings together an array of different languages that are reciprocally paraliterary and paraeconomic. In essence, what he is doing is articulating the many elements of a *ch'enko,* or messy, culture. One of these odd relations is the nexus between *presterío,* power, and the conspicuous consumption of the cholo bourgeoisie.

Prestes are the sponsors of festivities that often commemorate the annual celebrations of patron saints. These festivities are localized celebrations of the artisans who dwell in the popular quarters of the city. Sometimes, however, festivities grow beyond the limits of specific quarters and neighborhoods to become the patron festivals of the city, thus seizing power through ritual. In these cases, the preste must be a successful urban entrepreneur, a newly rich cholo who assumes the financial burden of the dancing, eating, and drinking. As Toranzo puts it:

> Si el "presterío" como la cultura popular, expresiva de algunos sectores del cholaje, era un acto "marginal," que debía vivir oculto en las "laderas" y en la periferia, hoy ya es un hecho perfectamente citadino, ya tomó calles y plazas de las principales ciudades del país. No en balde, la Fiesta del Gran Poder no es sino la metáfora real de uno de los presteríos ur-

banos más grandes del país. Es aquí donde nuevos actores sociales, en especial la burguesía chola, dicen que sí existen y no sólo desparraman cultura sino que también hacen ostentación de su poder económico. (Prologue, 13)

[If the "presterío" as popular culture, and a manifestation of some sectors of the cholos, was a "marginal" act that had to live hidden in the outskirts and in the periphery, now it is an expression of the center of the city because it invaded the streets and parks of the main cities. It is not gratuitous, then, that the Fiesta del Gran Poder be the real metaphor of one of the biggest "presteríos" in the country. It is here that the new social actors, particularly the cholo bourgeoisie, say that they exist by disseminating their culture and by showing their economic power.]

Some important issues concerning the postmodern aestheticization process must be discussed here.[5] First, the surface animation of presteríos and other festivities. Making the Fiesta del Gran Poder the real metaphor of the city of La Paz is a way of transforming the urban into the domain of experience. Indeed, "experience" is a central watchword in these processes of enhancement and animation. No longer a marginal act hidden in the outskirts of the city, the festive nature of the new popular movements is an active experience of open social participation where aestheticization means the furnishing of reality with carnal elements, a sugar-coating of the real with aesthetic flair. This certainly re-engages, as Wolfgang Welsch has noted, "an old and elemental need for a more beautiful reality corresponding to our senses and feelings for form" (2). With the carnal nature of this aestheticization process — I am thinking here on Albó's understanding of the silhouette — comes the symbolism of ethnic progress: "Look, we are no longer being molded by the dominant seigneurial order because we have developed 'structures of feeling' of our own." The old dream, that of improving life and reality through the introduction of aesthetics, seems to be being brought to bear by the new social actors. However, in this aestheticization of everyday life, which has nothing to do with the avant-garde programs that break down the limits of art, the colorful dancing attributes of the new social actors are carried over into reality, and daily life is pumped full of artistic character. This surface aestheticization, then, is increasingly determining the form of our culture as a whole, and Toranzo aptly registers it in his sociopolitical studies, thus introducing the "carnal knowledge" that was ignored by the vertebral analysis of social engineering.

Second, embellishment and animation are linked to the smoothing and antistructural nature of marginality. By linking presterío with the center/periphery dichotomy, Toranzo indicates that marginals and parvenus traditionally occupied the periphery in relation to the contextually determined center. Indeed, the rural indigenous cultures of the Andes, repressed for centuries by the dominant urban sectors of society, have always been the uncomfortable other located outside the social body. Nevertheless, as Toranzo indicates, the migrants have found their way into the center of the city through their patron festivities. The parade, which represents an important part of the festivity, penetrates every year the heart of La Paz, giving the migrants and newly rich cholos, usually excluded from the inner sanctums of upper mestizo/criollo society, a way to express prosperity and cultivate status. Migrants, therefore, invade the city with their jubilant dances that I am tempted to label as "ecstatic."

By "ecstasy," Peter Berger refers not to some abnormal heightening of consciousness in a mystic sense, but rather, quite literally, to the act of standing or stepping out of the taken-for-granted routines of society. In the passage from rural to urban cultures, ecstasy signals permanence instead of, or in addition to, transience. On anthropological grounds, ecstasy indicates the liminal position of these festivities, thus promoting the spatial relationship between a center and its periphery (Berger, 53–55).

Third, the Fiesta del Gran Poder does not stress a vertical or structurally ideal relationship with power, but the real way in which society articulates the rise of new actors within their struggle to attain social and political signification. In this sense, the surface aestheticization of the Fiesta del Gran Poder is the carnal, festive way in which the migrants and newly rich cholos combine an ambiguous reassertion of their ethnic heritage through the medium of folklore with the ostentatious display of wealth. But the spread of aestheticization today is no longer merely superficial; it reaches into deeper economic and political tiers as well. Allow me to indicate some very important aspects of this deep-seated aestheticization.

In the real world, the cholos are the unwanted product of the revolution of 1952. If the revolution could not create a national bourgeoisie of its own, it was also incapable of destroying both the seigneurial mental structure and the strong oligarchic constitution of society. Carlos Toranzo has indicated that the main achievement of this revolution may have been the unsolicited promotion of the cholos to the stature of bourgeoisie, thereby overstepping the barrier of seigneurialism ("Elementos ideológicos," 87–92). Until recently, this new entrepreneurial class did not have any political representation, nor did it partake in economic decision making. It could be said that although cholos had achieved the level of an economic bourgeoisie, the oligarchic sectors of society — both on the Right and on the Left — managed to keep them away from the center. Furthermore, it would be too simplistic to place cholos within capitalism and forget their complexity, their cultural ch'enko. Behind this ch'enko lies the clashing combination of economic, ethnic, and cultural factors that makes it impossible to treat cholos in a linear way. In economic terms, for instance, this new bourgeoisie shows a modality of accumulation of capital that is quite different from the seigneurial bourgeoisie. Indeed, this new sector was not born under the protection of the state; it reinvests its capital gains within Bolivia and does not privilege high consumption, but spends in ritual ceremonies and festivities such as the one I have been discussing so far. Simply put, cholo bourgeoisie defines the rising indigenous Aymara or Quechua entrepreneurs whose economic credentials seek to compensate for their lack of genealogical luster.[6]

Finally, Toranzo places great emphasis on people's self-understanding. Theory must start with the agent's description of his/her own practices in everyday life. This self-understanding must be previous to any attempt to construct definitions. Toranzo, then, would agree with Éscobar on the need to research interpretive approaches grounded on how people understand themselves as creators and practitioners of their world. More important than finding definitions, it is necessary to study the concreteness of everyday life. And it is this concreteness that indicates the country's real articulation as a messy culture, a cultura ch'enko. Only by combining the many intertwined aspects of the social texture will we be able to overcome the dogmas and prejudices, both on the Left and the Right, that have been clouding our understanding of social reality. Messy cultures, then, have no vertebral structure; they follow the ethnic, economic, and cultural undulations of everyday life.

There are undoubtedly great insights in Toranzo's attempt to reaffirm identity within diversity. Insights, however, carry their blindspots. Toranzo finishes his prologue with a certain exultation that brackets the contradictions between the dominant and the dominated. He writes: "Sabemos que este último (el futuro) no conducirá a mantener las fingidas y autoproclamadas purezas, antes bien, nos mezclará cada vez más, nos 'cholificará' de modo creciente; es decir, nos hará mestizos de un modo contemporáneo, pero mestizos diversos, diferentes, pero mestizos asumidos, sin necesidad de ocultar nuestro pasado y sin la obligación de ser iguales u homogéneos" (17). [We know that the future will not keep the faked and self-proclaimed purity; on the contrary, the future will mix us all even more, it will increasingly "hybridize" us; in other words, it will turn us into mestizos, but diverse, different mestizos, without any need to hide our past and without the obligation to be equal or homogeneous.]

The festive connotation of these words reminds me of the production of a postmodernist "sublime" that could also involve the aesthetic fetishization of the social, cultural, and economic status quo. There is, indeed, a certain fantasy in Toranzo's desire for the heterogeneous that obviates the long-standing colonial forms of oppression that displace and undermine the indigenous social organization and political practice. Let me, then, turn now to the studies of internal colonialism in order to balance the postmodern intent to sort out the difficult and messy nature of Bolivian reality.

Since the early 1970s the political voices of indigenous people and the rise of a significant layer of theoreticians and native intellectuals in search of new models for civil society have penetrated the discourse of academic social science monopolized by the traditional elites of the dominant culture.[7] Just as Stefano Varese has registered for the Latin American context, Bolivia is facing a process of Indian reappropriation of its historical past, and linking this initiative to the broader ethnopolitical mobilization of other colonized people of the Third World (Varese, 65).

We know that the model of modernity introduced by social scientists privileged pragmatic categories of analysis over a broader cultural critique of Indian movements. It is therefore not an exaggeration to say that social scientists gave a reduced version of Indian political struggles when explaining them as manifestations of a generic peasantry subordinated to the more rational proletarianized sectors of society. Given this simplistic explanation of indigenous movements, social science missed certain elements of traditionalist Andean organization that are still prevalent in the Bolivian highlands. Juliana Ströbele-Gregor has noted that "modern social organizational structures based on Western models such as the peasant confederation and the rural cooperative in practice incorporated many traditional Andean structural features." As Ströbele-Gregor also indicates, "one of the reasons was that to a considerable extent these highland communities were in fact not new but based on former ayllus that had been incorporated into the hacienda system for the purpose of maximizing profits" (77). Indeed, the 1953 agrarian reform was set up to allow small-scale peasant agriculture as an integral part of a far-reaching communal self-administration, which, in turn, was often viewed by scientific and political discourse as a model for grassroots democracy.

Not until the restoration of formal democracy did we have a full interpretation of these *comunidades originarias*. It is through the research of Silvia Rivera Cusicanqui—who considers "ayllu democracy" as an alternative to the democracy now being practiced in Bolivia—and of William Carter and Xavier Albó—who speak of a "rotating democratic organization"—that we can now understand that communal political organization cannot be conceptualized exclusively in Western models of thought. Consequently, I would like to focus this final part of the essay on the following aspects of Rivera's scholarship: the collision between the concepts of citizenship and ethnicity, and the interaction between modern and premodern categories of thought.

In her essay "Democracia liberal y democracia de ayllu en Bolivia: El caso del norte de Potosí" [Liberal democracy and ayllu democracy in Bolivia: The case of northern Potosí], Rivera shows that there is a long-term historic constant that runs through the successive phases of reform and modernization staged by the dominant creole/mestizo society. Rivera indicates that "the original colonial clash between two cultures and two world views in mutual confrontation became particularly acute during mobilizations to protest the late-nineteenth-century tributary reform, the revolution and agrarian reform of 1953, and, most recently, the promotion of trade unions by NGOS" (115).

If, in colonial times, forced Christianization was the way of turning Indians into rational beings, this religious rationalization was replaced during the republican period by social Darwinism. Sent to the bottom of the scale of human evolution, the Indians would either be subjugated or would perish. Creole society treated Indians with a double standard that recognized the indigenous as citizens, but denied them the same rights as the creole minority (for example, by keeping the Indian population in the countryside and the urban poor at a disadvantage and discriminating against them at all levels of social life). In turn, the revolution and the agrarian reform of 1953, just like the liberal reforms of the nineteenth century, denied the indigenous peasantry the right to preserve their ayllus and communities, imposing smallholding for commodity production as the only option in the distributive process.

This imposition of the liberal ideal of citizenship on the indigenous population was to be catastrophic because it denied Indians all vestiges of their ethnic identity. Indeed, if the nation of citizens finds its identity not in ethnic and cultural commonalities but in the practice of citizens who actively exercise their rights to participation and communication, the denial of these very same civil rights left the Indians at the mercy of the clientelist co-optation of the mestizo/creole minority. For Rivera, "clientelism served as an intermediate structure which gave the appearance of modernity to the new political system, while reproducing the tenacious structural patterns inherited from the colonial past" ("Democracia liberal," 116).

Let me reinforce here the unique nature of internal colonialism. The colonial transformations, just like the liberal and populist reforms, mark the successive ways in which the dominant groups invaded the social, territorial, economic, and cultural forms of the indigenous organizations. Indians, however, did not observe this process of destruction and acculturation passively. On the contrary, they fought and resisted. It is in this violent dialectic between the invaders and the invaded that we find the main mechanism of identity formation and transformation. In this way, the multiple ethnic identities were subdued to a process of homogenization that created new identities signaled by deep traces of racial and cultural intolerance. In other words, Indians and cholos may be citizens from the outside as a consequence of the liberal and populist transformations of the past two centuries. Their rebellion and resistance, however, comes from the inside, as a result of the long historic struggle that started after the Conquest and colonization and lasts until today. If, from the outside, cholos and Indians are modern citizens with membership in a state, from the inside they keep an unruly, visceral rebelliousness, tied to the long memory of their communal traditions and their ethnic past.

We must not forget that citizenship develops out of the concept of individual self-determination. At odds with ethnic and cultural commonalities, the nation of citizens finds its identity in individual performance rather than in communal values. Of the Aymara population, Albó writes: "In the midst of the apparent solitude of the Puna [the Aymara] could not live isolated. He lives submerged in his primary group: the family and the community. He could neither make decisions, nor organize his work . . . if it were not in reference to these relevant groups."[8] The contrast between citizenship and ethnicity could not be more striking. For political scientists who have not paid much attention to ethnicity, it is impossible to conceive citizenship away from the centrally administered nation-state. This state formation secures the boundary conditions under which the capitalist economic system can develop. That is, the nation-state provides the infrastructure for an administration disciplined by the rule of law, and it guarantees a realm of individual and collective economic action free from state interference. Moreover, the nation-state lays the foundation for the ethnic and cultural homogeneity that makes it possible, albeit at the cost of excluding and oppressing minorities.

The Western organization of the nation-state could not be more alien to the ideology of community. Indeed, the notion of community, as applied to premodern cultures, comprises several sets of elements that Rivera is well aware of. There are kinship relations as an organizing device for stabilizing social ties across time-space; there is the local community as a place, providing a familiar milieu; and there are the religious cosmologies as modes of belief and ritual practice providing a providential interpretation of human life and of nature. In contrast, the nation-state relies on economic relationships of a contractual nature; on abstract systems as a means of stabilizing relations across indefinite spans of time-space; and future-oriented, counterfactual thought as a mode of connecting past and present. Consequently, the vast extension of abstract systems (including nation-states and the commodified markets) is totally alien to the very nature of the ideology of community, which is found in, and reproduced in, the immediate process of production in the form of reciprocal labor arrangements as well as, external to the process of production, in the form of religious celebrations or rituals.

Mutually exclusive, the opposition between citizenship and ethnicity has for Rivera important theoretical and practical implications. First, the citizenship ideal of trade unions, political parties, and electoral systems undermines the autonomy of the ayllus. There is, then, a latent tension between the forms of direct democracy exercised by the ayllus, and the representative democracy implied by the model of modernization that relies on political parties and in the parliamentary and municipal democracy. Simply put, political science, based on the citizenship model, denies the ayllu territoriality as a jurisdictional space for political representation.

Second, the tensions between the communal model and the liberal citizenship model are rooted in the economic sphere and in modes of production. Since the citizenship model is the political expression of a petty-commodity regime, it does not go well with the ethnic model oriented toward the social and economic reproduction of the collectivity. At the end of her essay, Rivera indicates that "all this obliges us to reconsider the ideological basis of our democratic institutions. If the ideal of equality continues to be based on the Western model of citizenship . . . then it must likewise continue to prolong and reproduce this process of exclusion which, ultimately, is at the crux of the colonial experience" ("Democracia liberal," 117). I should add here that for Rivera, authentically democratic reform would have to imply some form of articulation between direct and representative democracy, "where citizenship may be reconceptualized in accordance with the multicultural nature of Bolivian reality" (ibid.).

Finally, I turn to the interaction between ethnic and class-oriented categories of thought. In her long essay "La raíz," published in the volume on *Violencias encubiertas en Bolivia* [Hidden violences in Bolivia], Rivera articulates ethnicity with class analysis to give a comprehensive discussion of internal colonialism. In the first chapter, titled "Pachacuti: Los horizontes históricos del colonialismo interno" [Pachacuti: The historical horizons of internal colonialism], Rivera outlines the present-day coexistence of layers of historical memories: the colonial cycle, the liberal cycle, the populist cycle. As we have seen before, these are not successive and unilinear stages of development, but coexisting temporalities that reproduce colonial domination, thus becoming the modalities of an internal colonialism that explains structural violence in Bolivia.

Referring to the chapter's title, Walter Mignolo asks: "Why 'Pachacuti' and not simply 'Los horizontes históricos del colonialismo interno'?" He adds: "Because the Aymara concept 'Pachacuti' (literally, 'teoría del vuelco'; metaphorically 'catastrophe theory'), is started as a category of thought that coexists and interacts with the Western notion of 'revolution'" (61). Indeed, what does the merging of "Pachacuti" with "revolution" teach us? Why is this articulation so important?

If Rivera would have theorized contemporary Bolivia exclusively from the historical horizons of the revolution, she would have engaged her discussion from a vertebral and systemic point of view of society in which the relevant categorizations are defined by the observer, by the "mind's eye" of the social scientist. Rivera, however, articulates very shrewdly the class-based modern dimension with the analysis based on the undulations of ethnic identity. Consequently, she seems to see the need of solving the country's problems "with both eyes": that is, "to see them both as a problem of exploited social classes, and as a problem of oppressed nations (peoples, ethnic groups) within a common Bolivian state" (oo). I must point out, however, some very important epistemological reasons why I think that Rivera's research goes beyond this theory of both eyes and does not abide by Albó's metaphors of the skeleton and the silhouette.

As Albó describes it, the class and ethnic nature of the theory of both eyes is in part a reaction against the "rational" point of view of the social sciences ("From MNRistas to Kataristas to Katari," 402). In this sense, rather than borrowing a model of modernity, capitalist or socialist, to understand Bolivian society, political sociologists use both eyes to solve the intricacies of a movement that runs in the opposite direction: to provide an understanding of society from its living experience, thus countering the experience of metropolitan centers whose theories we must borrow in order to understand ourselves. Carlos Toranzo's view of the plurilingual and multicultural nature of Bolivian society fits well within this description. Indeed, his constant vigilance of contemporary Bolivia places the source and resource of all knowledge and action in life-worldly experience. For good reason, we could describe him as an analyst of experience who, by way of bodily politics, gives a carnal interpretation of society. Replacing borrowed "theoria" with local and festive "aisthesis," Toranzo's approach gives primacy to the real perception of things. Consequently, if social engineers such as Mayorga and Malloy acknowledge the lack of importance of the body, Toranzo, by contrast, takes carnal enjoyment in signifying not only the aesthetic appreciation of bodily politics but also the subversion of Western rationalization as an epistemocratic pursuit of "clear and distinct ideas." Here "enchantment" subverts "enlightenment," and the theory of both eyes modifies the Cartesian rationality of the "mind's eye."

Indeed, the process no longer relies solely on the social scientist's "active" molding of reality through class-based abstractions, but, as we have seen before, on his "experiencing" reality through the carnal elements of ethnicity. The theory of both eyes moves us, then, beyond a narrow understanding of the social body as an object. The centrality afforded to ethnic intersubjectivity in this understanding of subjectivity, moreover, is mirrored in Toranzo's understanding of the Bolivian social world. The social cannot be thought of as an object of skeletal institutions or as an object of thought. It is a real, concrete intersubjective structure, reproduced through embodied action; it consists in sites of shared meaning (festivities, for example) and mutual interaction, where bodies act and are acted upon—where they are agents and targets of power.

There are, however, issues in Toranzo's as well as Albó's approach to reality that are problematic and should be questioned. Though modified, the ocular-centrism of the theory of both eyes is still tied to the process that goes from the outside into the inside. In this process, the carnal aspects of everyday life remain at a surface level—the process of aestheticization—where superficial aesthetic values dominate: desire, amusement, enjoyment without struggle against oppression. This animatory trend is dangerously determining the form of our culture as a whole, and giving the illusion that a society of experience is served by an expanding culture of festivals. It seems as if practitioners of cultural criticism often identify symptoms but shrink at identifying the disease. It is at this point that Rivera's research introduces the notion of "internal colonialism" as the malady that the "pluri-multi" conception of society fails to recognize.

Why "Pachacuti"? Because the teoría del vuelco, or catastrophe theory, goes beyond the theory of both eyes with a visceral process that does not emphasize the "higher" and ecstatic regions of the body (Albó's observer still bears a distant resemblance to its Cartesian predecessor), but the hidden depths of domination fully fleshed out with bone and guts. Colonialism, then, is not just a carnal knowledge that we see from the outside; it is a discomforting or painful sensation that we must eradicate from the inside. Decolonization, then, is always a violent phenomenon, much like catharsis, which in ancient times referred to the medicinal activity of purgation and cleansing.

Finally, the viscerality of internal colonialism overcomes the perils often linked to the instrumental usage of the social sciences, making research the agency for subaltern disintegration and defeat. As Rivera indicates, "Develar y desnudar lo que se conoce del 'otro'—sea éste un pueblo indio colonizado o cualquier otro sector 'subalterno' de la sociedad—equivale entonces a una traición" ("Sendas y senderos," 101) [To reveal the secrets of the "other"—be it a colonized Indian people or any other "subaltern" sector of society—amounts to treason.] What Rivera is doing here is intertwining ethics and the social sciences in such a way that researchers may neither assume a position of superiority or a position of power before the subaltern, nor make them objects of study and manipulation. Rivera's epistemological position clearly coincides with John Beverley's indications that: "What was at stake in our move to subalterns studies was, in other words, a growing sense of the inadequacy of the models of intellectual and political protagonism in which many of us were in fact formed. . . . What we liked about the South Asian Group was its acute sense of the limitations of elite discourse, whether historiographic, anthropological, or literary, colonial, liberal, or even Marxist—limits imposed, as Guha suggests, by the inescapable fact that elite discourse and the institutions that contain it, like the university or literature, are themselves complicit in the construction and maintenance of subalternity" ("Writing in Reverse," 272–273).

What Beverley envisions, as does Rivera, is a new type of intellectual as the protagonist of decolonization. Paradoxically, then, the function of the intellectual project is to displace the centrality of intellectuals. As Rivera affirms:

> Las ciencias sociales bolivianas se enfrentan hoy a una delicada opción: la de servir de instrumento legitimador de nuevas formas de dominación y de cooptación de las demandas indígenas en los nuevos proyectos políticos liberales y autoritarios de dominación; o la de caminar por la senda abierta de las reinvindicaciones indígenas, contribuyendo con elementos de análisis y sistematización, pero sin intentar suplantar a los propios indios como protagonistas organizativos y políticos de dichas reivindicaciones. ("Sendas y senderos," 101)

> [Bolivian social sciences encounter today a difficult decision: whether to become the legitimizing instrument of new forms of domination and manipulation of the indigenous demands in the new liberal and authoritarian political projects of domination. Or whether to walk the open path of the indigenous revindications, thus contributing with elements of analysis and systematization, but never trying to displace Indians as the political agents of said revindications.]

I opened this paper with some general comments regarding the skeletal, the carnal, and the visceral. It might be fitting to close it in the same tone. The skeletal, I would contend, remains within the Cartesian epistemology based on the *cogito,* which is logocentric and ocularcentric. As a metaphor, it expresses the rational organization of political institutions. In this sense, the skeletal is the structural and systemic engineering of modernity. In the case of Bolivia, the skeletal represents nowadays the qualitative transformation of the political system. That is why political scientists concentrate their research on the vertical relationship between society and the state. The skeletal, then, is the vertical construction of the appropriate institutional framework guaranteeing the stability and the governability of the political system. This rational way of seeing society through the mind's eye gives added emphasis to the political party system as the main vertebral linkage between the state and civil society. As I indicated before, the malfunctioning of the skeleton and the striae of society have important cultural implications. Indeed, the lack of a solid politi-

cal backbone created a distorted body that I have labeled as the "social grotesque." Let me say here that it is impossible to explain Bolivian literary production after the revolution of 1952 without relying on this notion. And the
grotesque — the aesthetic expression of the motivational crisis of society — is
deeply tied to the failures of the engineering of political structures in modern
Bolivia.

The carnal, on the other hand, implies a certain subversion of the Cartesian
cogito in the following sense: the question of the body has been an odd
marginalis or a thorn in the flesh of ongoing Western philosophical discourses
due mainly to the hegemony and prejudice of logocentrism. Consequently,
there is a deep necessity to rethink political theory by relating the skeleton
with the carnal silhouette. The carnal, then, introduces a cultural approach
that is inimical to traditional political thinking.

Viscerality, finally, demands that we take sides with the oppressed. Beyond
the theory of both eyes, the insides-out epistemological process of viscerality
wishes us to confront the subaltern not only as a "represented" subject but as
an agent of a transformative project that one day may become hegemonic.
And I accentuate here the "may," the uncertainty of such a project. Nevertheless, even at the risk of one-sidedness, the project must recover some of the
dichotomies of modernity, namely the unsolved struggle between the op-
pressors and the oppressed. As John Beverley has noticed, "While the theoretical force of dependency theory is certainly long spent, some of its underlying
assumptions are still very much with us. One is that it is somehow the responsibility of the left . . . to carry forward the project of elaboration of a national
culture left incomplete by the bourgeoisies" ("Writing in Reverse," 275).
Silvia Rivera also takes this challenge seriously. Speaking of Aymara intellectuals who have studied in Bolivia and in prestigious research institutions,
Rivera says:

> El planteamiento aymara del estado multinacional abordaba, por una
> parte, el problema de democracia y derechos humanos y en este sentido
> interpelaba a los aspectos liberales de la institucionalidad del país. Por
> otra parte, tenía — sin proponérselo — un tono postmodernista incompa-
> tible con las formulaciones nacionalistas y estanilistas. Y finalmente, abor-
> daba explícitamente el problema de la descolonización, que a mi juicio
> constituye el elemento crucial que diferencia el caso boliviano del peru-
> ano. Las implicaciones de estos hechos para la investigación no pueden
> pasar desapercibidas. ("Sendas y senderos," 94)

> [The Aymara proposal of a multinational state tackled, on one hand, the
> problematics of democracy and human rights, and interpellated, in that
> sense, the most liberal aspects of Bolivian institutions. On the other hand,

the proposal had—rather unintentionally—a postmodernist tone that was incompatible with the nationalist and Stalinist formulations. Finally, it tackled explicitly the problematics of decolonization, an aspect that, to my belief, was crucial to the differentiation of the Bolivian from the Peruvian case. The implications of all these facts cannot go unnoticed in research.]

The skeletal, the carnal, and the visceral are metaphors of Bolivia's contemporary social reality. The first can only be seen with the mind's eye. It is an invisible, ocularcentric metaphor for the institutional infrastructure beneath the disturbing tides of ethnicity and other elements of soft pathology. The carnal, on the other hand, modifies this ocularcentrism with both eyes: it sees both the institutional, class-based analysis of society, and the ethnic problems of identity formation. The view, however, is still exogenous, through an epistemological movement that goes from the outside into the inside. Last, but not least, the visceral shows a countermovement that goes from the insides-out. It gives us an understanding of the long-standing endogenous practices of the peasantry which lead to a necessary reconceptualization of democracy that is more in line with subalternity and with the multicultural nature of our societies.

Notes

An earlier version of this essay appeared as "The Skeletal, the Carnal, and the Visceral: Metaphors We Live By in Contemporary Bolivia," *Dispositio/n* 21, 48 (1996): 183–218.

1   I follow here Michael Hardt's indications that the striae of civil society are the skeleton that defines and supports the figure of the social body. See his essay "The Withering of Civil Society."

2   This is one of the main arguments of my book *Literatura contemporánea y grotesco social en Bolivia*.

3   I have freely interpreted Michael Hardt's notion of the "smoothing of social space" as opposed to disciplining it through the "striae of civil society"; see Hardt, "Withering of Civil Society." I will come back to this notion of a "messy culture" when discussing Carlos Toranzo's work on multiculturalism.

4   For an analysis of the culture-neutral aspects of the theories of modernity, see Charles Taylor, "Inwardness and the Culture of Modernity."

5   I follow here Wolfgang Welsch's "Aestheticization Processes: Phenomena, Distinctions, and Prospects."

6   I find striking similarities between these cholos and the postmodern reading of the *pícaros*. See Giancarlo Maiorino, "Renaissance marginalities," xi–xxvii, and Francisco José Sánchez and Nicholas Spadaccini, "The Picaresque in the Postmodern Times," 292–307.

7   I refer to Joanne Rappaport's mimeography "Andean Indigenous Intellectuals in the Nineties," written in collaboration with Luis de la Torre, Marcelo Fernández, Margarita Huayhua, and Esteban Ticona.

8   Quoted and translated into English by Dwight R. Hahn. See Hahn, "The Use and Abuse of Ethnicity: The Case of the Bolivian CSUTCB"; and Wolfgang Welsch, "Aestheticization Processes: Phenomena, Distinctions, and Prospects."

Works Cited

Albó, Xavier. "From MNRistas to Kataristas to Katari." In *Resistance, Rebellion, and Consciousness in the Andean Peasant World,* ed. Steve J. Stern. Madison: University of Wisconsin Press, 1987.

———. "Our Identity Starting from Pluralism in the Base." In *The Postmodernism Debate in Latin America,* John Beverley and José Oviedo. Special issue of *boundary 2* 20, 3 (fall 1993): 18–33.

Berger, Peter. "Sociological Perspectives: Society as Drama." In *Life as Theater: A Dramaturgical Sourcebook,* ed. Dennis Brissett and Charles Edgley. New York: Aldine de Gruyter, 1990: 51–61.

Beverley, John. *Against Literature.* Minneapolis: University of Minnesota Press, 1993.

———. "Writing in Reverse: On the Project of the Latin American Subaltern Studies Group." Special issue of *Dispositio/n* 19, 46: 271–288.

Boyte, Harry C. "The Pragmatic Ends of Popular Politics." In *Habermas and the Public Sphere,* ed. Craig Calhoun. Cambridge, Mass.: MIT Press, 1992.

Éscobar, Arturo. "Culture, Economics, and Politics in Latin American Social Theory and Research." In *The Making of Social Movements in Latin America: Identity, Strategy, and Democracy,* ed. Arturo Éscobar and Sonia E. Alvarez. Boulder: Westview Movements Press, 1992.

Giddens, Anthony. *The Consequences of Modernity.* Stanford, Calif.: Stanford University Press, 1990.

Hahn, Dwight R. "The Use and Abuse of Ethnicity: The Case of the Bolivian CSUTCB." *Latin American Perspectives* 23, 2 (spring 1996): 91–106.

Hardt, Michael. "The Withering of Civil Society." *Social Text* 45, (winter 1995): 27–44.

Ilie, Paul. *Literature and Inner Exile.* Baltimore: Johns Hopkins University Press, 1980.

Maiorino, Giancarlo. *The Picaresque: Tradition and Displacement.* Minneapolis: University of Minnesota Press, 1996.

Malloy, James M., and Eduardo Gamarra. *Revolution and Reaction: Bolivia 1964–1985.* New Brunswick, N.J.: Transaction Books, 1988.

Mignolo, Walter D. "Are Subaltern Studies Postmodern or Postcolonial? The Politics and Sensibilities of Geo-Cultural Locations." *Subaltern Studies in the Americas.* Special issue of *Dispositio/n* 19, 46 (1994) [1996]: 45–73.

Rivera Cusicanqui, Silvia. "Democracia liberal y democracia de ayllu en Bolivia: El caso del norte de Potosí." In *El difícil camino de la democracia,* ed. Carlos Toranzo. La Paz: ILDIS, 1990.

———. "La raíz: Colonizadores y colonizados." In *Violencias encubiertas en Bolivia.* Vol. 1. Ed. Xavier Albó and Raúl Barrios. La Paz: CIPCA-AYUWIYIRI, 1993: 27–139.

———, "Sendas y senderos de la ciencia social andina." *Autodeterminación* 10 (October 1992): 83–108.

Sanjinés C., Javier. *Literatura contemporánea y grotesco social en Bolivia.* La Paz: BHN-ILDIS, 1992.

Ströbele-Gregor, Juliana. "Culture and Political Practice of the Aymara and Quechua in Bolivia." *Latin American Perspectives* 23, 2 (spring 1996): 72–88.

Taylor, Charles. "Inwardness and the Culture of Modernity." In *Philosophical Interventions in the Unfinished Project of Enlightenment,* ed. Axel Honneth, Thomas McCarthy, Clauss Offe, and Albrecht Wellmer. Cambridge, Mass.: MIT Press, 1992: 88–93.

Toranzo, Carlos. "Elementos ideológicos y conductas de la nueva derecha." In *Nueva derecha y desproletarización en Bolivia,* ed. Carlos Toranzo Roca and Mario Arrieta Abdalla. La Paz: UNITAS-ILDIS, 1989: 87–111.

———. Prologue to *Lo pluri-multi o el reino de la diversidad.* La Paz: ILDIS, 1993.

Varese, Stefano. "The Ethnopolitics of Indian Resistance in Latin America." *Latin American Perspectives* 23, 2 (spring 1996): 58–71.

Welsch, Wolfgang. "Aestheticization Processes: Phenomena, Distinctions, and Prospects." *Theory, Culture, and Society* 13, 1 (February 1996): 1–24.

V. CITIZENSHIP: RESISTANCE, TRANSGRESSION, DISOBEDIENCE

The Teaching Machine for the Wild Citizen

BEATRIZ GONZÁLEZ STEPHAN

The inner side of civilized bodies, subject to a bulk of discourse practices that have given rise to the distribution of medical and anthropological knowledge, leaks out of the writing machine. Thus, it remains outside as a prepolitical resistance to the very process of technological and cognitive modernization, which wanted only to eliminate or, in the best of cases, recognize that inner side in order to domesticate it or explain it. These are the bodies and languages of the "other," of things resisting to enter the grammar and law of the enlightened city, to enter the Western order of the world and the reticulum of academic knowledge. Discourse can hardly either name or articulate these individuals and languages into its own logic of hierarchic differential distribution without them being punished under the slogan of "barbarism," "illiteracy," or "degeneration."

Discourse naturally orders, controls, and subjects sensibilities within its own boundaries. This is why the building of modern citizenship — cannot be thought of and designed except on the basis of a series of writings that establish, found, and circumscribe the human body. From treatises on medicine, health, and hygiene to manuals of conduct, courtesy, rhetoric, and grammar, passing through catechism books for children, including constitutions, and not forgetting about beauty tips, fashion, and body aesthetics, techniques, standards, rules, and practices: they all build up the nation's hegemonic body. Writing can only hold within its printed thickness what really departs from it: that other body which cannot be written, that lies in fandango, samba, tamunangue, carnival, *santería* (image worshipping), jargon, *quilombos* (shelters for runaway slaves), servants, children, peasants, gauchos, cowboys, cholos, white and mestizo craftsmen, and in female bodies convulsive and hyperaesthetic as a result of the repression they have been submitted to. These are the bodies of an impossible subalternity in a writing that can hardly draw its dull silhouettes in the back lights of its own logic.

Medical as well as philological narratives constructed their building of "positivities" on a background of "negativities." The production of a true effect of the illustrated elite should, in the same operation of writing, authenticate its proposal on the basis of a disqualifying representation of what was being validated. That is to say, in taking up the values of a society marked by accumulation, saving, ruled by constraint, they hid their own fears and passions, thus remaking in their discourses a satanized idea of subjects and cultures which not only did not understand but also that should be kept within limits. The modeling writing of civilized bodies operated simultaneously in two completely opposite directions: at the time it defined bodies within rules, constrained impulses, and homogenized languages, it spread new distinctions on the basis of habits and composure, or better, on the outer side of words, and it also reflected the body of hegemonic citizenship, representing the enlightened management of the national state, although on the back side of that same writing, words imprinted deep prints, such as those in a photo negative filled by the body of a subalternity built as a threatening instance of the official body, drawn also by the reverse of writing itself.

Obviously, the obverse of writing showed its prolific reflection on the clean, pure, and ruled body of citizenship at the time that its reverse wrote the "barbarization" of the other's body. What's more: the body became the surface on which discipline's technologies were shot. In one of its angles, the discourse device was substantially ordering and distributing boundaries. Meanwhile, on the other side, beyond discourse boundaries, a counterculture of enlightened disciplining emerged. Beyond the cataloging, analytical, and correcting word, a wide range of subalternities as such did not fit the order of discourse, except for its diminishing and Manichean representation on the part of the lord of words. In order to be controlled by the imaginary, the subaltern were subdued to "illiteracy" since they could not speak or read. They were considered "bandits" because they were not subjected to an exploitation economy. They were treated by physicians as "insane," "hysteric," or "furious" because they did not repress themselves. They were considered "ragged," "dirty," and "syphilitic" as a result of their own different subsistence modes. Besides, it was a strategy for "scientifically" ensuring their marginalization from the official political scenario.

The production of a citizenship within the framework of the new republican legality, which paved the way to an inevitable democratization process of the new era, had to be restrained with the reintroduction of new interclass distinction mechanisms. As the urbanity of lords was founded upon Christian virtues to give a democratic appearance to a system of distinctions based on old possessions and nobility degrees, its modern version lacks that moral root and faith in the creation of habits and in a complex code of manners and appearances, aiming at strengthening pragmatic and utilitarian components instead of being oriented toward civic and communicative goals. The discourse of good manners, of hygiene and education, pointed to body possibilities as a modern leverage for social positioning. Today it has become a mechanism of power that can, by means of its own modeling, distribute the bodies of hegemony and social subalternity merely with the "know how to say" and manners sweetened by courtesy.

The body of modern times is the result of printed technology, much in the same way that the body of "barbarism" was given a name, so that later, in a second turn, it was possible to disembody or dematerialize citizenship's legal body. Regarding this, not far from these attacks were the texts *La Quijotita y su prima* (published in fascicles in 1918) by Mexican José Joaquín Fernández de Lizardi; *Facundo, civilización, y barbarie* (published in parts, attached to the periodical *El Progreso* in 1845) by Argentinean Domingo Faustino Sarmiento; and the script of Venezuelan Gerónimo Pompa, *El Libertino arrepentido* (1838), all of which featured from the point of view of fiction undesirable body impulses that would become part of an alternative citizenship's counterhegemony.

Covert in these texts of the enlightened culture — just like in-between lines in manuals of conduct, hygiene, and grammar — on the reverse of the fabric the shadow of subaltern sensibilities was gaining shape. The postmodern look, by inquiring into a citizen's body which can no longer be restrained within the boundaries of writing because it overflows it, preaches this body's prison of language. Now both sides of discourse can be read, and the thin fabric building the fiction of the disciplined (and no less castrated) body of official citizenship can be separated at the time that it also drew with the force of fiction itself the dull body of subjects whose historical pressure have called into doubt the discourses that distorted them or crossed them out. Let us see then this double game of light and shadow, high and bas-relief of the devices of the modern citizen's body.

One of the critical goals of the political and pedagogical institutions of the nineteenth century was to change the habits and customs of urban populations and to generalize the use of correct words. The education of citizens and the standardization of the national language were issues that concerned most scholars as part of the complex modernizing agenda the new Latin American nations had to implement. The emergence of utilitarian thought would unite the civilizing project with the development of a reactive sensibility when faced with certain situations (expressions and behaviors) that are now perceived as pollution, dirt, obscenity, and perversion, which could hinder the effectiveness of the modernizing project if the right measures were not taken to eradicate them. Progress generated a new functional mentality that enabled and transmitted scientific knowledge, which, as one of its several implications, generalized a compulsion for cleanliness among the learned sectors and the incipient bourgeoisie. This had many consequences, pragmatic — from the cleanliness of streets to the new directions of personal hygiene — as well as metaphorical — from cordoning off certain sectors of the population, like prostitutes, to purging language of "indecent" words.

Portraits of customs and hundreds of chronicles describe social practices as confined to a sensibility that is now regarded as barbaric and discordant compared to the desired model of civilization — of European make. Obviously, the creation of new urban spaces, such as the theater, demanded rules of conduct that were still unknown to the users who were mostly illiterate and more used to entertainment where unrestraint, laughter, violence, and lack of inhibitions were the usual language. How could we go from the usual uproar and hooting of the cockpits or the unrestraint of the carnivals to a theater house that demanded silence, stillness, constraint, and just applause? During the first decades of the century, it seemed that police regulations and the endeavors of scholars concerned about redirecting sensibilities were tilling in a field of resistance to change. Among the activities carried out by theatergoers in Caracas in 1836 were urinating, defecating, farting, and fornicating inside the theater. Any dark corner, any dark place, any empty box (which was not momentarily transformed into a gambling den) would do. And if desire and impatience were pressing, one only had to make space between two seats, where, disregarding any possible comment by others, they freely performed the "natural" and civic sin. If the ladies did not want to smell it, they could hold their noses; if they did not want to see, they could close their eyes.[1] And it was not only in places of entertainment where spirits displayed this lack of constraint. In all registers of social life, human expressions were tinged with prominent tonalities: physical punishment, games, spontaneous sexuality, lack of hygiene, the natural expression of intimacy (tears, laughter, pain, rage), the cohabitation with death and disease.[2]

On another level, after the wars of independence the physiognomy of the continent's main cities was, if not dilapidated, then at the mercy of an unstable political life that did not offer a way out of the economic crisis nor the fineries of the urban landscape. From Buenos Aires to Caracas, the tales of travelers and the portraits of customs seem to describe the same place: the houses drained their sewers onto the streets; in the downtown area, pigs wallowed in putrid puddles; the peeling walls of houses gathered a filthy crust of rotten eggs, indigo, and sewage water, a remnant of semibarbaric carnivals; slum dwellers went barefoot, their toes deformed by chiggers. In paupers' cemeteries, corpses were often only half buried, decomposing among marauding dogs and pigs. In the market, the butchers slaughtered animals in plain view and *mondongo* (tripe) and vegetables were sold on the floor under makeshift stands. Very few carriages traveled over the stone pavement, which had gaping holes opened by the rain, where travelers had to wade between fetid swamps, waste, and a gallery of artisans who performed their trades outdoors. Vendors sold pork rinds, peanuts, and cups of *chicha* in the theaters, competing with the actors' speeches, as well as in the inns and slums, which were infested with bedbugs and fleas. Perhaps this scenario, which followed other patterns of cleanliness and human cohabitation, was inherited from colonial times.[3]

It is not strange, therefore, that as the century progressed and secularization modified perspectives on these situations, the new sensibility developed a phobia against dirt, disease, and even physical contact, followed by a compulsion for hygiene, cleanliness, and correctness. A severe and constrained morality united with advances in medicine and biology, and very directly with grammar. Language and body, flesh and spirit, individual and group, citizens and cities, began to be stigmatized by police, teachers, physicians, and scholars, who sought to repress, corset, discipline, or wash bodies, streets, and languages to eliminate miasma, mud, and "uncivilized deviations."

Among the known epidemics, the modern era was mostly concerned about cholera, as if it concentrated all the forms of "barbarism." At times, recommendations to eradicate cholera morbus took the most curious, not to mention irrational, turns. It served many followers of progress and of the new bourgeois ethics to associate disease not only with the deterioration of cities, stench, and carrion, but also with vagrancy and public idleness (i.e., peddlers), vandalism, begging (i.e., those with an active trade), unruliness, prostitution, or a bohemian life (probably poor artists). The issue of good habits and health, as the flipside of the same repressive discourse, was a main topic of countless publications. On January 20, 1834, *El Monitor* of Buenos Aires published a chronicle where cholera speaks out:

> I will look for the vicious and depraved, those who surrender to intoxication or gluttony and make these excesses the pleasure of their existence, and those who neglect hygiene and cleanliness and lay in filth. . . . Those whose constitutions are ravaged by the disorders of a dissolute lifestyle, the professional loafers who spend their time in the most absolute indolence, and who don't practice any rational occupation . . . and finally, those who ruin their health through contamination with sordid and pernicious diseases. . . . Be it also known that I prefer to live in dirty narrow streets with poor ventilation; in small, filthy, overcrowded rooms, and even better, in low areas which are close to garbage dumps, stagnant and corrupted waters, and similar filth. But I must admit *that I will have nothing to do with, nor will I come close to those who are industrious, sober and well behaved.* If they rise early, open the windows so that air circulates,

wash and clean themselves, have their house cleaned, work on their trade, and use the necessary nourishment with moderation . . . I will not enter their peaceful abode, and I will treat myself to the damaged liver of a drunkard, stir the bitter bile of the ill-tempered and troublemaker, and feast on those I mentioned before.[4]

This long quote helps us visualize — regardless of the obvious implications cholera had and still has — the persuasive and punitive operations that scholarly authorities undertook to attack, under the pretext of a feared disease, a concept of life that would not benefit capitalist ethics: the key point was not filth or the disease itself, nor a less moral sexual behavior, but the need to instill a new ethics based on commercial values where the individual's energies (sexual, emotional, and temporal) were redirected toward greater labor profitability. Capital stock — if the goal is to build modern nations with all kinds of luxury goods — could not be wasted in endless orgies, feasts, carnivals, and bullfights, which not only decreased the time needed for production, but also threatened Cartesian reasoning, which strived to impose composure and an orderly lifestyle. Therefore, those activities that were not imbued with acquisitive value were perceived as morally execrable or illegal. The way of being and speaking in a world centered on a more contemplative and less economical view had to change.

Biological and clinical metaphors allowed many conceptual maneuvers where *disease* (in this case, cholera, as we saw in the previous quote) was associated with dirt, indigence, crowding, poverty, homosexuality, masturbation, adultery (particularly feminine), prostitution, and lonely and vehement temperaments. On the other hand, *hygiene,* besides involving historically accepted habits of cleanliness (not necessarily related to water), is paired with the notion of physical and moral asepsis, which would lead to imposing controlled and constrained behaviors. In this sense, hygiene was equated with Victorian ethics, with marriage as the cell of society, with austere table and bedroom manners, with rich sectors, and with the biological distribution of sexual roles; and in the area of discourse, hygiene shares with manuals of conduct, grammars, and the law the tendency to establish boundaries between heterogeneous entities, to regulate the dynamics of contact, and to prevent contamination. In short: the boundaries of citizenship coincide with the boundaries imposed by the parameters of bodily hygiene, passions, cities, and languages. The language of the body had to silence its needs, and the body of language had to cleanse itself of its dialecticisms. It is this latter category which carried stiffer penalties for citizens who did not polish and purify the Spanish language, purging it of the vices of expression. Therefore, body and language had to be cleansed and fitted to the disciplinary writings of manuals of conduct and the art of speaking.[5]

Schools and the whole educational system (which includes many publications, their distribution, and reading), with a view to forming individuals who can be integrated and summoned as citizens, were a goal of liberal nationalism. Free public education, as established in the constitutions, was the slogan of the state, and the hope was to articulate, always within a hierarchic structure, the greatest number of individuals through a culture that summarized its codes in writing. It was within the framework of the process of writing/reading as a mechanism that produces symbolic values that individuals were to adapt a clean and disciplined body to the good use language. This assumed that the actions of the body (i.e., our behavior towards others) as well as the spoken word (i.e., conversation) had to be anchored, or regulated, by a previous mastery of written practices. Manuals of conduct, just as rhetoric, grammar, orthography, and pronunciation manuals, including hundreds of brochures and flyers with recommendations about health, hygiene, diseases, and home remedies, required the ability to read, whether the silent and private reading of urban sectors or the oral and collective reading by those who transmitted these texts to their communities. Citizenship implied the acquisition of fine and affable manners, as well as a "correct" language; being a citizen meant having a body and a language adjusted by rules, patterns, and laws established in writing—a writing that trapped bodies and languages, returning them to practical life as mirrors of bodies and written languages.[6]

From this perspective, education establishes "otherness": clearly Indians, blacks, "mestizos" and all those who were not part of the interests of the politically powerful (masters of writing, oratory, and finances) swelled the nation's margins. To read and write in national terms meant having control, specifically over "barbaric" freedoms. It assumed a standard destined to unify that geographic, ideological, social, and political expanse over, and despite, which the nation was being built. It implied a tacit agreement with those who led the national project. There could be no "impolite" words; everything had to be said within the new written order; that is, keeping an aesthetic and ideological position, knowing how to say things in the language of bureaucrats, of virtuous and enlightened men, of the model citizen.

Citizens had to be shaped through a series of disciplinary exercises—in schools, by instructors, and in seminaries, by priests—so that they became automatically used to a constrained moderation and a programmed eloquence. In the beginnings of the newly founded republics, the most abundant publications were grammars—not only of Spanish language, but also Latin, English, and French: dictionaries and manuals to teach people to speak and write properly.[7] The concern, particularly of the educated class, to speak correctly was essential to consolidate the nation-state because stabilization of the national language is a key element in giving a single meaning to the language of the law and contracts in a transparent, clean and clear, manner.[8]

At this time, however, I do not want to focus on the "cleansing" operation as standardizing language by means of grammars and dictionaries (the most well known manual of conduct throughout Latin America was titled *Manual de urbanidad y buenas maneras*, by Venezuelan Manuel Antonio Carreño). Grammar books, dictionaries, and manuals of good conduct served a very practical double purpose: they pointed out in a didactic way the proper bodily conduct, for the self as well as for others, as well as the patterns that good citizens were to follow in verbal exchanges.[9] All these manuals refer their users to more specific texts, including grammars, books on the art of conversation, treatises on hygiene and venereal diseases, cookbooks, collections of home remedies, women's beauty books, and fashion magazines.[10]

The Hygiene of the Body of Citizens

During the nineteenth century, owning manuals of conduct became more common among individuals in urban sectors, and even though they were not fully familiarized with them, they made the effort to acquire them, as a sign of comfort and "culture," to share the space on their modest bookshelves with a Bible, the lives of the saints, almanacs, brochures, and perhaps a book on national history. Throughout the century, didactics as well as historic and literary publications (novels and poems) progressively changed the taste for religious works as the public and private makeup of the citizen took on greater importance, both as the protagonists of the republican demos and the narcissistic heroes of their own subjectivity. The goal of these manuals was to capture individuals from their early childhood. Schools were the primary means of dissemination, and their goal was, and is, to "straighten" the body and the soul of the child to avoid undesirable twists. In the nineteenth century, this genre became popular among the bourgeoisie, whereas earlier it had been in the hands of the nobility and the upper class.

In Europe this tradition was inaugurated in 1530 with the first treatise of Erasmus of Rotterdam, *De civilitate morum puerilium*, which at the time was a smashing success, in number of editions (eighty in the sixteenth century, and at least thirteen in the eighteenth century) as well as in translations (in 1531 it was translated into high German; in 1532 into English; in 1537 into Czech and French; and in 1546 into Dutch). Erasmus immediately wrote a second version for children: *Declamatio de pueris statim ac liberaliter instituendis*, since that was indeed the ideal destination for the civilizing project of modern times.[11]

Since then, passing through the equally important rules of Jean-Baptiste de la Salle (*Regles de la bienséance et de la civilité chrétienne divisé en deux parties a l'usage des école chrétiennes,* with twenty editions published at regular intervals between 1793 and 1789), which successfully implemented efficient coactive standards among the lower levels of society, manuals of conduct became the panacea of the new bourgeois sensibility from the Enlightenment, and definitely after the French Revolution. Undoubtedly, de la Salle's rules were one of the most efficient, and timely, agents for establishing the behavior models of the elite in other sectors of society because they foresaw a "civilizing" program that combined control with respect for the social order: an ethics capable of controlling individual loneliness and caring for appearances.

This is not the place to trace the history of these manuals, how they traveled from Europe to Latin America, or who had an influence over whom. I only want to underscore that this practical literary genre had an amazing rise in popularity throughout the nineteenth century because it was essential for the nation's project to pay attention to the body, in its medical dimensions of physical and mental health, to achieve the appropriate demographic numbers that would guarantee not only a "civilized" population in terms of "civility," but also a "healthy" one in terms of labor effectiveness. The issues of "health," "cleanliness," and "hygiene" linked to "sexual morality" became the obsessions, and by the end of the century, it could be said that 40 percent of printed commercial advertisements were related to physical energy (remember the famous Scott Emulsion) and hygiene habits (the use of toothpaste and fragrances for the body). The intention was, on one hand, to increase physical energy, but on the other, to redirect energy through the ethics of guilt toward work and (re)production.

The body is a key element in the disciplining agendas of teachers, physicians, and priests. Without forgetting the soul altogether, modernization turns away from a metaphysical conception of the individual and tends toward a relationship where physical aspects — organic life, health, cleanliness — are going to deeply affect morality. In other words, the influence of physical aspects on morality establishes the value of cleanliness and orderliness. The body is punished — or disciplined, castrated, corseted, disinfected — because it is regarded as the source of feared "deviations." In fact, bourgeois sensibility pauses at bodily desires; it is obsessed with hiding and negating them, trapped between asceticism and a fascination with perversion, and an almost sacred respect for what is forbidden and its transgression, between blame and uninhibited confession. Therefore, they devote themselves to ridding the body of its excretions and its impulses to soften its outward manners, the hypertrophy of appearances, and to tame impulses, the repression of Eros, to achieve the affability and propriety that the dominating civilizing model appreciated so much.

Hands and Face. The success of the infectionist theory hypertrophied the regulation of contacts: hands, fingers, mouth, and face became the tentacles that were more prone to contamination. The golden rule of the new civic regime proposed that "the truly refined man is never in contact with other bodies" (MC, 23). The persistence in having our hands "perfectly clean every time we are going to shake them" (34) pointed toward a policy that preferred to avoid all direct contact: "we should never use our fingers to clean our ears, eyes, teeth and much less our noses" (25), food was not to be touched with mouths and hands if it had been already touched by someone else, and the use of gloves at balls was compulsory.

The prevailing concept of cleanliness during the nineteenth century did not necessarily associate cleanliness with the frequent use of soap and water, or with the daily bathing of the body.[12] The normal practice was a fragmented hygiene, where it was more important to control obvious excretions and filth of parts of the body (sweat, beards, nails, bad breath, eye secretions, belching, and spittle), to wear a proper attire, to ventilate rooms, and to take care of the home. The idea of cleanliness was associated first with controlling appearances and with manners (caring for hair and teeth, and having clean shoes), and second "with order and method, and a sensible economy of time" (MC, 18); that is, with policies of saving. Third, cleanliness was associated with pure categories, and in this sense the relationship between health and clean air, hygiene, and pure environments was to become very important.[13]

Hiding Disease. Riding the train of progress, particularly after 1860, meant making a pact with a program of personal and urban hygiene, which frequently implied presenting a good front. The modern era also built a physical body for the new bourgeois citizen: slimmer rather than pudgy, robust, mature, virile, strong, without premature baldness, and with all the teeth. Health promised success in business, ensured the increase of public wealth, and was the banner of morality. Disease meant failure, poverty, and physical and ethical ugliness. Consequently, disease had to be hidden. It was kept silent as something shameful ("whenever we have a disease that requires us to blow our noses, spit, etc., we should avoid going to meetings and receiving visitors" (MC, 33; "we should not visit or receive visits when we are sick or have suffered an accident, if we cannot follow strict hygiene rules," 163). The sick had to be cordoned off or locked up in health centers. Their emanations were feared because they were presumed to be contaminated, just as the emanations of wastes, waste waters, and slaughterhouses. In this sense, prostitutes met the same fate because a publicly degraded body was regarded as "putrid" and infected matter. The diseased body of society was assimilated directly (a necessary drainage), clearly relocated in certain "low" communities of the city.

Prostitution was hidden by the night, just as the dark object of bourgeois sexual desire was repressed and flagellated.[14]

In another sequence, sex, disease, and death had to be kept away from the daylight, and contact with them restricted. For "barbaric" sensibilities, co-habitation with disease and the dead was normal within the family: individuals' deaths and wakes took place at home. The modern era separated death from life, and sexuality from normality. Therefore, it is not strange that directly proportional to this morality was a simultaneous emergence of certain practices such as necrophylia, which as a transgression proves the tension between a more fluid and less caged sensibility and another that is punitive and aseptic. Modern literature was the ideal space for this imagination divided between the law and perversion.[15]

"Cover Yourself So They Do Not See You Naked!" The basic concern of manuals, rather than disciplining the body (although they refer to that all the time), was to create discourse areas that on one hand resist the open admission of sexuality, yet on the other talk about it all the time. Most of their norms deal constantly with Eros. The fear of physical impulses etches each gesture into an erotic grammar that must be counteracted by a disciplining grammar. On the back side of the page, they talk about the sexual potential of each segment of the body, of the erotic charge of every insinuation, touch, glance or close social exchanges.

The initial impression might be that in the nineteenth century the prevailing trend was to disembody impulses. If we analyze words carefully, however, an appalling number of discourses that rationalize the social, individual, biological, psychic, and moral body spans the whole century, analyzing, classifying, and counting sexual impulses in order to regulate ratios of population to wealth and to workforce, births, life expectancy, public health, frequency of diseases, eating habits, reproduction, and housing. The individual or social sexual body acquired an unusual presence that in some areas induced its repression (silencing), while in others it tended to its reconversion. Never is the sexual body subject to so much prohibition as when it triggers several discourses and disciplines to learn about it.[16]

The new discourse technologies, like the pastoral discourse, agreed when they blamed the needs and desires of the body; following the same Christian mapping of high and low, they stigmatized the "lower" parts of the human body just as they did a city's "outskirts." Any mention of genitals was carefully avoided; the functions of the reproductive cycle (sexual cohabitation, menstruation, gestation, and delivery) were nonexistent; the physiological need to evacuate (urinating and defecating) was explicitly denied. (Carreño states that "the habit of getting up at night to relieve physical needs is highly disapproved; and the individuals who don't know everything that education can ask from nature are those who justify it in vain" [MC, 48]). Desire also had to be tamed at the deepest and most intimate levels: "It is also a bad habit to make *strong movements* during our sleep, which at times make bed coverings fall from the bed and make us assume *offensive postures that go against honesty* and propriety" (ibid., emphasis added). Just as a prudent privacy was recommended for resting, changing clothes, and cleaning, readers were warned against the possible risks of individual solitude, which incites masturbation and hence deviance — in men, particularly, because the "unproductive" loss of semen equaled the waste of raw materials and a possible attempt to avoid the creation of a heterosexual couple.[17]

Readers were warned against discovering their own bodies (and, obviously, another person's body). The naked body was feared and prohibited: "A man is not allowed to be at home without a tie, jacket, socks, or wearing improper shoes" (MC, 55). And "when a married couple lives together, the room is even more inviolable for any of them; and only a rare and serious accident may justify entering it" (56). Censorship is even tighter when it is legal because of the inoculation of fear toward sexuality (understood as deviation, lack of constraint, and disease), and the body is always regarded as a wild animal despite the most systematic discipline.

In the nineteenth century the sexual potential of a child's body was discovered, and it was almost a paranoid perception ("We must also be careful of the clothes that other children wear at home, and we should never allow them to be naked or in rags" [57]). Children were carefully observed because any innocent gesture was regarded, in the eyes of a deeply repressed adult, in terms of sexual perversion. This was the reason for prohibiting physical contact (hand games) at school, and for police surveillance in dormitories and in public fairways. Pedagogy aimed its battery at young children to tame their liveliness as the first step toward redirecting or castrating sexual energy.

On the other hand, regarding the tradition of personal hygiene in the wealthy, a number of servants or slaves cared for the bath of the master or mistress. The new bourgeois sensibility inhibited the exposure of the body before anyone else, so bathing and cleaning parts of the body were strictly private ("For this reason, when delicate persons live with others in the same room, they try to be alone to clean their bodies or to change clothes" [MC, 56]). The intimacy of the individual was born: Deciphering the self — body and soul — and also its control. However, privacy of the body does not necessarily mean accepting it. Faced with their own excretions, the individuals were forced to deny themselves ("Dignity and propriety demand that we don't call the attention of anyone before or after we perform those acts that are or may be repulsive, regardless of how natural and necessary they are" [66]; and

"Some have acquired the terrible habit of closely observing the handkerchief they used after blowing their noses. This and any other similar acts are not allowed" [25]).

The nineteenth century observed the body with new eyes, at the edge of a sharp bifurcation: it discovered its magnitude as a source of wealth and social power: it cleaned, covered, and made it into a fetish.

The Control of Emotions. If cleanliness and asepsis were hygienizing measures for bodies and cities, containing and withdrawing drives to achieve an affable and sweet expression were the tasks to correct temper. It was a matter of cleaning behavior of roughness, violence, familiarity, and incontinence. Taking care of manners basically implied observing outward forms. What mattered were restrained appearances, with faces preferably inexpressive ("when a person is so rude that offends us intentionally, we must act with an inalterable serenity and we must control ourselves to the point that our countenance does not show our anger" [MC, 260]), revealing neither happiness nor repressed pain ("when we have an internal reason to be sad, we must overcome this while at the table so that we appear at least attentive and affable" [240]), with an immutable serenity ("we must be specially careful of never losing our serenity when we are in public, because nothing tarnishes more than a word or a movement that show exaltation or anger" [108]), ready to use a social mask ("because it always shows civility and culture when we openly express our pain for the afflicted persons that are with us" [223]). Like a steamroller, the modern urban habits would destroy the rainbow of premodern volitions, or at least that was the civilizing program that would take a century to be imposed: at the table one should avoid noises, crackling sounds, and belching, and keep elbows, arms, and legs together; at the theater one should refrain from laughter, exclamations, applause, and whistles; at balls and reunions one should control approaches, contacts, glances, jokes, and turns for speaking.

Although inhibiting "wild" passions as well as familiar gestures might have created citizens that were as polite as they were cold, in other areas, softening manners was undoubtedly welcome. Physical punishment of servants, children, and spouses was progressively eliminated ("Regarding homeowners, they must not speak to servants in an imperative or bitter tone of voice, and they must not scold them for any reason, no matter how serious their mistakes. . . . Whenever we speak to servants, we must use a soft tone of voice and words that avoid familiarity as well as harshness and arrogance" [MC, 210]). Violence decreased at schools, asylums, and hospices; the death penalty was no longer enforced at the public square; and people were condemned for taking sadistic pleasure in harming animals (except for bullfights and cockfights, which were strongly fought against, but to no avail). One of the chief concerns was to eliminate games of chance (or at lease their bad reputation) because besides the "feelings of greediness and cynicism" that they aroused, they are "immoral" because they "snatch away the product of work," "ruin the innocent family," and "mercenize the heart" (249).

The political economy spanned social life as a whole: restraining emotions, food, words, and pollution would, it was hoped, result in the unfolding of labor capital. However, a constrained spirit (which also led to the development of a guilty and self-flagellating conscience) was a substantial part of urban civility (etiquette, courtesy, and education) and would come from "all the sacrifices needed to please others . . . relinquishing our comforts, desires or the idea of enjoying any pleasure whatsoever" (14).

On one hand, manuals "cleansed" visible behaviors; on the other, the birth of psychiatry as a corollary would open the space for a rationalization and redirection of the hidden and no less dangerous "barbarism" that each good citizen carried inside. It is no wonder that diaries acquired so much importance at the end of the century: this type of written confession allowed the analysis of guilt and the expression of unconventional sexuality and hidden passions.

The Pure Categories. Like all utopias, the modern era was envisioned as a space of canceled heterogeneity and reduced impurities: from the identification of technological progress by whitening the skin, eliminating microbes (Indians and bandits were regarded as the same thing), following genetic laws up to the separation of the sexes, isolating the sick and the insane, and adopting a new urban plan in which the previous centers would slowly become poor peripheries and dangerous areas.

A future Arcadia would be disinfected of all polymorphism. We could therefore think that air purification ("The habit of rising early favors our health, because it allows us to breathe the pure morning air"; "we should see that clean air circulates in bedrooms and other rooms. This rule is at the same time a hygiene prescription, because the ventilation of rooms greatly contributes to the preservation of health" [MC, 51, 30]) or water purification was a basic symbolic rite. The grammar of boundaries and controlled contacts was the basis of citizenship-building discourses. We should remember that the truly refined and delicate man was *never in contact with other bodies.* The compulsion for purity contended with the phobia of otherness ("it would be uncivilized to drink from a glass used by another person, eat the food they left, take with our hands what came out from their mouths, or wear used clothes" [36]) due to the possibility of contamination from another ("In the most convenient part of the house, there must always be a water jug for the exclusive use of servants. If we do not supply this, they will be forced to have dirty hands, and when they wash them . . . they will dry them on the towels used to clean the silverware, if not on their own clothes" [61]).

Purist dogmatism reduced relationship with bodies to a minimum ("It is vulgar and uncivilized to touch the clothes or the body of those we are talking with. The woman that touches a man . . . will seem immodest and bold; but even more serious and rude is when a man allows himself to touch a woman" [MC, 120]) as well as parts of the body itself, because otherness is disturbing. Touching meant contamination; it meant relating to accidents. Hygiene — controlled contacts — would guarantee the moral purity of the "national being" and with it, the perfection of progress ("fulfilling our social duties . . . sacrificing our pleasures when necessary . . . being clean and composed . . . is the principle of preservation and progress of the people" [6]). Uncontrolled contacts would cause a moral septicemia and, as a result, backwardness, paralysis, loss of civility, and expulsion from the promised "paradise" of the modern era.

Following these categories, in regard to "legitimate and rational inequalities," the new societies had to see that homogeneous entities stayed together, guarding any asymmetrical relationship between them. Carreño insists that in order to have a healthy cohabitation, we must be polite to persons that are not our equals, but never familiar. In the end, the republic was conceived for citizens who are equal among themselves, and legitimate contact could occur only between analogous units.

Undesirable Social Bodies. Every civilizing project, every historical period proposed its sexed model of the human being as the ideal keeper of the values esteemed by the community. In other times, patriarchal societies preferred to acknowledge in the body of the elderly power as well as the human paradigm to be followed. However, modern times have another ideal: an adult man, without the damage of the years, young, dynamic, robust. The desired prototype is "the business man" ("As a general rule, we should never detain businessmen during working hours" or "our gait should not be too slow or too fast; but businessmen are allowed to speed it up during working hours" [MC, 81–83]). From the middle of the nineteenth century he had the leading role in the public life of national history. The new hero/heroine must look young (the market will provide all sorts of cosmetics and rejuvenating creams), well dressed (the importance of fashion will serve to swipe the prolongation of the past), thin (diets respond to a control of feeding habits), and agile (the beginnings of sports). Old age, disease, senility, and loss of energy could be a blow to the success of the bourgeois development program: "We must never tell another person that they look *dejected* or that they look *ill*, nor should we ask them what type of *disease* they have, just because they look *emaciated* or *pale*, nor should we tell them that they look a *little chubby*"; "We should avoid talking about a person's *age* as much a possible" (267; emphasis added).

The modern body reactivated the Adamic myth, with no childhood, no senility, no disease, no deformities. It is proposed as a timeless foundation project, as the last stages of history, and paradoxically as the end of history. The discourse on health versus disease is related to canceling the corrosion of time, preserving a selected group of citizens in a pure and immaculate state. Happiness goes hand in hand with this state of "eternal youth," with social escalation, financial success, marriage, and the multiplication of real state.

From this point, any other biological, sexual, social, or economic state was regarded as an accident, a blow to good state. Children were to disappear from the public and the domestic scene ("We must not allow our children to go out on the street to play"; "We must never take children or servants to parties"; "We should avoid having children in the drawing rooms. . . . Only young ladies and grown men can accompany their parents to do the honors of the house: *everything else is an unbeareble vulgarity*" [MC, 71, 196, 187; emphasis added]). Servants, and therefore the least favored sectors (*"because of defects or natural deformities"* [69]) were only allowed in the lower social levels. The working class or indigent sectors — not without increasing tensions — ended up assuming that "deformity" created by the bourgeois imagination to avoid the escalation of that "thousand headed monster." Children, the diseased, the insane, homosexuals, and the elderly could be isolated, but servants could not: it was essential to have them, with their dirty hands, close by (although not making contact with them). The issue was how to keep them in their place ("the individual is not responsible of correcting his defects") and at the same time soften the contradictions of this new situation ("We must approach servants so that they provide us with everything we need. . . . We must speak quietly, in a soft tone and using words that exclude familiarity as well as harshness and arrogance" [210]).

The urban centers that became modernized at the end of the century were not created for other bodies (the blind, mutilated, and in another sense, foundlings and unwed mothers). The creation of hospices, workshops, funeral parlors, hospitals, and geriatric institutions relieved urban life from those "accidents." The new nations wanted perfect bodies, and in the midst of the multiple paradoxes of modern life (handled not very innocently), impure and dirty categories were linked to poverty and misery as forms of a necessary and shameful otherness that existed despite progress, allowing a glorification of the civilizing program based on the cleanliness of a certain civil body.

The apology of hygiene as a moral issue, where health and vigor are identified with a disciplined life, is just one of the ideological angles of a commercialized society that sees no morality in the material appraisal of another body, but rather a purist and dogmatic alienation that is appropriate.

The Cleanliness of the Body of Language

Literacy indices — specifically, those indicating writing proficiency — are numbers that can reveal official satisfaction for the stages of development of a country. It is one of the fetishes of modernity, but it also has allowed for the legitimization of subordinate differential categories based on grammatical laws: "If we do not know the *rules of grammar* of the language we speak, *it is impossible to express* ourselves with the necessary *purity of language*" (MC, 116, emphasis added). Those who speak without following the law must keep quiet. Those languages outside a hegemonic standard, free within the cadences signed by its group verbalism, are "vicious and repulsive" (117). The Enlightenment will punish orality, and its written modality, "verbaliture." The virtual space of citizenship, and of national literature, will be supported by the symbolic order created by the written, purified, stabilized word. The standard inscribes individuals within the framework of the law and makes them "well-behaved" citizens. The disciplining of language overdetermines the boundaries of the citizen. In other words, the constitution within the individual — with the appropriate legality to be part of the public power — is only possible within the framework of writing as a prerequisite for the acknowledgement of citizenship.

Knowing how to speak became the key to the republic, not only because it was consubstantial to the narratives that legalized the national state (writing was a political activity because it inscribed chaos within the order of discourse), but also because it became essential symbolic capital for the rise of new social sectors (speaking correctly was an economic investment that guaranteed success in business). Studied language, like any other good, determined an individual's movement within the "opinion market" (MC, 106): the more eloquent and polished it was (disciplined and adapted to rhetorical rules), the higher the position of its owner, and the better paid its writer.

Andrés Bello thought that the standardization of language implied the double mission of articulating under a code common to the several national regions for commercial purposes and to transmit the law unequivocally (which meant cleansing the language of its "irregular, dissolute and barbaric dialects").[18] In the second half of the century, having a disciplined language (purged of "low" jargon) was the passport to citizenship: it had become important to value forms and to care for outward manners — *opinions*. Language would also become an empty shell, a high-flow sound; the upcoming literary modernism would have all these deformities.

Language and city would be clean of "mud" and "other filth." The grammarian no less than the prince "descends to the latrines to cleanse them. . . . From shit emerges a treasure: the treasure of language; of the king, the State."[19]

Soon after the wars of independence, a surprising number of grammars and treatises on orthography, lexicography, and particularly rhetoric started circulating (at least in Venezuela, published in Caracas). The aim was to establish a *single* national language that conserved ties to the language of the metropolis. Perhaps this was a conservative operation, but it could guarantee — through language — the legitimacy of the individual and the law. The language of the individual who knew how to speak had not been born recently, under the turbulent passions of the war. The new citizenship had to have a language with a pure tradition, decanted through the centuries and with a prestigious origin. Not by chance were "Latin grammars" published simultaneously with "Spanish grammars."[20] Teaching Latin and Greek was emphasized, together with Spanish rhetoric. The presence of Latin was just the wish to expand the frontiers of an imaginary European community that used Latin as a tool to reinsert its national project within Western history.[21] Latin, as the maximum disciplinarian, flexibilized language for the standard: within the new economies of language, the gift of language acquired a commercial value. In its wild state, like dirt and barbarity, it was worthless.

The Bad, the Dirty, and the Ugly. The criteria that guided the hygienization of the dark areas of language — "uncivilized," "vulgar," and "repulsive" — according to Carreño corresponded to socially undesirable bodies and spaces. In this sense, language and body formed an entity that was difficult to separate. If only the language that is within the limits established by the rules is acceptable ("it is essential to study grammar in order to spell properly . . . and to have good pronunciation, articulating words clearly and harmoniously . . . according to orthoepic and prosodic rules" [MC, 116–117]), then all other languages are at "fault." Therefore, the heterogeneity of the ethnolects is excluded from the civil circuit: "adages, popular sayings, and amphibological phrases are not accepted in good society. . . . Our language must always be refined . . . using the best sounding words: *pork* instead of *hog, breathing* or *inhaling* instead of *puffing*" (122, 123, 125).

Following the vertical and Manichean distribution of orders, a "bad society" would be formed by the popular and middle/low classes: those individuals who don't know any other way of communicating except for the familiar or spontaneous form (servants, employees, children, women, and the indigent). In this sense, language canonized the most serious and severe (high) discursive genres, and execrated the least rigorous forms (low, quotidian, and domestic): "The habit of speaking always in *humorous* or *mocking* terms is intolerable"; "There is nothing more vulgar and rude than the habit of using *jokes* and *insinuations*"; "We must truly exclude *irony* from all discussions, from all serious business . . . any ironic phrase will be regarded as an expression of contempt, and therefore as an insult" (MC, 110, 127, 128, emphasis added). All those expressive modes that worked in a destructuring double register — which allow a discrepant bivocal voice — were unauthorized in order to protect the unity of the androcentric individual's language.

Other springs that fostered the cleanliness of language, perhaps more subtly, point to the discrediting of the coexistence of polyphonic modalities because they would allow and legalize subordinate individuals and genres. They would also block the virile authority of foundational narratives, which should be monolithic and irrefutable. Gossip was commonly associated with the feminine subject, as was the confession of feelings and private secrets. The subject's disciplining silenced these "indiscreet and malignant revelations" and "restrained those emotional states that can alter the order and harmony of the environment."[22] The word must only be supported by the "arms of logic" (MC, 95), which will only show "a peaceful and friendly conversation" (107), restraining wild communication forms: discussions, exaltations, or anger ("The most serious of faults is to contradict a person" [139]), laconic replies and interjections, offensive words, "trying to use a language that neutralizes the strength of impressions" (256).

The phobia of impurity seriously delimited public and private spaces, and their respective transgressions were considered a contamination of the aseptic settings that the modern era preferred. Public words prohibited any reference to familiar or personal issues, as well as any mention of the body, except for those parts that are never covered (MC, 113, 124). The new discourse assigned these topics to psychological or intimist novels, to the soap operas and lyrics (areas where writing inscribes and controls passions), and the body to medicine ("leaving the property of names to anatomical science" [125]). In this sense, there was an increasing emphasis on the fact that reading should be an individual and solitary activity. There could be a connection between the development of private reading and the deepening of confessional literary genres, as well as with the social distribution of the public/private use of language: that is, the incidence of censorship and discipline in relation to the use of genres and topics, and public and private spaces.

There seemed to be a prevailing consensus in conservative sectors of the society at the end of the century about the risk of certain narratives that could condense, and channel, an overflow of passions that also lurked in the disciplining of these barbaric emotions. Like a pendulum, the public light of language wanted to get rid of those dark words and things, placing them in the private words of literature. At this point, we could risk the idea that literature moves within impure areas, negotiates with contaminated spaces/individuals/discourses, apparently in disagreement with the hygienic ideals of the century. For this reason, during this period the novel escaped these harsh categories and moved to the margins, enabling the reinsertion of issues displaced from hegemonic enunciation centers into the field of writing. Nevertheless, a second turn of the screw allowed another reflection in the opposite direction: the division of intellectual work opened a new function for literature, where language acquired a commercial value: the workmanship of language, the pure word. The bourgeois idea of "art for art's sake" embraced a sort of aesthetic asepsis. In this sense, literary modernism, particularly pure poetry, and hygienist compulsions do not degenerate.

Orthopedic Details: Synchronization of Body and Language. Speaking correctly demands a carefully calculated reconciliation between the cadences of the spoken word and the movement of the body: "The movements of the body must be so identified with the nature of our ideas, and with the energy of our expression, that they form a whole with words" (MC, 119). The forms are disciplined: voice and body constitute an essential target that prepares the participation of the political subject in the public arena: Congress would be the privileged setting.

Tone, timbre, rhythm, and volume not only became lower in intensity, but also every facial muscle, hand gesture, and chest position learned new constraints and smoothed any harshness: "The game of the mouth must be natural. Those who barely separate their lips to emit a sound, those who separate them too much, and those who move their mouths with studied and extravagant movements, are ridiculous"; "the hands perform movements that are more noticeable . . . and they need to be carefully studied. . . . We must see that our hand movements are not exaggerated, lest we show little culture"; "When we speak in a general conversation, we must alternatively speak to every one present" (MC, 118–120).

The use of words became closely related to their representation ability, to their power of convening and of convincing. We are aware of its materiality and malleability. Therefore, this disciplinary action points to its histrionic construction: Language (prosodic and lexicographic) is made up for its representation in the social theater. Speaking correctly meant being an actor-citizen. The disciplined language is a spectacle in itself for the large listening audience.

At another level, canceling the spontaneous movements of communication (body language) implied attitudes that were equally phobic of uncontrolled events. Unforeseen events and nomadic gestures were feared. The desire to regulate movements was also part of cleansing policies. Pure categories were in harmony with lack of movement, with static categories. Purity is a good ally of expressive paralysis. The war machine was interrupted: free movement was politically suspicious ("We must be very discreet when we give political news" [MC, 135]). Vehemence became part of the communication of subordinate forces (anarchist and socialist) that did not obey the compound theater of forms.

The grammaticalization of expressive gestures tended to erase differences, and in its unifying drive, forced the travestism of bodies and languages. We present what we are not; we say what we don't want to say: "The physiognomy of the speaker must give the same impression as his ideas; thus, it must contain the features of pain or compassion if we are talking about sad events; . . . and the features of happiness if the issue at hand is pleasant or funny" (MC, 118). This imposition of controlled univocal codes intensifies the masquerade, the ambiguity of codes, and a smooth surface that is also full of folds and cracks.

The Order of the Discourse. "*An inferior individual cannot address his superiors, even if he isn't authorized by a glance . . . etiquette establishes that an inferior cannot address his superior* before the latter does so first" (MC, 149–150 emphasis added). Not everyone can speak under the new laws established by the national utopia. By ensuring the democratization of certain processes, modernization places once again the old hierarchic categories within the dynamics of contacts, movements, and social participation — even as a mask. The right to spell is restricted because the game of this law is precisely the establishment of an equation between keeping silent — if you do not have the legal condition to speak — and civility. In this case, it would be barbaric to speak outside the law, without permission, and outside the limits of the area of silence assigned to the socially "inferior" individual. On the other hand, however, those expelled from the speech circuit form a "cloaked" part of the order of discourse: the silence of those who cannot or do not know must be standardized for the purposes of the bilateral spectacle of communication. It must seem as if they formally participate in this order: "Good manners demand that we show a perfect interest in the conversation, even when we don't feel moved by it. . . . Likewise, our attention must always correspond to the topic of the speaker . . . showing admiration, surprise . . . or sadness" (136–137).

Discipline hides its own discriminatory grammar by softening its undemocratic contradictions toward those who are now allowed to speak — because they do not know the "rules of grammar"; because they are not "home owners," "businessmen," or "degree holders"; because they do not know "literature, history, science, and the arts." The technique of travestism (doing as if . . .) smooths these rough edges. The body of the silent interlocutor (women, servants, children, the young, or other subordinates) in a specular synchronization with the speaker must make believe that he participates in the discourse: "Whenever we feel unable of feeding the conversation . . . we must avoid participating actively in it, and we must limit ourselves to following the movement established by others, so that we don't reveal our insufficiency" (MC, III).

The order of the discourse only recognizes one register, one valid individual ("When two people speak simultaneously, the inferior one must always yield to the superior one" [MC, IIO]), thus unauthorizing the second one. Other voices are shifted to a very "sufficient" sub-otherness, as we recognize it today. The speaker divides his knowledge into a double discourse: one that is simplified for those "insufficient" masses ("We must never speak in society of those topics that are beyond the scope of our listeners" [109]) and another for the initiates, for the "elite." The distribution of fields of knowledge will also follow a hierarchy, where the darkness of language will protect the knowledge that only a few can access.

The "democratic" effect of the hegemonic discourse system demands several strategies to avoid noise and dissonance: mimicry, explanations, and pretense among unequals. It is possible to think that these modalities preserve the "speaking proficiency" of the "other," and that this silence is only a forced position of active resistance before a policy that wants to wipe them off the map; and their pretense is a counterstrategy to avoid disciplinary alienation. In this sense, we revert to a previous observation: it is as if narrative became the file of differential voices, and allowed the exploration of a heterogeneous linguistic hierarchy.

The Narrative Logos: The Foundational Purpose. The citizen's space is ordered through a rigid distribution of pure changes, elucidating hybridations as much as possible; for example, a clear distinction between what belongs to public and to private spaces. Likewise, discourse modes will follow their respective enunciative spaces, with some belonging to the home, others to the public square.

Hard categories are going to dominate the public arena, as demanded by its dynamics: Cartesian logic, androcentric perspectives, objective representations, causal logistics, arboreal coherence schemes, epicity, and a reference system of an institutionalized knowledge. All this fosters the preference of the narrative genre as the best suited to the tone of the masculine public individual, and it is also in tune with the foundational sense of the state, which at the time required a rhetorical strategy that was capable of modeling — to be objective, describe, imprint, and fix — the basic coordinates of a social imagery. They needed foundational narratives that were previously disciplined, free from "rhyzomatic" elements and anti-Cartesian subjectivities.[23]

Society demands narrative to be knowledge. One cannot just narrate ("Anecdotes should not be told freely and without thought . . . certain gifts are essential to underline the merit of what we are telling with the art and charm of the account" [MC, 134]). The narrative must be subject to a series of rules that might make it *the* logocentric expression par excellence: *"Reasoning must be clear;* coordinating ideas so that the proposition precedes the consequence; using for every idea the words that represent it properly and accurately; *linking thoughts so that they are analogous and coherent; eliminating long digressions;* . . . and limiting the discourse so that there is no diffusion, which weakens and confuses it" (115, emphasis added).

The enlightened logic of the modern era organizes many of its representations through the macrostory, whose basic axioms are articulated on causal sequences, analogic progressions, cancellation of amphibologies, and the control of "grassy" thoughts, because everything must have a teleologic purpose ("We must never start a narration if we are not sure that we remember perfectly everything we are going to say, because it is annoying and clumsy to stop in the middle to search in our minds, and in the end give up our intent because we forgot some important points" [MC, 131]), where beginning and end structure the horizon of sensibilities, just as the illusion of progress.

The art of "hard narratives" also prefers to corset the "detours" and "inaccuracies" of imagination, and recommends "being careful" when we give an account of events so that we "never commit the serious fault of exaggeration or changing facts" (MC, 135). This is why there is a pedagogic idea for the national novel, which must show the customs, geography, and history of the country, and never meander into passions and individual intimacies which could exacerbate other antidisciplinarian logics. Even though the narrative genre was the most fertile laboratory of transgressions — because it allowed a renegotiation of a large amount of material that was excluded or considered "dirty" by manuals, grammars, and poetry — hygienist trends (which were also official) banned the mixture of times and genres desired for it. Jokes, puns, satire, irony, familiar allusions, flattery, and compliments would diminish the reliability of these state narratives ("Those who are in the habit of nourishing society with funny anecdotes, show that they are empty and with an unelevated character" [133]), which intend to fill the foundational vacuum. The modern project cannot run the risk of discredit; its masks must appear authentic. Only postmodern times gave the green light to laughter as one of the sharpest ways to alter the guarantees of that modernity.

Now, in the end of this century, all the accumulated and repressed "dirt" is appearing and expanding on the national body: citizenship is becoming an ailing body, and pure language is turning to subjectivities, ambivalences, and egotistic histories. The grammars of nationality ask to be rewritten in order to imagine other citizens that express themselves in other languages.

The enlighted city is now torn to pieces under the influence of voices and bodies of counterhegemonic cultures that have survived almost out of the boundaries of a mimetic game within writing. These cultures progress with their hybridized languages, free movements, resonant voices, without pedagogic and governmental establishments being able to stereotype them into one single model. The ideals of progress and nation, with their models of pure citizenship, restrained and castrated, are most likely in their death throes: not in vain in recent times, discipline's punitive eye has been devoted to increased hunting and monitoring, thus offering grotesque and pathetic inquisitive spectacles that ridicule their own mechanisms of power. Repressed lust can only break free from its own logorrhea within its own prison of language.

Notes

A version of this chapter appeared as "Políticas de Higienización: la limpieza del cuerpo y lengua nacionales (siglo XIX)," in *Asedios a la Heterogeneidad Cultural. Libro de Homenaje a Antonio Cornejo Polar,* eds. José Antonio Mazzotti and U. Juan Zevallos Guilar (Asociación Internacional de Peruanistas, 1996).

1   From "El Apuntador," in *El Constitucional* (Caracas), 2 November 1836, pp. 2–3.

2   See José Pedro Barrán, *Historia de la sensibilidad en el Uruguay,* vol. 1, *La cultura "bárbara" (1800–1860),* and vol. 2, *El disciplinamiento (1860–1920).* Montevideo: Ediciones de la Banda Oriental, 1992.

3   Cf. José Pedro Barrán, ibid.; Paul Verdevoye *Costumbres y costumbrismo en la prensa argentina, desde 1801 hasta 1834* (Buenos Aires: Academia Argentina de Letras, 1994; Mariano Picón Salas, *Antología de costumbristas venezolanos del siglo XIX* (Caracas: Monte Ávila Editores, 1980; Aquiles Nazoa, *Caracas física y espiritual* (Caracas: Editores Panapo, 1987); Alba Lía Barrios, *Primer costumbrismo venezolano* (Caracas: Ediciones La Casa de Bello, 1994); Dunia Galindo, *En las fronteras de una sensibilidad: Teatro, cuerpo, y nación,* Caracas: Monte Ávila Editores, 2000. These texts have supplied very eloquent information on the state of cities, inhabitants, and customs of Latin America during the first half of the nineteenth century.

4   Quoted in Verdevoye, pp. 71–75, emphasis added.

5   From the first national constitutions, it was almost a law to know grammar and to be competent in writing/reading. Article 7 of the third section of the Venezuelan Constitution of 1819 (designed by Simón Bolívar) says: "It is the realm of the Chamber to establish, organize and direct primary schools, of boys and of girls, teaching them to pronounce, read and write correctly, as well as the most common arithmetic rules and grammar principles" (Luis Mariñas Otero, *Las constituciones de Venezuela.* Madrid: Ediciones Cultura Hispánica, 1965, vol. 17, p. 193).

6   Cf. Ángel Rama, *La ciudad letrada* (Montevideo: F.I.A.R., 1984) and Julio Ramos, *Desencuentros de la modernidad en América Latina* (Mexico City: Fondo de Cultura Económica, 1989).

7   In Venezuela, grammar and orthography books, as well as dictionaries and elocution books, were published in the country since 1809, revealing a deep concern for "good language use." Among them we find *Análisis ideológico de los tiempos de la conjugación*

castellana of 1809 and published in 1841, by Andrés Bello; *Gramática castellana,* by José Luis Ramos, of 1820. In 1824, Bello translated the *Arte de escribir con propiedad,* by Etienne Condillac; in 1826 an anonymous author published *Elementos de gramática castellana, dispuestos en forma de diálogo para el uso de las escuelas de la república;* and in 1829, the book *Tratado de elocución o del perfecto lenguaje y buen estilo respecto al castellano,* by Mariano Madramani y Calatayud, was published in Caracas. These are some pioneer examples of the later avalanche of these type of books.

8   See Julio Ramos "El don de la lengua," *Casa de las Américas* 193 (October–December 1993), and *"Saber decir:* Literatura y modernización de Andrés Bello," *Nueva Revista de Filología Hispánica* 35, 2 (1987); Renée Balibar and Dominique Laporte, *Le français national* (Paris: Hachette, 1974); Beatriz González Stephan, "Las disciplinas escrituradas de la patria: Constituciones, gramáticas, y manuales," *Estudios* 5 (1995): 19–46.

9   The *Manual de urbanidad y buenas maneras,* used by the youth of both sexes, contains the main civilizing and etiquette rules to be observed in diverse social situations; it is preceded by a brief treaty on desires by Manuel Antonio Carreño (Caracas, 1812; Paris, 1874), which appeared as fascicles in Caracas newspapers in 1853; it was published as a book in New York by D. Appleton and Co. in 1854. The importance and transcendence of this work at that time, as well as that of the author, motivated the national Congress to make a special recommendation on March 14, 1855, to use this work. For this essay, we used the corrected and enlarged edition of 1927, published in Paris by Garnier Brothers. All the quotes come from this edition, and I will use the acronym MC to refer to this edition of the manual.

10 See the interesting book by Roger Chartier, *Libros, lecturas, y lectores en la edad moderna* (Madrid: Alianza, 1993).

11 Ibid. See specifically the chapter entitled "Los manuales de civilidad: Distinción y divulgación: La civilidad y sus libros," pp. 246–283.

12 From the recommendations in Carreño's *Manual* ("We should get used to the so-called cleaning baths, those where we introduce the whole body in the water in order to clean ourselves," p. 20), we assume that the usual practice was to clean the body by parts; whole-body baths had a therapeutic use, with very cold or very hot water.

13 Carreño emphasized that air was a possible way of transmitting diseases: rooms must be ventilated; the body emanates exhalations that must be diluted; the breath must be controlled; and we must take care that when sneezing we do not impregnate the air with our breath. These ideas correspond to theories of infection via the air which predominated in the nineteenth century.

14 See *Los bajos fondos: El antro, la bohemia, y el café* (Mexico City: Cal y Arena, 1990), by Sergio González Rodríguez; see also Catherine Gallagher and Thomas Laquer, *The Making of the Modern Body* (Berkeley: University of California Press, 1987).

15 Decades before, romanticism nurtured morbid sensibilities. In Venezuela, two poets, José Antonio Maitín (1804–1874) and José Heriberto García de Quevedo (1819–1871) mention in their poetic texts issues that have a certain sensual imagery surrounding death; particularly Maitín, in his long poem "Canto fúnebre" (1851), dedicated to his dead wife, takes delight in death, with images that are erotic, nostalgic, and necrophilic.

16 See Michel Foucault, vol. 1 of *Historia de la sexualidad: La voluntad de saber* (Mexico City: Siglo XXI Editors, [1977] 1985).

17 "The error caused by individual sexual practices constitutes a precious index of the scope of hypocrisy.... The publication in 1770 of the famous *Onania,* by Dr. Tissot, constantly re-published until 1905, is a decisive event. ... The struggle against plague is the respon-

sibility of parents, priest and above all, physicians. . . . In the dormitory of feminine pensions there is a sister in charge of watching that 'modesty' is practiced when they go to bed and when they rise. . . . The structure of equipments and, if necessary, of orthopedia concur in prevention. Some physicians hail the use of long shirts with slits, in the case of boys. In asylums, nymphomaniac women are handcuffed, or they must wear breast plates of devices between the legs so that they cannot close them. When the evil persists, surgery can be used. Cauterization of the urethra seems to be widely used." From *Historia de la vida privada,* vol. 8, chap. 2, "Entre bastidores," by Alain Corbin and Michelle Perrot (Madrid: Taurus, 1989), pp. 155, 156, 157.

18   See Bello's prologue to the *Gramática de la lengua castellana destinada al uso de los americanos* (1847) and "Advertencias sobre el uso de la lengua castellana," both collected in *Antología de Andrés Bello,* by Raúl Silva Castro (Santiago de Chile: Editorial Zig-Zag, 1965). See also "El don de la lengua," by Julio Ramos.

19   In Dominique Laporte, *Historia de la mierda* (Valencia: Pre-textos, 1980), pp. 15, 25.

20   In the Venezuelan case, a few years after independence, the following works were published in Caracas: *Elementos de lengua latina* (1829) by Pablo Arroyo Pichardo; in 1833 a reprint of *De institutione grammaticae,* by Antonio de Nebrija; in 1834, *Gramática latina,* by Juan de Iriarte; in 1835, *Breve explicación de las oraciones latinas para empezar a traducir,* by Demetrio Aguerrevere, and *Construcción de nombres y verbos latinos,* by José María Rodríguez; in 1849, Manuel Antonio Carreño himself, together with Manuel María Urbaneja, published the *Método para estudiar la lengua latina;* and in 1849, as an example, the *Tratado sintético de las oraciones latinas,* by Egidio Montesinos, was published together with French, English, and German grammars, languages that began dominating in the modern era.

21   In his *Orientalismo* (Madrid: Editorial Libertarias, [1978] 1990), Edward Said explains that the emergence of comparative philology in the nineteenth century belongs to the modern era as a symbolic gesture of European superiority, and that it works as a discourse intended as a representation of the "truth" (because it is supported by institutions, traditions, and conventions). It imposes a disciplined order to a specific material, thus offering power based on erudition, and the legitimate domination of European knowledge about the Orient. Likewise, I think that the correlation between Latin and Spanish grammars during the creation of the national order provides the representation of power through words to a certain social individual. Latin here worked as an implicit device for philologic operation, with the European library emerging as the model for the law.

22   See "Linguistic Utopias," in *The Linguistics of Writing: Arguments between Language and Literature,* by Mary Louise Pratt. Ed. Nigel Fabb (New York: Manchester University Press, 1987).

23   The book *Mil mesetas: Capitalismo y esquizofrenia* (Valencia: Pre-textos, 1988), by Gilles Deleuze and Félix Guatteri, offers suggestive concepts in this sense. The concepts of "rhyzome" and "war machine" can be tools with a multiple interpretative capacity.

Works Cited

"El Apuntador." *El Constitucional (Caracas),* 2 November 1836, pp. 2–3.

Armstrong, Nancy, and Leonard Tennenhouse. *The Ideology of Conduct.* New York: Methuen, 1987.

Balibar, Renée, and Dominique Laporte. *Le français national.* Paris: Hachette, 1974.

Barrán, José Pedro. *Historia de la sensibilidad en el Uruguay.* Vol. 1, *La cultura "bárbara,"* *1800–* *1860;* vol. 2, *El disciplinamiento, 1860–1920.* Montevideo: Ediciones de la Banda Oriental, 1992.

Barrios, Alba Lía. *Primer costumbrismo venezolano.* Caracas: Ediciones La Casa de Bello, 1994.

Bello, Andrés. "Advertencias sobre el uso de la lengua castellana." *Antología de Andrés Bello.* Ed. Raúl Silva Castro. Santiago de Chile: Editorial Zig-Zag, 1965: 184–206.

———. *Gramática de la lengua castellana destinada al uso de los americanos.* Ed. Ramón Trujillo. 1847. Reprint, Tenerife: Instituto Universitario de Lingüística Andrés Bello, 1981.

———. Prologue to *Gramática de la lengua castellana destinada al uso de los americanos.* 1847. Reprinted in *Antología de Andrés Bello.* Ed. Raúl Silva Castro. Santiago de Chile: Editorial Zig-Zag, 1965: 207–216.

Carreño, Manuel Antonio. *Manual de urbanidad y buenas maneras para el uso de la juventud de ambos sexos, en el cual se encuentran las principales reglas de civilidad y etiqueta que deben observarse en las diversas situaciones sociales precedido de un breve tratado sobre los deseos.* 1854. Reprint, Paris: Casa Editorial Garnier Hermanos, 1927.

Chartier, Roger. *Libros, lecturas, y lectores en la edad moderna.* Madrid: Alianza, 1993.

Corbin, Alain, and Michelle Perrot. *Historia de la vida privada.* Madrid: Taurus, 1989.

Deleuze, Gilles, and Félix Guattari. *Mil mesetas: Capitalismo y esquizofrenia.* 1980. Reprint, Valencia: Pre-textos, 1994.

Foucault, Michel. *Hermenéutica del sujeto.* Madrid: Ediciones de La Piqueta, 1994.

———. *Historia de la sexualidad.* 1977. Reprint, Mexico City: Siglo XXI Editores, 1985.

Microfísica del poder. Madrid: Ediciones de La Piqueta, 1978.

———. *Vigilar y castigar: Nacimiento de la prisión.* 1976. Mexico City: Siglo XXI Editores, 1988.

Galindo, Dunia. *En las fronteras de una sensibilidad: Teatro, cuerpo, y nación.* Caracas: Monte Ávila Editores, 2000.

Gallagher, Catherine, and Thomas Laquer. *The Making of the Modern Body.* Berkeley: University of California Press, 1987.

González Rodríguez, Sergio. *Los bajos fondos: El antro, la bohemia, y el café.* Mexico City: Cal y Arena, 1990.

González Stephan, Beatriz. "Las disciplinas escriturarias de la patria: Constituciones, gramáticas, y manuales." *Estudios: Revista de Investigaciones Literarias y Culturales* 5 (1995): 19–46.

———. "Escritura y modernización: La domesticación de la barbarie." *Revista Iberoamericana* 166–167 (1994): 109–124.

Hilkey, Judy. *Character is Capital: Success Manuals and Manhood in Gilded Age America.* Chapel Hill: University of North Carolina Press, 1997.

Laporte, Dominique. *Historia de la mierda.* Valencia: Pre-textos, 1980.

Lyon, David. *El ojo electrónico: El auge de la sociedad de la vigilancia.* Madrid: Alianza Editorial, 1995.

Mariñas Otero, Luis, de. *Las constituciones de Venezuela.* Madrid: Ediciones Cultura Hispánica, 1965.

Muchembled, Robert. *L'invention de l'homme moderne.* Paris: Librairie Arthéme Fayard, 1988.

Nazoa, Aquiles. *Caracas física y espiritual.* Caracas: Editores Panapo, 1987.

Picón Salas, Mariano. *Antología de costumbristas venezolanos del siglo XIX.* Caracas: Monte Ávila Editores, 1980.

Pratt, Mary Louise. "Linguistic Utopias." In *The Linguistics of Writing: Arguments between Languages and Literatures,* ed. Nigel Fabb. New York: Manchester University Press, 1987.

Rama, Ángel. *La ciudad letrada.* Montevideo: F.I.A.R., 1984.

Ramos, Julio. "El don de la lengua." *Casa de las Américas* 193 (1993): 13–25.

———. *Desencuentros de la modernidad en América Latina: Literatura y política en el siglo XIX.* Mexico City: Fondo de Cultura Económica, 1989.

———. *"Saber decir:* Literatura y modernización en Andrés Bello." *Nueva Revista de Filología Hispánica* 35, 2 (1987): 675–694.

Said, Edward. *Orientalismo.* 1978. Reprint, Madrid: Editorial Libertarias, 1990.

St. George, Andrew. *The Descent of Manners: Etiquette, Rules, and the Victorians.* London: Chatto and Windus, 1993.

Verdevoye, Paul. *Costumbres y costumbrismo en la prensa argentina, desde 1801 hasta 1834.* Buenos Aires: Academia Argentina de Letras, 1994.

Vigarello, George. *Concepts of Cleanliness: Changing Attitudes in France Since the Middle Ages.* New York: Cambridge University Press; Paris, Éditions de la Maison des Sciences de L'Homme, 1988.

Apprenticeship as Citizenship
and Governability

ILEANA RODRÍGUEZ

At the end of the eighteenth century and the beginning of the nineteenth (1770–1830), as debates on the abolition of the slave trade and of slavery glutted the space of English legislature, travel narratives registered a disengagement. Their opening pages establish a divide between natives and citizens: home and not-home — abroad and overseas; nations and natural geographies — the English state, the West Indies plantation estate.[1] These narratives are situated in the liminal zone of a structural change understood, in economic and political terms, as a transition between mercantilism and laissez-faire. Their task was to theorize the chasm of these in-betweens and to mark new frontiers.[2] My claim is that these divides are established through the proper management of aesthetics — literary references and styles, tropes, furniture, gardens, and taste — as well as by the economic narratives of research and development describing soil erosion, balances, losses, and yields. Both aesthetics and economy are in charge, not only of describing the material conditions of production, but also of suggesting the new relationships between peoples: masters and slaves, English and Creoles. I have selected as instances the works of R. R. Madden and Matthew Gregory Lewis. One is more concerned with the relationship between material production and culture, the other is more inclined to a discussion of the civic rights of people and the distribution of justice.[3] Both, however, engage the relation connecting nature, nation, and culture. As a counterpoint, I use the narratives of William Beckford, a Jamaican-born resident planter who went bankrupt.

English Citizens and Native Creoles

[Creoles are] all the ethnic groups which make up Caribbean society . . . moving through the period of settlement, through slavery and the post-emancipation period and the arrival of new ethnic immigrants, into the more recent phenomenon of vicarious culture contact through tourist, book, magazine, film, television. (Brathwaite, 204–205)[4]

The new era must discuss the nature of colonial culture as productive land-scapes. As debates move from the semantics of paradise, gardens, and aes-thetics into the social relationships between people, the central question is over the divide between native and citizen, as native (slave) is becoming the divide between citizen (an English freeman) and citizen (a white Creole native). The unraveling of this dilemma brings forth either the naming of people in reference to geographies, as spaces distinct from nations, or the unlikely opposite, the naming of nations in terms of natural spaces. Nation-ality (English, Spanish, Portuguese), we know, names a divide between na-ture and culture, one which in the sixteenth century was argued as a dis-tinction between animals (Indians/Africans) and *gentes de razón* — European peoples — and which the nineteenth century can neatly contain in its new specialized lexeme, as provided by social Darwinism — species.

Given that what is pivotal to this moment is the nature of production, which discusses the relationship native/citizen through the administration of justice in relation to the organization of labor, any discussion on any of the current theoretical divides here in question will return to labor as it relates to productivity and prosperity. This way of thinking presumes the possibility of vacillating from the geographic to the national and from narratives of nature to narratives of politics, and back. That is, it presumes thinking the pre- and postnational as postcolonial. Inasmuch as citizens and natives place each other in a relationship of opposition, so also do writings and writers who must make the transition from being seigniorial and local to being imperial and intellec-tual, to becoming colonial cultural managers and cadres.

In the case of Madden, he was a well-seasoned traveler, a man who, like John Lloyd Stephens from the United States (who was to set the conditions for the debate between cultures and geographies in the Guatemalan highlands), wan-dered through the Orient and wrote about it. Madden authored *Travels in the East* and *A Twelvemonth Residence in the West Indies,* twin texts which contrib-ute to the unravelings of colonialism and the analogic relation the imperial mind establishes between East and West. A glossary of terms at the end of the West Indian book explains the "Affinities in the manners, customs, supersti-tions, arts, character, and historical traditions of the natives of America and those of the East" — quite useful for those interested in the study of oriental-ism and colonialism, à la Edward Said. Madden was an abolitionist who translated the autobiography of the Cuban slave Juan Francisco Manzano to make it available, like Olaudah Equiano's, to the English public during the abolitionist debate; he was an English consultant who came to the West Indies to observe the state of the countries.[5] He inspected the material conditions of production, described the nature of soils, and discussed prosperity and labor as the cultural idiosyncracies of people who impinge upon production.

If in Madden we have the expertise of a voyager-voyeur, in Lewis we have that of an absentee planter, one who argues in favor of "the good aspects of slavery." Matthew Gregory Lewis constructs himself as a gentleman, the new liberal democrat who accepts the fact that slavery has come to an end. He declares himself an abolitionist. His *Journal of a West Indian Proprietor* can be read as a treatise on governance, although not necessarily on citizenship. Lewis touches all matters concerning the relationship between civil rights and labor. Fairness and justice are broached through a comparison between forms of labor, free versus slave. In this comparison, a profitable theoretical chasm separates politics from cultures, and English citizens from natives. The contrast is disfavorable to the former. His narrative produces the evidence to prove his point.

Citizenship rights in reference to slaves were about to be reformulated in England through the debates on the organization of labor and commerce within laissez-faire parameters. Insofar as white citizens' concerns at home, human labor relations were already in the hands of the state and had been coded into law. The state mediated all relations between people and prohibited any and all personal exercise and execution of justice. Justice was not a private but a public matter. Perhaps this constitutes the essence of citizenship. In the West Indies, plantations were small republics, small places, the borders of which marked the limits of estate and state. Inside the plantation, there was no distinction between the execution of justice and the management of labor. White authority often crossed the boundaries, and in the particular case of absentee owners, slaves could appeal to other slave owners for justice. In his journal, Lewis speaks from the position of a plenipotentiary statesman. He writes: "I gave [the slaves] a holiday for Saturday next" (63); "This was the day given to my negroes as a festival on my arrival" (73); when they show ingratitude and bad manners, "they are treated like English soldiers and sailors" (119).

The nature of Lewis's intervention is a hypothetical abstract indicating the difference it would have made to have practiced a more liberal administration of slavery. His skewed interest is the construction of the English subject as a liberal democrat. In his text, probity and humanity define English character. He feels proud to have "positively forbidden the use of [the cart-whip] on Cornwall; and if the estate must go to rack and ruin without its use, to rack and ruin the estate must go" (119). Inhumanity and abuse are related to class and education, and thereby projected onto the proverbial behavior of less illustrious whites, bookkeepers, and attorneys who act in flagrant disobedience of the orders of their more liberal (absentee) masters, such as Lewis's father, "one of the most humane and generous persons that ever existed. . . . his letters were filled with the most absolute injunctions for [the] good treatment [of slaves]" (115). Justice, then, is related to residency as well; injustice is constituted as the mediation of plantation managers between masters and slaves.

My readings of these records are located in the intersection of the personal and the political. Inasmuch as production determines venality and penalty, it writes into law the distinction between native (as slave) and citizen (as free-laborer). That diligence and indolence are categories related to labor; that diligence only works within the context of freedom understood as the freedom to sell one's own labor power; that slavery begets timid, feeble, as well as despondent human beings; and that flamboyance and moderation are simply two types of human behavior whose full meaning is only displayed within the narratives of modes of production are finally some of the redeeming aspects of Lewis's (re)construction of subjectivities, his way of discussing natives and citizens through entitlement, civic rights, and the distribution of justice.

It is obvious that the personalized and privatized application of justice signals the absence of a well-structured state and the presence of a strong real estate — plantation or hacienda. What is both absent and at stake in Lewis is the strict mandates of organized capital, which in turn make possible the sharp contrast between the narrated lax personal governance conditioning the administration of justice in the West Indies at the end of slavery, and the stern rules of governance of English laborers. The distribution of justice is not any better; it is just different. A gentle lord is paternalistic; a harsh state, tyrannical. In comparison, he finds the former more humane.

When we come to William Beckford, what is being discussed is dissent and the rights of planters as citizens of England, what Brathwaite calls "Creolization," "the intercultural process . . . the possibility of describing it in terms not of a 1 : 1 give and take act of gift or exchange, resulting in a new or altered product, but as a process, resulting in subtle and multiform orientations from or inwoards (sic) ancestral origins. . . . A model which allows for blood flow, fluctuations, the half-look, the look both/several ways; which allows for and contains the ambiguous, and rounds the sharp edges off the dichotomy. . . . a process which is particularly interesting since here we find an increasing reaction to external stimulus from the segmented orders as a whole (Brathwaite, 204–205). Beckford was a Jamaican-born citizen, a freeman who, once slavery had been abolished, became a merchant and ship owner in London and served twice as lord and mayor of that city. He inherited his father's estate and became a leading landholder in Jamaica. He owned about 22,000 acres, an amount he increased in 1762 with the purchase of Drax Hall Estate, "in a manner that excited the indignation of every honest man who became acquainted with the transaction" (Higman 100).[6]

Beckford embodied the type of mentality of governing colonial elites, whose styles and modes of domination and traditions would be reproduced by his white and mulatto heirs. As an Englishman native to one of the West Indian islands, Beckford was suffering from a rupture in paradigm. His world had collapsed. There was nothing in sight for him but ruins. At that moment, there was no nation being thought about in the West Indies. However, a rift had occurred between natives of England in England and English natives of the West Indies. West Indian Englishmen were looked down upon as natives, Creoles; that is, semicolonial subjects. As a native of England, residing in and being employed by England, Madden himself personified this difference.

The twentieth-century Creole intelligentsia finds itself in a similar predicament, if not the same one. The English Creole becomes a split self; his Creole interests are divided from his English interests. That they are called "Creoles" further reinforces the concept, for in the twentieth century all native-born West Indians were called Creoles. The term "native" (or "citizen"), then, suited both Beckford and his slaves, the two extreme positions of the socius. Equality between English subjects is what was being dislodged, since equality was no longer established by birthright alone. To be a citizen demanded the implementation of home policies abroad, at the risk of self-interest. Citizen rights demarcated a confluence between home and not-home, or a radical disengagement between nations and geographies. Citizenship is a right of birth stemming from the place of birth and always made extensive, in the case of imperial nations, to the place of residence. Echoes of this discussion, in reverse, could be heard in former debates on migrant intellectuals of the diaspora in the English Caribbean (Jamaica Kincaid versus Edna Brodber); in deterritorialized Cubans in exile (Roberto González Echeverría versus Roberto Fernández Retamar); and in migrant Mexican workers, which produced subsequent generations of intellectuals (Octavio Paz versus Gloria Anzaldúa).

There is no question that the free/slave labor debate profoundly and decisively affected the relationship native/citizen and created deep resentment in the planter class. West Indian resident planters such as Beckford, Edwards, and Long begrudged English policies and determination, which they held responsible for their bankruptcy. Manuel Moreno Fraginals documented these feelings of ambiguity in the Cuban planter class.[7] He sets their apocalyptic views side by side the paradisiacal names given to their *ingenios*. Some of the plantations' names in Jamaica—"Lucky Valley" (Edward Long's), "Friendship" and "Greenwich" (William Beckford's), "Parnassus" (Henry Dawkings'), "Worthy Park" (John Price's) — parallel the Cuban and the French; both portray sugar cane fields as gardens, linking their aesthetic tradition to the sublime of the commercial narratives of the Spanish Golden Age. The names given to their slaves — Plato, Priam, Pam, Hercules, Minerva, Psyche, Venus, Vulcan — invoke the orient via Greece.

The predicament for planters such as Beckford was either to go native or to go back to England. Many chose to return. But what Beckford's book demonstrates is that a white native Creole intelligentsia was here in the making. In the planters' views, their imperial nation was betraying them. It was tampering with their rights and withdrawing its protection over their wealth and property. In their dystopic narratives of decay, they had to make amends and ground their arguments not in nationality but in territoriality, property rights, in a seedling "native land" nativism.[8] That from here a sense of nationhood and nationality might be developed explains the shift from plantation (estate) to *factoría* (state) — as it is called in the Spanish Caribbean. This is the predicament of the sugar planters elsewhere. In Cuba, their ilk — Arango y Pareño, Domingo del Monte, José Antonio Saco — harbored ideas of a troubled independence.[9] The paradigmatic fiction addressing this moment in Cuba is Cirilo Villaverde's *Cecilia Valdés*.[10]

Madden, Lewis, and Beckford represent the English national and the Creole native as opposing forces in the Caribbean. They engaged in the civic debate by focusing their representation of nature on plains, plantations, and native lands not as recreational grounds, Columbus's gardens of Hesperides, but industrial sites producing sugar cane. Sugar fields, planting sites, and plantation geographies are narrated in a legalistic tone through the close scrutiny of labor as culture. Culture is understood as habits and habitat, peoples' characters and manners, the host of idiosyncratic types of Creole societies placed in the position of subaltern nonsubjects within their own natural geographies. Negroes, blackies, sambos, niggers, mulattoes, octoroons, quarteroons, mestee, mustefee, poor whites — that is, the vast array of social types — provide the tropes, moods, and styles found in the description of the divide between colonial West Indian Caribbean / Antillean societies and home.

Not-Home: The Picturesque Aesthetic Divide

[Picturesque is] giving the sense "in the style of a picture." . . . like or having the elements of a picture, fit to be the subject of a striking or effective picture; possessing pleasing and interesting qualities of form and color (but not implying the highest beauty or sublimity); said of landscapes, buildings, custom, scenes of diversified action . . . also of circumstances, situations, fancies, ideas, and the like. (*Oxford English Dictionary*)

Lewis's opening remarks introduce not-home, the West Indies, as a semiurban, semirural geography, an animal farm with pigs squealing, ducks quacking, fowls screaming. The world of primary needs — food, meals, the guts — is narrated as a gay presence. Living animals, their sounds, noises, and smells, will later become the delights of West Indian cuisine — pigs and ducks, turtles, quails, snipes. But animal sounds remind the passengers on board the ship to the West Indies that they are no longer home. All kinds of crawling bugs—a centipede that makes its way among the logwood, and then the scorpion and cockroach—are all tropes of discomfort narrating not-home. For the most part, environments abroad are grotesque compositions mixing undesirable living and eating habits with irritating sounds, to which is added the overbearing presence of insects. In one of Madden's funniest scenes, English gentlemen hit themselves in the face mercilessly all night to fend off insects only to come out the next morning all swollen, showing in their monstrous selves traces of their wanting acculturation.

Both Lewis and Madden illustrate the articulation home/not-home, and both describe exactly the same geographies—landscapes, architecture, cultural incidents—but they do so differently. In both we find all the tropes of arrival, the description of the John Canoe festivities, a dinner party at a planter's house, and the anthropological and ethnological layout of a plantation. But whereas for Lewis, social data is pleasure, for Madden it only illustrates asymmetries, a word he uses to signal the divide home/not-home. For Lewis, the experience of not-home life is not dramatic. On the contrary, he enjoys the new geographies; he is so enthralled by the sights that he wants to establish residence there; furthermore, he wants to die there. Writing joy and enjoyment, pleasure and beauty into his journal underscores his own sensibility in relationship to the people; likes and dislikes account for taking a side, for positioning. As was Christopher Columbus, he has been bewitched by the Caribbean Andalusian April-like gardens—a dreamed image of his plantations in bloom. In many ways, his narrative acts as a bridge between two sensibilities and two economic and political perspectives, those of the quasi-native buckra creoles and those of his English compatriots at home.

It is through enjoyment, I argue, that the use of irony as a technique for distancing is employed. In pleasure, the imperial "I" relaxes, and the imperious image of home as a model that regulates perception gives in. When this happens, the English subject dares to imagine the new geographies as possible new homes. "I am as yet so much enchanted with the country, that it would require no very strong additional inducements to make me establish myself here altogether; and in that case my first care would be to build for myself a cottage among these mountains, in which I might pass the sultry months (Lewis, 68). Via the sensual and sensuality, what Jane Austen would establish as the well-circulated trope of "sense and sensibility," the high mimetic yields to the picturesque. The picturesque is the agreeable appearance of a landscape that has been converted into a picture, a minimalist technique to represent societies in miniature. In the nineteenth century, pictures representing cultural landscapes were drawn in ink and pen; in the twentieth, they used bright colors. Their tropes are small villages, fruit trees, clusters of birds, hillsides, lovely plains, luxuriant fields, guinea grass, laurel-looking coffee plants, sugar mills, rarefied air, wagons, oxen, puffs of smoke, seaside views, noble harbors, vessels, merchantmen, people going about their daily chores. E. G. Squier's texts on the geographies of Central America are all fully illustrated using these techniques, which represent what the culture of politics has labeled "Banana Republics."[11] In the West Indies both the nature of geographies and the nature of humans are so quaint that they firmly stand for the picturesque: "light-coloured houses with their lattices and piazzas completely embowered in trees" (Lewis, 51); places which, like Montego Bay, "exceed in beauty all that [Lewis has] ever seen" (65).

Picturesque is also the figure of a much-too-pretty mulatto girl: "her form and features were the most statue-like. . . . her complexion had no yellow in it. . . . it was more of an ash-dove colour. . . . her teeth were admirable. . . . her eyes equally mild and bright; and her face merely broad enough to give it all possible softness and grandness of contour: her air and countenance would have suited Yarico. . . . only that Mary Wiggins was a thousand times more beautiful" (Lewis, 69); "Mary Wiggins and an old Botton-tree are the most picturesque objects that I have seen for these twenty years" (70). Picturesque enframes Mary Wiggins into a picture, a technique that laminates the view and the composition alongside the human relationship. It recasts her figure within the sentimental against the background of Yarico, the "good black woman" sensualized. In reference to Yarico, Peter Hulme claims that her story with Inkle is the product of a society that chose to tell and retell itself a romantic episode at a time when "the purity of true love would often be the product of a 'natural' society destroyed by some form of European corruption, calculation or double-dealing" (229).[12] In his opinion, the story of these two lovers makes a cogent political point and lends the lexemes of feeling to the political debate. The contemplation of Mary Wiggins can be read as a cross between literary moods expressing a shifting political sensibility via the sentimental picturesque, but it can also be read as a trope, the permissive white massa's gaze contemplating his mulatto women slaves. What his fixed look selects, white teeth, eyes, his careful rendering of body parts, crisscrosses the economic narratives of slavery that record the purchasing habits of masters with the semantics of sentimental and picturesque romanticism.

Nevertheless, my aim here is to argue that in this, as in many other subsequent scenes, the picturesque provides the clue that this gaze leaves no doubt that a man is looking at a woman: a white man looking at a mulatto woman, very much like Cirilo Villaverde saw his characters looking at Cecilia Valdés, the icon of Cuban liberal nationalism. Neither in Madden nor in Beckford is such sensual transgression allowed. There is an attraction in Lewis's gaze. Who if not Eros speaks when he tells us that Psyche, a creole girl, smells of orange blossoms emanating from an orange bough she brought to fan away disturbing insects?

Counterpoint: The Ludicrous Barbaresque

bucra nebber, nebber catch a death of cold in salt water, 'less, Massa, buckra happen to be drowned in it. (Madden, 43)

Sentimental and romantic sensibilities expressed through the picturesque always verge on the ludicrous barbaresque. The break begins upon arrival, when the interrelationship between people becomes one, if not the central, variable defining not-home. The real hermeneutical exercise commences at the moment of contact, when English intellectuals must define the terms of the new covenant regulating the native/citizen divide, which brings the culture of slavery to the forefront. Lewis's cultural background is the discussion on free versus slave labor undertaken by the English legislature. His diary projects the nation/geography disjunction, natives/citizens over and against the discrepancy between the details of slavery and the cruelties of plantation life put forth by the abolitionist society at home and his own experience abroad. What disturbs him is the lack of congruency between political, historical, and cultural narratives. Since experience and knowledge are at odds, doubt becomes the regulating practice of thinking, and Lewis confesses to not knowing who the slaves really are, or how to interpret them. Direct observation is to mediate the conflict between premeditated ideas and his own practice gathering social data. He then begins wondering about the relationship between what slaves think, say, and feel. His concern with feelings supports my contention that it is in the area of emotions that romantic sensibility places the divide between human beings, apes, slaves; only in the recognition of the slave's emotional side can liberal democracies constitute slaves into free laborers, human servants, and maids.

How slaves feel about slavery and what kind of relation they are willing to establish with their master is then a key question. To answer it, Lewis first observes the gap between words and behavior. The enunciating subject simultaneously grants and denies. From this observation, Lewis concludes that "unless a negro has an interest in telling the truth, he always lies" (129). To his great bewilderment, he becomes aware that his slaves seem to like him. He is moved when they offer their babies to him: "him nice lilly neger for Massa" (61). Although in excess, Lewis is pleased by the demonstration of their affection, albeit he honestly admits that his own pleasure comes from pure egotism, from "the consciousness that all these human beings were [his] slaves" (61–62). Yet he doubts them, since negroes "are excellent cajolers, and lay it on with a trowel" (120). In the laughter and happiness they show, he finds a hermeneutical riddle he encodes in the barbaresque: "The shouts, the gaiety, the wild laughter, their strange and sudden bursts of singing and dancing . . . formed an exact counterpart of the festivity of the witches in Macbeth" (61). The rituals of welcoming the "massa" are for him totally out of context—unexpected activities that point to the yawning chasm between what is put forth at home and what is experienced abroad.

The gap between knowledge and reality, which accounts for misunderstandings and puzzlements, explains why demeanor, veneer, countenance, body postures, and speech (in other words, the culture of everyday life) must be kept under strict surveillance; why transcribing the phonetics and syntax of Creole English becomes a favorite pastime: "hedicating the negroes is the only way to make them appy; indeed, in his umble hopinion, hedication his hall in hall!" (3). It is in the interstices of language, in the in-between of dialect, that masters suspect the answer lies.[13] But Creole language is unwieldy and sounds disturbing and irritating, a reason why environments abroad are considered grotesque, undesirable tableaux. Writing about them is a controlling device and a way of developing some parameters and criteria of management. As in the case of Gonzalo Fernández de Oviedo in the sixteenth century, doubt indicates a threshold.[14]

There is a perception governing the citizen/native interaction, that of an invisible dividing line between being and pretending.[15] Good management consists in knowing where the divide lies, because then knowledge will provide the criteria dividing what works from what does not; for instance, it will tell the difference between illness and health, likings and dislikings, working and idling. This invisible line that makes knowledge blurry is the space of negotiation: freedom for the slave, an area of ungovernability for the massa. For a laissez-faire mentality, which relies on counting, gauging, and measuring, the difference in between is rendered inoperative. How does one know if slaves are taking advantage of a kind massa, or if they are simply taking a break? How does one know if they are tired or despondent? Thus, interpretation, negotiation, and hermeneutics fuse.

Now, it is one thing to be lost in the codes; it is another to refuse to accept them. Whereas Lewis accepts the existence of alternative codes, Madden simply overlooks them, and Beckford positions himself within absolute denial. In the portrayal of people, as in writing hygiene, mapping festivities, and enjoying beauty, Lewis, Madden, and Beckford are at odds. For Lewis, the "negro" character is subject to a more ambiguous set of predications. They are:

always laughing and singing, and . . . seem to perform their work with so much nonchalance, taking up their baskets as if it were perfectly optional whether they took them up or left them there; sauntering along with their hands dangling; stopping to chat with every one they meet; or if they meet no one, standing still to look round, and examine whether there is nothing to be seen that can amuse them, so that I can hardly persuade myself that it is really work that they are about.

About six o'clock . . . the negroes are going to the field. . . . and all seem to be going to their employments, none to their work, the men and the women just as quietly and leisurely as the pigs and the poultry. The sight is really quite gay and amusing, and I am generally out of bed in time to enjoy it, especially as the continuance of the cool north breezes renders the weather still delicious. (101, 113)

Negro people and mulattoes constitute different sets. The former are inserted within economic narratives and accounted for as elements of production, spare parts. Mulattoes are already part of the discussion on citizenship. Beckford speaks about Negro people as he speaks about fields, sugar cane, and curing or boiling houses. For instance, he stresses the need for surveillance: "The negro-houses are, in general, at some distance from the works, but not so far removed as to be beyond the sight of the overseer" (20). In the provision grounds the slaves "scatter themselves over the face, and form themselves into distinct parties at the bottom of the mountains; and being . . . much divided, their general exertions can be only observed from a distance" (155). Madden ascribes women and the mores of colored people to the low mimetic and makes them the object of derision. But in the following quote, he strikes a contrast between the services of black slaves and freemen.

The defects of the Creole character are more than counterbalanced by its virtues. If they are easily moved to anger, they are still more easily incited to kindness and generosity; if they are "devils being offended," they are frank and honest to their enemies, and faithful beyond any people I know, to their friend. I wish they were less proud, because their noble qualities would be more appreciable, and I would be glad to find them less captious, because their personal courage has no need of such demonstration on slight occasions (81). It cannot be denied that they are addicted to lying, prone to dissimulation, and inclined to dishonesty. . . . [But] what weapons beside falsehood, cunning, and duplicity, has the slave to oppose to oppression? (104)

For Madden and Beckford, "the negro character" is either comedy or an economic figure, with one exception, that of the literate Africans, the "wronged captive kings."[16] Instances of restraint, moderation, but mainly endurance, are never lacking in them. They are written in the epic-heroic mood reserved for narrating home. Students of testimonial literature would find many opportunities in the African testimonials gathered by the historians Edward Long, Bryan Edwards, Jean Baptiste du Tertre, and Pere Labbat, which Madden reproduces. As usual, aesthetics works the divide between northern Africans of noble ancestry and others.[17] What is undergirded in these exhibits is a moral resiliency that directly contradicts the picturesque and projects the "negro character" into the sublime; terror—in this case, the terror of effective rebellion, as in Haiti—is an ingredient that must always enter into its composition. As a narrative transgression, the sublime is attenuated by the weight of the picturesque and the barbaresque. In Lewis, it is counterbalanced by disclaimers, for instance when his own readings and feelings become the way he fancies himself a "Sancho in Barataria" (79).

I want to argue that transgression in Lewis consists in the (re)construction of subject. His "I" resembles that of a modern anthropologist in that he has the ability, and the willingness, to disengage, to distance himself and somewhat bracket home categories. He is a sensualist who lets his body feel and his pen write his delight in contemplating geographies: the physical landscape, the merriment of black people, the beauty of mulatto women. But the strongest sign of his transgression is located in his narratives of leniency encompassing both "laziness" and "cheating." His leniency is also grounded in doubt. Because he doubts, he stops and reflects; he suspends judgement. He lets his readers know there might be another interpretive mode to properly assess what he does not understand in the mores of slaves. He insinuates that there is intelligence in cunning, and the will to resist in the slowing down of work. Within the genre of plantation narratives encoded by the English intelligentsia residing in England, Lewis's *Journal* is the closest we come to a transgression. He transgresses in the plotting of the subjectivities of Negro people, in the depiction of inner and outer spaces, in his ideas of justice. Slaves are not production ciphers, as in Beckford and Madden, but real flesh and blood people.

Exhibit 1: "Him nice lilly neger for massa!"

Their greatest fear is not having a master whom they know. (Lewis, 68)

Paralleling this instance of laughter, there is the laughter of the slaves. Lewis swears, upon his honor, he has never seen "people who appeared to be so unaffectedly happy" (58). The massa's laughter and that of the slaves meet at the same place, one being rendered as genuine, while the other is unqualified. But are both genuine? Here, a contrast between two cultures and the distance between genuine and transgressed emotions is being foregrounded.

On his arrival in Savannah la Mar, Lewis is first startled by noise. A reception committee is waiting for him at the gate. His trustee has gathered some people, and the scene resembles a rally, with people running around and saluting him as a statesman. "The works were instantly all abandoned" (60); even hogs, dogs, geese, and fowl and turkeys "all came hurrying along by instinct, to see what could possibly be the matter" (60). "Uproar and confusion," which defies description, are the words that come to his mind capturing his first impression of the new geographies. It is all beyond what he had experienced or expected. Disorder, asymmetry, confusion and uproar, the disruption of labor, and the mixing of humans and animals do not speak favorably to the eyes of a well-controlled observer. In all appearances, this population has learned to negotiate the massa's emotions, to collaborate with the attorney's wishes to appear welcoming to the owner of the plantation.[18]

The merriment of the welcome serves two purposes: to stop working and to pretend to be pleased. Such hullabaloo introduces the first hermeneutical puzzle: are they sincere? Once more, expressions of feelings coupled with body gestures split the otherwise secure hermeneutics, plotting topographies that divide genuine from feigned behavior, authenticity from performance. This is not ordinary behavior. He knows that whether his slaves like him or not, they would serve him the same. Slavery is a compulsory system, and the owner suspects the expression of feelings is also compulsory. In fact, predication and gestures coincide: they are written as kind-hearted, flamboyant, boisterous, boastful, drinkers, noisy, insincere, cunning, promiscuous, thoughtless, unrestrainable, heedless, inattentive, and understandable only through the lexicon of literature: the witches in Macbeth. What Lewis wishes for is symmetry, well-regulated and proper behavior. What he really wants is hegemony — that is, persuasion, the power to subordinate ethnicities to accept English norms and values and to behave accordingly. Nevertheless he is touched by this performance because they are his slaves. Ownership gives pleasure, happiness, doubt. Overall, the interaction makes him feel embarrassed, for there is a contrast between what he sees and what he hears. The word "slave" makes him feel "a pang at the heart" (62). So he wants to substitute the word "negro": "say that you are my negro, but do not call yourself my slave," he says (62). The shift from "slave" to "negro" as signifiers of a social condition denotes the transition between slavery and free-labor, and between being encoded solely as class or ethnicity.

Looking at it from the perspective of the slaves, there is a party when the massa comes, there is meat to eat, there is rum and sugar, and entertainment away from the drudgeries of work. They dress in their holiday clothes: "the blacks wore jackets, the mulattos generally wore cloth coats; and inasmuch as they were all plainly clean instead of being shabbily fashionable, and affected to be nothing except that which they really were, they looked twenty times more like gentlemen than nine tenths of the bankers' clerks who swagger up and down Bond Street" (Lewis, 74). Essence, being who they really are or are not, is a trope. Lewis confesses he has no key to that hermeneutics. The grin of a slave is like that of the Sphinx. Being lost in the codes is what mars the interpretation of black cultures. Misinterpretation is a result of misreading the codes, and misreading, or doubt, is what becomes evident in the texts by these two well-meaning abolitionists, Lewis and Madden. That is why they aim and invent. Attempts at understanding led to the creation of the premodern stereotypes that still legislate ethnic interrelationships. As we have witnessed above, stereotypes are the results of doubt, one which refuses to accept the codes provided by black cultures, one which upholds and institutionalizes a misguided interpretation of their cultural behavior.

Welcoming parties offer the mistaken impression that slaves are well cared for. Since the end of slavery brought the plantation economies to a virtual halt, the argument of the welfare estate is pronounced mainly by "benevolent" slaveholders who hold hearings to listen to the slaves' problems concerning health, quarrels, Obeah, miscarriages, childbirth, and related matters. Long-standing social scores are being settled. These narratives include entire sections on the good treatment slaveholders proffered to slaves, as well as scores of unusual information on what to do with the sick, the old, the runaway — incidents which speak to the humanity of slaves, their sorrows and happiness.

To be a slave owner is to be judge and government. Lewis takes this mandate upon himself. Since he is the authority, his aim is fair and equal distribution of justice, giving the slave every encouragement to confide in him, whereas always keeping in mind what Madden upholds, that "unless a negro has an interest in telling the truth, he always lies" (Madden, 129). The master is in charge of distributing equal sums and allowances of clothes and provisions; he gives mothers presents, thus making them receive a larger portion than the rest. Their first fault committed is forgiven for bringing more slaves into the world. In the context of good government, ingratitude is simply bad manners.

Lewis argues that freedom under slavery means destitution, that a slave without a master is like a boat cast adrift, how the death of his master, who has promised freedom to a family, can signify eternal slavery for an offspring about to be freed during his lifetime. Not having a massa has legal and economic consequences, for in an economy that only hires blacks as slaves, where the condition of ethnicity and that of labor is identical, where is the slave to labor? The problem of manumission is related to the spaces of insertion: where in the slave economy can they belong? Given that slave society is predicated on providing basic needs, what kind of occupation can a free person lacking a master obtain? The sick one, the lame, dropsical, aging—all share the same problem of allocation. "I rather be an under-work-man on Cornwall, than a head carpenter any where else," and "me wish make it good neger for massa" (77, 78), Lewis has them say.

In Villaverde's *Cecilia Valdés,* readers can find some answers to Lewis's economic concerns. In his society, the artisans, tailors, carpenters, and masons are groups constituted by free "coloreds." In Lewis, the festivities of John Canoe also speak of the labors of a free population. In Madden, innkeeping is a self-employment area for "brown ladies." In addition, tradition of self-subsistence economies already exists in the small plots of land, or gardens, that constituted the main West Indian landscape during the nineteenth century. These forms had always run parallel to plantation and hacienda economies. They constituted the internal market, the site of their industry, the description of which is a source of pleasure for Lewis as well as it is for Claude McKay and Jamaica Kincaid.[19] McKay states, "In our village we were poor enough but very proud peasants. We had plenty to eat. We had enough to wear, a roof against the rain, and beautiful spreading trees to shade us from the sun" (3). Christophine cultivates her own plot of land in Jean Rhys's novel, and this capacity to feed oneself constitutes the autonomy from law enforcement agents upon which these characters depend.[20] Good government and productive labor are the last bequests of the slaveholder to inform the debate over slave societies and their limits. Either labor has come to a complete halt, or the narratives overdramatize the lack of discipline. Being merry is related to labor in that it is interpreted as being "thoughtless and improvident." Slaves do not foresee the future; they know they will have something somehow. Many old slaves, seventy or over, were still able, healthy, strong, and cheerful, but did not work. Previous happiness turns into doubt and suspicion, and is then argued within the sphere of labor and productivity.

Narratives of soil production keep the body and its movements and expressions under surveillance. Dancing, for instance, is under the vigilant eye of the master. Lewis notices that they are not rhythmic, their "movements [are] entirely dictated by the caprice of the moment" (79), however "there is a regular figure, and that the least mistake, or a single false step, is immediately noticed by the rest" (79). But it is the Obeah practices of black culture that elicit the most distrust.

[The function of capital is] to create a world market; subjugate all antecedent modes of production, and replace all jural and institutional concomitant of such modes and generally the entire edifice of pre-capitalist cultures. . . . To suspect the production of direct use values not entering into exchange, i.e., precisely to posit production based on capital in place of earlier modes of production which appear primitive. (Guha, 222–223)

In Madden's narrative, home and nation are braided together from the very beginning. Their complicity is embedded in the portrait of English character, which "implicate[s] the character of a nation" (110). I will argue here that the paradigmatic axis of Madden's report is character, the constitution of the English imperial "I," which is simultaneous with the metaphor standing for his twelve-months' residence in the West Indies. The metonymy is of home. Aboard the ship, the Englishman speaks from at least two spaces: one is nation, and the other is high culture. Both make up citizenship, the platform from which he speaks. Nation and nationality also stand for empire, because speaking from aboard an English ship is speaking from a floating nation, simultaneously home and not-home. England is in the ship, as it is elsewhere; here just as there.

But what is the essence of English nationality or character? The model put forth is made up of loose and dispersed sets of predications which, brought together, constitute whatever makes up the new laissez-faire liberal democratic personality in the making, the free-trader who adventures into far-distant geographies guided by his spirit of enterprise, a fact that gives him joy and enhances his courage, which is his humanity. This type of narrative device is dispersed and repeated throughout the text and drilled into the reader, always serving the function of contrast and bridging. However, the trope of bridging is somewhat foggy, for "English character" does not represent itself outright as the negation of other characters, but simply as an affirmation of itself, a sample of instance of being — one among many, one within the marketplace of being; that is, it is a being constructed within laissez-faire parameters, hence Madden's productive ambiguity. Other character formations (i.e., the African) work through implicit contrast, which is another form of obscuring. What Madden says of the Irish priest helps to round out this point: "set of sleek, smooth-featured, stalwart, Irish parish-priest-faced fellows, tolerable well-fed looking whiglings (he must surely have viewed me through a magnifying lens of considerable power), sent out expressly to live on the fat of the land, and to feed and fatten at the expense of the poor colonists" (66).

Thus, narratives of laissez-faire national character formation are indeed technologies to assert the rights of the enunciating subject — here, the English character (nation, subject, citizen) over and against the other obscured characters, the Africans or the Irish — while concurrently constructing a simulated free space of being, where other beings can both exist and compete. The legality of the competition, we all know, is based on deception, for the winner is the one who has established the rules of control, whose power is the power to define and then to constitute those definitions into culture or law.

To be English means to be morally symmetrical: prudent, discrete, moderate. As a principle of character formation, of these three attributes, moderation is the golden rule. It constitutes the essence of Englishness as a nationality, as it also constitutes civilized behavior and citizenship. It refers to self-control, self-restraint, discipline — another significant difference marking English discursive zones in comparison with the space ascribed to other global natives (the East and West Indians). Moderation is a behavioral pattern that smooths out the functioning of society and in turn explains why the new geographies are so disturbing, being quite irritating asymmetries. The topographies of regularity (moderation and symmetry) betray the modalities of home as the structuring structure, although moderation, in the Caribbean context, can also be basically construed as repression. In Lewis's narrative, it is construed as anal retentiveness.

The opposite of moderation is excess, and in the case of the West Indian Negroes, flamboyance, which is here put forth as the art of enjoying life in eating, talking, laughing, with the women decked out in a profusion of beads, corals, and gold ornaments of all kinds. It is, as Lewis puts it, either joy or entertainment. In the description of the Negro character as well as in those of the character of West Indian Creoles (that is, whites) flamboyance is underscored, and it is in the behavioral resemblances between masters and slaves that the essence of going native is predicated.

Reduction: West Indian Innkeepers — Dull, Fat, Angry

[In Africa,] the jealousy of their chiefs, and the fanaticism of their priests, have unfortunately opposed the progress of European discovery, and been the occasion of sacrificing the lives of travellers, whose admirable qualities, enterprise, and courage, humanity and amiability, are remembered by us with feelings of interest analogous to those of private friendships; and when we lament the fate of those who so worthily deserved our esteem, we are apt, I fear, to spread our indignation against their destroyers over too wide a surface, and to implicate the character of a nation in the barbarous acts of a few infatuated priests and ferocious chieftains. (Madden, 109–110)

Nationality is nothing unless it is defined in contrast with or in opposition to other forms of being; for instance, that of an African native, an Irish priest, or a West Indian woman. Whereas English character and nationality encompass progress, enterprise, courage, humanity, and amiability, African character is jealousy, fanaticism, and opposition to progress. But where Madden really sharpens his wit is in his descriptions of West Indian natives in the figures of two fat innkeepers, Miss Betsy Austin and Miss Hanna Lewis. The details about these two Creole women—and here "Creole" means colored—whom he calls "specimen of the species," serve to illustrate the opposition native/citizen. Labeling them "specimen of the species" situates him within social Darwinism, which places "these people" in transition between humans and apes—or, at best, pets. In and through these two women, he executes his reduction; that is, they are used as samples that embody the native.

The presentation of a society through the misbehavior of women is set against laissez-faire policies. Within laissez-faire parameters, misconduct consists in making adverse the rules of market competition and, in this case, disrespecting the freedom of choice. What is wrong with these two women is not only that they do not understand the rules of patronage and cannot abide by them, but that they extrapolate commercial transactions into personal drama. First, their display of strong feelings and, second, their dramatic style that is described as simplicity. For an Englishman, only laissez-faire conduct is fair game. Englishmen then find the mores of native geographies ridiculous, a reason for which they can oppose them in deriding them. The moral of the fable is that to behave un-English-ly is simply ridiculous. No local interpretation is written into the text. Dignity, or even West Indian hospitality, is not even entertained as a hypothesis to explain the behavior of these two women.

The character divide is most apparent in the area of feelings. Anger and aggravation, from now on two of the big markers of Creole behavior, establish the productive contrast between the Englishman and the Creole woman. The only permissible feeling for an Englishman is that of distancing through irony. To mock and deride are clear signs of being a proper citizen, ones which contrast with anger and drama. A distinguished Englishman cannot really engage in the habits of the country. He must dismiss them in his person and in his narrative. His narrative thus turns into one of dismissals, anti-drama, understatement, or comedy, one which fails to grasp and refuses to acknowledge the codes regulating local behavior. West Indian culture is bracketed off, elided. Every utterance, every body movement, the body in a state of repose, body weight and posture are acts of violence and a declaration of war. Mulattoes will not be able to budge without being pointed at. A state of siege or perennial surveillance is evident in a sharp tongue always at the ready to attack habit, habitat, and inhabitants. English perversity in humoring what hurts the most is amply put on display. Madden administers and compartmentalizes his discourse by allocating styles: one for West Indian cultural sites and services; another for official records of production; a third for traveling tips. The inn narratives are classified as service narratives and cataloged within the social and cultural ethnologies to illustrate indolence — that is, the opposite of labor.

But how the English mind moves from feelings to ethics, from anger to pride and prejudice, is our next question. To start, excessive demonstrations of feelings are construed as a lack of urbanity and decency, a kind of excitability that is explained in terms of climate and "climacterics." But then, other cultural habits are also brought in to complement English judgment. For instance, sitting in front of an open doorway is labeled indolence, one of the worst insults an Englishman can proffer. That the two innkeepers are seated with "indolent tranquility" (23) and "imperturbable repose" (24) becomes a trait of "the luxury of native indolence" (24). What is most amazing is the fact that the lady "specimens" display these gestures as correct posture, as an attitude appropriate to a landlady, although both posture and demeanor are easily disturbed. At the smallest opposition or contradiction, they can turn into its opposite, thus a lady's natural urbanity and gentleness of disposition is something ruffled by the squabbles with her guests, incidental to the bills, and the influence of the climate and the excitability of the Creole temperament conjoined (23).

An alternative hermeneutics will construe a different chain of meaning and will underline the relationship between "indolence," labor and laboring, accountability, deprivation, control, repression — that is, the proper activities of "the bustling . . . English landlady" (26). A more localized interpretation underscores Raymond Williams's distinction between the leisure class and the slaves, and their respective rights to free time and enjoyment because whereas ruins, monuments, and the picturesque are presented here as the settings for a leisure class, authorized to enjoy — à la Lewis — Creole tranquility and repose are proscribed. But what is clear is that there is no space available for West Indian Creoles to display their habits or to negotiate their cultures. The offered verdict, based on mercantilist values, is always negative, not pride but prejudice, not dignity but indolence, not urbanity and gentleness, but squabbles of another sort. All these indignities are added to figure, fatness, and age, which become the significant markers of natives being "a female member of the Creole aristocracy [tracing ancestry] back to the dusky antiquity of a century and a half ago" (Madden, 23). Reduction, in this case, turns human beings into specimens, museum pieces, and exhibits that through extension stand for a place "not-home."

What underlines the story of the two misses is that ignorance or neglect of the rules of competition turns citizens into native specimens: "The ferocious yet vacant gaze of baffled desperation of Miss Austin, the unmeaning yells of her slaves, and the uproarious merriment of the negroes outside, all combined, made a scene which Cruikshank might do justice to, but which I cannot. . . . The ill-mannered slaves all the time kept tittering and giggling, with an occasional 'hi! hi! you no hearie dat!' and 'MiGar Amighty, whara say misis! nebber in no passion!' " (30). This cultural situation is then encored in the depiction of a boardinghouse, where the writer takes the opportunity to bring his readers indoors and to expand the knowledge of the native characters. Descriptions of service are most hilarious because they dramatize the incompatibilities and idiosyncracies of two cultures at odds and the workings of slower-paced economics. Madden's remarks on Jamaican inns constitute an opportunity to comment on the character of natives through their habits of labor in delivering services. He begins by lambasting the inner comforts of West Indian buildings, whose sense of space and decoration relative to climate constitutes an insult to his sensibility. Mansions, he says, have "imposing exterior[s]," floors are "highly-polished." Entering a building is a hazard, "the stranger slides, at the risk of his neck" (68). But his real irritation is servants, whom he says are always seated, immovable, mute, dumb, to the point that "the stranger is afraid she is an invalid" (69). They refuse to speak with words, using their bodies as an alternative, as when they point their chins in the direction of another servant who supposedly responds for the services.

Speed is contrary to any and all sense of movement in the West Indies: "the brown waiters, like feathered Mercuries in a galloping decline, are doing violence to the laws of nature in the West Indies. . . . Once the stranger loses sight of the waiters, black or brown, he may bid adieu to the light of their greasy countenances, perhaps for hours to come. He may knock the table till he is tired, shout till he is hoarse — (ring a bell he cannot); he may call Ned, Frank, Cupi, or Columbus — ay, he may call niggers from the kitchen's depths, but, query, will they come? . . . 'Will nobody come there?' and lo and behold! at last everybody does come, at the rate of a brown-hunt, which is about a step and a half in ten seconds" (69–70). In contrast, when Madden dines at a merchant mansion in Kingston, accompanied by the attorney-general, the lawyers, and other distinguished guests, he observes that the service is impeccable, the hospitality, proverbial, the food and drink, superior. The point, then, is to contrast white and "colored" management and governance, free enterprise and service: "The black servants who wait at table in such houses as I have been alluding to, are a very different sort of attendants from those in such establishments as Miss Hannah Lewis, Miss Winter, and the innumerable brown misses who board, lodge, and 'bleed' *usque ad deliquium*. . . . I think there are no better waiters, or more competent butlers in the world than black ones" (146–147).

Speaking of English character, we stated above that it is the principal metaphor of Madden's book, the paradigmatic axis. Part of this characterology is completed by the display of wit. Body traits and cultural habits are enablers provoking Madden's humor and sense of irony. Mocking is a distancing device, a way of attenuating that which threatens, like stating that Miss Lewis is "verging on her grand climacteric; she was evidently conscious of her natural advantages—a sedate, sensible woman of some two hundred weight" (24). First Madden notices the lack of sophistication in the repetition of vocabulary "the same unvaried greeting, the same drawling courtesy, the same apathetic reply . . . the same moaning excuses. . . . she only drawled out a few sentences strung together for a similar occasions" (24). The captain's wit is honed by the women's dullness, his wit put at the service of their condition and linguistic idiosyncracies. It is an exchange in the most quaint and charming comedic style.

Other minor oddities are constituted through glossaries of mispronounced terms such as Sir/Sa; God/Gar; Almighty/Amighty; What do you/whara; never/nebber, first/fuss; thief/teef; master/massa; that is, "the vile French patois . . . is still spoken a great deal by the negroes" (46). Humor is achieved through the positioning of oneself separate and apart from the one who is mocked, scoffed, derided. In spite of the fact that Coleridge speaks highly of West Indian hospitality and "has done much to immortalize the brown ladies of the West Indies" (23–24), Madden says he probably did not meet specimens like these two ladies. Art and literature are made into the punch lines validating opinions, for both ladies and their idiosyncracies will make picturesque marble statues—decorations, miniatures, Aunt Jemimas.

Another principle of construction is the encore, which consists of repeating the same information to fix the idea. To repeat key words—for instance, indolence—will strike his readers right, and they will validate the factual observation. In the "Castle of Indolence," which is the metaphor he uses to describe "the two fat ladies" at the inns (what George Lamming turned into *In the Castle of My Skin*) makes the two women repulsive.[21] Thus encore serves memory. It reiterates European tropes, emphasizing the familiar and reinforcing the dynamics of acceptable/unacceptable. In this sample, the West Indies is a negation of England, the antipode. Paradoxically, the example also gauges the incapacity, or rather the unwillingness, of England to civilize, to make unlikes alike. Reduction and encoring make the sample extensive to the larger society made up of ladies and servants.

> There sat the pink of Barbadian dignity, the pride of the Creole aristocracy. . . . her head and the upper part of her body thrown back nearly in an angle of forty-five degrees with her lower extremities . . . elevated on a

foot-stool. A black damsel stood behind their chair, taking advantage of her situation to grin at the passengers instead of plying her large fan carefully and sedulously for the result of her grinning was flapping the said fan against the side of her mistress's head-gear, and receiving a volley of viragoism . . . that would have startled an adder, and a box on the ear that would have produced a vermilion suffusion on the skin of a white waiting-maid. . . . three or four very demure looking blackies were gravely drawn up in front of the landlady, and were occasionally dispatched on errands to the house, while their tardiness or stupidity got rebuked in all the discordant tones of a Creole termagant. (27–28)

Relaxation and enjoyment is transformed into laziness and scoffed at because it contradicts the philosophies of labor. Laziness is to work oneself into stupidity, and stupidity backs up the idea of women as specimens.

Ungovernability: Transgressing

I find it quite impossible to resist the fascination of the conscious pleasure of pleasing; and my own heart, which I have so long been obliged to keep closed, seems to expand itself again in the sunshine of the kind looks and words which meet me at every turn, and seem to wait for mine as anxiously as if they were so many diamonds. . . . All of this may be palaver; but certainly they at least play their parts with such an air of truth, and warmth, and enthusiasm, that, after the cold hearts and repulsive manners of England, the contrast is infinitely agreeable. (Lewis, 90)

"Ungovernability" is a term I use to introduce transgression; that is, a cultural behavior that does not conform or submit to the norms. Ungovernability constitutes an area that escapes the control of dominant hermeneutics, where subalterns are not lumped together under the generic names of "Negro" or "slave." In this section, I read Madden's and Lewis's narratives and look for places where they transgress: narrative spaces where the object of contemplation and understanding renders itself ambiguous to their gaze. At this point, I argue, sentimentalism, as Hulme defines it—the sadness felt for a cultural moment destroyed by the politics of colonialism—yields to solidarity, a feeling of compassion that involves transgressing. I would like to suggest that what is at stake in transgression is decolonization, or the possibilities of breaking colonial patterns by contradicting, however mildly, however incompletely, and however topically, the presuppositions of a relationship that are not necessarily unwavering. And that is why Lewis's narrative, more so than Madden's and Beckford's, is of interest to me.

We have learned to read these narratives to follow the discursive line along the macrotopics, from the cruelty of the masters to the despicable nature of the societies as observed by the "imperial eye." This manner of reading takes us directly into the path of white planter biographies and epistemologies, and thus we remain wedded to the epistemology of the writers and the critics, to the structuring structure or structural causality that induces a reading of the external and hegemonic. The areas belonging to the subaltern are thus neglected. But dominant cultures frequently appropriate materials from other cultures and transform them symbolically into something else. Reading them against the grain, we can suggest that ridicule, irony, and the sense of the despicable — that is, everything that falls into the asymmetrical and barbaresque, or that is labeled grotesque — is part of what we have called "distancing." In distancing, the enunciating subject as imperial reveals that what he sees in the colonies is, as Bakhtin would have it, carnival, a parody of his own society turned upside down. What they read in the characters and idiosyncrasies of people, what they see in their renditions of England, is the incapacity of the empire to reproduce itself, hence negative criticism and dialectics.

In the above quote, expressions of feelings take precedence over the logic of empire, and the emotional moment constitutes a disclaimer of imperial values. The English subject has found an agreeable society of gentle people, "kind looks and words," people who transform looks and words into diamonds, and whose ontology contrasts with "the cold hearts and repulsive manners of England." The contrast between the two places makes his "heart expand." With much the same conviction, Madden includes the story of Mary Logan, "an old brown woman in Annotto Bay," in which we find the same hermeneutical break. Mary Logan's story is a sample of the possibilities of a relationship between a washerwoman and an Englishman, one who, disgusted with the patriots of South America, came upon the Jamaican shores almost destitute. That she is given a name and a place of residence is already a sign of making her into a person, not "a negro woman" or a "slave." Mary Logan knows how to administer herbs; that is, she is positioned as a "doctor-feuille," as Simone Schwarz-Bart would call her character Ma Cia, or Jean Rhys would think of Christophine, two of the best personifications of West Indians in contemporary Caribbean writings by women.

In appreciation of her services, there is an exchange of gifts: Madden gives her a ring as a token of his gratitude, and in appreciation, she gratefully reassures him she is a servant by calling him "her good master." The exchange of the ring for the services prompts Madden to speculate on payments, exchanges, and services, and catapults him back to his laissez-faire frame of reference, expecting the washerwoman Mary to begin asking for more when she finds out the man she helped is back in Jamaica and no longer impoverished. Would she, he speculates, return the ring and ask for some pecuniary reward? Would she show her true character? To his pleasure, he finds the woman is truly pious: "the old brown woman had her own 'exceeding great reward,' in the satisfaction of knowing that she had done her duty to a fellow-creature [her equal] in sickness and distress, and to one who was not unworthy of her kindness, or forgetful of it" (Madden, 93).

As in Lewis's narrative, Madden establishes symmetry between people through Christian ideas that erase imperial distancing by recognizing feelings between people. In Madden, the example renders some utilitarian purposes. The image of a good black woman helps his proselytizing in favor of abolitionism. As a reward for being pious, for enabling the human condition in him, for providing an alternative to the otherwise degraded uses and customs of the place, Madden rewards her again by paying her a visit in her house and by sitting with her "for . . . a good hour" (94), until the neighbors begin looking at him as a "walk and nyam" (94), a very indigent white man without a horse. Mary Logan stands in sharp contrast to the innkeepers Miss Hanna Lewis and Miss Betsy Austin, whose portrayal serves to illustrate the undesirable in colonial women of color. But what is the real divide between them? In all appearance it is services, good versus bad. Being a person for a person of color then means being a good servant? Always a house slave? Is it the sense of duty with which the good woman performs?

Peter Hulme would see in this incident a repetition of the tropes established by sentimental literature, a rerun of Inkle and Yarico, of Robinson Crusoe and Friday. Stephen Greenblatt would support Hulme's position, branding the instance as another sample from the same set — that is, the magnificent rhetorical apparatus of the West. But both positions are more invested in asserting the power of colonialism than in bringing up the presence of the subaltern in the documents. I am invested in arguing here that the moments of solidarity must be rescued from the shoddy soil of Western colonial literatures and set apart in recognition of a subaltern presence that transcends its negation by making itself worthy of mentioning. This act of intrusion of subaltern humanity shifts the category of the "other" into "self." I think it is important for cultural critics to recognize these moments. Madden pays Mary Logan further due by including her in his narrative and by making her a paradigm of humanity. Mary Logan, the old brown washerwoman, and Plato, a young maroon, are just two patterns framing the transcendence of subaltern status.

Notes

1   William Beckford, *A Descriptive Account of the Island of Jamaica, with Remarks upon the Cultivation of the Sugar-Cane, throughout the Different Seasons in the Year, and Chiefly Considered in a Picturesque Point of View; also Observations and Reflections upon What Would*

Probably Be the Consequences of an Abolition of the Slave-Trade, and of the Emancipation of the Slaves (London: T. and J. Egerton, Whitehall, 1790). Edward Long, *History of Jamaica* (London: 1774). Bryan Edwards, *The History, Civil and Commercial, of the British Colonies in the West Indies* (London: 1794–1801).

2 Eric Eustace Williams, *Capitalism and Slavery* (Chapel Hill: University of North Carolina Press, 1944); *British Historians and the West Indies* (London: Deutsch, 1966); Selwyn R. Cudjoe, ed., *Speaks: Essays on Colonialism and Independence* (Amherst: University of Massachusetts Press, 1993); Orlando Patterson, *Ethnic Chauvinism: The Reactionary Impulse* (New York: Stein and Day, 1977); *The Sociology of Slavery: An Analysis of the Origins, Development, and Structure of Negro Slave Society in Jamaica* (Rutherford, N.J.: Fairleigh Dickinson University Press, 1969, 1967); Philip D. Curtin, *Two Jamaicas: The Role of Ideas in a Tropical Colony, 1830–1865* (Cambridge, Mass.: Harvard University Press, 1955); Elsa V. Goveia, *Slave Society in the British Leeward Islands at the End of the Eighteenth Century* (New Haven, Conn.: Yale University Press, 1965), and *A Study on the Historiography of the British West Indies to the End of the Nineteenth Century* (Washington, D.C.: Howard University Press, 1980, 1956); C. J. Bartlett, *The West Indian Slave Laws of the Eighteenth Century,* and *A New Balance of Power: The Nineteenth Century* (Barbados: Caribbean University Press, 1970); Immanuel Wallerstein, *"The Rise and Future Demise of the World Capitalist System:* Concepts for Comparative Analysis."

3 R. R. Madden, *Travels in the East,* and *A Twelvemonth Residence in the West Indies, During the Transition from Slavery to Apprenticeship; with Incidental Notices of the State of Society, Prospects, and Natural Resources of Jamaica and Other Islands* (Westport: Negro University Press, 1970; originally published in 1835 by Carey, Lea and Blanchard, Philadelphia); Matthew Gregory Lewis, *Journal of a West Indian Proprietor* (New York: Negro University Press, 1969; originally published in 1834 by John Murray, London).

4 Edward Kamau Brathwaite, "Caribbean Man in Space and Time," *Carifesta Forum: An Anthology of Twenty Caribbean Voices,* ed. John Hearne (Jamaica: Carifesta, 1976), pp. 199–208.

5 Juan Francisco Manzano, *The Autobiography of a Slave,* ed. Ivan A. Schulman, trans. Evelyn Picon Garfield (Detroit, MI.: Wayne State University Press, 1996); Olaudah Equiano, *The Life of Olaudah Equiano, or Gustavus Vassa, the African, Written by Himself* (New York: Negro University Press, 1969).

6 B. W. Higman, *Jamaica Surveyed: Plantation Maps and Plans of the Eighteenth and Nineteenth Centuries* (Kingston: Institute of Jamaica, 1988).

7 Manuel Moreno Fraginals, *The Sugarmill: The Socioeconomic Complex of Sugar in Cuba, 1760–1860,* trans. Cedric Belfrage (New York, Monthly Review Press, 1976).

8 Richard Pares, *Yankees and Creoles: The Trade between North America and the West Indies before the American Revolution* (Cambridge, Mass.: Harvard University Press, 1956).

9 Ileana Rodríguez, "Romanticismo literario y liberalismo reformista: El grupo de Domingo del Monte," *Caribbean Studies* 20, 1 (1980): 35–56.

10 Cirilo Villaverde, *Cecilia Valdés* (Havana: Cultural, 1941).

11 E. G. Squier, *The States of Central America: Their Geography, Topography, Climate, Population, Resources, Productions, Commerce, Political Organizations, Aborigines, etc., etc., Comprising Chapters on Honduras, San Salvador, Nicaragua, Costa Rica, Guatemala, Belize, the Bay Islands, The Mosquito Shore, and the Honduras Inter-Oceanic Railway* (New York: Harper and Brothers, 1858).

12 See the story of Inkle and Yaricoo. Peter Hulme, *Colonial Encounters: Europe and the Native Caribbean, 1492–1797* (London: Routledge, 1986).

13 Benita Parry, "Problems in Current Theories of Colonial Discourse," *The Post-Colonial Studies Reader,* ed. Bill Ashcroft, Gareth Griffiths, and Helen Tiffin (London: Routledge, 1995): 36–44.

14 See Antonello Gerbi, *The Dispute of the New World: The History of a Polemic, 1750–1900,* trans. and ed. Jeremy Moyle (Pittsburgh: University of Pittsburgh Press, 1973); *Nature in the New World: From Christopher Columbus to Gonzalo Fernández de Oviedo,* trans. Jeremy Moyle (Pittsburgh: University of Pittsburgh Press, 1985).

15 Sylvia Winter, "Beyond the Categories of the Master Conception: The Counterdoctrine of the Jamesian Poiesis," *C. L. R. James's Caribbean,* ed. Paget Henry and Paul Buhle (Durham, N.C.: Duke University Press, 1992), 63–91.

16 See Aphra Behn, *Oronooko: or, the Royal Slave,* in *Shorter Novels: Seventeenth Century* (Boston: Bedford/St. Martin's, 2000); Wylie Sypher, *Guinea's Captive Kings: British Anti-Slavery Literature of the Eighteenth Century* (New York: Octagon Books, 1969).

17 See Pere Labbat, *Nouveau voyage aux iles de l'Amerique* (Paris: 1722); Pere Jean-Baptiste Du Tertre, *Histoire general des Antilles habitees par les Francais (Paris: 1667–1671).*

18 This depiction of black cultures works in tandem with Mikhail Bakhtin's notions of the grotesque in which the images of the body acquire "a considerable and substantial development in the popular, festive. . . . the grotesque concept of the body forms the basis of abuses, oaths, and curses" (*Rabelais and His World,* trans. Helene Iswolsky [Bloomington: Indiana University Press, 1984], p. 24).

19 Jamaica Kincaid, *A Small Place* (Ontario: Penguin, 1988); Claude McKay, *My Green Hills of Jamaica* (Kingston, Jamaica: Heinemann, 1979).

20 Jean Rhys, *Wide Sargasso Sea,* with an introduction by Francis Wyndham (London: Deutsch, 1966).

21 George Lamming, *In the Castle of My Skin,* with an introduction by Richard Wright (New York: McGraw-Hill, 1953).

The Architectural Relationship between Gender, Race, and the Bolivian State

MARCIA STEPHENSON

The critical debates on governability and citizenship in Bolivia foreground the ongoing crisis of legitimacy that has haunted the modern state due to its inability to integrate productively the heterogeneous civil society into the political order. Instead of forging a unified social body that brings together the racial and cultural diversity of the country, the state has served the needs of a specific, privileged few, functioning more as a "guarantor of order" than as an "agent of change," as Jorge Lazarte observes (ILDIS 1992: 9–20).[1] Luis Antezana similarly points to the disjunction between the state and civil society to argue that their relationship, at least in part, is determined by an unbreachable verticality that positions the state above civil society. Political parties have been ineffectual at mediating the complex dynamics between the state and racially and ethnically diverse social actors. External pressures from international institutions such as the IMF and the World Bank further undermined the state's ability to govern (ILDIS, 64). As a result, the state never achieved the legitimacy of a nation-state or a common-sense perception of a *nosotros* predicated on the plurality of identities. The problem the state currently faces is how to overcome this "privatist" history so that it might reformulate itself according to the interests of the collective social body and develop a genuine public sphere that incorporates individual and collective subjects.

This essay examines further the nexus of relations between the Bolivian state and the heterogeneous social body, focusing on the ways by which the state, as a guarantor of order, has sought to contain civil society.[2] It argues that the practices of social enclosure and cultural fragmentation are implemented through hegemonic discourses of modernity and citizenship. In Bolivia, discourses of modernity and citizenship continue to be linked to histories of colonialism because they deploy a rhetoric structured by hierarchical notions of racial difference that produce and reproduce an idealized (mestizo) citizen-subject and its (indigenous) other.[3] These discursive practices are spatially structured, mapping fixed boundaries and demarcating clear-cut distinctions between inside and outside. Moreover, these racialized spaces of containment are also gendered because they require prevailing ideologies of womanhood for the reproduction of power.[4] My analysis, therefore, begins with the consideration of hegemonic depictions of the house, a compelling example of one enclosure where, in a stratified society such as Bolivia's, notions of space, race, and gender converge with the reproduction of power. I contend that the underlying architectural rhetoric of the house and the accompanying image of the Western white mother depicted as inhabiting this idealized space function as organizing principles of modernity. The door of the house thus serves as a threshold metaphor, one that marks the limit of the racialized space of the selfsame. To illustrate this process, I will include in the second section of the essay a reading of Ana María Condori's testimonial *Nayan Uñatatawi: Mi despertar* (1988).

Critical studies on the relationship between motherhood and the home in Bolivia, written by middle- and upper-class essayists, have changed little throughout the twentieth century. These accounts confirm the notion of an essential feminine nature that is fixed and unchanging, one that is biologically determined by woman's reproductive activities.[5] According to this prevailing representation, the domestic space of the home constitutes the fundamental core of womanhood. Normative depictions of the private, domestic realm emphasize a logic of interiority, a unified spatial order that is enclosed and timeless, where stasis, nostalgia, and security are troped in the figure of the mother.[6] Thus, the essence of womanhood, and therefore also of motherhood, is inextricably linked to the socio-spatial arena that is the home.

In his study of Bolivian housing, *El problema social de la vivienda* (1949), Alberto Cornejo elaborates on the metaphorical relationship between motherhood and the home, claiming that both can be linked to the notion of origin. Cornejo frames his argument by citing at length from the work of Ramón Clarés. Clarés, in turn, appears undoubtedly to have been influenced by Freud, who, in his essay on "The Uncanny," defines humankind's original home as the mother's womb (Freud 1955: 245). On motherhood, Clarés writes: "Madre es pues, síntesis viva de espacio y tiempo. . . . Más allá de la madre, el infante no siente la vida, porque madre es origen. . . . La madre es la mujer fundamental, simbólicamente llamada la casa, en el místico lenguaje de los libros sagrados" (Clarés, cited in Cornejo 1949: 6). [Mother is the living synthesis of space and time. . . . Beyond the mother, the infant does not feel life, because mother is origin. . . . The mother is the fundamental woman, symbolically called the "house" in the mystical language of the sacred books.] Premising his thesis on Clarés's ideas, Cornejo foregrounds the link between the foundational role of the house and motherhood in the development of humankind to contend that both influence the quality and condition of human character and of life itself (Cornejo 1949: 6).

Cornejo argues that legislators must address Bolivia's housing shortage, a shortage that already constituted a problem in 1949 because of the increasing growth of urban populations and economic limitations that prevented many people from buying their own homes (Cornejo 1949: 5). According to Cornejo, the solution to the problem is, simply put, more affordable housing. However, he cautions, the houses should be constructed according to certain specifics that would enable the reorganization of urban society: "Los barrios donde el conventillo ofrece capacidad de vivienda para multitudes policromas, va siendo proscrita por las necesidades sociales. Porque, no sólo basta construir casas, sino que ellas deben responder a las necesidades y finalidades de la vivienda" (18). [The districts where low-income projects offer housing for the polychromatic multitudes, these projects are becoming outdated due to social necessity. It is not enough to build houses; rather, these should meet the needs and objectives of a home.] If mother equals origin equals home, Cornejo clearly advocates a House (Mother) through which the polychromatic poor can be eliminated, thereby establishing a decisive link between motherhood, the home, and the racial formation of the modern nation-state.

In recent years, critical work in architectural theory, drawing from the practices of Derridean deconstruction, psychoanalytic theory, and gender studies, has begun to interrogate the political, cultural, and spatial order of the house. For example, Mark Wigley (1992) analyzes the production of gender by examining the spatial, structural, and psychic operations of the house. This work, in turn, has carried over into a detailed reading of the ways in which Western metaphysics constructs a "domestic regime" as it appropriates and delimits the logic of its domain. This analysis can be productive for understanding hegemonic representations of modernity in Bolivia, which, I will suggest in this essay, are organized according to an architectural logic that structures dominant understandings of race and gender relations. The equation of a particular kind of house with the formation of acculturated (mestizo) citizens suggests that, like clothing, architecture fashions the body politic. Consequently, the house constitutes both the gateway to citizenship and the condition of its possibility, functioning literally and symbolically in a continuous trajectory of identity formation.

As an overdetermined cultural and political site, the house is central to both hegemonic discourses of domesticity and counterhegemonic indigenous practices that continually resist criollo efforts to delimit the boundaries of the familiar and the selfsame. Both Wigley and Anthony Vidler address the violence of the house that is structured through the very act of domestication; domestication, in other words, delimits the realm of the familiar at the same time it represses the unfamiliar, the unhomely. The critical interrogation of the house from the point of view of its architecture and the implications this has for understanding social, political, and economic relations become a useful lens through which it is possible to read the racialized and gendered boundaries of modernity in the context of Bolivia. These current debates unequivocally indicate that hegemonic depictions of modernity in Bolivia are structured through a rhetoric of domestic space; the house functions as a spatial metaphor through which the "unruly play of representation" can be controlled precisely because it defines and differentiates the (modern or civilized) inside from the (uncivilized) outside (see Wigley 1993: 106–107).

The architectural rhetoric that is deployed insistently by criollo discourses through the anxious reiteration of boundaries suggests that this domestic regime constitutes both the condition and the very possibility of the hegemonic state itself. Dominant depictions of the house, emphasizing enclosure, the privatization of space, and individualization, become an important mechanism with which hegemonic discourses repeatedly attempt to order and discipline the racially heterogeneous social body throughout the second half of the twentieth century. So-called "normative" houses domesticate individual bodies and families by forcibly bringing them into the realm of the familiar; therefore, the physical layout of hegemonic houses structures processes of ethnic and racial acculturation at the same time that it organizes dominant constructions of gender. Moreover, because normative houses insistently delineate a series of boundaries between inside and outside, it soon becomes apparent that racially diverse groups position themselves and are positioned differently in relation to these same boundaries. Indeed, different or nonhegemonic houses suggest competing positions about boundaries.

The analysis in this essay goes beyond current debates in architecture because it introduces the question of racial formation. Indeed, while recent architectural discourse has enriched the understanding of the operations of gender construction, to date it has remained largely silent on race. If, however, the House is "a metonym of the prototypical Mother," as critics Heidi J. Nast and Mabel O. Wilson maintain (1994: 49), this essay suggests that the prototypical mother in Bolivia who inhabits the normative house is either white and from the upper class or an acculturated, Westernized mestiza. Consequently, the state constitutes itself through specific constructions that not only produce traditional gender roles but also promote racial assimilation by privileging white, Western norms. Nonhegemonic or resistant homes, therefore, have implications not only for gender roles but also for racial and political identities.

The architectural relationship between modernity and racial and gendered identities is at the forefront of architect Jorge Saravia Valle's study *Planificación de aldeas rurales* (1986). Saravia Valle contrasts a drawing of an alleged present-day rural house with a model of a proposed modernized house. In figure 1, labeled "vivienda actual" [present-day dwelling], the house depicted is run-down, in a state of advanced disrepair. The cracked walls, falling roof, and lack of a foundation suggest the fragility and permeability of boundaries that define and differentiate the interior from the exterior; the presence of a clay oven on the patio indicates that the woman carries out her domestic activities, literally, outside the confines of the house. A cow pictured in the front yard wanders freely, leaving in its tracks a pile of manure. A man can be seen just beyond the wall of the corral, squatting and defecating. Next to the house there is a mound of garbage.

In contrast, Saravia Valle's proposed model house (fig. 2) has been emptied of all human and animal presences. The modern house underscores the importance of private rooms, the enclosed latrine, the contained corral, and a state of cleanliness missing in the first drawing. According to the architect, this model house illustrates how "el MEJORAMIENTO, con asistencia técnica que requiere la vivienda campesina tiene como objetivo principal, hacer de ella un 'ambiente' cómodo, higiénico, agradable y orgánico dentro de su crecimiento progresivo" (Saravia Valle 1986: 82). [The principal objective of IMPROV-ING the *campesino* house with technical assistance is to make it a comfortable, hygienic, pleasant, and organic environment.]

The process by which the Indian woman's identity undergoes transformation is illustrated in a second group of drawings by Saravia Valle. Figures 3 and 4 contrast the interior space of an actual Indian house with that of an "improved" dwelling. The actual house consists of a single room that serves household needs. An Indian woman squats on the floor, cooking, while another person sleeps. A pig, rooster, and dog share the same domestic space with the family. In contrast, the improved house once again stands out because of the absence of people and animals. Internal walls have been added to emphasize architecturally the containment and privatization of space; now the living room and the kitchen are separate from the bedrooms. The drawings suggest that as the house is modernized and improved, the racial identity of its inhabitants is also transformed. The Indian woman present in the first drawing as a symbol of a collective, native identity but absent in the second, no longer has a place in the refurbished space; instead, we await the arrival of an acculturated housewife to take up residence there.

In their discussion of Minnie Bruce Pratt's work, Biddy Martin and Chandra Mohanty have suggested that a monolithic representation of home guarantees its own repeatability (or fixity) because it participates in and reproduces a series of "exclusions and repressions which support the seeming homogeneity, stability, and self-evidence of 'white identity,' which is derived from and dependent on the marginalization of differences within as well as 'without'" (Martin and Mohanty 1983: 193). This tension between represen-

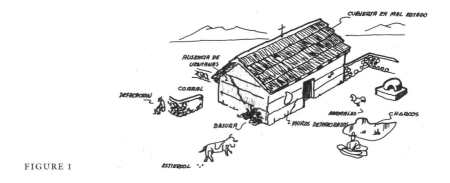

FIGURE I

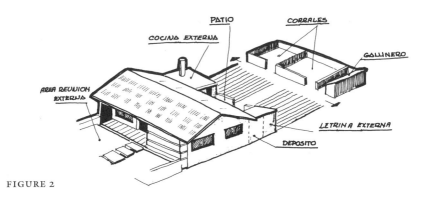

FIGURE 2

tation and repression is what Homi Bhabha identifies as the paradox that is central to fixity, precisely because, as a sign of difference in the "ideological construction of otherness," it connotes both "an unchanging order" *and* "disorder" (Bhabha 1983: 18). Thus, for example, when urban indigenous women and working-class *cholas* circulated freely outside the home, as in the instance of the militant anarchists of the 1930s and 1940s, their bodies threatened the social order because they were out of place (the home) and in the streets. According to the criollo oligarchy then, these disorderly, hence polluted and polluting racialized, female bodies were identified with (political) instability and consequently subjected to surveillance and discipline (see Stephenson 1997). By the 1960s and 1970s, hegemonic womanhood continued to be constructed according to a racial and economic logic that was spatially organized according to the constellation of signifiers ranging between "order" and "home" (property). This process is reminiscent of what French feminists have identified as the continuum of meanings between *propre–propriété*.[7]

For Hélène Cixous, the multiplicity of meanings embedded in the continuum between propre–propriété is inextricably bound up in the construction of the economy of masculine desire and the assurance of its repeatability:

"The opposition appropriate/inappropriate, proper/improper, clean/un-
clean, mine/not mine (the valorization of the selfsame), organizes the opposition identity/difference. Everything takes place as if, in a split second,
man and being had propriated each other. And as if his relationship to woman
was still at play as the possibility—though threatening, of the not-proper, not-
clean, not-mine: desire is inscribed as the desire to reappropriate for himself
that which seems able to escape him" (Cixous and Clément 1986: 80).[8] In an
influential study of the reciprocal relationship between gender and architecture, Mark Wigley argues that this economy of masculine desire for the selfsame, expressed through the play of meaning in propre-propriété, is produced
and reproduced spatially through the actual physical structure of the home,
the house. In other words, the house's "primary role is to protect the father's
genealogical claims by isolating women from other men. Reproduction is
understood as reproduction of the father. The law of the house is undoubtedly
no more than the law of the father. The physical house is the possibility of the
patriarchal order that appears to be applied to it" (Wigley 1992: 336). The
possibility of the patriarchal order depends on woman's sexuality being con-

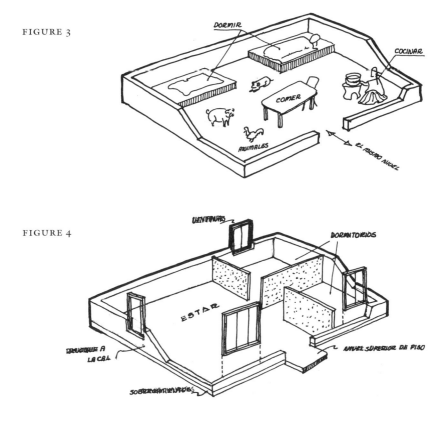

FIGURE 3

FIGURE 4

fined within the bounds of the house. Therefore, Wigley continues, "the house then assumes the role of the man's self-control. The virtuous woman becomes woman-plus-house or, rather, woman-as-housed, such that her virtue cannot be separated from the physical space" (337).

One might note that Peter Stallybrass has similarly commented in another context (Renaissance England) that close watch and supervision of women emphasized "the mouth, chastity, the threshold of the house. These three areas were frequently collapsed into each other" (Stallybrass 1986: 126). The law of the father, understood as the reproduction of the selfsame, requires, then, that the boundaries of the house be maintained and protected through a complex system of surveillance that includes controls that are both tangible (walls, doors, closed windows) and intangible (dress, manners, legal and cultural codes) (Wigley 1992: 338). For Wigley, the law of the father is therefore always already architectural: "it is itself understood as the intersection of a spatial system and a system of surveillance" (339).

Whereas Wigley's article convincingly analyzes the complicity between architecture and the construction of gender, Peter Stallybrass's work links the relationship between architecture and gender to the production and maintenance of state structures. Drawing from Bakhtin, Stallybrass suggests that the predominant signs of Woman include "the enclosed body, the closed mouth, the locked house" (Stallybrass 1986: 127). Therefore, "normative 'Woman' could become the emblem of the perfect and impermeable container, and hence a map of the integrity of the state" (129).[9] The architectural rhetoric that enables these metaphors of containment, enclosure, and interiority to slide between Home — Woman — State is one that fosters notions of safety and security, the condition of being at home and all that that implies (the familiar, family history, nostalgia, and so on) (see Vidler 1992: 17); this rhetoric is therefore grounded in the recognition of the selfsame, and bolstered with the deployment of multiple boundaries that necessarily reinforce differences between inside and outside.

Silvia Rivera Cusicanqui and Tristán Platt have argued that the binary inside/outside has constituted the spatial law of civilization-citizenship in Bolivia from the nineteenth century to the present. Platt, for example, links the discourse of civilization to positivist rhetoric that equated participation in the liberal market system with citizenship: "La incorporación del indio al mercado aparece como una medida humanitaria para lograr su incorporación a la sociedad 'civilizada'" (Platt 1982: 96). [The incorporation of the Indian into the market appears as a humanitarian measure in order to achieve his incorporation into "civilized" society.] This "humanitarian" process was sanctioned with the 1874 *Ley de exvinculación* that legalized the abrogation of the indigenous *ayllu* and implemented a new system of taxation. According to the first *revisitador,* Narciso de la Riva, the law was crucial because it would effect the dissolution of indigenous communities. "'La parte esencial . . . de la ley consiste en la exvinculación de la tierras de orijen, con el fin de disolver esos grupos de individuos rezagados' [los ayllus]." [The essential part of the law consists of the expropriation of indigenous territorial lands, the objective of which is to break up those groups of individuals lagging behind (the ayllus)] (cited in Platt 1982: 96). Consequently, de la Riva envisioned the law as a vehicle enabling a particular kind of "coming out," a passage across household thresholds: "[La *ley de exvinculación* es] un instrumento esencialmente móvil, que semejante al mar produzca flujos y reflujos, con cuyo poder el aboríjena salga de las grutas donde habita, se interpole con las masas ilustradas del país, y despierte a la vida del progreso" (cited in Platt 1982: 96). [(The Law of Expropriation is) an essentially dynamic instrument, which, like the sea, produces rising and ebb flows; empowered by it the aborigine can come out of the caves where he lives, mix in with the country's enlightened masses, and wake up to the life of progress.]

For de la Riva, the Indians that came forth out of their primitive houses (*grutas*), entered into knowledge and the realm of the civilized. This "outside/inside" location in which de la Riva's discourse positions indigenous peoples calls to mind Diana Fuss's observations regarding the particular situatedness of gays and lesbians today: "to be out . . . is precisely to be no longer out; to be out is to be finally outside of exteriority and all the exclusions and deprivations such outsiderhood imposes. Or, put another way, to be out is really to be in — inside the realm of the visible, the speakable, the culturally intelligible" (Fuss 1991: 4). De la Riva's commentary on the 1874 law suggests that an Indian could enter the "realm of the visible," the "speakable," and the "culturally intelligible," only by stepping "outside of exteriority" or crossing over the threshold of the Andean house into the criollo world.

Rivera Cusicanqui contends that within this particular historical context, citizenship has constituted a cultural and racial benchmark according to which individuals can be measured in terms of their "ontological" status. Rather than constituting a genuine democratic social pact, liberal citizenship has functioned as a form of cultural discipline that manifests itself with increasing violence the closer one comes to the indigenous pole on the horizontal axis of identities (Rivera Cusicanqui 1993: 76). A citizen, "he" (*sic*) who is "inside" the social contract (an acculturated mestizo), is oppositionally situated with respect to the noncitizen (Indian) who is "outside" the social contract. This fundamental opposition, "inside/outside," is tightly bound to the question of architecture and, more specifically, to the construction of the house. The spatial law of citizenship (inside/outside) is guaranteed and enforced through the architectural representation of the house. The house does not precede this argument; rather, it both constitutes and is constituted by the very condition of the possibility of each side of the binary. While depicted as representing "Order," the house in fact represents a specific criollo order (see Wigley 1992: 380).

Prevailing criollo notions of modernity emphasize the dividing line that marks the passage from the Aymara house to the interior space of the criollo home. For young Aymara women and girls, this passage takes place, generally, for reasons of economic necessity as they migrate to the city in search of work as domestics. Ana María Condori's *testimonio, Nayan Uñatatawi: Mi despertar* (1988), provides a compelling account of this journey across thresholds, from her parents' house in the rural province Carangas to that of her employers in the city of Oruro and later La Paz.

Condori's first job is cast as her entrance into the socio-symbolic contract when her father leaves her in her employer's house after having been assured by the *señora* that she will be treated just like another member of the family: "Nosotros le vamos a tratar como a una hija, no le va a faltar nada, ni comida ni ropa. Todo lo que comen mis hijos ella ha de servirse, el trato va a ser muy bueno" (56). [We will treat her like a daughter, she will not lack anything, neither food nor clothing. Everything that my children eat she will help herself to as well, the treatment will be very good.] Disregarding the sociocultural and economic differences that constitute the employer-employee relationship in this instance, the woman of the house emphasizes instead familial and homely relations which will supposedly determine their interaction; just like another daughter of the family, Condori will be "at home" in her new surroundings. The passage across thresholds therefore is presented as continuous and unfragmented; Condori was a daughter in her parents' house, and she will be a daughter in her employer's house.

As Anthony Vidler has observed, the homely house is associated with domesticity and the sense of being "at home" (1992: 24–25). The seemingly secure and innocent space of the house becomes, therefore, in Wigley's words, a "paradigm of interiority" (1993: 104). Nevertheless, the criollo house domesticates precisely because it insistently structures inside and outside spaces, thereby determining those places that are proper (the familiar and selfsame) and improper (the unfamiliar, the unrecognizable) (see Wigley 1993: 106–107). What is more, not all interiors are equal, nor does everyone inhabit the interior in the same way.

As Condori's testimonio demonstrates, one can be both inside and outside simultaneously. Condori's testimonio of her life as a domestic worker in the city discloses a Bolivian-criollo version of the "architectural drama of instituting and revealing the proper" (Ingraham 1988: 10). Thus, what at first appears to be a seamless transition between houses increasingly gives way to the violence of domestication as Condori begins to learn her proper place: "Al principio yo me imaginaba que almorzaría y cenaría con ellos en un solo lugar y que el plato también iba a ser de los que usaba toda la familia, pero después vi que yo tenía que comer en la cocina, separada de todos, que para mí el plato era reservado" (59). [At first I imagined that I would eat dinner and supper with them in the same place and that my dish would be from the set used by all the family. But later I saw that I had to eat in the kitchen, separated from everyone, and that for me there was a reserved plate.] Not only must Condori learn to eat apart from the others, she also discovers that she cannot sit on the family's chairs, nor on the sofa, nor on any of the beds; she may not use their shower nor their soap. Paradoxically, even when she occupies her proper place, she is always already improper: "Ellos creen que porque una es campesina es cochina, sucia y por eso dicen: 'No te sientes, no uses, me lo vas a ensuciar.'" (60–61). [They believe that because you're a campesina girl you're a pig, dirty, and so they say: "Don't sit down there, don't use that, you're going to get it dirty."] This interior, therefore, is not a homogeneous space inhabited equally by all. Within the house, Condori becomes further restricted to certain spaces such as the kitchen, beyond which she ventures only to clean and order the other rooms. The phrase "la empleada tiene que estar en su lugar" [the maid has to be in her place] resonates like a litany throughout the pages of *Mi despertar*.

Condori's new place is also marked by a hitherto unfamiliar language, a language exemplified by the phrase "set the table": "Después, 'pon la mesa' me decía, pero yo no sabía qué era poner la mesa. En el campo estaba acostumbrada a comer parada o sentada en cualquier lugar, porque hay que estar a la expectativa de los rebaños para que no se vayan al pastizal reservado para el invierno o a la chacra" (57). [Then, "set the table," she told me, but I didn't know what set the table meant. In the countryside I was used to eating while standing up or seated anywhere, because you have to be on the lookout for the flocks of sheep so that they don't wander into the grazing pasture reserved for the winter or into the garden.] Little by little, she explains, she had to learn this new language. Nevertheless, it is not a language to which she comes as a speaking subject. She herself cannot utter the phrase "set the table." Instead, Condori need only learn enough so that she can be commanded. She is always only this language's object, its other, and she will never occupy the place of subjectivity; she can never be "at home" in this language of domestication. Her place is that of silence.

Reflecting on her silence, Condori locates its origin in her upbringing: "Lo positivo del niño campesino es que conoce su realidad, está integrado al trabajo de la familia y además no se cría muy mimado de los padres; aprendemos a soportar muchas cosas. Pero lo negativo es que a veces uno se acostumbra a no protestar. Así era yo al principio: no decía nada en mi trabajo; calladita nomás aceptaba, tenía miedo de hablar de lo que quería" (60). [The positive thing about the campesino child is that she knows her reality; she is integrated into the family work and besides she is not raised by her parents to be spoiled; we learn to endure many things. But the negative thing is that sometimes one becomes used to not protesting. That's the way I was at first: I didn't say anything at work; with my mouth shut I accepted. I was afraid to talk about what I wanted.]

If the relation between language and silence she remembers from her own home was rooted in processes by which the child is brought into familial and communal practices, her silence in the employer's house results from a different structure of power relations. Analyzing her (im)proper place as a domestic worker, Condori recognizes that this supposedly familiar, homey interior, is, in fact, unfamiliar and unhomely: "Ya no esperaba comer con ellos; me di cuenta de que me hubiera sentido incómoda, de que se hagan la burla de mí: de lo que como, de mi manera de hablar. Sentarse en la misma mesa con ellos no es lo mismo que estar con un amigo o un familiar, sino que es tener que comer delante del patrón, del que manda" (60). [I no longer wished to eat with them; I realized that I would have felt uncomfortable, that they might make fun of me: of what I eat, of my way of speaking. Sitting at the same table with them is not the same as being with a friend or a family member; rather, it's having to eat in front of the boss, of the one who commands.] Condori is homeless in a home that continually reiterates the proper. She can never forget that her (im)proper place, that of economic dependence and racial difference, is apart from the familiar and the familial.

When Condori does speak up, at the end of her time working as a domestic employee, it is to talk back to the señora. Bell hooks defines "talking back," the transition for the oppressed from silence to speech, as a "gesture of defiance that heals, that makes new life and new growth possible. It is that act of speech, of 'talking back,' that is no mere gesture of empty words, that is the expression of our movement from object to subject—the liberated voice" (hooks 1989: 9).[10] Condori tells of how she argued with the señora over a period of two hours about her salary, which had been withheld from her for the past few months. The señora attempted to silence her on several occasions by crying out, "Esta india . . . , ¡vos eres una campesina que no sabes nada!" (Condori 1988: 103). [This Indian (girl). . . . You're a campesina who doesn't know anything!]

The señora's repeated use of the phrase "this Indian" calls attention to racial differences and constitutes an attempt to highlight Condori's impropriety within the house. Condori refuses to be silenced, however, and instead she continues to talk back, insisting on the relations that sanction economically and racially the señora's property/propriety and her own supposed impropriety: "Gracias a la india, gracias al campesino, tienes mercado aquí, que tienes donde comprar; gracias a todos los campesinos tienes toda la comodidad porque al final son ellos los que trabajan. —Así he empezado a hablar y ¡uhh! se ha desmayado" (104). ["Thanks to the Indian, thanks to the campesino, you have a market here, you have a place to go and buy; thanks to all the campesinos you have all the convenience because in the end they're the ones who work." —That's how I began to speak and oh! she fainted.] The señora, clearly shocked by Condori's unwelcome positioning as a speaking subject, is herself rendered speechless by fainting away.

Whereas Condori was invited into the house on the grounds of propriety, as a daughter, her testimonio is about the breakdown of the proper and how the proper can only improperly domesticate. Wigley has argued that "Architecture is no more than the strategic effect of the suppression of internal contradiction. It is not simply a mechanism that represses certain things. Rather, it is the very mark of repression" (Wigley 1993: 209). Condori's testimonio also reveals the contradictory and repressive operations of the hegemonic criollo house. For example, Condori is repeatedly warned about the dangers facing a young woman who ventures outside the house alone. Domestic workers live like caged birds, she explains. The door to the outside is often locked to them, "y aunque esté abierta y una podría irse el rato que quisiera, hay muchos obstáculos que impiden: el desconocimiento, el temor, el aislamiento" (84); [and even if the door were open and you could leave the moment you wanted, there are many obstacles that impede leaving: the unknown, fear, isolation]. She admits that she was afraid to leave the house at first: "Era muy acomplejada siempre; tenía miedo que me pase algo, que pueda aparecer embarazada" (73). [I always had a lot of hang-ups; I was afraid that something might happen to me, that I could end up pregnant.]

Her employers took advantage of her reluctance to go out because that way she worked even more for them. They affirmed her fears by contrasting the security of the interior with the dangers of the exterior: "Entonces ellos también me decían: 'No hay que salir, . . . no hay que tomar amistad, . . . no conviene porque con otras ha pasado que . . .' . . . Miles de cosas contaban y más me acomplejaban con eso" (74). [So they also told me: "You shouldn't go out, . . . you shouldn't make friends, . . . it's not advisable because with other girls it has happened that . . ." Thousands of things they told me and I felt even more afraid.]

What she discovers, however, is that the real danger lies *inside* the house, where she is sexually harassed on various occasions by the fathers of the families for whom she works. By revealing the fathers' attempts to assault her physically, Condori overturns prevailing depictions of the house as a "paradigm of security" and as the "abode of the familiar" (Wigley 1993: 118). In this manner, Condori insistently calls attention to the necessary violence with which the hegemonic interior must be policed so that the law and propriety of the Father (modern criollo state) prevail.

Notes

I gratefully acknowledge the University of Texas Press for granting permission to include portions of this chapter that appeared in my book *Gender and Modernity in Andean Bolivia* (1999).

1 These pressing issues have formed the basis of several important conferences, such as the 1991 seminar on the topic "Cultura de la crisis institucional en Bolivia," organized by the Instituto Latinoamericano de Investigaciones Sociales (ILDIS). At this gathering, Jorge Lazarte's preliminary remarks set the stage for the presentations that would follow. The papers from the conference were subsequently published under the title *Diversidad étnica y cultural* (La Paz: ILDIS, 1992). Please note that the papers presented in the ILDIS publication were not given titles. Sometimes the same panelist participated in a general debate, and as such, only the panelists' names have been indicated.

2 Javier Sanjinés has examined the process of social enclosure and cultural fragmentation with great insight through his analysis of the production of literary and cultural discourses in Bolivia (see ILDIS 1992: 109–110; Sanjinés 1992).

3 See Dhaliwal 1996 for an insightful discussion of the relationship between radical democracy and western colonialism.

4 Sonia Montaño also has called for a reexamination of how spaces have been gendered. For example, she eloquently argues for the need to create public awareness of domestic violence against women, an awareness that would lead inexorably to the politicization of the private, domestic realm. She insists that this cannot happen as long as politics and the public sphere continue to be perceived as exclusively masculine domains (ILDIS 1992: 102–103).

5 Only since the 1980s has work been published exploring the cultural construction of gender in Bolivia. Publications by nongovernmental organizations such as the Taller de Historia Oral Andina (THOA), Centro de Información y Desarrollo de la Mujer (CIDEM), and Taller de Historia y Participación de la Mujer (TAHIPAMU), as well as other women's organizations, interrogate traditionally held views of womanhood and motherhood. While by no means a complete bibliography, see, for example, THOA, *Mujer y resistencia comunaria: Historia y memoria* (La Paz: HISBOL, 1986). For an English version of the monograph, see Silvia Rivera Cusicanqui and THOA, "Indigenous Women and Community Resistance: History and Memory," in *Women and Social Change in Latin America*, ed. Elizabeth Jelin, 151–183 (London: Zed Books, 1990); see also Rosario León "Bartolina Sisa: The Peasant Women's Organization in Bolivia," in Jelin 1990: 135–150; Lucila Criales Burgos, *Mujer y conflictos socio-culturales: El caso de las migrantes de Caquiaviri en la ciudad de La Paz* (La Paz: Aruwiyiri, 1994); Ximena Medinaceli, *Alterando la rutina: Mujeres en las ciudades de Bolivia, 1920–1930* (La Paz: CIDEM, 1989); Beatriz Rossells, *La mujer, Una ilusión: Ideologías e imágenes de la mujer en Bolivia en el siglo XIX* (La Paz: CIDEM, 1988); Julieta Paredes and María Galindo, *¿Y si fuésemos una, espejo de la otria? Por un feminismo no racista* (La Paz: Ediciones Gráficas, 1992). See also Rossana Barragán's work, including "Entre polleras, ñañacas y lliqllas: Los mestizos y cholas en la

conformación de la 'Tercera República.'" In *Tradición y modernidad en los Andes,* ed. Henrique Urbano, 43–73 (Cusco: Centro de Estudios Regionales Andinos "Bartolomé de Las Casas," 1992); and *Espacio urbano y dinámica étnica: La Paz en el siglo XIX* (La Paz: HISBOL, 1990); Elizabeth Peredo Beltrán, *Recoveras de los Andes: La identidad de la chola del mercado: Una aproximación psicosocial.* La Paz: ILDIS-TAHIPAMU, 1992); Ineke Dibbits with Elizabeth Peredo, Magaly Terrazas, and Ruth Volgger, *Lo que puede el sentimiento: La temática de la salud a partir de un trabajo con mujeres de El Alto Sur* (La Paz: TAHIPAMU, 1994); Elizabeth Peredo, Ruth Volgger, and Ineke Dibbits, *Trenzando ilusiones: Reflexiones y propuestas para una metodología de trabajo con mujeres* (La Paz: TAHIPAMU, 1994).

6   This description fits what Doreen Massey considers to be the predominant understanding of space, one that "attempts to fix the meaning of places, to enclose and defend them." Such views, she continues, "construct singular, fixed and static identities for places, and they interpret places as bounded enclosed spaces defined through counterposition against the Other who is outside" (Massey 1994: 168). Criollo depictions of space in Bolivia have tended to emphasize a similar formulation, as the texts referred to demonstrate. Nevertheless, in her analysis of the relationship between identity and place, Massey argues that place has to be interrogated in the same way as personal identity (167–168).

7   This same cluster of signifiers has been deconstructed by French feminists. See for example, Luce Irigaray's *This Sex Which Is Not One,* and Hélène Cixous and Catherine Clément's *The Newly Born Woman.* In the Bolivian context, this cluster of signifiers is not only about the construction of gender; race and class or economic issues are similarly implicated in representations of "order," the "proper," the "improper," and so on.

8   Betsy Wing, the translator of *The Newly Born Woman,* writes that she rendered the French "propre" as "Selfsame: ownself. It has overtones of property and appropriation. It also means 'proper,' 'appropriate,' and 'clean'" (167). For an analysis of Cixous's reading of the propre, see also Brian Duren's article, "Cixous' Exorbitant Texts," 1981. *Sub-Stance* 32: 39–51.

9   Ileana Rodríguez has recently examined the relationship between gender, the house and the nation in the context of Latin America in her book *House/Garden/Nation: Space, Gender, and Ethnicity in Post-Colonial Latin American Literatures by Women,* 1994. Trans. Robert Carr and Ileana Rodríguez. Durham, N.C.: Duke University Press.

10   In her noteworthy study *Talking Back: Toward a Latin American Feminist Literary Criticism* (Ithaca: Cornell University Press, 1992), Debra A. Castillo employs the concept of talking back as a trope for Latin American feminist practices that critically engage and dialogue with other feminisms.

Works Cited

Bhabha, Homi K. 1983. "The Other Question. . . ." *Screen* 24, 6: 18–36.

Castillo, Debra A. *Talking Back: Toward a Latin American Feminist Literary Criticism.* Ithaca, N.Y.: Cornell University Press, 1992.

Cixous, Hélène, and Catherine Clément. *The Newly Born Woman.* Trans. Betsy Wing. Theory and History of Literature, vol. 24. Minneapolis: University of Minnesota Press, 1986.

Condori, Ana María, with Ineke Dibbits and Elizabeth Peredo. *Nayan Uñatatawi: Mi despertar.* La Paz: HISBOL/TAHIPAMU, 1988.

Cornejo S., Alberto. *El problema social de la vivienda.* Cochabamba: Imprenta Universitaria, 1949.

Dhaliwal, Amarpal K. 1996. "Can the Subaltern Vote? Radical Democracy, Discourses of Representation and Rights, and Questions of Race." In *Radical Democracy: Identity, Citizenship, and the State,* ed. David Trend. New York: Routledge, 1996.

Duren, Brian. "Cixous' Exorbitant Texts." *Sub-Stance.* 32 (1981): 39–51.

Freud, Sigmund. "The Uncanny." In *The Standard Edition of the Complete Psychological Works of Sigmund Freud,* trans. James Strachey with Anna Freud, Alix Strachey, and Alan Tyson, 17: 217–252. London: Hogarth Press and the Institute of Psychoanalysis, 1955.

Fuss, Diana. "Inside/Out." In *Inside/Out: Lesbian Theories, Gay Theories,* ed. Diana Fuss, 1–10. New York: Routledge, 1991.

hooks, bell. *Talking Back: Thinking Feminist, Thinking Black.* Boston: South End Press, 1989.

ILDIS. *Diversidad étnica y cultural.* La Paz: Instituto Latinoamericana de Investigaciones Sociales, 1992.

Ingraham, Catherine. "The Faults of Architecture: Troping the Proper." *Assemblage* 7 (1988): 7–13.

Irigaray, Luce. *This Sex Which is Not One,* trans. Catherine Porter. Ithaca, N.Y.: Cornell University Press, 1985.

Martin, Biddy, and Chandra Talpade Mohanty. 1986. "Feminist Politics: What's Home Got to Do with It?" In *Feminist Studies/Critical Studies,* ed. Teresa de Lauretis, 191–212. Bloomington: Indiana University Press.

Massey, Doreen. 1994. *Space, Place, and Gender.* Minneapolis: University of Minnesota Press.

Nast, Heidi J., and Mabel O. Wilson. 1994. "Lawful Transgressions: This Is the House that Jackie Built. . . ." *Assemblage* 24: 48–55.

Platt, Tristán. 1982. *Estado boliviano y ayllu andino: Tierra y tributo en el norte de Potosí.* Lima: Instituto de Estudios Peruanos.

Rivera Cusicanqui, Silvia. 1993. "La raíz: Colonizadores y colonizados." In *Violencias encubiertas en Bolivia,* ed. Xavier Albó y Raúl Barrios, 25–139. Cultura y política, vol. 1. La Paz: CIPCA-Aruwiyiri.

Rodríguez, Ileana. *House/Garden/Nation: Space, Gender, and Ethnicity in Post-Colonial Latin American Literatures by Women.* Trans. Robert Carr and Ileana Rodríguez. Durham, N.C.: Duke University Press, 1994.

Sanjinés C., Javier. 1992?. *Literatura contémporanea y grotesco social en Bolivia.* La Paz: Fundación BHN/ILDIS.

Saravia Valle, Jorge. 1986. *Planificación de aldeas rurales.* La Paz: Juventud.

Stallybrass, Peter. 1986. "Patriarchal Territories: The Body Enclosed." In *Rewriting the Renaissance: The Discourses of Sexual Difference in Early Modern Europe,* ed. Margaret W. Ferguson, Maureen Quilligan, and Nancy J. Vickers, 123–142. Chicago: University of Chicago Press.

Stephenson, Marcia. *Gender and Modernity in Andean Bolivia.* Austin: University of Texas Press, 1999.

Vidler, Anthony. 1992. *The Architectural Uncanny: Essays in the Modern Unhomely.* Cambridge, Mass.: MIT Press.

Wigley, Mark. 1993. *The Architecture of Deconstruction: Derrida's Haunt.* Cambridge, Mass.: MIT Press.

——. 1992. "Untitled: The Housing of Gender." In *Sexuality and Space,* ed. Beatriz Colomina, 327–389. Princeton Papers on Architecture. Princeton, N.J.: Princeton University School of Architecture.

Gender, Citizenship, and Social Protest:
The New Social Movements in Argentina

MARCELO BERGMAN AND MÓNICA SZURMUK

Introduction

On the morning of September 10, 1990, the naked body of María Soledad Morales was discovered on the outskirts of San Fernando del Valle de Catamarca, the capital city of the province of Catamarca in northwestern Argentina. She had been brutally raped and sodomized, and her body showed signs of battery and cocaine abuse. What could have been a piece of news relegated to the police section of a provincial newspaper for a few days triggered enough attention to make national and international headlines as María Soledad's disfigured dead body became an icon of resistance.

This essay studies the process whereby a murder on the outskirts of an impoverished province in the north of Argentina gave rise to a social movement that challenged the practices of recently established democratic governments in the region. To do this, we explore the complex relationships between the female body and the construction of the idea of citizenship. We show how the conflation of images of race, gender, and class play out in the construction of resistance embodied in the dead teenager. We argue that this movement was a new phenomenon in Argentina which, following the model of the Mothers of Plaza de Mayo, set out to claim civil rights and to dramatize this claim by situating it in the violated body. This essay examines the move toward the acquisition of civil rights by members of subaltern groups that characterizes this historical movement in the process of redemocratization in the Southern Cone. This claim for civil rights is also a hermeneutic movement toward a different reading of the corpse, one that extends citizenship to dark-skinned, sexually available, poor women. Since the particulars of the case are not well known outside of Argentina, we will start with an account of the "facts."

The Legal Narrative

In this section, we attempt a summary of the facts leading to María Soledad's death using information that became available through the legal process as well as the media. This account also relies on the three books that were published to document the case. Two of them — *No llores por mí, Catamarca* by Rey and Pazos, and Norma Morandini's *Catamarca* — are open indictments of Catamarca's ruling family written by journalists who covered the case. A third book — *Dieciocho años de Soledad* — is a pamphlet that plays on the connections between eroticism and violence in the case. We also conducted interviews with Fanny Mandelbaum, one of the journalists who covered the particulars of the case for Channel 11 in Buenos Aires, and with the nun Martha Pelloni, who organized the Marches of Silence. The account that follows attempts to include these different voices and to explore the gaps in the narratives, the places where prejudice takes over.

María Soledad was seventeen, an average student at the Catholic Colegio del Carmen y San José who dreamed of becoming a model. She was the second of seven children in a working-class family of the city of Catamarca. Her father, like almost half of the inhabitants of the city, is a public employee.

The city of Catamarca lies 1,200 kilometers northwest of Buenos Aires, in the heart of a valley where in the seventeenth century the Spaniards protected themselves from an uprising of the Calchaquí Indians. Half of the 240,000 inhabitants of the province of Catamarca live in this city. The Saadi family has governed the province almost uninterruptedly since 1949, when the first Vicente Saadi was elected governor during the first presidency of Juan Domingo Perón. In 1990, at the time of María Soledad's death, Vicente's son Ramón Saadi, a Peronist like his father, was the province's governor. The provincial government was characterized by nepotism, and every single member of the Saadi family had a position of power in the province. It is believed that María Soledad died at a party in the house of Angel Luque, a congressman who rose to power as Vicente Saadi's secretary. The party was organized by Luque's son, Guillermo, and attended by other young men who had grown up around the circles of power.

On the night of Saturday, September 8, María Soledad sent a message to her boyfriend Luis Tula asking him to pick her up from a high school fund-raising dance. She wanted to spend the night with him. Luis Tula was twenty-nine and married, but he and his wife kept their marriage a secret. Tula had lied about being single when he began his relationship with María Soledad, but by the time of her death, María Soledad knew about his marital status and had engaged in several heated arguments with Tula's wife. Tula and his wife were therefore the first suspects in the police investigation. Tula did go to see María Soledad that night but did not leave with her. According to his statement, he did not want to pick up a woman "who smelled of fish" (more about this later). María Soledad walked over to the bus stop. She was last seen getting into a car that belonged to Arnaldito Saadi, one of the cousins of the governor.

About thirty hours later, Alicia Cubas, Vicente Saadi's widow and the governor's mother, was quoted as remarking, "Se le murió una chinita al hijo de Luque" [a chinita died on Luque's son]. *Chinita* is a word pejoratively used to refer to a dark-skinned working-class woman from the provinces.[1] In her racist sarcasm, Alicia Cubas could not have suspected that the case would attract so much attention at the national and international level, and change the political map of Catamarca forever, with the central government having to intervene in the provincial administration, tacitly firing the constitutionally elected governor.[2] Three extensive investigations were conducted without reaching conclusive results. The Saadi family, which had managed to control the politics of Catamarca for more than forty years, lost the elections to the opposition in 1992 as a direct consequence of the scandal surrounding "el caso María Soledad," as the legal case came to be known. A trial in 1996 was annulled when every single provincial judge was declared incompetent to preside at the trial due to suspicious connections to the indicted. The final trial was conducted in 1998, eight years after the murder, and Luis Tula and Guillermo Luque were convicted.

For more than a year following her death, weekly protests were organized by Martha Pelloni, a nun and the director of the Colegio del Carmen y San José, and supported by local church hierarchy. The marches symbolized the emergence of a new type of mass mobilization. Thousands of protesters gathered in a pacific call for the clarification of the teenager's death and the sanctioning of the murderers in what have been called "marches of silence" (*marchas del silencio*). The suspicion that the traditional caudillo families had been involved in the murder and the cover-up that followed it generated a popular outrage that exceeded the estimation of the local authorities. At stake were the traditional clientelistic patterns of social control and the unusually empowered grassroots movement that successfully brought about the crumbling of the once hegemonic traditional and peripheric Peronist bastion. The quasi-feudal political system of the Saadi family, the Peronist labor trade union, and corrupt political leadership was challenged by the emergence of a social movement in which individuals for the first time felt entitled to the basic right of equal protection under the law. The María Soledad case epitomizes the emergence of a subaltern struggle for citizenship. The case also exemplifies new trends of counter-hegemony for popular mobilization, and a new narrative for the understanding of gender roles and the role of actual bodies in politics.

In this article, we analyze this case in light of major national and local developments. The case occurred seven years after the transition to democracy in Argentina, in the midst of the most acute economic crisis in the country's entire history, and at a juncture of major social and cultural transformations in both central cities like Buenos Aires and in the provinces. It is our contention that a case such as this one would not have had the ramifications it did if traditional political and cultural patterns had been in place. However, the demands for equal protection under the law and for accountability are among the new developments that called national attention to a case that might have been relegated to the police pages of provincial newspapers. The peculiarities of this case tapped into the issues at stake in the struggle for citizenship in post-dictatorship Argentina, such as the right for equal protection under the law and the end of the era of impunity. These are rights that states throughout Latin America are seldom able to deliver.

The María Soledad case has been analyzed in the context of the process of democratization in Argentina.[3] Our contention is that although political democratization influenced these events, a comprehensive explanation should transcend the discussion of democratization. The corpus of literature on transition to democracy in Latin America has been extensive.[4] Since the mid-1980s, scholars have theorized democracy as a procedural minimum, as an antidote to the failure of the policies of the 1970s, particularly the brutal repression of the military regimes (O'Donnell and Schmitter). These authors have conceived it as a "game" in which the actors (social and political forces) accept losses if, in the foreseeable future, they can expect a payoff. Democracy is the "only game in town" when the uncertainty of political outcomes becomes institutionalized (Przeworski).

In this paradigm, democratization is conceived as the process of building institutions capable of channeling and articulating interests and demands. Democracy is also understood as a competition for power and for accountability in governments. Democracies consolidate when the threat of a reversal to dictatorial regimes has been ruled out. This definition of democracy remains persuasive to explain transitions of military dictatorships to more stable regimes in Latin America. However, the institutionalization of democracies does not successfully account for the emergence of new social movements and, particularly, for the struggle for citizenship (Escobar and Alvarez; Foweraker). Democracy might be the "only game in town," but it may not meet the demands of social actors who, as a result of social and cultural transformations, begin to claim rights. In other words, the weak institutions of representation found in the new democracies throughout Latin America do not seem to threaten the stability of the political systems, but undermine its scope of governability. That is, democracies may be in the process of political consolidation, but they also show signs of their inability to meet basic social demands such as civil and economic rights. This leads to hybrid types of democracies, such as O'Donnell's delegative democracy or Touraine's tutelaged democracy.[5]

A major shortcoming of the democratization debate lies in its neglect of the state. Since political scientists have conceived of democracy basically as a regime, democracy as a system has never actually been read bottom up. Therefore, the emergence of noninstitutionalized challenges to central authority was conceived as insurgency. However, examples like the María Soledad mobilization, the Indian CONAIE uprising in Ecuador, or the neighborhood organizations in Brazil do not fit the category of insurgency, although they also represent challenges to the effectiveness of democracies. Consequently the current discussion of transitions to democracy must be transcended in order to account for the challenges posed by popular movements.

The problem of the state is central because in its ability to perform its duties lies the institutional design to meet the challenges posed by subaltern and marginal groups. In other words, state strength has become the key to analyzing social conflicts and resolutions. But how is such strength to be determined? We propose to define "state strength" as *a set of institutions capable of delivering goods and services according to the law*. This operative definition presumes a direct relationship between laws and their degree of enforceability. Through time, state expand their laws, and therefore they need to increase their capacity to enforce them. A state is considered strong inasmuch as it enforces laws within the very limits of the procedures those laws prescribe. States today are under pressure to provide a wide range of goods and services. The key to their strength is their ability to channel those pressures via deliverable laws, and to then act under the guidelines of those laws.

No state can be totally strong since no state delivers all the goods and services its laws prescribe, and, more important, no state uniformly enforces its laws. Therefore, strength is a matter of degree. Moreover, laws are the partial resolution of social conflict (Chambliss and Seidman; Cotterrel), and they change over time according to social configurations and power relations. Nonetheless, modern states are generally conceived of as providers of goods and services that, for practical reasons, may be encompassed in the ability to deliver civil, political, and social rights. Those are the basic services that allow the state to pass a threshold of strength. Such is the source of weakness of the Latin American states (O'Donnell 1993). Rights have not been historically met or respected. And more important, even when they were, legality was either marginal or consistently violated. Lawlessness is not a new phenomenon in Latin America. What is new is the demand by a larger population for more visible law enforcement.[6]

Scholars have recently noticed the apparent paradox of political democracies — that is, the reasonable prevalence of universal political rights coexisting with the denial of civil rights to large segments of the population. O'Donnell states: "Democracy is not only a political regime but also a particular mode of relationship between state and citizens, . . . under a kind of rule of law that, in addition to political citizenship, upholds civil citizenship and a full network of accountability" (1999: 321). Habermas has also emphasized that the role played by laws in democracies is paramount. Civil rights need to be universal and effectively protected by law in order to be considered compatible with democracy. The singularity of Latin American history is that political citizenship was granted before civil rights were effectively protected. This course was the reverse of the one undertaken by most western European nations, where civil rights and the protection of the law was universally granted before effective political rights (the right to vote and assembly) were enacted.[7] Moreover, in Argentina, some social rights were granted (particularly under populist governments) while civil rights were consistently infringed, and the rule of law was seriously undermined.

The protests around María Soledad's murder were precisely a call for the rule of law, civil rights, and accountability, and were, in this sense, in line with the protests inaugurated by the Mothers of Plaza de Mayo in their departure from traditional protest and mass mobilization in Argentina.

Social Movements

The foundational paradigm of collective action theory (Olson; Elster) emphasizes the goal-oriented motivations of the collective. Social agents or collective actors, including the popular movement of Catamarca, act according to goals. The ability to meet these goals defines the success of a movement. However, goals are shaped by expectations, which aggregate into concrete demands. What activates social agents is the articulation of those expectations, the way those shape a new discourse. The processes of modernization and globalization have carried with them a dramatic transformation of people's expectations. In other words, the cultural transformations introduced by modernization and globalization have activated a revolution of expectations. The state was expected to be capable of delivering what it has largely failed to provide over time: civil and social rights.

States in Latin America are very weak. Since the change of expectations tends to increase the pressure for a wide set of rights, and the states are unable to meet them, there is a rich ground for the emergence of collective actions that aim their mobilization at attainable concrete goals rather than major transformations such as social revolutions. Social movements in Latin America are generally responses of peripheral groups who feel entitled to unmet rights. To a large degree, their struggle represents the counterpart to the state's weakness.

The concept of rights, however, must be understood beyond the classical sociological formulation.[8] In such an approach, rights are state initiatives to include new social classes in the political order. This top-down explanation underestimates the fertile ground of subaltern groups and social processes that construct a different dimension of citizenship. Rights are not only a natural attribute granted by the state, but a demand for a space for and recognition of individuals.

In *Consumidores y ciudadanos,* Néstor García Canclini rightfully indicates that citizenship is not only the juridical concept of substantive rights. More than abstract values, rights must be conceived of as a construction process that changes in relation to practices and discourses. Therefore, citizenship and rights do not refer only to the formal structure of society but also to the fight of other individuals who have "valid interests, pertinent values and legitimate demands." Therefore, "rights are conceived as an expression of a state order and also a civil grammar" (García Canclini, 20).

In sum, social movements such as the one generated by the María Soledad case are neither prodemocratic nor antidemocratic, but clearly prorights. They indirectly enhance democracy since the claim for citizenship is, in the long run, in opposition to any dictatorial regime, but the movement is first and foremost a challenge to a weaker state. It is a mobilization of civil society that pursues a new agenda and, like almost every social movement, catches everybody by surprise precisely because it challenges traditional patterns of social control. The mobilization in Catamarca erupted as a break in the continuous trend of political clientelism, social conservatism, and pauperization epitomizing the discontinuity of the previous legacy. Democracy and modernization raised new expectations that challenged the traditional patterns of control. It developed into a crisis because the state was unable to meet the new demands of civil society.

New Actors and Motives

Mass mobilizations, social protest, and armed struggles mark the history of Argentina. Many of these movements have been able to stamp their mark and shape the political and social institutions of the country. This long tradition of social protest finds an element of continuity in the events of Catamarca; however, these events also are marked by a departure from traditional mass mobilization. The demand for an effective rule of law and accountability became one of the new modalities.

The Marches of Silence could not have happened in pre-1976 Argentina. Unlike the revolutionary movements of the 1960s and early 1970s, the Marches of Silence were the products of the emergence of new social actors championing specific civil rights without seeking radical social change. The protesters of

Catamarca are heirs to human rights organizations such as the Mothers of Plaza de Mayo and are the products of a society in which ideas of politics, law, and public action had radically changed. The brutality and sophistication that the military deployed against citizens in order to maintain power from 1976 through December 1983 required new strategies of resistance. The Mothers of Plaza de Mayo inaugurated a new way of doing politics. They fought against the force and the weapons of the military with their mere presence, which defied the prohibition of open demonstrations. Their walks around the Plaza de Mayo every Thursday came to symbolize a new type of resistance lodged within women's traditional roles — maternity, self-sacrifice — but which challenged essential characteristics of those roles such as privacy, passivity, and subservience.

The Mothers fought with their own bodies, which they offered as evidence of the existence of the children the regime had "disappeared." They had birthed those children, and now, in their absence, they had to speak for them and birth them again as words and as ideas. They set the lives they had given their children against the lives the military had taken away; since no one has claimed responsibility for their murders, they still use their slogan of the 1970s: "con vida los llevaron, con vida los queremos" [alive they were taken, alive we want them back]. To incorporate their children's presence into the life of the country, the Mothers have used strategies that actually bring their children's corporeality back. In different demonstrations, the women have used paper silhouettes, masks, paper hands, and human shapes drawn on the pavement to help the public perceive the children's absence physically.[9]

This insistence on the human body is not surprising in a country where the body had become a site of oppression. What the Mothers did was turn their own bodies, their own public presence into a memorial for their children, who had been tortured in clandestine camps. They responded to a system that had invaded their private lives and private places such as schools, homes, universities, and hospitals by reclaiming as their own the streets and a plaza at the center of the political and economic center of the city.

The political example offered by the Mothers of Plaza de Mayo and other human rights organizations, such as the Grandmothers of Plaza de Mayo, served to model new forms of resistance and also to inform the public of different ways of understanding oppression. When María Soledad Morales's body appeared in Catamarca, people used the model of the Mothers in two different ways: (1) It was through the information disseminated by human rights organizations that they could read María Soledad's death as a political event, and it was through education about the nature of human rights violations that they could understand that rape and mutilation were not only individual deviations but could also be means whereby the powerful exercised control; (2) Their ad hoc organization to demand justice took forms that echoed the Mothers' public struggle, such as the use of demonstrations in public spaces with nonpartisan slogans to demand justice. The Mothers also provided a model of public grieving and public suffering as political praxis.

Silence

> A la hora que el sol resbala entre los cerros y el atardecer es la tregua diaria del verano calcinante, el valle de Catamarca se llena de silencio. Recogida y muda, una pequeña multitud camina detrás de una monja de ojos clarísimos, Martha Pelloni, y de los dolidos padres de María Soledad. Apenas se oyen los pasos. Con la lentitud de una procesión salen del Colegio del Carmen y recorren las calles hasta detenerse en las escalinatas de la Catedral. Ni rosarios, ni rezos, tan sólo el grito de "justicia," profundo y grave resuena en el valle. Se cuela entre los huesos, recorre instintivamente la memoria y consigue un estremecimiento involuntario: son las "marchas del silencio."
> — Norma Morandini, *Catamarca*

> [At the time the sun glides between the hills and the sunset is the daily truce from the scorching summer weather, the Valley of Catamarca fills up with silence. Mute and solemn, a small multitude walks behind Martha Pelloni, a nun with light and clear eyes, and behind María Soledad's grieving parents. The steps can hardly be heard. Slowly like a procession, they leave the School and they walk the streets until they stop in the stairs in front of the Cathedral. No rosaries, no prayers, only the deep and grave scream for justice resonates in the valley. The scream gets into the bones, it instinctively travels through memory and creates an involuntary shudder: such are the "marches of silence."]

The Marches of Silence were an articulation of the resistance against an economic and political system. They criticized the government for its nepotism, its corruption, and its impunity. They broke down traditional patterns of social mobilization. Instead of the classic gatherings organized by political parties or trade unions, with their vociferous mobilizations complete with drumming, political slogans, and public shows of masculinity, the Marches of Silence remarkably resembled the collective actions the Mothers of Plaza de Mayo had started thirteen years earlier in the city of Buenos Aires. In Catamarca, the protesters engaged in peaceful walks around the downtown plaza of the city of Catamarca every Thursday demanding justice and accountability. These collective actions introduced a new mode of protest in this peripheral city. In a traditional society with overtones of quasi-feudal systems of domination, these collective actions defied the legitimacy of the public institutions. They were grassroots gatherings of working-class and middle-class citizens supported by charismatic Catholic leaders who denounced the corruption of the Saadi family and the political hierarchy. The marches did not pursue the accommodation of grassroots demands within the traditional scheme of power, but sought to install new patterns of political control based on an open system, the protection of civil rights, and the rule of law.

The first march was organized by a group of María Soledad's classmates a few days after her death. Martha Pelloni became their mentor and served as a clearinghouse for information on the murder that witnesses did not want to share with the police or the courts. The first three marches averaged 7,000 people. In a city of 122,000 people in which most families are economically dependent on the provincial government, this was a remarkable figure. But as soon as the cover-up became evident, the marches attracted 30,000 participants. During the first year following the murder, more than fifty marches took place. The public protest undermined the credibility of the entire judicial system, which was unable to provide a convincing account of the events. The demands that the marches championed included not only the replacement of the system of nepotism that ruled the province but also the enhancement of new criteria for public life. As a continuation of broader national processes, the private became public. The classical venues of representation became obsolete because citizenship was moved to center stage.

The marches were, above all, female endeavors. Women, some of them only seventeen or eighteen, organized them. A nun led them, and they dramatized the types of virtues associated with women: silence, temperance, endurance. Above all they displayed bodies — mostly female bodies of teenagers — in gray uniforms and wearing gold crosses. In these marches, María Soledad was portrayed as one more teenager in a gray school uniform, her dark hair in a ponytail. This image was opposed and juxtaposed to the portrayal of her as temptress that Luque and Tula unsuccessfully tried to establish. It is no coincidence, therefore, that Martha Pelloni always referred to her as *la nena* (the little girl), and that her classmates insisted on using the familiar "Sole" when talking to reporters. From the marches, the figure of María Soledad emerged as a teenager who, regardless of her flaws, deserved to be equally protected under the law while alive, and respectfully treated in death.

Strategies of Resistance

Social movements must be conceived of as social processes rather than particular groups of people seeking specific goals. Social movements are defined either by the identity of their members (new social movements theory) or by the capacities to organize collective action (resource mobilization theory). In the new-social-movement approach the crucial element of collective action is the question of who mobilizes, whereas the critical question that distinguishes social movements in the resource-mobilization approach is how collective action develops and transforms these movements.[10] In essence, the current debate on the formation of social protest and popular movements stresses the need to integrate these two approaches. Both the resources and organizational strategies and capacities to mobilize, and the construction of an identity through the sense of community generated by these collective actions are instrumental for new social actors to successfully challenge the mechanisms of social control.

In the new social movement of Catamarca, both elements can be traced. Without the leadership of Martha Pelloni, the support of a crucial institution like the Catholic Church, and the natural network of students, both cohorts of the victim and others, it would be virtually impossible to conceive of the marches. But there was an equally important source of empowerment to the protest. The citizens of Catamarca defied their role as "subjects" of the nepotist government. They constructed the collectivity of true citizens, a new notion of "we." The protection of rights was a banner, but their unifying principle was the construction of their new collective identity. In essence, it was the prologue of an initiation into citizenship.

Two significant groups were instrumental in the mobilization: women and students. As was the case with the Mothers of Plaza de Mayo, the mobilization of women in Catamarca departed from the model of gender-neutral participation in the public sphere. It was in their roles as daughters, wives, and mothers that they acquired their legitimization to claim the rights of protection for their children. Since the church could not insulate children from those dangers (María Soledad was, after all, a student in a Catholic school), there was a need to enter the public space from the traditional role of family protector, enhancing the claim for basic civil rights. In this process a new social solidarity was created among women.[11] Women felt entitled to challenge patterns of abuse and claim a new space. Their identities as daughters, wives, teachers, and mothers led them to participate in a new movement. Their participation, in turn, brought about the affirmation of such identities and their entitlement to a new voice. The sexually available chinita, poor and dark skinned, was a symbol that did not belong in the new era of equal rights. Students from the Colegio del Carmen y San José and from other Catholic and public schools also played a crucial role in the mobilization. Students provided the initial legions of participants. Moreover, the marches started from the school, generating a strong peer commitment. The students' central role facilitated the collective action enabling the social movement to gather strength. From the material and strategic perspective, student mobilization was a valuable leadership resource.

Students also were actively involved in the movement because they epitomized the radical changes that had occurred in Catamarca. As a peripheral city, it was extensively influenced by cultural trends emanating from Buenos Aires. Just a few years before María Soledad's murder, only one local television channel existed in the province. But by the mid-1980s television channels had multiplied, the number of video stores had grown, and consumer culture had permeated the more traditional patterns of what had been a quiet and peaceful town. With it came the transformation of rising expectations. Younger people from Catamarca, exposed to cultural products and social norms from Buenos Aires, became more connected to it because barriers to communication had been lifted by technological advances, allowing Catamarca to be included in the recently democratized imagined community.[12]

These transformations, however, clashed with a social reality that did not allow expectations of a modernized life to materialize. The occupational structure of the province and its depressed economy did not present an encouraging future to the younger generations. Catamarca has no university, and migration to the big cities seemed to be the best alternative for those who could afford it. Catamarca nonetheless remained the theater where everything seemed to function in opposition to the national processes. It did not have a dynamic economy, it lacked cultural attractions, and it functioned according to antiquated models of sexual morals.

Success for the sons of the privileged and wealthy citizens in Catamarca was to spend half of their time in Buenos Aires and then replicate patterns of consumption typical of the big cities in their visits to Catamarca. Drugs penetrated some of those circles. Catamarca has become a region of extensive drug trafficking and production, and some of the police and political figures are involved. For a new generation of adolescents in Catamarca, the effects of new patterns of consumption and expectations, along with a lack of opportunities, generated a new space for popular protest. Young people reacted immediately when they found out that María Soledad's boyfriend was not directly responsible for the murder, and that she had died at a party attended by the sons of wealthy public figures. By organizing and successfully raising local and national interest, the mobilization succeeded in breaking down the Saadi hegemony in the province and in bringing about the incarceration of privileged suspects.

These repercussions affected the political establishment and the church, and they symbolically presaged similar national processes. In today's Argentina judicial inefficiency impunity, and the dark prospects of a vastly unemployed younger generation are indeed embedded in the national agenda. In the long run, they may represent potential outbreaks of social unrest. At center stage is the weak enforcement of civil, social, and economic rights. Perhaps this is why the televised proceedings of the trials, almost six years after the murder, had extremely high ratings. The María Soledad case epitomizes a decisive cross-roads of Argentina's democracy. The murder exposed the weaknesses of a society in transformation — weaknesses that open-market capitalism and regular competitive elections have been unable to solve.

María Soledad's Death

In "Chandra's Death," Ranajit Guha analyzes a thirteenth-century Bengali legal text that records declarations given by a group of people regarding the death of a woman named Chandra after an abortion. Reading the document against the grain, Guha is able to construct a convincing argument of how patriarchal morals served to force Chandra into a dangerous abortion and then rewrite as criminal the effort of the women in her family to provide Chandra with abortive herbs and to nurse her through the abortion, her painful convalescence, and ultimate death. In providing this analysis, Guha is himself reclaiming as history the minute details of everyday life that do not make their way into history books but which document the history of the subaltern: "For when a victim, however timid, comes to regard herself as an object of injustice, she already steps into the role of a critic of the system that victimizes her. And any action that follows from that critique contains the elements of a practice of resistance" (165).

The intrinsic paradox on María's Soledad's notoriety — she wanted to be a rich and famous model, but she acquired fame in a brutal murder — is the germ itself of the practice of resistance that followed her death. This practice articulated a critique of the models of unequal development that we have come to associate with global capitalism and postmodernity. The public rendering of María Soledad's intimate journal portrayed an adolescent preoccupied with beauty and financial success. Her role models were the models from Buenos Aires whom she watched on television, not the courageous nun who led the fight to solve María Soledad's murder, or her impoverished mother raising seven children. María Soledad became a martyr not because she was a virgin, a saint, or an exceptional teenager, but because her murder symbolized a type of violence and impunity that the Mothers of Plaza de Mayo had taught Argentineans to recognize. And in their critique of the political elite, the protesters were also fighting against poverty, political corruption, the drug traffic, and an increasingly wider gap between the poor and the rich.

María Soledad's body was thrown in a ditch along a busy road between Catamarca and the small town in the valley where both María Soledad and her boyfriend Luis Tula lived. The body was meant to be found, and to tell a story that would protect those who had thrown it there. The disfigurement of the body, the excessive amount of cocaine it contained, and the brutality it exhibited were meant to suggest satanic rites or a drug lord's vengeance.[13] Since murder is rare in Catamarca, the police are not trained to work around a murder site. The murderers were close enough to the legal system to think that it did not threaten any sort of danger. They had to provide the press and the grapevines in Catamarca something to work with, and a naked woman who has been raped is somehow always suspected of wrongdoing. Or so they thought.

North American and Argentinean viewers of shows such as *Law and Order* are familiar with the dead body as text. A corpse is found, and within hours it tells a story that helps investigators figure out details of the death. It is the stuff of which mysteries are made: teeth, bones, and human flesh can tell stories that specialists interpret and codify in a narrative text that attempts to reconstruct the identity of the deceased and also the identity of the murderer. This narrative then becomes a legal document that can be used in a court of law.

Let us now go through the different steps. A body is found, the press reports on it, medical specialists "read" it, and a court of law uses the narrative in which this reading is recorded to determine guilt and innocence. Every step of this process is punctuated by the credibility of the professionals involved: reporters, forensic specialists, lawyers, judges. In Catamarca, mistrust and lack of credibility at every step tainted this process. The narrative that María Soledad's corpse produced for the legal system was not worthy of the trust of those who were close to her, and ultimately they resisted this narrative and created a narrative of resistance.[14]

When the circle who attended the parties in Guillermo Luque's house began to be questioned, they pointed their fingers back at María Soledad. They expected that their testimonies of María Soledad's promiscuity would necessarily prove she was to blame and that she had brought her tragedy onto herself by her loose morals. The provincial elite felt that María Soledad was disposable because she was a woman, because she was poor, because she was dark skinned. Catamarcans en masse felt that she had a right to be protected, and that the failure of the state to protect her or punish the murderers rendered them incompetent to govern. Nowhere is this difference of appreciation clearer than in the way that both groups talked about María Soledad.

Those close to the government always described María Soledad in sexual terms. At best she was presented as an oversexed teenager completely unsupervised by her parents. At worst she was described as a temptress whose body had a foul odor. In his declaration in front of the judge, Luis Tula claimed he refused to let her get in his car the night of her disappearance because she "smelled of fish." This reference to a woman's vaginal odor, usually reserved for men-only *machista* circles, implies that a woman is promiscuous and/or dirty—often both.[15] This car scene was repeated ad nauseam for the courts and the television cameras. The scene is always presented in the same way: María Soledad comes up to Tula's car and talks to him through the window but does not get into the car. He is horrified by her smell and leaves. The truth of the description notwithstanding, the narrative itself reeks of the worst kind of sexism. For much of Western history the female body has been seen as a repository of horror and monstrosity. The sexual depiction of María Soledad itself points back to what is absent from all of the narrations leading up to her tragic end: there is no tenderness in any of the depictions of the teenager given by the man who had consensual sex with her and the men who raped her. To oppose this monstrous image, the marches multiplied María Soledad into hundreds of similar teenagers whose presence alone reinforced María Soledad's absence.

In 1996 a large-scale demonstration was mobilized in Belgium, and more than 300,000 people defied the Belgian state. Two young sisters had been found starved to death in a basement after the police and other state agencies had failed to locate them even though they had concrete information that could have led them to the murderer. As in the case of María Soledad, but under completely different circumstances, a particular type of outrage mobilized people: the failure of the state to fulfill its duties.

In postindustrial and open-market capitalism, the expectation of protection and of justice has, in general, not vanished (Friedman). Habermas and Offe insist that the difficulty of reconciling mass democracy with capitalism creates a "crisis of ungovernability." Traditional forms of political representation (political parties, trade unions, and other corporate representations) seem unable to canalize new demands of citizenship. Although the new globalized savage capitalism has lowered citizens' expectations of state economic patronizing, the demonstrations also suggest that citizens' expectations of the protection of their civil rights in recently democratized countries have risen. Since the traditional channels of representation are not generally responsive to these new demands, two alternative scenarios are possible: a "withdrawal" from the state—that is, an atomization of subaltern groups who stop pursuing benefits and participation in national life, such as the uprising in Chiapas or the emergence of social movements in search of a responsive state able to deliver basic rights. This is the case of the Marches of Silence. They presaged a national search for a more responsive judicial system, the end of special privileges, and the demands for a state that is able to protect its citizens and enforce the law on an equal basis.

The political elite of Catamarca came up against new ways of understanding the role of women in the country and especially the role of poor young women. They expected to be able to construct María Soledad as a victim of her own choices. Catamarca read her instead as a victim of a corrupt system and likened her death to that of Jesus at the Cross. Other cases of murders involving young women in Argentina have since stirred emotional responses from citizens who have learned to read beyond official versions of events and to challenge the very institutions which are supposed to protect them.[16]

A couple of days before the military overthrew the constitutionally elected government of President Isabel Martínez de Perón in March 1976, the armed forces ran an advertisement in the major newspapers in the country. In it, a young blue-eyed soldier looked straight out of the picture into the reader's eyes. Above the picture were the words "está velando por nosotros." The translation of the verb *velar* itself sums up the very contradiction of the role of institutions in Argentina: *velar por* means to protect, to be awake and alert while somebody else sleeps; the soldier is therefore "watching after us, protecting us." *Velar,* however, has another meaning: *velar a* means to mourn, to be awake through the night before a dead person is buried. Taking the second meaning of "velar," the advertisement foreshadowed the rampant repression to follow: the soldier is "mourning us," anticipating the widespread destruction to follow. The movement that grew around the María Soledad case exemplifies the crisis of credibility of institutions in Argentina, institutions that claim to protect but which end up oppressing.

In the formation of Catamarca's social movement, new identities were shaped, old ones were reinforced, and new patterns of social organization were established. Popular protest in Catamarca transcended the tragic events of a victim and the political scandal that followed it. It was a crucial step in the symbolic construction of citizenship, testing the boundaries of governability.

Notes

1 Alicia Cubas's remarks are included in Rey and Pazos, and in Morandini.
2 President Menem used the constitutional figure of the "intervención provincial," whereby as president he could do away with constitutionally elected provincial authorities on the grounds of preserving "public order." In essence, President Menem, who had greatly benefited from the support of the Saadi family in his rise to power, had to give up on that political alliance in order to respond to parliamentary and public opinion pressure.
3 Newspaper articles and books that narrate the story relate the breakdown of the Saadi family hegemony in Catamarca to the broader process of political liberalization.
4 A good review of this literature can be found in Diamond, and Mainwaring et al.

5   Both O'Donnell (1993) and Touraine emphasize the limitations of a political system that is not able to be responsive to the economic and legal needs of large segments of the population. In Argentina, for instance, post-1983 democracy is more stable than previous democratic systems, but it does not resemble the integrative system of western Europe; in other words, it is a democracy with limited rights.

6   Other examples in Argentina include the Monday assemblies in front of the Buenos Aires courthouse organized by Memoria Activa to demand clarification of the bombing of the headquarters of the Jewish Social Services office in Buenos Aires, the demonstrations by relatives of victims of police brutality in the suburbs of Buenos Aires, and those in Cutral-Có after the closure of the state oil company in the town.

7   Two very important exceptions should be mentioned. First, women were, in many cases, granted civil rights after political rights were granted to men; and second, the institution of slavery in the United States coexisted with universal civil and political rights for white males.

8   The standard sociological formulation was advanced by T. H. Marshall. Rights in western European states followed a sequence in which first civil (bourgeois) rights were granted, followed by political rights (particularly the expansion of the right to vote), and finally, by the mid-twentieth-century, social rights (mainly education and social welfare entitlement). In Latin America, the expansion did not follow the same sequence.

9   In her article "Killing Nuns, Priests, Women, and Children," Jean Franco refers in similar terms to the space that the *desaparecidos,* such as her friend Alaíde Floppa, occupy: "To this day, Alaíde 'continues disappeared' in the words of the newspaper, like many other men, priests, nuns, and children in Latin America who no longer occupy space but who have a place" (420).

10 A good discussion of the two major theories of social movements can be found in Joe Foweraker.

11 For more on women's roles in social movements, see Safa and also Jelín.

12 García Canclini argues that in Latin America the discourse of modernism had a hopeful component of equality and progress represented by the attempt to educate people, open universities, and subsidize the arts. Postmodernism and the age of global capitalism, on the contrary, have been characterized by disdain for the very idea of education and establishment of cultural mores. In this era of market economies, consumers are supposed to decide what to consume, and educational projects are seen with distrust. Catamarca is an exemplary case of this trend: the city's only two movie theaters have been closed and television reigns. There is no attempt to create venues for cultural endeavors, and in an exacerbated instance of what happens in the rest of the country, gossip about the rich and the famous dominates the press. Communication specialists such as Silvio Waisbord are studying the creation of a political elite that consorts with members of show business and overdoses on sexual liaisons and expensive tastes. It is within this context of economic, cultural, and moral impoverishment and the glamorization of show business that the María Soledad case takes on new proportions; María Soledad becomes the "cordero de Dios que expía los pecados del mundo," and the ditch where her body was disposed of, a shrine for believers.

13 The second autopsy concluded that cocaine was injected into María Soledad's body after her death.

14 Public opinion in Argentina had been influenced by the debate on forensic pathology and the analysis of crime victims' corpses in the mid-eighties after the restitution of democracy. The Grandmothers of Plaza de Mayo championed forensic pathology and the poten-

tials of science for determining the identities of disappeared children and children born in captivity. They have also used the analysis of the corpses of kidnapped pregnant women to determine if these women birthed their babies in captivity. The practice of unearthing corpses from unmarked graves in clandestine cemeteries was supported by the Grandmothers of Plaza de Mayo, but staunchly opposed by a group of the Mothers of Plaza de Mayo, who claimed that recovering corpses would only serve to put a lid on the issue of disappearances by pointing attention to the victims of human rights abuses and not to the criminals. This issue divided the Mothers of Plaza de Mayo and ultimately produced a schism in the movement.

15   We believe that this disgust with bodily fluids produced by women is related to the fear of female desire, which the secretion of fluids evidences. Fluids are also physical, external manifestations of the interior of women's bodies. Page du Bois historicizes the understanding of the female body as a repository of a truth that needs to be extracted through violence: "The slave's body and the woman's body are marked off as the property of the master; the subject of history in the ancient city, the Greek male citizen, ruled over his subordinates, animals, barbarian slaves, and women, who were seen as like one another in their subordination. Like slave's bodies, tattooed with signs of ownership and origin, women's bodies were metaphorically inscribed by their masters. The veiled citizen woman, who conceals her true nature with cosmetics and drapery, remains an other, full of potential truth, uncannily resembling the slave, male and female, who awaits torture, who conceals truth" (90).

16   We are thinking mainly of the cases of Ximena Hernández and Nair Mostafá.

Works Cited

Bouvard, Marguerite Guzmán. *Revolutionizing Motherhood: The Mothers of the Plaza de Mayo.* Wilmington, Del.: Scholarly Resources, 1994.

Chambliss, W. J., and R. B. Seidman. *Law, Order, and Power.* Reading, Mass.: Addison-Wesley, 1982.

Cotterrell, Roger. *The Sociology of Law: An Introduction.* London: Butterworths, 1984.

Diamond, Larry. "Economic Development and Democracy Reconsidered." *The American Behavioral Scientist* 35, 4–5 (1992): 450–489.

du Bois, Page. *Torture and Truth.* New York: Routledge, 1991.

Elster, Jon. *The Cement of Society: A Study of Social Order.* Cambridge: Cambridge University Press, 1989.

Escobar, Arturo, and Sonia Alvarez, eds. *The Making of Social Movements in Latin America: Identity, Strategy, and Democracy.* Boulder, Colo.: Westview, 1992.

Filc, Judith. *Entre el parentesco y la política: Familia y dictadura, 1976–1983.* Buenos Aires: Biblos, 1997.

Foweraker, Joe. *Theorizing Social Movements.* London: Pluto, 1995.

Franco, Jean. "Killing Nuns, Priests, Women, and Children." In *On Signs,* ed. Marshall Blonsky. Baltimore: Md.: Johns Hopkins University Press, 1985.

Friedman, L. *Total Justice.* Boston: Russell Sage, 1985.

García Canclini, Néstor. *Consumidores y ciudadanos: Conflictos multiculturales de la globalización.* Mexico City: Grijalbo, 1995.

Guha, Ranajit. "Chandra's Death." *Subaltern Studies V.* New Delhi: Oxford University Press, 1988: 135–165.

Habermas, Jürgen. *Between Facts and Norms: Contributions to a Discourse Theory of Law and Democracy*. Cambridge, Mass.: MIT Press, 1996.

Jelín, Elizabeth. *Women and Social Change in Latin America*. London: Zed Books, 1990.

Mainwaring, Scott. "Transitions to Democracy and Democratic Consolidation: Theoretical and Comparative Issues." In *Issues in Democratic Consolidation*, eds. Mainwaring, O'Donnell, and Valenzuela.

Mainwaring, Scott, Guillermo O'Donnell, and Samuel Valenzuela, eds. *Issues in Democratic Consolidation*. Notre Dame, Ind.: U of Notre Dame Press, 1999.

Marshall, T. H. *Citizenship and Social Class*. Cambridge: Cambridge University Press, 1950.

Morandini, Norma. *Catamarca*. Buenos Aires: Planeta, 1991.

O'Donnell, Guillermo. "On the State, Democratization, and Some Conceptual Problems: A Latin American View with Some Glances at Post-Communist Countries." *World Development* 21, 8 (1993): 1355–1369.

———. "Polyarchies and the (Un) Rule of Law in Latin America: A Partial Conclusion." In *The (Un)Rule of Law and the Underprivileged in Latin America*, ed. Juan E. Méndez, Guillermo O'Donnell, and Paulo Sérgio Pinheiro. Notre Dame: University of Notre Dame Press, 1999: 303–339.

O'Donnell, Guillermo, and Philippe Schmitter. "Tentative Conclusions about Uncertain Democracies." *Transitions from Authoritarian Rule: Prospects for Democracies*. Pt. 4. Baltimore, Md.: Johns Hopkins University Press, 1986.

Offe, Claus. *Contradictions of the Welfare State*. Cambridge, Mass.: MIT Press, 1987.

Olson, Mancur. *The Logic of Collective Action*. Cambridge: Harvard University Press, 1965.

Przeworski, Adam. *Democracy and the Market: Political and Economic Reforms in Eastern Europe and Latin America*. Cambridge: Cambridge University Press, 1991.

———. "The Games of Transition." In *Issues in Democratic Consolidation*, ed. Mainwaring, O'Donnell, and Valenzuela.

Rey, Alejandra, and Luis Pazos. *No llores por mí, Catamarca: La intriga política de un crimen*. Buenos Aires: Sudamericana, 1991.

Safa, Helen. "Women's Social Movements in Latin America." *Gender and Society* 4, 3 (1990): 354–369.

Tilly, Charles. "Social Movements and National Politics." *State Building and Social Movements*. Ann Arbor: University of Michigan Press, 1984.

Touraine, Alain. *¿Qué es la democracia?* Trans. Horacio Pons. Buenos Aires: Fondo de Cultura Económica, 1995.

Waisbord, Silvio. *El gran desfile: Campañas electorales y medios de comunicación en la Argentina*. Buenos Aires: Sudamericana, 1995.

Zicolillo, Jorge. *Los Saadi, historia de un feudo: Del 45 a María Soledad*. Buenos Aires: Legasa, 1991.

Who's the Indian in Aztlán? Re-Writing Mestizaje, Indianism, and Chicanismo from the Lacandón

JOSEFINA SALDAÑA-PORTILLO

A number of years have passed since I first submitted this essay for publication in this anthology on subaltern politics. Since that time, negotiations between the Zapatistas and the Mexican government have been suspended, and a policy of low-intensity warfare against Zapatista civilian strongholds has been implemented in Chiapas with devastating human cost. Even though the Zapatistas have been contained geographically by the Mexican army, they — or, more precisely, zapatismo *— continue to be a dominant influence in Mexico politically, with indigenous and nonindigenous opposition groups identifying as Zapatistas in their quest for economic equity and democratic freedoms. This essay, written while negotiations were in full swing, is a preliminary theorization of the significance of the Zapatistas, drawn from field research conducted from 1994 to 1996. In it I argue that, contrary to popular representation, the Zapatistas are not a movement for broadened indigenous rights, but a movement for broadened citizens' rights. It is in this capacity that they threaten not only Mexico, but an occidental model of the nation-state and of racialized citizenship in the Americas. The course taken by the negotiations in Mexico further confirms this initial conclusion.*

The Zapatistas finished the first of four rounds of negotiations with the Mexican government in February 1996. During this first round of negotiations — on "Indigenous Culture and Rights" — they successfully negotiated communal autonomy for Chiapas's indigenous communities based on the model of indigenous autonomy already existing in the neighboring state of Oaxaca. It was not until the second round of talks — on "Democracy and Justice" — that the Mexican government broke off negotiations with the Zapatistas permanently, in 1997. Most political analysts argued that this break in negotiations demonstrated the Mexican government's true unwillingness to grant the communal autonomy and indigenous rights agreed on in the first accords. However, this analysis fails to explain why *the Mexican government would resist extending to Chiapas the communal autonomy it had already granted to the indigenous peoples of Oaxaca more than a decade ago. Instead, I would suggest that it was precisely at the moment that Zapatistas exceeded the terms of their own subalternization — the moment they attempted to negotiate democratic transparency in the form of a voter registration policy, referendum initiatives, recall votes, and so on, for the national community of Mexican citizens — that the government representatives balked. As the essay below demonstrates, it is precisely at the moment that the indigenous Zapatista subalterns exceed the particularly of their ethnicity to claim the presumably universal right of citizenship that the Mexican nation-state is most seriously threatened. By claiming the right to citizenship* as Indians, *they are fundamentally rewriting the terms of a citizenship based on the biological metaphor of* mestizaje, *a metaphor that formally excludes the Indian subaltern.*

In terms of the limits of mestizaje *as the dominant trope in the formation of Chicana/o identity, the critique offered in this essay remains timely. In 1999, at the annual* MEChA *conference, the Mexico Solidarity Network requested that the Chicana/o student delegates formally support the Zapatista movement. Student delegates choose four public advocacy projects each year, but the Zapatista cause was not among the four chosen in 1999. I believe this further illustrates how* mestizaje *fetishizes a residual Indian identity to the detriment of contemporary Indians in the United States and Mexico. A more exhaustive analysis of the impact of the Zapatista movement on revolutionary identity in the Americas, and on Chicana/o identity forms, is forthcoming in my book* The Age of Development: Colonizing the Revolutionary Imagination in the Americas *to be published by Duke University Press.*

I begin this essay with a brief overview of the scholarship of which this intervention on indigenism and nationalism in the Zapatista and Chicano movements is a small part. Such an overview will not only give some sense of my philosophical and political points of interest and departure, but will also, I hope, add nuance to the subject at hand. Quite specifically, I am concerned in my work with the analysis of the discourse of development and globalization, and with the placement within this discourse of the subaltern subject in Central America and southern Mexico, of the immigrant and minority subject in the United States, and of the concept of revolutionary consciousness. My interest in this subject came out of the troubling observation that the logic of development reasserts itself time and again in radical movements, often to the detriment of intended beneficiaries. And as James Ferguson has astutely pointed out, development — whether it be of the World Bank variety, the "alternative" variety, or the Zapatista variety — remains fiercely "anti-political," magically outside of ideology and before history in its self-representation.

As I myself have played handmaiden to this enchantress in another life, I decided, in this life, to make a valiant effort to expose it to history. Of course, I have found myself in good company.[1] Along with a growing number of Latin American and U.S. scholars, I became interested in the relevance of postcolonial scholarship to the study of (the failure of) decolonization in Latin America and the United States; the relevance, in short, of postcolonial theory to

American studies broadly conceived. My purpose in taking the intersection of postcolonial studies, development studies, Latin American studies, and U.S. minority discourse studies as a point of departure is not, however, to collapse the radical difference between Third World rural subaltern and First World marginal subject. Rather, to quote Gayatri Chakravorty Spivak, "It is through a critique of 'development' ideology that we can locate the migrant in the First World in a transnational frame shared by the obscure and oppressed rural subaltern. Otherwise, in our enthusiasm for migrant hybridity, Third World urban radicalism, First World marginality, and varieties of ethnographically retrieved ventriloquism, the subaltern is once again silent for us" (255). It is only through this rigorous and honest unraveling of the global nature of development that we can come to understand the definitely different — and at times opposed — position of the marginalized or minority subject in the First World and the rural subaltern in the Third World. My discussion of Mexican indigenous subjectivity and U.S. Chicana/o subjectivity in a transnational frame supports this effort. In the first half of this essay I examine the Zapatista movement and its critique of mestizaje and *indigenismo* as the basis for Mexican identity. I then proceed to discuss Gloria Anzaldúa and Richard Rodríguez's reappropriation of mestizaje and indigenismo in their theorization of Chicana/o identity.

On January 1, 1994, the Zapatistas emerged out of the Lacandón jungle of Chiapas into what appeared to be the postrevolutionary 1990s and a neoliberal new world order that, with the signing of NAFTA, had finally ceded to Mexico a position among the fraternity of "modern nations." But the '90s turned out to be not quite postrevolutionary, and Mexico has been quietly escorted to the antichamber of modernity to sit out this latest political (intraparty assassinations, indigenous insurrections, student strikes) and economic (collapsed financial markets, devaluations) fainting spell. The jungle, once imagined as a pristine preserve of flora, fauna, and traditional Mayan ways, has turned out to be a cosmopolitan hotbed of political discontent and reconstructed indigenous identities. From the jungle, via fax and cellular phone, the Zapatistas have denounced the limits of transnational agrobusiness and Mexican democracy; they have demanded an autonomy project that allows for the preservation of indigenous customs *and* the urbanization of the Lacandon; they have called for a reformulation of the relations between mestizos and indígenas, but they make this call *not* from the position of indigenous peoples, but from the position of citizens of Mexico (EZLN 189).

It is important to recognize that the Zapatistas are not an "Indianist movement," although their military command, rank and file, and base of support within the Lacandon jungle are 99 percent indigenous people (Camú Urzúa and Totóro Taulis, 19–33). Mexican intellectuals and political activists consistently describe the Zapatistas as an Indianist movement, though they are also described as an agrarian movement, a movement for modernization, a movement for democratization, an antipoverty movement. Most academics in the United States insist on reading the Zapatistas as an indigenous movement. The Zapatistas, however, do not define themselves as an Indianist movement (Casal et al., 9–10). Their project and their demands put forward in the peace negotiations are national in scope. Indeed, the earliest Zapatista declarations from the jungle made no mention of indigenous autonomy or special indigenous rights (ibid., 59–85). Although the Zapatistas are predominantly Indian, they launch their armed struggle from the subject position of "citizens of the nation" (Sarmiento). This refusal to define themselves as strictly "Indian," I suggest, is a refusal of the citizenship offered by mestizaje as the central trope in Mexican revolutionary identity formation.

The Zapatista uprising has brought the Mexican nationalist project to crisis and has challenged mestizaje as its dominant trope for citizenship. This challenge to mestizaje is launched not only on political grounds for democratic representation, but also on ontological grounds for figural re-presentation. "Mestizaje" is a concept with at least a five-hundred-year history in the Americas. Referring most literally to the biological mixture of Spanish and Indian peoples, the term gained linguistic currency with the advent of Creole independence movements in the first half of the nineteenth century. Creole elites, seeking independence from Spain, revalued the trope of the Indian in search of a justification for their own nationalist struggles. These elites claimed a direct lineage to those inhabitants of the Americas who originally encountered the Spaniards, and they rehabilitated these ancestral Indians who nobly struggled against colonial Spain as the origins of a retroactively constructed *patria*. Mestizaje as a theory of racial admixture adopted by these nationalist elites, however, also allowed them to claim an Indian ancestor while distancing themselves from their contemporary Indian counterparts, seen as fallen, decadent descendants of these ancestral warriors (Bonfil Batalla, 232–33; Knight 82).

It is not until the mid-twentieth century, however, in the aftermath of Mexico's 1910 revolution, that we see mestizaje fully ensconced as a principle of citizenship. José Vasconcelos, the Mexican intellectual who served as the minister of education from 1919 to 1925, defined the concept as the basis for revolutionary education with the publication of his book *La raza cósmica* (The Cosmic Race). In this essay he theorizes the Latin American people as closest to forging a universal race—the cosmic race—which will bring together the best qualities of the four great races: black, white, yellow, and red (Vasconcelos). The impact of the dissemination of this essay by a public figure during the early formation of the Mexican revolutionary state served to permanently link mestizaje and revolutionary citizenship. Under the administration of Lázaro Cárdenas (1934–1940), as part of his effort to modernize the nation, mestizaje was further institutionalized as the model for citizenship (Knight).

Unlike the Creole elites of the nineteenth century, revolutionary Mexican elites fully embraced the Indian aspect of mestizo identity. Representations of the Indian aspects of mestizaje did not disappear with the rise of the regime of mestizo citizenship. To the contrary, representations of Indian identity proliferated under the revolution's policy of *indigenismo*. Cárdenas and his administration played a pivotal role in ushering in a revival of indigenismo not just for Mexico, but for all of Latin America (Barre, 33–44). Indigenismo functioned as the twentieth-century cultural counterpart to the political construct of mestizaje. Indigenismo formally became part of state cultural policy for a select few of the Latin American countries attempting to modernize their economic and political systems (ibid., 45–85). Historically, the Indian has been understood as the cause for the failure of national cultures to congeal in Latin America. Thus, as state policy, twentieth-century indigenismo set out to modernize the Indian element in national cultures, integrating indigenous populations into mestizo life.

The intellectual architects of revolutionary indigenismo in Mexico, Manuel Gamio and Alfonso Caso, for example, believed that integration of the Indians could be enlightened rather than coercive, that intellectual and economic modernization of the Indians could proceed without the elimination of existing Indian culture (Knight, 80). They hoped this could be achieved through wide-spread educational programs, rather than the wholesale dispossession of Indian lands that took place during the nineteenth-century liberal era. Toward this effort, Gamio, who served as minister of education under Cárdenas, designed the rural school program. These rural schools were to infuse Indians with "the new 'religion' of the country — post-Revolutionary nationalism," while integrating Indian customs and history into revolutionary history (Gamio, 159 [Knight, 82]). Gamio believed these schools could preserve the positive elements of indigenous culture, integrating these elements into the national culture, while eliminating the negative aspects through education. Indian culture was reappraised by institutes set up for this purpose, such as the National Indigenist Institute (INI). Features of Indian culture were selectively put into national discourse by politicians and experts according to the cultural and economic needs of the modernizing project (Díaz Polanco). Indigenismo supplemented this early manifestation of developmentalist discourse in Mexico under the Institutional Revolutionary Party (PRI). Under the regime of these paired identity tropes of mestizaje and indigenismo, the "black" and "yellow" aspects of the cosmic race were systematically forgotten as mestizo identity was reduced to a Spanish and Indian binary. This identity binary, presumably overcome in mestizaje, remains disturbingly hierarchical, as it is always Indian cultural traits that are negative, that must be eliminated or subsumed to the "national" culture of mestizaje.[2]

The Zapatista movement insists that the current ideology of mestizaje, like its nineteenth-century counterpart, has incorporated the historical figure of the Indian in the consolidation of a nationalist identity in order to effectively exclude contemporary Indians from modernization. This process of exclusion is not exterior to mestizaje; in other words, it is not a simple oversight or a misinterpretation of mestizaje in the application of governmental policy. Rather, the erasure of the indigenous is interior to the logic of mestizaje, a concept that nevertheless has had moments of radical appropriation throughout the Americas. Certainly, prior to the popularization of the concept of mestizaje, Latin American elites repressed consciousness of the indigenous population as a cultural force in the Americas.[3] At issue, however, is the discursive process through which mestizaje brings the Indian to consciousness. The critique of this term and its counterpart, "indigenismo," by the Zapatista movement forces us to reconsider first the national deployment of mestizaje as a trope for citizenship, and second, the transnational deployment of mestizaje as the presumed intersection between Mexican indigenous identity and Chicano/a identity. Mapping mestizaje's inherent developmentalism will make evident not only its unviability as a model of citizenship, but will also locate the contradictory positionalities of the indigenous rural subaltern and the Chicana/o mestizo subject.

Mestizaje has served as the biological metaphor for the corporativist government policies of the PRI, policies that held sway in the country from the establishment of corporativism with the presidency of Lázaro Cárdenas to the introduction of neoliberal reforms with the presidency of De la Madrid in the 1980s (1982–1988). And just as PRI corporativist interest cling to political power in Mexico through increasingly violent means, mestizaje clings to its cultural power as the dominant trope for corporativist citizenship through systemic representational violence. In the trope of mestizaje, the Indian is posited as an originary movement in an evolutionary Mexican history. Biologically, the Indian dissolves into the formulaically more progressive mestizo. Unlike quantitative biological metaphors of race in the United States, where, for example, the "one drop" rule rigidly determines your status as African American, or the "one-eighth" rule your status as Native American, in mestizaje a third term gets produced in the mixture that subsumes previous categories. In the cultural extension of this logic, citations of the Indian in Mexico's art, architecture, and history are always citations of a noble yet tragic past: the heroic, yet inevitably unsuccessful, resistance of Montezuma, Cuahutemoc, and the Aztecs to the Spanish Conquest. Indeed, the revolutionary appropriation of mestizaje is not that different from the Creole elite's appropriation of the concept a hundred years earlier.

Indigenismo, then, as a counterpoint to mestizaje, is precisely the state-sponsored policy for the recuperation and celebration of this indigenous past *as past*. One needs only to visit the Diego Rivera murals at the National Palace or the National Anthropological Museum in Mexico City — presumably two of the finest moments of indigenismo in the revolution's cultural history — to understand the evolutionary logic of Mexican citizenship that subsumes the Indian as heroic past to the mestizo as heroic present. Or consider that further excavation of the center of the Aztec city, the Templo Mayor, is prevented by the fact that the ruins of the city lie directly beneath the Basilica and the National Palace — the center not only of colonial and church rule, but also of the PRI's secular power. In this architectural system of signs, Mexico's indigenism is always already under erasure by mestizaje.

Politically, mestizaje extends the biological metaphor to corporativist policy because the Mexican Revolution extended the rights of citizenship and representation to the indigenous population through agrarian reform and agrarian unionism (Cook and Joo). This extension of political enfranchisement, however, again placed indigenous subjectivity under erasure. Agrarian reform extended political citizenship to indigenous people *not* on the basis of their Indian identity, but on the basis of their peasant identity. Peasant identity, in the developmentalist logic of modernization, represents an advance in consciousness from indigenous identity because such an identity formation is contingent on the concepts of individual or family-based land ownership.[4] Agrarianism, as the grounds for political incorporation, privileges economic consciousness over other cultural or religious forms of consciousness. In fact, it performs the division between economic and ethnic subjectivity on which developmentalist notions of progress depend.

The agrarian reform statute in the 1917 Mexican Constitution, Article 27, extended land rights on the basis of separate *ejidos* and communal farms.[5] While thousands of farm titles were granted under Article 27, Indianist activists such as Araceli Burgette and Margarito Ruiz (both interviewed in 1994) believe the article was actually a hindrance to indigenous rights broadly conceived. Article 27 granted separate and discrete farms to clan-based structures, but recipients have limited economic rights and no political rights over these parcels. Specifically, they have no rights *as tribes* over their historical domains. Burgette and Ruiz argue that agrarian reform, as it took place, precluded the granting of territorial rights to historical domain to associations of indigenous people that existed, and continue to exist, beyond the family or village. Territorial rights to historical domains would have granted larger indigenous social formations much broader political, cultural, and economic control over extensive areas of land. In other words, they are suggesting that something akin to autonomy rights early in the revolution would have recognized other kinds of indigenous rights beside the right to land they did acquire as peasants. Another kind of territorial arrangement would have recognized other aspects of indigenous identity, rather than enacting a separation between indigenous economic and cultural identity.

Indian identity, as I have suggested, does not disappear with mestizaje. Rather, mestizaje depends on it for its self-definition. Historically, the PRI has adroitly incorporated indigenismo as the counterpart of mestizaje in two ways, both of which also placed contemporary Indians under erasure. First, the PRI has appropriated a fetishized form of indigenism in the figure of the cacique, the local strongman. The PRI regularly and ritualistically extended political subjectivity and enfranchisement to the local cacique — be he indigenous or mestizo — so long as the cacique guaranteed the semblance of democratic participation through the effective repression of it: through the coercion of votes for the PRI or through electoral fraud. Second, through public policy the PRI has appropriated another fetishized form of Indian identity: the Indian as living museum of historical culture. The PRI has provided economic support, through INI and its policy of indigenismo, for the performance of cultural practices as a folkloric backdrop for tourism, Mexico's second largest industry. The current split within INI reflects the rejection of the former fetishist function of the institute since the Zapatista uprising.

Let me clarify that I am using the PRI as a kind of shorthand for a series of discursive practices that function beyond the parameters of its institutions (see Foucault; Said). This collection of discursive practices serves to reinforce a hegemonic consciousness in which indigenous identity is always in a subordinate position to the dominant mestizo identity. Until January 1, 1994, for hegemonic mestizo consciousness, this translated into a veneration of noble Indian ancestors, but a general amnesia about the living Indian peoples of Mexico.

The Zapatistas reject biological representations in their call to arms precisely because biologized terms of representation, both mestizo and indigenismo, structurally deny them political subjectivity and enfranchisement (Stavenhagen, 47). Instead of recurring to their indigenous identity, they position themselves as guardians of the nation, defenders of the 1917 Constitution, and radical democrats. They reappropriate Zapata, founder of the revolutionary Mexican nation, and call upon their fellow citizens to fight for Mexico, to prove themselves to be at least as civic-minded as their poor and indigenous compatriots (Morquecho, interview). Their most theatrical performance of the Indian-as-good-citizen took place in August 1994 at the first National Democrat Convention held in the Zapatista-controlled jungle. Here

Zapatista representatives discussed how to ensure free and fair presidential and state elections for that year with six thousand representatives of various sectors of Mexican civil society. Thus, at the very moment that the Zapatista movement threw the Mexican nation into crisis — exposing the PRI's dictatorship and the country's lack of democracy, of equality, of a viable economy; in short, its lack of modernization — they paradoxically insisted on their claim to representative citizenship in that nation, not their exclusion from the nation. What the Zapatistas are doing that is radically new to Mexican hegemonic consciousness is reconceptualizing the Mexican constituency as a constituency that includes Indians as political agents in the nation-state.

Consequently, over the course of the last three years, a national Indianist movement has come together to press forward an autonomy plan.[6] Autonomy was added to the list of Zapatista demands in March 1994, largely in response to pressure from these Indianist groups outside of the EZLN. Some of these Indianist associations are new; however, most of them predate the Zapatista uprising in some form or another. These independent Indianist rights groups insist on the term Indi*anist* rather than Indi*genist* to differentiate their understanding of Indian subjectivity from the PRI's historical understanding of Indian subjectivity in indigenismo. These Indianist organizations from all over the country are loosely grouped together at the national level under the organization ANIPA, which is currently holding a series of state assemblies with respective Indianist organizations to devise a functional plan for autonomous regions that would necessarily encompass mestizo and indígena populations. These assemblies are taking place independently at the grassroots level while the Zapatistas conduct their negotiations with the government over indigenous rights and autonomous governmentality.

The preliminary plan for autonomy emerging from these assemblies is not a naive return to pre-Columbian ways. Rather, these groups are discussing an autonomy that is as new for the indigenous populations as it is for the rest of Mexican society. The step toward autonomy implies an acceptance of Western terms of political representation, although in combination with the institutionalization of heterogeneous traditions of Indianist representation. And certainly the legalization of Indianist democratic traditions would necessarily alter these traditional forms of representation. In very broad strokes, the institution of autonomous regions for these independent Indianist organizations would add a fourth tier of regionally based government to the vertical distribution of power that now exists: federal, state, municipal. These autonomous regional governments would themselves consist of three tiers of governance with a horizontal distribution of power: regional representative assemblies; regional executive branches, which would exist *below* the regional assemblies; and the authorities at the level of communities and municipalities, which would retain certain autonomy from the other two tiers. Theoretically, these regional government structures would be constituted according to the traditional rights and practices of the fifty-six different indigenous groups, or those interested in participating (Díaz Polanco, "La experiencia autonómica," 16).

Currently, state and municipal boundaries divide many indigenous groups. Thus a regional body would bring the numerical strength of these indigenous voices together, without, Indianist activists insist, excluding or segregating them from government at the other three levels (Burgette, interview). Obviously many challenging questions about jurisdiction, taxation, and distribution of resources would arise. And communities with a history of caciquismo would have to confront this political problem if autonomous zones are to avoid becoming a form of protection for illegitimate power. When I asked ANIPA representative Margarito Ruiz what autonomous government might look like at the local level, he responded that this was impossible to answer as the structure and meaning of "indigenous autonomy" must be determined community by community. Autonomy as a way of introducing indigenous forms of representation into Mexican governmentality presents the possibility of pushing the real limits of representation under liberal electoral democracies.

As one example of the balancing act necessary between Western and indigenous forms of democratic representation, independent Indianist women's groups in Chiapas insist that before the institutionalization of any model of autonomy takes place in Chiapas, the traditional patriarchal forms of representation within Mayan communities have to change to ensure the protection of indigenous women's rights. In May 1994, for example, the Grupo de Mujeres de San Cristóbal Asociación Civil held a workshop to discuss how the change made in 1992 to Article 4 of the Mexican Constitution would affect women. The change made to Article 4 was historic because it marked the first constitutional recognition of the rights of Indians, adding a paragraph that guaranteed their rights to their languages, customs, and forms of social, political, and legal organization. The indigenous women attending this workshop expressed concern that the interpretation of this constitutional guaranty for the cultural practices of the Maya could serve as a cover for the continued abuse of indigenous women if, for example, the government officially sanctioned the predominance of men as the recognized representatives of the community (Grupo de Mujeres de San Cristóbal Asociación Civil, 40–42). And these women's groups continue to express this concern through discussions of what autonomy might mean for them as women. According to Aída Hernández, a member of Grupo, indigenous women in Chiapas are very concerned that autonomy guarantee the rights of women that are not necessarily recognized by traditional forms of Mayan representation. These indigenous women's groups have used the first Zapatista Revolutionary Law — which recognizes a woman's right to be a representative of the community — to lend moral weight to their battle against sexism within their indigenous communities (interview). Thus, these women are constantly negotiating their identities between the rights available to them as subjects of Western democracy, potential rights available through autonomous forms of representation, and rights promised to them as subjects of a new revolutionary order.

The communal and regional autonomy projects currently under debate by the Zapatistas and other indigenous organizations (such as ANIPA) would require the decentralization of power at the current federal and state levels of government to redistribute resources, tax revenues, and responsibilities between the new tiers of government. Autonomy projects would require the rewriting of various constitutional articles and the refoundation of the nation-state from a federal entity into something new. It it not autonomy in itself, however, that would radically redefine Mexican citizenship; it is the insistence by indigenous peoples represented in the Zapatista movement that they have a say in the forms of government that rule them, including those forms of government that have nothing distinctly to do with indigenous identity, such as the restructuring of electoral law to enable greater transparency in the democracy in which all Mexicans participate. Thus, I would argue, the positionality of the indigenous subject in Mexico is shifting from the position of the subaltern who evades representation — when representation is understood in its political and literary guise — to the position of constitutional subject: the Indian as citizen as Indian. To put it in the terms of U.S. constitutionalists, the new Indianist movement is insisting on a subjectivity emphatically constituted in the representative "We" of "We the people" (Spivak, 259).

I would like to conclude that the Zapatistas have opened up this space for the discussion of new forms of governmentality. These forms of governmentality could combine indigenous forms of representation with Western forms of federal and state representation, and could allow for the indigenous subject to write her- and himself into being in a reconstituted model of citizen-subject. The Zapatista insurrection is an intervention into the discourse of democracy that has propped open a door, allowing other social formations to press forward their own visions of governmentality. While it is difficult to conceive of Indianist rights groups conducting regular statewide assemblies on autonomy prior to the Zapatista revolution, it is also clear that the vision of autonomy put forward by these civic Indianist groups exceeds Zapatista political vision (Monjardin, interview; Esteva, 2). Nevertheless, it is the Zapatistas' rejection of the biologistic terms of representation that provides the opening for indigenous subjects to constitute political exchange through a deessentialized trope of citizenship.

For the second half of this essay I turn to mestizaje and indigenismo in the context of theorizations of Chicana/o identity formations. Chicanos appropriated the discourse of mestizaje in the early 1970s when we claimed Aztlán as an indigenous nation historically anterior to the founding of the United States. Indeed, it is the concept of mestizaje that enabled us to claim a biological tie to this Aztec origin story and to place it in the U.S. Southwest. Aztlán lent a moral and historical legitimacy to our claims for economic and civil rights (Padilla). Aztlán constituted a space outside the U.S. nation, prior to the U.S. nation, from which to launch a critique of a hegemonic and racist system of representation. Aztlán-based Chicano nationalism has been eloquently and exhaustively critiqued by Chicana feminists and Chicana and Chicano poststructuralist scholars. Thus I will not rehash these arguments here. I would like to refocus our attention on the residual effect of this era of nationalism: the continued use of mestizaje as a trope for Chicana/o identity and the presumed access to indigenous subjectivity that this biologized trope offers us. I would like to suggest that mestizaje is incapable of suturing together the heterogeneous positionalities of Mexican, Indian, and Chicana/o that coexist in the United States, or, more importantly, of offering effective *political* subjectivity to these positionalities.

We must recognize that when we appropriate the tropes of mestizaje and indigenismo, we are necessarily operating within the logic of representation to which these tropes belong. We must take seriously the Zapatista movement's critique of mestizaje and indigenismo as parallel ideologies that incorporate the figure of Indian in the consolidation of a nationalist identity in order to effectively exclude contemporary Indians. Thus, in our Chicano reappropriation of the biologized terms of mestizaje and indigenismo, we are also always recuperating the Indian as an ancestral past rather than recognizing contemporary Indians as coinhabitants not only of this continent abstractly conceived, but of the neighborhoods and streets of hundreds of U.S. cities and towns. Why, in other words, do Chicanos in Austin dance to *tejano* music in one bar, mestizo Mexican migrants in another, and indigenous Mexican migrants in none at all? In mestizaje, we are reduced to searching for signs of our indigenous past and, more significantly, for a collective political future in some inherent tie to the land—in our "cosmic green thumb," as Guillermo Gómez Peña, the border *brujo,* has so ironically put it. To recognize this process is not to deny our indigenous ancestry; rather, to recognize this is to refuse to reduce indigenous subjectivity, and indeed Mexican mestizo identity, to biologistic representation that, in discursive and political terms, always already places the Indian under erasure.

I now turn to Gloria Anzaldúa and Richard Rodríguez to determine if either of them is able to recuperate a more sophisticated concept of mestizaje:

one that might possibly extend political enfranchisement or literary representation to the broad range of subject positions implied by a common Mexican heritage. I should warn the reader that Rodríguez is somewhat more successful in this regard than Anzaldúa.

In the opening pages of *Borderlands La Frontera* Anzaldúa movingly represents *la frontera,* the borderlands, in a way that indeed promises us a new paradigm of mestizaje: "The US-Mexican border *es una herida abierta* where the Third World grates against the first and bleeds. And before a scab forms it hemorrhages again, the lifeblood of two worlds merging to form a third country — a border culture. Borders are set up to define the safe and the unsafe, to distinguish *us* from *them.* A border is a dividing line, a narrow strip along a steep edge. A borderland is a vague and undetermined place created by the emotional residue of an unnatural boundary. It is a constant state of transition" (3). The border is a site of mestizaje, of a mixture. In this first image of the borderland, Anzaldúa unsettles the conventional usage of mestizaje by restaging the violence of the initial colonial encounter between Spaniard and Indian in the neocolonial encounter between the First World and Third World. This encounter, this mixture, "es una herida abierta" — an open wound, a wound that refuses to heal because the violence of the initial encounter continues, metamorphosing into new instances of wounding. The traditional usage of mestizaje sutures over the violence of the colonial encounter with the developmentalist logic implicit in it as a third term — the Indian and the Spaniard evolve into the mestizo.[7] Anzaldúa interrupts the teleological drive in mestizaje, however, with her image of the wound that has not healed: when the "lifebloods of two worlds" merge in the borderlands, they hemorrhage. Anzaldúa's "third country," her border culture, is not a plausible end of history, but a "constant state of transition."

In this passage Anzaldúa's borderlands promises to unsettle the conventional usage of mestizaje for Chicanos as well. For if Anzaldúa's borderland undoes the artificial duality of a border, of the "us" and "them," it does so in the service of recognizing the material violence of such artificial constructs. Thus, at this point in the text, Anzaldúa could proceed to resituate the Chicana/o as mestizo, the Mexican as mestizo, and the Indian as Mexican within a transnational frame that would address the power relations among such positionalities. In other words, whereas the mestizaje of Aztlán in the 1970s allied Mexicanos and Chicanos through a common past — through a dead indigenous ancestry — the mestizaje of Anzaldúa's borderlands could disrupt such assumption and place each of these positionalities in that uneasy and "constant state of transition" within a capitalist world-system that depends on our differences for its own reproduction.

Instead of taking up her own provocative challenge to do this, Anzaldúa quickly slips back into the historic usage of mestizaje, constructing Chicana/os in the borderlands as the "us" against the Anglo "them." She rallies mestizaje to access an indigenous ancestry that legitimates a prior claim to the Southwest for Chicanas and Chicanos, "The oldest evidence of humankind in the United States—the Chicanos' ancient Indian ancestors—was found in Texas and has been dated 35,000 BC" (4). Ignoring the contemporary Native American inhabitants of the Southwest and their very different mythogenealogies, Anzaldúa predictably claims this "oldest evidence of humankind" for Chicanos as evidence of the occupation of the Southwest by the Indian ancestors of the Aztecs. Consequently, a page and a few thousand years later, when the settlement of the Southwest by the Spaniards occurs in her book, she continues: "Our Spanish, Indian and mestizo ancestors explored and settled parts of the United States Southwest as early as the sixteenth century. For every gold hungry conquistador and soulhungry missionary who came north from Mexico, ten or twenty Indians and mestizos went along as porters or in other capacities. For the Indians this constituted a return to the place of origin, Aztlán, thus making Chicanos originally and secondarily indigenous to the Southwest" (5). Let us trace the circuitous route by which mestizaje makes Chicanos "originally and secondarily indigenous to the Southwest." According to Anzaldúa Chicanos are originally indigenous to the area because of our biological tie to the first Indians who inhabited it some 37,000 years ago (her date), that mythical Indian tribe that traveled from Aztlán in the Southwest to Mexico City and subsequently formed the Aztec Empire. And we are secondarily indigenous through our "return" to this homeland with the Spaniards as Indians and mestizos. Once again mestizaje is deployed to produce a biological tie with pre-Aztec Indians rather than a political tie with contemporary U.S. Native Americans or Mexican Indians. Consequently, in this system of representation, indigenous subjectivity is once again put under erasure. The condition of possibility for Chicana/o nostalgia over our indigenous subjectivity made evident in this passage is the rarefaction of indigenous peoples as past.

Of course, this is mestizaje with a feminist, queer twist. In a refreshing contradistinction to earlier Chicano deployments of mestizaje, Anzaldúa draws from the female deities in the Aztec pantheon to explain a variety of Chicana-mestiza customs, to explain patriarchy in Chicano culture, to explain Chicana sexuality. Thus, throughout the book, Anzaldúa links Chicana artistic creativity to Coatlique, the goddess of fertility; Chicana sexual expression or freedom to Tlazolteyotl, a goddess of the underworld; and Chicana mourning or sorrow over oppression in all its guises with Cihuocowatl, a goddess of war. To access our mestiza consciousness as Chicanas, we must open ourselves up to the connections in our everyday lives to this pantheon of female deities, to our psychobiological links with the matriarchal Aztec culture of some five hundred years ago: "The new *mestiza* copes by developing a tolerance for contradictions, a tolerance for ambiguity. She learns to be an Indian in Mexican culture, to be Mexican from an Anglo point of view. She juggles cultures. She has a plural personality, she operates in a pluralistic mode" (79). Anzaldúa is certainly correct when she suggests that in her model of mestiza consciousness, one "learns to be an Indian in Mexican culture," because in Anzaldúa's model we are right back where we started—the PRI's state-sponsored mestizaje and indigenismo. What Anzaldúa does not recognize is that her very focus on the Aztec female deities is, in fact, an effect of the PRI's statist policies to resuscitate, through state-funded documentation, this particular, defunct Mexican Indian culture and history to the exclusion of dozens of living indigenous cultures. When she resuscitates this particular representation of indigenous subjectivity to be incorporated into contemporary mestiza consciousness, she too does so to the exclusion and, indeed, erasure of contemporary indigenous subjectivity and practices on both sides of the border.

Turning to Rodríguez, despite his misinterpretation of contemporary Mexican politics and culture, he misinterprets the tropes of mestizaje and indigenismo in provocative ways for Chicanos and Mexicans. He begins his chapter "India" in *Days of Obligation:*

> I used to stare at the Indian in the mirror. The wide nostrils, the thick lips. . . . Such a long face—such a long nose—sculpted by indifferent, blunt thumbs, and of such common clay. No one in my family had a face as dark or as Indian as mine. My face could not portray the ambition I brought to it. What could the United States of America say to me? I remember reading . . . the Kerner Report in the sixties: two Americas, one white, one black—the prophecy of an eclipse too simple to account for the complexity of my face.
>
> *Mestizo* in Mexican Spanish means mixed, confused. Clotted with Indian, thinned by Spanish spume.
>
> What could Mexico say to me?
>
> Mexican philosophers powwow in their tony journals about Indian "fatalism" and "Whiter Mexico?" *El fatalismo del indio* is an important Mexican philosophical theme; the phrase is trusted to conjure the quality of Indian passivity as well as to initiate debate about Mexico's reluctant progress toward modernization. Mexicans imagine their Indian part as deadweight, stunned by modernity; so overwhelmed by the loss of what is genuine to him—his language, his religion—that he sits weeping like a medieval lady at the crossroads; or else he resorts to occult powers and

superstitions, choosing to consort with death because the purpose of the world has passed him by. (1–2)

In this passage Rodríguez eloquently captures the failure of literary and political representations of race in the United States and Mexico to capture the complexities of a face. The hegemonic black/white paradigm of race relations in this country precludes the recognition — much less the reward — of a face like his, so he turns to Mexico. But Mexico has nothing to offer his ambition either. If black/white relations in this country eclipse the complexities of his mestizaje, Mexican philosophical ruminations on mestizo identity deny him and his Indian features any futurity. The Indian in mestizaje is dead weight, modernity incomprehensible to him. Indeed, Mexican pundits shackle the Indian and his lack of futurity with the responsibility of the failure of a system that was predicated on his erasure to begin with.

In this first passage, Rodríguez synopsizes the history of Indian representation in mestizo Mexico: in mestizaje the Indian is feminized and prehistoric as a "medieval lady" (indeed, she gives birth to the mestizo race only to disappear, with Malinche, from the script of history), passive and resigned in his "weeping," incomplete in his loss of truth (symbolized by his language and religion). Alternately, he is treacherous in his fraternizing with the devil through the occult, but he is nevertheless impotent in his rebellion as he is always already consorting with death. Ultimately Anzaldúa finds nothing but a celebratory hybridity in the concept of mestizaje, but Rodríguez recognizes and reveals mestizaje as the repressive apparatus that it is for indigenous peoples. For the remainder of the chapter Rodríguez resists traditional representations of mestizaje precisely because any future that incorporates the reality of his face depends on it. Instead, Rodríguez inverts the power relations implicit in mestizaje by insisting that the mestizo is not the evidence of the triumph of the Spanish colonizer over the colonized Indian, but the evidence of the triumph of the colonizing Indian over the colonized Spaniard.

Rodríguez begins with a rejection of the construction of Malinche, the representational birthplace of mestizaje, as either the victim of a Spanish rape or the betrayer of her indigenous past. She is instead the curious seductress of Spain, with all of the agency that postmodern feminism has restored to the power of seduction:

Because Marina was the seducer of Spain, she challenges the boast Europe has always told about India.

I assure you that Mexico has an Indian point of view as well, a female point of view:

I opened my little eye and the Spaniard disappeared.

*Imagine a dark pool; the Spaniard dissolved; the surface triumphantly
smooth.*

My eye!

*The spectacle of the Spaniard on the horizon, vainglorious, the shiny surfaces,
clanks of metal; the horses, the muskets, the jingling bits.*

Cannot you imagine me curious? Didn't I draw near?

European vocabularies do not have a silence rich enough to describe
the force within Indian contemplation. (22)

The "boast" that Europe tells itself is, of course, that the Spaniards discovered
the Indians. Instead, Marina casts her gaze of discovery upon the Spaniard.
Just as millions of Indians "disappeared" from disease upon "discovery," the
Spaniard immediately disappears within the gaze of discovery. The complexity
of his subjectivity — his heritage, his culture, his history — is immediately dissolved into the dark pool of a mestizaje that swallows him and is "triumphantly smooth" afterward, leaving no trace of Spanish culture. Marina is
unconcerned with the depth of the Spaniard: what she is enamored of is the
surface; what she is after in her seduction are the jingly trinkets. The Spaniard
is the spectacle here, not the Indian. And yet, this is not a simple anticolonialist
inversion of the identity terms. It is more complicated than an inversion, as
Malinche is only accessible to us through her Spanish given name, Marina —
through the language of the colonizer.

Nevertheless, the Indian does not simply return the gaze: the Indian is the
gaze. And while the European hears the silence as a vanquished enemy, the
silence is not an absence but a presence filled with centered and active contemplation: "The Indian stands in the same relationship to modernity as [Ma-
rina] did to Spain — willing to marry, to breed, to disappear in order to ensure
her inclusion in time; refusing to absent herself from the future. The Indian
has chosen to survive, to consort with the living, to live in the city, to crawl on
her hands and knees, if need be, to Mexico City or L.A." (24). The weapons
available to the Indian in the colonial and postcolonial encounters have been
the weapons of the weak; to remain visible, you disappear; to survive, you
crawl; to win, you breed (Scott). Modern Indians find agency in the only way
possible, through resistive adaptation. And by making assiduous use of the
weapons of the weak, the Mexican Indian not only survived in mestizaje, but
eventually consumed his other, the Spaniard, the European:

> Look once more at the city from La Malinche's point of view. Mexico is
> littered with the shells and skulls of Spain, cathedrals, poems, and the
> limbs of orange trees. But everywhere you look in this great museum of
> Spain you see living Indians.

Where are the *conquistadores?*

Postcolonial Europe expresses pity or guilt behind its sleeve, pities the Indian the loss of her gods or her tongue. But let the Indian speak for herself. Spanish is now an Indian language. Mexico has captured Spanish. (Rodríguez, 23–24)

The mestizo is now an Indian. The Spaniard is the museum. Through mestizaje a thoroughly modern Indian has cannibalized the Spanish markers of identity. The Indian has absorbed the European terms of subjectivity, and consequently these terms are turned into indigenous markers of identity from the inside out. The European is silent; the Indian is speaking.

I believe Rodríguez's reworking of the representational tropes of mestizaje and indigenismo is the most fruitful to date. It refuses the erasure of the Indian by putting the Spaniard under erasure—by insisting on the Indian as the primary term in the trope of mestizaje. He recognizes not only the Indian presence in the contemporary world, but the Indian as the agent of modern Mexican history. However, Rodríguez also ends up at a biological representation of indigenism—one that is exciting and new but has its own set of limits. Ultimately for Rodríguez, the signs of indigenous identity are reduced to the surface signifiers of facial features, to genetics: the "beak nose," the dark skin, the almond eyes. And the only avenue to political agency for the modern-day Indian is the avenue of this newly configured domain of mestizaje. While Rodríguez's mestizaje radically reconstructs power relations between the colonizer and the colonized, it nevertheless requires the Indian to give up his or her language, religious practices, and other forms of cultural and social organization.

In other words, Spanish is not an "Indian" language precisely because most Indians living in Mexico and the rest of Latin America do not speak Spanish as a first language. And for a further understanding of the underlying biologism in both Anzaldúa's and Rodríguez's re-presentation of tropes of indigenism and mestizaje, we need to turn to Rigoberta Menchú. Menchú insists time and again in her autobiography that indigenous identity is not biological. Any person born an Indian, with all the genetic Indian features, can become Ladinized by refusing to practice his or her indigenous identity in the hopes of accessing the limited amount of power made available to poor Ladinos. ("Ladino" is roughly equivalent to mestizo in Guatemalan culture.) Indigenous identity, for Menchú, depends not simply upon biology, but on the rigorous practice of cultural, linguistic, social, religious, and political forms that constitute one as Indian. And these are not forms that exist in a kind of pastiche grab bag of Indian spiritual paraphernalia, as they seem to exist for

Anzaldúa. Instead they are forms of culture that are shared with a practicing community of indigenous people. And we need to return to the autonomy movement in Mexico to remember that Indianist groups *do* appropriate Spanish as the constitutional language, but they appropriate that language precisely to construct a space for legitimating themselves as multilingual, multicultural citizens of the body public. In other words, they appropriate the Spanish of the mestizo to insist on their inclusion in the body politic not as mestizo, but as radically other: as coterminously citizen and Indian.

I would like to end this essay with a personal anecdote. I remember coming home on some college vacation and asking my dark-skinned mother which great-grandmother or great-grandfather on her side of the family had been Indian. My mother laughed, and intuiting, as she always does, what I was after, she refused to answer my question and dismissed me simply with, "Ay, m'ija, if you want to believe you're Indian, go right ahead." At the time, I felt sorry for my mother, and felt her pain — her internalized racism. Now I realize that my mother, born and raised in Oaxaca among living Indians, understood what it would take me years of education to understand: the meaning of radical difference within a context of radical humanity.

Ultimately, Anzaldúa's model of representation reproduces liberal models of choice that privilege her position as a U.S. Chicana: she goes through her backpack and decides what to keep and what to throw out, and she chooses to keep signs of indigenous identity as ornamentation and spiritual revival. But what of the living Indian who refuses mestizaje as an avenue to political and literary representation; what of the indígena that demands new representational models that include her among the living?

Notes

1 As only three of the most recent examples, see James Ferguson, *The Anti-Politics Machine;* Arturo Éscobar, *Encountering Development: The Making and Unmaking of the Third World;* and Akhil Gupta, *Postcolonial Developments.*
2 For a full discussion of the history of mestizaje, from its emergence as a colonial strategy of governmentality in the Indian township to its deployment by the PRI as a development strategy, please see my forthcoming article "Reading a Silence: The 'Indian' in the Era of Zapatismo" (Saldaña-Portillo), forthcoming.
3 Even during these radical moments of appropriation, however, mestizaje cannot escape the racial hierarchy that it inevitably produces. In *Nuestra América,* for example, José Martí summons mestizaje as the focal point of Latin American unity while simultaneously describing it in the metaphorical terms of the human body, with the head as the metaphorical equivalent of the white race and the body as the metaphorical equivalent of the Indian and black races.
4 For a thorough discussion of the developmentalist logic inherent in agrarian reform and the role of agricultural policy in the consolidation of modernization and nationalist iden-

tity, see Saldaña-Portillo, "Developmentalism's Irresistible Seduction: Rural Subjectivity under Sandinista Agricultural Policy," in *The Politics of Culture in the Shadow of Capital*, ed. David Lloyd and Lisa Lowe.

5   A communal farm is a geographically restricted farm that is granted to members of a single indigenous ethnic group that have historically formed a community, such as a village or town, and were formally recognized by the Spanish Crown in colonial times. An ejido farm is granted to groups of farmers, either indigenous or mestizo, with some geographic or historical ties to each other. In both cases, the land is granted under the presumption that the land will be worked communally by the members of the cooperative. Such communal farming does not generally take place, even on the farms communally granted to indigenous peoples. Generally, the members are granted individual plots of land within the ejido or communal farm, and they may or may not pool their labor for certain seasonal work.

6   I do not mean to imply that the Indianist movement is born of the Zapatista movement. The Indianist movement's organization certainly predates the Zapatista uprising of 1994. Since the 1990s, Mexico's Indianist population had been participating through the Comisión Coordinadora de Organizaciones y Naciones Indígenas del Continente (the Coordinating Commission for the Indigenous Organizations and Nations of the Continent/ CONIC) in preparations for the protest of the 1992 quincentennial Columbus Day celebrations. Various Mexican Indianist groups attended the Continental Conference of Indigenous People held in Quito, Equador, in 1992 (CONIC, 53–62). However, it was as a consequence of the Zapatista uprising that the Indianist movement in Mexico gained a national profile. Prior to January 1, 1994, the growing Indianist movement received little or no publicity. Since the uprising, the Indianist movement has not only received increased publicity, it has gained members and cohesion in its political platform (Ruiz, interview).

7   It is interesting to consider the representation of the rape/betrayal of Malinche as the displacement of the violence that is sutured over by mestizaje as national origin story. In order to transcend the differences of the heterogeneous populations of Mexico in its formation as a nation-state, it is necessary to place the memory of the violence on Malinche and contain it precisely in her marginality.

Works Cited

Anzaldúa, Gloria. *Borderlands/La Frontera*. San Francisco: Spinsters/Aunt Lute Press, 1987.

Barre, Marie-Chantal. *Ideologías indigenistas y movimientos indios*. Mexico City: Siglo XXI, 1983.

Bonfil Batalla, Guillermo. "Historias que no son todavía historia." In *Historia ¿para qué?* ed. Carlos Pereyra et al. Mexico City: Siglo XXI, 1980.

Burgette, Araceli. Interview conducted by the author in September 1994.

——. Interview conducted by the author in July 1996.

Camú Urzúa, Guido, and Dauno Totóro Taulis. *EZLN: El ejército que salió de la selva*. Mexico City: Grupo Editorial Planeta, 1994.

Casal, María Luz, Rafael Jacob, Mario Monroy, and Carlos Zarco, eds. *Los hombres sin rostro*. Mexico City: Centro de Estudios Ecuménicos and Servicios Informativos Procesados, 1994.

CONIC. *"Memoria de la Comisión Coordinadora de Organizaciones y Naciones Indígenas del Continente CONIC."* Mexico City: J. C. Impresores, Junio 1994.

Cook, Scott, and Jong-Taick Joo. "Ethnicity and Economy in Rural Mexico: A Critique of the Indigenista Approach." *Latin Research Review* 30, 2 (1995): 33–59.

Díaz Polanco, Hector. "La experiencia autonómica: Problemas y perspectivas." In *Ojarasca* 38–39 (November–December 1994): 14–17.

——. *Indigenous Peoples of Latin America: The Quest for Self-Determination.* Trans. Lucía Rayas. Latin American Perspective Series, 18. Boulder, Colo.: Westview Press, 1997.

——. Interview conducted by the author in April 1994.

Éscobar, Arturo. *Encountering Development: The Making and Unmaking of the Third World.* Princeton, N.J.: Princeton University Press, 1995.

Esteva, Gustavo. "La cuestión indígena: ¿Más allá del estado-nación?" *La Jornada Semanal* 69 (30 June 1996): 2–3.

EZLN. "Plan de 34 puntos." In *Los hombres sin rostro,* ed. María Luz Casal, Rafael Jacob, Mario Monroy, and Carlos Zarco. Mexico City: Centro de Estudios Ecuménicos and Servicios Informativos Procesados, 1994.

Ferguson, James. *The Anti-Politics Machine.* Cambridge: Cambridge UP, 1990.

Foucault, Michel. *The Order of Things.* New York: Vintage, 1973.

Gamio, Manuel. *Forjando Patria.* Mexico City: Editorial Porrúa, 1960.

Gilly, Adolfo. *La revolución interrumpida.* Colleción Problemas de México. Mexico City: Ediciones Era, 1994.

Grupo de Mujeres de San Cristóbal Asociación Civil. "Memorias del encuentro—Taller 'Los derechos de las mujeres en nuestras costumbres y tradiciones.'" Manuscript. San Cristóbal de las Casas, 1994.

Gupta, Akhil. *Postcolonial Developments: Agriculture in the Making of Modern India.* Durham, N.C.: Duke University Press, 1998.

Hernández Castillo, Aída. Interview conducted by the author in September 1994.

——. Interview conducted by the author in July 1996.

Hernández, Luís. Interview conducted by the author in September 1994.

——. Interview conducted in July 1996.

Knight, Alan. "Racism, Revolution, and Indigenismo: Mexico, 1910–1940." In *The Idea of Race in Latin America, 1910–1940,* ed. Richard Graham. Austin: University of Texas Press, 1990.

Martí, José. *Nuestra América.* Buenos Aires: Editorial Losada, 1939.

Mogel, Reyna. "Autonomía y las poblaciones indígenas de Chiapas." Manuscript. San Cristóbal de las Casas: CIES, 1994.

——. Interview conducted by the author in October 1994.

Monjardin, Adriana. Interview conducted by the author in July 1996.

Morquecho, Gaspar. Interview conducted by the author in July 1996.

Padilla, Genaro. "Myth and Comparative Cultural Nationalism: The Ideological Uses of Aztlán." In *Aztlán: Essays on the Chicano Homeland,* ed. Rodolfo A. Anaya and Francisco A. Lomeli. Albuquerque: University of New Mexico Press, 1989: 111–134.

Pereyra, Carlos, et al. *Historia ¿para que?* Mexico City: Siglo XXI, 1980.

Rodríguez, Richard. *Days of Obligation: An Argument with My Mexican Father.* New York: Penguin, 1992.

Ruiz, Margarito. Interview conducted by the author in September 1994.

Said, Edward. *Orientalism.* New York: Vintage, 1978.

Saldaña-Portillo, María Josefina. "Reading A Silence: The 'Indian' in the Era of Zapatismo." *Nepantla,* forthcoming.

——. "Developmentalism's Irresistible Seduction: Rural Subjectivity under Sandinista Agricultural Policy." In *The Politics of Culture in the Shadow of Capital,* ed. David Lloyd and Lisa Lowe. Durham, N.C.: Duke University Press, 1997: 132–172.

Sarmiento, Sergio. Interview conducted by the author in July 1994.
Scott, James. "Everyday Forms of Resistance." In *Everyday Forms of Peasant Resistance,* ed. Forrest D. Colburn. London: M. E. Sharpe, 1989.
Spivak, Gayatri Chakravorty. *Outside in the Teaching Machine.* New York: Routledge, 1993.
Stavenhagen, Rodolfo. "Las lecciones del diluvio zapatistas." *La Cronica* 2, 5 (February 1994): 43–47.
Vasconcelos, José. *La raza cósmica.* Los Angeles: Centro de Publicaciones, Department of Chicano Studies, University of California, 1979.

Coloniality of Power and Subalternity

WALTER D. MIGNOLO

In the fall of 1996 Ranajit Guha was invited to Houston to dialogue with members of the Latin American Subaltern Studies Group, where he read the essay published in this volume. At the time of Guha's visit, he was familiar with the "Founding Statement" and with *Postmodernism in Latin America,* the volume of *boundary 2* edited by John Beverley, José Oviedo, and Michael Aronna in which it was included. On this ground he established, first, a dialogue between South Asian and Latin American subaltern studies projects, highlighting "postmodernism" as portrayed in the special issue of *boundary 2.* Attempting to identify the common grounds of the two projects, Guha observed that it is not territoriality but temporality that connects South Asian and Latin American projects. By "temporality" he means that "collapsing of local and global times — the time of the Naxalbari uprising in India and that of the Cultural Revolution in China, the time of the Nicaraguan elections and that of the fall of the Berlin Wall — is of course one of the most salient features of capital's 'self-realization process in the course of which it strives to annihilate space with time, as Marx has argued" (Guha, this volume).

It is indeed interesting that Guha framed "temporality" as "modernity," situated modernity in the second half of the eighteenth century, and highlighted Immanuel Kant's "What is Enlightenment?" Guha's reference to Michel Foucault's interpretation of Kant's classical piece allowed him to frame temporality in two extremes, modernity and postmodernity. Reflecting on the Latin American encounter with postmodernism as it is explored in the special issue of *boundary 2* already mentioned, Guha noted that this engagement is "displayed clearly enough *to make it stand well apart from similar engagements such as the Anglo-European and South Asian ones*" (emphasis added). Guha made a reference to India's "two hundred years of solitude" and to the fact that coloniality and postcoloniality, rather than modernity and postmodernity, are the issues at stake. This is precisely the point I would like to expand on in this belated dialogue with Guha's statement.

My intention here is two-fold. The first is to intervene in and contribute to a conversation between both projects.[1] The second is to bring a third party into the conversation, the contribution of Latin American scholars and intellectuals who, since the 1970s, have been reflecting on coloniality, capitalism, modernity, and, indirectly, on subalternity in the Americas.[2] It is not my intention to establish priorities such as who was first and who deserves the honor of first arrival. On the contrary, I want to emphasize that if this dialogue was not established before (say, in the early 1980s), it was due to the historical structure of modernity/coloniality and the geopolitics of knowledge.

Latin American and South Asian scholars looked toward Europe for the "source" of knowledge, simultaneously ignoring each other or assuming that there was nothing to be learned from each other beyond the epistemic tradition of Western modernity. Last, but not least, by bringing together coloniality of power and subalternity, two particular responses to two particular colonial histories, my intention is to underline epistemic diversity and to keep on arguing for diversality as a universal project beyond the disciplinary epistemic legacies of North Atlantic modernity and the ideological underpinnings of area studies. This argument is also compelling at present with the logic of area studies being reproduced and "applied" to Latino/a studies.[3]

Subalternity and Coloniality in British India

Guha's observation that "engagements such as the Anglo-European and South Asian" with postmodernity stand well apart from those of the Latin-European and South American deserves some attention. The comparison is between British India and Spanish America, or, if you prefer, between Anglo India and Latin America. He characterizes the temporality of the former (Anglo-European and South Asian) as "postcolonial" and underlines three "salient aspects of modernity's intersection with colonialism":

> First, that the phenomenon of post-Enlightenment colonialism is *constitutive* of and presupposed in modernity even if it is not always explicitly acknowledged to be so; secondly, that postmodernism as a critique can never be adequate to itself unless it takes colonialism into account as a historic barrier that reason can never cross; thirdly, that the colonial experience has outlived decolonization and continues to be related significantly to the concerns of our time. (Guha, this volume)

I would like, first, to support Guha's remarks by bringing similar perspectives on modernity/coloniality to the foreground, and second, to depart from the historical limits he set in the eighteenth century. The issues implied in Guha's remarks are not explicitly mentioned in the "Founding Statement" or reflected upon in Beverley et al.; however, such perspectives have been signifi-

cantly debated in Latin America at least since the 1970s. The following observations are aimed at explaining two basic assumptions on which these debates
emerged and stand (still today) in harmony with the project of the South
Asian Subaltern Studies Collective. First, coloniality is constitutive of modernity, and modernity/coloniality should be located in the sixteenth century
with the emergence of the Atlantic circuit and the consolidation of capitalism;
second, subalternity is not only a question of social classes, but is instead a
larger issue embedded in the coloniality of power and in the formation of the
modern/colonial world-system; third, although "colonialism" or "colonial
periods" refers to specific historical stages of coloniality, coloniality of power is
intrinsic to modernity, and, consequently, coloniality at large goes beyond decolonization and nation building: coloniality is the machine that reproduces
subalternity today in the form of global coloniality in the network society.

   The links between subalternity and coloniality have been explored in great
detail in one of Guha's classic works, "Dominance without Hegemony and Its
Historiography." It's clear in his argument that subalternity is not only a
question of a subordinate class within an industrial country, but of subordinated social organizations and histories within the interstate structure of
power, such as that between England and India until 1947. Guha's opening
sentences reveal that subalternity and the colonial difference presuppose each
other: "There was one Indian battle that Britain never won. It was a battle for
appropriation of the Indian past. It began with the East India Company's
accession to *diwani* in 1765" (210). He continues: "A colonialist knowledge,
its function was to erect that past as a pedestal on which the triumphs and
glories of the colonizers and their instrument, the colonial state, could be
displayed to best advantage. Indian history, assimilated to the history of Great
Britain, would henceforth be used as a comprehensive measure of difference
between the peoples of these two countries. Politically that difference was spelt
out as one between rulers and the ruled" (211). Colonialism under the British
Empire went together with a particular stage of capitalism, no longer mercantile capitalism as in the sixteenth century, but industrial capitalism. Guha is
here making three interrelated points: one about colonialism, one about capitalism, and the third about intellectual and academic critiques (in his case,
historiography) of hegemony and domination.

   "Coloniality of power" is not a term used by Guha but one introduced by
Peruvian sociologist Anibal Quijano (1992, 1997a, 1997b). My aim is to find
the point of articulation between coloniality of power and Guha's conceptualization of power as a complex matrix of Dominance (D) by Coercion (C) and
by Persuasion (P) and of Subordination (S) by Collaboration (C*) and by
Resistance (R). Let's remember the general configuration of power as described by Guha in the following matrix:

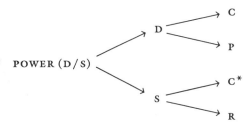

$$\text{POWER (D/S)} \nearrow \begin{array}{c} D \nearrow C \\ \searrow P \end{array} \searrow \begin{array}{c} S \nearrow C^* \\ \searrow R \end{array}$$

Crucial in Guha's proposal is the double articulation of the matrix. One level is the interstate system primed by capitalism and colonial expansion. The second level is the internal situation in colonial India once the interstate system is put in place through colonial dominance. The matrix describes a general structure of power that can be implemented to understand both England and India before colonialism as well as British dominance over India during the colonial period. Guha uses the word "paradigm" (instead of "cosmology" or "worldview") to describe two kind of discourses articulated in the colonial structure of power (or, if you prefer, articulated by the coloniality of power). Rather than a contact zone, what we have here is the violence of border (lands).

The English "idiom" of "Improvement" and the Indian "idiom" of "*Danda*" which was central to all indigenous notions of dominance) intersect. "Improvement" carries all the weight, and the belief in that progress and "improvement" was the point of arrival *for* India. The point of arrival itself was enunciated *from* England. "Danda" Guha explains, instead "emphasizes force and fear as the fundamental principles of politics. The source and foundation of royal authority, *Danda* is regarded as the manifestation of divine will in the affairs of the state" (1989: 238). The idiom of "improvement" was employed by British *indigenous* government (in England) as well as by the British *foreign* government (in India). It was supposed to be implemented in a *foreign* country as a political strategy to Persuade (P) the *indigenous* elite (in the country where the British were *foreign*) "to 'attach' themselves to the colonial regime" (242).

If, then, there were two independent idioms to articulate power and dominance (danda and improvement), coloniality of power emerged at the moment in which capitalism and colonial expansion acquired the face of "improvement" as the building block of the idiom of modernization, civilizing mission, and the like. However, while danda was the paradigm of dominance in India before British colonialism, improvement was the paradigm of dominance in England, also before colonialism. It was introduced by the bourgeoisie to detach itself from the feudal order and to introduce a new form of domination of subaltern communities in England. Subalternity, in this argu-

ment, becomes a *connector* of different local histories and structures of domination in the modern/colonial world-system, which is further complicated by
the double articulation of the structure of power under colonial regimes. In
the modern/colonial world, however, subalternity is not only a question that
affects the relationship between sectors of the civil society and the state, but it
is also ingrained in the interstate system structured by the coloniality of power.

Guha's focus on the conflictive "conversation" between two paradigms
clearly locates subalternity in the hierarchical structure of the interstate system.
He goes through a detailed philological work in order to explain the idioms of
Improvement and Order in one paradigm and of Dharma and Danda in the
other. However, there is a moment of his analysis in which the "temporalization" in the encounter and the conflict between the two paradigms become the
focus. Allow me to transcribe the two paradigms and the constituent elements
organized by Guha in order to understand his point about "temporalization"
(see Guha 1989: 271):

Paradigms		
Constitutent elements	Contemporary, British, liberal	Precolonial, Indian, semifeudal
C	Order	Danda
P	Improvement	Dharma
C*	Obedience	Bhakti
R	Rightful Dissent	Dharmic Protest

I will not comment here on the dangers of reproducing British historiographic chronology when contrasting contemporary British India with precolonial India. But it is important to remember that there was both a precolonial and feudal England that the bourgeois revolution was attempting to
overcome, as there was a precolonial India that was overtaken by the British
bourgeoisie that overcame feudalism in a precolonial England. In other words,
two independent local histories were intercrossed and articulated by coloniality of power.

Guha's effort to understand the relationships between D and S under interstate colonial structures in tension, and the conflicts between two paradigms
(or cosmologies) that are hegemonic in each of the states in question, is the
pillar of his argument. The conditions of Dominance and Subordination are,
for Guha, *"specific and adequate to the conditions of colonialism* an ensemble of
overdetermining effects" that he explains through Lacan's concept of "double
meaning" (see Guha 1989: 271). Guha describes double meaning as the "pro-

cess of condensation and displacement by which the ideological moments of social contradictions in pre-colonial India and modern England [also pre-colonial] were fused with those of the living contradictions of colonial rule to structure the relation D/S" (ibid.).

[What is of interest for my argument is the fact that] one could explain the same phenomenon from a subaltern perspective (instead of from a "scientific" one) by invoking W. E. B. Du Bois's "double consciousness" (1990: 8–9) and finding the parallels between double consciousness in the Afro-American experiences and double consciousness in British India. The explanatory power of "double consciousness" instead of "double meaning" would have supported and strengthened the argument that British colonialism in India was dominance without hegemony. Why? Because "double consciousness" carries in and with it the weight of the colonial experience, of which "double meaning" is deprived. "Double meaning" carries the weight of the bourgeois individual experience in nineteenth-century Europe. However, and as I said before, the geopolitics of knowledge (and the hegemony of certain types of knowledge) prevented the dialogue between different experiences of coloniality as both subalternity and double consciousness were mediated by the "common ground" provided by European production of knowledge, theories, and disciplinary fields. None of the "constituent elements" of the diagram (C, P, C*, and R) remain the same: "improvement" comes to mean something else, and "dharma" also changes its meaning: "Thus C as an element of D/S is not identical with the notion of Order in the lexicon of eighteenth- and nineteenth-century British politics nor with the notion of Danda in that of classical Hindu polity, although its formation owes much to both. Again, P., though a product of the interaction of Improvement and Dharma, is characterized by properties only some of which it shares with those idioms, while the rest are uniquely its own. And so for each element" (Guha 1989: 271).

Guha's explanation of "double meaning" in each of the "constituent elements" introduces the perspective of the observer, while a concept such as Du Bois's "double consciousness" allows, instead, for an understanding of double meaning from the perspective of the colonial subaltern who can understand and has to deal with both improvement and dharma. What remains to be underlined here is that double consciousness is unthinkable from the hegemonic perspective of Western epistemology, while double meaning is acceptable as a "scientific" conceptualization. However, from a subaltern perspective, double consciousness could be articulated in various forms. Indian liberals (in Guha's terminology) will embrace improvement, while Indian nationalists will restitute and embrace dharma. The first proposes assimilation; the second, resistance.

There is a third possibility, however, that I call "border thinking" or "border epistemology," and its outcome "critical assimilation." The assimilation of improvement from the perspective of dharma means a radical transformation of the former from the perspective of the latter, and the transformation of the latter because of the unavoidable presence of the former. This is, in the last analysis, what Du Bois's "double consciousness" implied: a critical assimilation to Anglo hegemonic culture from and into the perspective of the Black Soul.[3] Because double consciousness is a necessary outcome of colonial subalternity, it is precisely why colonialism in India, and everywhere else, was dominance without hegemony: a dominance that could never colonize the past. (The present planetary order mapped by the exercise of the coloniality of power and subalternity in the interstate system requires diversality (diversity as a universal project) as a project for the future. The Zapatistas' dictum "Because we are all equal we have the right to the difference" could be taken as the platform for a diversal or pluriversal project that takes the place of the existing abstract universals in which coloniality of power and colonial subalternity have been engrained.)

This line of argument explains, also, that British historians operated (and they could hardly have done otherwise) on a "single consciousness," the consciousness of improvement and order (and presupposed the expansion of British universal assumptions). Evaluating British historiography in India, Guha suggests: "The strategy of the Cambridge approach is to credit that mediation with complete success in this regard and represent the colonized subject's relation to the colonizer as one in which C* triumphed effectively over R. In other words, *it is a strategy aimed at characterizing colonialism as a hegemonic dominance*" (1989: 296).

British colonial, as well as Marxist, historiography (exemplified in Guha's article with the works of David Wasbrook) "surgically removed the subaltern domain" (Guha 1989: 305). Consequently, "all initiative other than what emanates from the colonizers and their collaborators strictly ruled out, all elements of resistance meticulously expelled from its political processes, *colonialism emerges from this historiography as endowed with a hegemony which was denied to it by history*" (ibid.). And he concludes this statement by observing that "the Cambridge approach achieves this feat by an act of bad faith — by writing up Indian history as a 'portion' of the British History" (ibid.).

The bottom line of Guha's argument is that subalternity is inextricably linked to coloniality. And this was not the case in Gramsci's original conceptualization of subalternity in the context of class hierarchy in Europe under industrial capitalism. Guha's contribution was to link subalternity to coloniality and to redefine it as a structure of power in the (modern/colonial) interstate system. Capitalism and coloniality, as Guha's argument amply demonstrates, have a different (although complementary) articulation than capitalism and modernity. Future conversations between the South Asian and Latin American Subaltern Studies groups should be more attentive to the similarities-in-difference that are engraved in a singular local histories of modernity / coloniality.

Coloniality is of the essence in the modern / colonial trajectory whose history is the history *of* Latin America and the history that *made* Latin America, although it has been hidden from view through two hundred years of nation building and national ideology. The two hundred years of (colonial) solitude that Guha refers to for British India have been five hundred years of solitude for Ibero America and the Caribbean. The different temporalities of colonial British India and Ibero America and the Caribbean makes the conversation between scholars in both groups (and between them and intellectuals and scholars in Latin America) difficult but at the same time exciting. India was falling under British administration approximately at the time that the British were expelled from the River Plate in South America. Nation building, in the Americas and up to World War II, coexisted with the British Empire's dominance in Asia and Africa.

In the period after World War II, post-partition India had to solve the problems presented by decolonization (and the South Asian Subaltern Studies Collective emerged as a consequence of such process), while in Latin America the problems unfolded around modernization and development (roughly 1950–1970), but also with the wave of dictatorships during the period in which transnational corporations began to rise (roughly 1970–1990). If this is the "history" of the two regions, the "encounter" between South Asian and Latin American Subaltern Studies belongs to a post-Cold-War period. Interestingly enough, the "Founding Statement" was published in 1992, the year of the conflictive celebration of the Spanish "discovery" of America. And that coincidence allows me to bring into the conversation the concerns of and the contributions made by those in Latin America who since the seventies have been attentive to coloniality, Eurocentrism, and the rise of U.S. imperialism.

Coloniality and Subalternity in Latin America

To enlarge the scope of the conversations between Latin American intellectuals and South Asian and Latin American Subaltern Studies groups let me now change the scenario slightly. During the 1970s when Ranajit Guha and various collaborators were formulating the South Asian project in response to the postcolonial situation in India and South Asia, a similar set of concerns was being attended by Latin American intellectuals. In Latin America what needed attention was not a short-lived postcolonial condition, as in India, but the failures—after more than 150 years of decolonization—of development and modernization coupled with the critical situation prompted by the Cuban Revolution and the consequent reaction of the U.S. government. There was a chronological coincidence between the New Left in England and in Latin America, particularly in Argentina. The concerns with decolonization that prompted the emergence of South Asian subaltern studies were parallel to those that in Latin America were expressed through dependency theory, philosophy of liberation, internal colonialism, and the dialogue between Latin American and African philosophers, historians, and sociologists working on decolonization.[4] The Cold War and the Cuban Revolution added an important, complex element once the initial enthusiasm of the Left for the decolonization of Cuba was converted into the suspicions that it was a recolonization under a different ideology of planetary expansion.

Thus, the intellectual parallelisms shall be complemented with the historical parallelisms between the five hundred years of coloniality in Latin America and the Caribbean and the two hundred years in British India. In the Americas, the year 1992 (more so in Latin America and the Caribbean) was a significant date from both the perspective of the state as well as from the perspective of the indigenous population. The "official story" commemorated the "discovery," while the indigenous population denounced five hundred years of colonization. Somewhat in the middle, Creole and immigrant intellectuals expressed their solidarity with anticolonial manifestations, although with a certain distance and caution toward a historical event that did not have (in the eyes of most of them) any bearing in an ascending neoliberal society and the demise of the nation-state.

For Guha, and in general for the South Asian Subaltern Studies group, there was no choice but to locate the "beginning" of coloniality in the emergence of British India. For Latin American intellectuals interested in understanding coloniality and coloniality of power embedded in nation building, there was no choice but to locate the "beginning" in the emergence of Spanish (and later on Latin) America. It is not by coincidence that Anibal Quijano and Immanuel Wallerstein coauthored an article titled "Americanity as a concept, or the Americas in the Modern World-System" (1992). While Guha emphasized (on the experience of British colonialism in India) the "universalizing tendency of capital and its limitations" (1989: 222) and referred to colonialism as "the failure of the universalist project" (272), Quijano and Wallerstein emphasized (based on the experience of Ibero colonialism in the Americas) the emergence and consolidation of capitalism and of colonialism. In the sixteenth century the universalist project was not so much a bourgeois as it was a Christian one. The "model," so to speak, was already in place when Britain enacted and transformed it into the colonization of India.

In the parallels I am exploring between the 1970s and 1990s, it should be remembered that Wallerstein's first volume on the modern world-system was published in 1974. This publication was a landmark on several fronts. The ones I am here interested in are those that connect with the British and Latin American New Left, and those that locate the "beginning" of modernity/ coloniality in the sixteenth century with the emergence of the Atlantic commercial circuit and the "discovery" of America. Let's remember how Quijano and Wallerstein traced the interrelations between capitalism, coloniality and modernity: "The modern world-system was born in the long sixteenth century. The Americas as a geosocial construct were born in the long sixteenth century. The creation of this geosocial entity, the Americas, was the constitute act of the modern world-system. *The Americas were not incorporated into an already existing capitalist world economy. There could not have been a capitalist world economy without the Americas*" (549).

The Americas were conceived as the "New World," Quijano and Wallerstein state, because the New World became "the pattern, the model, of the entire world-system" (550). They describe a four-fold pattern; namely, coloniality, ethnicity, racism, and "newness" itself. Coloniality is, for Quijano and Wallerstein, something that transcends the particularities of historical colonialism and that does not vanish with independence or decolonization. Coloniality is also embedded in national formation because, in their thesis, coloniality is constitutive of modernity and, therefore, of the modern/colonial world system. The difference is that for Guha modernity/coloniality is located in the eighteenth century, and for Quijano and Wallerstein in the sixteenth century.[5] British capitalism and colonial expansion to India under the banner of the civilizing mission that Guha explored in "Dominance without Hegemony" is, for Quijano and Wallerstein, a variation of the pattern of the modern/colonial world articulated in the sixteenth century.

Latin American independence, obtained during the same period that Britain was colonizing India, is another variation of coloniality of power in the formation and transformation of the modern/colonial world-system. I do not have time here to go into the four aspects discussed by Quijano and Wallerstein, even less to discuss some shortcomings of their formulation. I will limit myself to what I consider relevant for a triangular discussion between the project of some Latin American scholars and intellectuals, Latin (and Latin/ o/a American) subaltern studies in the United States, and the South Asian Subaltern Studies group. Let's then focus on coloniality:

> Coloniality was an essential element in the integration of the interstate system, creating not only a ranking order but also a set of rules for the interactions of states with each other. *Thus it was that the very efforts of those*

at the bottom of the rank order to overcome their low ranking served in many ways to secure the ranks further. The administrative boundaries established by the colonial authorities had had a certain fluidity in that, from the perspective of the metropole, the essential boundary line was that of the empire vis-à-vis other metropolitan empires. It was decolonization that fixed the stateness of the decolonized states. Spanish viceroyalty were carved up in the process of the war of independence to yield, more or less, the states we know today. (Quijano and Wallerstein, 551)

Thus, coloniality has been explored and expanded (chiefly by Quijano) in order to grasp a dimension that has been left in the dark in the conceptualization of the modern world-system as well as, in a parallel line of reflections, by discussion and debates on modernity and postmodernity. Coloniality is, for Quijano (as well as, and independently, for Guha) not only constitutive of modernity but also a locus of enunciation defined by the epistemic colonial difference. As such, it transverses the end of the first wave of decolonization and nation building (for example, the decolonization from England and the formation of the United States, Haiti's independence from France, and Latin American Iberian colonies' from Spain and Portugal). Nation building cannot be detached from, and it is indeed a particular stage of, the modern/colonial world. From the perspective of coloniality nation building is simply a new phase of modernity/coloniality and not the end of colonialism. "Internal colonialism," therefore, was a necessary concept introduced to describe and explain, precisely, the colonial dimension of modern nation building after decolonization, whether in the first stage (late eighteenth to early nineteenth centuries) or second stage (after World War II) of decolonization. In other words, decolonization and nation building became a new form of articulation of the coloniality of power in the Americas (in the nineteenth century) and in Asia and Africa (in the second half of the twentieth century).

Quijano's conception of coloniality of power links race, labor, and epistemology. First of all, the pattern of colonial domination and labor in the sixteenth century presupposed, for Quijano, the concept of "race." This key concept allowed for a social classification and the creation of new identities around the planet that were established as historically necessary permanent relations and not as a justification for the control and exploitation of labor (see Quijano 1997a: 29). "Indians" and "blacks" became two overarching categories that displaced and obscured the historical and ethnic diversity of people inhabiting the Americas and those transported from Africa to the Americas. Such a distribution of social identities (to which should be added the background of the classification of Jews and Moors in the Iberian Peninsula) was, for Quijano, the foundational move for the classification of the population in the Western Hemisphere. (And of the planet if we consider the Moors and the Jews and, later on, the emergence of "orientalism.") Epistemology was endowed with the power to organize the planet by identifying people with territories and differentiating Europe from the other three continents (according to the four continents [imaginary] since the sixteenth century). Epistemology was endowed, indeed, with the coloniality of power (see Quijano 1997a: 29–31).

It should be observed, in passing, that the word "race" did not exist in the sixteenth century and that the classification of people was largely based on religion. However, the underlying principle was racial. "Purity of blood," which served to establish the distinction between Christians, Moors, and Jews, was indeed religious but based on biological "evidence." In the nineteenth century, when science replaced religion, racial classification was no longer based on blood mixture but on skin color. Beyond the changing faces of racial configurations, the underlying principle of the modern/colonial world for the classification of people in epistemic hierarchies is racial in the sense that it is based on physical features, whether blood or skin, linked to either religious or national communities.

The alliance between Quijano and Wallerstein — in spite of their differences — is not surprising. It is well known that Wallerstein's concept of the modern world-system owes much to the work of Fernand Braudel's history of the Mediterranean in the sixteenth century, while his notion of center-periphery owes much to Argentinean economist Raul Prebisch (reflecting on the limits of modernization in the Third World) and to dependency theory advanced by Brazilian sociologists Fernando Henrique Cardoso and Enzo Faletto (see Wallerstein 1979: 69–94; Grosfogel 1997). However, while Wallerstein proposed a new map of the modern world as a system, he perceived colonialism but not coloniality.

Colonialism ended with independence (in Latin America, Asia, or Africa), but not coloniality. And this is precisely the trust of Quijano's contribution. The "idiom" or the "paradigm" (to borrow Guha's terms) of coloniality makes visible both the geopolitics of knowledge from colonial perspectives and the strength of critical reflections on modernity from the perspective of coloniality. Although these reflections were happening simultaneously in the 1970s, the hegemonic power of modern epistemology managed to keep them hidden from each other. Poststructuralism and postmodernity functioned as orange cones blocking the road that connected Southeast Asia with South America. Furthermore, and because of the hegemonic power of modern epistemology, Indian and Peruvian intellectuals had their backs to the Pacific and were looking toward France, England, and Germany.

The identification of the sixteenth century as the beginning of modernity/coloniality is not only a narrative from the social sciences in both their northern (Wallerstein) and southern (Quijano) versions, but something that is ingrained in a different colonial experience. Indigenous movements also have been emphasizing, lately, the five hundred years of colonization. The first paragraph of the Zapatistas' first declaration from the Lacandón jungle is, in a nutshell, a cartography of coloniality of power, through nation building, and subalternity in the interstate modern/colonial world:

> We are a product of 500 years of struggle: first against slavery, then during the War of Independence against Spain, then to avoid being absorbed by North American imperialism, then to promulgate our constitution and expel the French empire from our soil; later the dictatorship of Porfirio Díaz denied us the just application of the Reform laws and the people rebelled and leaders like Villa and Zapata emerged, poor men just like us. We have been denied by our rulers the most elemental conditions of life, so they can use us as cannon fooder and pillage the wealth of our country. They don't care we have nothing, absolutely nothing, not even a roof over our heads, no land, no work, no health care, no food or education. Nor are we able to freely and democratically elect our political representatives, nor is there independence from foreigners, nor is there peace or justice for ourselves and our children. (García de León, 33–36)

It would not be surprising to find the "Declaration from the Lacandon Jungle" in the second edition of *Postmodernism in Latin America* (Beverley et al.). Indeed, one can take this declaration as a second "Founding Statement," particularly because it is a historical, theoretical, and political statement coming from people in a subaltern position that breaks away from the directionality of studying or theorizing subalternity in academia only. The Zapatistas have shown that the subaltern may not be able to speak, but they are certainly able and willing to think.

I do not have time to pursue this line of reasoning here, which I have done elsewhere (Mignolo 1997). I will instead close this section by going back to the relevance of the sixteenth century in thinking modernity/coloniality from Latin America, to which, of course, the Zapatista movement is no exception. Argentinean Enrique Dussel, a key figure of philosophy of liberation, could help in underlining the geopolitical and interdisciplinary perspectives of colonial expansion and of the link between capitalism and knowledge. I am also particularly interested in those cases in which power and subordination connect two ethos, cosmologies, or paradigms (in Guha's terminology). Knowledge becomes, on one side of the spectrum, part of the social reality that shall be improved, managed, or domesticated. Dussel conceptualized the formation of the Eurocentric paradigm in the early 1970s, and his version of liberation philosophy very much presupposed a geopolitics of knowledge that now we can understand within Guha's matrix of P(ower)/S(ubordination).

Let's now move from the sociohistorical perspective on coloniality introduced by Quijano to the philosophical critique of modernity developed by Dussel. When Dussel published *Philosophy of Liberation* in 1977, he reflected on "modern European philosophy" in the following terms:

> Beginning with the fourteenth century, the Portuguese and then the Spanish began to control the North Atlantic (which from the end of the fifteenth century until today will be the center of history). Spain and Portugal opened Europe to the west; Rusia will do it to the east. In the sixteenth century Spain discovered the Pacific to the west and Russia did the same to the east. Now the Arab world is enclosed and loses the centrality it had exercised for almost a thousand years. Later Spain and Portugal will give way to the British Empire. Now Europe is the center. From the experience of this centrality gained by the word and by power, Europe began to consider itself the archetypal foundational "I." (8)

More recently, Dussel has rearticulated his early conceptualization of the geopolitics of knowledge and power in a slightly different but consistent frame: "Two opposing paradigms, the Eurocentric and the planetary, characterize the question of modernity" (1998: 3). The first paradigm was constructed from a Eurocentric horizon. Modernity in this paradigm was conceived as exclusively a European phenomenon. The second paradigm instead underlines the planetary contribution to modernity and, therefore, "conceptualizes modernity as the culture of the *center* of the world-system, of the first world-system, through the incorporation of Amerindia as a result of the *management* of this centrality. In other words, European modernity is not an *independent,* autopoietic, self-referential system, but instead is *part* of a world-system: in fact, its center" (4). Anyone familiar with some of the writing of the South Asian Subaltern Studies group would soon realize the parallelisms of their motivations and goals with the project of philosophy of liberation and decolonization of knowledge in Quijano and Fals Borda.

Gender and Internal Colonialism

The recent translation into Spanish (and in Bolivia) of a collection of articles by members of the South Asian Studies group made visible another story that originated in the 1970s (see Rivera Cusicanqui and Barragán). This story has coloniality also as a main character in the colonial horizon of modernity. In the late 1960s and early 1970s a discussion about the transition from feudalism to capitalism in Latin America occupied several pages and a considerable amount of energy. Two classic examples were the differing points of view advanced by sociologist Andre Gunder Frank on the transition from feudalism to capitalism, and its refutation by Argentinean philosopher Ernesto Laclau (see also Stern). On the other hand, the intervention of argentine economic historians Enrique Tandeter, Sempat Assadurian, and Carlos Garavaglia placed the debate in a different domain, that of colonialism (see Rivera Cusicanqui and Barragán; Larson). As Argentine historians studying the exploitation of the silver mines in Potosí (Bolivia), they were looking toward the Andes instead of toward Europe, as were Frank and Laclau.

The economic historians saw a different story: not the replica of Western linear macronarratives universalizing feudalism and capitalism, but the story of colonialism and the emergence of the Atlantic commercial circuit and the consolidation of capitalism. The silver mines of Potosí were not just one mine among many. The only other comparable silver mine was in Zacatecas, Mexico. It was, indeed, one of the major sources of silver for Europe. The reaches of the Indies contributed to the dissolution of feudalism in Europe, to engrossing the reservoir of European countries north of the Pyrenees and to the emergence of Holland and England as capitalist/colonialist leading countries in the seventeenth and eighteenth centuries, respectively (Arrighi 1994). However, if the silver mines of Potosí contributed to the dissolution of feudalism in Europe and the transition to capitalism, that was not the case in the Andes. There was no room in the Andes for a transition from feudalism to capitalism since there was no feudalism to be overcome by the emergence of the European bourgeoisie. The Incas and the Aztecs were not living in the Middle Ages before the arrival of the Spaniards! The Middle Ages were an invention of the Renaissance and of Western modernity, and not a planetary reality.

The economic historians revealed, on one hand, the expanding noncapitalistic and nonmarket economy of Inca social organization, and on the other, that there was a population (elite and masses) that had to make the transition from an economy based on reciprocity to an economy based on pillage and individualism; that is, a transition to a market economy with all the consequences this transition implied.[6] The complexities that Guha described in the structure P/S could be rehearsed here, although in a different kind of colonial domination that was inventing itself in the process of its emergence. The emergence of the modern/colonial world-system in the sixteenth century, and the articulation of its matrix, led the foundations of modernity/coloniality of which the British Empire in India is nothing less than the adaptation of previous patterns put in place in the sixteenth century.

Parallel to the contribution made by argentine historians, two Mexican sociologists, Pablo González Casanova and Rodolfo Stavenhagen, introduced the notion of "internal colonialism" in the debate on national development.

The social sciences faced therein the conflict that, later on, would be faced by subaltern historiography in India by confronting the limits and tensions between coloniality, nation building, and the disciplines. "Internal colonialism" not only underlined the relevance of colonialism embedded in the nation state but also modified the taken-for-granted idea that independence of Spanish American countries in the nineteenth century was the end of colonialism. It may have been the end of the colonial period (like 1947 was for India), but it was not the end of coloniality and of coloniality of power. The Creole elite, of Spanish descent, obtained political independence from Spain but entered a process of nation building economically dependent on new ascending colonialism, chiefly by England during the nineteenth century and increasingly the United States during the twentieth century. Nation building, in other words, reproduced the colonial rules vis-à-vis the indigenous population and concentrated the power in the Creole elite.

The very existence of a Creole elite in the Americas that went through the process of decolonization from European colonial powers (approximately between 1776 and 1831) is one of the crucial differences between coloniality in India and in the Americas. Decolonization in the Americas was in the hands of Creoles (Anglo, African, and Iberian), while in India it was in the hands of the indigenous population. The diverse Creole elite in the Americas (of Anglo-Saxon descent in the U.S. decolonization from England; of African descent in Haiti's decolonization from France; and of Iberian descent in Latin America decolonization from Spain and Portugal) reproduced coloniality of power in the form of internal colonialism. Contrary to what happened in India, the indigenous population in the Americas was not in a position to accomplish the type of "collaboration" Guha analyzed for the indigenous population in India in complicity with the officers of the British Empire (240–245). Today "internal colonialism" may sound out of place. The fact that globalization is undermining state sovereignty and transnational corporations by passing frontier regulations does not mean, necessarily, that internal colonialism is no longer in force. First of all, it is important to understand the differences between nation-states in Europe and in the Third World. And second, it should be rethought in terms of the new forms of coloniality in a global and transnational world.

Silvia Rivera Cusicanqui has inscribed her work since the mid-1980s at the intersection of coloniality and internal colonialism. As founder of the Taller de Historia Oral, Rivera Cusicanqui worked with indigenous scholars and intellectuals, always emphasizing coloniality over modernity or, if you wish, the fact that "peripheral" modernities in the modern/colonial world have been and are "colonial" modernities. Her crucial essays on the epistemological potential of oral history and its relevance to, in her own words, "decolonization of history" (1991) mesh very well with Guha's crucial essays on dominance and hegemony that I have been analyzing here, and also with Dipesh Chakrabarty's follow-up on history as a subaltern discipline when practiced in/from the Third World (1992). The fact, then, that Rivera Cusicanqui and Rossana Barragán coedited the volume I mentioned above, *Debates post coloniales: Una introducción a los estudios de la subalternidad,* can be understood as a confluence of a well-established political and research program in Bolivia with South Asian subaltern studies. Why Bolivian scholars had enough interest in translating South Asian contributions to Spanish and not vice versa is a question that cannot be explored here. I will say, however, that one of the reasons for a one-direction translation goes beyond the individual or collective contributions of each group. It has to do with the larger picture of coloniality of power; with language, translation, and knowledge in the colonial horizon of modernity; with the force of coloniality of power that permeates even intellectual work and dialogues, almost imperceptibly. (And with the hegemony of the English language in cultures of scholarship, even when it is a colonial English, as in South Asia, the Caribbean, and sub-Saharan Africa.)

Ileana Rodríguez, in her introduction to this volume, maps the story and describes the motivations for the formation of the Latin American Subaltern Studies Group. In this belated conversation with Ranajit Guha, and as a member of the Latin American group, my intention was to examine the relations between subalternity and coloniality as they have been discussed in Latin America since the 1970s, and, therefore, to contribute to a triangular dialogue between, on one hand, South Asian and Latin American critical reflections on modernity, coloniality, and Eurocentrism, and on the other, between South Asian and Latin American intellectual production and Latin American and Latino/a intellectuals in the U.S. Some members of the Latin American Subaltern Studies Group have been working on colonialism since the 1980s (mainly Patricia Seed, José Rabasa, Sara Castro-Klarén, and I). The emphasis on postmodernity instead of postcoloniality that Guha underlines in his contribution to this volume has more to do with the differential historical rhythms in the Americas and in South Asia, with the temporal distance from decolonization , and with their location in the world order during the nation-building period. The early decolonization in the Americas and the Caribbean (Haiti) coincided with the emergence of the Enlightenment and the bourgeois revolution, while the late decolonization of India and other countries in South Asia coincided with the emergence of the Cold War, with the ideology of development and modernization, and with the inception of transnational corporations — in other words, with the five hundred and two hundred years of solitude, respectively.

How can these different perspectives benefit from each other? In my view, critical social theory in Latin America and in U.S. Latin American subaltern studies could benefit from the detailed type of analysis of colonial relations of power (e.g., coloniality of power) that Guha put forward in studies such as "Dominance without Hegemony." South Asian subaltern studies, on the other hand, could benefit from the articulation of modernity/coloniality advanced by Latin American scholars such as Quijano, Dussel, and Rivera Cusicanqui, among others. The South Asian perspective takes as its point of departure the Enlightenment, which explains Guha's reference to Kant. The Latin American perspective takes as a point of departure the sixteenth century, which explains the importance of Bartolomé de Las Casas, of Vitoria and the School of Salamanca (for philosophy of liberation, Dussel) and the emergence of the Atlantic commercial circuit (Quijano, Mignolo). Vitoria set up an agenda for international relations (or the interstate system, in Quijano's vocabulary), cosmopolitanism, and group rights that was ignored during the Enlightenment with the emphasis on nation building and individual (man and citizen) rights. The sixteenth century is not "out" of modernity, a pre-modernity fighting to liberate itself from the Middle Ages. On the contrary, the eighteenth century is a "new" moment of the modern/colonial world-system that tried to deny its past and built itself as the newness of "new" — that is to say, the "modern." There was certainly an interval between the end of the seventeenth century and the end of the eighteenth century when the Spanish Empire was in decay and the British Empire was not yet in place. That was the moment of the Europe of Nations, of the bourgeois revolution, and of an idea of modernity centered on France, England, and Germany. That very moment was the moment of the construction of the "south" of Europe and of orientalism. There was, indeed, a new moment within the modern/colonial world, and not a new, modern world.

The encounter between South Asian subaltern studies and Latin American critiques of modernity and colonialism have one thing in common: their conception that subalternity is not only a question of social groups dominated by other social groups, but of the subalternity in the global order, in the interstate system analyzed by Guha and by Quijano. Dependency theory was clearly an early reaction to this problematic. This is no doubt a crucial and relevant point today, when coloniality of power and subalternity are being rearticulated in a postcolonial and postnational period controlled by transnational corporations and by the network society.

One of the difficulties that Latin American and South Asian intellectuals will have to overcome is the legacy of the "Black Legend" — the idea that modernity is a question of the Enlightenment and that the Iberian Peninsula was steeped in the darkness of the Middle Ages. Consequently, Latin America was the inheritor not of northern, but of southern Europe, closely connected with

Africa and the Islamic world. This image is part of the very self-fashioning of the Enlightenment, and the self-fashioning modernity, but also of the impossibility of understanding that the Haitian revolution was an implementation of the very liberating principles that the Enlightenment was putting forward.

One of the concerns shared by Latin American and South Asian subaltern studies is coloniality at large, an issue that has been investigated independently by each group since the 1970s. But this topic has also been a common concern among north and sub-Saharan African intellectuals since decolonization. One of the future avenues of subaltern studies would be, perhaps, to work toward a mutual understanding of the history, as well as of the rearticulation, of global coloniality being enacted in the network society.

Notes

There is a related and interesting parallelism to be pursued between Latin American critical reflections on coloniality and South Asian subaltern studies. One would be Quijano's "coloniality of power" and Partha Chaterjee's description of power in his description of the "colonial state" (Chaterjee 1993: 15–34). The other would be between Chaterjee's "rule of colonial difference" (1993: 16–18) and my redefinition of "the colonial difference" on the basis of coloniality of power (Mignolo 2000: 15–35). The connections could be pursued by considering José Rabasa's engagement with Dipesh Chakrabarty's "time of history" and "time of gods" (Chakrabarty 1997) in the epilogue of Rabasa's *Writing Violence in the Northern Frontier* (2000).

1 The conversation that began at Houston continued at Duke with Dipesh Chakrabarty, Gyan Prakash, Ishita Dube, and Saraubh Dube in the fall of 1998 during the conference "Cross Genealogies and Subaltern Knowledges."

2 See Mignolo, "The Larger Picture: Hispanics / Latinos in the Colonial Horizon of Modernity," in Gracia and De Grieff 2000.

2 Ibid.

3 Du Bois [1905] 1990: 8–9: "One ever feels his two-ness, — an American, a Negro; two souls, two thoughts, two unreconciled strivings; two warring ideals in one dark body, whose dogged strength alone keeps it from being torn asunder."

4 For instance, Samir Amin and Pablo González Casanova in sociology; and Kwasi Wiredu, Enrique Dussel, and Leopoldo Zea in philosophy.

5 There is significant difference between Quijano and Wallerstein, which I explore elsewhere (Mignolo 2000) from the perspective of the geopolitics of knowledge. Wallerstein and Quijano are at different ends of the colonial difference, although both of them offer a critique of capitalism and colonialism.

6 See Larson 1995 for an update on this issue.

Works Cited

Arrighi, Giovanni. *The Long Twentieth Century*. London: Verso, 1994.

Beverley, John, José Oviedo, and Michael Aronna, eds. *The Postmodernism Debate in Latin America*. Durham, N.C.: Duke University Press, 1995 [1992].

Braudel, Fernand. *The Mediterranean and the Mediterranean World in the Age of Philip II.* Trans. Sian Reynolds. 2 vols. Berkeley: University of California Press, 1995 [1948].

Cardoso, Fernando Henrique. "Les Etats-Unis et la théorie de la dépendance." *Revue Tiers Monde* 17, 68 (1976): 805–825.

Cardoso, Fernando Henrique, and Faletto Enzo. *Dependencia y desarrollo en América Latina.* Mexico City: Fondo de Cultura Económica, 1969.

Chakrabarty, Dipesh. "Provincializing Europe: Postcoloniality and the Critique of History." *Cultural Studies* 6, 3 (1992): 337–357.

——. "The Time of History and the Time of God." In *Politics of Culture in the Shadow of Capital,* ed. L. Lowe and D. Lloyd. Durham, N.C.: Duke University Press, 1997.

Chaterjee, Partha. *The Nation and Its Fragment: Colonial and Postcolonial Histories.* Princeton, N.J.: Princeton University Press, 1993.

Du Bois, W. E. B. *The Souls of Black Folk.* New York: Vintage, 1990 [1905].

Dussel, Enrique. *Philosophy of Liberation.* Trans. from Spanish by A. Martinez and C. Morkovsky. New York: Orbis, 1985 [1977].

——. "Marx's Economic Manuscripts of 1861–63 and the 'Concept' of Dependency." *Latin American Perspective* 17, 1 (1990): 62–101.

——. *Historia de la filosofía latinoamericana y filosofía de la liberación.* Bogota: Nueva América, 1994.

——. "Eurocentrism and Modernity (Introduction to the Frankfurt Lectures)." In Beverley, Oviedo, and Aronna, eds. 65–76.

——. *The Underside of Modernity: Apel, Ricoeur, Rorty, Taylor, and the Philosophy of Liberation.* Atlantic Highlands, N.J.: Humanities Press, 1996.

Fals Borda, Orlando. *Ciencia propia y colonialismo intelectual: Los nuevos rumbos.* Bogota: C. Valencia Editores, 1971.

Founding Statement. *boundary 2* 20, 3 (1992).

Frank, Andre Gunder. *Capitalism and Underdevelopment in Latin America: Historical Studies of Chile and Brazil.* New York: Monthly Review Press, 1967.

García de León, Antonio. *EZLN: Documentos y comunicados.* Vol. 1. Mexico: Ediciones Era. English translation in Beverley et al., 1994.

González Casanova, Pablo. "Internal Colonialism and National Development." *Studies in Comparative International Development* 1, 4 (1965): 27–37.

Gracia, Jorge, and Pablo De Grieff. *Ethnicity, Race, and Rights.* New York: Routledge, 2000.

Grosfogel, Ramon. "A TimeSpace Perspective on Development: Recasting Latin American Debates." *Review* 20, 3–4 (1997): 465–540.

Guha, Ranajit. "Dominance without Hegemony and Its Historiography." In *Subaltern Studies VI.* New Delhi: Oxford University Press, 1989.

Laclau, Ernesto. "Feudalism and Capitalism in Latin America." *New Left Review* 67 (1971): 19–38.

Larson, Brooke. "Andean Communities, Political Cultures, and Markets: The Changing Contours of a Field." In *Ethnicity, Markets, and Migration in the Andes at the Crossroads of History and Anthropology,* ed. Brooke Larson and Olivia Harris (with Enrique Tandeter). Durham, N.C.: Duke University Press, 1995.

Mariátegui, José Carlos. *Textos Basicos.* Selección, prólogo, y notas introductorias de Ánibal Quijano. Mexico City, Fondo de Cultura Económica, 1990.

Mignolo, Walter D. "The Zapatistas' Theoretical Revolution: Its Epistemic, Political, and Ethical Consequences." Keynote address at the conference "Comparing Colonialisms." Binghamton: Center for Medieval and Renaissance Studies (Binghamton University).

Forthcoming in the conference proceedings. A Spanish version is in *Orbis Tertius: Revista de Teoría y Crítica Literaria* (1997): 5, 63–81.

——. *Local Histories/Global Designs: Coloniality, Subaltern Knowledges, and Border Thinking.* Princeton, N.J.: Princeton University Press, 2000.

——. "Geopolitics of Knowledge and the Colonial Difference." Forthcoming in the proceedings, edited by Agustín Lao-Montes and Ramón Grosfogel.

Quijano, Anibal. "Colonialidad y modernidad-racionalidad." In *Los conquistados: 1492 y la población indígena de las Américas.* Comp. Heraclio Bonalla. Bogota: Tercer Mundo Editores, 1992.

——. 1995. "Modernity, Identity, and Utopia in Latin America." In Beverley, et al.

——. "The Colonial Nature of Power in Latin America." In *Sociology in Latin America,* ed. R. Briceño-León and H. R. Sonntag. International Sociological Association, precongress volume, 1997.

——. "Colonialidad del poder, cultura, y conocimiento en América Latina." *Anuario Mariateguiano,* 9, 9 (1997b): 113–121.

——. 1998. "Estado-nación, ciudadanía, y democracia: Cuestiones abiertas." In *Democracia: Un modelo para armar.* Caracas: Nueva Sociedad, 1998.

Quijano, Anibal, and Immanuel Wallerstein. 1992. "Americanity as a Concept, or the Americas in the Modern World-System." ISSA1 134: 549–557.

Rabasa, José. *Writing Violence in the Northern Frontier.* Durham, N.C.: Duke University Press, 2000.

Rivera Cusicanqui, Silvia. "Democracia liberal y democracia de *ayllu:* El caso del norte de Potosí, Bolivia." In *El difícil camino hacia la democracia,* ed. Carlos F. Toranzo Roca. La Paz: ILDIS, 1990.

——. "El potencial epistemológico de la historia oral: De la lógica instrumental a la descolonización de la historia." In *Temas Sociales.* revista de Sociología, Universidad Mayor de San Andrés 11 (1991): 5–38.

——. "Sendas y senderos de la ciencia social andina." En *Autodeterminación: Análisis Histórico Politico y Teoría Social* 10 (1992): 83–107.

——. "La noción de 'derecho' o las paradojas de la modernidad postcolonial: Indígenas y mujeres en Bolivia." *Temas Sociales* (revista de Sociología, Universidad Mayor de San Andrés) 19 (1997): 27–52.

Rivera Cusicanqui, Silvia, and Rossana Barragán, eds. *Debates post coloniales: Una introducción a los estudios de la subalternidad.* La Paz: SEPHIS/Aruwiyiri, 1997.

Stavenhagen, Rodolfo. "Classes, Colonialism, and Acculturation." *Studies in Comparative International Development* 1, 7 (1965): 53–77.

Stern, Steve. "Feudalism, Capitalism, and the World-System in the Perspective of Latin America and the Caribbean." *American Historical Review* 93, 4 (1988): 829–872.

Wallerstein, Immanuel. *The Modern World-System.* Vol. 1, *Capitalist Agriculture and the Origins of the European World-Economy in the Sixteenth Century.* New York: Academic Press, 1974.

——. "Dependence in an Interdependent World: The Limited Possibilities of Transformation within the Capitalist World-Economy." In *The Capitalist World-Economy.* Cambridge: Cambridge University Press, 1979.

Contributors

MARCELO BERGMAN teaches sociology and Latin American studies at the University of Oregon. He has published articles on rising crime and criminal law. He is coordinating a collaborative project on public policy and tax compliance in Latin America. He is also compiling a collection of articles on empirical assessments of new crime waves in the region.

JOHN BEVERLEY teaches Spanish and Latin American literature and cultural studies at the University of Pittsburgh. His most recent books include *Against Literature* (1993), *The Postmodernism Debate in Latin America* (coeditor; 1995), *Una modernidad obsoleta: Estudios sobre el barroco, Subcultura homogeneización* (with Phil Cohen and David Harvey; 1998), *Subalternity and Representation,* and *Arguments in Cultural Theory* (1999). He is a founding member of the Latin American Subaltern Studies Group. With Sara Castro-Klarén he coedits a new series for the University of Pittsburgh Press, *Illuminations: Cultural Formations of the Americas.* He is currently working on a book about Miami.

ROBERT CARR studied and taught in the United States until 1998. He has a Ph.D. in literature and is currently a graduate student in the Department of Sociology, Psychology and Social Work at the University of the West Indies, Mona, Jamaica. His publications include "The New Man in the Jungle: Chaos, Community and the Margins of the Nation-State," in *Callallo,* "Notes on Crossing the Third World/First World Divide: Testimonial, Transnational Feminisms, and the Postmodern Condition" in *Scattered Hegemonies,* and "Palabras/Cuerpos/Capital: El Discourso de Poder y la Lucha para Representación en el Amazona" in *Discurso y Poder.* He was also a coeditor of *Latin American Subaltern Studies: A Special Issue of Dispositio/n* with Jose Rabasa and Javier Sanjinés for the Latin American Subaltern Studies Collective. His current project is "Tangled Skeins," a manuscript on West Indian and African-American nationalist strategizing.

SARA CATRO KLAREN is Professor of Latin American Culture and Literature at The Johns Hopkins University. She has published books and numerous articles in English and Spanish on the work of José María Arguedas, Mario Vargas Llosa, Guamán Poma, Garcilaso de la Vega Inca, Julio Cortazar, and Diamela Eltit. Her interdisciplinary approach weaves critical theory together with anthropology and history. Her most recent work on historiography and subaltern subjects has appeared in *Dispositio/n, Representations, Nepantla, Social History, Revista de Literatura Iberoamericana, Borders and Margins: Post-Colonialism and Post-Modernism* (1995), and *El debate de la postcolonialidad en Latinoamérica* (2000).

MICHAEL T. CLARK is Executive Director of the U.S.-India Business Council. He earned his A.B. in Government at Harvard University (1979), an M.A. in Latin American studies and international economics (1986), and a Ph.D. in international relations (1990) at the Johns Hopkins School of Advanced International Studies. During more than twenty years of practice and six years of teaching in the field of international relations, Dr. Clark has consistently been concerned with altering the terms of public (national, international, and local) discourse on salient topics of contemporary transnational politics. He has frequently been at the cusp of major international controversy, whether by advising four Sandinista ambassadors in Washington, organizing senior policy studies groups on Latin American debt, or contriving a meeting of Israeli and Palestinian finance and industry ministers with Oslo negotiator Yair Hirschfeld. Much of Clark's practice and thought has involved positions of political and moral complexity, which he regards as an unavoidable consequence of entry into the political field. In his present position, he is responsible for organizing policy dialogue between Indian economic and political elites and their U.S. counterparts. Many of his published writings have been concerned with U.S. foreign policy toward Nicaragua, Cuba, and Latin American debt. He has also written on the fifth-century B.C.E. Athenian democracy and empire, and on U.S. relations with Russia and Europe after the Cold War.

BEATRIZ GONZÁLEZ STEPHAN is Professor at the Universidad Simòn Bolìvar and, from 2001, Lee Hage Jamail Chair Professor at Rice University, Department of Hispanic and Classical Studies. She has served as the director of the journal *Estudios: Revista de Investigaciones Literarias y Culturales* since 1993. In 1987, her book *La historiografía literaria del liberalismo hispanoamericano del siglo XIX* was awarded the Casa de las Américas Prize. Her books include *La duda del Escorpión: la tradición heterodoxa en la narrativa latinoamericana* (1992); *Crítica y descolonización: el sujeto colonial en la cultura latinoamericana* (1992, in collaboration with Lúcia Helena Costigan); *Esplendores y miserias del siglo XIX. Cultura y sociedad en América Latina* (in collaboration with Javier Lasarte and Graciela Montaldo, 1995); *Cultura y Tercer Mundo* (1996). *Fundaciones: Canon, Historia y Cultura Nacional* (Fondo de cultura Económica y Universidad Simón Bolivar, forthcoming) and *Escribir la historia literaria: capital simbólico y monumento cultural* (Barquisimeto, Venezuela, forthcoming).

RANAJIT GUHA is a historian and founder of the South Asian Subaltern Studies Group. His publications include *Elementary Aspects of Peasant Insurgency in Colonial India* (Duke University Press, 1999), *A Subaltern Studies Reader* (University of Minnesota, 1997), *Subaltern Studies: Writings on South Asian History and Society* (Oxford University Press, 1982), *Selected Subaltern Studies* (Oxford University Press, 1982), *An Indian Historiography of India: A Nineteenth-Century Agenda and its Implications* (Calcutta: Center for Studies in Social Science, 1988), *A Rule of Property for Benal: An Essay on the Idea of Permanent Settlement* (Paris: Mouton, 1963), and *Dominance without Hegemony: History and Power in Colonial India* (Harvard University Press, 1997).

WALTER D. MIGNOLO is William H. Wannamaker Professor of Romance Studies and Professor of Literature and Cultural Anthropology at Duke University. His recent publications include *The Darker Side of the Renaissance: Literacy, Territoriality, and Colonization* (University of Michigan Press, 1995) and *Local Histories/Global Designs: Coloniality, Subaltern Knowledge, and Border Thinking* (Princeton University Press, 2000). With Elizabeth Hill Boone, he coedited *Writing without Words: Alternative Literacies in Mesoamerica and the Andes* (Duke University Press, 1994). He is the founder and coeditor of *Dispositio/n: American Journal of Comparative and Cultural Studies* and cofounder and coeditor of *Nepantla: Views from South.*

MARIA MILAGROS LOPEZ was a sociologist. She edited *Más allá de la bella (in)diferencia: revisión postfeminista y otras escrituras posibles* (San Juan, Puerto Rico: 1994), with Madeline

Roman and Heidi J. Figueroa-Sarrieta; and with Ricardo Zúñiga Burmester, *Perspectivas cíticas de la psicología social* (Rio Pedras, Puerto Rico, 1988).

ALBERTO MOREIRAS is Anne and Robert Bass Associate Professor of Romance Studies and Literature and Director of Graduate Studies in the Literature Program at Duke University. He is the author of *Interpretación y diferencia* (Madrid: Visor, 1992), *Tercer espacio: Duelo y literatura en América Latina* (Santiago: ARCIS/Lom, 1999), and *A Exaustão da diferença* (Belo Horizonte: Minas Gerais University Press, 2000). He is the executive editor of *Nepantla — Views from the South* and coeditor of *Journal of Spanish Cultural Studies*.

ABDUL KARIM MUSTAFA is a graduate student in Literature and Romance Studies at Duke University.

JOSÉ RABASA is Professor of Latin American Literature in the Department of Spanish and Portuguese at the University of California, Berkeley. He is the author of *Inventing America: Spanish Historiography and the Formation of Eurocentrism* (University of Oklahoma Press, 1993) and *Writing Violence on the Northern Frontier: The Historiography of Sixteenth-Century Florida and New Mexico and the Legacy of Conquest* (Duke University Press, 2000). Rabasa coedited with Javier Sanjinés and Robert Carr the special issue of *Dispositio/n on Subaltern Studies in the Americas* 46 (1994).

ILEANA RODRÍGUEZ is Professor of Latin American Literatures and Cultures at Ohio State University. She has authored several books including *Women, Guerrillas, and Love: Understanding War in Central America* (University of Minnesota Press, 1999), *House, Garden, Nation* (Duke University Press, 199); *Registradas en la Historia: 10 años de quehacer feminista en Nicaragua* (Nicaragua: CIAM, 1990), *Primer Inventario del Invasor* (Editorial Nueva: Nicaragua, 1984). She has also coedited two volumes: with Marc Zimmerman, *The Process of Unity in Caribbean Society* (Minneapolis: Institute for the Study of Ideologies and Literatures, 1983), and with William L. Rowe, *Marxism and New Left Ideology* (Minneapolis: Marxist Educational Press, 1977).

MARÍA JOSEFINA SALDAÑA-PORTILLO is Assistant Professor with the English Department and the Ethnic Studies Program at Brown University. Her forthcoming manuscript is entitled "The Age of Development and the Colonization of the Revolutionary Imagination in North America." Her recent publications include "Developmentalism's Irresistible Seduction: Rural Subjectivity under Sandinista Agricultural Policy" in *The Politics of Culture in the Shadow of Capital*, and "Consuming Malcolm X: Prophecy and Performative Masculinity," in *Novel: A Forum on Fiction*.

JAVIER SANJINÉS C is Assistant Professor in the Department of Romance Languages and Literatures at University of Michigan, Ann Arbor. He has written *Estética y Carnival: Essays de Sociología de la Cultura* (1984), *Literatura contemporanea y grotesco social en Bolivia* (1992); and in collaboration with Fernando Calderon, *El gato que ladra* (1999). He has edited *Tendencias actuales en la literatura boliviana* (1985) and coedited with Jose Rabasa and Robert Carr *Subaltern Studies in the Americas* a special issue of *Dispositio/n* 46.

PAT SEED, a historian, teaches at Rice University and is the author of *American Pentimento: The Invention of Indians and the Pursuit of Riches, 1492–1640* (University of Minnesota Press, forthcoming); *Ceremonies of Possession in Europe's Conquest of the New World, 1492–1640* (Cambridge University Press, 1995), *Amar, honrar, y obedecer en el México colonial* [Spanish translation of *To Love, Honor, and Obey*] (Mexico: Editorial Patria, 1991), *To Love, Honor, and Obey in Colonial Mexico: Conflicts Over Marriage Choice, 1574–1821* (Stanford University Press, 1988), which received the 1989 Bolton Prize. Recent articles include "Caliban and Native Title: 'This Island's Mine'" in Peter Hulme and William Sherman, eds. *The Tempest and Its Travels* (Philadelphia: University of Pennsylvania Press, 2000); "Jewish Scientists and the Origin of Modern Navigation" in Norman Fiering and Paolo Bernardini, eds. *Jews in the Expansion of Europe* (Oxford: Berghahn, 2000); "Carlos V y las Americas" in Juan Hernandez, ed. *Carlos V* (Madrid, 1999).

DORIS SOMMER, Professor of Romance Languages at Harvard University, is author of *One Master for Another: Populism as Patriarchal Rhetoric in Dominican Novels* (University Press of America, 1983), *Foundational Fictions: The National Romances of Latin America* (University of California Press, 1991), and *Proceed with Caution, When Engaged by Minority Writing in the Americas* (Harvard University Press, 1999). Currently she is writing on bilingual aesthetics.

MARCIA STEPHENSON is Associate Professor of Spanish and the Associate Director of Women's Studies at Purdue University-West Lafayette. She publishes in Andean literary and cultural studies. Her book, *Gender and Modernity in Andean Bolivia*, published by the University of Texas Press, received the A. B. Thomas Award from the South Eastern Council on Latin American Studies for the best book published in Latin American Studies in 1999. She has published articles in *Mln, Revista de estudios hispánicos, Dispositio,* and *Chasqui.*

MÓNICA SZURMUK teaches Latin American literature at the University of Oregon. She has published articles on women's literature in Mexico, Argentina, and Catalonia. She has compiled a collection of travel writing by women, *Mujeres en viaje: Escritos y Testimonios* (Buenos Aires: Alfaguara, 2000). Her book *Gender, Ethnicity, and Community in Women's Travel Writing* will be published in 2001 by the University of Florida Press.

GARRETH WILLIAMS is Assistant Professor of Latin American Literature at Wesleyan University. He is the author of *The Other Side of the Popular: Neoliberalism and Subalternity in Latin America* (Duke University Press, forthcoming).

MARC ZIMMERMAN is Professor and Director of the Latin American Studies graduate program at the University of Illinois at Chicago, he holds a doctorate in comparative literature from the University of California, San Diego (1974). He has made innumerable presentations throughout the United States and Latin America and has published articles in a wide variety of journals. His books and editions in collaboration include *Processes of Unity in Caribbean Societies, Ideologies, and Literatures* (with Ileana Rodríguez, 1983), *Lucien Goldmann y el estructuralismo genético* (1985), *The Central American Quartet* (1980–1998). *Literature and Politics in the Central American Revolutions* (with John Beverley 1991), *U.S. Latino Literature* (1992), *Literature and Resistance in Guatemala (1995),* and *New World [Dis]Orders and Peripheral Strains: Cultural Dimensions in Latin American and Latino Studies* (1998). Zimmerman worked for several years with migrant farmworkers. In 1979–1980, he served in the literature section of Nicaragua's Ministry of Culture, today he directs the Latin American/Latina Cultural Activities and Studies Arena (LACASA Chicago).

Index

Abrams, Philip, 265
Achugar, Hugo, 8, 115
Acosta, José de, 148, 151–160, 164
Adorno, Rolena, 88
Adorno, Theodor, 182
Afghanistan, 60
Africa, 8, 50, 129, 199, 434–435, 442
Agrarianism, 408
Agrarian reform (Mexico), 408
Ak'abal, Humberto, 117, 119–121
Alarcón, Norma, 1
Alaska Native Claims Settlement, 133
Albó, Xavier, 23–24, 289–290, 297, 300, 302, 304–305
Albornoz, Cristobal de, 159
Algeria, 59, 131
Almazán, Germán, 203
Althusser, Louis, 81–83, 100
Alvarez, Sonia, 386
Amazon Basin, 137
America(s), 8, 19, 129, 137–138, 150, 152, 163, 227, 229, 238, 342, 402–407, 416, 425, 431–440
America (nuestra), 88–89
American Revolution, 230
Andahuaylas (Peru), 270
Andamarca (Peru), 269
Andes, 144–148, 158–160, 163–164, 269–272, 276, 298, 438
Ann Arbor (Michigan), 191, 193

Anonymous Jesuit (Blas Valera), 145, 147, 162
Antezana, Luis, 367
Anzaldúa, Gloria, 28, 345, 404, 413–420
Apollo, 267, 270
Appadurai, Arjun, 97–99, 214
Arango y Parreño, José, 346
Arbenz, Jacobo, 112
Arendt, Hannah, 178, 182
Arévalo, Juan José, 124
Argentina, 27, 131, 383–389, 394–398, 432
Arguedas, José María, 269
Aridjis, Homero, 203
Aristide, Jean Bertrand, 253
Aristotle, 150–152
Aroca, Santiago, 122
Aronna, Michael, 424
Aronowitz, Stanley, 66
Arrighi, Giovanni, 438
Asia, 50, 129, 434
Assadurian, Sempat, 438
Asturias, Miguel Angel, 121
Atusparia (Peru), 274
Austin (Texas), 413
Australasia, 19
Australia, 131–138; House of Representatives, 13
Ayacucho (Peru), 274
Aymara, 290, 299

Aztecs, 407, 438
Aztlán, 413–415

Bahamas, 253
Bakhtin, Michael, 182, 363, 374
Balibar, Etienne, 64
Barbero, Jesús Martín, 9, 29
Barnet, Richard, 99
Barragán, Rossana, 7–8, 437–438, 440
Barragán Gutierrez, Pedro Margarito, 207
Barre, Marie-Chantal, 406
Barthes, Roland, 179
Baudrillard, Jean, 68, 97, 228–229, 238
Beckford, William, 341–350, 352, 362
Belgium, 397
Bello, Andrés, 25, 329
Benjamin, Walter, 176, 182, 263, 273, 279
Berger, Peter, 298
Bergman, Marcelo, 24, 27
Bergquist, Charles, 1
Berlin, 39
Berlin Wall, 36, 424
Berry, Wendell, 67
Beverley, John, 1–2, 5, 15–17, 75, 95, 200–
    201, 212, 290, 293–294, 305–307, 424–
    425, 436
Bhabha, Homi, 94–95, 176, 372
Bhadra, Gautam, 197–198, 242
Black Legend, 441
Black Panther Party, 237
Black Power Movement, 235–236
Blades, Rubén, 181
Blair, Tony, 48
Blanco Aguinaga, Carlos, 2
Blue Lake (New Mexico), 132
Bolivia, 5, 26, 97, 136, 288–290, 291–300,
    301–307, 367–370, 437–438, 440
Bonfil Batalla, Guillermo, 405
Bourdieu, Pierre, 245–246, 249
Boyte, Harry C., 291–292
Brading, David, 149
Brathwaite, Edward Kamau, 341, 344
Braudel, Fernand, 435
Brazil, 8, 131, 137, 387
Brazilian Worker Party (PT), 57
Bright, Charles, 81, 86–87, 91–92
Britain, 43, 48, 422, 432–433

Brittin, Alice A., 126
Brodber, Edna, 345
Brown, Elaine, 237
Bruce Pratt, Minnie, 371
Brunner, José Joaquín, 60
Buenos Aires, 289, 316–317, 384, 386, 391,
    394–395
Burgette, Araceli, 408, 411
Butler, Judith, 52, 98

Cajamarca (Peru), 159
Cajiga, Tomás, 203–204
Calchaquí Indians, 384
Calderón, Fernando, 289
Caliban, 29
California, 2
California, San Diego, University of, 2
California, Santa Cruz, University of, 2
Camberra, 130
Canada, 19, 131, 133–134
Cándido, Antonio, 53
Canoe, John, 347, 355
Caracas, 316, 330
Carangas (Bolivia), 376
Cárdenas, Lázaro, 406–407
Cardoso, Fernando Henrique, 435
Cardoza y Aragón, Luis, 117–118, 120–121
Caribbean Basin, 76
Carr, Robert, 1–2, 5, 21–22
Carreño, Manuel Antonio, 320–330
Carrillo Olea, Jorge, 207
Carson National Forest (New Mexico),
    132
Carter, Jimmy, 134
Carter, William, 23, 300
Casal, María Luz, 405
Casas, Bartolomé de las, 148, 150, 157, 441
Caso, Alfonso, 406
Cassirer, Ernst, 39
Castañeda, Jorge, 17, 94–96, 116
Castro-Klaren, Sara, 7, 18–19, 159, 440
Catalan Greenheads, 99
Catamarca (Argentina), 383–390, 391–398
Cedillo Méndez, Asciano, 208
Central America, 27, 348, 403
Central Unica de Trabajadores (CUT) (Mex-
    ico), 207–208

Centro de Estudios para América Latina (CEPAL), 2
Centro Latinoamericano de Ciencias Sociales (CLACSO), 289
Cerezo, Marcos Vinicio, 112, 116
Chakrabarty, Dipesh, 9, 15, 49–51, 53, 55, 58, 440
Chambliss, William J., 387
Charles V (emperor), 152
Chatterjee, Partha, 199
Chiapas, 116, 125, 136, 191–195, 201–208, 397, 402, 404, 411
Chile, 48, 137
China, 36, 47, 424
Chuquisaca (Peru), 158
Cihuocowatl, 415
Civil rights (U.S.), 21, 235, 388
Civil War (U.S.), 21, 229–230, 232
Cixous, Hélène, 372–373
Clandestine Indigenous Revolutionary Committee General Command (CCRICG) (Mexico), 201
Clarés, Ramón, 368
Clark, Michael, 5, 7, 21–22
Clément, Catherine, 181, 373
Clinton, William J., 48, 123, 253
Coatlique, 415
Cohn, Robert, 1
Cold War, 21, 48, 114–115, 214, 231, 262, 431–432, 440
Colegio del Carmen y San José (Catamarca, Argentina), 384–385, 391, 393
Collins, Joseph, 260–261
Colón, Willie, 181
Columbian Votán, 193
Columbia University, 30, 59
Columbus, Christopher, 25, 114, 346–347
Comandnacia General del Ejército Zapatista de Liberación Nacional, 201
Comité de Unidad Campesina (CUC) (Guatemala), 114, 119, 123–126
Communist Party, 13, 48
Concha, Jaime, 2
Condori, Ana María, 26, 368, 376–380
Congress: Brazilian, 131; Guatemalan, 122–123; U.S., 133; Venezuelan, 332

Constitution: Bolivian, 136; Brazilian, 130; Canadian, 133; Guatemalan, 122; Mexican, 208, 408–409, 411; Philippine, 136; U.S., 21, 48, 67, 229
Constitutional Convention (U.S.), 230
Consulta Nacional e Internacional (Chiapas, Mexico), 202
Cook, Scott, 408
Coordinating Committee of Civil Sectors (CSC) (Guatemala), 122
Cornejo, Alberto, 368–369
Cornejo Polar, Antonio, 17, 88–92, 103
Cornell, Drucilla, 178
Coronil, Fernando, 7, 227, 230
Corrigan, Philip, 246
Cortázar, Julio, 177
Cotterrell, Roger, 387
Councils of Lima and Cuzco, 158
Cresap, Steven, 267
Cruz, Celia, 181
Cruz, Sor Juana Inés de la, 177
Cuahutemoc, 407
Cuba, 47, 346, 432; missile crisis, 36; revolution, 432
Cubas, Alicia, 385
Cuenca del Caribe, 76
Cultural Revolution (China), 36, 424
Cultural studies, 53, 57, 85, 93
Curtis, Fred, 67
Cuzco (Peru), 144–145, 158, 269
Cuzqueño, El (Cristobal de Molina, Friar), 148, 162

Dakota, 135
Dawkings, Henry, 345
de Certeau, Michel, 295
Declaration from the Lacandon Jungle (Mexico), 436
Degregori, Carlos Ivan, 264–265
Deleuze, Gilles, 10, 147–148
de Man, Paul, 178
Demesa Padilla, Gerardo, 207
Department of Justice (U.S.), 133
Department of the Treasury (U.S.), 76
Derrida, Jacques, 4, 6, 50–51, 53, 175, 217, 243–244, 260, 275–280
Descombes, Vincent, 192

Díaz, Porfirio, 436
Díaz del Castillo, Bernal, 276
Díaz Polanco, Hector, 406, 411
Dionysus, 268, 273
Douglass, Frederick, 231
Drax Hall Estate (Jamaica), 344
Dreyfus, Hubert L, 146
D'Souza, Dinesh, 176
Du Bois, W. E. B., 229, 429–430
Dussel, Enrique, 436–437, 441
Dutton, Charles, 236–237
Duvalier, Papa Doc, 250

East India Company, 426
Ecuador, 387
Edwards, Bryan, 345, 352
Ejército Guerrillero de los Pobres (EGP)
    (Guatemala), 124, 126
Ejército Zapatista de Liberación Nacional
    (EZLN) (Mexico), 191–192, 201–202,
    206, 404, 410
Elias, Norberto, 249
Elster, Jon, 388
Engels, Frederick, 17, 214, 268
England, 53, 67, 130, 132, 343–346, 352,
    356, 361–363, 374, 426–429, 432–439,
    441
English Caribbean, 345
Enlightenment, 9, 13, 15, 38–41, 44–45, 99,
    159, 180, 265, 314, 321, 329, 424, 440–442
Equiano, Olaudah, 342
Erasmus of Rotterdam, 320
Eros, 175, 321, 323, 349
Escobar, Arturo, 294–295, 299, 386
Espino Salguero, Gustavo, 123
Esquipulas II (Guatemala), 112
Estefan, Gloria, 180–181
Esteva, Gustavo, 412
Europe, 3, 9, 12, 49, 75, 163–164, 193, 227,
    230, 233, 260, 418–419, 425–430, 435–
    438, 441

Fabian, Johannes, 247
Facultad Latinoamericana de Ciencias Soci-
    ales (FLACSO), 2
Faletto, Enzo, 435
Fals Borda, Orlando, 437
Farmer, Paul, 252

Ferguson, James, 403
Fernández de Lizardi, José Joaquín, 315
Fernández de Oviedo, Gonzalo, 350
Fernández Retamar, Roberto, 345
Fiesta del Gran Poder (Bolivia), 296–298
First World, 64–65, 75, 82, 404, 414
Flores, Lauro, 1
Foucault, Michel, 4, 6, 10, 39, 54, 146–147,
    163–164, 212, 245–246, 409, 424
Foweraker, Joe, 386
Fox, Vicente, 208
France, 3, 53, 66, 207, 434–435, 439, 441
Franco, Jean, 2, 99
Frankel, Boris, 214
Frankfurt School, 53
Fraser, Nancy, 98
Frederick II (Prussia), 39
French Revolution, 44, 178, 321
Freud, Sigmund, 368
Friedman Mier, Lawrence, 397
Fujimori, Alberto, 114–115, 121
Fukuyama, Francis, 262
Fusco, Coco, 5
Fuss, Diana, 375

Gamarra, Eduardo, 291–292
Gamio, Manuel, 406
Gandhi, Mohandas K., 14, 44
Garavaglia, Carlos, 438
García, Alan, 274
García, Nineth, 121
García Canclini, Nestor, 9, 12–17, 54–55,
    72, 94–95, 195, 389
García de León, Antonio, 205, 436
García Escobar, Carlos René, 120–121
Garrido, Luis Javier, 202
General Telephone and Electronics (GTE),
    193
George Mason University, 1, 7, 29
Germany, 435, 441
Geyer, Michael, 81, 86–87, 91–92
Gidden, Anthony, 293, 295
Gitksan, 133
Golden Age, 23, 345
Gomez-Peña, Guillermo, 102, 413
González Casanovas, Pablo, 202, 206, 438
González Echeverría, Roberto, 345
González Stephan, Beatriz, 24

Gorbachev, Mikhail, 115
Gordon, Colin, 147, 164
Graham, Julie, 67
Gramsci, Antonio, 3–4, 6, 14–15, 20, 49,
  51–57, 61, 121, 157, 195–199, 201, 203,
  206, 213–219, 263, 430
Grandmothers of Plaza de Mayo (Argen-
  tina), 390
Greenblatt, Stephen, 153, 364
Grosfogel, Ramón, 435
Grupo de Apoyo Mutuo(GAM)
  (Guatemala), 125
Grupo de Mujeres de San Cristóbal Asocia-
  ción Civil (Mexico), 411
Grupo KS (Mexico), 203, 207
Guamán Poma de Ayala, Felipe, 19, 144,
  147, 159–163, 265
Guatemala, 18, 11–120, 121–126, 175
Guha, Ranajit, 2–9, 11–20, 30, 143, 197,
  199, 211, 220–222, 235, 237, 242, 306,
  356, 395, 424–441
Gulbenkian Commission, 84–87, 102–104
Gunder Frank, Andre, 12, 438

Habermas, Jürgen, 49, 52, 56–57, 292, 388,
  397
Haiti, 22, 241–243, 247–254, 352, 434, 439–
  440
Haitian Revolution, 22
Hardiman, David, 4
Hardt, Michael, 268
Harrington, Michael, 48
Harris, David, 68
Hegel, George Wilhelm Fredrich, 50, 192–
  193
Heidegger, Martin, 40
Heilbrunn, Jacob, 86–87
Herder, Johann Gottfried, 40
Hernández, Aida, 411
Hesperides (garden of), 346
Higman, B.W., 344
Hindness, Barry, 216
Hirst, Paul, 216
Hispaniola, 252
Hobsbawm, Eric, 6, 13, 325
Holland, 438
hooks, bell, 5, 378
Houston (Texas), 116, 424

Huamanga, 274–275
Hulme, Peter, 348, 362, 364
Huntington, Samuel, 53

Iberian Peninsula, 434, 441
Iberoamerica, 19, 136–137, 431
Ileto, Reynaldo, 193
Ilie, Paul, 293
India, 6, 8, 13–14, 20, 36, 42, 44, 197, 220,
  416–417, 424–433, 438–440
Indian Mission Council, 130
Indian Subaltern Studies Group, 7, 195,
  197–200
Indigenous Communities Statute of Para-
  guay, 135
Indigenous Peoples World Summit, 122
Indonesia, 8, 131
Ingraham, Catherine, 376
Inquisition, 146, 162
Institute of Black Parenting, 236
Institute of Ideologies and Literature
  (II&L), 2
Institutional Revolutionary Party (PRI), 28,
  192, 208, 406–410, 416
Institute for Social Research (ILDIS), 289,
  295, 367
Instituto de Investigación Nutricional (IIN)
  (Peru), 274
Instituto Nacional Indigenista-National
  Indigenist Institute(INI), 406, 409
International Monetary Fund (IMF), 261,
  264, 367
Inuit (aboriginal group, Alaska), 133
Italian Risorgimento, 3, 197
Italy, 3, 20, 195, 197, 201

James, C. L. R., 215
Jameson, Fredric, 1–2, 55, 58, 87, 262
Jonas, Suzzane, 116

Kant, Immanuel, 38–40, 44, 424, 441
Katari, Tupac, 288
Kawash, Samira, 69
Kerner Report, 416
Kincaid, Jamaica, 345, 355
Kingston (Jamaica), 360
Kirk, Robin, 264–265
Kladt Sobrino, Juan, 203

Knack, Martha C., 137
Knight, Alan, 405–406
Konner, Melvin, 65
Kraniauskas, John, 7, 83, 273
Kristeva, Julia, 51, 179
Kroker, Arthur, 70

Labbat, Pere, 352
Lacan, Jacques, 178, 428
Laclau, Ernesto, 5–6, 9, 12–17, 56–60, 111,
    121, 124, 126, 180, 196, 247, 279–281, 438
Lamming, George, 361
Lancaster, Roger, 1
La Paz (Bolivia), 297–298, 376
La Perriere, Guillome de, 163
Larráinzar VI (Mexico), 191
Latin American Council of Social Sciences,
    289
Latin American Cultural Studies, 9, 17, 87,
    97, 102–103
Latin American Institute for Social
    Research, 289, 295, 367
Latin American studies, 12, 17, 25, 30, 35,
    87, 404
Latin American Subaltern Studies, 4–6, 9,
    12, 30, 36, 45, 199, 202, 211–212, 278,
    424, 431, 433, 441–442; in the U.S., 433
Latin American Subaltern Studies Group, 2,
    3, 7, 29–30, 35, 195, 200, 206, 212, 228,
    424, 431, 440; founding statement, 424–
    425, 431, 436; projects, 4–5, 8, 30, 195,
    200, 424, 440
Latino studies, 1, 425
Law of Expropriation (Bolivia), 375
Lazarte, Jorge, 367
Lear, John, 260–261
Lechner, Norbert, 261
León Carpio, Ramiro de, 122–126
Levinas, Emmanuel, 178–179, 182
Lévi-Strauss, Claude, 243, 249
Lewis, Matthew Gregory, 341–350, 352–
    359, 362, 364
Lida, Clara, 2
Lienhard, Martin, 88
Lima, 158, 263–264, 271–276
Lincoln, Abraham, 234
Littlefield, Alice, 137

Lomas, Clara, 1
Lomnitz, Claudio, 194, 203
Long, Edward, 345, 352
López, María Milagros, 5, 7, 16–17, 23, 29
Losada, Alejandro, 2
Los Angeles, 21, 418
Louis XIV, 249
Ludmer, Josefina, 9
Lukacs, Georg, 215–216
Luque, Angel, 384–385, 392
Luque, Guillermo, 384–385, 396
Lyotard, Jean-Francois, 43

Machiavelli, Niccolo, 162–164
Mack, Helen, 121, 123
Mack, Mirna, 121
Macondo, 275
Madden, R. R., 341–343, 345–352, 354–364
Madrid, Miguel de la, 407
Maffesoli, Michel, 66
Malinche, La, 417–418
Mallon, Florencia, 3–8
Malloy, James, 291–293, 295, 304
Mamdani, Mahmood, 59–60
Manchay Tiempo, 264, 277
Mandelbaum, Fanny, 384
Manley, Michael, 5
Mann, Michael, 245
Manzano, Juan Francisco, 342
Maori, 133, 135
Mapuche, 137
Marches of Silence, 27, 384, 389, 391, 397
Marcuse, Herbert 2, 56
María Soledad, 27, 383–385, 387–398
Mariátequi, José Carlos, 23, 144, 266–268,
    270–280
Márquez, Roberto, 2
Martin, Randy, 66–67
Martínez de Perón, Isabel, 398
Marx, Karl, 17, 36, 51, 70, 82, 211–219, 260,
    265, 268
Marxist Literary Group (MLG), 1–2
Maryland, University of, 2
Matienzo, Juan de, 148, 150–151, 154, 156–
    162, 164
Matos Mar, José, 265–266, 279
Matsuda, Mari J., 181

Maya, 411
Mayorga, René, 295, 304
Mazzotti, José Antonio, 1
McKay, Claude, 355
Menchú, Rigoberta, 18, 99, 111–114, 116–126, 129, 175–179, 182, 200, 419
Mesoamerica, 113
Mexican Revolution, 193, 405, 408
Mexico, 5, 8, 27, 122, 124, 131, 137, 177, 195, 199, 201–208, 402–409, 412–420, 438
Mexico City, 5, 191, 193, 203, 207, 403, 408, 418
Mexico Solidarity Network, 403
Mignolo, Walter, 7, 28–30, 88, 303, 436, 441
Mintz, Sidney W., 248
Mohanty, Chandra, 371
Molina, Cristobal de, Friar, 148, 156, 162, 276
Monjardin, Adriana, 412
Montaigne, Michel, 151, 177
Montana, University of, 2
Monte, Domingo del, 346
Monteforte Toledo, Mario, 117, 119
Montego Bay (Jamaica), 348
Montesquieu, Michel, 177, 179
Montezuma, 407
Morales, María Soledad, 383, 390
Morales, Mario Roberto, 117–118, 121
Moraña, Mabel, 8–9
Morandini, Norma, 384, 391
Moreiras, Alberto, 7, 17–18, 21, 30, 212, 216
Morelos, José María, 193–194, 205, 207
Moreno Fraginals, Manuel, 345
Morote Best, Efraín, 274
Morquecho, Gaspar, 409
Morrison, Toni, 176, 181
Mothers of the Plaza de Mayo, 27, 383, 388, 390–391, 393, 395
Mouffe, Chantal, 5–6, 12–17, 56–60, 111, 121, 124, 126
Movimiento Estudiantil Chicano (MECHA) (U.S.), 403
Movimiento Nacional Revolucionario (MNR-National Revolutionary Movement), 291

Moylan, Tom, 1
Mustafa, Abdul, 7, 21

Naccos (Peru), 269–270
Nast, Heidi J., 370
National Anthropological Museum (Mexico), 408
National Archives of Mexico, 136
National Indigenist Institute (INI) (Mexico), 406
National Palace (Mexico), 408
National Public Radio (NPR), 203–204
National Revolutionary Movement (Bolivia), 291
Navajo (U.S.), 134
Navajo Forest Products Industry, 134
Naxalbari uprising (India), 36, 424
Near Eastern studies (U.S.), 30
Negri, Antonio, 18, 21, 193, 268
Nevada (U.S.), 135
New International Order, 192
New World, 114, 229, 433
New Zealand, 131, 133–135
Nicaragua, 1, 5, 36
Nicaraguan elections, 424
Nietzsche, Friedrich, 23, 77, 266–268
Nobel Peace Price, 18, 113–120, 122, 125
Nongovernmental organizations (NGOs), 98, 301
North American Free Trade Agreement (NAFTA), 28, 116, 125, 404
Nuestra America, 88–89
Nueva York, 181
Nunavut (Canada), 133

O'Donnell, Guillermo, 386–387
O'Gorman, Edmundo, 144
Oaxaca, 402, 420
Obeah, 354–355
October Revolution of 1944 (Guatemala), 120
Offe, Clauss, 397
Oklahoma, 132, 134
Olmedo Gutierrez, Marcos, 207
Olson, Mancur, 388
Ondegardo, Polo, 144–150, 156, 158, 161–162

Organization of American States (OAS), 122
Organization of American States International Civil Mission, 22
Organization of Petroleum Exporting Countries (OPEC), 131
Ortiz, Renato, 9
Oviedo, José, 424

Pachacutec (Inca ruler), 148
Pachacuti (catastrophe theory), 303, 305
Padgen, Anthony, 151–158
Padilla, Genaro, 413
Palancares, Jesusa, 179
Partido Revolucionario Democrático (PRD) (Mexico), 208
Partido Revolucionario Institucional (PRI) (Mexico), 28, 192, 208, 406–410, 416
Passamaquoddy (aboriginal group, U.S.), 133, 136–137
Payeras, Mario, 112
Paz, Octavio, 345
Pazos, Luis, 384
Peabody Coal (U.S.), 134
Pelloni, Martha, 27, 384–385, 391–393
Penobscot Tribes (U.S.), 133–136, 137
Perón, Juan Domingo, 384
Peru, 8, 19, 23, 47, 148, 157, 161, 163, 176, 263–268, 271–276
Perus, Françoise, 2
Phillip II (king), 149, 154, 156
Piccone, Paul, 216
Piura (Peru), 271
Plato, 150–160, 163, 222
Platt, Tristán, 374–375
Plaza de Mayo (Argentina), 390
Pletsch, Carl E., 91–92
Pompa, Gerónimo, 315
Poniatowska, Elena, 176–177
Popular Front, 16, 57
Porras Barrenechea, Raúl, 148–149
Portocarrero, Gonzalo, 273–275
Portugal, 434, 437, 439
Potosí (Bolivia), 97, 301, 438
Prebisch, Raúl, 435
Presidencia Municipal (Tepoztlán, Mexico), 203, 205
Prestes, Luis Carlos, 296
Prewitt, Kenneth, 85–86

Prices, John, 345
Princeton University, 1
Prudhoe Bay (Alaska), 33
Przeworski, Adam, 386
Puerto Rican Socialist Party, 5
Puerto Rican Women Movement, 5
Puerto Rico, 7, 17, 65, 67, 72–77
Puna (Bolivia), 302
Purity of blood, 435
Pyrenees, 438

Quechua, 144, 148, 264, 270–271, 275, 299
Quijano, Anibal, 426, 432–437, 441

Rabasa, José, 1, 2, 5, 20, 157, 193, 195, 202, 212–213, 440
Rabinow, Paul, 146
Rainbow Coalition (U.S.), 57–58
Rama, Angel, 293
Ramona (Zapatista commander), 201
Ramos, Julio, 1, 12
Ranciere, Jacques, 222
Ranger, Terence, 199–200
Reich, Robert, 234–235
Representación Unitaria de la Oposición Guatemalteca (RUOG), 122
Revolution of 1944 (Guatemala), 117, 120
Rey, Alejandra, 384
Rhys, Jean, 355, 363
Richard, Nelly, 9, 113, 116
Rio de la Plata, 8
Ríos, José de los, 207
Rios Montt, Efrain, 126
Riva, Narciso de la, 375
Rivera, Diego, 408
Rivera Cusicanqui, Silvia, 7–9, 17, 23–24, 97–98, 103, 290, 300–307, 374–375, 437–441
Rodríguez, Ileana, 234–235, 238, 440
Rodríguez, Richard, 28, 176–179, 404, 413–419
Rodríguez Castañeda, Lázaro, 205, 208
Rojas, Raúl, 112
Rojas, Rosa, 204
Ross, Andrew, 74
Ruiz, Margarito, 408, 411
Ruiz, Samuel, 125
Ruta 100 (strike, Mexico City), 202

Saadi family, 384–385, 394
Saadi, Arnaldito, 384
Saadi, Ramón, 384
Saadi, Vicente, 384–385
Saco, José Antonio, 346
Saharan Africa, 440–442
Said, Edward, 66, 262, 342, 409
Salamanca, 148, 151, 154
Saldaña-Portillo, Josefina, 7, 27–28
Salle, Jean-Baptiste de la, 321
San Andrés Larráinzar (Mexico), 191
San Andrés Sacamch'en de los Pobres (Mexico), 191
San Fernando del Valle de Catamarca (Argentina), 383
Sandinista(s), 1, 5, 36
Sandoval, Chela, 17, 100–103
Sanjinés, Javier, 1–2, 5, 21, 23, 212–213
Santiago, Silviano, 17, 93–96
Saravia Valle, Jorge, 370–371
Sardinia, 198
Sarlo, Beatriz, 12, 17, 92
Sarmiento, Domingo Faustino, 315
Sarmiento, Sergio, 405
Sarmiento de Gamboa, Pedro, 144–148, 154–158, 161–164, 266–268
Savannah la Mar (Jamaica), 353
Schmitter, Philippe, 386
School of Salamanca, 151, 154, 441
Schutte, Ofelia, 267
Schwartz, Roberto, 12
Schwartz-Bart, Simone, 363
Scott, James, 418
Second International, 13
Second World, 82, 227
Seed, Patricia, 1, 5, 18–19, 440
Seidman, Robert B., 387
Selva Lacandona (Mexico), 201
Sendero (Peru), 269–270
Sendero Luminoso, 47, 264, 268–269, 273–274
Sepúlveda, Ginés de, 149
Serrano Elías, Jorge, 114–118, 120–125
Sheperd, George, 158
Shining Path, 270
Shoshone (aboriginal group, U.S.), 135
Siegel, Robert, 203–204
Sierra de Vilcaza, 276

Sklair, Leslie, 87
Smith, Carol, 1
Smith, Paul, 101–102
Social Darwinism, 301, 342, 358
Social Science Research Council, 85
Sommer, Doris, 19–20, 111, 124, 126, 200–201
Sommers, Joseph, 2
Soto, Hernando de, 260–261, 276
South America, 363, 431, 435
South Asia, 4, 15, 28, 35–38, 41–45, 59, 195, 242, 424–425, 431, 440–441
South Asian Collective, 1, 3
South Asian Group, 1–8, 144, 195, 242, 305
South Asian Project, 6, 242, 424, 431
South Asian studies, 42, 437
South Asian Subalternists, 7, 198
South Asian Subaltern Studies, 5, 29, 143, 195, 241, 424, 426, 431–432, 440–442
South Asian Subaltern Studies Collective, 1, 3, 4–5
South Asian Subaltern Studies Group, 30, 431–437
Southeast Asia, 435
Southeast Asian Subaltern Group, 206
Southern Cone, 383
Soviet Union, 47–48, 60
Spain, 157, 207, 276, 405, 417–418, 434–439
Spanish America, 135, 137, 425
Spanish Caribbean, 346
Spanish Conquest, 150, 153, 276, 407
Spanish Empire, 143, 145, 149, 441
Spanish Golden Age, 345
Spivak, Gayatri, 1, 3, 6, 10–20, 26, 30, 51–52, 57, 199, 242, 262–263, 275, 279, 404
Squier, E. G., 348
Stalin, Joseph, 47
Stallybrass, Peter, 374
Stanford University, 176
Starn, Orin, 264–265
State Department (U.S.), 85
Stavenhagen, Rodolfo, 409–438
Stephens, John Lloyd, 342
Stephenson, Marcia, 7, 26, 372
Stern, Steve, 438
Stoll, David, 126
Ströebele-Gregor, Juliana, 300

Subaltern studies, 9, 30–38, 41, 49–50, 53, 197, 199, 213, 229, 241–242, 277
Subaltern Studies Group, 1, 30, 195
Subaltern Studies in the Americas, 36
Subcomandante Marcos, 201
Sub-Saharan Africa, 440, 442
Supreme Court (Guatemala), 122–123, 133, 135
Szeminski, Jan, 276
Szurmuk, Mónica, 24, 27

Tacho (Zapatista commander), 201
Tagore, Rabindranath, 44
Taino, 76
Taller de Historia Oral (Bolivia), 439
Tandeter, Enrique, 438
Taos Pueblos, 132
Taqui-Oncoy movement (1564), 159
Taulis, Totóro, 404
Taussig, Michael, 274, 276
Templo Mayor (Mexico), 408
Tepozteco, El, 205
Tepoztlán, 191–195, 201–208
Tertre, Jean Baptiste du, 352
Texas, 132, 415
Third International, 13
Third Way, 58
Third World, 10, 192, 220, 227, 250, 261, 300, 404, 414, 435, 439–440
Third World Feminists, 99, 102
Thompson, E. P., 6
Tlaltizapán, 207
Tlazolteyotl, 415
Todorov, Tzevtan, 177, 179
Toledo, Francisco de, 19, 143–154, 156, 158–164
Toranzo, Carlos, 289, 295–299, 304–305
Touraine, Alain, 386
Trippett, Frank, 136
Tula, Luis, 384–385, 392, 396
Tupac Amaru, 144, 148–149
Tupac Yupanqui, 148
Tuyuc, Rosalina, 119, 121

Unión Revolucionaria Nacional Guatemalteca (URNG), 112, 114, 122–125
United Arab Emirates, 131
United Nations, 129–130, 261

United Nations Organization for the Study of Science and Culture (UNESCO), 192
United Nations-Organization of American States International Civil Mission, 22
United States, 3, 5, 6–7, 19, 21, 27, 35, 47, 58–59, 65–68, 76, 85, 94, 99, 102, 115, 122, 124, 131–137, 191–193, 195, 227–231, 234–236, 243, 249, 253, 342, 403–405, 407, 412–420, 431–434, 439–441; Congress, 76 ; Constitution, 21, 48, 67, 229; Department of the Treasury, 76; Supreme Court, 133
Universidad Nacional Autónoma de México, 202
University Student Asociacion (Guatemala), 121, 123
Urúa, Camú, 404
Uruguay, 8

Valcarcel, Luis E., 145, 149, 154
Valdés, Cecilia, 348, 355
Valera, Blas ("the anonymous Jesuit"), 19, 147, 162–163
Valley of Catamarca, 391
Varese, Stefano, 300
Vargas Llosa, Alvaro, 122
Vargas Llosa, Mario, 23, 177, 261–270, 272–277
Vasconcelos, José, 405
Vazquez Calzada, José, 75
Vega, Garcilaso, 19, 147, 163, 176–177
Venezuela, 227, 230, 330
Venezuelan National Assemblly, 227
Vicente Menchú Foundation, 114
Vidal, Antonio, 2
Vidler, Antonio, 369, 374, 376
Vietnam War, 36
Vilas, Carlos M., 96
Villa, Francisco, 436
Villaverde, Cirilo, 346, 348, 355
Virgen de Guadalupe, 205
Virgen de la Natividad, 205
Virnmo, Paolo, 52
Vitoria, Francisco de, 148, 151–158, 164, 441
Vodoun, 248–249

Wachtel, Nathan, 159, 273
Wacquant, Loïc J. D., 245

Washington, D.C., 1, 29, 203
Washington, Denzel, 231–234
Washington, George, 133, 136
Welna, David, 203–204
Welsch, Wolfgang, 297
West Indies, 341–348, 356, 360–361
Wet'suwet'en (aboriginal group, British
  Columbia), 133
Wigley, Mark, 369, 370–380
Williams, Gareth, 7, 21–23, 212
Williams, Raymond, 359
Wilson, Mabel O., 370
Wittgenstein, Ludwig, 8, 20, 37, 178, 247
Womack, John, 193
World Bank, 261, 367, 403
World War I, 43
World War II, 43, 45, 47, 264, 431, 434

Yakima Indians, 132
Yanomani (aboriginal group, Brazil),
  137
Yúdice, George, 9, 94, 96
Yup'ik (aboriginal group, Alaska), 133

Zacatecas (Mexico), 438
Zahareas, Antonio, 2
Zapata, Emiliano, 193, 205, 207, 409, 436
Zapatismo, 192–193, 195, 199, 402
Zapatista Revolutionary Law, 412
Zavala, Iris, 2
Zedillo Ponce de León, Ernesto, 207
Zimmerman, Marc, 18–19, 112
Žižek, Slajov, 56
Zunkel, Osvaldo, 2

Library of Congress Cataloging-in-Publication Data
The Latin American subaltern studies reader / edited by Ileana Rodríguez.
p. cm. — (Latin America otherwise)
Includes bibliographical references.
ISBN 0–8223–2701–5 (cloth : alk. paper) — ISBN 0–8223–2712–0 (pbk. : alk. paper)
1. Marginality, Social — Latin America. 2. Minorities — Latin America. 3. Poor — Latin
America. I. Rodríguez, Ileana. II. Series.
HN110.5.Z9 M2643 2001   305.5'6'098 — dc21   2001023932